W9-CUA-672

SOLIDWORKS 2016
Basic Tools

Introductory Level Tutorials
Getting started with Parts, Assemblies and Drawings

Written by: Sr. Certified SOLIDWORKS Instructor
Paul Tran, CSWE, CSWI

SDC Publications
P.O. Box 1334
Mission, KS 66222
913-262-2664
www.SDCpublications.com
Publisher: Stephen Schroff

ISBN-13: 978-1-63057-001-9
ISBN-10: 1-63057-001-X

Printed and bound in the United States of America.

Acknowledgments

Thanks as always to my wife Vivian and my daughter Lani for always being there and providing support and honest feedback on all the chapters in the textbook.

I would like to give a special thanks to Karla Werner and Rachel Schroff for their editing and corrections. Additionally thanks to Kevin Douglas, Dave Worcester and Peter Douglas for writing the forewords.

I also have to thank SDC Publications and the staff for their continuing encouragement and support for this edition of **SOLIDWORKS 2016 Basic Tools**. Thanks also to Zach Werner for putting together such a beautiful cover design.

Finally, I would like to thank you, our readers, for your continued support. It is with your consistent feedback that we were able to create the lessons and exercises in this book with more detailed and useful information.

Foreword

For more than two decades, I have been fortunate to have worked in the fast-paced, highly dynamic world of mechanical product development providing computer-aided design and manufacturing solutions to thousands of designers, engineers and manufacturing experts in the western US. The organization where I began this career was US CAD in Orange County CA, one of the most successful SOLIDWORKS Resellers in the world. My first several years were spent in the sales organization prior to moving into middle management and ultimately President of the firm. In the mid-1990s is when I met Paul Tran, a young, enthusiastic Instructor who had just joined our team.

Paul began teaching SOLIDWORKS to engineers and designers of medical devices, automotive and aerospace products, high tech electronics, consumer goods, complex machinery and more. After a few months of watching him teach and interacting with students during and after class, it was becoming pretty clear – Paul not only loved to teach, but his students were the most excited with their learning experience than I could ever recall from previous years in the business. As the years began to pass and thousands of students had cycled through Paul's courses, what was eye opening was Paul's continued passion to educate as if it were his first class, and students in every class, without exception, loved the course.

Great teachers not only love their subject, but they love to share that joy with students – this is what separates Paul from others in the world of SOLIDWORKS Instruction. He always has gone well beyond learning the picks & clicks of using the software, to best practice approaches to creating intelligent, innovative and efficient designs that are easily grasped by his students. This effective approach to teaching SOLIDWORKS has translated directly into Paul's many published books on the subject. His latest effort with SOLIDWORKS 2016 is no different. Students that apply the practical lessons from basics to advanced concepts will not only learn how to apply SOLIDWORKS to real world design challenges more quickly, but will gain a competitive edge over others that have followed more traditional approaches to learning this type of technology.

As the pressure continues to rise on U.S. workers and their organizations to remain competitive in the global economy, raising not only education levels but technical skills is paramount to a successful professional career and business. Investing in a learning process towards the mastery of SOLIDWORKS through the tutelage of the most accomplished and decorated educator and author in Paul Tran will provide a crucial competitive edge in this dynamic market space.

Kevin Douglas
Vice President Sales/Board of Advisors, GoEngineer

Foreword

I first met Paul Tran when I was busy creating another challenge in my life. I needed to take a vision from one man's mind, understand what the vision looked like, how it was going to work and comprehend the scale of his idea. My challenge was I was missing one very important ingredient, a tool that would create a picture with all the moving parts.

Research led me to discover a great tool, SOLIDWORKS. It claimed to allow one to make 3D components, in picture quality, on a computer, add in all moving parts, assemble it and make it run, all before money was spent on bending steel and buying parts that may not fit together. I needed to design and build a product with thousands of parts, make them all fit and work in harmony with tight tolerances. The possible cost implications of failed experimentation were daunting.

To my good fortune, one company's marketing strategy of selling a product without an instruction manual and requiring one to attend an instructional class to get it, led me to meet a communicator who made it all seem so simple.

Paul Tran has worked with and taught SOLIDWORKS as his profession for 30 years. Paul knows the SOLIDWORKS product and manipulates it like a fine musical instrument. I watched Paul explain the unexplainable to baffled students with great skill and clarity. He taught me how to navigate the intricacies of the product so that I could use it as a communication tool with skilled engineers. *He teaches the teachers*.

I hired Paul as a design engineering consultant to create the thousands of parts for my company's product. Paul Tran's knowledge and teaching skill has added immeasurable value to my company. When I read through the pages of these manuals, I now have an "instant replay" of his communication skill with the clarity of having him looking over my shoulder - *continuously*. We can now design, prove and build our product and know it will always work and not fail. Most important of all, Paul Tran helped me turn a blind man's vision into reality and a monument to his dream.

Thanks Paul.

These books will make dreams come true and help visionaries change the world.

Peter J. Douglas
CEO, Cake Energy, LLC

Images courtesy of C.A.K.E. Energy Corp., designed by Paul Tran

Preface

The modern world of engineering design and analysis requires an intense knowledge of Computer Aided Design (CAD) tools. To gain this deep understanding of unique CAD requirements one must commit the time, energy, and use of study guides. Paul Tran has invested countless hours and the wealth of his career to provide a path of easy to understand and follow instructional books. Each chapter is designed to build on the next and supplies users with the building blocks required to easily navigate SOLIDWORKS 2016. I challenge you to find a finer educational tool whether you are new to this industry or a seasoned SOLIDWORKS veteran.

I have been a part of the CAD industry for over twenty five years and read my share of instructional manuals. I can tell you Paul Tran's SOLIDWORKS books do what most promise but what others don't deliver. This book surpasses any CAD instructional tool I have used during my career. Paul's education and vast experience provides a finely tuned combination, producing instructional material that supports industry standards and, most importantly, industry requirements.

Anyone interested in gaining the basics of SOLIDWORKS to an in-depth approach should continue to engage the following chapters. All users at every level of SOLIDWORKS knowledge will gain tremendous benefit from within these pages.

Dave Worcester
System Administer
Advanced Sterilization Products - A Johnson & Johnson Company

Author's Note

SOLIDWORKS 2016 Basic Tools, Intermediate Skills, and Advanced Techniques are comprised of lessons and exercises based on the author's extensive knowledge on this software. Paul has 30 years of experience in the fields of mechanical and manufacturing engineering; 20 years were in teaching and supporting the SOLIDWORKS software and its add-ins. As an active Senior SOLIDWORKS instructor and design engineer, Paul has worked and consulted with hundreds of reputable companies including; IBM, Intel, NASA, US-Navy, Boeing, Disneyland, Medtronic, Terumo, Toyota, Kingston and many more. Today, he has trained nearly 9,000 engineering professionals, and given guidance to nearly half of the number of Certified SOLIDWORKS Professionals and Certified SOLIDWORKS Expert (CSWP & CSWE) in the state of California.

Every lesson and exercise in this book was created based on real world projects. Each of these projects have been broken down and developed into easy and comprehendible steps for the reader. Learn the fundamentals of SOLIDWORKS at your own pace, as you progress from simple to more complex design challenges. Furthermore, at the end of every chapter, there are self test questionnaires to ensure that the reader has gained sufficient knowledge from each section before moving on to more advanced lessons.

Paul believes that the most effective way to learn the "world's most sophisticated software" is to learn it inside and out, create everything from the beginning, and take it step by step. This is what the **SOLIDWORKS 2016 Basic Tools, Intermediate Skills, and Advanced Techniques** manuals are all about.

About the Training Files

The files for this textbook are available for download on the publisher's website at **www.SDCpublications.com/downloads/978-1-63057-001-9**. They are organized by the chapter numbers and the file names that are normally mentioned at the beginning of each chapter or exercise. In the <u>Built Parts folder</u> you will also find copies of the parts, assemblies, and drawings that were created for cross references or reviewing purposes.

It would be best to make a copy of the content to your local hard drive and work from these documents; you can always go back to the original training files location at anytime in the future, if needed.

Who this book is for

This book is for the mid-level user who is already familiar with the SOLIDWORKS program. It is also a great resource for the more CAD literate individuals who want to expand their knowledge of the different features that SOLIDWORKS 2016 has to offer.

The organization of the book

The chapters in this book are organized in the logical order in which you would learn the SOLIDWORKS 2016 program. Each chapter will guide you through some different tasks, from navigating through the user interface, to exploring the toolbars, from some simple 3D modeling to advancing towards more complex tasks that are common to all SOLIDWORKS releases. There is also a self-test questionnaire at the end of each chapter to ensure that you have gained sufficient knowledge before moving on to the next chapter.

The conventions in this book

This book uses the following conventions to describe the actions you perform when using the keyboard and mouse to work in SOLIDWORKS 2016:

Click: means to press and release the mouse button. A click of a mouse button is used to select a command or an item on the screen.

Double Click: means to quickly press and release the left mouse button twice. A double mouse click is used to open a program or show the dimensions of a feature.

Right Click: means to press and release the right mouse button. A right mouse click is used to display a list of commands, a list of shortcuts that is related to the selected item.

Click and Drag: means to position the mouse cursor over an item on the screen and then press and hold down the left mouse button; still holding down the left button, move the mouse to the new destination and release the mouse button. Drag and drop makes it easy to move things around within a SOLIDWORKS document.

Bolded words: indicate the action items that you need to perform.

Italic words: Side notes and tips that give you additional information, or explain special conditions that may occur during the course of the task.

Numbered Steps: indicates that you should follow these steps in order to successfully perform the task.

Icons: indicates the buttons or commands that you need to press.

SOLIDWORKS 2016

SOLIDWORKS 2016 is a program suite, or a collection of engineering programs that can help you design better products faster. SOLIDWORKS 2016 contains different combinations of programs; some of the programs used in this book may not be available in your suites.

Start and exit SOLIDWORKS

SOLIDWORKS allows you to start its program in several ways. You can either double click on its shortcut icon on the desktop, or go to the Start menu and select the following: All Programs / SOLIDWORKS 2016 / SOLIDWORKS, or drag a SOLIDWORKS document and drop it on the SOLIDWORKS shortcut icon.

Before exiting SOLIDWORKS, be sure to save any open documents, and then click File / Exit; you can also click the X button on the top right of your screen to exit the program.

Using the Toolbars

You can use toolbars to select commands in SOLIDWORKS rather than using the drop down menus. Using the toolbars is normally faster. The toolbars come with commonly used commands in SOLIDWORKS, but they can be customized to help you work more efficiently.

To access the toolbars, either right click in an empty spot on the top right of your screen or select View / Toolbars.

To customize the toolbars, select Tools / Customize. When the dialog pops up, click on the Commands tab, select a Category, then drag an icon out of the dialog box and drop it on a toolbar that you want to customize. To remove an icon from a toolbar, drag an icon out of the toolbar and drop it into the dialog box.

Using the task pane

The task pane is normally kept on the right side of your screen. It displays various options like SOLIDWORKS resources, Design library, File explorer, Search, View palette, Appearances and Scenes, Custom properties, Built-in libraries, Technical alerts and news, etc.

The task pane provides quick access to any of the mentioned items by offering the drag and drop function to all of its contents. You can see a large preview of a SOLIDWORKS document before opening it. New documents can be saved in the task pane at anytime, and existing documents can also be edited and re-saved. The task pane can be resized, closed or moved to different locations on your screen if needed.

Table of Contents

Setting the System Parameters

Basic Modeling Topics

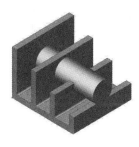

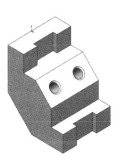

Table of Contents

Bottom Up Assembly Topics

Drawing Topics

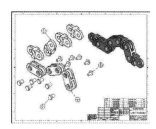

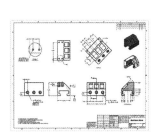

Chapter 18:

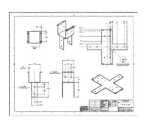

CSWA Preparation Practice (Certified SOLIDWORKS Associate)

Glossary

Index

SOLIDWORKS 2016 Quick-Guides:

Quick Reference Guide to SOLIDWORKS 2016 Command Icons and Toolbars.

Introduction

SOLIDWORKS User Interface

The SOLIDWORKS 2016 User Interface

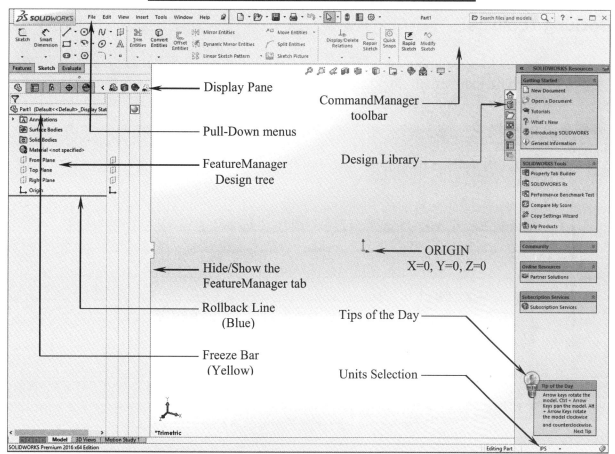

The 3 reference planes:

- The Front, Top and the Right plane are 90°
  apart. They share the same center point
  called the Origin.

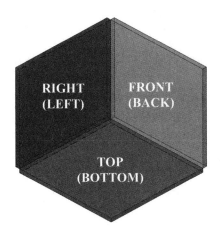

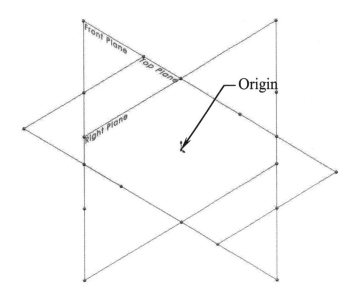

—Origin

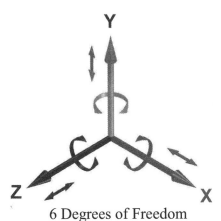

6 Degrees of Freedom

Docking Toolbars:

- The docking behavior of toolbars and the CommandManager have changed to
  eliminate inadvertent docking and undocking. The move zone for toolbars and
  the CommandManager are now more specific so you are less likely to undock
  accidentally.

- The move zone is the area of the toolbar or CommandManager where the move
  pointer becomes active.

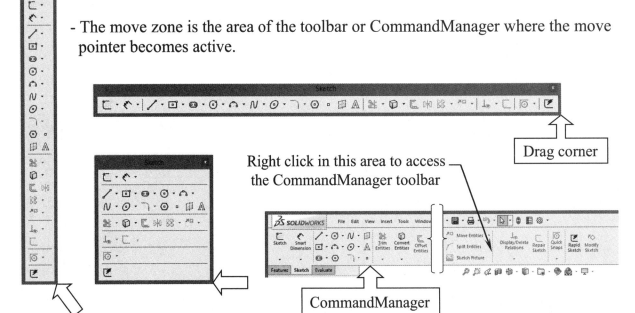

Drag corner

Right click in this area to access
the CommandManager toolbar

CommandManager

Introduction

- If the CommandManager is not used, toolbars can be docked or left floating.

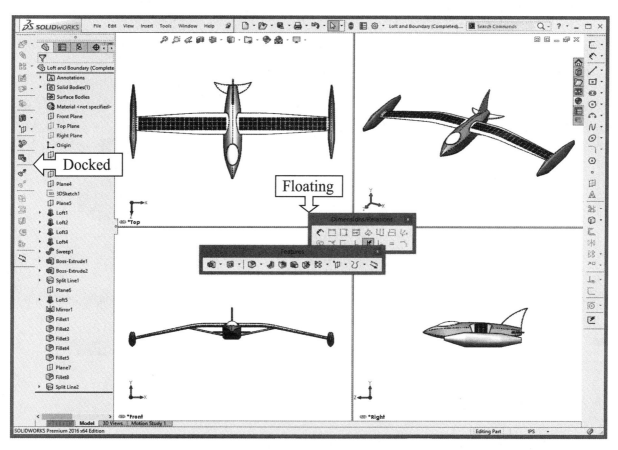

- Toolbars can be toggled off or on by activating or de-activating their check boxes:

- Select **Tools / Customize / Toolbars** tab.

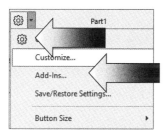

- The icons in the toolbars can be enlarged when its check box is selected.

The View ports: You can view or work with SOLIDWORKS model or an assembly using one, two, or four view ports.

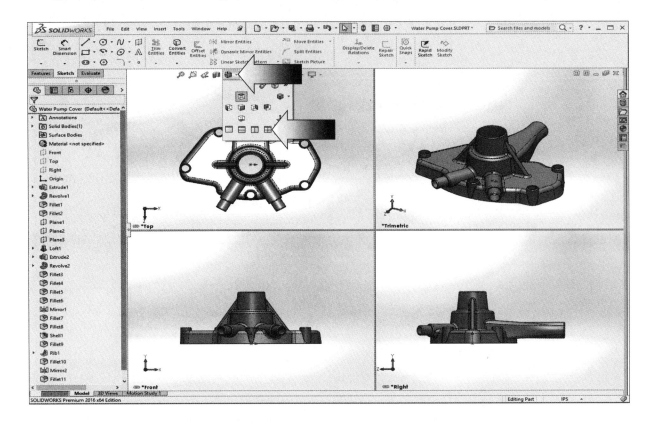

- Some of the **System Feedback symbols** (Inference pointers):

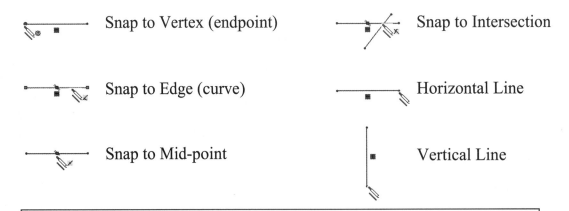

Snap to Vertex (endpoint)

Snap to Intersection

Snap to Edge (curve)

Horizontal Line

Snap to Mid-point

Vertical Line

The Status Bar: (View / Status Bar)

Displays the status of the sketch entity using different colors to indicate:

Green = Selected   **Blue** = Under defined
Black = Fully defined   **Red** = Over defined

<u>2D Sketch examples:</u>

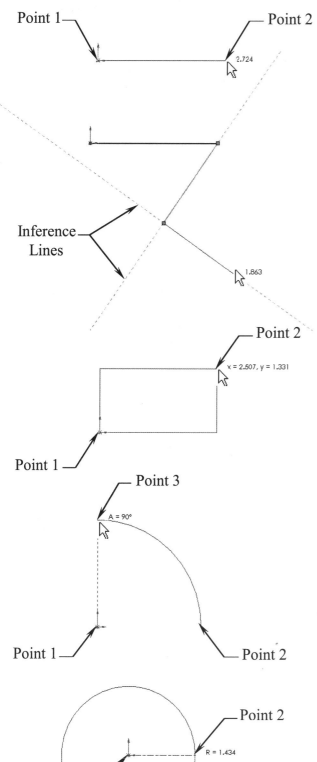

Click-Drag-Release: Single entity.

(Click Point 1, hold the mouse button, drag to point 2 and release.)

Click-Release: Continuous multiple entities.

(The Inference Lines appear when the sketch entities are Parallel, Perpendicular or Tangent with each other.)

Click-Drag-Release: Single Rectangle

(Click point 1, hold the mouse button, drag to Point 2 and release.)

Click-Drag-Release: Single Centerpoint Arc

(Click point 1, hold the mouse button and drag to Point 2, release; then drag to Point 3 and release.)

Click-Drag-Release: Single Circle

(Click point 1 [center of circle], hold the mouse button, drag to Point 2 [Radius] and release.)

3D Feature examples:

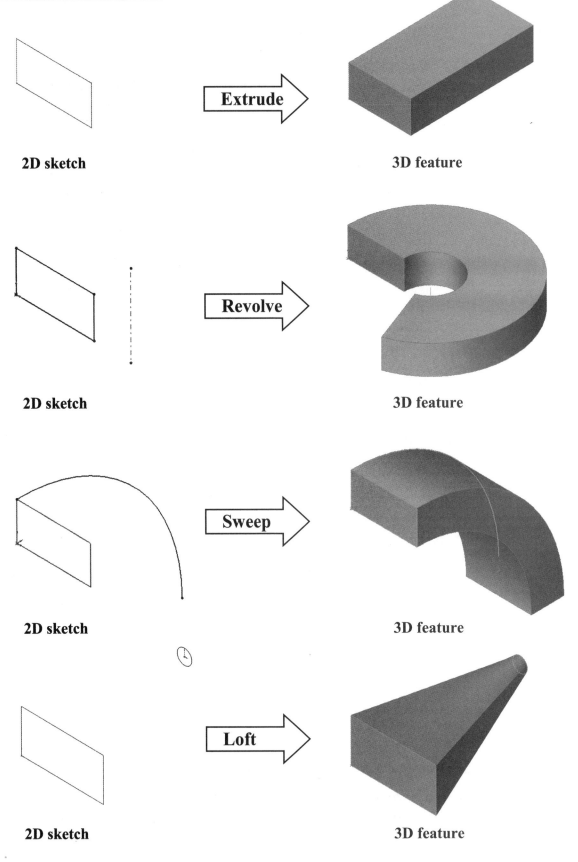

2D sketch   Extrude   **3D feature**

2D sketch   Revolve   **3D feature**

2D sketch   Sweep   **3D feature**

2D sketch   Loft   **3D feature**

Box-Select: Use the Select Pointer to drag a selection box around items.

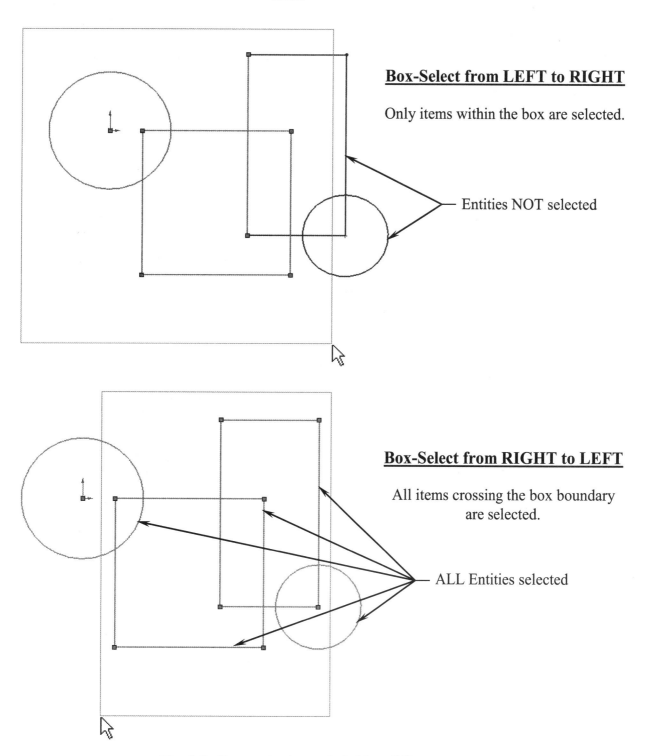

Box-Select from LEFT to RIGHT

Only items within the box are selected.

Entities NOT selected

Box-Select from RIGHT to LEFT

All items crossing the box boundary are selected.

ALL Entities selected

The default geometry type selected is as follows:

* Part documents – edges * Assembly documents – components * Drawing documents - sketch entities, dims & annotations. * To select multiple entities, hold down **Ctrl** while selecting after the first selection.

The <u>Mouse Gestures</u> for Sketches, Drawings and Parts

- Similar to a keyboard shortcut, you can use a Mouse Gesture to execute a command. A total of 8 keyboard shortcuts can be independently mapped and stored in the Mouse Gesture Guides.

- To activate the Mouse Gesture Guide, **right-click-and-drag** to see the current eight-gestures, then simply select the command that you want to use.

Mouse Gestures for Sketches   **Mouse Gestures for Parts & Assemblies**   **Mouse Gestures for Drawings**

- To customize the Mouse Gestures and include your favorite shortcuts, go to:

Tools / Customize.

- From the **Mouse Gestures** tab, select **All Commands** and enable the **Show only commands with Mouse Gestures assigned** check box.

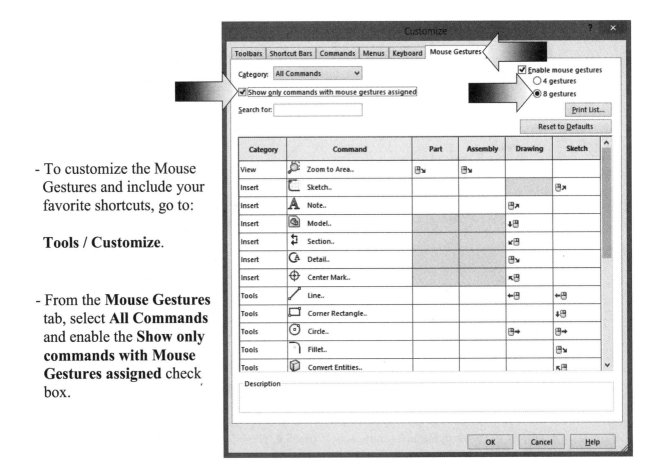

Fit to Left display ⎯⎯⎯⎯⎯⎯⎯⎯   ⎯⎯ Fit to Right display

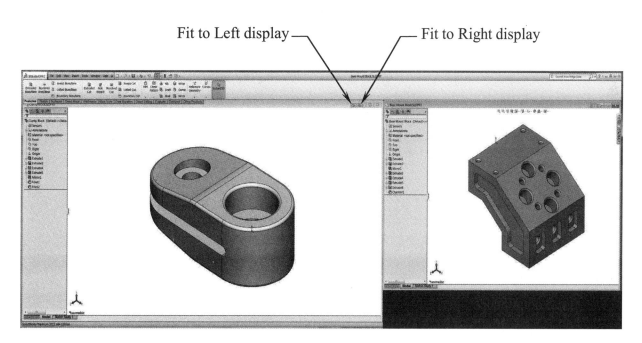

Dual monitors display

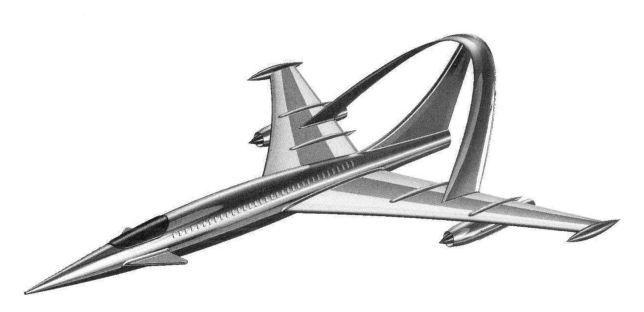

Text and images created using Windows 7-SP1 and SOLIDWORKS 2016-64bit SP0

CHAPTER 1

System Options

Setting Up The System Options

One of the first things to do after installing the SOLIDWORKS software is to set up the system options to use as the default settings for all documents.

System Options such as:

- Input dimension value, Face highlighting…

- Drawing views controls, edge and hatch display.

- System colors, errors, sketch, text, grid, etc.

- Sketch display, Automatic relation.

- Edges display and selection controls.

- Performance and Large assembly mode.

- Area hatch/fill and hatch patterns.

- Feature Manager and Spin Box increment controls.

- View rotation and animation.

- Backup files and locations, etc.

The settings are all set and saved in the **system registry**. While not part of the document itself, these settings affect all documents, including current and future documents.

This chapter will guide you through some of the options settings for use with this textbook; you may need to modify them to ensure full compatibility with your applications or company's standards.

System Options

The **General** Options

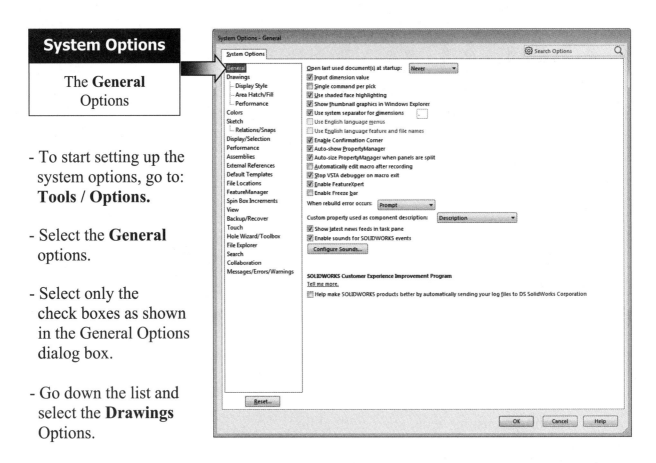

- To start setting up the system options, go to: **Tools / Options.**

- Select the **General** options.

- Select only the check boxes as shown in the General Options dialog box.

- Go down the list and select the **Drawings** Options.

System Options

The **Drawings** Options

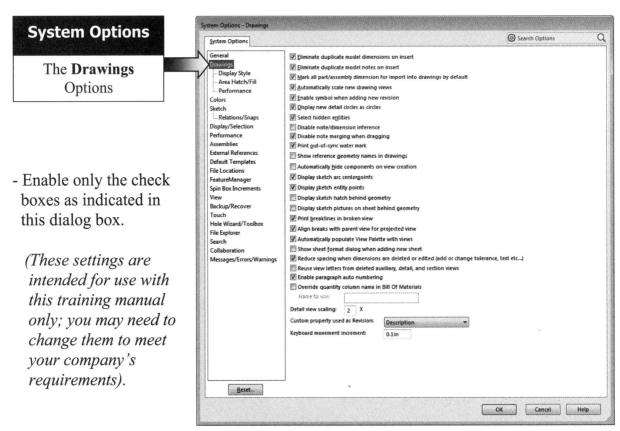

- Enable only the check boxes as indicated in this dialog box.

(These settings are intended for use with this training manual only; you may need to change them to meet your company's requirements).

System Options

The **Display Style** Options

- Continue going down the list and follow the sample settings shown in the dialog boxes to set up your System Options.

- For more information on these settings click the Help button at the lower right corner of the dialog box (arrow).

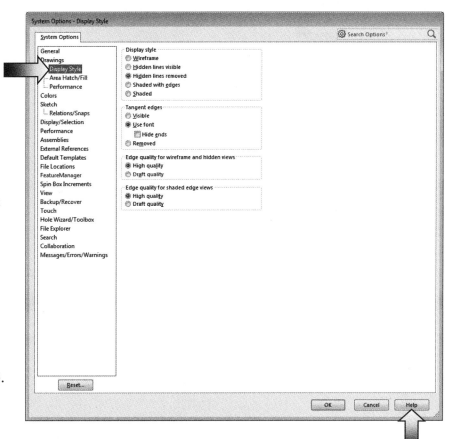

System Options

The **Area Hatch/Fill** Options

- The Area Hatch/Fills option sets the hatch pattern and Spacing (Scale).

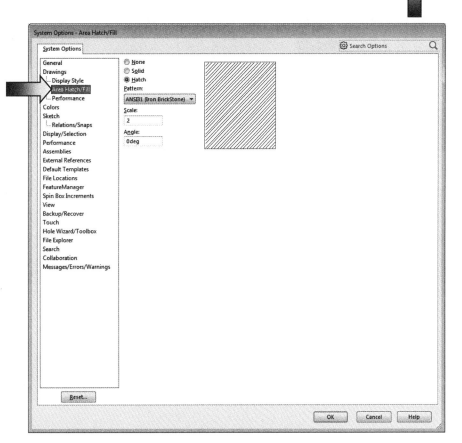

System Options

The **Performance** Options (Drawing)

- Preview and High Quality display options take extra memory, which affects the performance of the computer. (Use the Automatically Load Components Lightweight option in large assembly mode.)

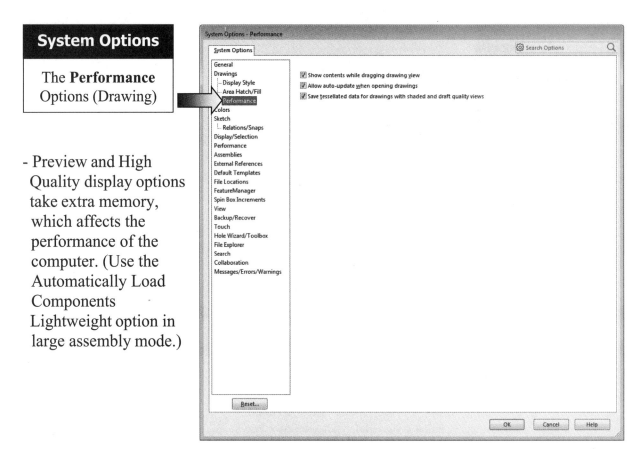

System Options

The **Colors** Options

- The Colors options set the colors of the background and the Feature-Manager Design tree.

- For Background-Appearance select the PLAIN option, and for Viewport Background color click Edit and select the White color.

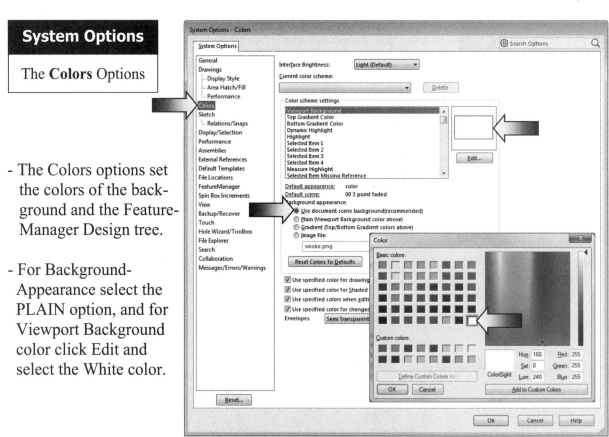

System Options

The **Sketch** Options

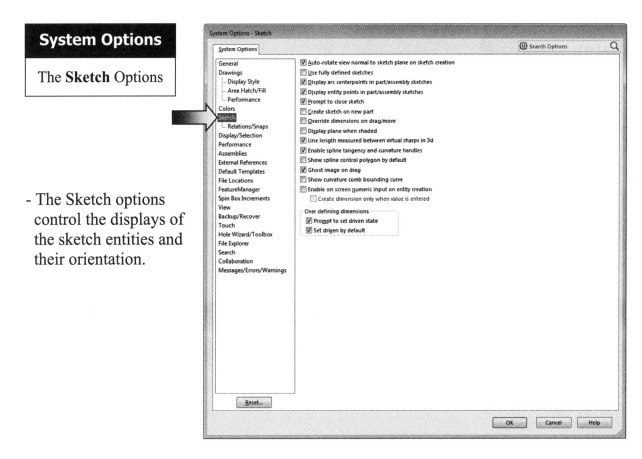

- The Sketch options control the displays of the sketch entities and their orientation.

System Options

The **Relations / Snaps** Options

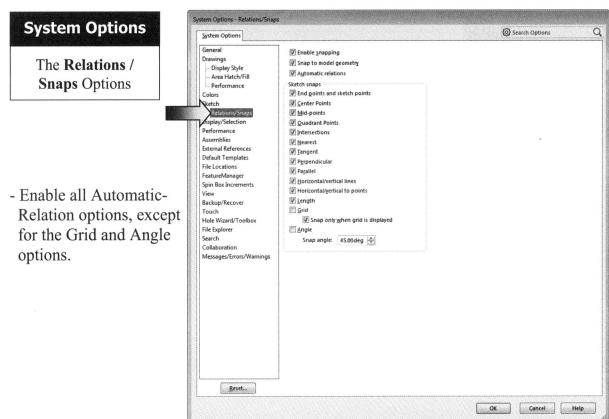

- Enable all Automatic-Relation options, except for the Grid and Angle options.

System Options

The **Display /
Selection** Options

- The controls for Display
and Selection options in
the Part, Assembly, and
Drawings modes.

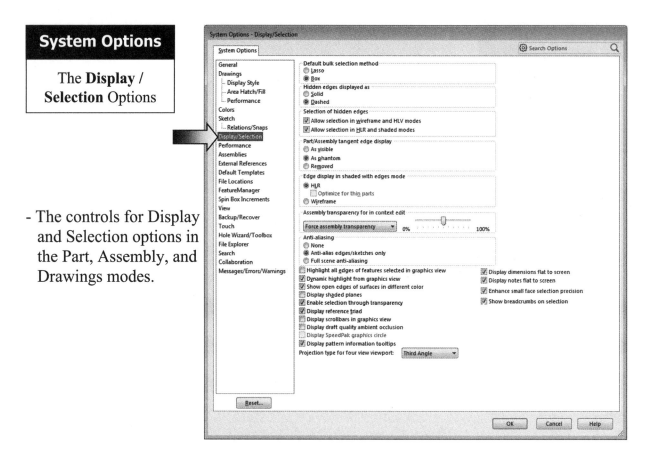

System Options

The **Performance**
Options (Assembly)

- Preview and High
Quality display options
take extra memory,
which affects the
performance of the
computer. (Enable the
Automatically Load
Components
Lightweight option.)

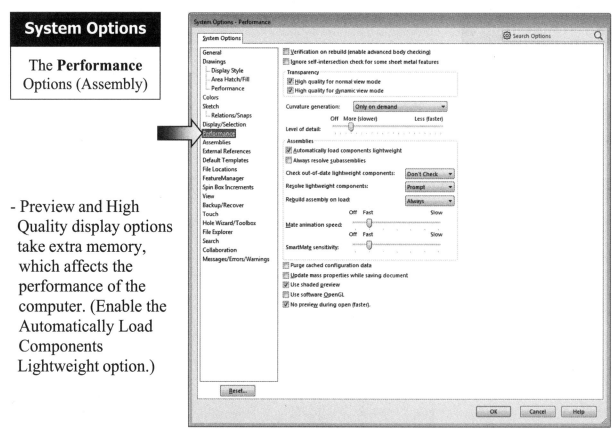

System Options

The **Assemblies** Options

- Use the Large Assembly option to help speed up the process of opening and saving large assemblies.

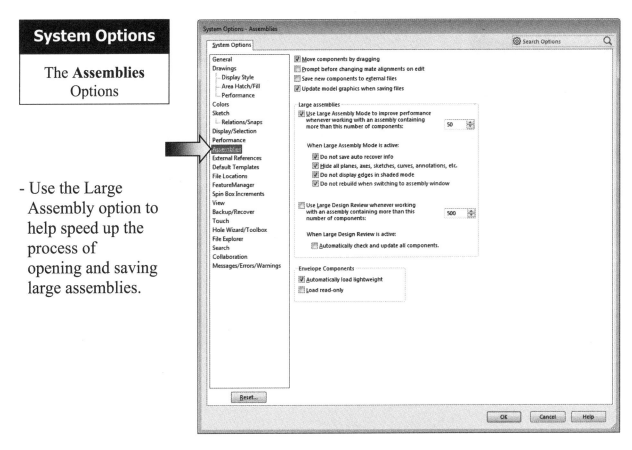

System Options

The **External References** Options

- Select the options that help locate file references and update component names.

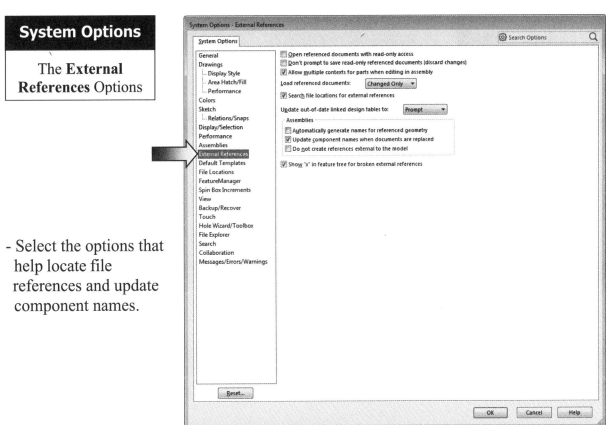

System Options

The **Default Templates** Options

- Set the default Template for Parts, Assemblies, and Drawings.

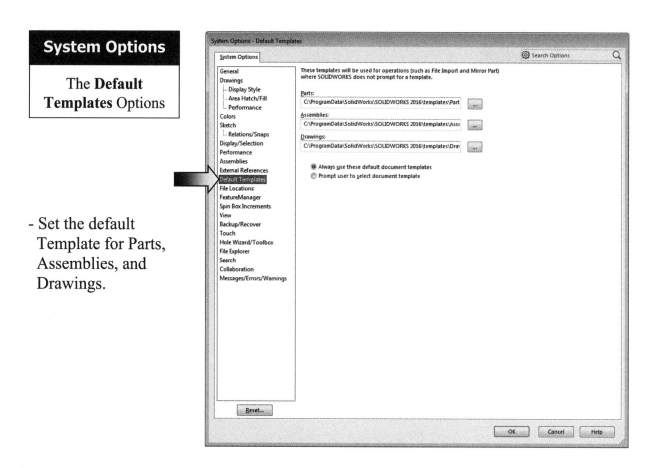

System Options

The **File Locations** Options

- Select and Add the files and folders: Design Library, Holes Table Templates, Weldments, etc.

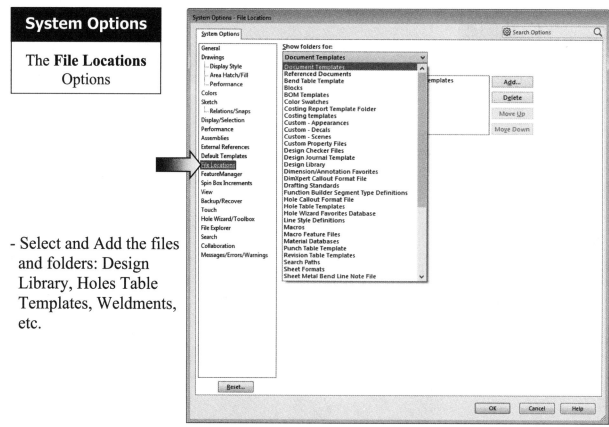

System Options

The **Feature-Manager** Options

- Select the Folders that you want to show on the FeatureManager Design tree.

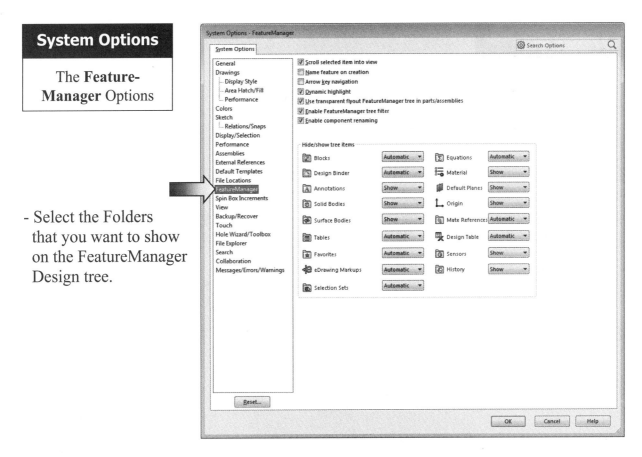

System Options

The **Spin Box Increments** Options

- Set the default increments for the Modify Spin Box (when creating or Editing dimensions).

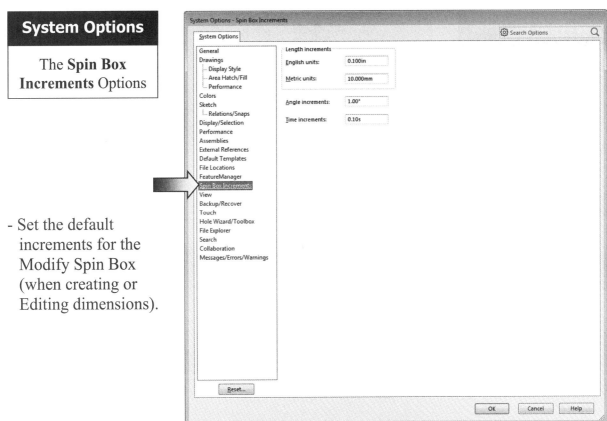

System Options

The **View** Options

- Set the Rotation,
Mouse Speed,
and Transitions
of the view.

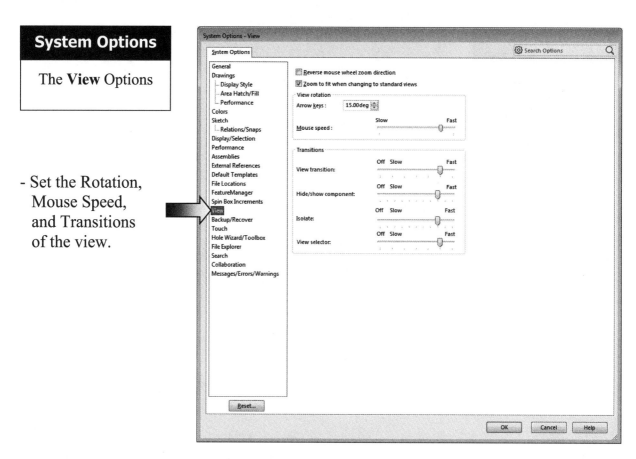

System Options

The **Backups /
Recover** Options

- Set the Auto-
Recover Location,
Time and the Number
of Backup Copies.

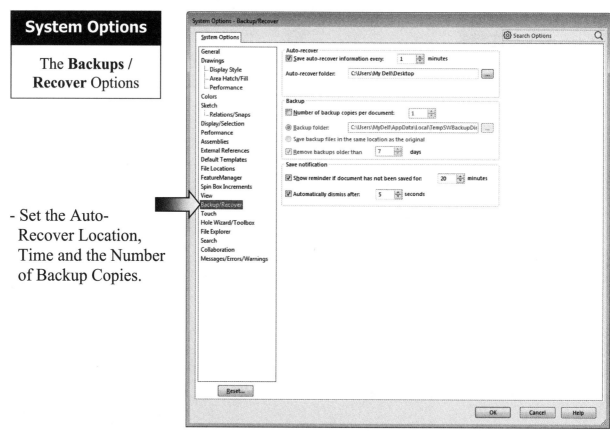

System Options

The **Touch**
Options

- With a Touch-enabled
computer, you
can use flick
touch and multi-
touch gestures in
SOLIDWORKS 2016.

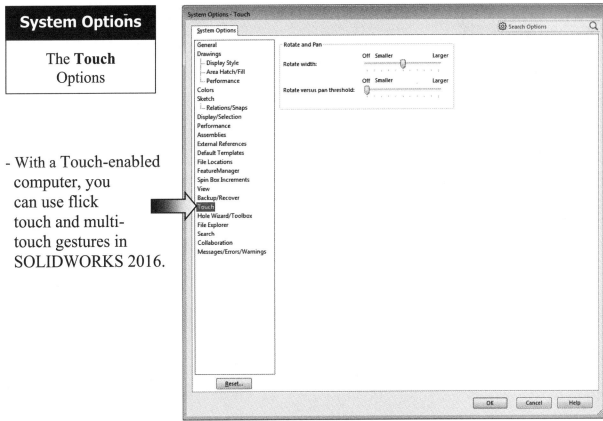

System Options

The **Hole-
Wizard/Toolbox**
Options

- Locate the Hole
Wizard and
Toolbox folder.

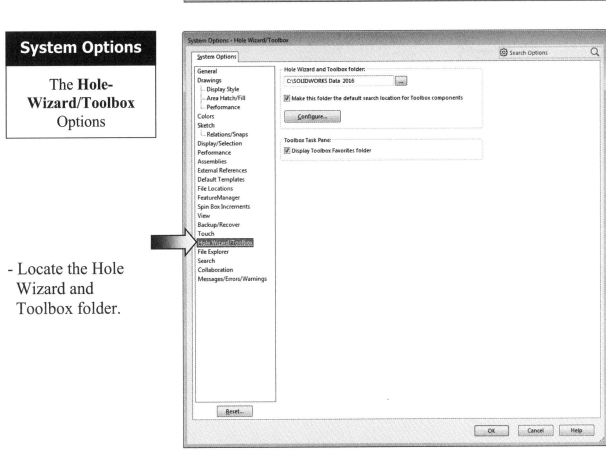

System Options

The **File Explorer** Options

- Enable the File Locations for accessing the SW documents.

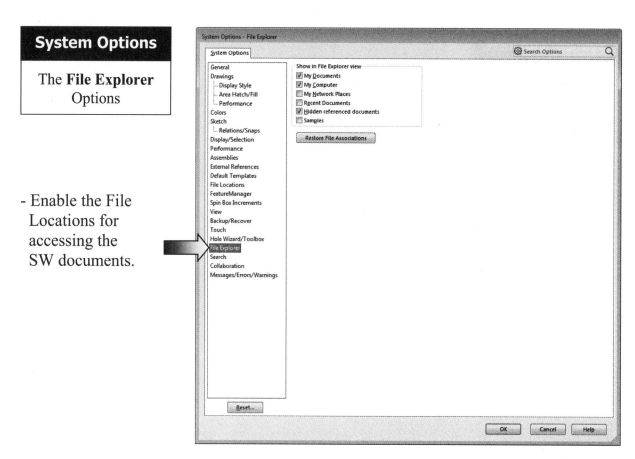

System Options

The **Search** Options

- Set the Search options.

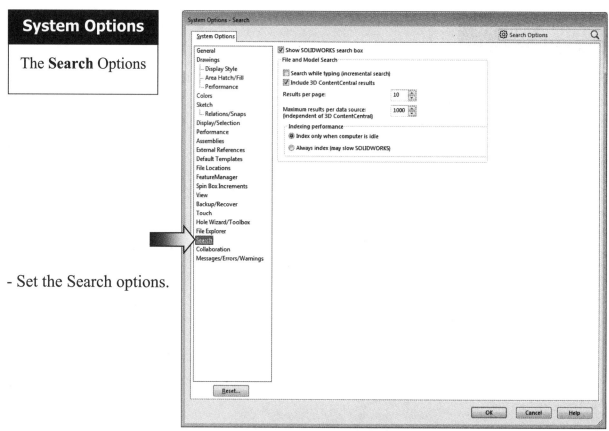

System Options

The **Collaboration**
Options

- Enable / Disable
the Multi-User
Environment.

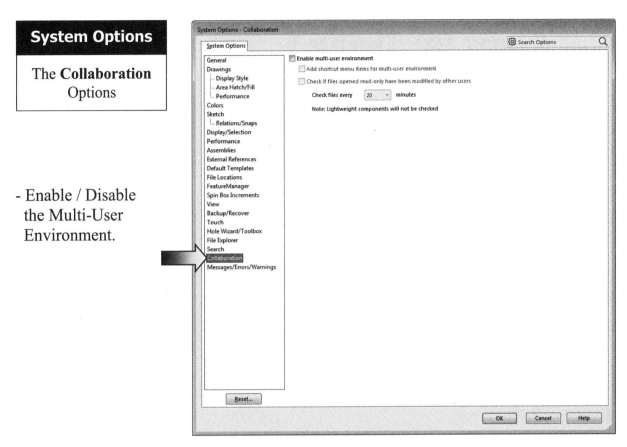

System Options

The **Messages
/Errors/Warnings**
Options

- Set the Error and
Warning messages.

- Continue to set up the
Document Properties
in Chapter 2...

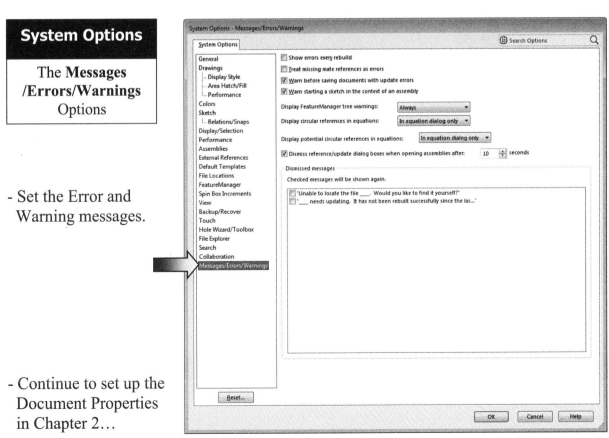

Questions for Review

System Options

1. The settings in the System Options affect all documents including the current and the future documents.
   - a. True
   - b. False

2. The sketch display and automatic relations are samples of System Options.
   - a. True
   - b. False

3. The background colors cannot be changed or saved in the System Options.
   - a. True
   - b. False

4. The mouse wheel zoom direction can be reverse and saved.
   - a. True
   - b. False

5. Default document templates can be selected and saved in the System Options.
   - a. True
   - b. False

6. The spin box increment is fixed in the System Options; its value cannot be changed.
   - a. True
   - b. False

7. The number of backup copies for a document can be specified and saved in the System Options.
   - a. True
   - b. False

8. The System Options can be copied using the SOLIDWORKS Utility / Copy Settings Wizard.
   - a. True
   - b. False

7. TRUE   8. TRUE
5. FALSE 6. FALSE
3. FALSE 4. TRUE
1. TRUE   2. TRUE

CHAPTER 2

Document Templates

Setting Up The Document Properties

After setting up the System Options, the next task is to set up a document template where drafting standards and other settings can be set, saved, and used over and over again as a template. The Document Properties such as:

- Drafting Standard (ANSI, ISO, DIN, JIS, etc.).

- Dimension, Note, Balloon, and Fonts Sizes.

- Arrowhead sizes.

- Annotation display.

- Grid spacing and grid display.

- Units (Inches, Millimeters, etc.) and Decimal places.

- Feature Colors, Wireframe, and Shading colors.

- Material Properties.

- Image quality controls.

- Plane display controls.

These settings are all set and saved in the templates; all settings affect only the **current document** (C:\Program Data\SOLIDWORKS\SOLIDWORKS 2016\ Templates) OR (C:\ProgramFiles\SOLIDWORKSCorp\SOLIDWORKS\ Lang\ English\Tutorial).

The following are examples of various document settings which are intended for use with this textbook only; you may need to modify them to ensure full compatibility with your applications.

Document Properties

The **Drafting Standard** options

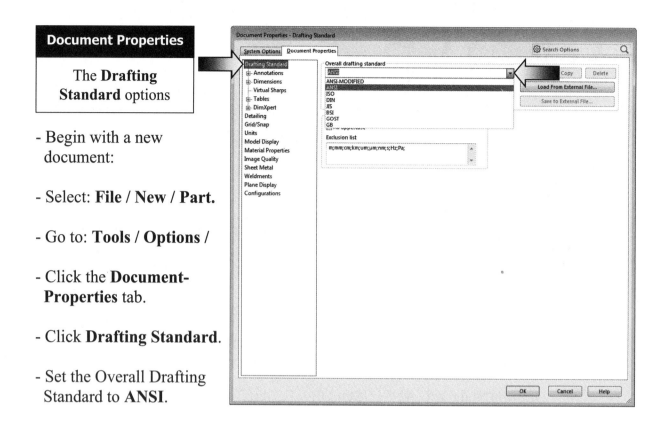

- Begin with a new document:

- Select: **File / New / Part.**

- Go to: **Tools / Options /**

- Click the **Document-Properties** tab.

- Click **Drafting Standard**.

- Set the Overall Drafting Standard to **ANSI**.

<u>Note</u>: *If your Units are in Millimeters, skip to the Units options on page 2-13 and set your units to IPS, then return to where you left off and continue with your template settings.*

Document Properties

The **Annotations** options

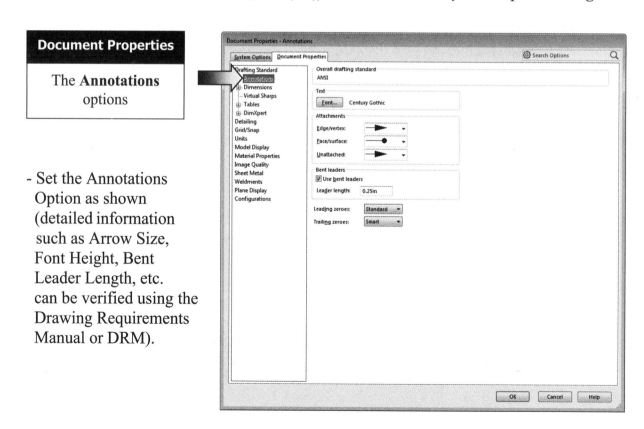

- Set the Annotations Option as shown (detailed information such as Arrow Size, Font Height, Bent Leader Length, etc. can be verified using the Drawing Requirements Manual or DRM).

Document Properties

The **Annotations / Balloons** options

- Set the Balloons standard to ANSI and the other options as shown.

- Click on the Help button at any time to access the information on these topics.

Document Properties

The **Annotations / Datums** options

- Set the Datums standard to ANSI and other options as shown.

Note:

1982 Datum symbol $\boxed{-\text{A}-}$

1994 Datum symbol $\boxed{\text{A}}$

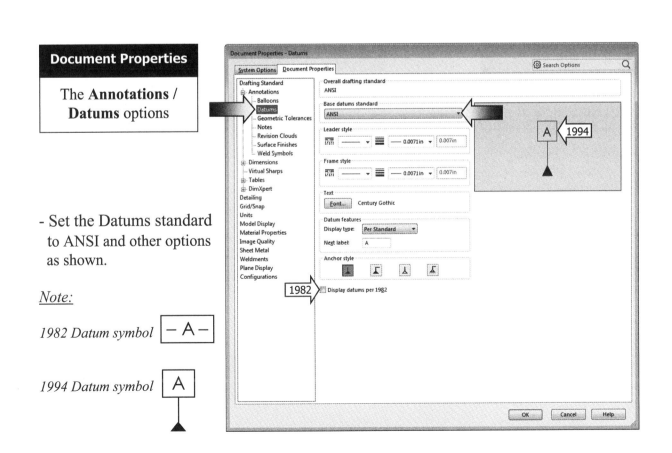

Document Properties

The **Annotations / Geo. Tol.** options

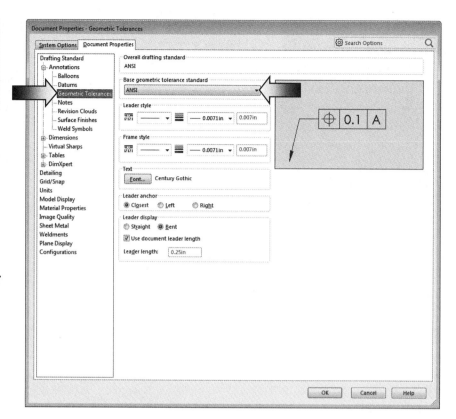

- Set the Geometric-Tolerance standard to ANSI.

- The Font selection should match the other options for all annotations.

Document Properties

The **Annotations / Notes** options

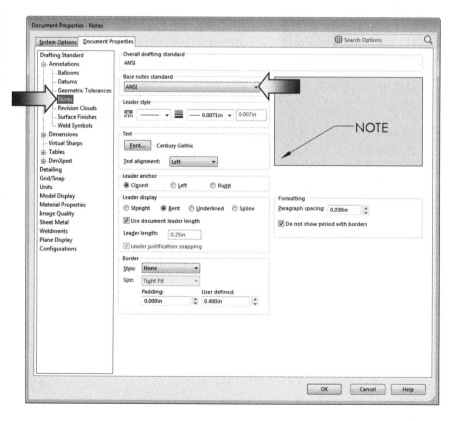

- Set the Notes standard to ANSI.

- Use the same settings for Font and Leader display.

SOLIDWORKS 2016 I Basic Tools I Document Templates

Document Properties

The **Revision Clouds**
options

- Use Revision Clouds to
call attention to geometry
changes in a drawing.

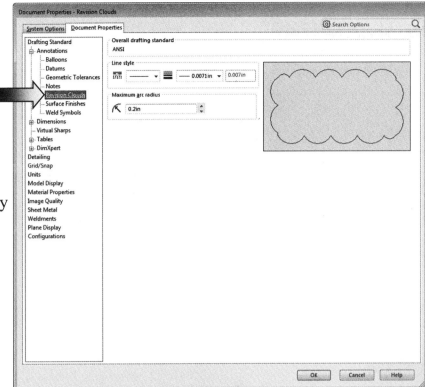

Document Properties

The **Surface Finishes**
options

- Set the Surface Finish
standard to ANSI and
set the Leader Display
to match the ones in
the previous options.

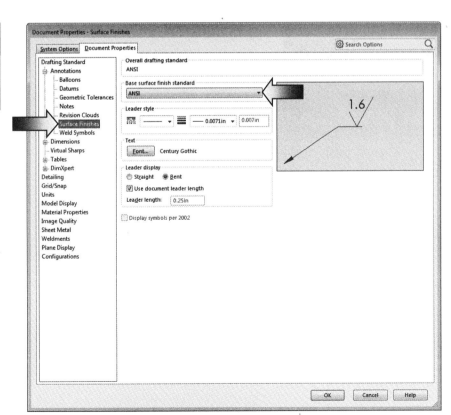

Document Properties
The **Annotations /** **Weld Symbols** options

- Set the Weld Symbols standard to ANSI.

- Clear the Fixed Size Weld Symbols check-box to scale the size of the symbol to the symbol font size.

Document Properties
The **Dimensions** options

- Continue with setting the options as shown in the next dialog boxes.

- The document-level drafting standard settings for all dimensions are set here.

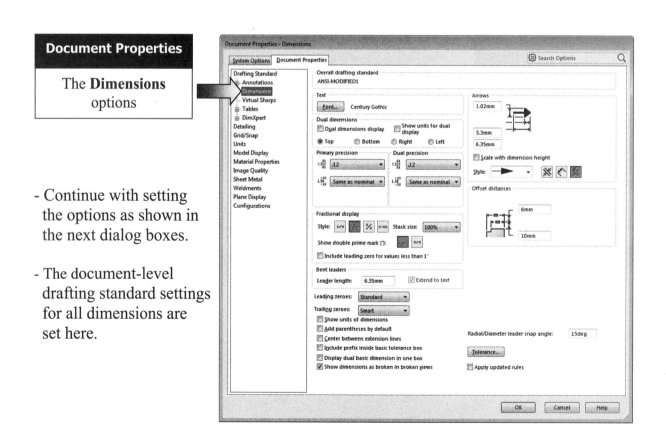

Document Properties

The **Dimensions** /
Angle options

- Set the Angle Dimension
standard to ANSI and set
the other options shown.

- Set the number of decimal
places for angular
dimensions based on your
company's standard
practices.

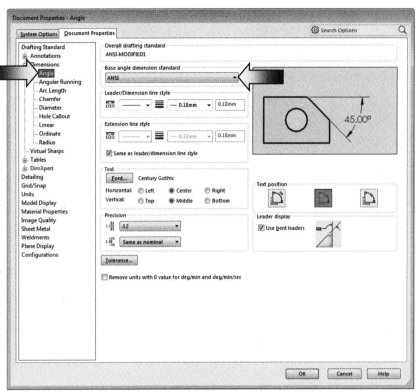

Document Properties

The **Angular
Running** options

- A set of dimensions
measured from a zero-
degree dimension in a
sketch or drawing.

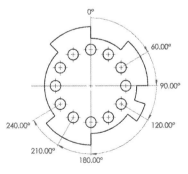

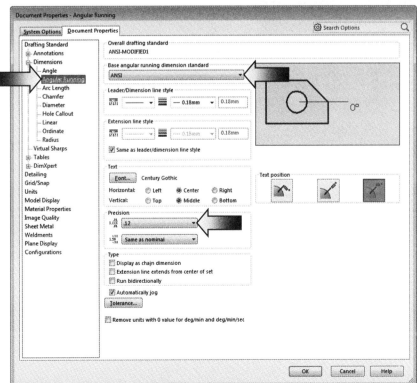

- Set Precision to 3 decimals.

Document Properties

The **Dimensions / Arc Length** options

- Set the Arc Length dimension standard to ANSI, Primary Precision to 3 decimals, and Dual Precision to 2 decimals.

- The Arc Length dimension is created by holding the Control key and clicking the arc and both of its endpoints.

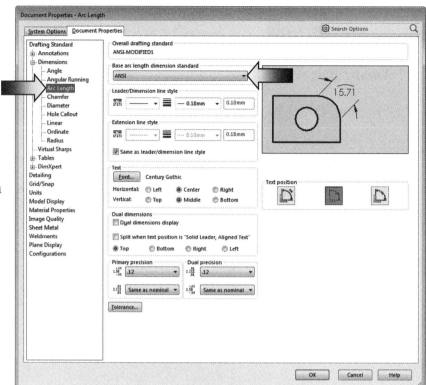

Document Properties

The **Dimensions / Chamfer** options

- Set the Chamfer-Dimension standard to ANSI and the Primary-Precision to 3 decimals.

- Set other options shown.

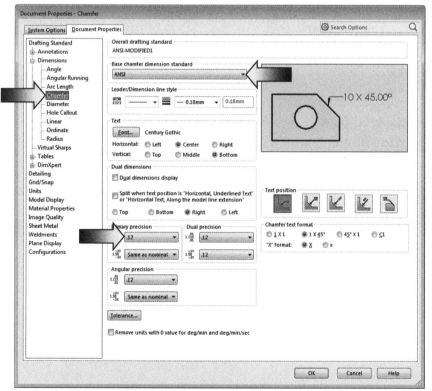

Document Properties

The **Dimensions** /
Diameter options

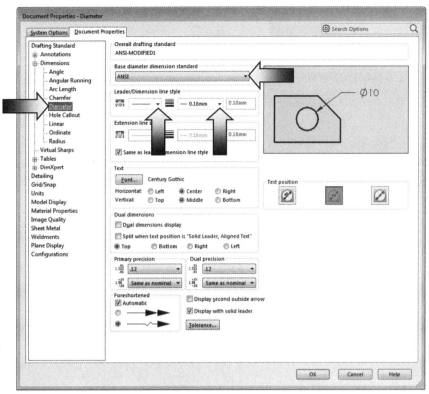

- Set the Diameter-
Dimension standard to
ANSI.

- Set the Leader Style and
thickness here.

- Set other options shown.

Document Properties

The **Dimensions** /
Hole Callout options

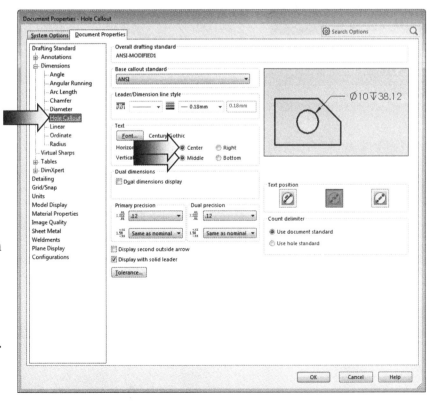

- Set the Hole Callout
Dimension standard
to ANSI.

- Set the Text justification
positions to Center and
Middle.

- Set other options shown.

Document Properties

The **Dimensions /
Linear** options

- Set the Linear Dimension
standard to ANSI.

- Enable the Use Bent-
Leader checkbox.

- Set other options shown.

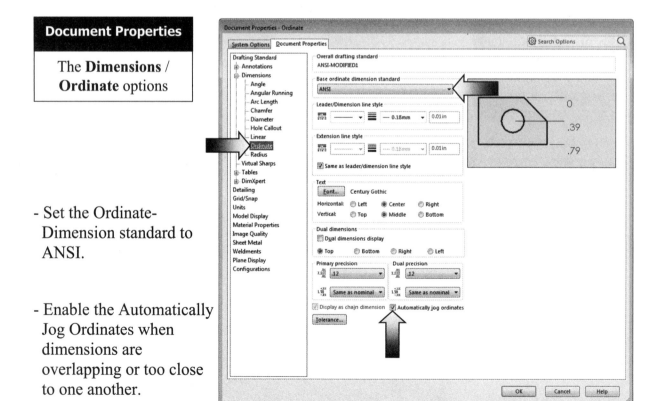

Document Properties

The **Dimensions /
Ordinate** options

- Set the Ordinate-
Dimension standard to
ANSI.

- Enable the Automatically
Jog Ordinates when
dimensions are
overlapping or too close
to one another.

Document Properties

The **Dimensions /
Radius** options

- Set the Radius-
Dimension standard
to ANSI.

- Enable the Display With
Solid Leader Checkbox.

- Set other options shown.

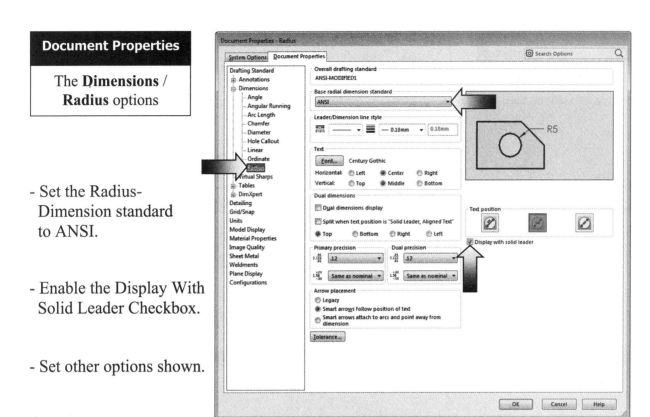

Document Properties

The **Virtual Sharps**
options

- Select the Plus
symbol for Virtual
Sharp (the intersection
between the two
entities).

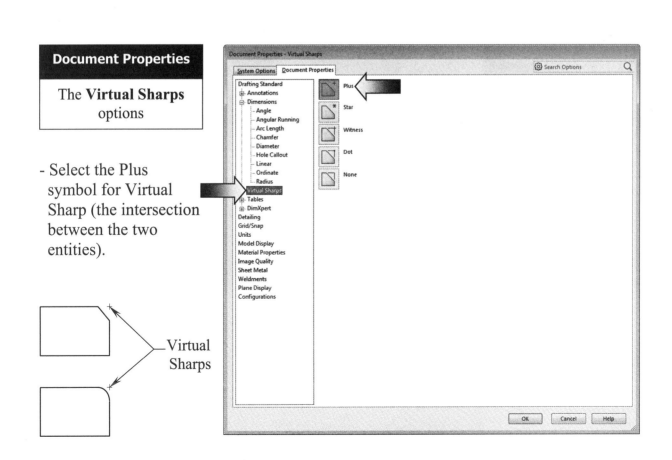

Virtual
Sharps

Document Properties

The **Tables** options

- Set the Font Style to Century Gothic and Font Size to 12 Points (or whichever font options you selected earlier for Annotations and Dimensions).

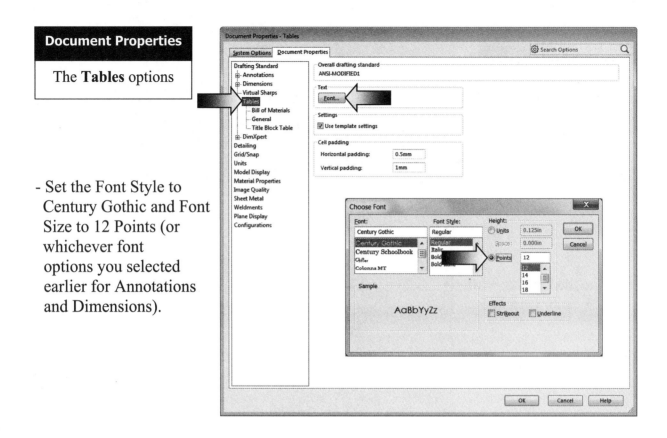

Document Properties

The **Bill of Materials** options

- Set the border for the Bill of Materials (BOM).

- Enable the Automatic Update of BOM check-box.

- Set other options shown.

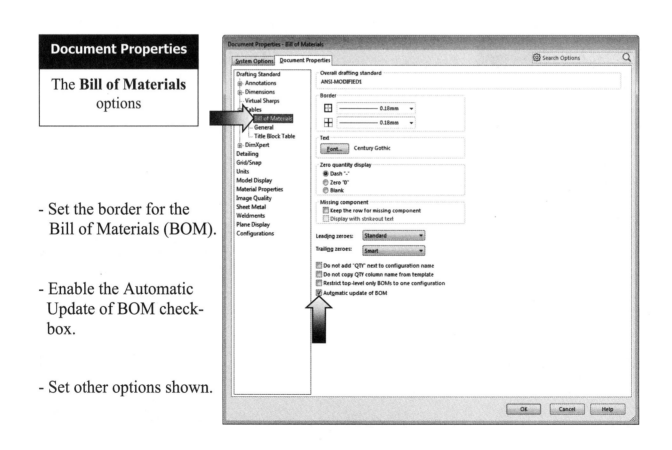

Document Properties

The **General** options

- Create a General Table to use in a drawing. The user inputs data in the cell manually.

- Set the line thickness for the border of the table here.

Document Properties

The **Title Block Table** options

- Set the border for the Title Block Table.

- Set the Thickness and the Font for the Title Block Table to match the BOM border.

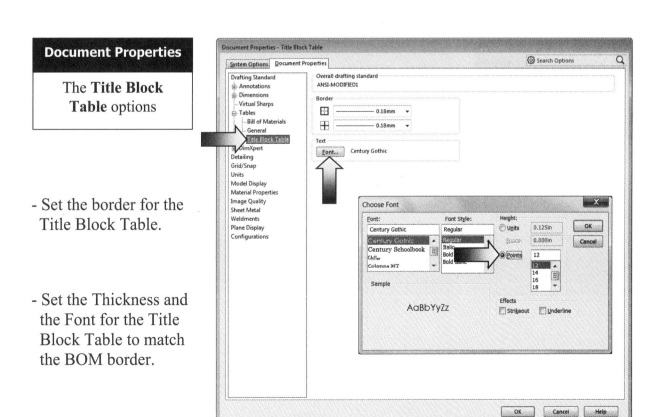

Document Properties

The **DimXpert**
options

- Set the DimXpert to
  your company's
  specifications.

- **Block Tolerance** is a
  common form of
  tolerancing used with
  inch units.

- **General Tolerance** is a
  common form of
  tolerancing used with
  metric units in conjunction
  with the ISO standard.

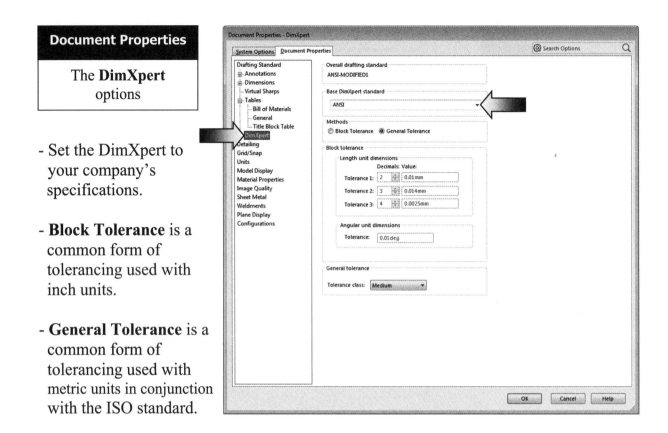

Document Properties

The **Size Dimension**
options

- Set per company Std.

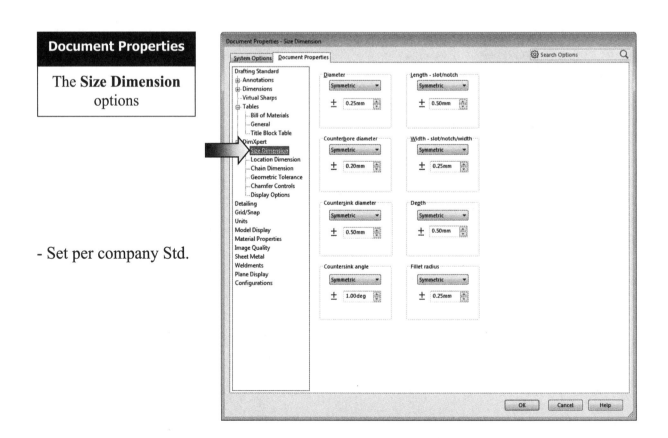

Document Properties

The **Location-Dimension** options

- Set per company Std.

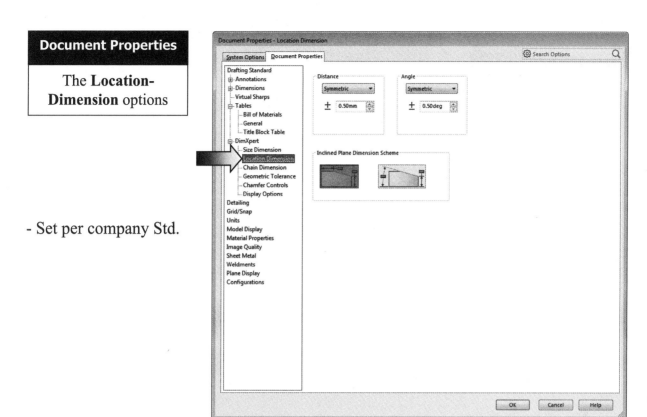

Document Properties

The **Chain Dimension** options

- Set per company Std.

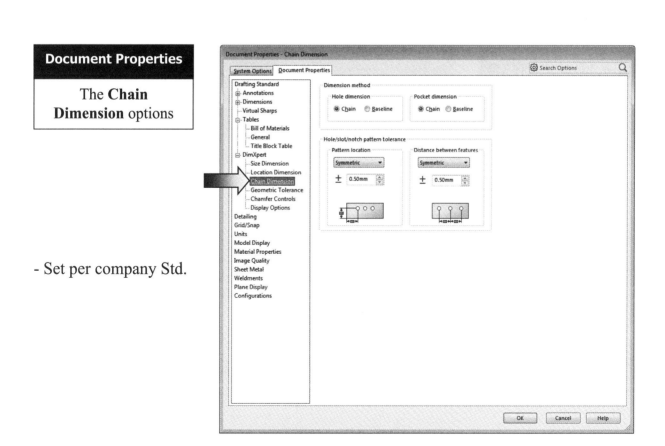

Document Properties

The **Geometric-Tolerance** options

- Set per company Std.

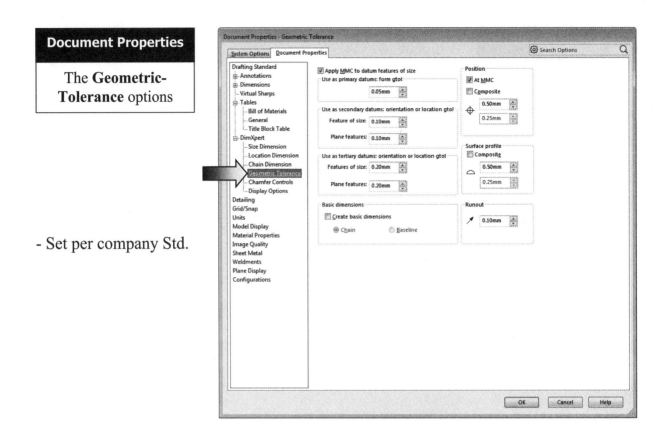

Document Properties

The **Chamfer-Controls** options

- Set per company Std.

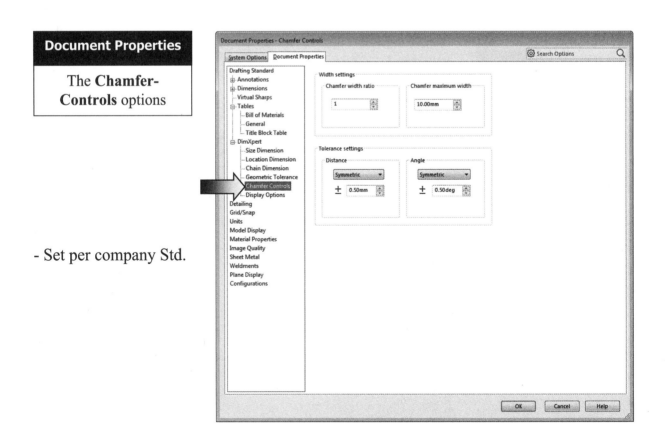

Document Properties

The **Display** options

- Set per company Std.

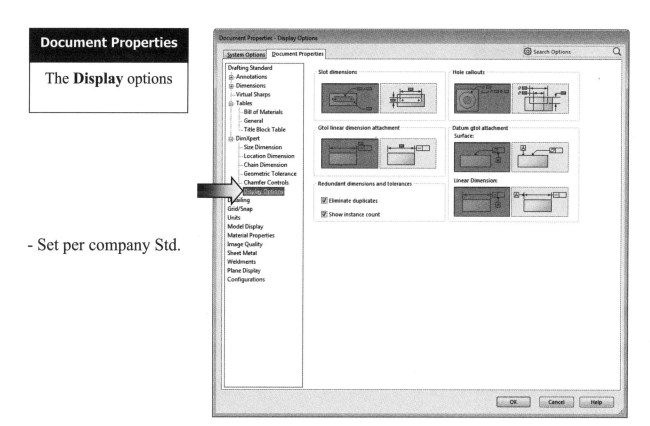

Document Properties

The **Detailing** options

- Set the Detailing options.

- The option that keeps
the text from changing
its size when zooming in
or out should be enabled.
(Always display text at
the same size.)

- Set other options shown.

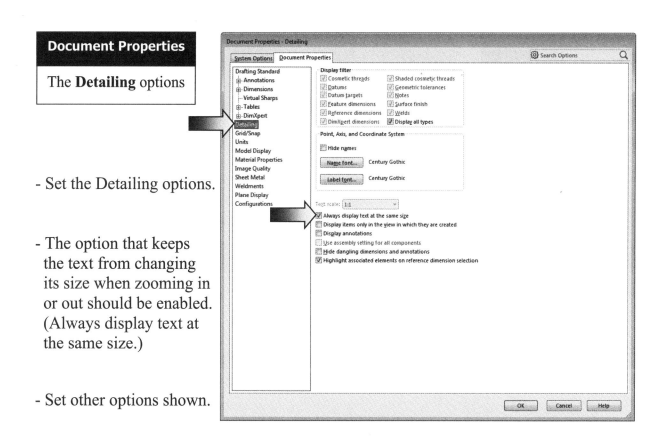

Document Properties

The **Grid/Snap** options

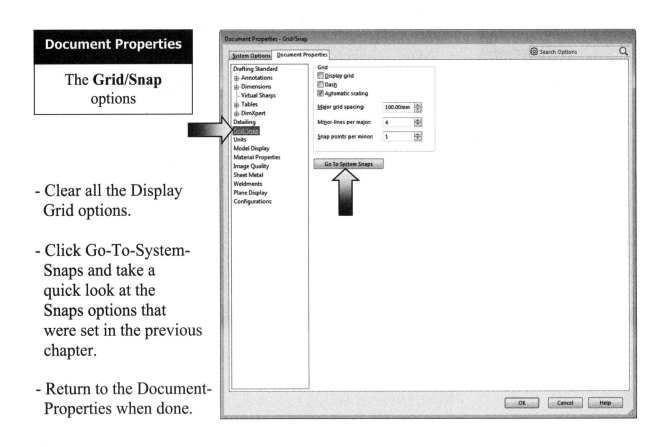

- Clear all the Display Grid options.

- Click Go-To-System-Snaps and take a quick look at the Snaps options that were set in the previous chapter.

- Return to the Document-Properties when done.

Document Properties

The **Units** options

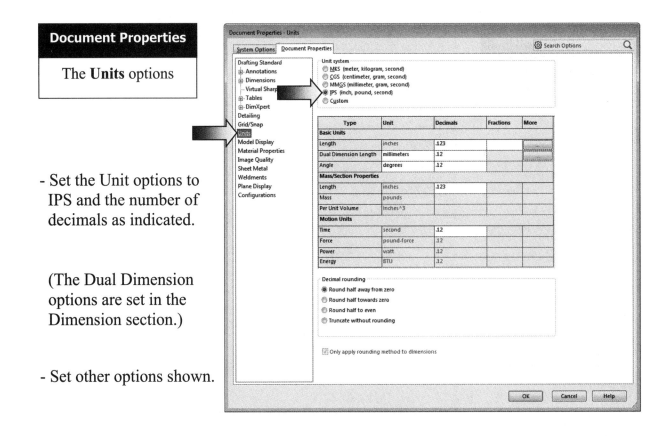

- Set the Unit options to IPS and the number of decimals as indicated.

(The Dual Dimension options are set in the Dimension section.)

- Set other options shown.

Document Properties

The **Model Display** options

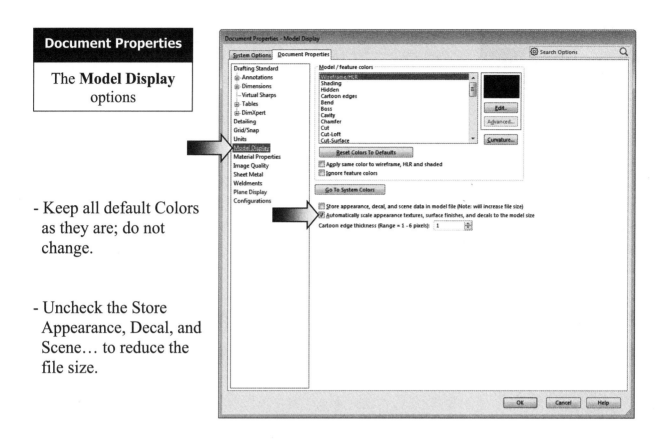

- Keep all default Colors as they are; do not change.

- Uncheck the Store Appearance, Decal, and Scene… to reduce the file size.

Document Properties

The **Material Properties** options

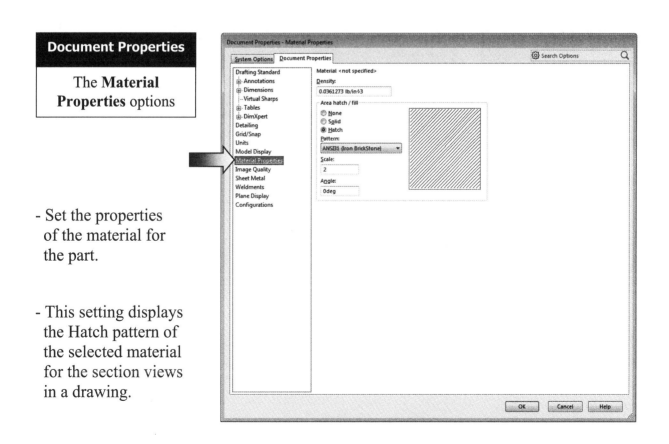

- Set the properties of the material for the part.

- This setting displays the Hatch pattern of the selected material for the section views in a drawing.

Document Properties

The **Image Quality** options

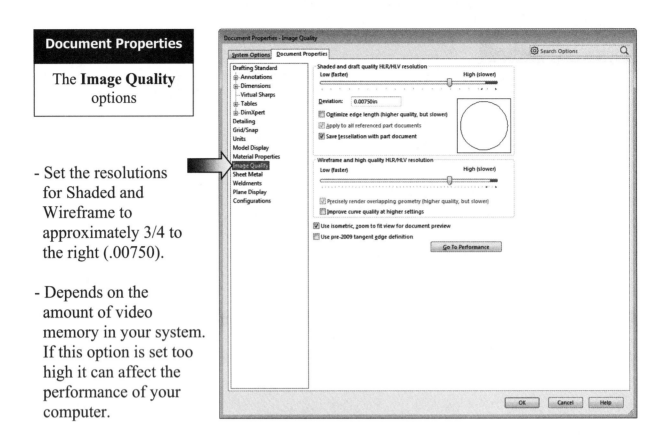

- Set the resolutions for Shaded and Wireframe to approximately 3/4 to the right (.00750).

- Depends on the amount of video memory in your system. If this option is set too high it can affect the performance of your computer.

Document Properties

The **Sheet Metal** options

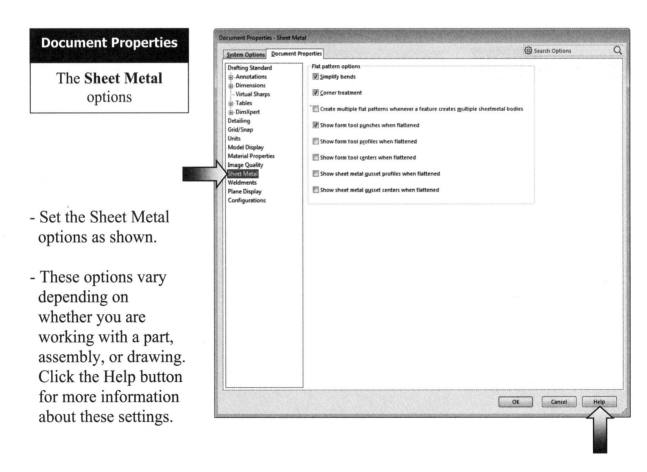

- Set the Sheet Metal options as shown.

- These options vary depending on whether you are working with a part, assembly, or drawing. Click the Help button for more information about these settings.

Document Properties

The **Weldments**
options

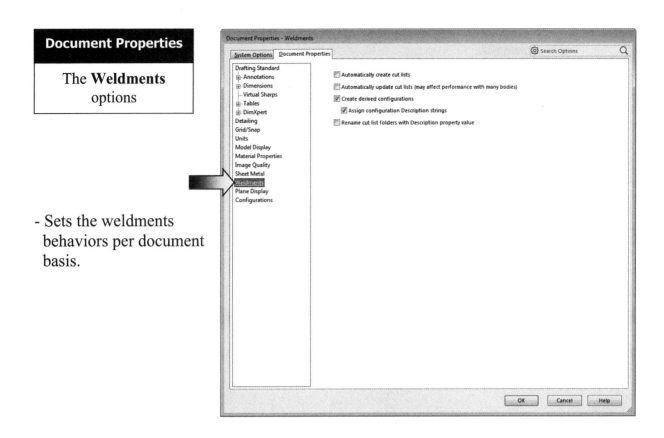

- Sets the weldments
behaviors per document
basis.

Document Properties

The **Plane Display**
options

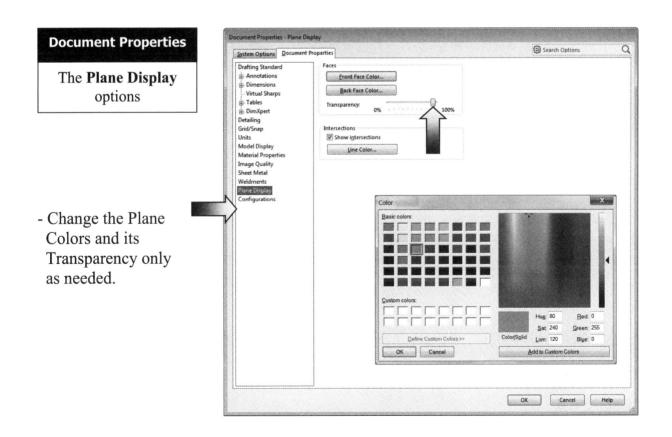

- Change the Plane
Colors and its
Transparency only
as needed.

Document Properties
The **Configurations** option

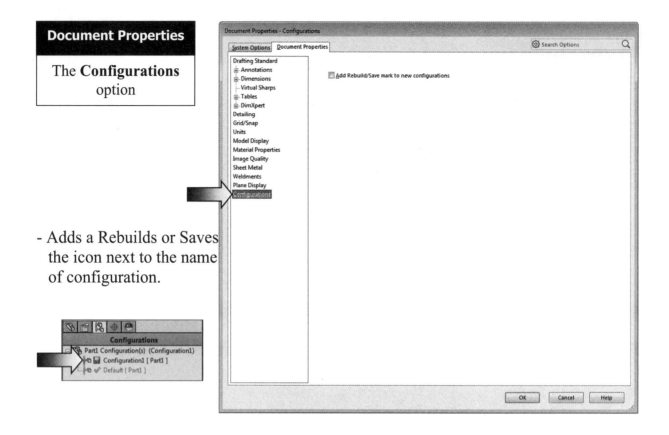

- Adds a Rebuilds or Saves
  the icon next to the name
  of configuration.

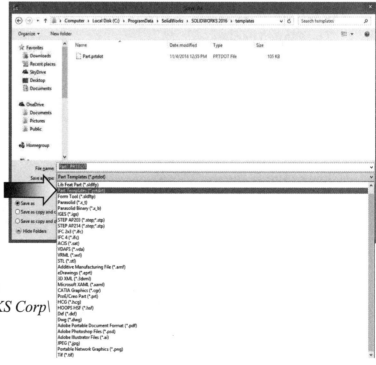

Saving the settings as a Part Template:

- These settings should be saved
  within the Document Template
  for use in future documents.

- Click **File / Save As.**

- Change the Save-As-Type to
  Part Templates (*.prtdot or
  part document template).

- Enter **Part-Inch.prtdot** for
  the file name.

- Save either in the default Templates
  folder *(C:\ProgramData\SOLIDWORKS Corp\
  SOLIDWORKS\Data\ Templates).*

- Click **Save**.

Questions for Review

Document Templates

1. The ANSI dimensioning standard (American National Standards Institute) can be set and saved in the System Options.
   - a. True
   - b. False

2. The size of dimension arrows can be controlled globally from the Document Templates.
   - a. True
   - b. False

3. The balloon's size and shape can be set and saved in the Document Templates.
   - a. True
   - b. False

4. Dimension and note fonts can be changed and edited both locally and globally.
   - a. True
   - b. False

5. The Grid option is only available in the drawing environment, not in the part or assembly.
   - a. True
   - b. False

6. The number of decimal places can be set up to 10 digits.
   - a. True
   - b. False

7. The feature colors can be pre-set and saved in the Document Templates.
   - a. True
   - b. False

8. The display quality of the model can be adjusted using the settings in the Image Quality option.
   - a. True
   - b. False

9. The plane colors and transparency can be set and saved in the Document Templates.
   - a. True
   - b. False

	9. TRUE
8. TRUE	7. TRUE
6. FALSE	5. FALSE
4. TRUE	3. TRUE
2. TRUE	1. FALSE

CHAPTER 3

Basic Solid Modeling – Extrude Options

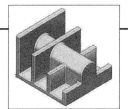

Basic Solid Modeling
Extrude Options

- Upon successful completion of this lesson, you will be able to:

  * Sketch on planes and/or planar surfaces.

  * Use the sketch tools to construct geometry.

  * Add the geometric relations or constraints.

  * Add/modify dimensions.

  * Explore the different extrude options.

- The following 5 basic steps will be demonstrated throughout this exercise:

  * Select the sketch plane.

  * Activate Sketch pencil ▢ .

  * Sketch the profile using the sketch tools ▢ ▢ ▢ .

  * Define the profile with dimensions ▢ or relations ▢ .

  * Extrude the profile ▢ .

- Be sure to review the self-test questionnaires at the end of the lesson, prior to moving to the next chapter.

Basic Solid Modeling
Extrude Options

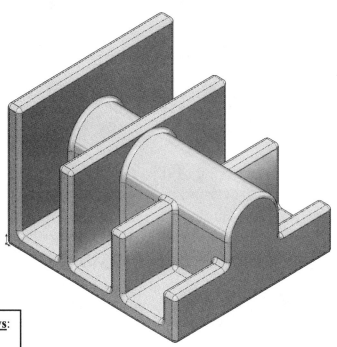

View Orientation Hot Keys:

Ctrl + 1 = Front View
Ctrl + 2 = Back View
Ctrl + 3 = Left View
Ctrl + 4 = Right View
Ctrl + 5 = Top View
Ctrl + 6 = Bottom View
Ctrl + 7 = Isometric View
Ctrl + 8 = Normal To
        Selection

Dimensioning Standards: **ANSI**

Units: **INCHES** – 3 Decimals

Tools Needed:

 Insert Sketch

 Line

 Circle

 Add Geometric Relations

 Dimension

 Sketch Fillet

 Trim Entities

 Boss / Base Extrude

1. Starting a new Part:

- From the **File** menu, select **New / Part**, or click the **New** icon.

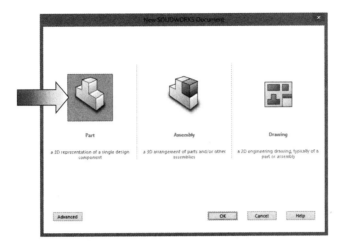

- Select the **Part** template from either the Templates or Tutorial folders.

- Click **OK** [OK]; a new part template is opened.

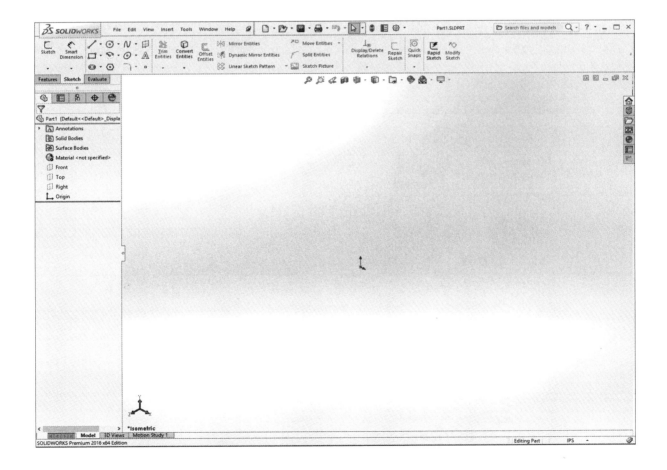

2. Changing the Scene:

- From the View (Heads-up) toolbar, click the Apply Scene button (arrow) and select the **Plain White** option (arrow).

- By changing the scene color to Plain White we can better see the colors of the sketch entities and their dimensions.

- To show the Origin, click the **View** dropdown menu and select **Origins**.

- The Blue Origin is the Zero position of the part and the Red Origin is the Zero position of a sketch.

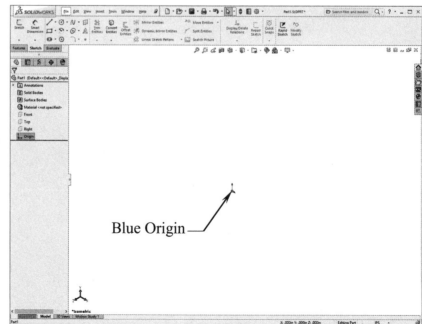

3. Starting a new Sketch:

- Select the <u>Front</u> plane from the Feature-Manager tree and click the **Pencil** icon  to start a new sketch.

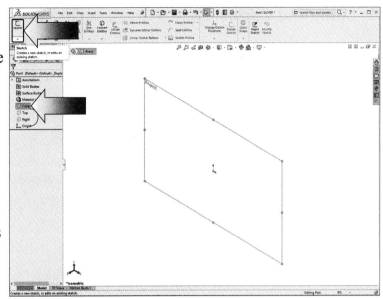

- A sketch is normally created first, relations and dimensions are added after, and then it gets extruded into a 3D feature.

- From the Command-Manager toolbar, select the **Line** command.

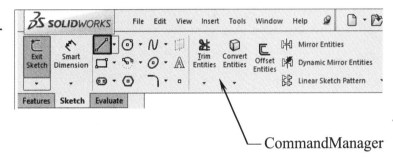

CommandManager

Mouse Gesture

OPTION:
Right-Drag to display the Mouse Gesture guide and select the Line command from it. (See the Introduction section, page XVIII for details on customizing the Mouse Gesture.)

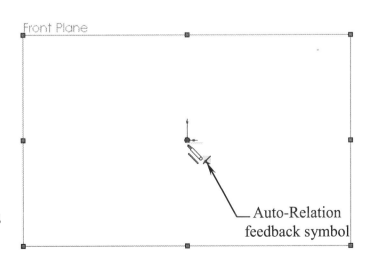

Auto-Relation feedback symbol

- Hover the mouse cursor over the Origin point; a yellow feedback symbol appears to indicate a relation (Coincident) is going to be added automatically to the 1st endpoint of the line. This endpoint will be locked at the zero position.

4. Using the Click + Hold + Drag technique:

- Click at the Origin point and *hold* the mouse button to start the line at point 1, *drag upwards* to point 2, then release the mouse button.

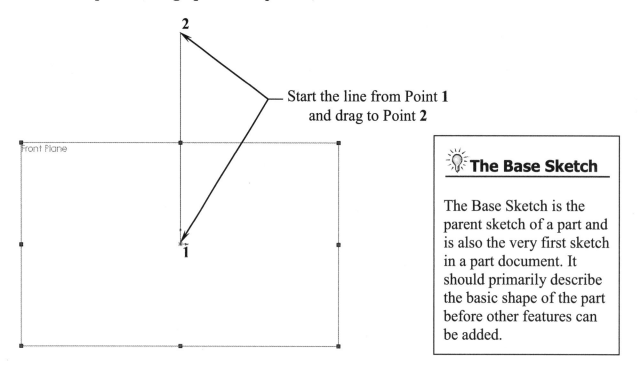

Start the line from Point **1**
and drag to Point **2**

> ### 💡 The Base Sketch
>
> The Base Sketch is the parent sketch of a part and is also the very first sketch in a part document. It should primarily describe the basic shape of the part before other features can be added.

- Continue adding other lines using the *Click-Hold-Drag* technique.

- The relations like Horizontal and Vertical are added automatically to each sketch line. Other relations like Collinear and Equal are added manually.

- The size and shape of the profile will be corrected in the next few steps.

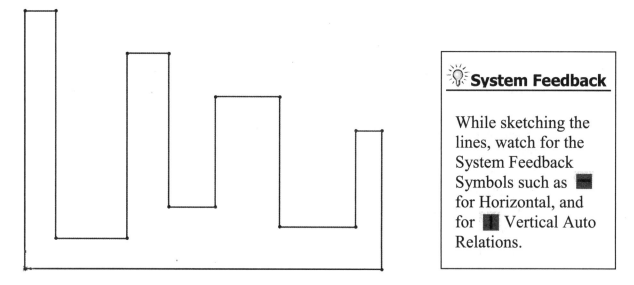

> ### 💡 System Feedback
>
> While sketching the lines, watch for the System Feedback Symbols such as ▬ for Horizontal, and for ▌ Vertical Auto Relations.

5. Adding Geometric Relations*:

- Click **Add Relation**  under Display/Delete Relations - OR - select **Tools / Relations / Add**.

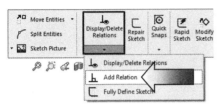

- Select the 4 lines shown below.

- Click **Equal** from the Add Geometric Relation dialog box. This relation makes the length of the two selected lines equal.

* Geometric relations are one of the most powerful features in SOLIDWORKS. They're used in the sketch level to control the behaviors of the sketch entities when they are moved or rotated and to keep the associations between one another.

When applying geometric relations between entities, one of them should be a 2D entity and the other can either be a 2D sketch entity or a model edge, a plane, an axis, or a curve, etc.

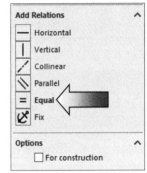

Equal Relations

Adding the EQUAL relations to these lines eliminates the need to dimension each line.

Geometric relations can be created manually or automatically. The next few steps in this chapter will demonstrate how geometric relations are added manually.

Select the top 4 lines and click Equal relation.

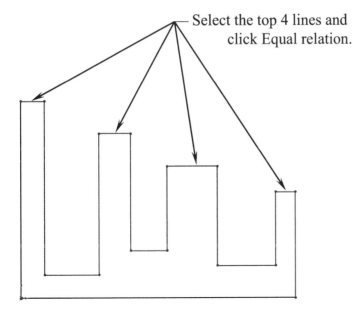

The top 4 lines are now Equal in size.

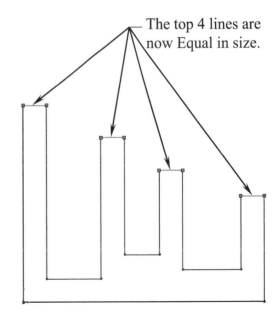

6. Adding a Collinear relation**:

- Select the **Add Relation** ⌐h command again.

- Select the 3 lines as shown below.

- Click **Collinear** from the Add Geometric Relations dialog box.

- Click **OK** ✅.

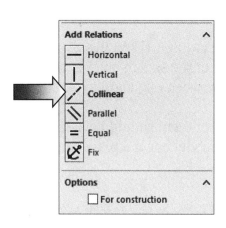

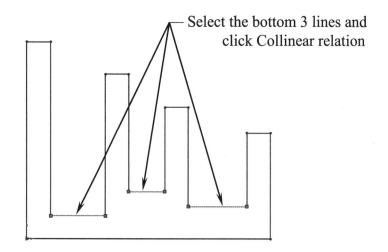

Select the bottom 3 lines and click Collinear relation

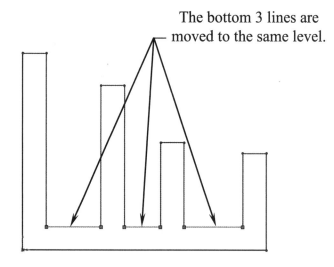

The bottom 3 lines are moved to the same level.

💡 Collinear Relations

Adding a Collinear relation to these lines puts them on the same height level; only one dimension is needed to drive the height of all 3 lines.

** Collinear relations can be used to constrain the geometry as follows:

- Collinear between a line and another line(s) (2D and 2D).

- Collinear between a line(s) to a linear edge of a model (2D and 3D).

Geometric Relations Examples

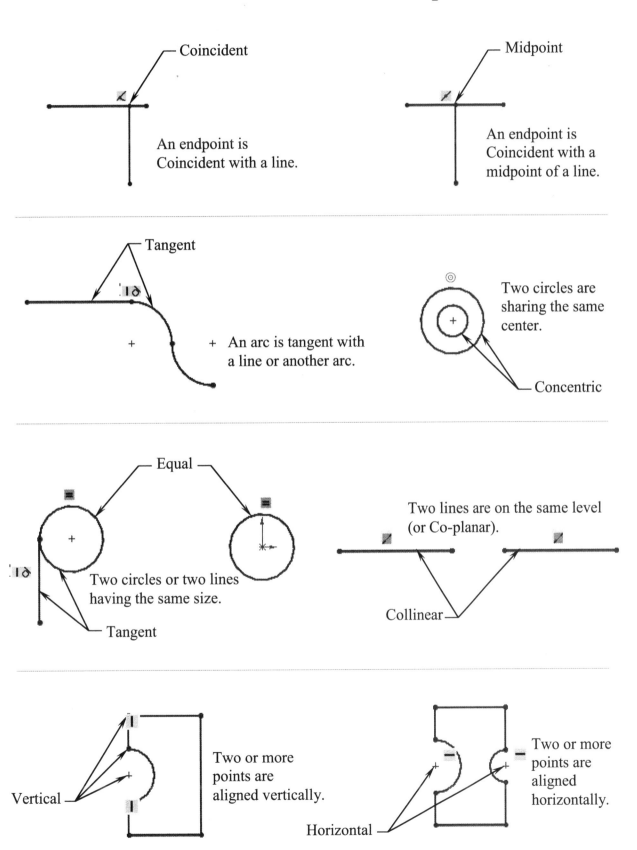

Coincident

An endpoint is Coincident with a line.

Midpoint

An endpoint is Coincident with a midpoint of a line.

Tangent

An arc is tangent with a line or another arc.

Two circles are sharing the same center.

Concentric

Equal

Two circles or two lines having the same size.

Tangent

Two lines are on the same level (or Co-planar).

Collinear

Vertical

Two or more points are aligned vertically.

Horizontal

Two or more points are aligned horizontally.

7. Adding the horizontal dimensions:

- Select 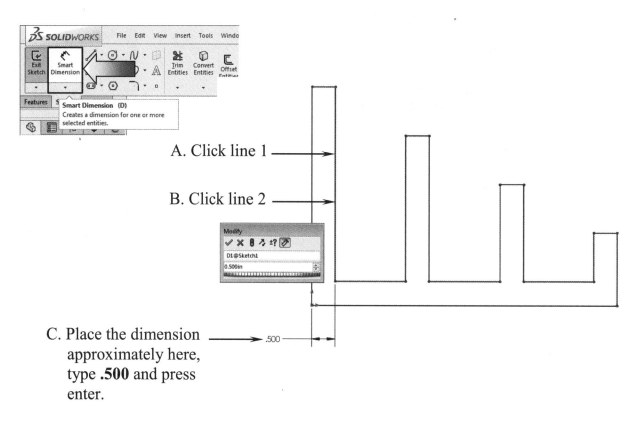 from the Sketch toolbar - OR - select **Insert / Dimension**, and add the dimensions shown below (follow the 3 steps A, B and C).

A. Click line 1

B. Click line 2

C. Place the dimension approximately here, type **.500** and press enter.

- The Inch-Units is filled in automatically because it has been set previously to Inches, 3 decimal places.

- Continue adding the horizontal dimensions as shown here.

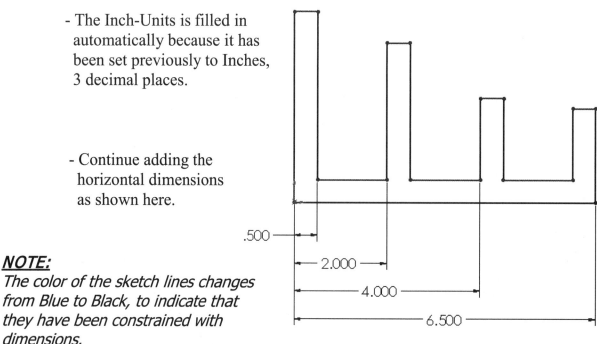

NOTE:
The color of the sketch lines changes from Blue to Black, to indicate that they have been constrained with dimensions.

8. Adding the Vertical dimensions:

- With the Smart-Dimension tool still selected, click on line 1 and line 2; place the dimension approximately as shown, and change the value to **.500 in**.

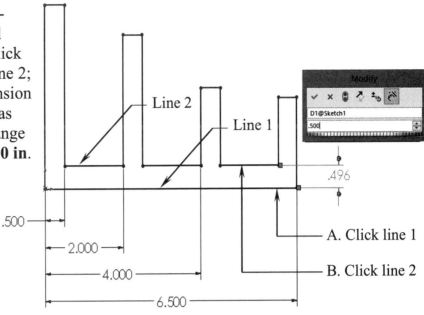

- Continue adding other dimensions until the entire sketch turns into the Black color.

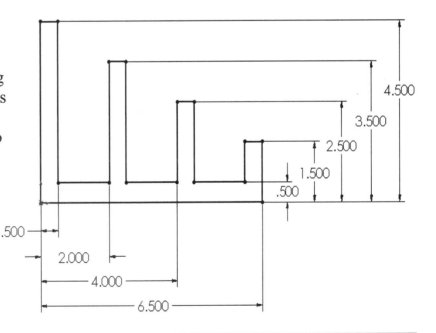

The Status of a Sketch:

The current status of a sketch is displayed in the lower right corner of the screen.

Fully Defined	=	**Black**	Fully Defined
Under Defined	=	**Blue**	Under Defined
Over Defined	=	**Red**	Over Defined

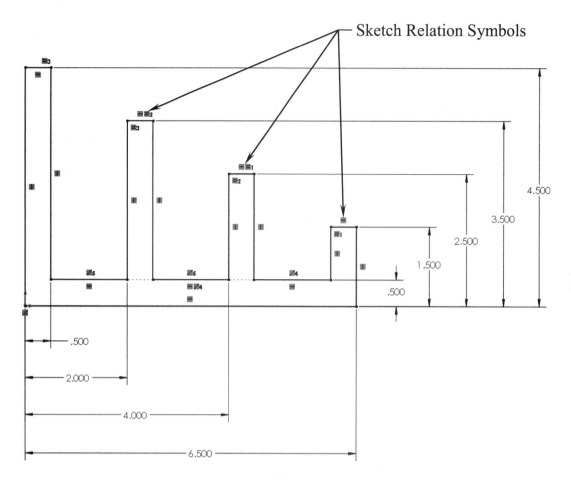

Sketch Relation Symbols

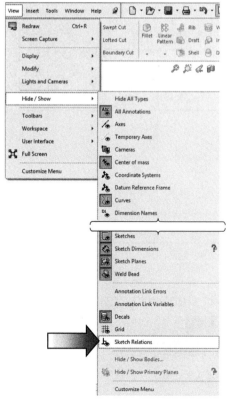

9. Hiding the Sketch Relation Symbols:

- The Sketch Relation Symbols indicates which geometric relation a sketch entity has, but they get quite busy as shown.

- To hide or show the Sketch Relation Symbols, go to the **View** menu and Click off the **Sketch Relations** option.

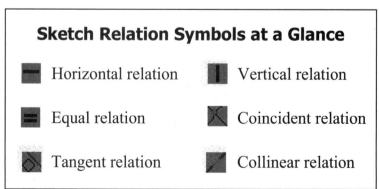

Sketch Relation Symbols at a Glance

▬	Horizontal relation	▌	Vertical relation
▬	Equal relation	✕	Coincident relation
◈	Tangent relation	◢	Collinear relation

10. Extruding the Base:

- The **Extrude Boss/Base** command is used to define the characteristic of a 3D linear feature.

- Click ⬚ from the Features toolbar OR select **Insert / Boss Base / Extrude**.

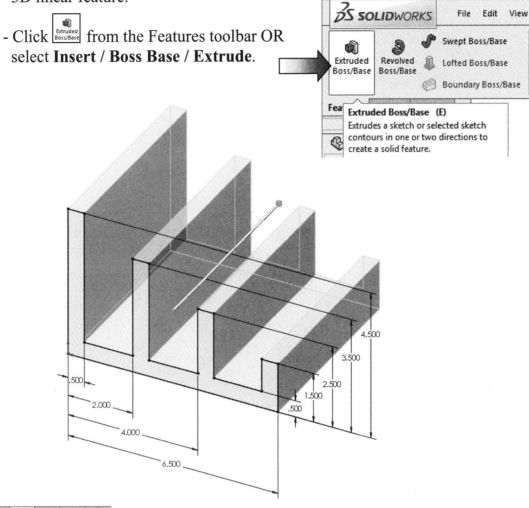

- Set the following:

- Direction: **Blind**.

- Depth: **6.00 in**.

- Enabled **Reverse** direction.

- Click **OK** ✅.

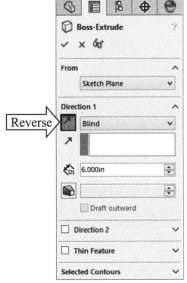

11. Sketching on a Planar Face:

- Select the face as indicated.

- Click [Sketch] or select **Insert/Sketch** and press the shortcut keys **Ctrl+7** to change to the Isometric view.

- Select the **Circle** command [⊙] from the Sketch Tools toolbar.

Select the
Sketch Face

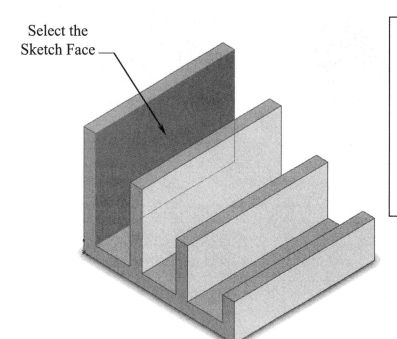

> 💡 **Planar Surfaces**
>
> - A planar surface of the model can also be used as a Sketch Plane.
>
> - The Sketch will then be extruded normal to the selected surface.

- Position the mouse cursor near the center of the selected face, and click and drag outward to draw a circle.

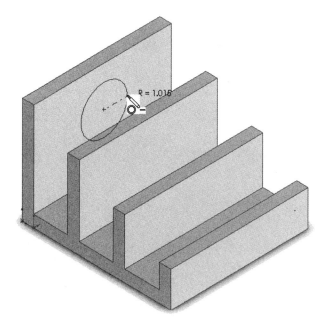

- While sketching the circle, the system displays the radius value next to the mouse cursor.

- Dimensions are added after the profile is created.

- Select the **Smart Dimension**
command 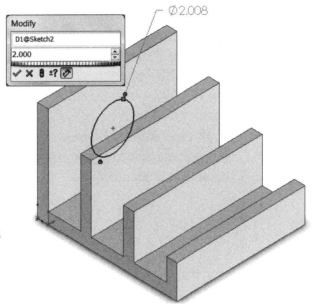 and add a
diameter dimension to the
circle.

(Click on the circle and move
the mouse cursor outward at
approximately 45 degrees, and
place the dimension).

- To add the location dimensions
click the edge of the circle and
the edge of the model, place
the dimension, then correct
the value.

- Continue adding the location
dimensions as shown to fully
define the sketch.

- Select the Line command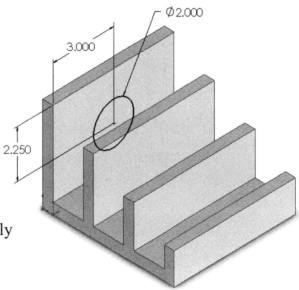
and sketch the 3 lines as shown
below. Snap to the hidden edge
of the model when it lights up.

- The color of the sketch should
change to black at this point (Fully
Defined).

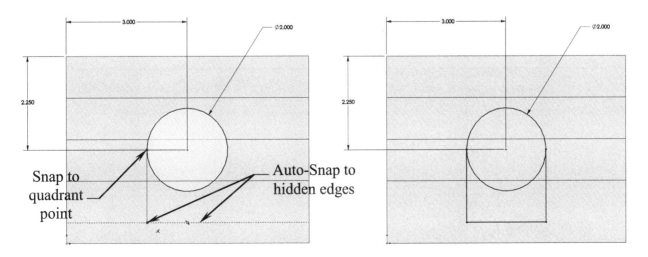

Snap to quadrant point — Auto-Snap to hidden edges

12. Using the Trim Entities command:

- Select the **Trim Entities** command from the Sketch toolbar (arrow).

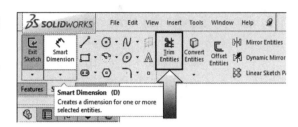

- Click the **Trim to Closest** option (arrow). When the pointer is hovered over the entities, this trim command highlights the entities prior to trimming to the next intersection.

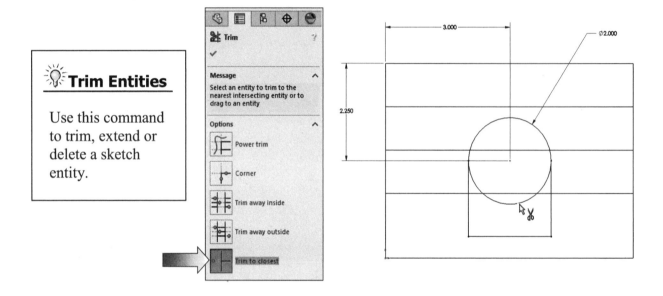

> **Trim Entities**
>
> Use this command to trim, extend or delete a sketch entity.

- Hover the pointer over the lower portion of the circle, the portion that is going to be trimmed-off lights up. Click the mouse button to trim.

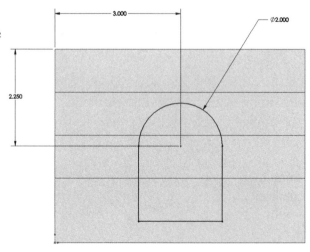

- The bottom portion of the circle is trimmed, leaving the sketch as one-continuous-closed-profile, suitable to extrude into a feature.

- Next, we are going to look at some of the extrude options available in SOLIDWORKS.

13. Extruding a Boss:

- Switch to the Feature toolbar and click 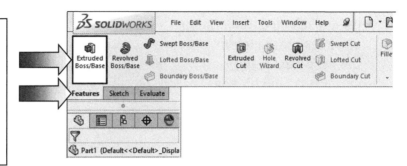 or select:
Insert / Boss-Base / Extrude.

> ### ☼ Extrude Options...
>
> Explore each extrude option to see the different results.
> Press Undo to go back to the original state after each one.

(A) Using the Blind option:

- When extruding with the Blind option, the following conditions are required:

    * Direction

    * Depth dimension

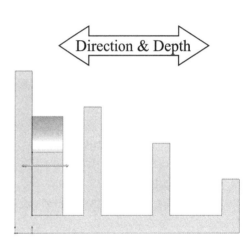

Blind
Condition

- Drag the direction arrow on the preview graphics to define the direction, then enter a dimension for the extrude depth.

(B) Using the Through All option:

- When the Through All option is selected, the system automatically extrudes the sketch to the length of the part, normal to the sketch plane.

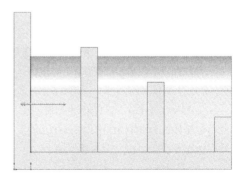

Through All
Condition

ⒸUsing the Up To Next option:

- With the Up To Next option selected, the system extrudes the sketch to the very next set of surface(s), and blends it to match.

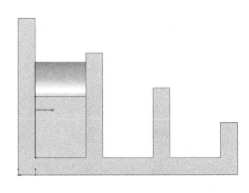

Up To Next
Condition

ⒹUsing the Up To Vertex option:

- This option extrudes the sketch from its plane to a vertex, specified by the user, to define its depth.

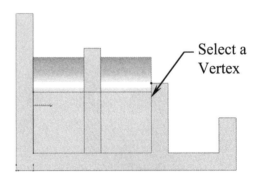

Select a Vertex

Up To Vertex
Condition

ⒺUsing the Up To Surface option:

- This option extrudes the sketch from its plane to a single surface, to define its depth.

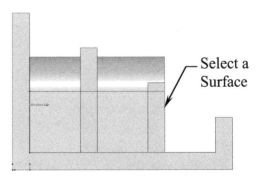

Select a Surface

Up To Surface
Condition

(F) Using the Offset From Surface option:

- This option extrudes the sketch from its plane to a selected face, then offsets at a specified distance.

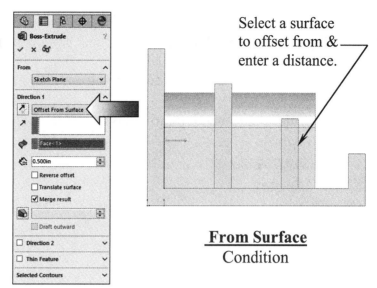

Select a surface to offset from & enter a distance.

From Surface
Condition

(G) Using the Up To Body option:

- This option extrudes the sketch from its sketch plane to a specified body.

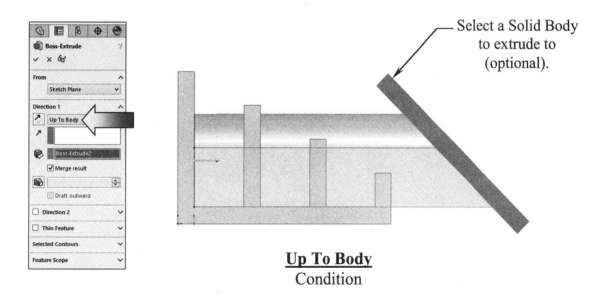

Select a Solid Body to extrude to (optional).

Up To Body
Condition

- The Up To Body option can also be used in assemblies or multi-body parts.

- The Up To Body option works with either a solid body or a surface body.

- It is also useful when making extrusions in an assembly to extend a sketch to an uneven surface.

(H) **Using the Mid Plane option:**

- This option extrudes the sketch from its plane equally in both directions.

- Enter the Total Depth dimension when using the Mid-Plane option.

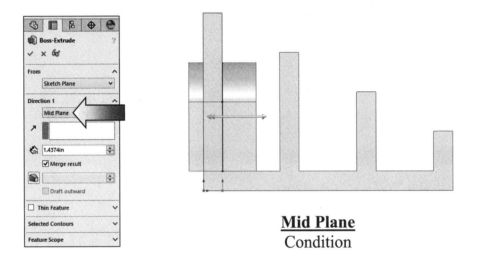

Mid Plane
Condition

- After you are done exploring all the extrude options, change the final condition to **Through All**.

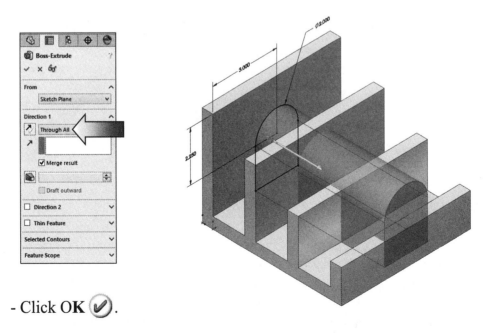

- Click OK ✔.

- The system extrudes the circle to the outermost surface as the result of the Through All end condition.

- The extra material between the first and the second extruded features is removed automatically.

- Unless the Merge Result checkbox is cleared, all interferences will be detected and removed.

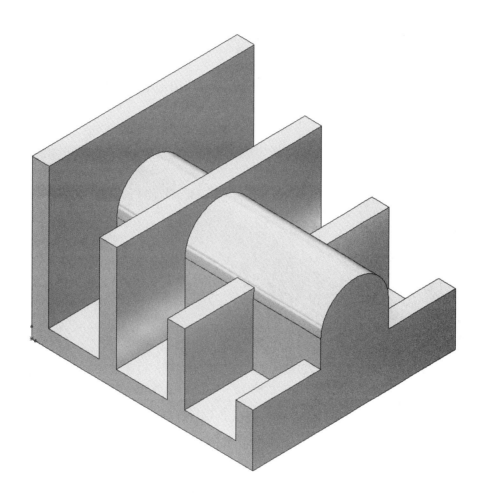

Extrude summary:

* *The Extrude Boss/Base command is used to add thickness to a sketch and to define the characteristic of a 3D feature.*

* *A sketch can be extruded in both directions at the same time, from its sketch plane.*

* *A sketch can also be extruded as a solid or a thin feature.*

14. Adding the model fillets by Lasso*:

- Fillet/Round creates a rounded internal or external face on the part. You can fillet all edges of a face, select sets of faces, edges, or edge loops.

- The **radius** value stays in effect until you change it.
  Therefore, you can select any number of edges or faces in the same operation.

- Click 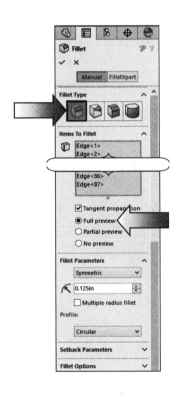 or select **Insert / Features / Fillet/Round**.

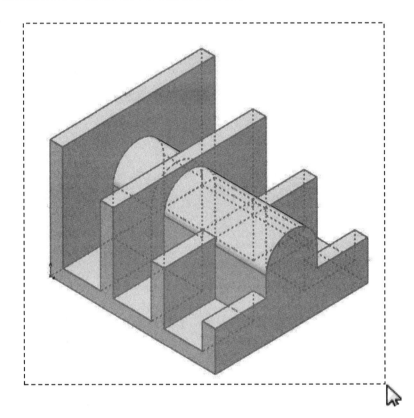

- Select the **Constant Size Fillet** button (Arrow).

- Either "drag-select" to highlight all edges of the model or press the shortcut key **Control+A** (select all).

- Enter **.125 in**. for radius size.

- Enable the **Full Preview** checkbox.

- Click **OK** ✅.

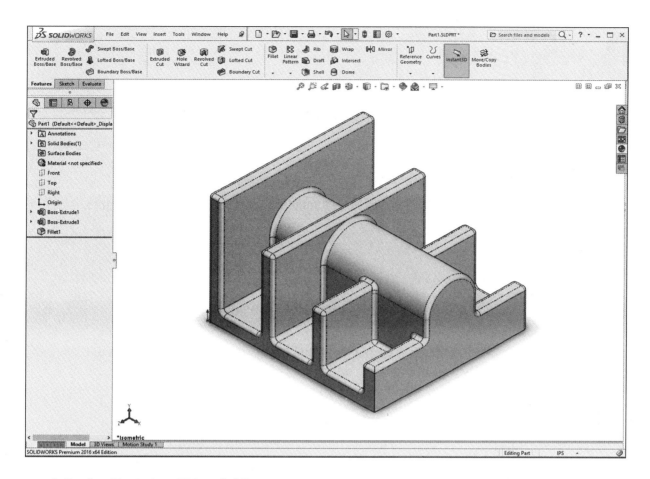

In the Training Files folder, in the <u>*Built Parts folder*</u> *you will also find copies of the parts, assemblies, and drawings that were created for cross referencing or reviewing purposes.*

* **Fillets and Rounds:**

Using the same Fillet command, SOLIDWORKS "knows" whether to add material (Fillet) or remove material (Round) to the faces adjacent to the selected edge.

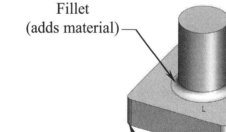

Fillet
(adds material)

Round
(removes material)

15. Saving your work:

- Select **File / Save As**.

- Change the file type to **Part** file (.sldprt).

- Enter **Extrude Options** for the name of the file.

- Click **Save**.

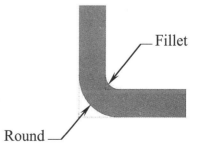

Fillet

Round

Questions for Review

Basic Solid Modeling

1. To open a new sketch, first you must select a plane from the FeatureManager tree.
    a. True
    b. False

2. Geometric relations can be used only in the assembly environments.
    a. True
    b. False

3. The current status of a sketch is displayed in the lower right area of the screen as Under defined, Fully defined, or Over defined.
    a. True
    b. False

4. Once a feature is extruded, its extrude direction cannot be changed.
    a. True
    b. False

5. A planar face can also be used as a sketch plane.
    a. True
    b. False

6. The Equal relation only works for Lines, not Circles or Arcs.
    a. True
    b. False

7. After a dimension is created, its value cannot be changed.
    a. True
    b. False

8. When the UP TO SURFACE option is selected, you have to choose a surface as an end-condition to extrude up to.
    a. True
    b. False

9. UP TO VERTEX is not a valid Extrude option.
    a. True
    b. False

1. TRUE 2. FALSE
3. TRUE 4. FALSE
5. TRUE 6. FALSE
7. FALSE 8. TRUE
9. FALSE

Using the Search Commands:

The Search Commands lets you find and run commands
from SOLIDWORKS Search or locate commands in the user interface.

These features make it easy to find and run any SOLIDWORKS command:

- The results are filtered as you type and typically find the
  command you need within a few keystrokes.

- When you run a command from the results list for a query, Search Commands
  remembers that command and places it at the top of the results list when you
  type the same query again.

- Search shortcuts let you assign simple and familiar keystroke sequences to
  commands you use regularly.

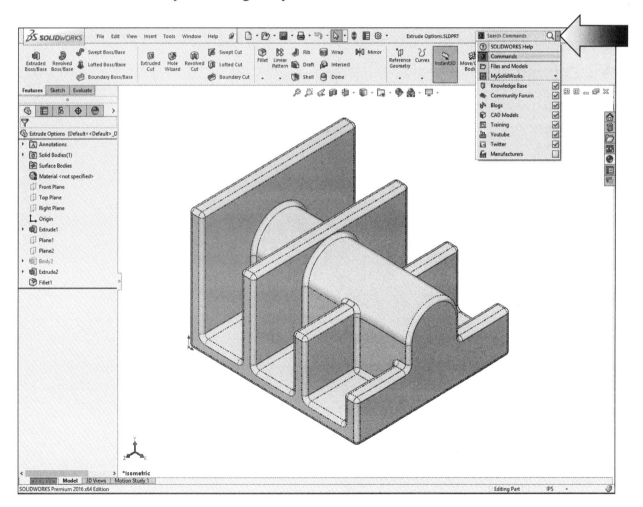

- Click the drop down arrow to see the search options (arrow).

1. Search Commands in Features Mode:

- The example below shows how you might use Search Commands to find and run the **Lasso Selection** command in the Feature Mode.

- With the part still open, start typing the command **Lasso Selection** in Search Commands. As soon as you type the first few letters of the word Lasso, the results list displays only those commands that include the character sequence **"lasso,"** and **Lasso Selection** appears near the top of the results list.

- Click **Show Command Location** ; a **red arrow** indicates the command in the user interface.

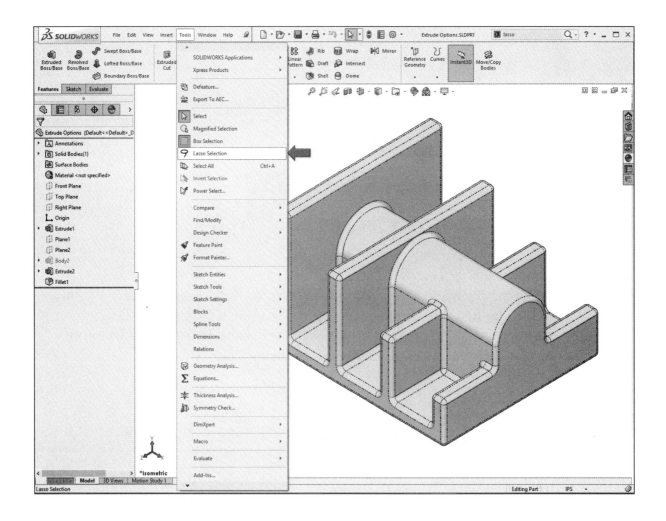

2. Search Commands in Sketch Mode:

- The example below shows how you might use Search Commands to find and run the **Dynamic Mirror** command in the <u>Sketch Mode</u>.

- Using the same part, open a **new sketch** on the <u>side face</u> of the model as noted.

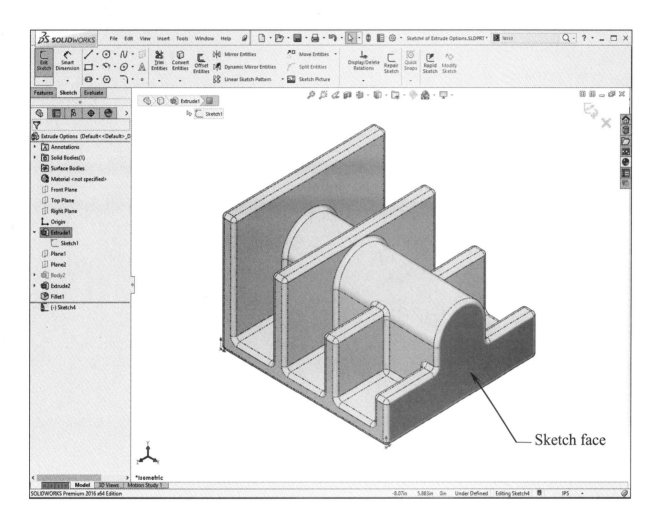

Sketch face

- Start typing the command **Dynamic Mirror** in Search Commands. As soon as you type the first few letters of the word Dynamic, the results list displays only those commands that include the character sequence **"dyna,"** and **Dynamic command** appears near the top of the results list.

- Click **Show Command Location** ; a red arrow indicates the command in the user interface.

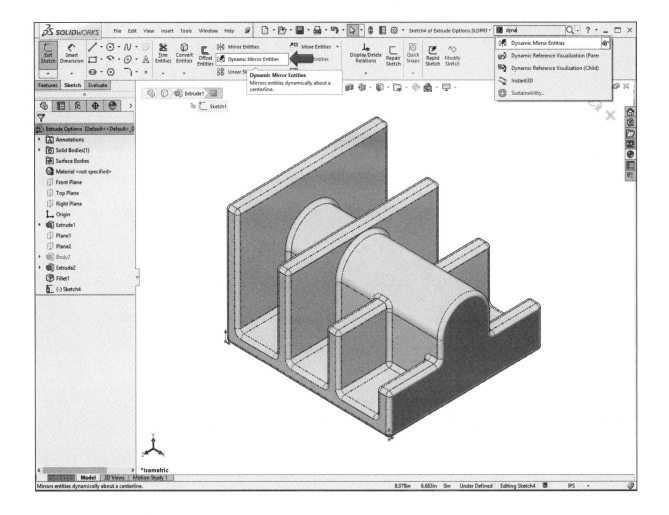

- Additionally, a Search Shortcut can be assigned to any command to help find it more quickly (see Customize Keyboard in the SOLIDWORKS Help for more info):

    1. Click **Tools / Customize**, and select the **Keyboard** tab.
    2. Navigate to the command to which you want to assign a search shortcut.
    3. In the Search Shortcut column for the command, type the shortcut letter you want to use, then click OK.

- **Save** and close all documents.

Exercise: Extrude Boss & Extrude Cut

NOTE: *In an exercise, there will be less step-by-step instruction than those in the lessons, which will give you a chance to apply what you have learned in the previous lesson to build the model on your own.*

1. Dimensions are in inches, 3 decimal places.
2. Use Mid-Plane end condition for the Base feature.
3. The part is symmetrical about the Front plane.
4. Use the instructions on the following pages if needed.

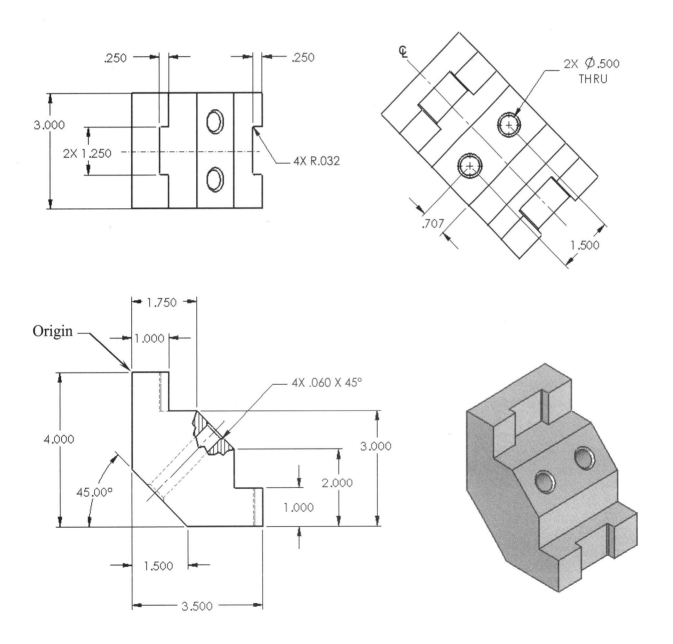

1. Starting with the base sketch:

- Select the <u>Front</u> plane and open a new sketch.

- Starting at the top left corner, using the line command, sketch the profile below.

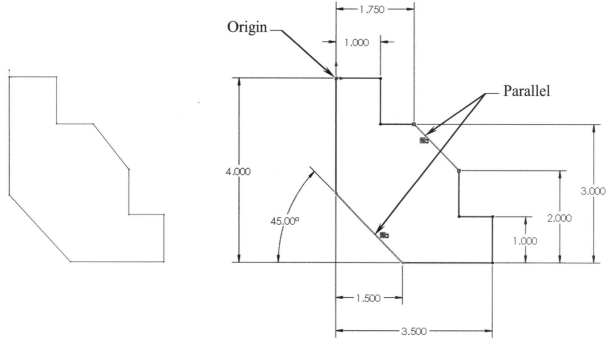

- Add the dimensions shown.

- Add the Parallel relation to fully define the sketch.

- Extrude Boss/Base with **Mid Plane** and **3.000"** in depth.

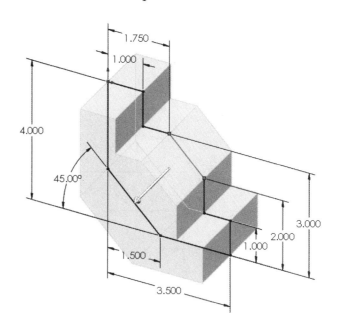

SOLIDWORKS 2016 | Basic Tools | Basic Solid Modeling – Extrude Options

2. Adding the through holes:

- Select the <u>face</u> as indicated and click the Normal-To button.

- This command rotates the part normal to the screen.

- The hot-key for this command is **Ctrl + 8**.

Select this face and click the Normal-To button

- Open a new sketch and draw a centerline that starts from the origin point.

- Sketch 2 circles on either side of the centerline.

- Add the diameter and location dimensions shown. Push Escape when done.

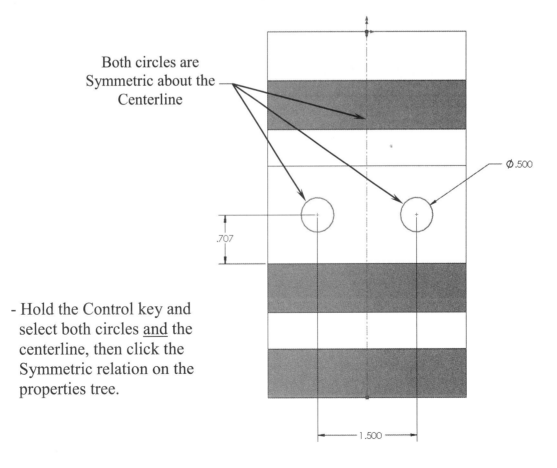

Both circles are Symmetric about the Centerline

Ø.500

.707

1.500

- Hold the Control key and select both circles <u>and</u> the centerline, then click the Symmetric relation on the properties tree.

3-31

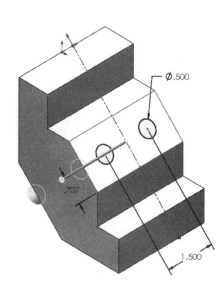

- Create an extruded cut using the **Through-All** condition.

3. Adding the upper cut:

- Select the <u>upper face</u> and click the Sketch pencil to open a new sketch.

- Sketch a centerline that starts at the Origin.

Both lines are Symmetric about the Centerline

- Sketch a rectangle as shown.

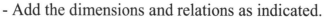

- Add the dimensions and relations as indicated.

- Create an extruded cut using the **Up-To-Vertex** condition (up-to-surface also works).

- Select the Vertex indicated.

Select Vertex

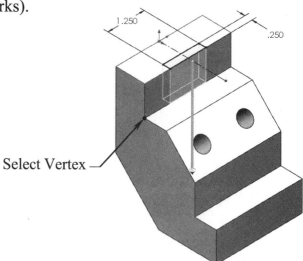

- Click **OK**.

4. Adding the lower cut:

- Select the <u>lower face</u> of the part and open a new sketch.

- Sketch a rectangle on this face.

- Add a Collinear <u>and</u> an Equal relations to the lines and the edges as noted.

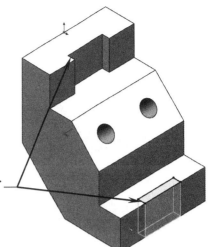

The line is Collinear <u>and</u> Equal with the edge on both sides.

- Extrude a cut using the **Through All** condition.

5. Adding fillets:

- Select the **Fillet** command from the Features toolbar.

- Enter **.032in**. for radius size.

- Select the **4 vertical edges** on the inside of the 2 cuts.

- Keep all other options at their default settings.

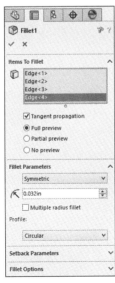

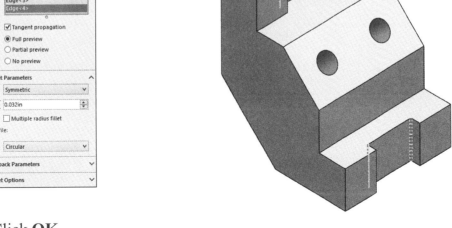

- Click **OK**.

6. Adding chamfers:

- Click **Chamfer** under the Fillet button.

- Enter **.060** for depth.

- Select the 4 circular edges of the 2 holes.

- Click **OK**.

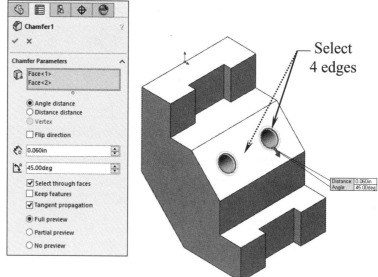

Select
4 edges

7. Saving your work:

- Click **File / Save As**.

- Enter **Extrudes_Exe1** for the file name.

- Select a location to save the file.

- Click **Save**.

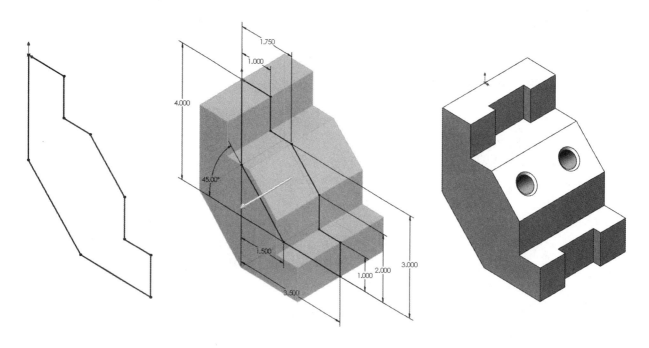

CHAPTER 4

Basic Solid Modeling – Extrude & Revolve

Basic Solid Modeling
Extrude & Revolve

- Upon successful completion of this lesson, you will be able to:

* Perform basic modeling techniques.

* Sketch on planar surfaces .

* Add dimensions  .

* Add geometric relations or constraints .

* Use extrude with Boss / Base  .

* Use Extruded Cut  .

* Create revolved features  .

* Create Fillets and Chamfers .

- The components created in this lesson will be used again later in an assembly chapter to demonstrate how they can be copied several times and constrained to form a new assembly, check for interferences, and view the dynamic motion of an assembly.

- Be sure to review self-test questionnaires at the end of the lesson, prior to going to the next chapter. They will help to see if you have gained enough knowledge required in the following chapters.

Link Components
Basic Solid Modeling

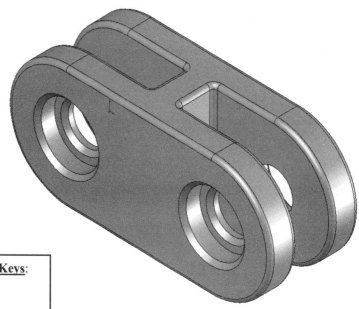

Dimensioning Standards: **ANSI**

Units: **INCHES** – 3 Decimals

Tools Needed:

	Insert Sketch		Line		Straight Slot
	Circle		Mirror		Dimension
	Add Geometric Relations		Fillet		Chamfer
	Extruded Boss/Base		Extruded Cut		Boss/Base Revolve

1. Sketching the first profile:

- Select the <u>Front</u> plane from the FeatureManager tree.

- Click ⬜ (Insert Sketch) and select the **Straight Slot** command ⬜ .

- Sketch a slot following the 3 steps as indicated. Steps 1 and 2 defines the length of the slot, and step 3 defines the slot's radius.

- Add 2 circles on the same centers of the arcs.

- Add Dimensions ⬜ and Relations ⬜ as shown.

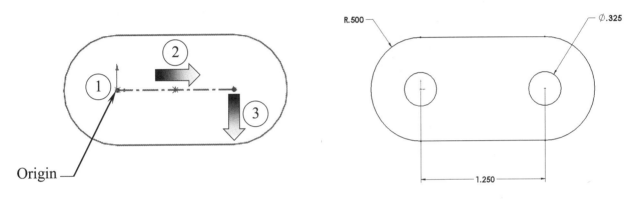

Origin

2. Extruding the first solid:

- Click ⬜ on the Features toolbar or select **Insert / Boss-Base / Extrude**.

- End condition: **Mid Plane**

- Extrude depth: **.750 in**.

- Click **OK** ⬜ .

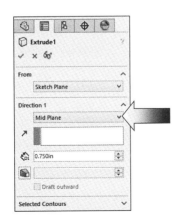

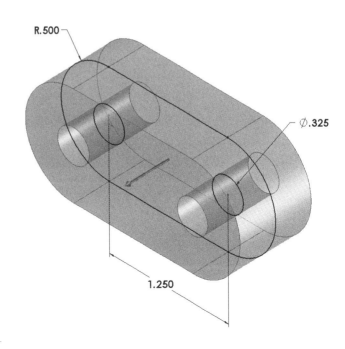

3. Creating the Bore holes:

- Select the front <u>face</u> as indicated and click  (Insert / Sketch).

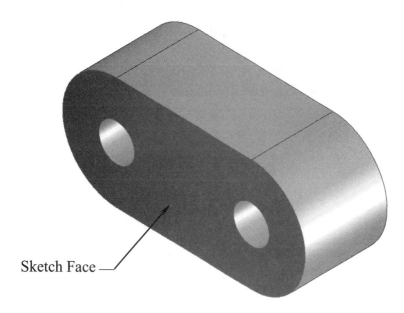

Sketch Face —

> ### 💡 Planar Surfaces
>
> The planar surfaces of the model can also be used as sketch planes; sketch geometry can be drawn directly on these surfaces.

(The Blue origin is the Part's origin and the Red origin is the Sketch's origin).

- Sketch a **circle**  starting at the center of the existing hole.

- Add **Ø.500** dimension as shown.

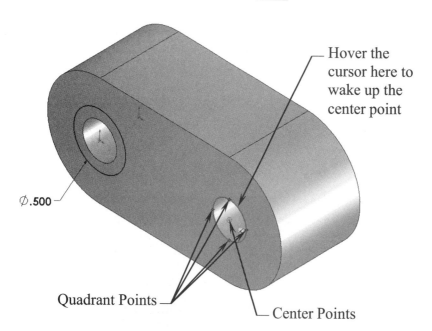

Hover the cursor here to wake up the center point

⌀.500

Quadrant Points —

Center Points

> ### 💡 Wake-Up Entities*
>
> To find the center (or the quadrant points) of a hole or a circle:
>
> * In the Sketch mode, select one of the sketch tools (Circle, in this case), then hover the mouse cursor over the circular edge to "wake-up" the center point & its quadrant points.

- Sketch the 2nd **Circle** and add an **Equal** relation between the 2 circles.

- Click off the Circle command. Hold the **Control** key, select the 2 Circles and click the **Equal** relation (arrow).

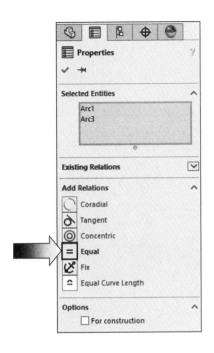

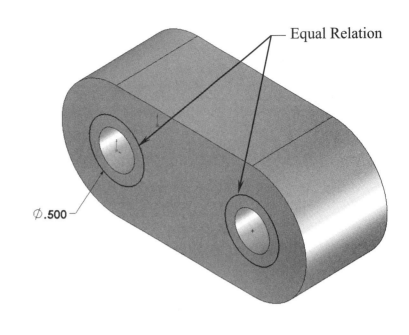

Equal Relation

⌀.500

4. Cutting the Bore holes:

- Click **Extruded Cut** [icon] or select **Insert / Cut / Extrude**.

- End Condition: **Blind**

- Extrude Depth: **.150 in**.

- Click **OK** ✔.

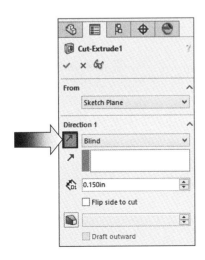

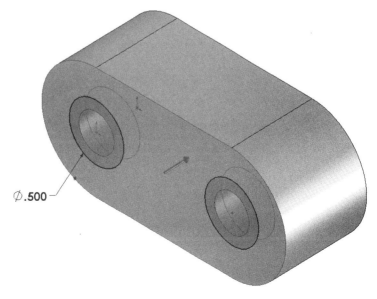

⌀.500

5. Mirroring the Bore holes:

- Select the <u>Front</u> plane from the FeatureManager Tree as the Mirror Plane.

- Click **Mirror** 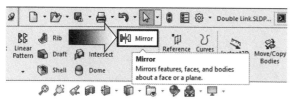 or select **Insert / Patent Mirror / Mirror**.

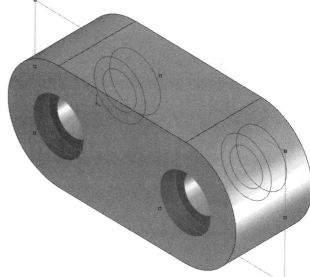

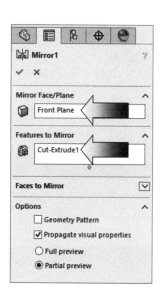

- The Mirror command copies one or
  more features about a plane or a planar face.

- Select the **Cut-Extrude1** from the FeatureManager Tree, or
  click one of the Bore holes from the graphics area.

- Click **OK** ✔.

Sketch face

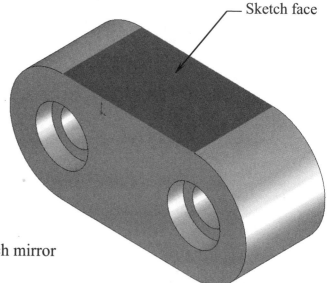

6. Adding more Cuts:

- Select the <u>face</u> as
  indicated and
  open a new sketch [icon].

- We will learn to use the sketch mirror
  entities in the next step.

- Sketch a vertical centerline  and a horizontal centerline as shown.

- To rotate the part normal to the screen, hold the ALT key, and press the LEFT Arrow key 6 times.

- The default angle was set to 15° for each key stroke. This setting can be changed by going to Tools / Options / System Options / View / Arrow Keys.

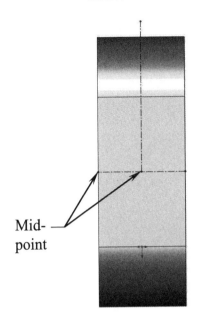

Mid-point

- Select the vertical centerline and click the **Dynamic Mirror** command or click **Tools, Sketch Tools, Dynamic Mirror**.

- Sketch a Rectangle on one side of the centerline; it will get mirrored to the other side automatically.

- Click off the Dynamic mirror button. Add a Symmetric relation to the 3 lines as noted.

- Add dimensions  to fully define the sketch.

- Click **OK** ✅.

.230

Mid-Point

.300

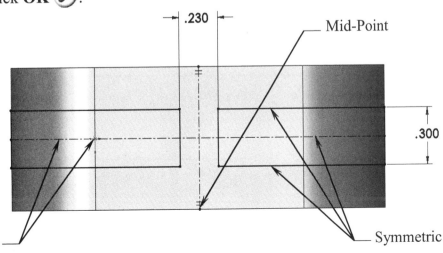

Coincident

Symmetric

7. Extruding a Through All cut:

- Click 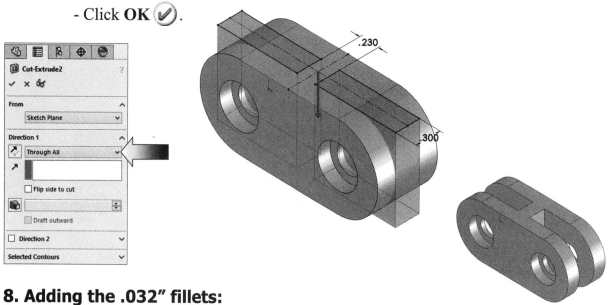 (Extruded Cut) or select **Insert / Cut / Extrude**.

- Direction 1: **Through All**.

- Click **OK** ✓.

8. Adding the .032" fillets:

- Click **Fillet** or select **Insert / Features / Fillet/Round**.

- Enter **.032 in.** for radius size.

- Select the edges as indicated below.

- Click **OK** ✓.

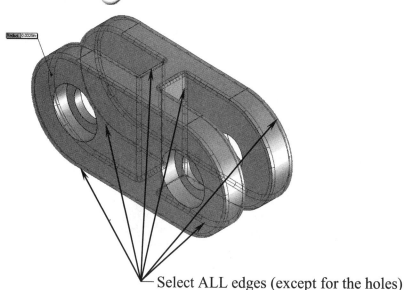

Select ALL edges (except for the holes)

9. Adding the .032" chamfers:

- Click **Chamfer** 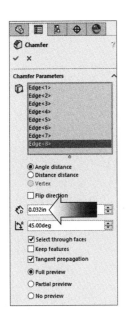 or select **Insert / Features / Chamfer.**

- Enter **.032 in.** for the depth of the chamfer and select the <u>edges</u> of the 4 holes.

- Click **OK** ✅.

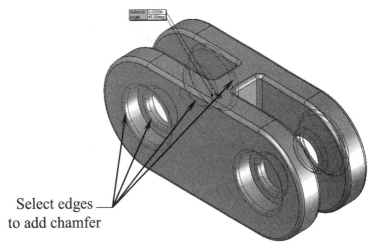

Select edges
to add chamfer

10. Saving your work:

- Select **File / Save As / Double Link / Save**.

11. Creating the Sub-Components:

- The 1st sub-component is the **Alignment Pin**.

- Select the <u>Right</u> plane from the FeatureManager Tree.

- Click  or select **Insert / Sketch**.

- Sketch the profile below using the Line tool .

- Add dimensions as shown to fully define the sketch.

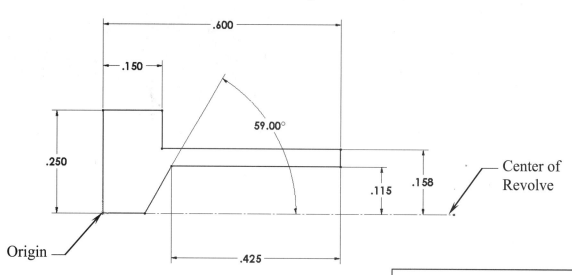

.600

.150

59.00°

.250

.115   .158

Center of Revolve

Origin

.425

12. Revolving the base feature:

- Click or select **Insert / Boss-Base / Revolve**.

- Revolve Type: **Blind**.

- Revolve Angle: **360 deg**. (default).

- Click **OK** .

> ### Center of Revolve
>
> A centerline is used when revolving a sketch profile.
>
> A model edge, an axis, or a sketch line can also be used as the center of the revolve.

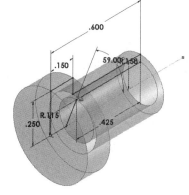

13. Adding chamfers:

- Click **Chamfer**  or select **Insert / Features / Chamfer**.

- Enter **.032** for Distance.

- Enter **45 deg**. for Angle.

- Select the 2 Edges as indicated.

- Click **OK** ✅.

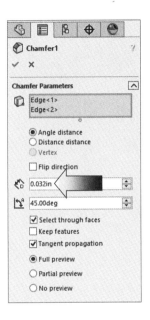

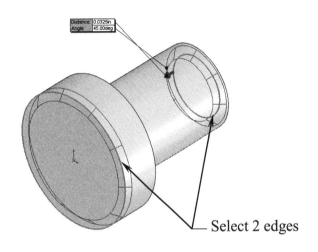

Select 2 edges

14. Saving your work:

- Select **File / Save As / Alignment Pin / Save**.

15. The 2ⁿᵈ Sub-Components:

- The 2ⁿᵈ sub-component is the **Pin Head**:

- Select the <u>Front</u> plane from the FeatureManager Tree.

- Click [⌐] or select **Insert / Sketch**.

- Sketch the profile below using the Centerline [✎] and the Line tools [✎] .

- Add dimensions [✎] as shown to fully define the sketch.

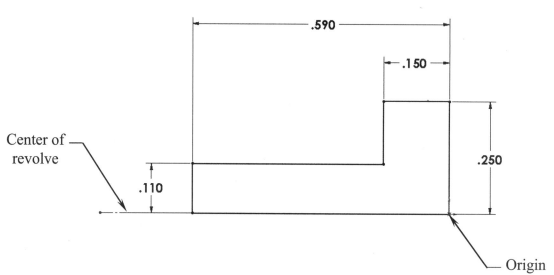

Center of revolve

.590

.150

.250

.110

Origin

16. Revolving the base feature:

- Click [🥄] or select **Insert / Boss-Base / Revolve**.

- Revolve Type: **Blind**.

- Revolve Angle: **360 deg**. (default).

- Click **OK** ✅.

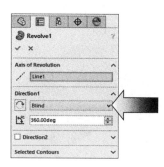

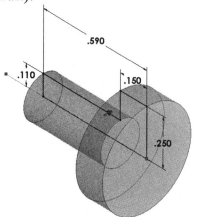

.590

.110

.150

.250

17. Adding chamfer:

- Click **Chamfer** or select **Insert / Features / Chamfer**.

- Enter **.032** for Distance.

- Enter **45 deg**. for Angle.

- Select the <u>Edge</u> as indicated.

- Click **OK** .

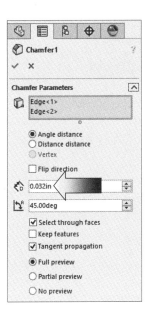

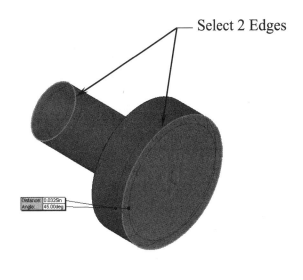

Select 2 Edges

18. Saving your work:

- Select **File / Save As / Pin Head / Save**.

19. Creating the 3rd Sub-Components:

- The 3rd sub-component is the **Single Link**:

- Select <u>Front</u> plane from FeatureManager Tree.

- Click 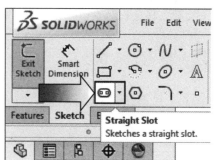 Insert Sketch and select the **Straight Slot** . command.

- Enable the **Add Dimensions** checkbox (arrow below).

- This command requires 3 clicks. Start at the origin for point 1, move the cursor horizontally and click the point 2, then downward to make the point 3.

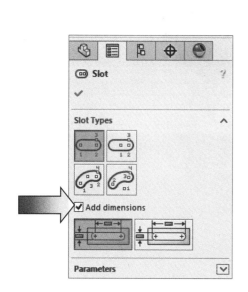

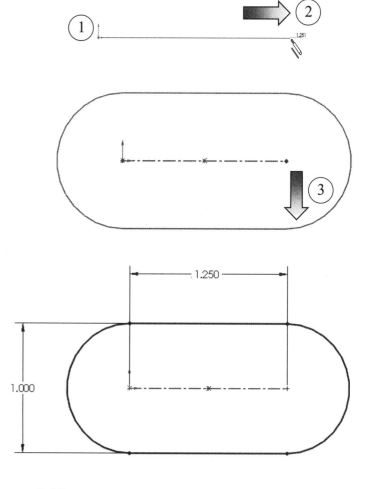

- Click **OK** to exit the Straight Slot command and modify the dimension values to fully define the sketch.

20. Extruding the base:

- Click **Extruded Boss-Base** or select **Insert / Boss-Base / Extrude**.

- End condition: **Mid Plane**

- Extrude depth: **.750 in**.

- Click **OK** ✅.

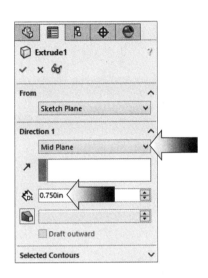

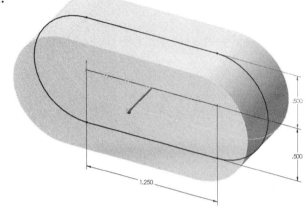

21. Sketching the Recess Profiles:

- Select the <u>face</u>
  indicated and
  open a new sketch .

Sketch Face —

- Sketch 2 Circles ⊙ at the
  centers of the circular edges
  (with the Circle command
  already selected, hover over
  the circular edge to see its center).

⌀**1.020**

- Add a Ø**1.020 in.** dimension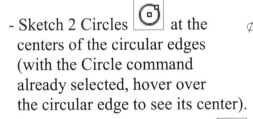
  to one of the circles. (The circles
  are slightly larger than the part.)

- Add an **Equal** relation 🔳
  between the 2 circles.

Equal Relation —

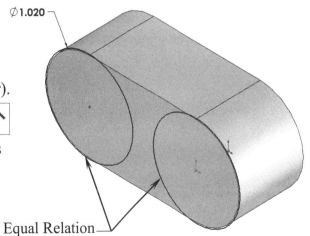

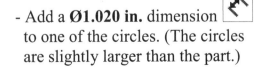

22. Extruding a blind cut:

- Click **Extruded Cut** 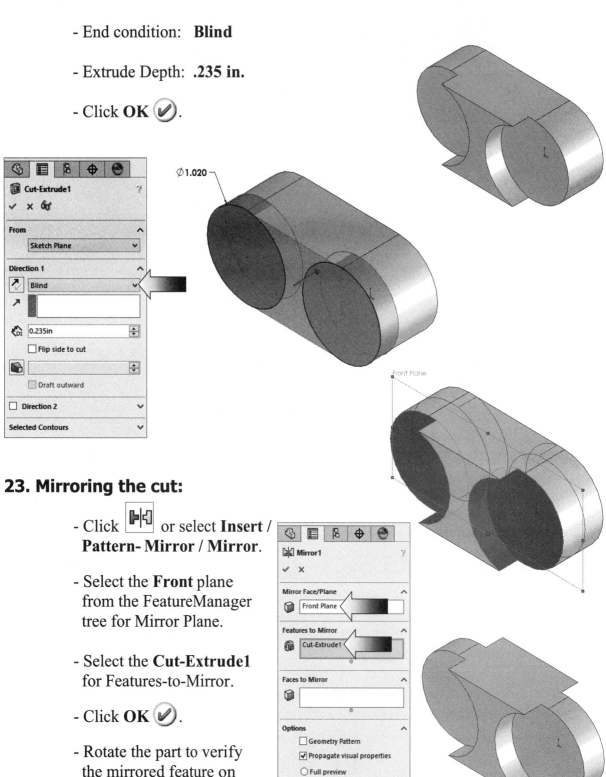 or select **Insert / Cut / Extrude**.

- End condition: **Blind**

- Extrude Depth: **.235 in.**

- Click **OK** ✓.

23. Mirroring the cut:

- Click ⊞ or select **Insert / Pattern- Mirror / Mirror**.

- Select the **Front** plane from the FeatureManager tree for Mirror Plane.

- Select the **Cut-Extrude1** for Features-to-Mirror.

- Click **OK** ✓.

- Rotate the part to verify the mirrored feature on the opposite side.

24. Adding the Holes:

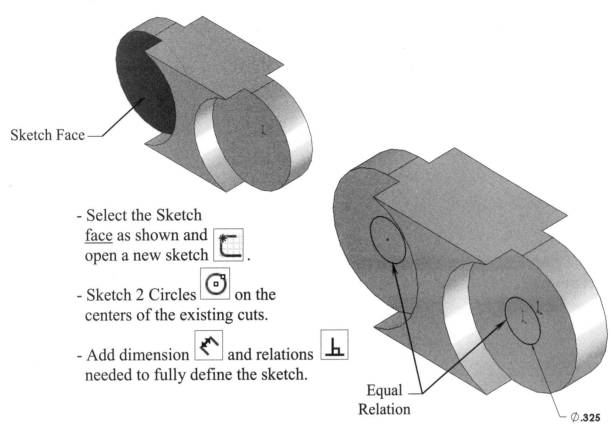

Sketch Face

- Select the Sketch <u>face</u> as shown and open a new sketch .

- Sketch 2 Circles on the centers of the existing cuts.

- Add dimension and relations needed to fully define the sketch.

Equal Relation

⌀.325

25. Cutting the holes:

- Click **Extruded Cut** or select **Insert / Cut / Extrude**.

- End condition: **Through All**

- Click **OK** .

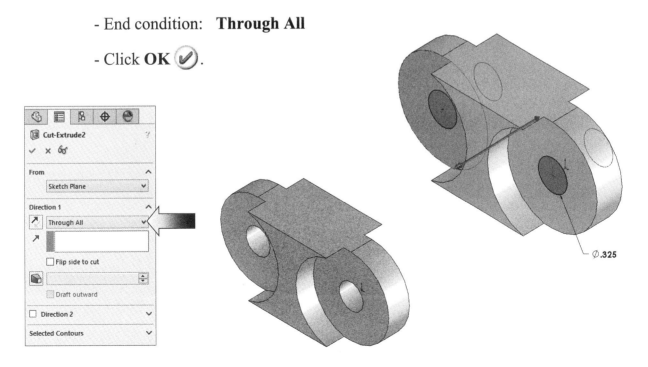

⌀.325

26. Adding the .100" fillets:

- Click **Fillet** 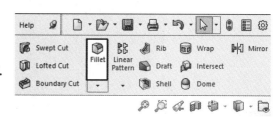 or select **Insert / Features / Fillet/Round**.

- Enter **.100 in.** for Radius.

- Select the <u>8 edges</u> as indicated below.

- Click **OK** ✓.

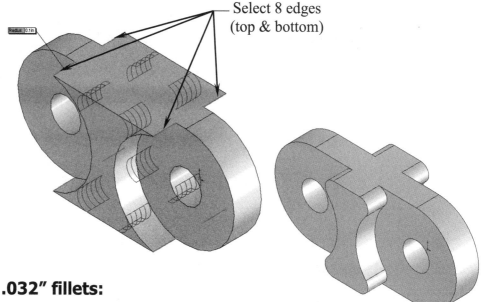

Select 8 edges
(top & bottom)

27. Adding the .032" fillets:

- Click **Fillet** or select **Insert / Features / Fillet/Round**.

- Enter **.032 in.** for Radius.

- Select the <u>edges</u> as shown.

- Click **OK** ✓.

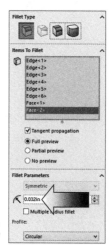

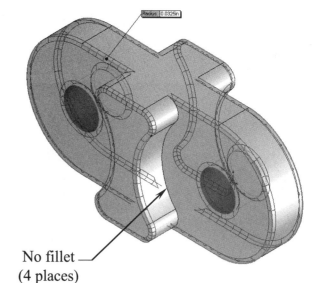

NOTE:

There are no fillets on the 4 edges as indicated.

No fillet
(4 places)

28. Saving your work:

- Click **File / Save As / Single Link / Save.**

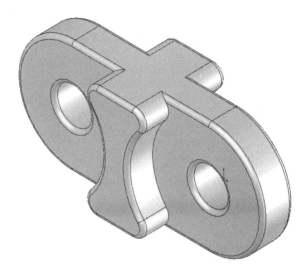

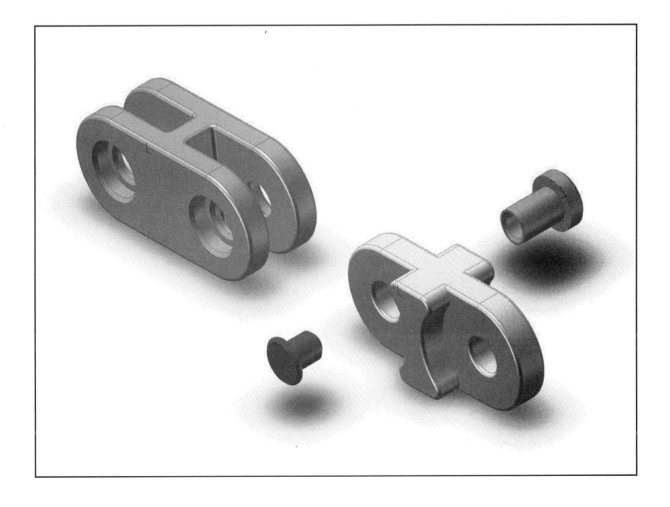

Questions for Review

Basic Solid Modeling

1. Tangent relations only work with the same type of entities such as an arc to an arc, not between a line and an arc.
   - a. True
   - b. False

2. The first feature in a part is the parent feature, not a child.
   - a. True
   - b. False

3. The dimension arrows can be toggled to flip inward or outward when clicking on its handle points.
   - a. True
   - b. False

4. The Shaded with edges option cannot be used in the part mode, only in the drawing mode.
   - a. True
   - b. False

5. The Concentric relations make the diameter of the circles equal.
   - a. True
   - b. False

6. More than one model edge can be selected and filleted at the same time.
   - a. True
   - b. False

7. To revolve a sketch profile, a centerline should be selected as the center of the revolve.
   - a. True
   - b. False

8. After a sketch is revolved, its revolved angle cannot be changed.
   - a. True
   - b. False

7. TRUE   8. FALSE
5. FALSE   6. TRUE
3. TRUE   4. FALSE
1. FALSE   2. TRUE

Exercise: Extrude Boss & Extrude Cut

1. Create the solid model using the drawing provided below.
2. Dimensions are in Inches, 3 decimal places.
3. Tangent relations between the transitions of the Arcs should be used.
4. The Ø.472 holes are Concentric with R.710 Arcs.
5. Use the instructions on the following pages, if needed.

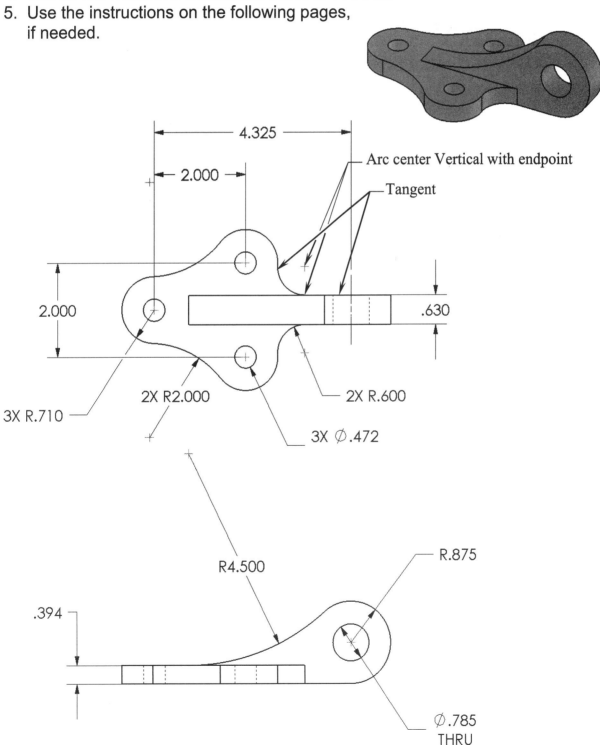

1. Creating the Base sketch:

- There are many ways to create this part, but let's try this basic method first.

- Select the <u>Top</u> plane and open a new sketch.

- Create the construction circles (toggle the **For Construction** checkbox), then create the Sketch Geometry over them.

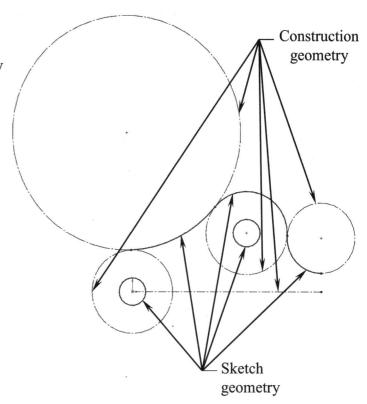

Construction geometry

Sketch geometry

- Either re-create the rest of the geometry or mirror them as noted.

- To mirror the sketch geometry, hold the Control key and select the entities that you want to mirror <u>AND</u> the centerline as noted, then click the Mirror-Entities command.

(*) Add a Tangent Arc to the left side of the profile.

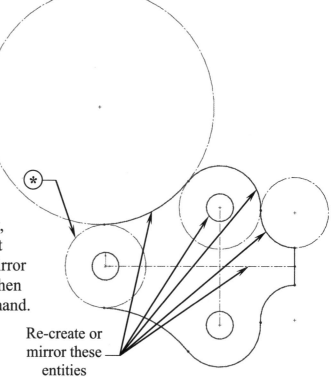

Re-create or mirror these entities

- Add the geometric relations as indicated. Remember to add the Equal relations to the circles and the arcs.

- Add the Smart-Dimensions to fully define the sketch.

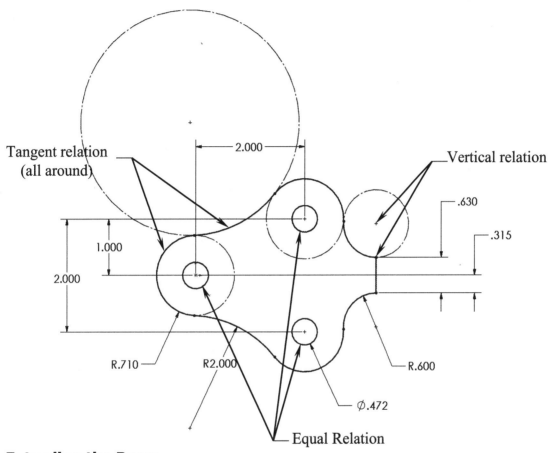

2. Extruding the Base:

- Click **Extruded Boss-Base**.

- Use the **Blind** type for Direction1.

- Enter **.394"** for extrude Depth.

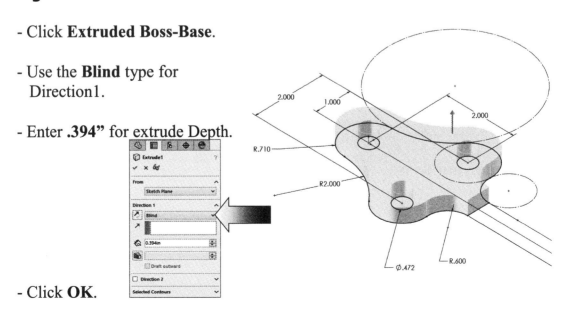

- Click **OK**.

3. Creating the Tail-End sketch:

- Select the <u>Front</u> reference plane from the Feature tree and open another sketch.

- Sketch the construction circles and add the sketch geometry right over them.

- Add the Tangent relation as noted.

- Add the Smart Dimensions to fully define the sketch.

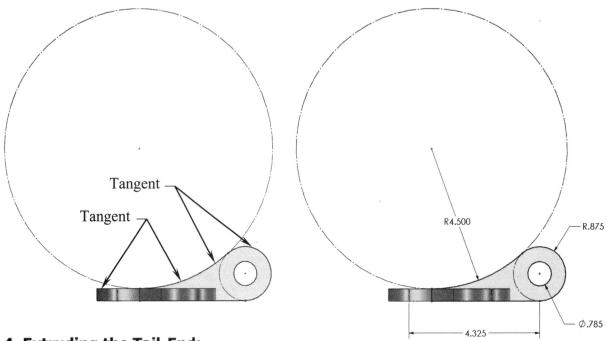

4. Extruding the Tail-End:

- Click **Extruded Boss-Base**.

- Use the **Mid Plane** type for Direction1.

- Enter **.630"** for extrude Depth.

- Click **OK**.

5. Saving your work:

- Click **File / Save As**.

- Enter **Extrudes_Exe2**.

- Click **Save**.

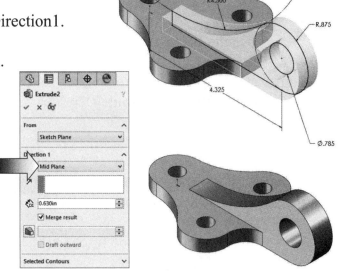

CHAPTER 5

Revolved Parts

Revolved Parts
Ball Joint Arm

- The Revolve command rotates one or more sketch profiles around a centerline, up to 360° to create a <u>thin</u> or a <u>solid</u> feature.

Open profile
= Thin Feature

Closed profile
= Solid Feature

- The revolved sketch should have a continuous closed contour and it can either be a polygon, a circle, an ellipse, or a closed spline.

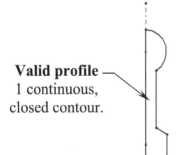   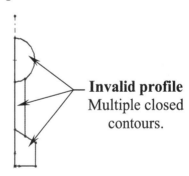

Valid profile
1 continuous,
closed contour.

Invalid profile
Multiple closed
contours.

- If there is more than one centerline in the same sketch, the center of rotation must be selected when creating the revolve.

- In the newer releases of SOLIDWORKS, the center of the revolve (centerline) can be replaced with a line, an axis, or a linear model edge.

- The revolve feature can be a cut feature (which removes material) or a revolve boss feature (which adds material).

- This chapter will guide you through the basics of creating the revolved parts.

Ball Joint Arm
Revolved Parts

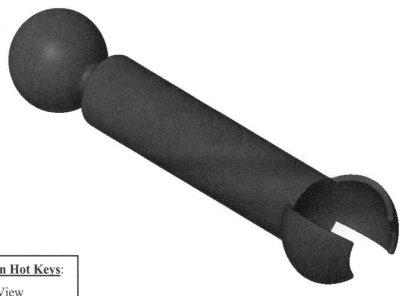

Dimensioning Standards: **ANSI**

Units: **INCHES** – 3 Decimals

Tools Needed:

	Insert Sketch		Line		Circle
	Rectangle		Sketch Fillet		Trim
	Add Geometric Relations		Dimension		Centerline
	Base/Boss Revolve		Fillet/Round		Mirror Features

1. Creating the Base Profile:

- Select the <u>Front</u> plane from the FeatureManager tree.

- Click 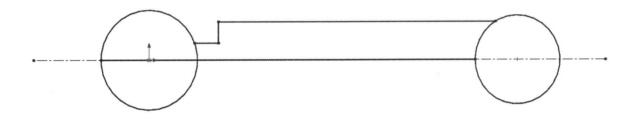 or select **Insert / Sketch**.

- Sketch the profile using the Line and Circle commands.

- Trim the circles as shown.

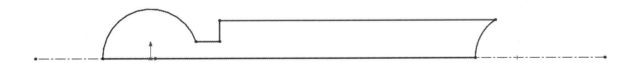

- Add Dimensions and Relations needed to fully define the sketch.
(It is easier to add the R.050" fillets after the sketch is fully defined.)

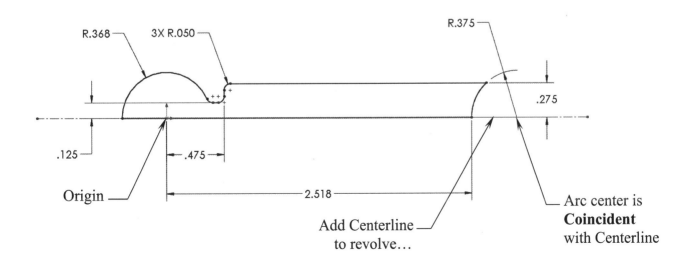

R.368   3X R.050   R.375

.275

.125   .475   2.518

Origin

Add Centerline to revolve…

Arc center is **Coincident** with Centerline

2. Revolving the Base Feature:

- Click **Revolve**  or select **Insert / Boss-Base / Revolve**.

- Revolve Type: **Blind**.

- Revolve Angle: **360 deg**.

- Click **OK** ✅.

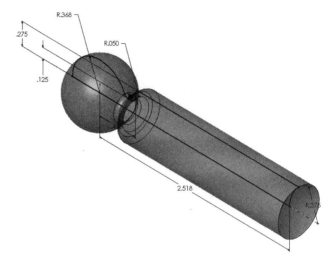

3. Sketching the Opened-End Profile:

- Select the <u>Top</u> plane from the FeatureManager tree.

- Click ⬚ or select **Insert / Sketch**.

- Switch to Hidden Lines Visible mode: click ⬚ on the VIEW toolbar.

- Sketch 2 circles ⊙ as shown.

- Add a **Coradial** relation ⊥ between the small circle and the hidden edge.

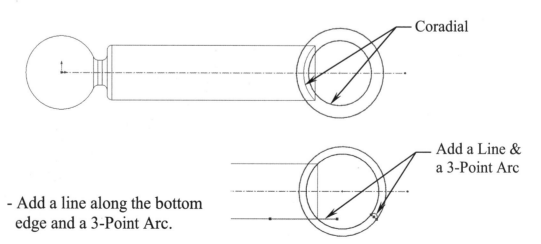

Coradial

Add a Line &
a 3-Point Arc

- Add a line along the bottom
edge and a 3-Point Arc.

- Add a <u>tangent</u> relation between the two small and the large arcs. Repeat the same relation to the other side.

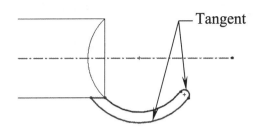

- Trim ⊞ the line and the 2 circles.

- Add a Collinear relation ⊥ between the line and the bottom edge of the part.

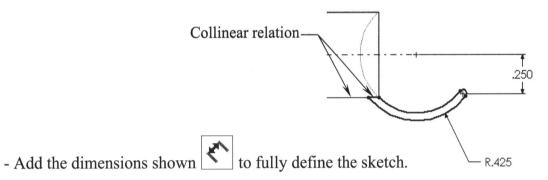

- Add the dimensions shown 🗅 to fully define the sketch.

4. Revolving the Opened-End Feature:

- Click **Revolve** or select **Insert / Boss-Base / Revolve**.

- Revolve Type: **Mid Plane**.

- Revolve Angle: **75 deg**.

- Click **OK** ✓.

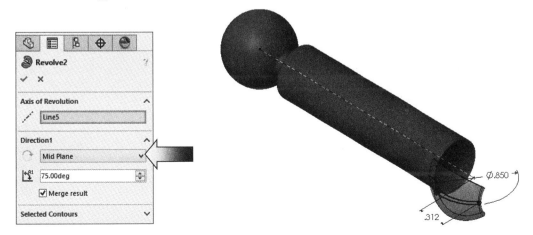

5. Mirroring the Revolved feature:

- Click **Mirror**  or select **Insert / Pattern Mirror / Mirror**.

- Select the <u>Front</u> plane from the FeatureManager tree as mirror plane.

- Select the Revolve2 feature either from the graphics area or from the Feature-Manager tree, as Features to Mirror.

- Click **OK** ✓.

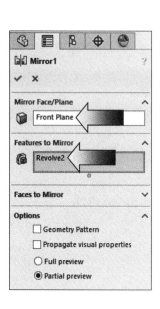

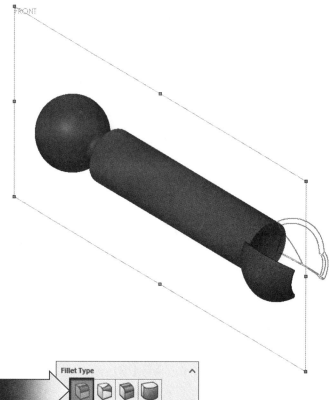

6. Adding the .080" Fillets:

- Click **Fillet** ⬜ or select **Insert / Features / Fillet / Round**.

- Enter **.080** in. as the Radius.

- Select the <u>two edges</u> as shown for Items to Fillet.

- Click **OK** ✓.

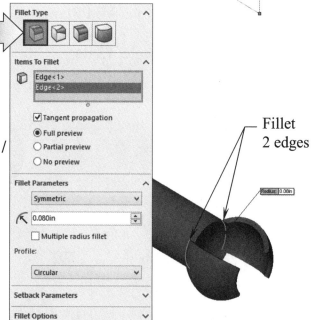

Fillet 2 edges

7. Adding the .015" Fillets:

- Click **Fillet** 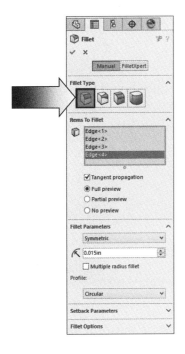 or select **Insert / Features / Fillet / Round**.

- Enter **.015** in. as the Radius.

- Select the <u>edges</u> of the 2 revolved features as shown.

- Click **OK** ✓.

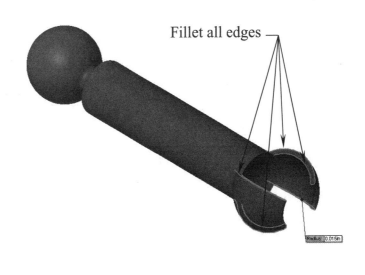

Fillet all edges

8. Saving Your Work:

- Select **File / Save As / Ball-Joint-Arm / Save**.

Questions for Review

Revolved Parts

1. A proper profile for use in a revolved feature is a single closed contour created on one side of the revolved centerline.
   - a. True
   - b. False

2. If there is more than one centerline in the same sketch, one centerline should be selected prior to revolving the sketch.
   - a. True
   - b. False

3. A revolve feature should *always* be revolved a complete 360°.
   - a. True
   - b. False

4. The Sketch Fillet command can also be used on solid features.
   - a. True
   - b. False

5. To mirror a 3D feature, a plane or a planar surface should be used as a mirror plane.
   - a. True
   - b. False

6. To mirror a series of features, a centerline can be used as a mirror plane.
   - a. True
   - b. False

7. After a fillet feature is created, its parameters (selected faces, edges, fillet values, etc.) cannot be modified.
   - a. True
   - b. False

8. Either an axis, a model edge, or a sketch line can be used as the center of the revolve. (Newer releases of SOLIDWORKS only).
   - a. True
   - b. False

7. FALSE	8. TRUE
5. TRUE	6. FALSE
3. FALSE	4. FALSE
1. TRUE	2. TRUE

Exercise: Flat Head Screw Driver

1. Create the part using the drawing provided below.
2. Dimensions are in inches, 3 decimal places.
3. The part is symmetrical about the Top plane.
4. Unspecified radii to be R.050 max.
5. Use the instructions on the following pages, if needed.

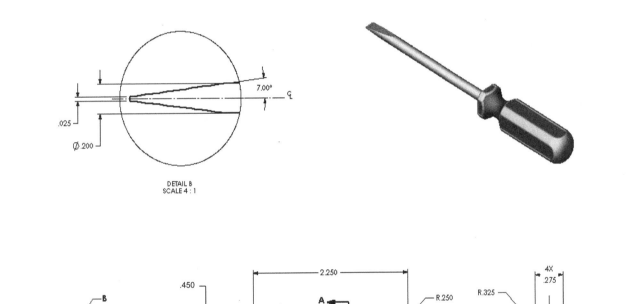

6. Save your work as **Flat Head Screw Driver**.

1. Creating the base sketch:

- Select the <u>Front</u> plane and open a new sketch.

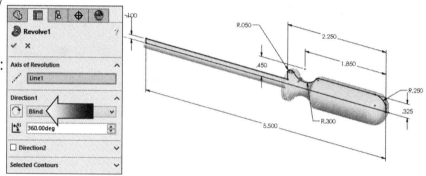

- Sketch the profile shown and add the dimensions noted.
(Note: Only add the Sketch Fillets after the sketch is fully defined.)

2. Revolving the base:

- Click **Revolve / Boss-Base**.

- For Direction 1: Use **Blind**.

- Angle = **360°**

- Click **OK**.

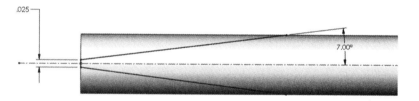

3. Creating the flat head:

- Select the <u>Front</u> plane and open another sketch.

- Sketch the lines as shown and add the dimensions to fully define the sketch.

- Create an **extruded cut** using **Through-All** for both directions.

- Since the sketch was open, Through All is the only extrude option in this case.

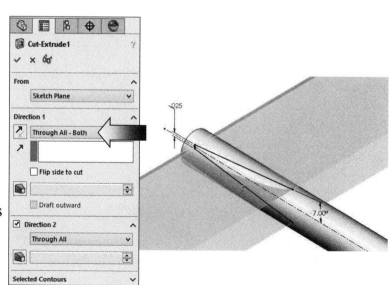

4. Creating the flat handle:

- Select the <u>flat surface</u> on the right end of the handle and open a new sketch.

- Sketch a rectangle and <u>mirror</u> it using the vertical and horizontal centerline (the sketch can be left under defined for this example).

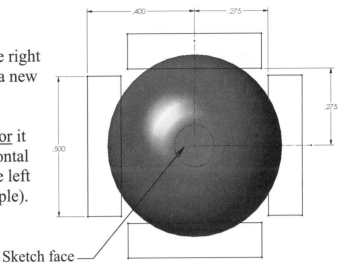

Sketch face

- Create an extruded cut using the opposite end of the handle as the end condition for the Up-To-Surface option (Through-All can also be used to achieve the same result).

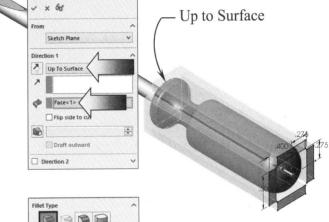

Up to Surface

5. Adding the .050" fillets:

- Apply a **.050"** fillet to the 2 faces as indicated. (It is quicker to select the faces rather than the edges to add the fillets. If a face is selected, SOLIDWORKS applies the fillet to all edges on that face).

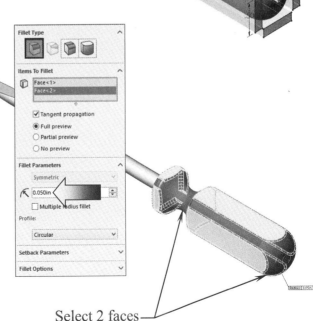

Select 2 faces

6. Saving your work:

- Save your work as **Flat Head Screw Driver**.

Revolved Parts (cont.)

Derived Sketches

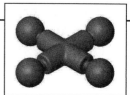

Derived Sketches
Center Ball Joint

- The derived sketch option creates a copy of the original sketch and places it on the same or different plane within the same part document.

  * The derived sketch is the child feature of the original.

  * The derived sketch (copy) cannot be edited. Its size and shape are dependent on the parent sketch.

  * Derived sketches can be moved and related to different planes or faces with respect to the same model.

  * Changes made to the parent sketch are automatically reflected in the derived sketches.

- To break the link between the parent sketch and the derived copies, right click on the derived sketch and select **Underived**.

- After the link is broken, the derived sketches can be modified independently and will not update when the parent sketch is changed.

- One major difference between the traditional copy / paste option and the derived sketch is:

  * The copy/paste creates an Independent copy. There is no link between the parent sketch and the derived sketch.

  * The derived sketch creates a dependent copy. The parent sketch and the derived sketch are fully linked.

Center Ball Joint
Derived Sketches

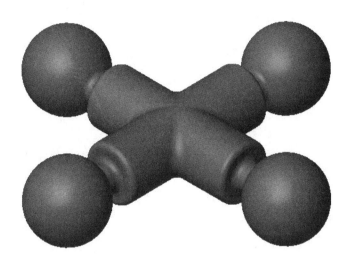

Dimensioning Standards: **ANSI**

Units: **INCHES** – 3 Decimals

Tools Needed:

Insert Sketch	Line	Centerline
Circle	Sketch Fillet	Trim
Add Geometric Relations	Dimension	Plane
Derived Sketch	Fillet/Round	Base/Boss Revolve

1. Creating the Base Profile:

- Select the <u>Front</u> plane from the Feature Manager tree.

- Click ⌐ or select **Insert / Sketch**.

- Sketch the profile using Lines ╱ , Circles ⊙ , Sketch Fillets ⌐ and

the Trim Entities ✂ tools (refer to step 1 on page 5-3 for reference).

- Add the Dimensions ⌐ and Relations ⊥ needed to fully define the sketch.

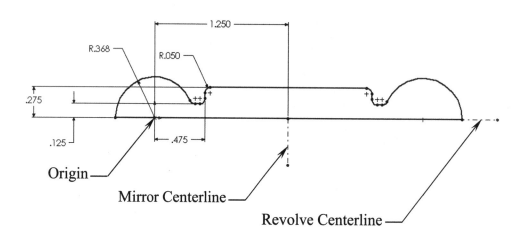

2. Revolving the Base Feature:

- Click **Revolve** or select **Insert / Boss-Base / Revolve**.

- Revolve Type: **Blind**.

- Revolve Angle: **360 deg**.

- Click **OK** ✔.

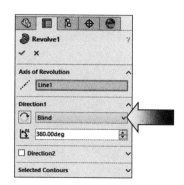

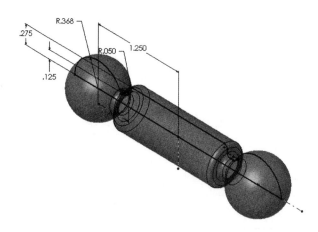

3. Creating a new work plane*:

- Click **Plane** or select **Insert / Reference Geometry / Plane**.

- Select the <u>Right</u> plane from the FeatureManager tree.

- Choose the **Offset Distance** option.

- Enter **1.250** in. (place the new plane on the right side).

- Click **OK** .

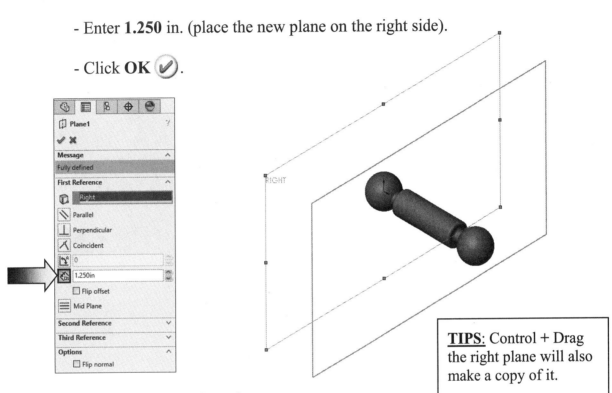

> **TIPS**: Control + Drag the right plane will also make a copy of it.

4. Creating a Derived Sketch:

- Hold the **Control** key, select the new plane (**Plane1**) and the **Sketch1** (under Base-Revolved1) from the FeatureManager tree.

- Select **Derived Sketch** under the **Insert** menu.

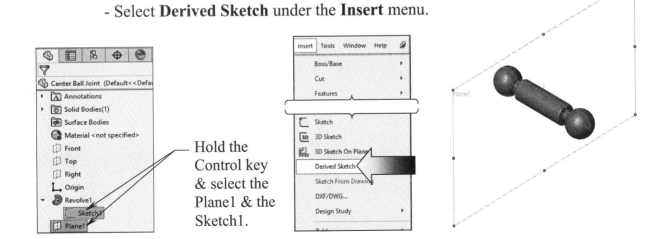

Hold the Control key & select the Plane1 & the Sketch1.

- A copy of Sketch1 is created and placed on Plane1 and is automatically activated for positioning.

5. Positioning the Derived Sketch:

- Add a **Collinear** relation between the Top plane and the Line as indicated. (Select the plane from the FeatureManager tree.)

- Add a **Collinear** relation between the Front plane and the Centerline as shown.

- Click **OK** .

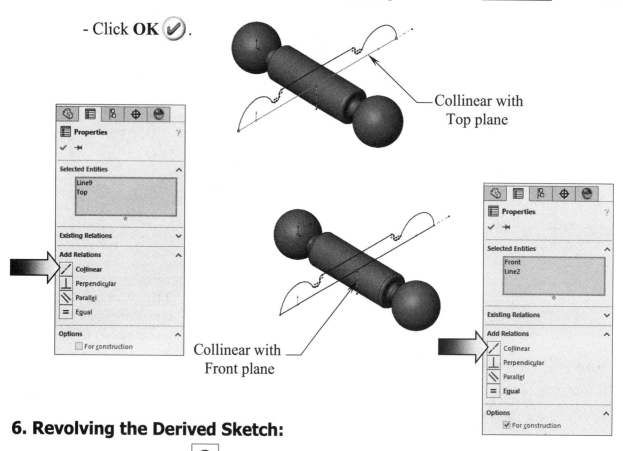

Collinear with
Top plane

Collinear with
Front plane

6. Revolving the Derived Sketch:

- Click **Revolve** or select **Insert / Boss-Base / Revolve**.

- Revolve Type: **Blind**.

- Revolve Angle: **360 deg**.

- Click **OK** .

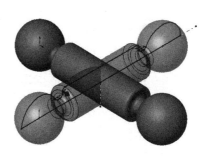

7. Adding Fillets:

- Click **Fillet** 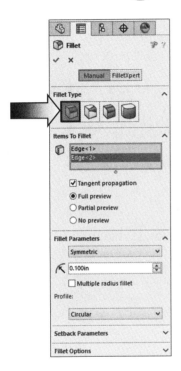 or select **Insert / Features / Fillet / Round**.

- Enter **.100 in.** for radius size.

- Select the 2 <u>edges</u> shown.

- Click **OK** ✅.

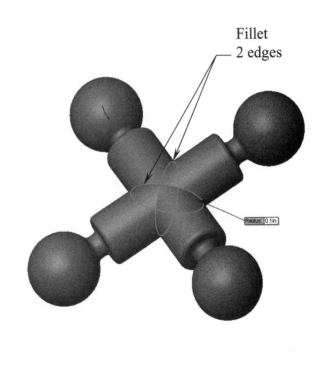

Fillet
2 edges

8. Saving Your Work:

- Select **File / Save As / Center Ball Joint / Save**.

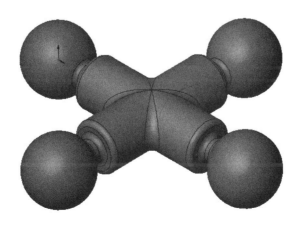

Questions for Review

Derived Sketches

1. The first feature in a part is the parent feature.
   a. True
   b. False

2. More than one centerline can be selected at the same time to revolve a sketch profile.
   a. True
   b. False

3. A parallel plane can be created from another plane or a planar surface.
   a. True
   b. False

4. A derived sketch can be copied and placed on a different plane / surface.
   a. True
   b. False

5. A derived sketch can be edited just like any other sketch.
   a. True
   b. False

6. A derived sketch is an independent sketch. There is no link between the derived sketch
   and the parent sketch.
   a. True
   b. False

7. A derived sketch can only be positioned and related to other sketches / features.
   a. True
   b. False

8. When the parent sketch is changed, the derived sketches will be updated automatically.
   a. True
   b. False

7. TRUE   8. TRUE
5. FALSE   6. FALSE
3. TRUE   4. TRUE
1. TRUE   2. FALSE

Exercise: Revolved Parts - Wheel

1. Create the 3D model using the drawing provided below.
2. Dimensions are in inches, 3 decimal places.
3. The part is Symmetrical about the horizontal axis.
4. The 5 mounting holes should be created as a Circular Pattern.
5. Use the instructions on the following pages if needed.

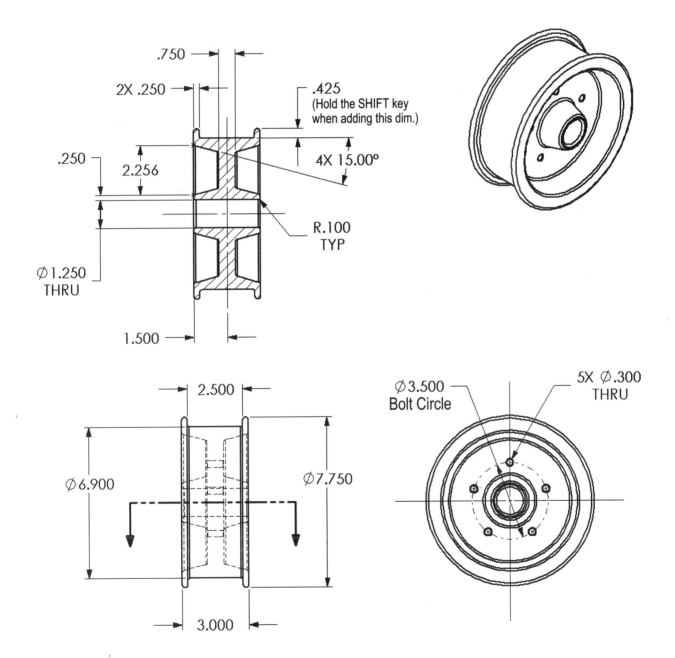

6. Save your work as **Wheel_Exe**.

1. Start with the Front plane.

- Sketch 2 centerlines and use the vertical centerline for Dynamic Mirror.

- Sketch the profile as shown.

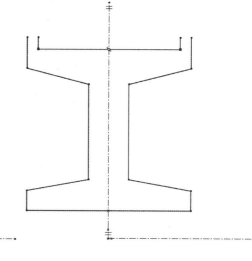

- Add a tangent arc to close off the upper portion of the sketch.

- Add the dimensions and relations as indicated.

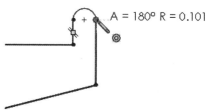

A = 180° R = 0.101

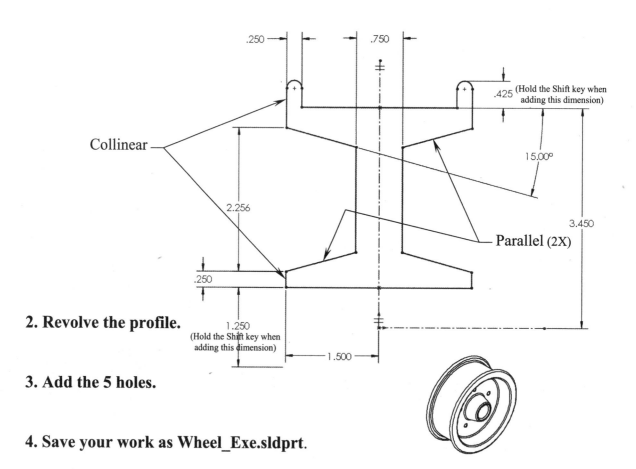

.250

.750

.425 (Hold the Shift key when adding this dimension)

Collinear

15.00°

2.256

Parallel (2X)

3.450

.250

1.250
(Hold the Shift key when adding this dimension)

1.500

2. Revolve the profile.

3. Add the 5 holes.

4. Save your work as Wheel_Exe.sldprt.

Exercise: Plastic Bottle
Extrude / Revolve / Sweep and Circular Pattern

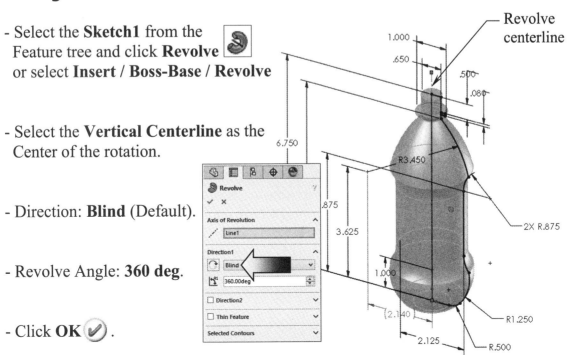

1. Copying the document:

__Go to:__
Training Files folder, and browse
to the file named
__Basic Solid Modeling_
Bottle EXE.sldprt__

__Make a Copy__ of this file
and __Open the copy__.

(To review how this part
was made, open the sample
part from the Training Files
folder in the Built-Parts
folder).

2. Revolving the Base feature:

- Select the __Sketch1__ from the
Feature tree and click __Revolve__
or select __Insert / Boss-Base / Revolve__

- Select the __Vertical Centerline__ as the
Center of the rotation.

- Direction: __Blind__ (Default).

- Revolve Angle: __360 deg__.

- Click __OK__.

3. Adding fillets:

- Click the **Fillet** 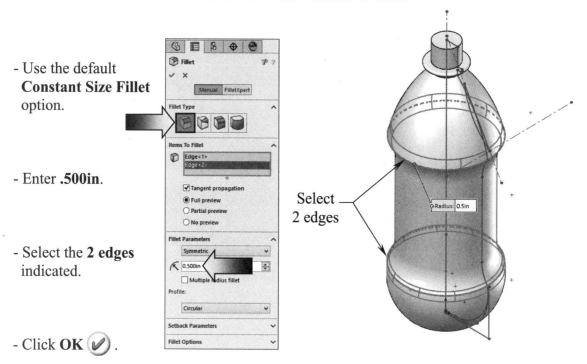 command from the Features toolbar.

- Use the default **Constant Size Fillet** option.

- Enter **.500in**.

- Select the **2 edges** indicated.

Select 2 edges

Radius: 0.5in

- Click **OK** .

4. Creating the upper Cut:

- Select the **Sketch2** and click **Revolved Cut** or select **Insert / Cut / Revolve**.

- Select the **Angular Centerline (30°)** as the Center of the rotation.

- Use the default **Blind** option.

- Revolve Angle: **360 deg**.

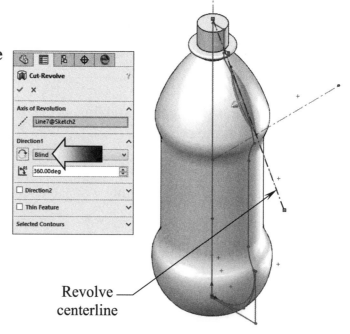

Revolve centerline

- Click **OK** .

5. Creating the lower cut:

- Select the **Sketch3** from the Feature-Manager tree and click **Revolved Cut** .

- Revolve Direction: **Mid-Plane**

- Revolve Angle: **40 Deg**.

- Click **OK** .

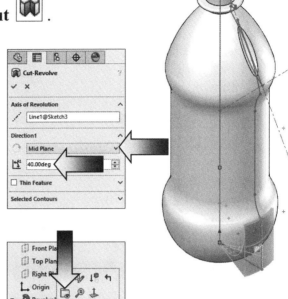

- Expand each feature on the tree and hide all 3 sketches by clicking on each sketch name and selecting **Hide** (arrow).

6. Adding the .062" fillets:

- Click the **Fillet** command from the Features toolbar.

- Use the default **Constant Size Fillet** option.

- Enter **.062in**. for radius size.

- Select the 4 edges as noted.

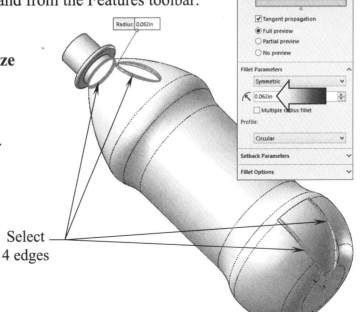

Select 4 edges

- Click **OK** .

7. Adding the .125" Fillets:

- Click the **Fillet** command.

- Use the default **Constant Fillet Size** option once again.

- Enter **.125in** for radius size.

- Select the 2 edges shown.

- Click **OK** .

Select 2 edges

8. Creating a Circular Pattern:

- Click **Circular Pattern**  or select **Insert / Pattern-Mirror / Circular Pattern**.

- Select the **Circular Edge** to use as the pattern direction.

- Pattern Angle: **360deg**.

- Number of Copies: **6**

- **Equal Spacing** enabled.

- Select the **Cut-Revolved1**, the **Cut-Revolved2**, the **Fillet2**, and **Fillet3**, either from the graphics or from the feature tree.

- Click **OK** 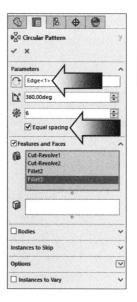.

Pattern direction

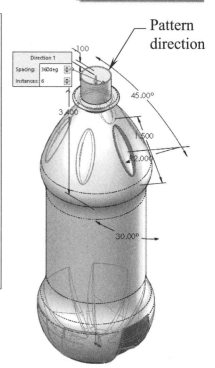

9. Shelling with Multi-Wall thicknesses:

- Click the **Shell** command (arrow).

- Enter **.025in** for the 1st wall thickness.

- For Faces-to-Remove select the <u>upper face</u> as noted.

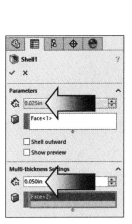

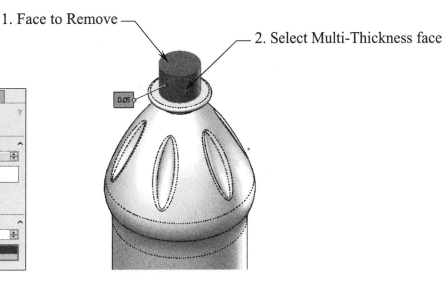

1. Face to Remove

2. Select Multi-Thickness face

- For Multi-Thickness face, select the <u>side face</u> of the circular boss as indicated.

- Change the 2nd wall thickness to **.050in.**

- Click OK.

10. Creating a section view:

- Click **Section View** from the View (Heads-Up) toolbar (arrow).

- Use the default Front plane to make the cut with.

- Zoom in to verify the wall thicknesses and <u>EXIT</u> the section command when done.

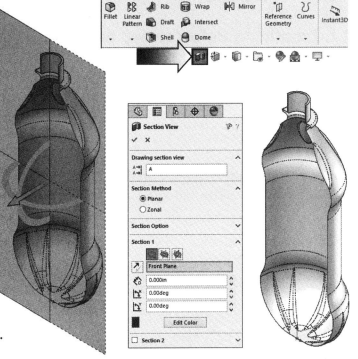

11. Creating an Offset-Distance plane:

- Click the <u>upper face </u>shown and select the **Plane** command .

- Enter **.400in**. for offset distance.

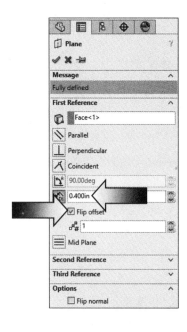

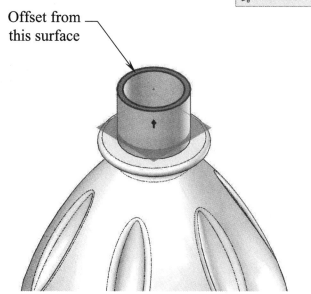

Offset from this surface

- Enable the **Flip Offset** checkbox to place the plane <u>below</u> the upper surface.

- Click **OK** 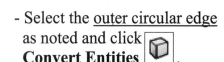 .

12. Creating a Helix (sweep path):

- A helix curve is normally used as a sweep path for a swept feature. A sketch profile is swept along the path to define the feature's shape and size.

- Select the <u>new plane</u> and open a **new sketch** 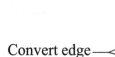 .

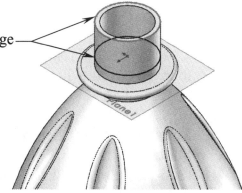

- Select the <u>outer circular edge</u> as noted and click **Convert Entities** .

Convert edge

- The selected edge is converted into a fully-defined circle.

- The circle will be converted to a helix in the next step.

- Change to the Features toolbar and click **Curves**, **Helix-Spiral** .

- Use the default **Constant Pitch** option.

- Change the Pitch to **.125in**.

- Change the Revolutions to **2.5**.

- Set Start Angle to **0.0deg**.

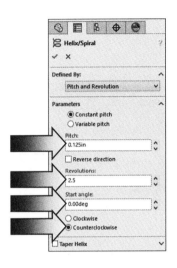

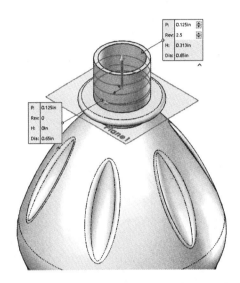

- Set Direction to **Counterclockwise**.

- Click **OK** ✓.

13. Sketching the Thread contour (Sweep Profile):

- Select the <u>Right</u> plane and open a **new sketch**.

- Zoom in on the neck area, closer to the helix.

- Sketch a **horizontal centerline** and **two normal lines** as shown.

- Push **Esc** to turn off the line command and Box-Select all three lines to highlight them (drag the cursor across the lines to select them).

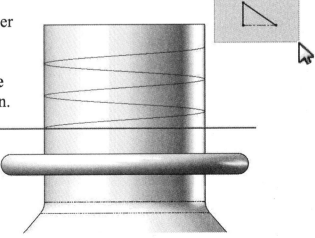

- Click the **Mirror Entities** command 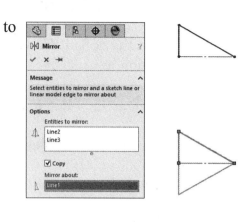 to mirror the selected lines.

- Add the dimensions shown below.

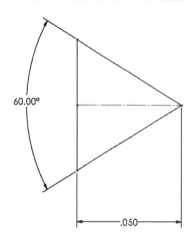

- Add a Sketch Fillet of **.005in** to the right corner of the sketch.

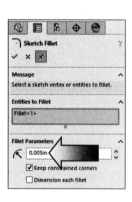

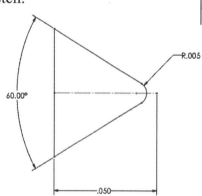

- Add a **Pierce** relation between the endpoint on the left side of the centerline and the helix. The Pierce relation snaps the sketch endpoint to the closest end of the helix.

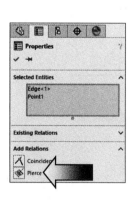

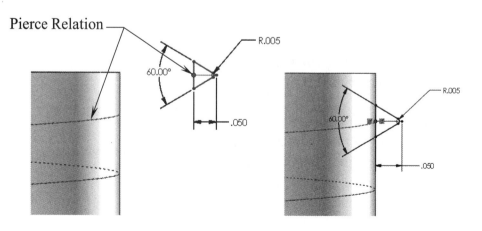

Pierce Relation

14. Adding the Threads:

- Click **Swept Boss Base** 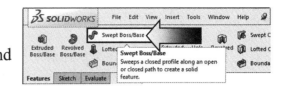 command on the Features toolbar.

- For Sweep Profile, select the <u>triangular profile</u> either from the graphics area or from the Feature tree.

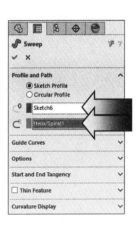

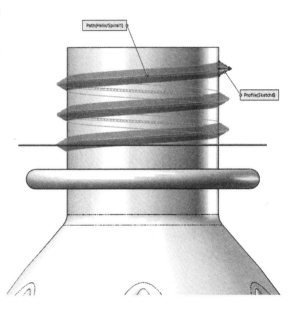

- For Sweep Path, select the <u>Helix</u>.

- The preview graphic shows the profile is swept along the path as shown above.

- Click **OK** ✔.

Hide the plane

Need to close off the ends

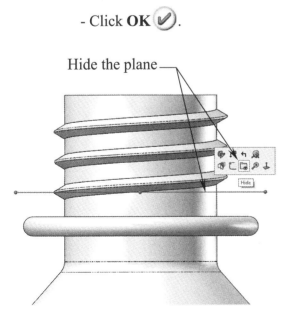

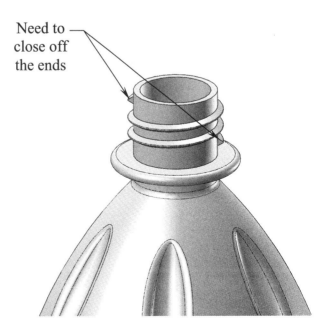

15. Closing the ends:

- Select the flat-<u>end</u> of the Swept feature and open a new sketch.

- While the selected face is still highlighting click **Convert-Entities**.

Convert face ⸺

- Add a **Vertical Centerline** as shown.

- Click **Revolve** 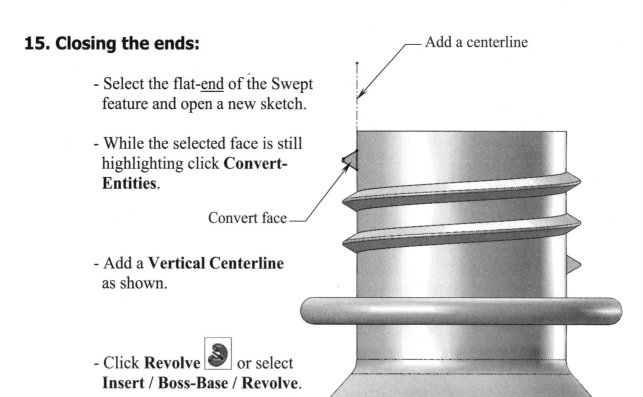 or select **Insert / Boss-Base / Revolve**.

Add a centerline

- Revolve **Blind** (Default), and click Reverse if needed.

- Revolve Angle: **100 deg**.

- Click **OK** ✓.

- *Repeat Step 15 to round off the other end of the threads.*

16. Saving your work:

- Click **File / Save As /**

- For the file name, enter **Basic Solid Modeling_Bottle EXE**

- Click **Save**.

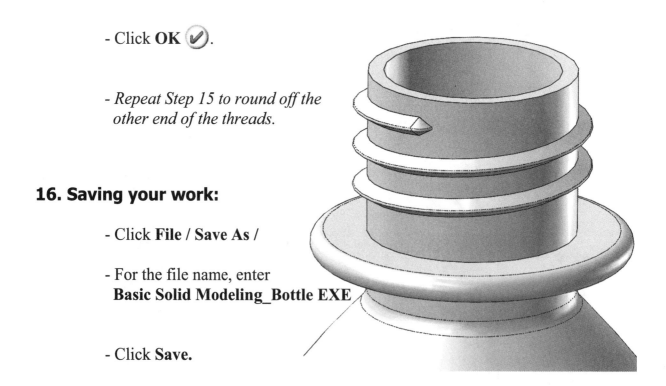

CHAPTER 6

Rib & Shell Features

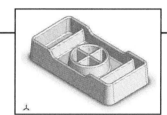

The Rib 🔲 and Shell 🔲 Features
Formed Tray

* A **Rib** is a special type of extruded feature created from open or closed sketched contours. It adds material of a specified thickness in a specified direction between the contour and an existing part. A rib can be created using single or multiple sketches.

    - Rib features can have draft angles applied to them either inward or outward.

    - The **Detailed Preview** 🔲 Property Manager can be used with multi-body parts to enhance detail and select entities to display.

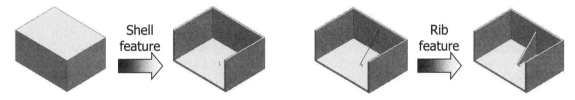

* The **Shell** tool hollows out a part, leaves the selected faces open, and creates thin walled features on the remaining faces. If nothing (no face) is selected on the model, a solid part can be shelled, creating a closed hollow model.

    - Multiple thicknesses are also supported when shelling a solid model. In most cases, the model fillets should be applied before shelling a part.

    - One of the most common problems when the shell fails is when the wall thickness of the shell is smaller than one of the fillets in the model.

    - If errors appear when shelling a model, you can run the **Error Diagnostics**. The shell feature displays error messages and includes tools to help you identify why the shell feature failed. The diagnostic tool **Error Diagnostics** is available in the **Shell** Property Manager.

Formed Tray
Rib & Shell Features

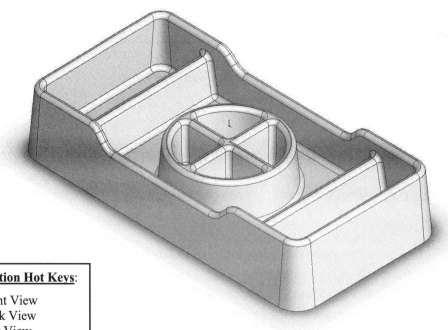

Dimensioning Standards: **ANSI**

Units: **INCHES** – 3 Decimals

Tools Needed:

 Insert Sketch

 Line

 Circle

 Add Geometric Relations

 Dimension

 Fillet

 Boss/Base Extrude

 Rib

 Shell

1. Sketching the Base Profile:

- Select the <u>Top</u> plane from the FeatureManager tree.

- Click Sketch or select **Insert / Sketch**.

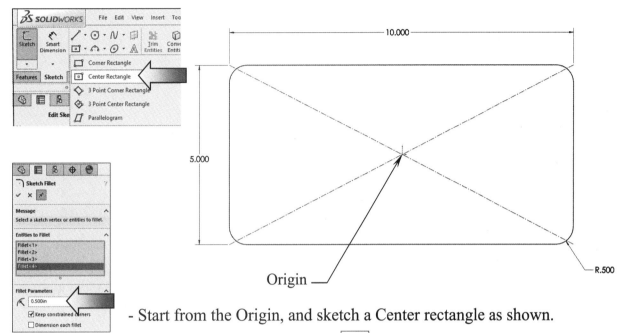

Origin

- Start from the Origin, and sketch a Center rectangle as shown.

- Add sketch fillets and dimensions to fully define the sketch.

2. Extruding the Base feature:

- Click **Extruded Boss-Base** or select **Insert / Boss-Base / Extrude**.

- End condition: **Blind (Reverse)**

- Extrude depth: **2.00 in**.

- Draft angle: **5.00 deg.**

- Click **OK**.

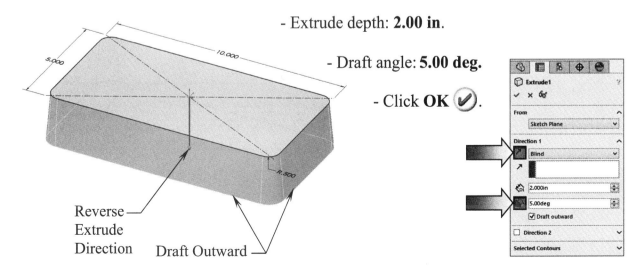

Reverse
Extrude
Direction   Draft Outward

3. Adding the Side Cutouts:

- Select the <u>Front</u> plane from the FeatureManager tree.

- Click Sketch or select **Insert / Sketch.**

- Sketch the profile as shown and add Dimensions / Relations necessary to fully define the sketch.

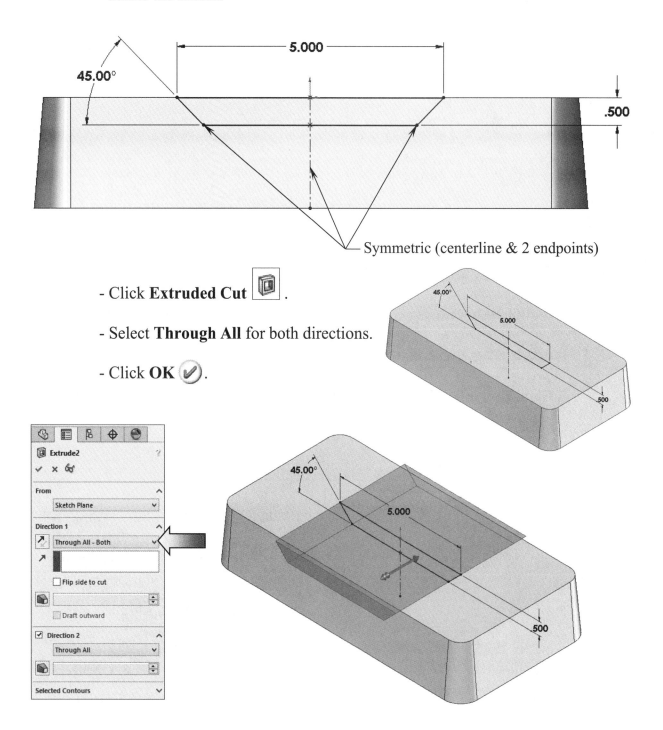

- Click **Extruded Cut** .

- Select **Through All** for both directions.

- Click **OK** .

4. Removing more material:

- Select the <u>upper surface</u> and open a new sketch.

- Select the <u>outer edges</u> and create an **offset** of **.250in** as indicated.

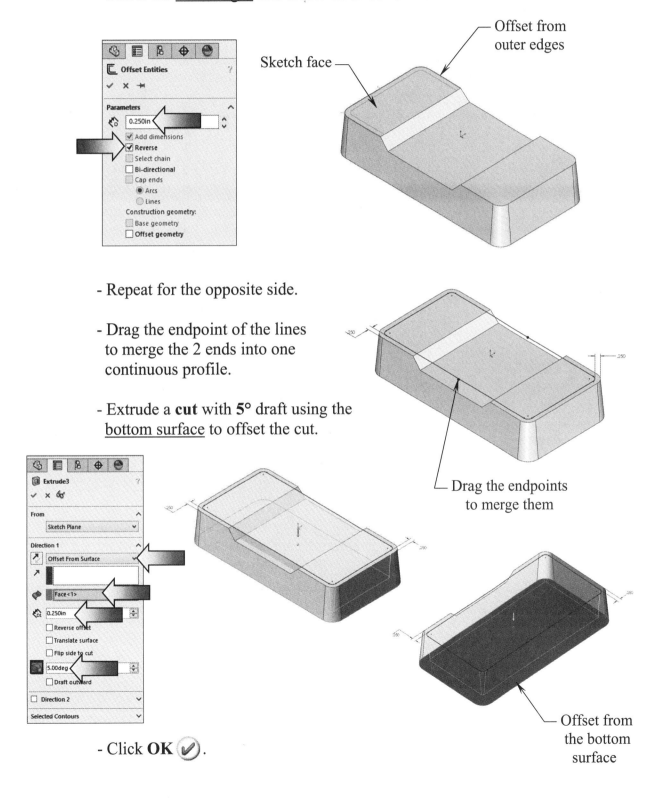

Offset from outer edges

Sketch face

- Repeat for the opposite side.

- Drag the endpoint of the lines to merge the 2 ends into one continuous profile.

- Extrude a **cut** with **5°** draft using the <u>bottom surface</u> to offset the cut.

Drag the endpoints to merge them

Offset from the bottom surface

- Click **OK** .

5. Creating the Rib Profiles:

- Select the <u>face</u> as indicated and open a new sketch .

- Sketch the profile and add dimensions / relations needed to fully define the sketch.

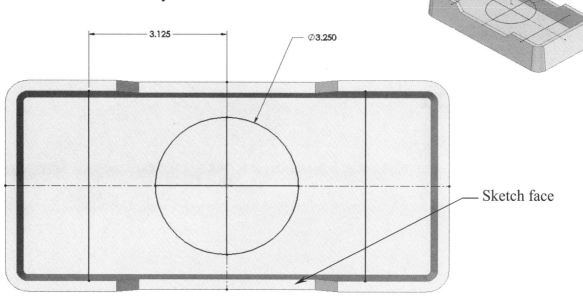

Sketch face

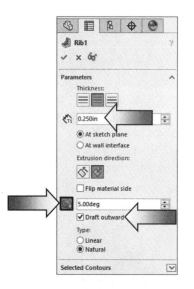

- Click **Rib** or select **Insert / Features / Rib**.

- Select the Both-Sides option and enter **.250 in.** for thickness.

- Select the **Normal To Sketch** option.

- Click the **Draft** option and enter **5.00** deg.

- Enable **Draft Outward** checkbox.

- Click **OK** .

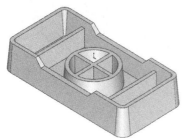

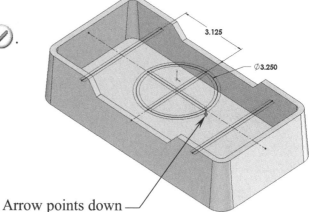

Arrow points down

6. Adding the .500" Fillets:

- Click **Fillet** 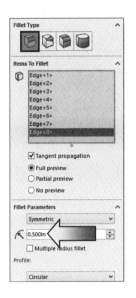 or select **Insert / Features / Fillet-Round**.

- Enter **.500 in.** as the Radius and select the <u>8 Edges</u> as shown.

- Click **OK** ✅.

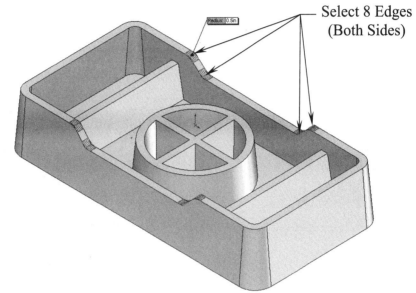

Select 8 Edges
(Both Sides)

7. Adding the .125" Fillets:

- Click **Fillet** 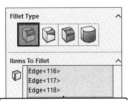 or select **Insert / Features / Fillet-Round**.

- Enter **.125 in.** for radius size and select <u>all edges</u> **except** for the bottom edges.

- Click **OK** ✅.

Box select

Select All-Edges
except for the bottom

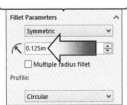

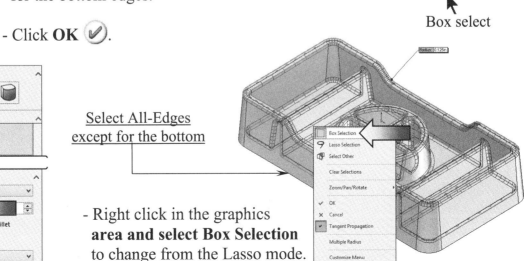

- Right click in the graphics **area and select Box Selection** to change from the Lasso mode.

8. Shelling the lower portion:

- The Shell command hollows out a part, and leaves open the faces that you select.

- Click **Shell** 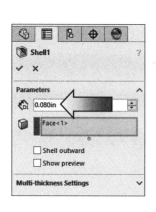 or select **Insert / Features / Shell**.

- Select the <u>bottom face</u> and enter **.080** in. for Thickness.

- Click **OK** ✅.

Select this face to remove

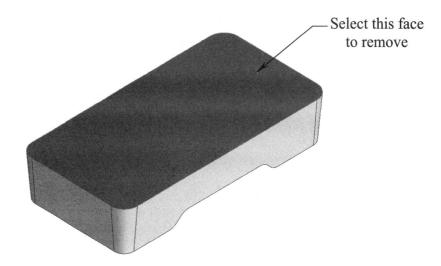

9. Saving Your Work:

- Click **File / Save As**.

- Enter **Rib and Shell** for file name.

- Click **Save**.

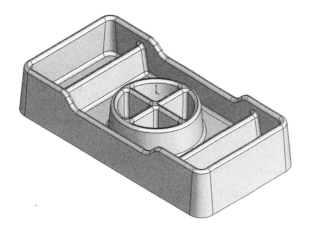

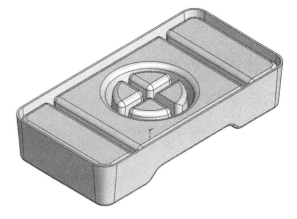

Questions for Review

Rib & Shell Features

1. A fully defined sketch can be repositioned after its relations/dimensions to the origin have been removed.
   - a. True
   - b. False

2. The Mid-Plane extrude option extrudes the profile in both directions and with equal thickness on both sides.
   - a. True
   - b. False

3. Draft Outward is the only option available; the Draft Inward option is not available.
   - a. True
   - b. False

4. The Shell feature hollows out the part starting with the selected face.
   - a. True
   - b. False

5. If nothing (no faces) is selected, a solid model cannot be shelled.
   - a. True
   - b. False

6. A Rib is a special type of extruded feature; no drafts may be added to it.
   - a. True
   - b. False

7. A Rib can only be created with a closed-sketch profile; opened-sketch profiles may not be used.
   - a. True
   - b. False

8. The Rib features can be fully edited, just like any other feature in SOLIDWORKS.
   - a. True
   - b. False

7. FALSE
5. FALSE
3. FALSE
1. TRUE
8. TRUE
6. FALSE
4. TRUE
2. TRUE

CHAPTER 6 (cont.)

Using Shell & Mirror

Using Shell & Mirror
Styrofoam Box

- In most cases, creating a model as a solid and then shelling it out towards the end of the process would probably be easier than creating the model as a thin walled part from the beginning.

- Although the model can be made as a thin walled part in the newer releases of SOLIDWORKS, this lesson will guide us through the process of creating the solid model, and the shell feature will be added in the end.

- The shell command hollows out a model, deletes the faces that you select, and creates a thin walled feature on the remaining faces. But if you do not select any faces of the model, it will still get shelled, and the model will become a closed hollow part. Multi-thickness can be created at the same time.

- Mirror, on the other hand, offers a quick way to make a copy of one or more features where a plane or a planar surface is used to mirror about.

- These are the options that are available for mirror:

    * Mirror Features: used to mirror solid features such as Extruded Boss, Cuts, Fillets, and Chamfers.

    * Mirror Faces: used when the model, or an imported part, has faces that make up the features but not the solid features themselves.

    * Mirror Bodies: used to mirror solid bodies, surface bodies, or multibodies.

- If Mirror bodies option is selected, the Merge Solids and the Knit Surfaces options appear, requiring you to select the appropriate checkboxes prior to completing the mirror function.

Using Shell & Mirror
Styrofoam Box

View Orientation Hot Keys:

Ctrl + 1 = Front View
Ctrl + 2 = Back View
Ctrl + 3 = Left View
Ctrl + 4 = Right View
Ctrl + 5 = Top View
Ctrl + 6 = Bottom View
Ctrl + 7 = Isometric View
Ctrl + 8 = Normal To
          Selection

Dimensioning Standards: **ANSI**

Units: **INCHES** – 3 Decimals

Tools Needed:

 Offset Entities   Extruded Boss-Base   Extruded Cut

 Mirror   Shell   Fillet/Round

1. Starting a new part:

- Click **File / New / Part**. Set the Units to Inches and number of Decimal to 3.

- Select the <u>Top</u> plane and open a new sketch .

- Sketch a **rectangle** a little bit to the right of the Origin as shown below.

- Add a reference centerline from the origin and connect it to the mid point of the line on the left.

- Add the dimensions as pictured to fully define this sketch.

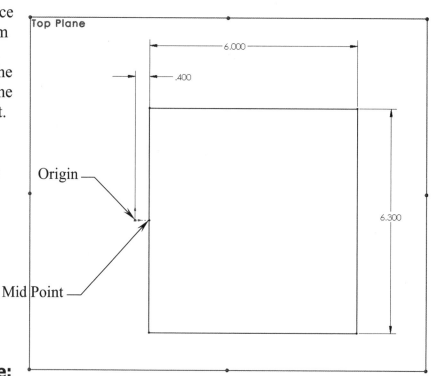

2. Extruding the base:

- Click **Extruded Boss-Base** .

- Direction: **Blind**

- Click **Reverse** (arrow).

- Depth: **1.000**in.

- Draft: **10deg**.

- Click **OK** .

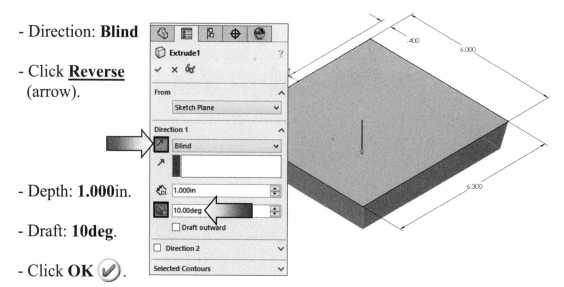

3. Adding the .750" fillets:

- Click the **Fillet**  command from the Features toolbar.

- Enter **.750in** for radius.

- Select the **4 edges** as noted.

- Click **OK** ✓.

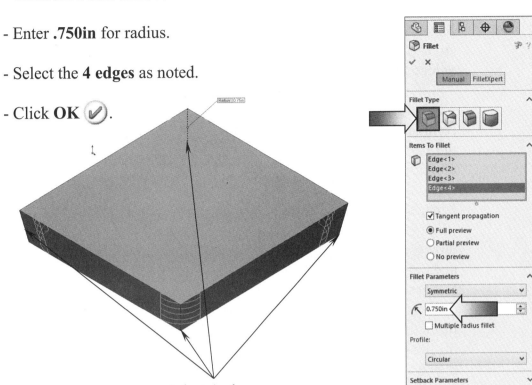

Select 4 edges

4. Adding the .250" fillets:

- Press **Enter** to <u>repeat</u> the previous command or click the Fillet command again.

- Enter **.250in** for radius.

- Select one of the edges at the <u>bottom</u> of the part. The fillet should propagate automatically because the Tangent Propagation checkbox was enabled by default.

- Click **OK** ✓.

5. Creating an offset sketch:

- Open a new sketch on the <u>bottom face</u> as indicated.

- Right click on one of the edges as noted and pick **Select Tangency**.

- Click the **Offset Entities** command on the Sketch toolbar.

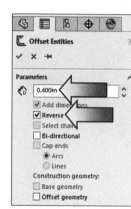

- Enter **.400in** for offset dimension and click the **Reverse** checkbox to place the new profile on the <u>inside</u>.

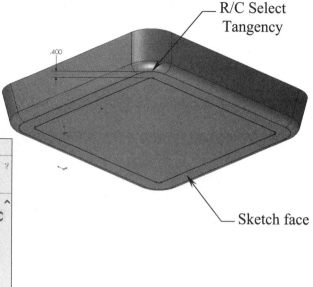

R/C Select Tangency

Sketch face

6. Creating a recess:

- Click **Extruded Cut**.

- Use the default **Blind** type.

- Enter **.200in** for extrude depth.

- Enable the draft button and enter **10.00deg.** for angle (arrow).

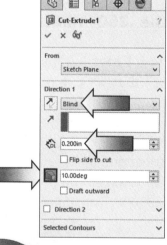

- Click **OK**.

7. Adding the .125" fillets:

- From the Features toolbar, click the **Fillet** command .

- Enter **.125in** for radius value.

- Select the rectangular <u>face</u> of the recess instead. The fillet propagates along all edges of the selected face.

Select face

- Click **OK** .

8. Adding the .200" fillets:

- Press **Enter** to repeat the last command (or click the Fillet command again).

- Enter **.200in** for radius.

- Select <u>one</u> of the <u>upper edges</u> of the recess. The fillet propagates around the recess feature.

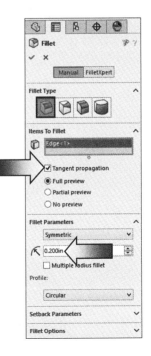

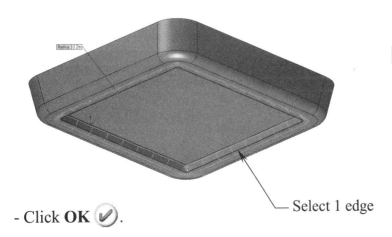

Select 1 edge

- Click **OK** .

9. Creating the rim:

- Select the <u>upper face</u> of the part and open a new sketch .

- The selected face should still be highlighted.

Sketch face

- Click the **Offset Entities** command on the Sketch toolbar.

- Enter **.600in** for offset dimension.

- Click Reverse if needed to flip the offset to the <u>outside</u>.

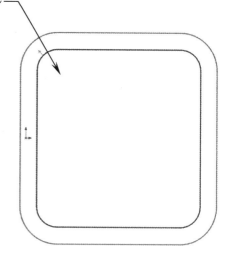

- Click **OK** .

- Delete the 2 corner radiuses and extend the lines by dragging and dropping the endpoints or by using the Merge relation to close off both ends of the profile.

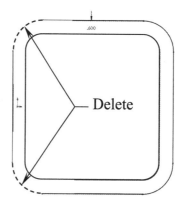

Delete

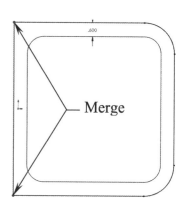

Merge

- Click **Extruded Boss**

- Use the **Blind** type.

- Enter **.400in** for extrude depth.

- Enter **10deg** for draft angle and enable the Draft Outward checkbox.

- Click **OK** .

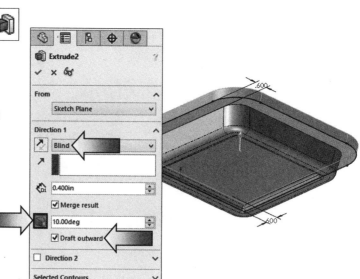

10. Adding another .125" fillet:

- Click the **Fillet** command from the Feature toolbar.

- Enter **.125in** for radius.

- Rotate the part and select one of the edges of the last extruded boss.

- The fillet propagates around the boss automatically.

- Click **OK**.

Select 1 edge

11. Creating the fold feature:

- Select the <u>Front</u> plane and open a new sketch . Press **Ctrl + 8** to rotate the view normal to the sketch.

- Sketch a triangle using the **Line** tool. Add the dimensions shown.

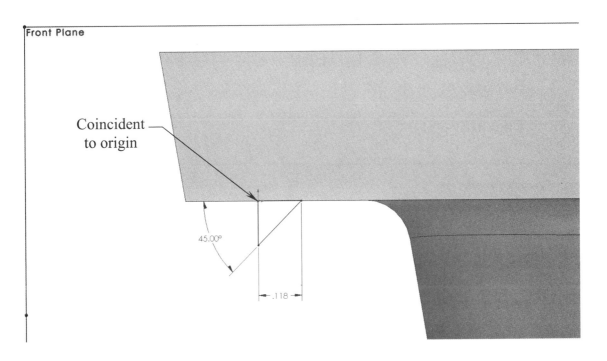

Coincident to origin

45.00°

.118

- Click **Extruded Boss-Base**.

- For **Direction 1**, select
  the **Up-To-Surface**
  option from the
  list and click
  the face on
  the right side
  of the part.

- For Direction 2,
  also select the **Up-To-
  Surface** option, and click
  the face on the left side.

- This way the width of the fold feature is
  linked to the width of the part, allowing
  them to change at the same time.

- Click **OK** ✅.

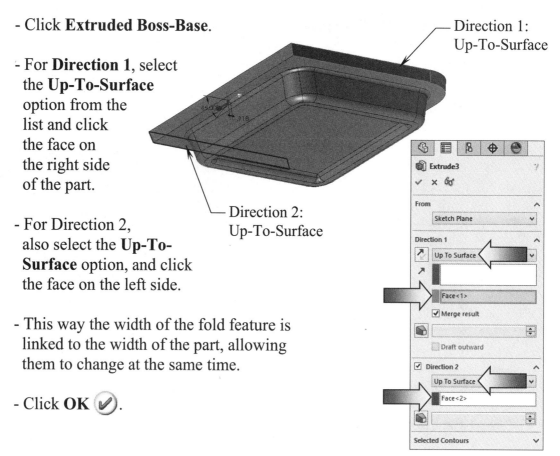

Direction 1:
Up-To-Surface

Direction 2:
Up-To-Surface

12. Mirroring the solid body:

- Select the <u>Right</u> plane from the Feature tree and click the **Mirror** button.

- Expand the **Bodies to Mirror** section and click the part in the graphics area.

- Enable the
  Merge Solid
  checkbox.

- Click **OK** ✅.

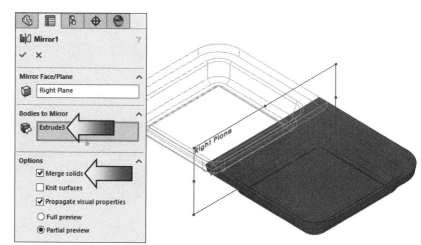

Notes: To mirror one or
more features of a
part, use the
Features To-Mirror
option.

- To mirror the entire
  part, use the Bodies-to-Mirror option.

13. Creating the lock feature:

Sketch
face

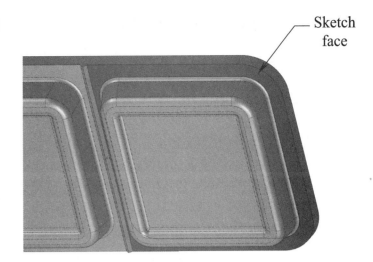

- Rotate the part, select the <u>bottom face</u> of the rim and open a new sketch .

- Sketch a centerline from the origin and use it as the mirror line.

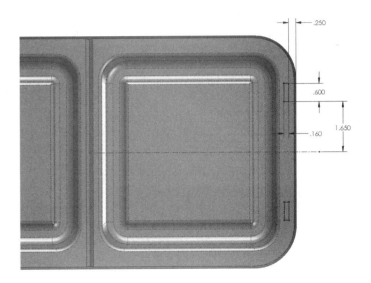

- Sketch a small rectangle above the centerline.

- Use one of the mirror options to mirror the rectangle below the centerline.

- Add the dimensions shown to fully define the sketch.

- Click **Extruded Cut** [icon].

- Use the default **Blind** type.

- Enter **.150in** for depth.

- Enable the Draft checkbox and enter **3deg** for taper angle.

- Click **OK** [icon].

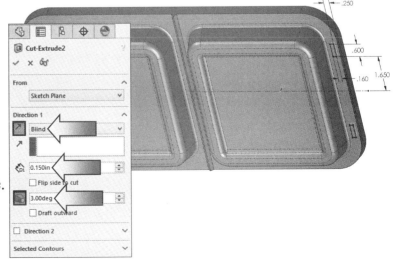

14. Creating the lock cavity:

- Select the <u>bottom</u> <u>face</u> of the rim & open a new sketch 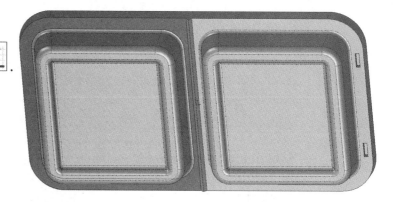.

- Similar to the last step, sketch a center-line from the origin and create a small rectangle above it.

- Mirror the rectangle to the opposite side of the centerline.

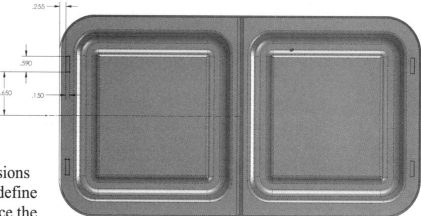

- Add the dimensions shown to fully define the sketch (notice the rectangles are slightly smaller than the last ones).

- Click **Extruded Boss-Base** .

- Use the default **Blind** type.

- Enter **.140in** for depth.

- Enable the Draft checkbox and enter **3deg** for taper angle.

- Click **OK** ✅.

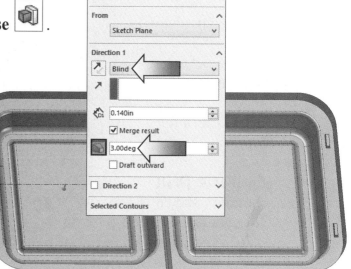

15. Adding the .032" fillets:

- Click the **Fillet** command from the Features toolbar.

- Enter **.032in** for radius.

- Expand the FeatureManager tree (push the arrow symbol) and select the last 2 features, the **Cut-Extrude2** and the **Extrude4**.

- This method is a little bit quicker than selecting the edges individually.

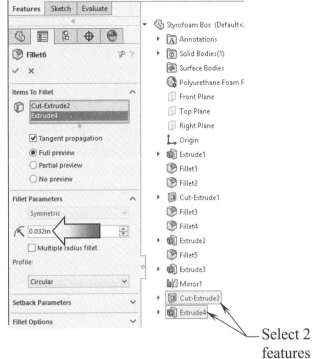

Select 2 features

- All edges of the selected features are filleted using the same radius value. You should create the fillets separately if you want the features to have different radius values.

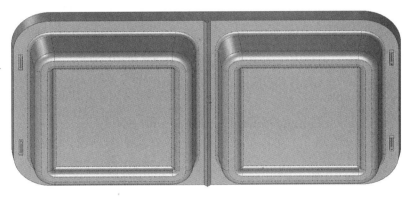

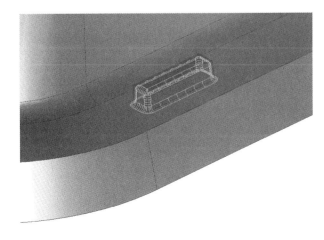
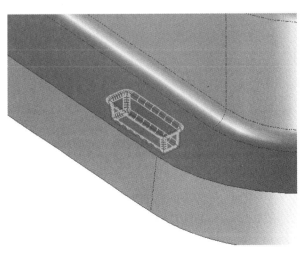

- Rotate and zoom closer to verify the fillets on both features.

16. Shelling the part:

- The shell command hollows a solid model, deletes the faces you select, and creates thin walled features on the remaining faces.

- During the shell mode, if you do not select any face of the model, the part will still be shelled, creating a closed hollow model.

- The first selection box is used to specify the faces of the model to remove, and the second selection box is used to specify different wall thicknesses.

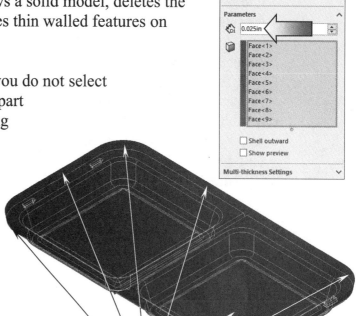

Select 9 faces

- Click the **Shell** command from the Features toolbar.

- Enter **.025in** for wall thickness.

- Select the <u>upper face</u> of the model and the <u>8 faces</u> of the rim to remove.

- Click **OK**.

- Compare your model with the image shown below. Edit the shell to correct it if needed.

17. Adding the .050" fillets:

- Zoom in on the fold section in the middle of the part.

- Click **Fillet**

- Enter **.050in** for radius.

- Select the 3 edges as noted (2 on the top and 1 on the bottom).

- Click **OK** .

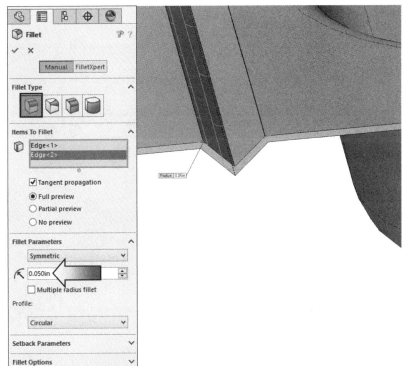

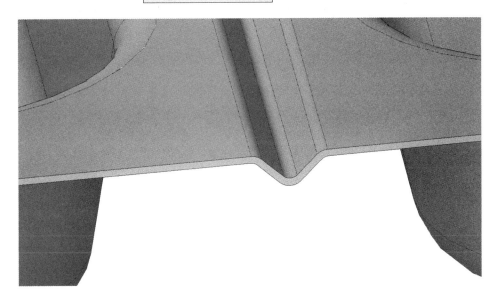

- Verify the resulting fillets.

- We could have used the Multiple Radius option to create both fillets, the .050" and the .032" (in the next step), but the screen will get very busy, making it hard to identify which edges should be used to apply the correct fillets.

- Instead, we are going to create the two fillets separately; that will also give you a chance to practice using the fillet command once again.

18. Adding the .032" fillets:

- Click the **Fillet** command again.

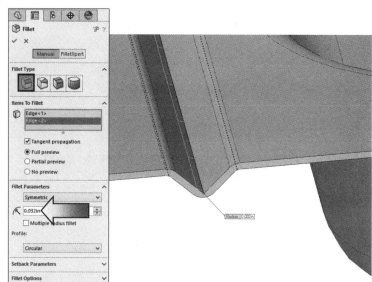

- Enter .032" for radius size.

- Select the 3 edges as indicated (one edge on the top and two edges on the bottom).

- Click **OK** ✅.

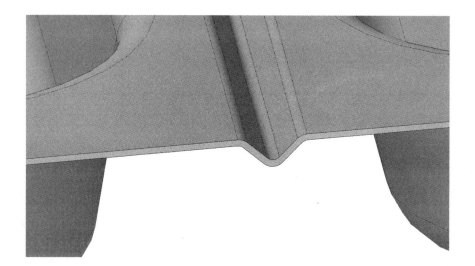

19. Saving your work:

- Save your work as **Using Shell_ Mirror**.

Questions for Review

Using Shell & Mirror

1. It is easier to create a thin walled part by making it as solid and then shell it out in the end.
     a. True
     b. False

2. The shell command hollows out a solid model and removes the faces that you select.
     a. True
     b. False

3. If you do not select any faces of the model, the part will still be shelled into a closed volume.
     a. True
     b. False

4. Only one wall thickness can be created with the shell command.
     a. True
     b. False

5. To mirror a feature, you must use a centerline to mirror about.
     a. True
     b. False

6. To mirror one or more features, a planar face or a plane is used as the center of the mirror.
     a. True
     b. False

7. To mirror the entire part you must use mirror-features and select all features from the tree.
     a. True
     b. False

8. To mirror the entire part you must use mirror-body and select the part from the graphics area or from the Solid Bodies folder.
     a. True
     b. False

7. FALSE   8. TRUE
5. FALSE   6. TRUE
3. TRUE   4. FALSE
1. TRUE   2. TRUE

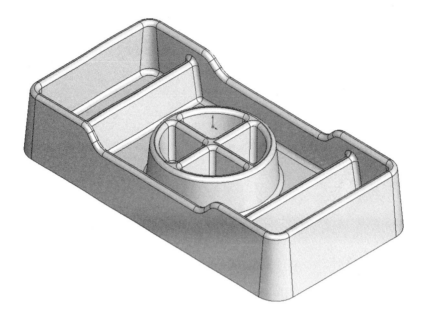

CHAPTER 7

Linear Patterns

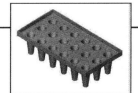

Linear Patterns
Test Tray

- The Linear Pattern is used to arrange multiple instances of selected features along one or two linear paths.

- The following 4 references are needed to create a linear pattern:

    * Direction of the pattern (linear edge of the model or an axis).

    * Distance between the pattern instances.

    * Number of pattern instances in each direction.

    * Feature(s) to the pattern.

- If the features used to create the pattern are changed, all instances within the pattern will be updated automatically.

- The following options are available in Linear Patterns:

    * Pattern instances to skip. This option is used to hide / skip some of the instances in a pattern.

    * Pattern seed only. This option is used when only the original feature gets repeated, not its instances.

- This chapter will guide you through the use of the pattern commands such as Linear, Circular, and Curve Driven Patterns.

Test Tray
Linear Patterns

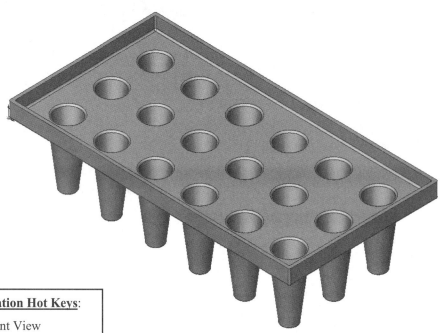

Dimensioning Standards: **ANSI**

Units: **INCHES** – 3 Decimals

Tools Needed:

 Insert Sketch   Rectangle   Circle

 Dimension   Add Geometric Relations   Base/Boss Extrude

 Shell   Linear Pattern   Fillet/Round

1. Sketching the Base Profile:

- Select the <u>Top</u> plane from the FeatureManager tree.

- Click 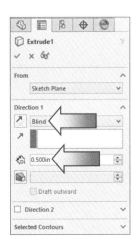 or select **Insert /Sketch**.

- Sketch a **Corner Rectangle** starting at the Origin.

- Add the dimensions shown.

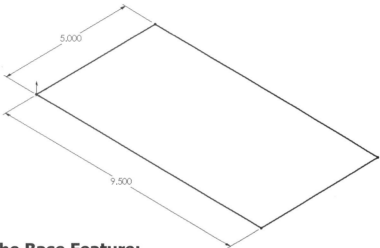

5.000

9.500

2. Extruding the Base Feature:

- Click or select **Insert / Boss-Base / Extrude**.

- End Condition: **Blind.**

- Extrude Depth: **.500 in**.

- Click **OK**.

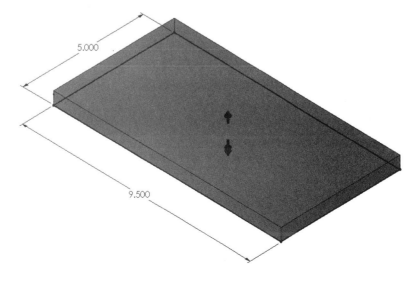

5.000

9.500

3. Sketching the seed feature:

- Select the <u>face</u> indicated as the sketch plane.

- Click  or select **Insert / Sketch**.

- Sketch a **circle** and add dimensions as shown.

Ø1.000

1.000

1.000

Sketch Face

4. Extruding a seed feature:

- Click or select **Insert / Boss-Base / Extrude**.

- End Condition: **Blind, Reverse Dir**.

- Extrude Depth: **2.00 in**.

- Draft On/Off: **Enabled**.

- Draft Angle: **7 deg**.

- Click **OK** .

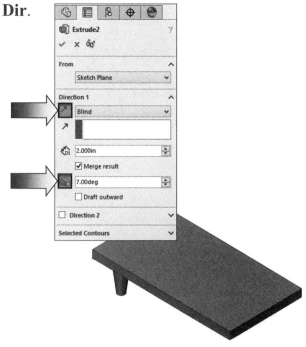

5. Creating a Linear Pattern:

- Click  or select **Insert / Pattern Mirror / Linear Pattern**.

For **Direction 1:**

- Select the bottom **horizontal edge** as Pattern Direction1.

- Enter **1.500** in. as the Spacing.

- Enter **6** as the Number Of Instances.

For **Direction 2:**

- Select the **vertical edge** as Pattern Direction2.

- Enter **1.500** in. as the Spacing.

- Enter **3** as the Number of Instances.

- Select **Extrude2** as the Features to Pattern.

- Click **OK** ✅.

> 💡 **Linear Patterns**
>
> The Linear Pattern option creates multiple instances of one or more features uniformly along one or two directions.

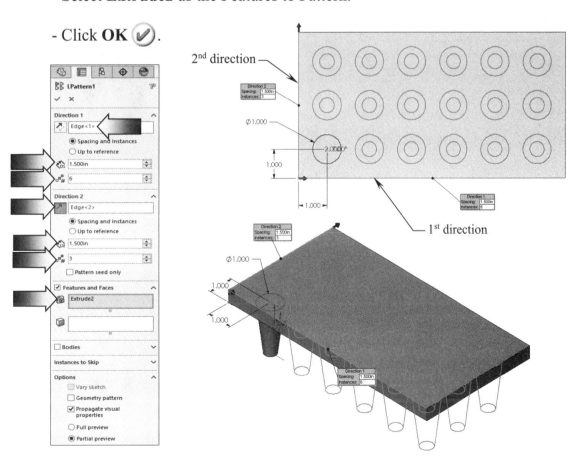

6. Shelling the Base feature:

- Select the <u>upper face</u> as shown.

- Click or select **Insert / Features / Shell**.

- Enter **.100** in. for the Thickness.

- Click **OK** ✅ .

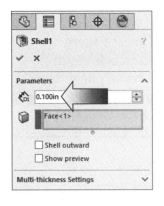

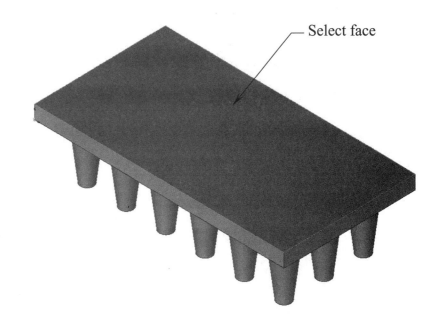

Select face

- The shelled part.

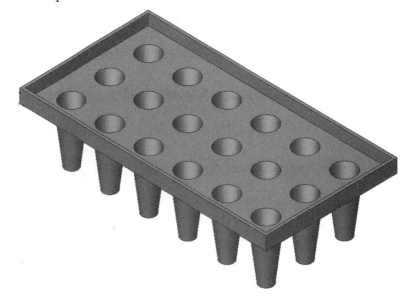

> ### Shell
>
> The Shell command hollows out the part, starting with the selected face.
> Constant or multi-wall thickness can be done in the same operation.

7. Adding Fillets:

- Click **Fillet**  or select **Insert / Features / Fillet / Round.**

- Enter **.050** in. for Radius size.

- Select the <u>all edges</u>.
  (To use Box-Select method right click in the graphics area and select Box-Selection.)

- Click **OK** ✅.

> 💡 **Fillets**
>
> A combination of faces and edges can be selected within the same fillet operation.
> (Box-select the entire part to select all edges.)

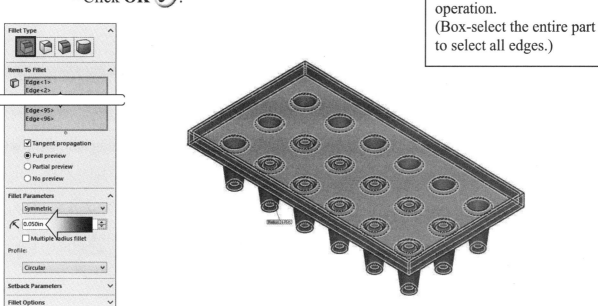

8. Saving your work:

- Select **File / Save As / Test Tray / Save**.

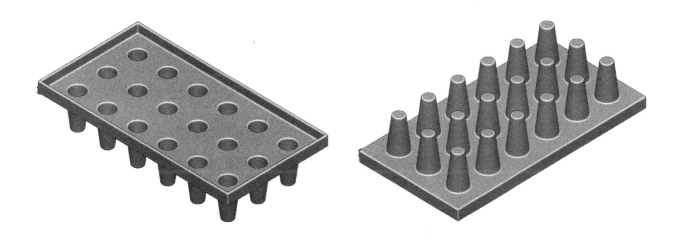

Questions for Review

Linear Patterns

1. SOLIDWORKS only allows you to pattern one feature at a time. Patterning multiple features is not supported.
   - a. True
   - b. False

2. Only the spacing and number of copies are required to create a linear pattern.
   - a. True
   - b. False

3. SOLIDWORKS does not require you to specify the 2nd direction when using both directions option.
   - a. True
   - b. False

4. The Shell feature hollows out the part using a wall thickness specified by the user.
   - a. True
   - b. False

5. After the Shell feature is created, its wall thickness cannot be changed.
   - a. True
   - b. False

6. A combination of faces and edges of a model can be selected in the same fillet operation.
   - a. True
   - b. False

7. The value of the fillet can be changed at any time.
   - a. True
   - b. False

8. "Pattern a pattern" is not supported in SOLIDWORKS.
   - a. True
   - b. False

7. TRUE   8. FALSE
5. FALSE 6. TRUE
3. FALSE 4. TRUE
1. FALSE 2. FALSE

CHAPTER 7 (cont.)

Circular Patterns

Circular Patterns
Spur Gear

- One or more instances can be copied in a circular fashion or around an Axis.

- The center of the pattern can be defined by a circular edge, an axis, a temporary axis, or an angular dimension.

- In the newer releases of SOLIDWORKS, a circular edge can be used as the center of the pattern instead of an axis.

- These are the references required to create a circular pattern:

    * Center of rotation.

    * Spacing between the instances.

    * Number of copies.

    * Feature(s) to copy.

- Only the original feature can be edited; changes made to the original are automatically updated within the pattern.

- The features to the pattern can be selected directly from the graphics area or from the Feature Manager tree.

- The instances in a pattern can be skipped. The skipped instances can be edited during or after the pattern is made.

Spur-Gear
Circular Patterns

Dimensioning Standards: **ANSI**

Units: **INCHES** – 3 Decimals

Tools Needed:

 Insert Sketch   Line   Center Line

 Dynamic Mirror   Add Geometric Relations   Dimension

 Convert Entities   Trim Entities   Base/Boss Revolve

 Circular Pattern   Base/Boss Extrude   Extruded Cut

1. Sketching the Body profile:

- Select the <u>Front</u> plane from the FeatureManager Tree.

- Click 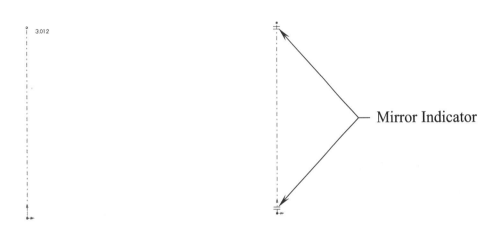 or select **Insert / Sketch**.

- Sketch a **Centerline** starting at the Origin.

- Select the **Mirror** tool and click the centerline to activate the Dynamic Mirror mode (or select **Tools / Sketch Tools / Dynamic Mirror**).

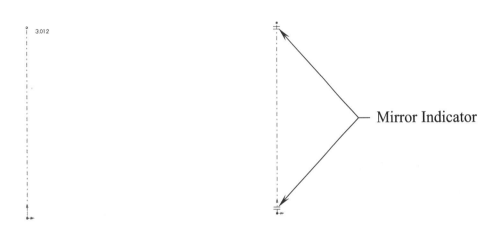

Mirror Indicator

- Sketch the profile below using the Line tool .

To cancel Auto-Relations (dotted inference lines), either hold down the Control key while sketching the lines – OR – just simply avoid sketching over the dotted lines.

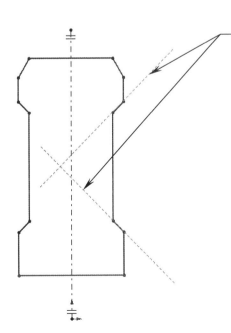

Using the Dynamic Mirror:

- Sketch on one side of the centerline only.

- The sketch should not cross the centerline.

- SOLIDWORKS creates **Symmetric** relations between all mirrored sketch entities.

- Add the following Geometric Relations to the entities indicated below:

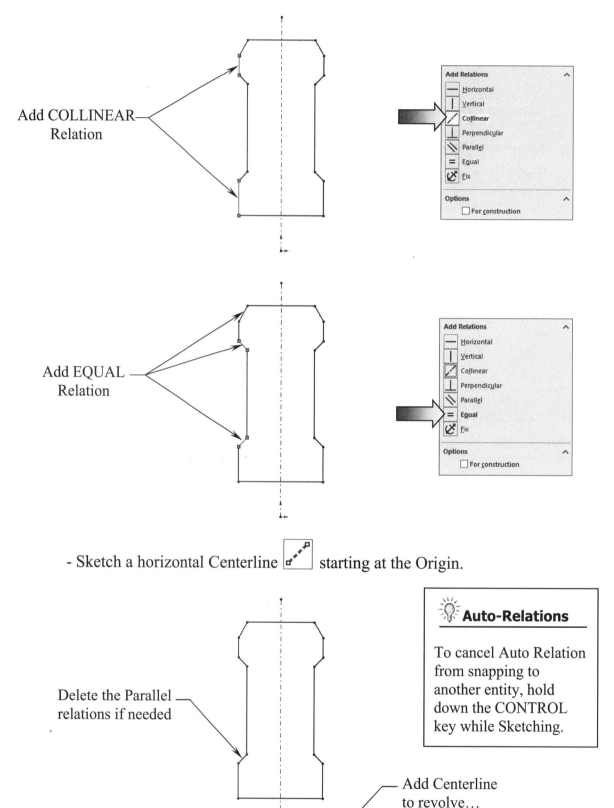

Add COLLINEAR
Relation

Add EQUAL
Relation

- Sketch a horizontal Centerline starting at the Origin.

Delete the Parallel
relations if needed

Auto-Relations

To cancel Auto Relation
from snapping to
another entity, hold
down the CONTROL
key while Sketching.

Add Centerline
to revolve...

- Add the **dimensions** 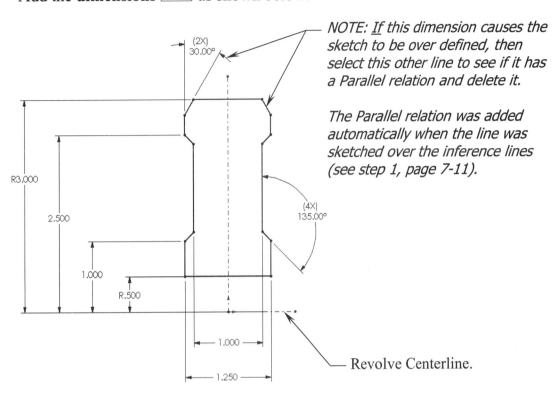 as shown below:

NOTE: _If_ this dimension causes the sketch to be over defined, then select this other line to see if it has a Parallel relation and delete it.

The Parallel relation was added automatically when the line was sketched over the inference lines (see step 1, page 7-11).

Revolve Centerline.

2. Revolving the Base Body:

- Select the horizontal centerline as indicated above.

- Click  or select **Insert / Boss-Base / Revolve**.

- Revolve direction: **One Direction**

- Revolve Angle: **360°**

- Click **OK** .

3. Sketching the Thread Profile:

- Select the <u>face</u> as indicated and click ⬚ or select **Insert / Sketch**.

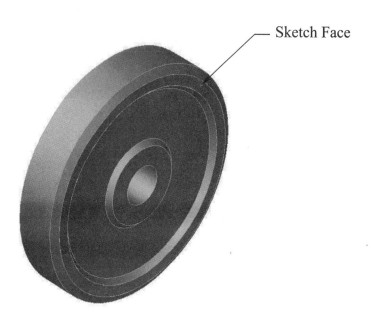

—— Sketch Face

- Click **Normal To** ⬚ from the Standard View Toolbar.

- Sketch a vertical **Centerline** ⬚ starting at the origin.

- Select the **Mirror** tool ⬚ and click the centerline to activate the Dynamic-Mirror mode.

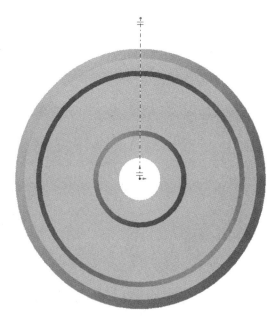

- Sketch the profile using the Line and the 3-Point-Arc tools.

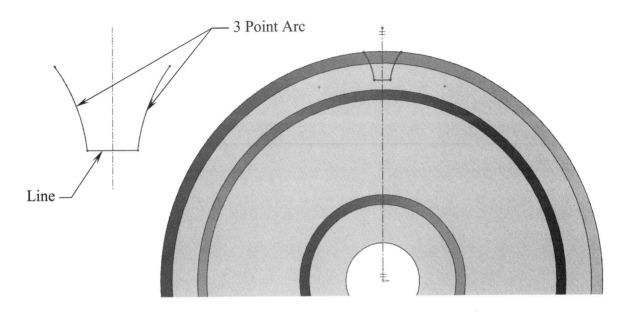

4. Converting the entities:

- Select the **outer edge** of the part and click **Convert Entities** from the Sketch toolbar.

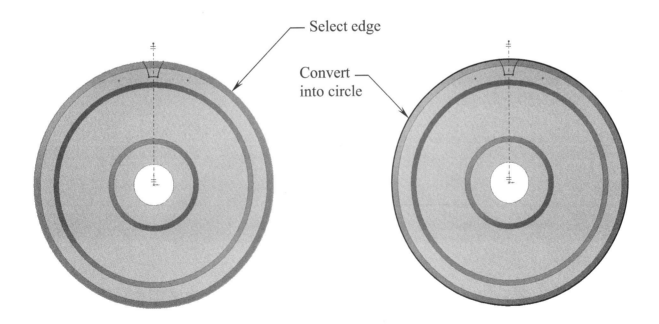

- The selected edge is converted to a circle.

5. Trimming the Sketch Entities:

- Select the **Trim** tool from the Sketch toolbar; select the **Trim-to-Closest**

option , and click on the **lower right edge** of the circle to trim.

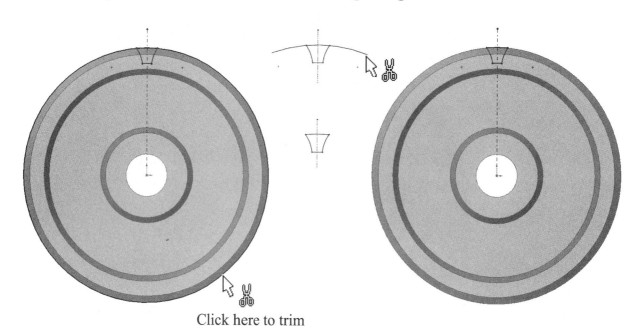

Click here to trim

6. Adding Dimensions:

- Select the **Dimension** Tool from the Sketch-Tools toolbar and add the
dimensions shown.

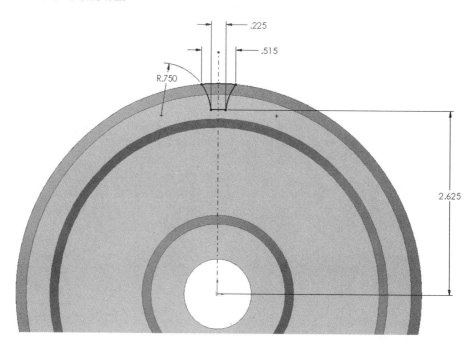

- Switch to the Isometric View 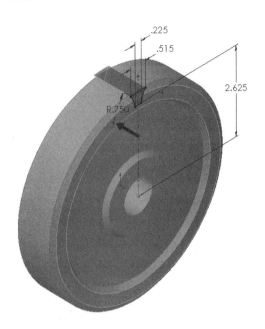 or press **Ctrl + 7**.

7. Cutting the First Tooth:

- Click **Extruded Cut** from the Features toolbar.

- End Condition: **Through All**.

- Click **OK** .

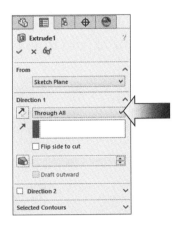

8. Circular Patterning the Tooth:

- Click the drop-down arrow under the **Hide/Show Items** (arrow) and select the Temporary Axis command (arrow). A temporary axis in the center of the hole is created automatically; this axis will be used as the center of the pattern.

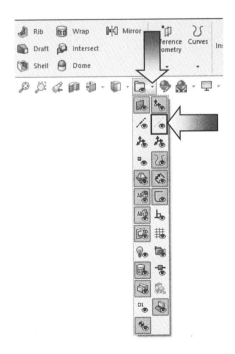

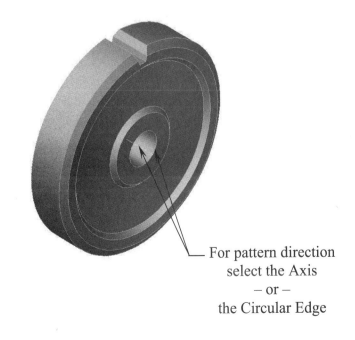

For pattern direction
select the Axis
– or –
the Circular Edge

- Click **Circular Pattern** from the Features toolbar.

- Click on the center **axis** as Direction 1.

- Click the **Equal Spacing** check box.

- Set the Total Angle to **360°**.

- Set the Number of Instances to **24**.

- Click inside the Features to Pattern box and select one of the faces of the cut feature (or select the previous **Extruded-Cut** feature from the tree).

- Click **OK**.

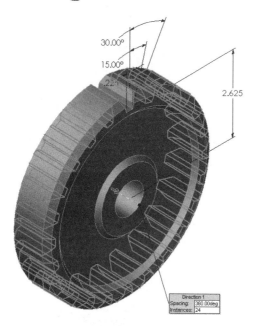

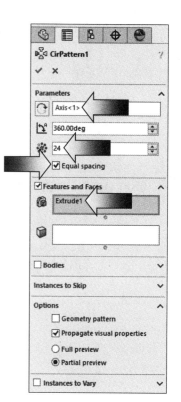

- The resulting circular Pattern.

9. Adding the Keyway:

- Select the <u>face</u> indicated and open a new sketch or select **Insert / Sketch**.

Sketch Face

- Click **Normal To** from the Standard Views toolbar (Ctrl + 8).

- Sketch a vertical **Centerline** starting at the Origin.

- Select the **Mirror** tool and click the centerline to activate the Dynamic-Mirror mode.

💡 **Sketch Mirror**

Use the Mirror option in a sketch to make a symmetrical profile.

When a sketch entity is changed, the mirrored image will also change.

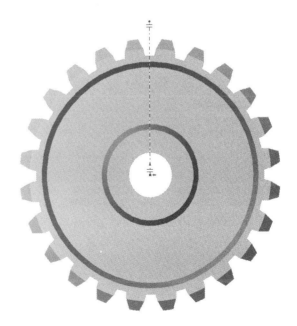

- Sketch the profile of the keyway and add dimension as shown:

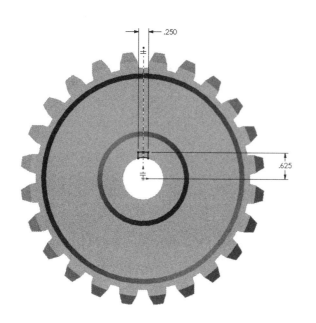

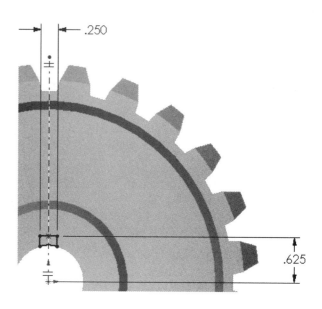

10. Extruding a Cut:

- Click on **Extruded Cut** from the Features toolbar.

- End Condition: **Through All**

- Click **OK** .

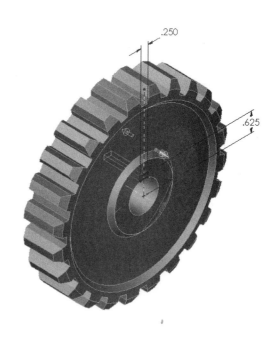

11. Saving Your Work:

- Select **File / Save As**.

- Enter **Spur Gear** for the file name.

- Click **Save**.

Questions for Review

Circular Patterns

1. The Revolve sketch entities should not cross the Revolve centerline.
    a. True
    b. False

2. The system creates **symmetric** relations to all mirrored sketch entities.
    a. True
    b. False

3. An Equal relation makes the entities equal in size.
    a. True
    b. False

4. The system creates an On-Edge relation to all converted entities.
    a. True
    b. False

5. The Trim tool is used to trim 2D sketch entities.
    a. True
    b. False

6. The center of the circular pattern can be defined by an axis, a linear edge, or an angular dimension.
    a. True
    b. False

7. The center of rotation, spacing, number of copies, and features to copy are required when creating a circular pattern.
    a. True
    b. False

8. When the original feature is changed, all instances in the pattern will also change.
    a. True
    b. False

7. TRUE   8. TRUE
5. TRUE   6. TRUE
3. TRUE   4. TRUE
1. TRUE   2. TRUE

CHAPTER 7 (cont.)

Circular Patterns

Circular Patterns
Circular Base Mount

- As mentioned in the 1st half of this chapter, the Circular Pattern command creates an array of feature(s) around an axis.

- These are the elements required to create circular patterns:

   * Center axis (Temporary Axis, Axis, an Edge, etc.)

   * Spacing between each instance

   * Number of instances in the pattern

   * Feature(s) to the pattern

- Only the original feature may be edited and changes made to the original feature will automatically be passed onto the instances within the pattern.

- The features to the pattern can be selected directly from the graphics area or from the Feature Manager tree.

- Instances in a pattern can be skipped. The skipped instances can be edited during or after the pattern is complete.

- The Temporary axis can be toggled on or off (View/Temporary Axis).

- This 2nd half of the chapter will guide you through the use of the Circular Pattern command as well as the Curve Driven Pattern command.

Circular Base Mount
Circular Patterns

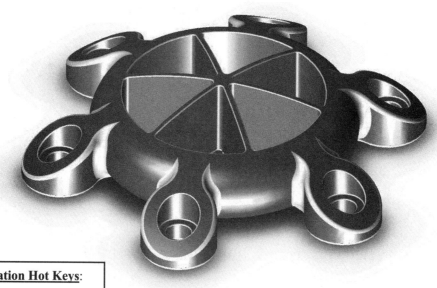

Dimensioning Standards: **ANSI**

Units: **INCHES** – 3 Decimals

Tools Needed:

Insert Sketch	Line	Mirror Dynamic
Add Geometric Relations	Dimension	Base/Boss Revolve
Revolve Cut	Circular Pattern	Fillet/Round

1. Creating the Base Sketch:

- From the <u>Front</u> plane, start a new Sketch .

- Sketch the profile on the right side of the revolve centerline as shown.

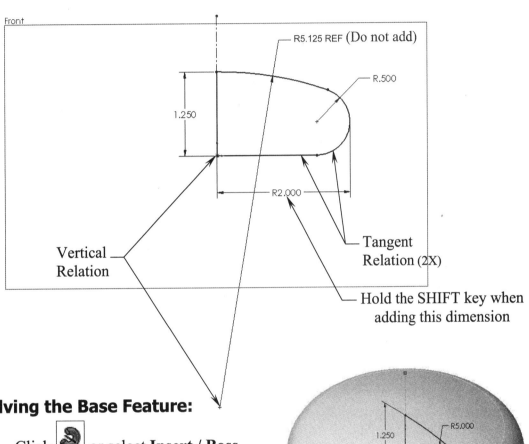

Front

R5.125 REF (Do not add)

R.500

1.250

R2.000

Vertical Relation

Tangent Relation (2X)

Hold the SHIFT key when adding this dimension

2. Revolving the Base Feature:

- Click 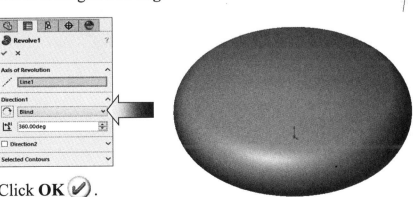 or select **Insert / Boss-Base / Revolve**.

- Revolve Direction: **Blind**.

- Revolve Angle: **360 deg**.

Revolve1

Axis of Revolution
Line1

Direction1
Blind
360.00deg

Direction2

Selected Contours

- Click **OK** .

3. Creating the first Side-Tab sketch:

- Select the <u>Top</u> plane and open a new Sketch.

- Sketch the profile as shown; add the dimensions and relations needed to fully define the sketch.

- Add the **R.250** after the sketch is fully defined.

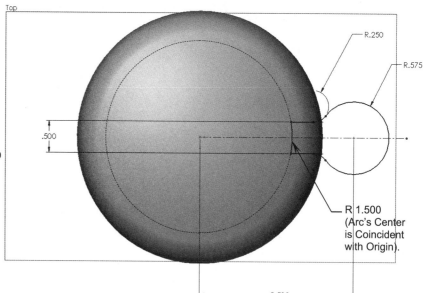

4. Extruding the Side-Tab:

- Click 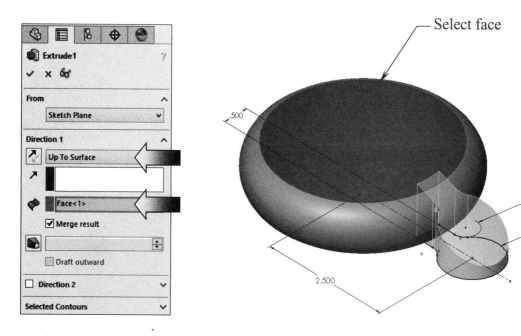 or select **Insert / Boss-Base / Extrude**.

- Direction 1: **Up To Surface**.

- Select the <u>upper surface</u> for End Condition.

Select face

- Click OK.

5. Adding a Counterbore Hole:

- Using the "traditional Method," sketch the profile of the Counter-Bore on the <u>Front</u> plane.

(To create the "Virtual Diameter" dimensions, 1st click the centerline then any other entity and place the dimension on the other side of the centerline.)

Virtual Diameter: Add dimension from the center-line to the end point of the line on the left of the profile.

- Add the 2 Diameter and the 2 Depth dimensions.

- Add the relations needed to fully define the sketch.

Mid-Point Relation

6. Cutting the C'Bore:

- Click 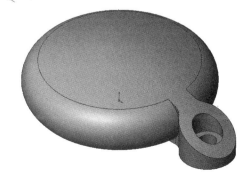 or select **Insert /Cut / Revolve**.

- Revolve Direction: **Blind**.

- Revolve Angle: **360 deg**.

- Click **OK** ✅ .

7. Creating the circular pattern:

- Click 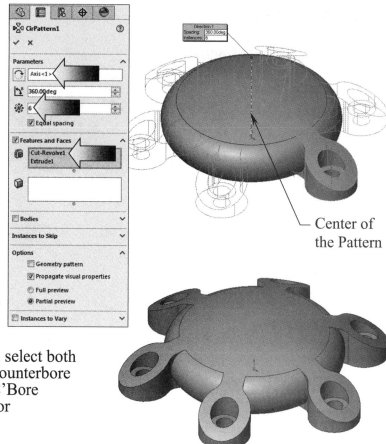 Circular Pattern (below Linear).

- From the **View** menu, select the **Temporary-Axis** option.

- Select the **Axis** in the middle of the part as noted.

- Set Pattern Angle to **360°**

- Enter **6** for the Number of Instances.

- For Features to Pattern, select both the **Side Tab** and the Counterbore hole (either select the C'Bore from the graphics area or from the Feature tree).

- Click **OK**.

Center of the Pattern

8. Creating a new Plane:

- Click or select **Insert / Reference Geometry / Plane**.

- Select **Offset Distance** option.

- Enter **1.300 in.** as the distance.

- Select the **TOP** reference plane from the FeatureManager tree to offset from.

- Click **OK**.

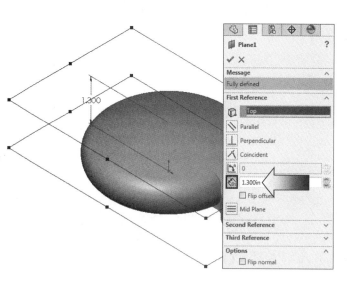

9. Creating the Pockets Sketch:

- Select the <u>new plane</u> (Plane1) and open a new sketch.

- Use the **Dynamic Mirror** 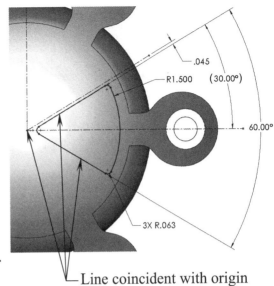 and sketch the profile as shown.

- Add the dimensions and relations as needed to fully define the sketch.

- Use **Circular Sketch Pattern** to make a total of 6 instances of the pocket.

.045
R1.500   (30.00°)
60.00°
3X R.063
Line coincident with origin

10. Cutting the Pockets:

- Click 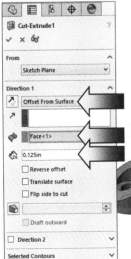 or select **Insert / Cut / Extrude**.

- For direction 1, use **Offset From Surface**.

- Select the **bottom surface** to offset from.

- Enter **.125 in**. for Depth.

- Click **OK** ✓.

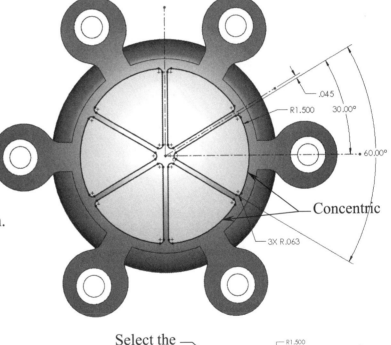

.045
R1.500   30.00°
60.00°
Concentric
3X R.063

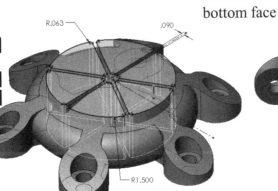

Cut-Extrude1
From
Sketch Plane
Direction 1
Offset From Surface
Face<1>
0.125in
☐ Reverse offset
☐ Translate surface
☐ Flip side to cut
☐ Draft outward
☐ Direction 2
Selected Contours

R.063   .090
R1.500

Select the bottom face

R1.500

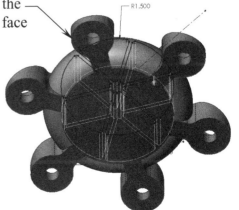

11. Adding the .0625" Fillets:

- Click **Fillet**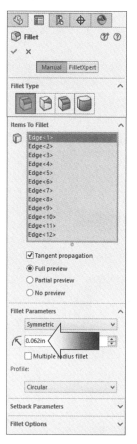
  or select **Insert /
  Features / Fillet-
  Round**.

- Enter **.062 in**.
  for radius size.

- Select all upper
  and lower edges
  of the <u>6 tabs</u>.

- Click **OK** ✔.

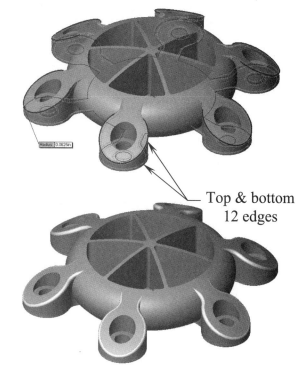

Top & bottom
12 edges

12. Adding the .125" Fillets:

- Click **Fillet** or select
  **Insert / Features / Fillet-
  Round.**

- Enter **.125 in**. for Radius.

- Select all edges on the sides
  of the <u>6 tabs</u> or select the
  6 faces as noted.

- Click **OK** ✔.

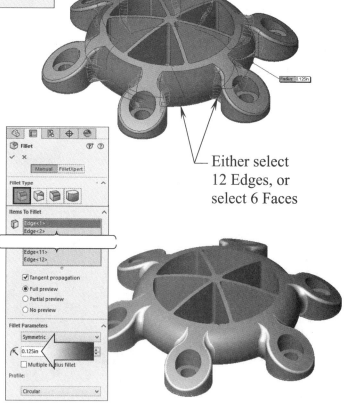

Either select
12 Edges, or
select 6 Faces

13. Adding the .015" Fillets:

- Click **Fillet**  or select
  Insert / Features / Fillet-Round.

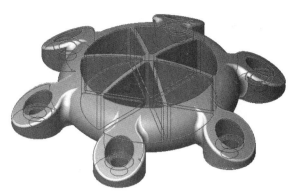

- Enter **.015 in**. for
  radius size.

- Select <u>all edges</u>
  of the 6 Pockets
  and the 6
  Counterbores.

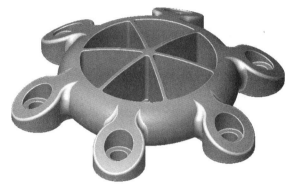

- Click **OK**.

14. Saving your work:

- Click **File / Save As**.

- Enter **Circular Base Mount** for file name.

- Click **Save**.

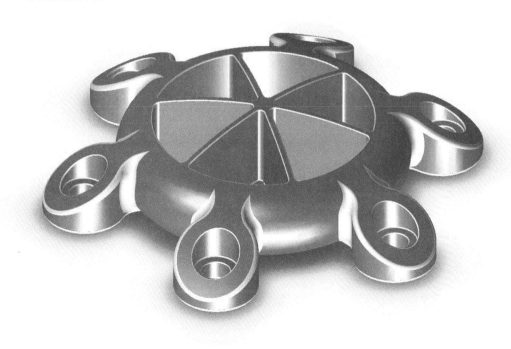

Questions for Review

Circular Patterns

1. The Circular Patterns command can also be selected from Insert / Pattern Mirror / Circular Pattern.
    a. True
    b. False

2. A Temporary Axis can be used as the center of the pattern.
    a. True
    b. False

3. A linear edge can also be used as the center of the circular pattern.
    a. True
    b. False

4. The Temporary Axis can be toggled ON / OFF under View / Temporary Axis.
    a. True
    b. False

5. The instances in the circular pattern can be skipped during and after the pattern is created.
    a. True
    b. False

6. If an *instance* of the patterned feature is deleted, the whole pattern will also be deleted.
    a. True
    b. False

7. If the *original* patterned feature is deleted, the whole pattern will also be deleted.
    a. True
    b. False

8. When the Equal spacing check box is enabled, the total angle (360°) must be used.
    a. True
    b. False

7. TRUE   8. FALSE
5. TRUE   6. FALSE
3. TRUE   4. TRUE
1. TRUE   2. TRUE

CHAPTER 7 (cont.)

Curve Driven Patterns

Curve Driven Patterns
Universal Bracket

- The **Curve Driven Pattern** PropertyManager appears when you create
 a new curve driven pattern feature or when you edit an existing curve driven pattern feature.

- The PropertyManager controls the following properties:

   Pattern Direction: Select a curve, edge, sketch entity, or select a sketch from the
   FeatureManager to use as the path for the pattern. If necessary, click Reverse Direction to
   change the direction of the pattern.

   Number of Instances: Set a value for the number of instances of the seed feature in the
   pattern.

   Equal spacing: Sets equal spacing between each pattern instance. The separation between
   instances depends on the curve selected for Pattern Direction and on the Curve method.

   Spacing: (Available if you do not select Equal spacing.) Set a value for the distance between
   pattern instances along the curve. The distance between the curve and the Features to Pattern
   is measured normal to the curve.

Curve method: Defines the direction of the pattern by transforming how you use the curve selected
for Pattern Direction. Select one of the following:

   * **Transform curve**. The delta X and delta Y distances from the origin of the selected curve
     to the seed feature are maintained for each instance.

   * **Offset curve**: The normal distance from the origin of the selected curve to the seed feature
     is maintained for each instance.

Alignment method: Select one of the following:

   * **Tangent to curve**: Aligns each instance tangent to the curve selected for Pattern direction.

   * **Align to seed**: Aligns each instance to match the original alignment of the seed feature of
     Curve method and **Alignment method** selections.

   * **Face normal:** (For 3D curves only.) Select the face on which the 3D curve lies to create the
     curve driven pattern.

Curve Driven Pattern and Hole Wizard
Universal Bracket

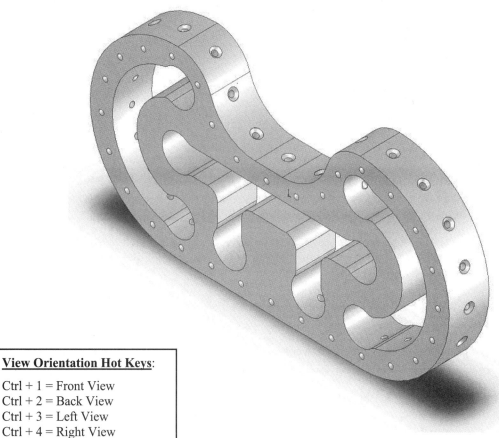

Dimensioning Standards: **ANSI**

Units: **INCHES** – 3 Decimals

Tools Needed:

 Insert Sketch

 Convert Entities

 Offset Entities

 Boss Base Extrude

 Hole Wizard

 Curve Driven Pattern

1. Opening the existing file:

- Go to: The Training Files folder
            <u>Open</u> a copy of the file named
            Curve Driven Pattern.sldprt

- **<u>Edit</u>** the **Sketch1.**

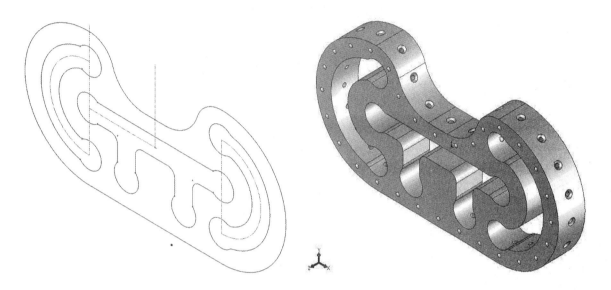

- Make sure the sketch1 is fully defined before extruding.

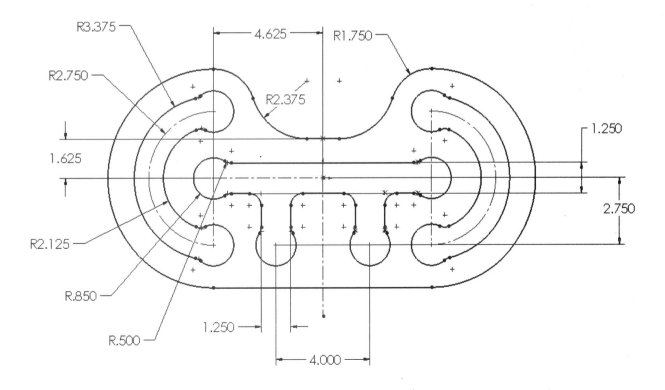

2. Extruding the Base:

- Click 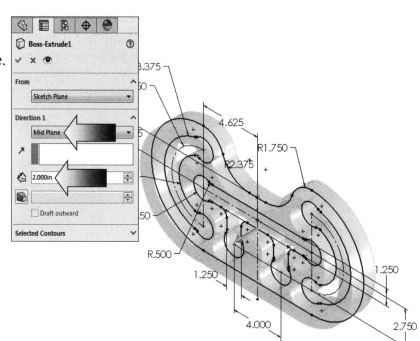 or select **Insert / Features / Boss Base Extrude**.

- Use **Mid Plane** for Direction1.

- Enter **2.00 in**. for Depth.

- Click **OK** ✓.

3. Creating the sketch of the 1st hole:

- Select the <u>face</u> as indicated and open a new sketch.

- Sketch a Centerline at the Mid-Point of the two arcs.

- Add a Circle on the Mid-Point of the centerline.

- Add a **Ø.250 in**. dimension.

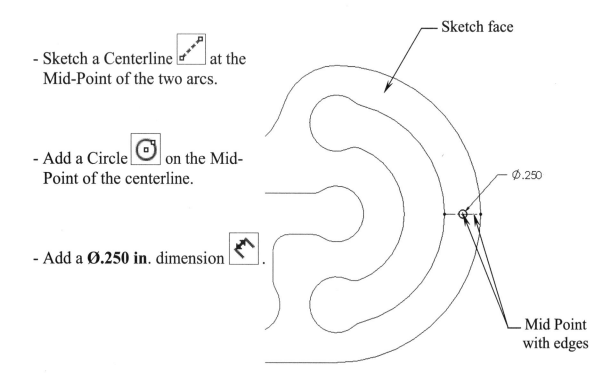

Sketch face

Ø.250

Mid Point with edges

4. Cutting the hole:

- Click 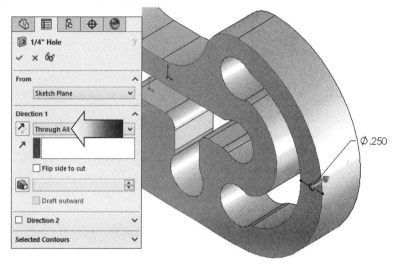 or select **Insert / Cut / Extrude**.

- Select **Through All** Direction1.

- Click **OK** .

5. Constructing the Curve-Sketch to drive the Pattern:

- Select the <u>face</u> as noted* and open a new sketch .

- Select all Outer-Edges of the part (Right click on an edge & Select Tangency).

- Click or select **Tools / Sketch Entities / Offset Entities**.

- Enter **.563 in**. for Offset Distance.

- Click Reverse if necessary to place the new profile on the **<u>inside</u>**.

- **Exit** the sketch mode and change the name of the sketch to **CURVE1**.

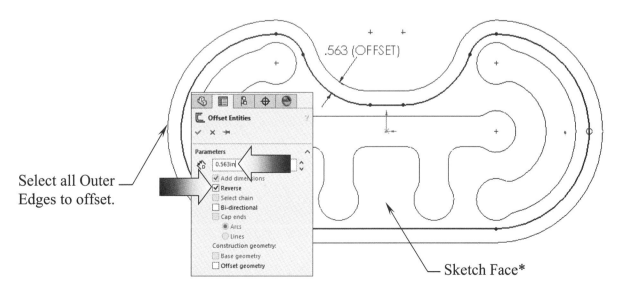

Select all Outer Edges to offset.

Sketch Face*

.563 (OFFSET)

6. Creating the 1st Curve-Driven Pattern:

- Click 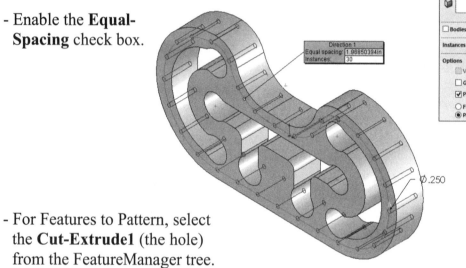 or select **Insert / Pattern Mirror / Curve Driven Pattern**.

- For Direction1, select the **Curve1** from the Feature-Manager tree.

- For Number of Instances, enter **30**.

- Enable the **Equal-Spacing** check box.

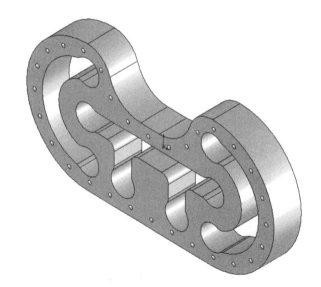

- For Features to Pattern, select the **Cut-Extrude1** (the hole) from the FeatureManager tree.

- Click **OK** ✓.

- Hide the Curve1.

7. Constructing the 2nd Curve:

- Select the <u>Front</u> plane and open a new sketch 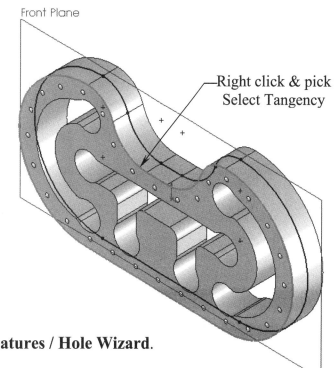.

- Select all **Outer-Edges** of the part and click or select **Tools / Sketch Entities / Convert Entities**.

- **Exit the Sketch** and change the sketch name to **CURVE2**.

Front Plane

—Right click & pick Select Tangency

8. Adding the Hole Wizard:

- Click or select **Insert / Features / Hole Wizard**.

- Select the **Counter-Sink** option and set the following:

* Standard: **Ansi Inch**
* Type: **Flat Head Screw** (100)
* Size: **1/4**
* Fit: **Normal**
* End Condition: **Blind**
* Depth: **1.250 in**.

- Select the **Position** tab (arrow) and click the **3D Sketch** button `3D Sketch`; this option allows the holes to be placed on non-planar surfaces as well.

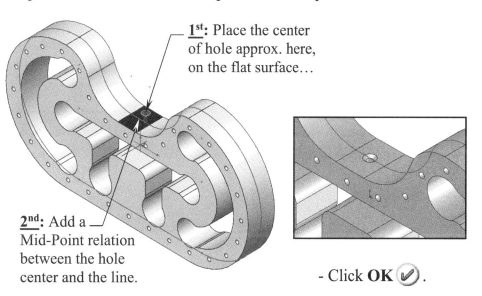

1st: Place the center of hole approx. here, on the flat surface...

2nd: Add a Mid-Point relation between the hole center and the line.

- Click **OK** ✓.

9. Creating the 2nd Curve Driven Pattern:

- Click 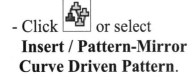 or select
Insert / Pattern-Mirror Curve Driven Pattern.

- For Direction1, select the **Curve2** from the FeatureManager tree.

- For Number of Instances, enter **30**.

- Enable **Equal Spacing** option.

- Select the **Tangent To Curve** option.

- For Features to Pattern, select the **CSK-Hole** from the FeatureManager tree.

- Click **OK** ✓.

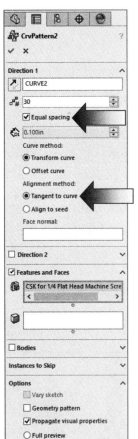

10. Saving a copy of your work:

- Click **File / Save As**.

- Enter **Curve Driven Pattern** for file name.

- Click **Save**.

CHAPTER 8

Part Configurations

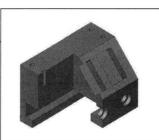

Part Configurations
Machined Block

- This chapter reviews most of the commands that were covered in the previous chapters plus the use of configurations in the part level. Upon successful completion of this lesson, you will have a better understanding of how and when to:

* Sketch on planes and planar surfaces.

* Sketch fillets and model fillets.

* Dimensions and Geometric Relations.

* Extruded Cuts and Bosses.

* Linear Patterns.

* Using the Hole-Wizard option.

* Create new Planes.

* Mirror features.

* Create new Part Configurations, an option that allows the user to develop and manage families of parts and assemblies.

- Configuration options are available in Part and Assembly environments.

- After the model is completed, it will be used again in a drawing chapter to further discuss the details of creating an Engineering drawing.

Machined Block
Part Configurations

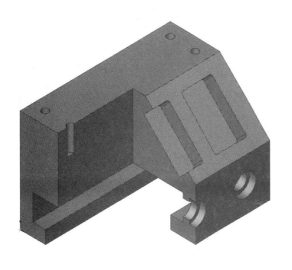
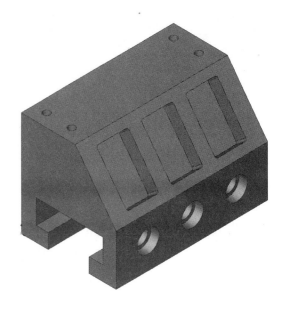

View Orientation Hot Keys:

Ctrl + 1 = Front View
Ctrl + 2 = Back View
Ctrl + 3 = Left View
Ctrl + 4 = Right View
Ctrl + 5 = Top View
Ctrl + 6 = Bottom View
Ctrl + 7 = Isometric View
Ctrl + 8 = Normal To
             Selection

Dimensioning Standards: **ANSI**
Units: **INCHES** – 3 Decimals

Tools Needed:

Insert Sketch	Line	Rectangle
Circle	Sketch Fillet	Dimension
Add Geometric Relations	Extruded Boss/Base	Extruded Cut
Hole Wizard	Linear Pattern	Fillet

1. Sketching the base profile:

- Select the <u>Front</u> plane from the FeatureManager tree.

- Click 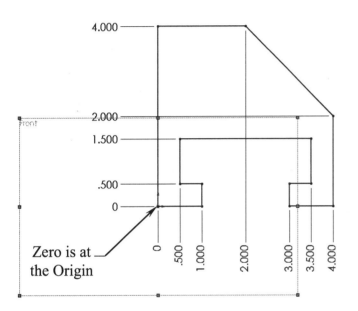 or select **Insert / Sketch**.

- Sketch the profile below using the Line tool .

- Add the dimensions shown.

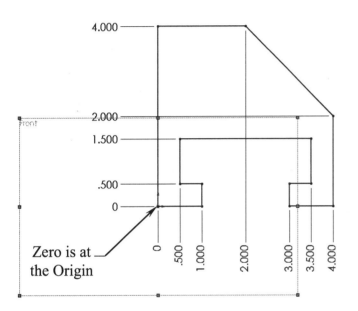

Zero is at the Origin

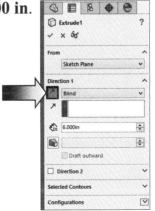

Ordinate Dimensions

To create Ordinate dimensions:

1. Click the small drop down arrow below the Smart-Dimension command and select either Vertical or Horizontal Ordinate option.

2. First click at a vertex to determine the Zero dimension, then click the next entity to create the next dimension.

3. Repeat step 2 for the other entities / dimensions.

2. Extruding the base feature:

- Click or select **Insert / Boss-Base / Extrude**.

- End Condition: **Blind**.

- Extrude Depth: **6.00 in**.

- Click **OK** .

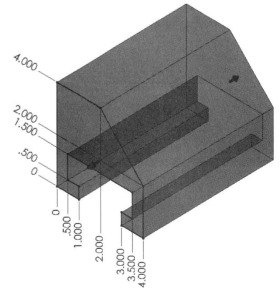

3. Creating the pocket profiles:

- Select the <u>face</u> as indicated below for sketch plane.

- Click 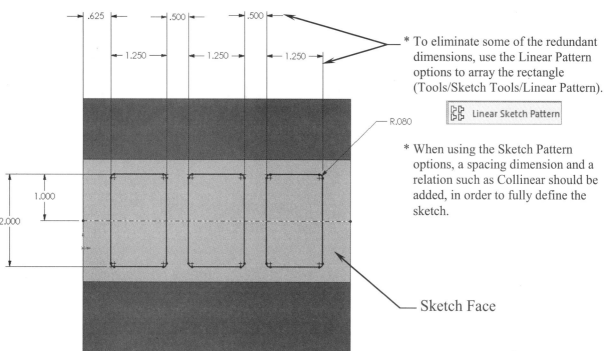 or select **Insert / Sketch**.

- Sketch the profile below using Rectangle and Sketch Fillet tools.

- Add dimensions or Relations needed to fully define the sketch*.

* To eliminate some of the redundant dimensions, use the Linear Pattern options to array the rectangle (Tools/Sketch Tools/Linear Pattern).

Linear Sketch Pattern

* When using the Sketch Pattern options, a spacing dimension and a relation such as Collinear should be added, in order to fully define the sketch.

R.080

Sketch Face

4. Cutting the pockets:

- Click  or select
Insert / Cut / Extrude.

- End Condition: **Blind**.

- Extrude Depth: **.500 in**.

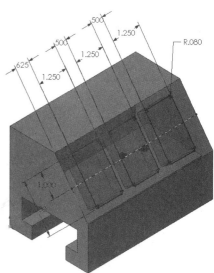

- Click **OK** .

5. Adding a CounterBore from the Hole Wizard:

- Select the <u>face*</u> as shown for sketch plane.

- Click 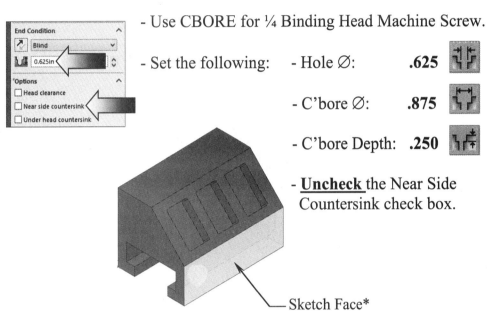 or select **Insert / Features / Hole / Wizard**.

- Click the **Counterbore** button (Circled).

- Use CBORE for ¼ Binding Head Machine Screw.

- Set the following: - Hole ∅:   **.625**

- C'bore ∅:   **.875**

- C'bore Depth: **.250**

- **<u>Uncheck</u>** the Near Side Countersink check box.

Sketch Face*

- Select the **Positions Tab** (arrow). (Note: We need to review the pattern and mirror commands, so only one hole will be created and then pattern it to create the others).

- Add Dimensions 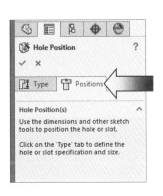 as shown to position the C'bore.

- Click **OK** ✓.

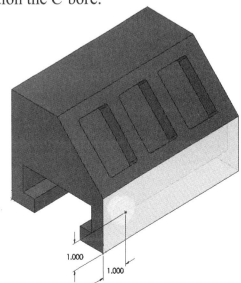

1.000

1.000

6. Patterning the Counterbore:

- Click 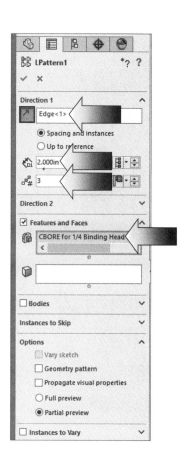 or select **Insert / Pattern Mirror / Linear Pattern**.

- Select the **bottom edge** as direction.

- Enter **2.00 in**. for Spacing.

- Type **3** for Number of Instances.

- Select the **C'bore** feature as Features to Pattern.

- Click **OK** ✓.

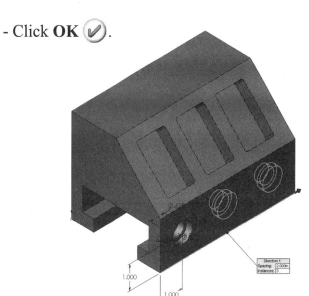

7. Creating the Mirror-Plane:

- Click 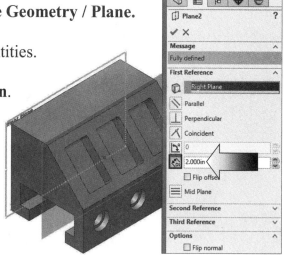 or select **Insert / Reference Geometry / Plane.**

- Select the <u>Right</u> plane as Reference Entities.

- Click **Offset Distance** and enter **2.00 in**.

- Use the Flip option if needed to place the new plane on the **right side**.

- Click **OK** ✓.

8. Mirroring the C'bores:

- Click [icon] or select **Mirror** under **Insert / Pattern Mirror menu**.

- Select the <u>new plane </u>(Plane1) as Mirror Face/Plane [icon] .

- Choose the C'bore and its Pattern as Features to Pattern [icon] .

- Click **OK** [icon].

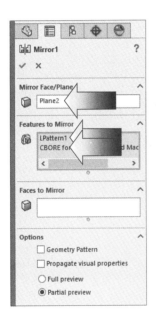

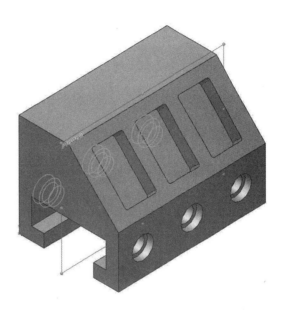

- Rotate [icon] the model around to verify the result of the mirror.

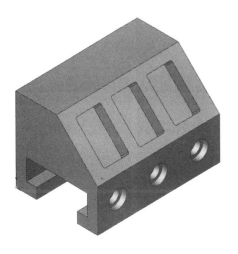

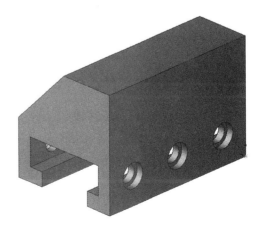

9. Creating the blind holes:

- Select the <u>top face</u>* as the new sketch plane.

- Click 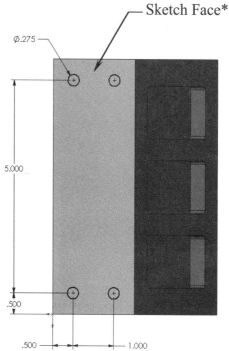 or select **Insert / Sketch**.

- Sketch 4 Circles as shown.

- Add Dimensions and Relations needed to fully define the sketch.

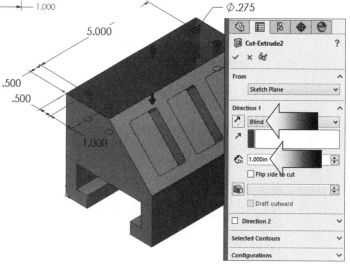

10. Cutting the 4 holes:

- Click or select
Insert / Cut / Extrude.

- End Condition: **Blind**.

- Extrude Depth: **1.00 in**.

- Click **OK** .

11. Creating a Cutaway section: (in a separate configuration).

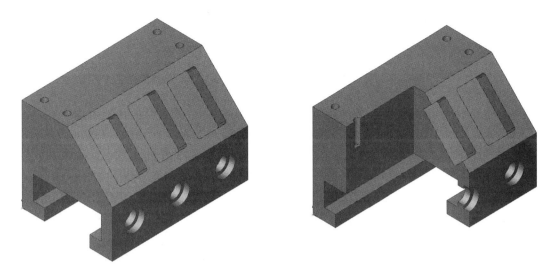

Default Configuration   **New Cutaway Configuration**

- At the top of the FeatureManager tree, select the **Configuration tab**.

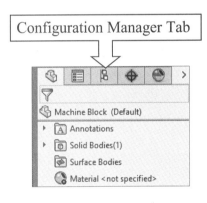

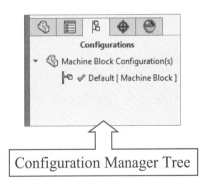

- Right click on the name of the part and select **Add Configuration**.

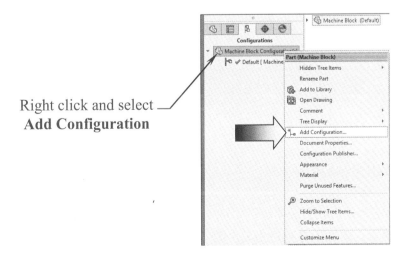

Right click and select ——
Add Configuration

- Under Configuration Name, enter **Cutaway View.**

- Click **OK** OK

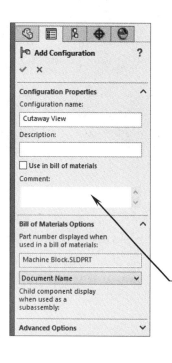

── Optional: enter a comment to
reference the changes
in this configuration.

┌─────────────────────────────────────┐
│ 🔆 **Configurations**   │
│   │
│ The Configuration option   │
│ allows you to create   │
│ multiple variations of a   │
│ part or assembly and save   │
│ all changes within the   │
│ same document.   │
└─────────────────────────────────────┘

── Sketch face

12. Sketching a profile for the cut:

- Select the face indicated as the new
  sketch plane.

- Click [ ] or select **Insert / Sketch.**

- Sketch the profile as shown using

  the Corner Rectangle [ ] tool.

- Add the dimensions or relations
  needed to fully define the sketch.

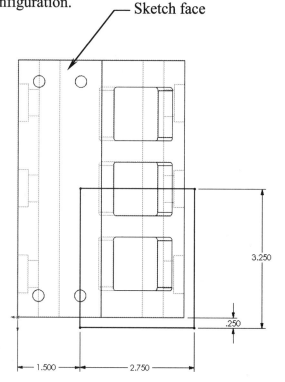

13. Creating the section cut:

- Click 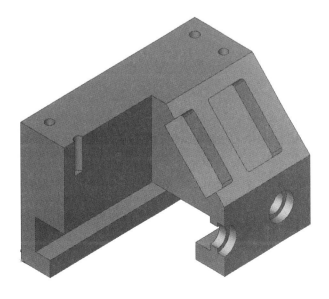 or select **Insert / Cut / Extrude**.

- End Condition: **Through All.**

- Click **OK** ✅.

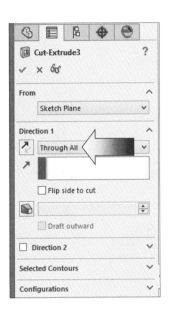

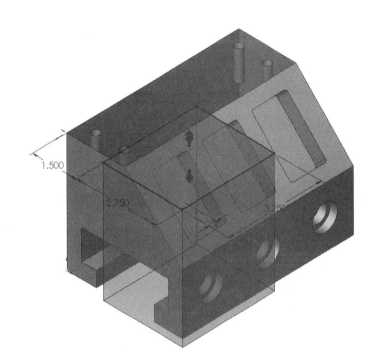

- The Cutaway section view.

14. Switching between the Configurations:

- Double-click on Default configuration to see the original part.

- Double-click on Cutaway View configuration to see the cut feature.

Double-click to toggle between Configurations*

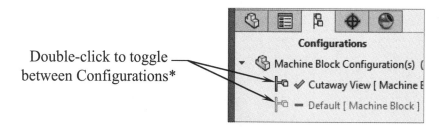

* The **Yellow** icon next to the name of the configuration means it is **active**.

* The **Grey** icon next to the name of the configuration means it is **inactive**.

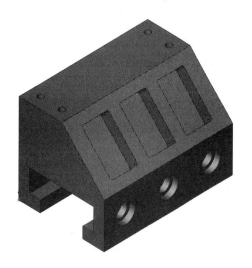

Cutaway Configuration

Default Configuration

- The Cutaway configuration will be used again in one of the drawing chapters.

- There is no limit on how many configurations can be created and saved in a part document.

- If a part has many configurations, it is might be better to use a design table to help manage them (refer to chapter 20 in this textbook for more infomation on how to create multiple configurations using the Design Table option).

15. Splitting the FeatureManager pane:

- Locate the Split Handle on top of the FeatureManager tree and drag it down about half way.

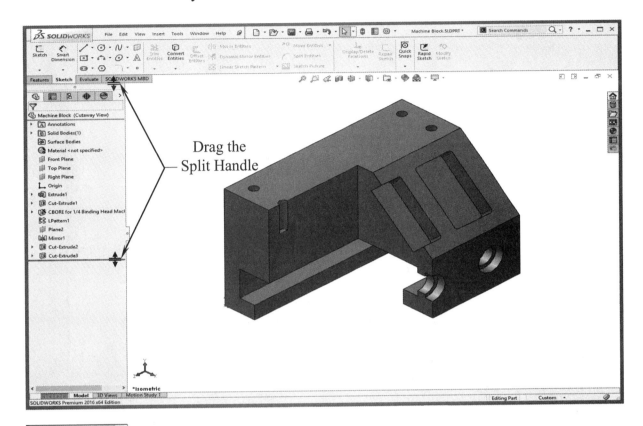

Drag the
Split Handle

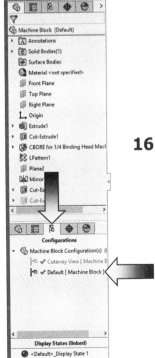

- Click the ConfigurationManager tab (arrow) to change the lower half to ConfigurationManager.

- Double click on the **Default** configuration to activate it.

16. Creating a new configuration:

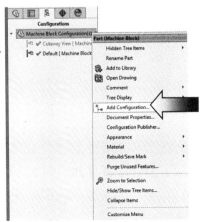

- Right click the name of the part and select **Add Configuration** (arrow).

- For the name of the new configuration, enter **Machine Features Suppressed**.

- Click **OK** to close the config. dialog (see next page)...

- Hold the Control key and select the following cut features from the tree: **Cut-Extrude1, C'Bore for 1/4 Binding Head, LPattern1, Mirror1,** and **Cut-Extrude2**.

- Release the Control key and click the **Suppress** button from the pop-up window.

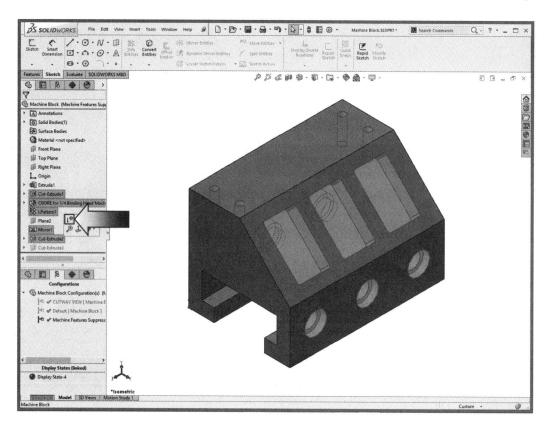

- The machine features are now suppressed and their feature icons are diplayed in grey color on the feature tree.

The machine features are now suppressed

- Double click on each configuration to see the changes between each one.

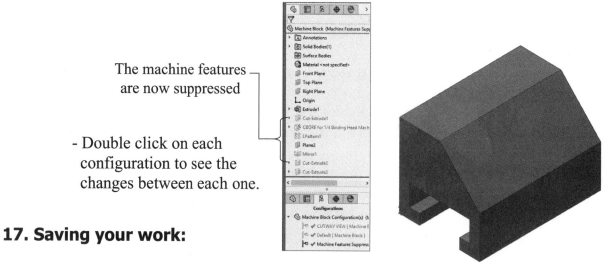

17. Saving your work:

- Select **File / Save As / Machined Block / Save**.

18. Optional:

- Create 3 additional configurations and change the dimensions indicated below: (Select **This Configuration** option from the pull-down list after each change).

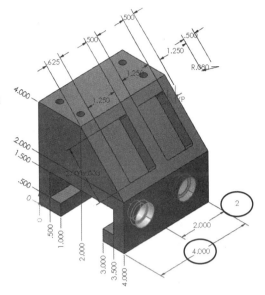

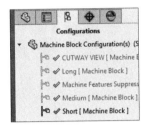

Short Configuration:

* Overall length: **4.00in**
* Number of Pockets: **2**
* Number of holes: **2**

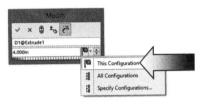

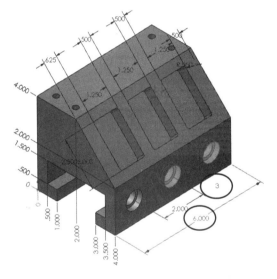

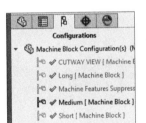

Medium Configuration:
(Change from Default)
* Overall length: **6.00in**
* Number of Pockets: **3**
* Number of holes: **3**

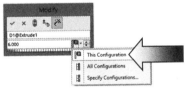

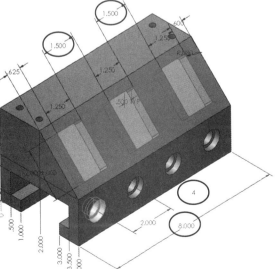

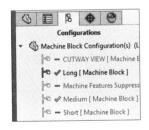

Long Configuration:

* Overall length: **4.00in**
* Number of Pockets: **2**
* Number of holes: **2**

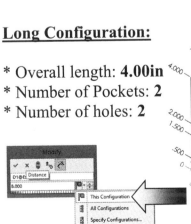

Questions for Review

Part Configurations

1. The five basic steps to create an extruded feature are:
    - Select a sketch Plane OR a planar surface
    - Activate Sketch Pencil (Insert / Sketch)
    - Sketch the profile
    - Define the profile (Dimensions / Relations)
    - Extrude the profile
        a. True
        b. False

2. When the extrude type is set to Blind, a depth dimension has to be specified as the End-Condition.
        a. True
        b. False

3. More than one closed sketch profiles on the same surface can be extruded at the same time to the same depth.
        a. True
        b. False

4. In the Hole Wizard definition, the Counterbore's parameters such as bore diameter, hole depth, etc. cannot be changed.
        a. True
        b. False

5. Holes created using the Hole Wizard cannot be patterned.
        a. True
        b. False

6. Configurations in a part can be toggled ON / OFF by double clicking on their icons.
        a. True
        b. False

7. Every part document can only have *one* configuration in it.
        a. True
        b. False

7. FALSE

5. FALSE   6. TRUE

3. TRUE   4. FALSE

1. TRUE   2. TRUE

Exercise 1: Using Vary-Sketch

1. Opening an existing part:

- Browse to the training folder and
open a part document named
Vary Sketch.sldprt

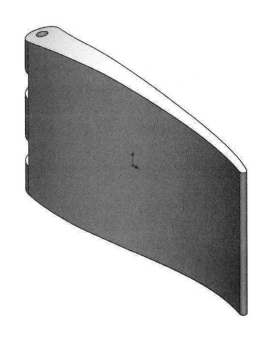

2. Creating a new configuration:

- Change to the ConfigurationManager
tree.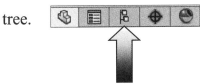

- Create a new configuration called **With Cutouts**.

3. Creating the cutouts:

- Open a new sketch on the <u>Front</u> plane.

- Create 2 separate
Offset-Entities at
.275in each.

- Place the new
entities on the
<u>inside</u>.

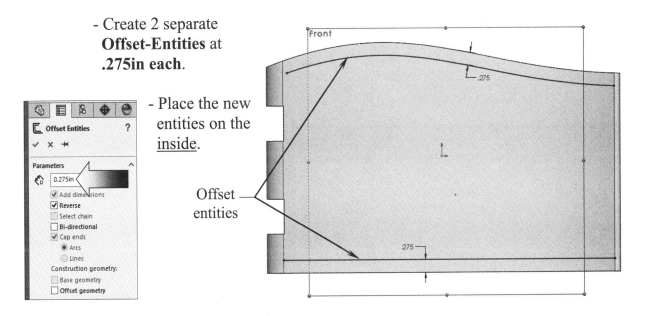

Offset
entities

- Drag the endpoints
  outward to extend
  the spline and the
  line.

Drag endpoints
outward

- Every converted
  entity will have an
  On-Edge relation
  added to it to reference
  the model edge that
  it was created from.

- Add 2 additional lines.
  Make the lines a little
  longer so that
  trimming them will
  be easier.

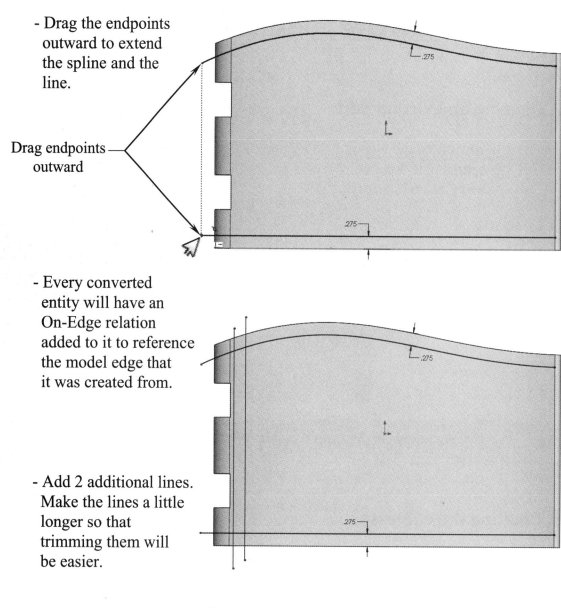

- Trim the entities.

Trim entities

- The profile should be
  closed and fully defined.

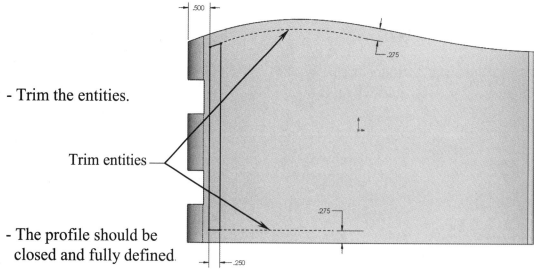

- Click **Extruded Cut**.

- Use **Through All-Both** to cut through both sides.

- Click **OK**.

4. Creating a linear pattern:

- Change to the Features toolbar and select the **Linear Pattern** command.

Pattern direction

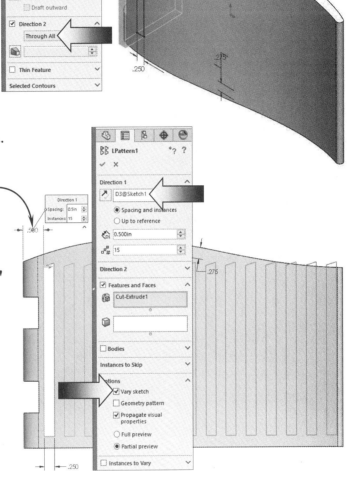

- For Pattern Direction select the dimension **.500"**

- Enter **.500in** for spacing.

- Enter **15** for number of instances.

- For Features and Faces to pattern select **Cut-Extrude1**, the rectangular cut from the previous step.

- Enable the **Vary Sketch** checkbox.

- Click **OK**. Toggle between the 2 configurations to see the differences.

- Save your work as **Vary Sketch_Exe1**.

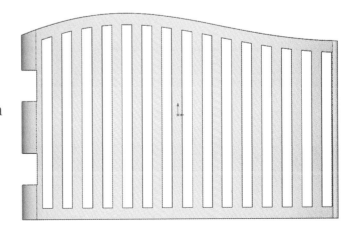

Exercise 2: Using Vary-Sketch

1. The Vary Sketch allows the pattern instances to change dimensions as they repeat.
2. Create the part as shown, focusing on the Linear Pattern & Vary-Sketch option.

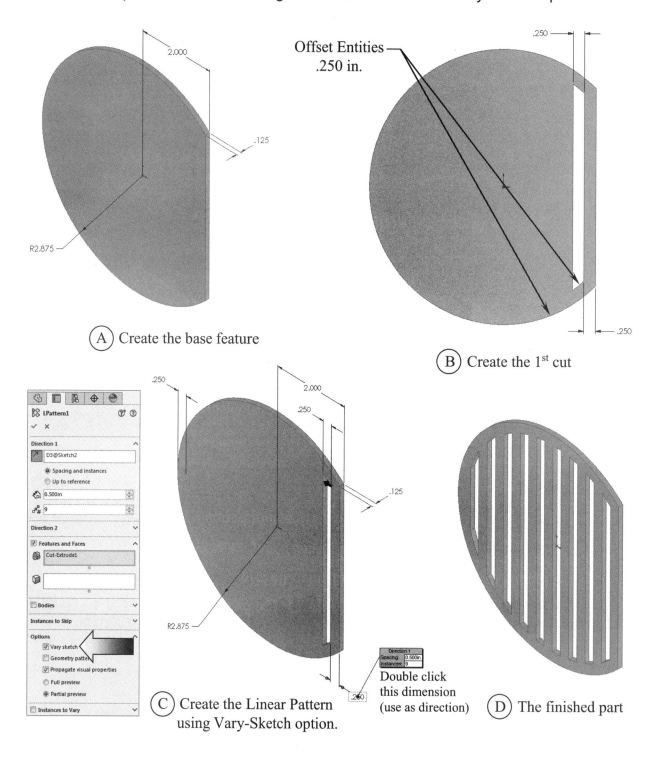

(A) Create the base feature

(B) Create the 1st cut

(C) Create the Linear Pattern using Vary-Sketch option.

Double click this dimension (use as direction)

(D) The finished part

3. Save your work as **Vary Sketch_Exe.**

CHAPTER 9

Modeling Threads

Modeling Threads - External
Threaded Insert

- Most of the time threads are not modeled in the part, instead they are represented with dashed lines and callouts in the drawings. But for non-standard threads they should be modeled in the part so that they can be used in some applications such as Stereo Lithography for 3D printing or Finite Element Analysis for simulation studies, etc.

- The traditional method that was used to create the threads required two sketches to make the threads:

  * A sweep path (a helix that controls the pitch, revolutions, starting angle, and left or right hand threads).

  * A sweep profile (shape and size of the threads).

- Most of the time the sweep cut command is used when creating the threads but in some cases, the sweep boss command can also be used to add material to the sweep path when making the external threads.

- The new thread feature creates the thread profile and the helical path based on the user's inputs. The on-screen parameters allows you to define the start thread location, specify an offset, set end conditions, specify the type, size, diameter, pitch and rotation angle, and choose options such as right-hand or left-hand thread.

- This chapter and its exercises will guide you through some special techniques on how internal and external threads can be created in SOLIDWORKS.

Modeling Threads – External
Threaded Insert

Dimensioning Standards: **ANSI**

Units: **INCHES** – 3 Decimals

Tools Needed:

 Insert Sketch

 Line

 Thread Feature

 Dimension

 Add Geometric Relations

 Helix/Spiral

 Extruded Base / Revolve

 Cut Sweep

 Mirror

1. Sketching the base profile:

- Select the <u>Front</u> plane from the FeatureManager tree.

- Click **Sketch** or select **Insert / Sketch**.

- Sketch the profile as shown below using the **Line** tool .

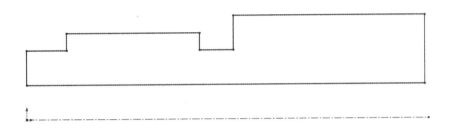

- Add the **Ordinate** dimensions shown below to fully define the sketch.

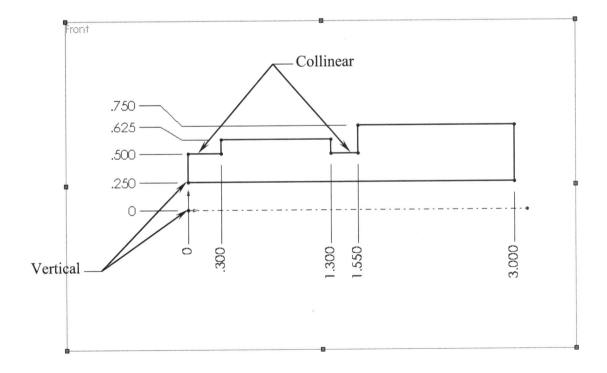

(The Ordinate dimension options are under the Smart Dimension command.)

2. Revolving the base feature:

- Click **Revolve**  or select **Insert / Base / Revolve**.

- Revolve Direction: **Blind**.

- Revolve Angle: **360°**

- Click **OK** ✓.

💡 **Axis of Revolution**

The center of a revolved feature can now be an axis, a centerline, a sketch line, or a linear model edge.

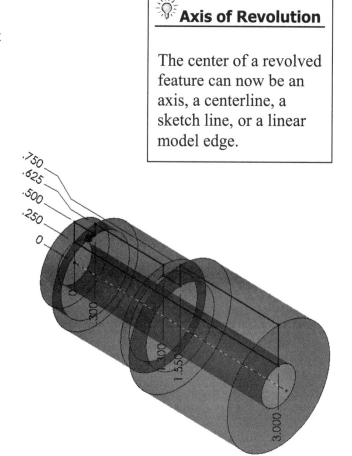

3. Creating the right hand threads:

- Using the traditional method you can create helical threads on cylindrical faces by sweeping a thread profile along a helical path. This option requires a little bit more work than the new Thread feature.

- The new thread feature creates the thread profile and the helical path based on the user's inputs. The on-screen parameters allows you to define the start thread location, specify an offset, set end conditions, specify the type, size, diameter, pitch and rotation angle, and choose options such as right-hand or left-hand thread.

- Click **Threads** 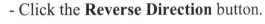 or select **Insert / Features / Threads**.

- For Edge of Cylinder, click the **circular edge** as noted.

- For Start Location, select the **face** shown.

- Enable the **Offset** checkbox.

- For Offset Distance, enter **.0625in**.

- Click the **Reverse Direction** button.

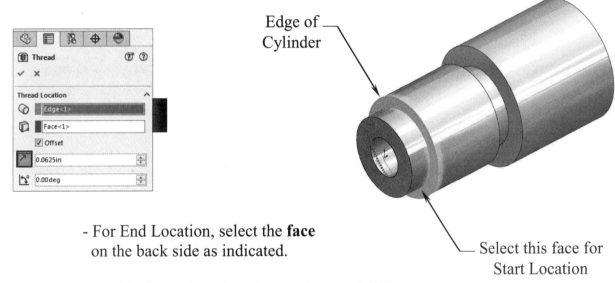

Edge of Cylinder

Select this face for Start Location

- For End Location, select the **face** on the back side as indicated.

- Enable the **Offset** checkbox and enter **.0625in.** for Offset Distance.

- Click the **Reverse Direction** button.

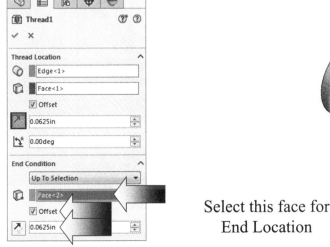

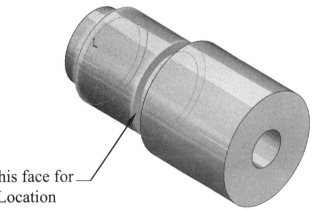

Select this face for End Location

- Under the Specification section, keep the Type at its default **Inch Die**.

- For Size, select **1.2500-12** from the list.

- For Thread Method, select the **Cut Thread** option.

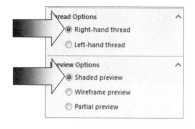

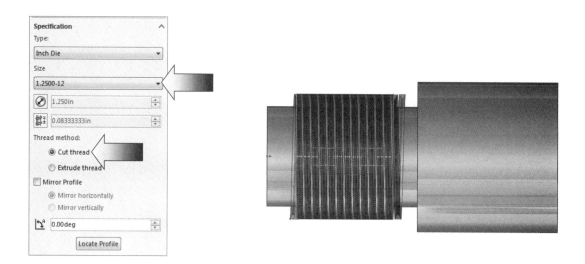

- Select the **Right-Hand Thread** under the Thread Options.

- Select **Shaded Preview** under the Preview Options.

- Click **OK** ✓.

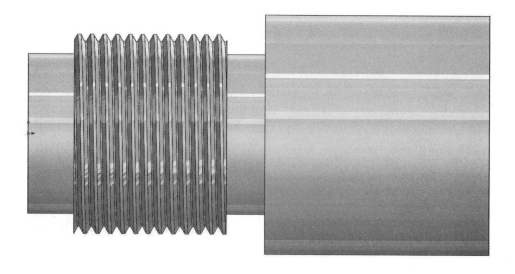

4. Using the Mirror Bodies option:

- Select **Mirror** from the Features tool tab or click **Insert / Pattern-Mirror / Mirror**.

- For Mirror Face/Plane, select the **face** indicated.

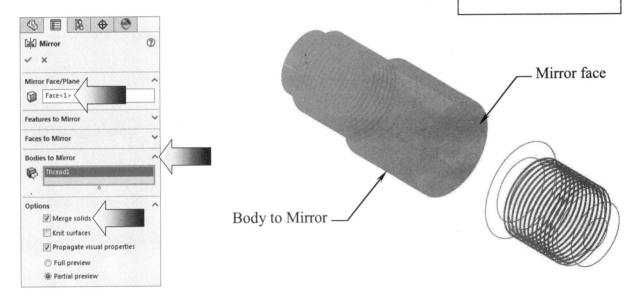

Mirror face

Body to Mirror

- Expand the Bodies to Mirror section and select the **model** in the graphics area as noted.

- Enable the Merge Solids checkbox. This option will join or combine the two bodies into a single solid.

- Click **OK**.

Right Hand Threads

Left Hand Threads

5. Adding chamfers:

- Click **Chamfer** 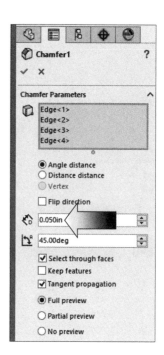 or **Insert / Features / Chamfers**.

- Select the **4 edges** as indicated.

- Enter **.050 in**. for Depth.

- Enter **45°** for Angle.

- Click **OK** ✅.

Select 4 edges

6. Saving the finished part.

- Select **File / Save as**.

- Enter **Threaded Insert** for the name of the file.

- Click **Save**.

Questions for Review

Modeling Threads

1. It is proper to select the sketch plane first before activating the sketch pencil.
   - a. True
   - b. False

2. The ordinate dimension options can be found under the smart dimension drop down menu.
   - a. True
   - b. False

3. The center of a revolve feature can now be an axis, a centerline, a line, or a linear model edge.
   - a. True
   - b. False

4. Threads cannot be modeled; they can only be represented with dashed lines and callouts.
   - a. True
   - b. False

5. Either a planar surface or a plane can be used to perform a mirror-bodies feature.
   - a. True
   - b. False

6. Several model edges can be chamfered at the same time if their values are the same.
   - a. True
   - b. False

7. The mirrored half is an independent feature; its geometry can be changed and the original half will get updated accordingly.
   - a. True
   - b. False

8. The mirror function will create the left-hand threads from the right-hand threads.
   - a. True
   - b. False

7. FALSE	8. TRUE
5. TRUE	6. TRUE
3. TRUE	4. FALSE
1. TRUE	2. TRUE

Exercise: Modeling Threads - Internal

1. Dimensions provided are for solid modeling practice purposes
2. Dimensions are in Inches, 3 decimal places.
3. Use the instructions on the following pages, if needed.
4. Save your work as **Nut_Internal Threads**.

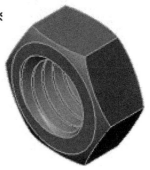

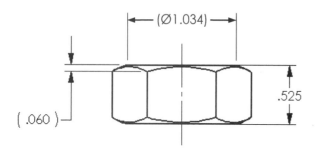

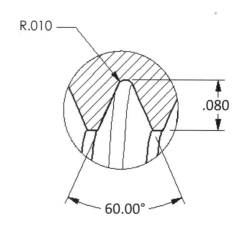

DETAIL B

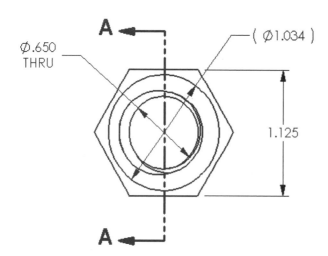

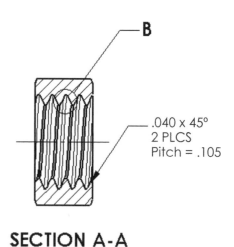

SECTION A-A

1. Starting with the base sketch:

- Select the <u>Front</u> plane and open a new sketch.

- Sketch a 6 sided Polygon and add the dimensions and relation shown.

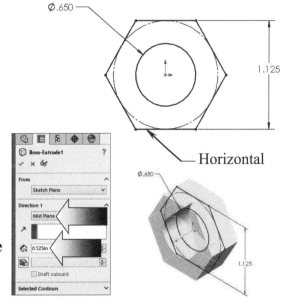

Horizontal

2. Extruding the base:

- Extrude the sketch using **Mid Plane** and **.525"** thick.

3. Removing the Sharp edges:

- Select the <u>Top</u> plane and open another sketch.

- Sketch the profile shown.
  * See the note on page 9-14 about Virtual Diameter dim.

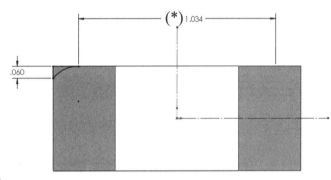

Tangent

- Add the dimensions and the Tangent relation as noted.

- Mirror the profile using the horizontal centerline.

- Revolve Cut with **Blind** and **360°** angle.

- Click **OK**.

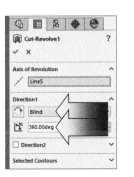

4. Creating a new plane:

- Select the <u>front face</u> of the part and click **Insert / Reference Geometry / Plane**.

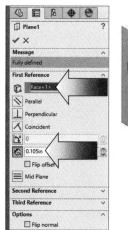

- The **Offset Distance** should be selected automatically; enter **.105"** for distance.

- Click **OK**.

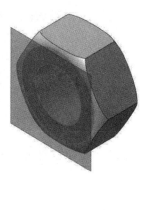

5. Creating the sweep path:

- Select the <u>new plane</u> and open a new sketch. (Starting from this offset location will prevent an undercut from happening where the thread starts.)

Convert this edge

-Select the circular edge as indicated and click **Convert Entities**.

- The selected edge turns into a sketch circle.

- Click the **Helix** command or select **Insert / Curve / Helix-Spiral**.

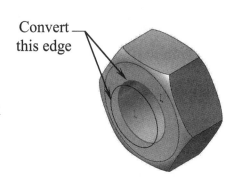

- Enter the following:
  * Pitch = **.105"**
  * Reverse Direction: **Enabled**.
  * Revolutions: **7**
  * Start Angle: **0.00 deg**.
  * **Clockwise**

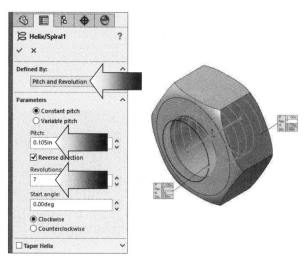

- Click **OK**.

6. Creating the sweep profile:

- Select the <u>Top</u> plane, open a new sketch and sketch the profile using Dynamic Mirror.

- Add the dimensions as shown to fully define the sketch before adding the fillet.

- Add a **.010"** sketch fillet to the tip.

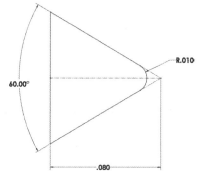

- Add a **Pierce** relation between the endpoint of the centerline and the 1st revolution of the helix.

- **Exit** the sketch.

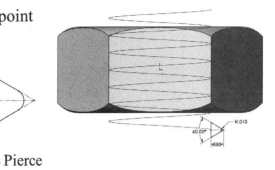

Pierce

7. Creating the swept cut:

- Using the traditional method we will sweep the thread profile along the helix.

- Change to the **Features** toolbar.

- Click **Swept Cut**.

- Select the triangular sketch for Profile.

- Select the Helix for Path.

- The Profile is Swept along the Path.

- Click **OK**.

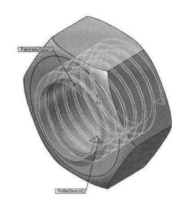

8. Saving your work:

- Select **File / Save as**.

- Enter **Nut_Internal Threads** for the file name.

- Click **Save**.

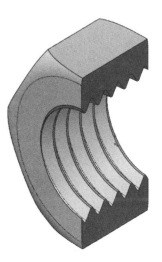

Exercise: Internal & External Thread

A. Internal Threads:

1. Creating the Revolve Sketch:

- Select the <u>Front</u> plane and open a new sketch plane as shown.

- Sketch the profile and add relations & dimensions as shown.

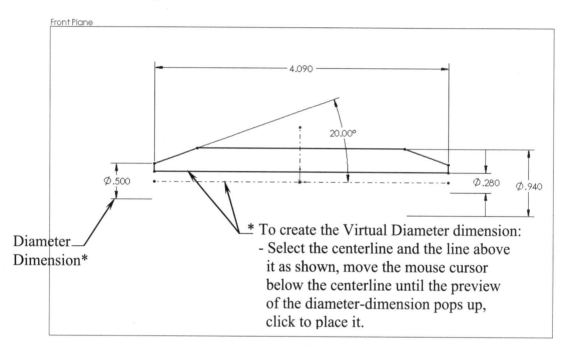

Front Plane

4.090

20.00°

∅.500

∅.280

∅.940

Diameter Dimension*

* To create the Virtual Diameter dimension:
- Select the centerline and the line above
  it as shown, move the mouse cursor
  below the centerline until the preview
  of the diameter-dimension pops up,
  click to place it.

2. Revolving the Body:

- Revolve the sketch a full 360 deg. and click **OK** ✅.

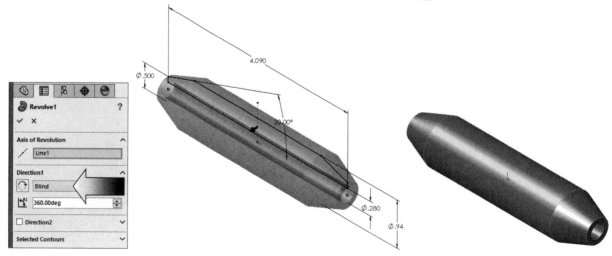

3. Creating the cutout features:

- From the Front plane, sketch the profiles of the cutouts.

- Use the Mirror function where applicable. Add Relations & Dimensions to fully define the sketch.

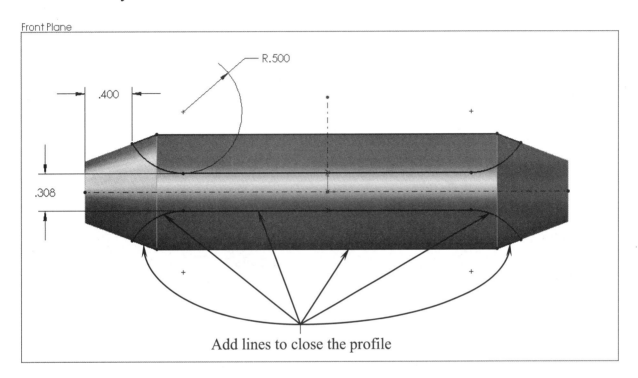

Add lines to close the profile

4. Extruding the Cutouts:

- Click **Extruded Cut** and select **Through All-Both**.

- Click **OK** .

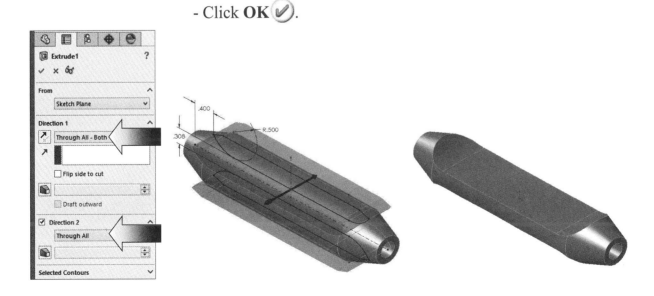

5. Sketching the Slot Profile:

- From the <u>Top</u> plane, sketch the profile of the slot (use the Straight Slot options).

- Add Relations & Dimensions to fully define the sketch.

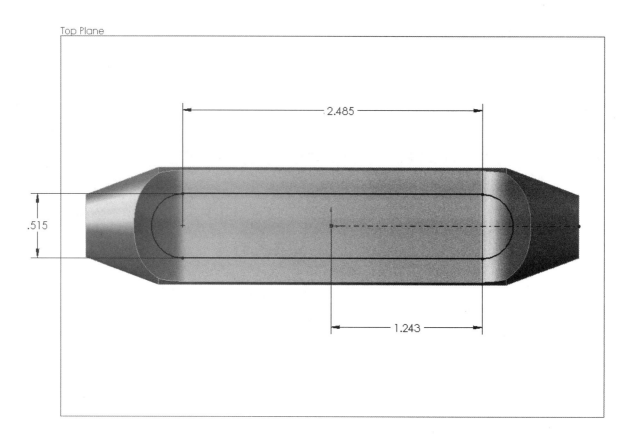

6. Cutting the Slot:

- Click **Extruded Cut** and select **Through All-Both**.

- Click **OK** ✓.

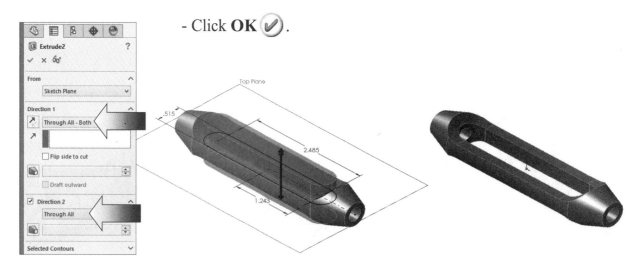

7. Adding Chamfers:

- Add a **chamfer** to both ends of the holes.

- Chamfer Depth = **.050 in**.   - Chamfer Angle = **45 deg**.

- Click **OK** ✅.

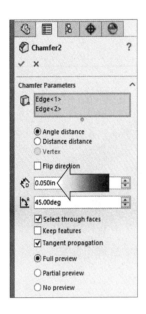

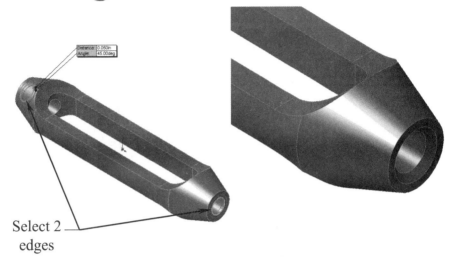

Select 2
edges

8. Adding Fillets:

- Add **fillets** to the **4 edges** as noted.

- Radius = **.250 in**.

- Click **OK** ✅.

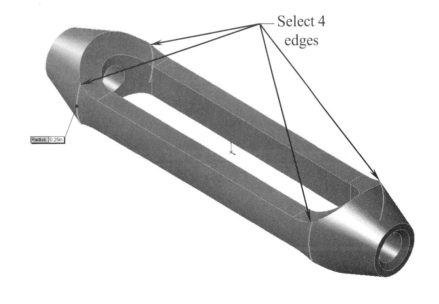

Select 4
edges

9. Filleting all edges:

- Box-Select the entire part and add a fillet of **.032in**. to all edges (or use the shortcut Control+A to select all edges of the model).

- Click **OK** ✅.

10. Creating an Offset-Distance Plane:

- Click **Plane** or select **Insert / Reference Geometry / Plane**.

- Click **Offset-Distance** option and enter **2.063 in**.

- Select the <u>Right</u> plane to copy from; place the new plane on the right side.

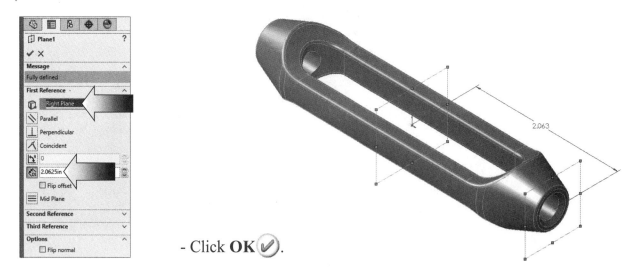

- Click **OK** ✅.

11. Creating the Helix (the sweep path):

- Select the <u>new plane</u> to open a new sketch.

- Convert the **Inner Circular Edge** into a Circle.

(Using an offset of "1-pitch" can help prevent the under-cut from showing where the thread starts.)

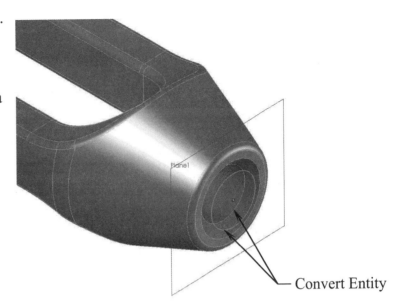

Convert Entity

- Click **Helix** or select **Insert / Curve / Helix-Spiral**.

- Pitch: **.055 in**.   - Revolutions: **11**

- Start Angle: **0 deg**.   - Direction: **Clockwise**

- Click **OK** 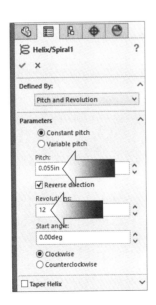.

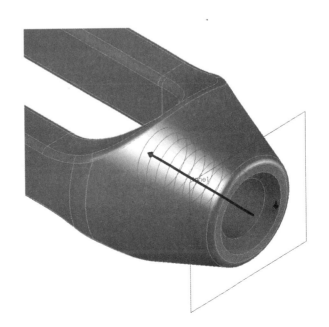

12. Sketching the Thread Profile:

- Select the <u>Top</u> reference plane and open a new sketch.

- Sketch the thread profile as shown. Add the relation and dimensions needed to define the profile.

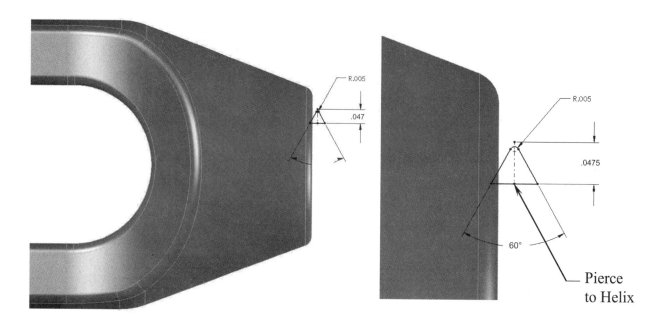

- **Exit** the Sketch.

13. Sweeping the Cut:

- Click **Cut-Sweep** or select **Insert / Cut / Sweep**.

- Select the triangular sketch as Profile and select the helix as Sweep Path.

- Click **OK** .

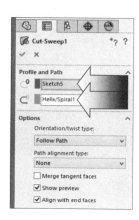

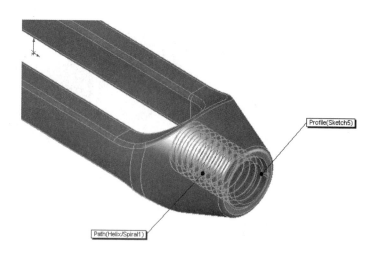

14. Mirroring the Threads:

- Click **Mirror** or select **Insert / Pattern Mirror / Mirror**.

- Select the **Right** plane as the Mirror Plane.

- For Features to Mirror select the **Cut-Sweep1** feature.

- Click **OK** 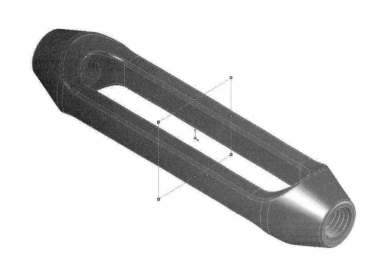.

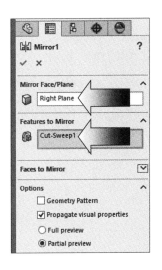

15. Creating the Cross-Section to view the Threads:

- Select the Front plane from the FeatureManager tree.

- Click **Section View** or select **View / Display / Section**.

- Zoom in on the threaded areas and examine the thread details.

- Click **Cancel** when you are done viewing.

- Save the part as **Internal Threads**.

B. External Threads:

1. Sketching the Sweep Path:

- Select the <u>Front</u> plane and open a new sketch.

- Sketch the profile shown; add Relations & Dimensions needed to fully define the sketch.

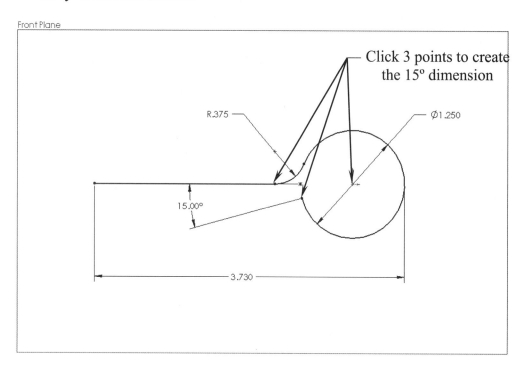

Front Plane

Click 3 points to create the 15° dimension

R.375

Ø1.250

15.00°

3.730

2. Creating a plane Perpendicular to a line:

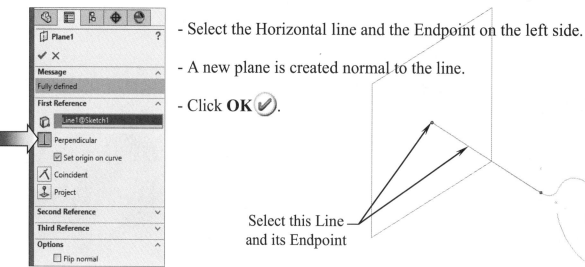

- Click **Plane** or select **Insert / Reference Geometry/ Plane**.

- Select the Horizontal line and the Endpoint on the left side.

- A new plane is created normal to the line.

- Click **OK**.

Plane1

Message
Fully defined

First Reference
Line1@Sketch1
Perpendicular
☑ Set origin on curve
Coincident
Project

Second Reference
Third Reference
Options
☐ Flip normal

Select this Line and its Endpoint

3. Sketching the Sweep Profile:

- Select the <u>new plane</u> and open a new sketch.

- Sketch a **Circle** as shown and add a diameter dimension.

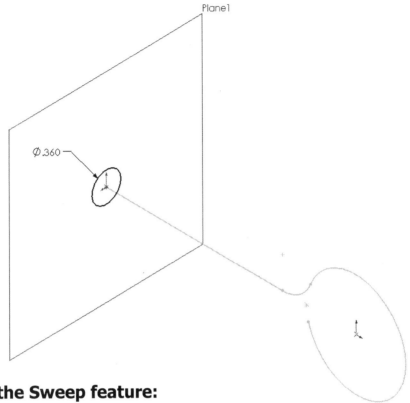

4. Creating the Sweep feature:

- Click **Swept Boss-Base** or select **Insert / Features / Sweep**.

- Select the **Circle** as Sweep Profile and select the **Sketch1** as Sweep Path.

- Click **OK** .

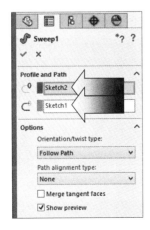

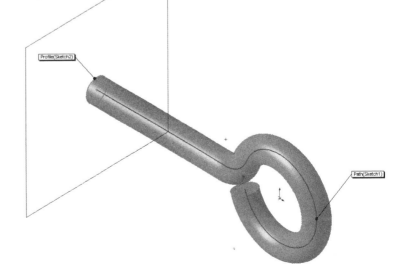

5. Adding Chamfers:

- Click **Chamfer** or select **Insert / Features / Chamfer**.

- Select the **2 Circular Edges** at the 2 ends.

- Enter **.050 in**. for Depth.

- Enter **45 deg**. for Angle.

- Click **OK** ✓.

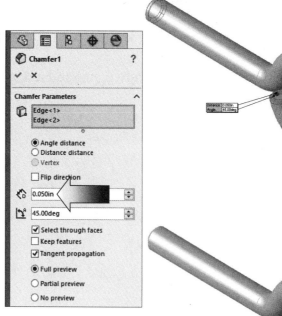

— Sketch face

6. Creating the Helix:

- Select the <u>face</u> as indicated and open a new sketch.

- Select the **circular edge** at the end as shown and click Convert Entities or select **Tools/Sketch Tools/Convert Entities**.

- Click **Helix** or select **Insert/ Curve/Helix-Spiral**.

- Enter **.055** in. for Pitch.

- Enter **39** for Revolutions.

- Enter **0 deg**. for Start Angle.

- Click **OK** ✓.

Convert Entity

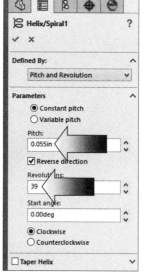

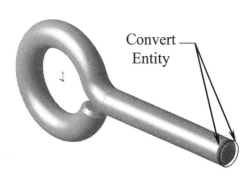

7. Creating the Thread Profile:

- Either copy the previous thread profile or recreate it.

- Add a **Pierce** relation to position the thread profile at the end of the helix.

- Click **OK** .

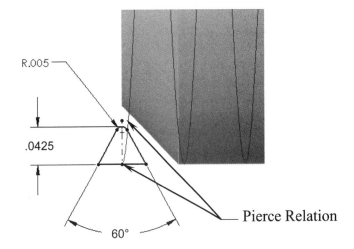

NOTE:
There should be a clearance between the 2 threaded parts so that they can be moved back and forth easily.

Pierce Relation

8. Sweeping Cut the Threads:

- Click **Swept Cut** or select **Insert / Cut / Sweep.**

- Select the **triangular sketch** as the Sweep Profile.

- Select the **Helix** as the Sweep path.

- Click **OK** .

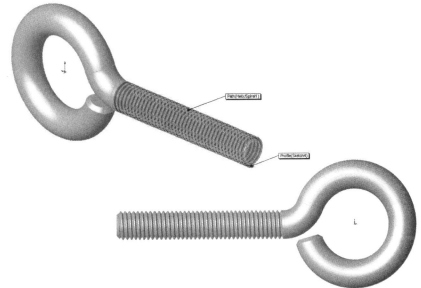

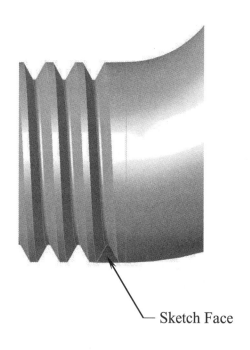

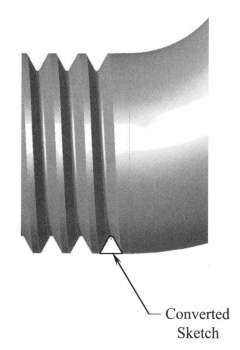

Sketch Face

Converted Sketch

9. Removing the Undercut:

- Select the <u>face</u> as noted and open a new sketch.

- **Convert** the selected **face** into a new triangular sketch.

- Click Extruded-Cut or select **Insert / Cut / Extrude**.

- Select **Through All** for End Condition.

- Click **OK** .

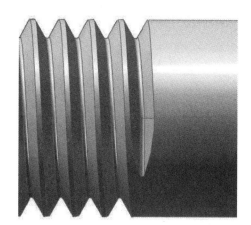

10. Saving your work:

- Save a copy of your work as **External Threads**.

11. Optional:

(This step can also be done after completing the Bottom Up Assembly chapter.)

- Start a New Assembly document and assemble the 2 components.

- Create an Assembly Exploded View as shown below.

- Save the assembly as **TurnBuckle.sldasm**

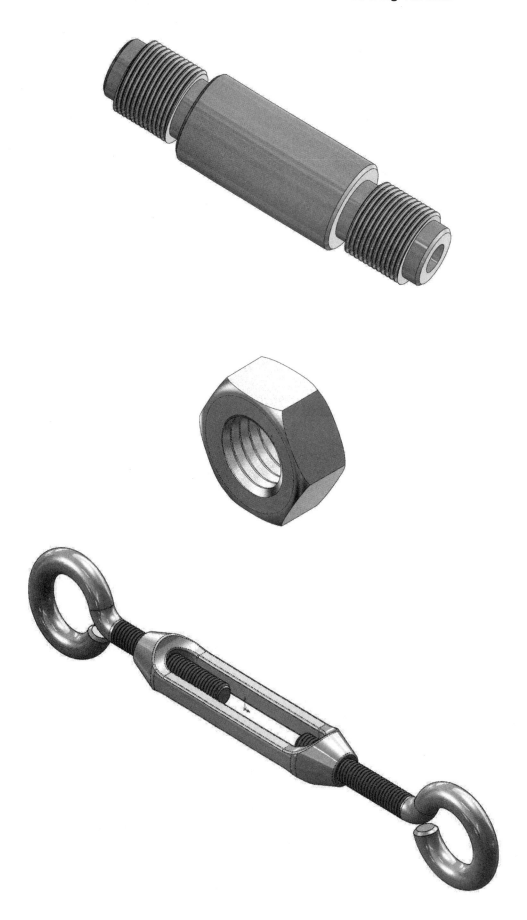

CHAPTER 10

Bottom Up Assembly

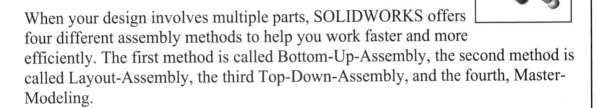

Bottom Up Assembly Overview
Ball Joint Assembly

When your design involves multiple parts, SOLIDWORKS offers four different assembly methods to help you work faster and more efficiently. The first method is called Bottom-Up-Assembly, the second method is called Layout-Assembly, the third Top-Down-Assembly, and the fourth, Master-Modeling.

We will explore the first two methods, the Bottom-Up and the Lay-Out Assemblies, in this textbook.

When you insert components into an assembly document and mate them together (assemble), this method is called Bottom Up Assembly.

The first component inserted into the assembly will be fixed by the system automatically. If it is placed on the Origin, then the Front, Top, and the Right planes of the first component will automatically be aligned with the assembly's Front, Top, and Right planes.

Only the first part will be fixed by default; all other components are free to move or be reoriented. Each component has a total of 6 degrees of freedom; depending on the mate type, once a mate is assigned to a component one or more of its degrees of freedom are removed, causing the component to move or rotate only in the desired directions.

All Mates (constraints) are stored in the FeatureManager tree under the Mates group. They can be edited, suppressed, or deleted.

This lesson and its exercises will discuss the use of the Standard Mates, Advanced Mates, and Mechanical Mates.

Ball Joint Assembly
Bottom-Up Assembly

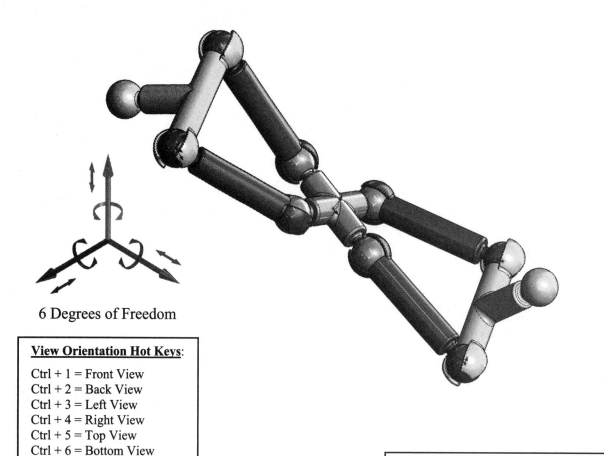

6 Degrees of Freedom

Dimensioning Standards: **ANSI**

Units: **INCHES** – 3 Decimals

Tools Needed:

 Mates

 Move Component

 Rotate Component

 Concentric Mate

 Inference Origins

 Placing New Component

1. Starting a new Assembly template:

- Select **File / New / Assembly / OK**.

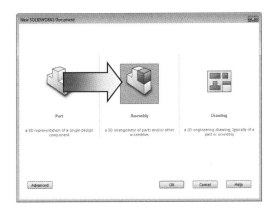

- In the Insert Component dialog, click Browse .

- Select the **Center Ball Joint** document from the training folder and click **Open**.

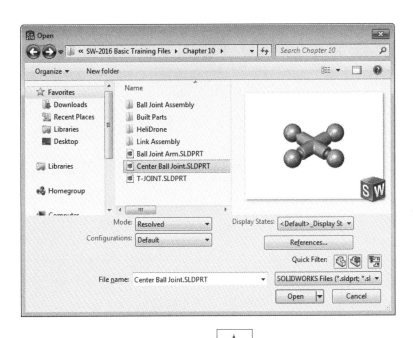

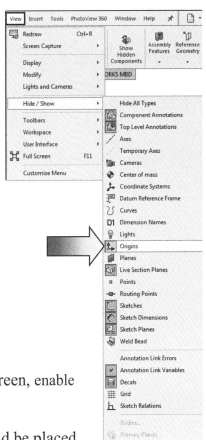

2. Showing the Origin:

- If the Origin symbol is not yet shown on the screen, enable it by selecting **View / Hide / Show / Origins**.

- It is recommended that the 1st component should be placed on the Origin.

3. Inserting the 1ˢᵗ component (the Parent) on the Origin:

- Hover the pointer over the origin; an Origin-Inference symbol 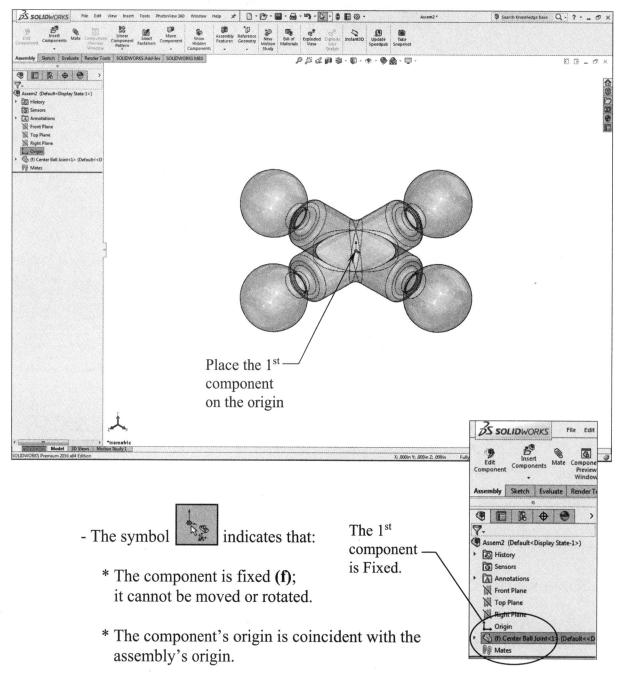 appears to confirm the placement of the 1ˢᵗ component.

- Click the **Origin** point to place the component.

Place the 1ˢᵗ
component
on the origin

The 1ˢᵗ
component
is Fixed.

- The symbol indicates that:

  * The component is fixed (**f**);
    it cannot be moved or rotated.

  * The component's origin is coincident with the
    assembly's origin.

  * The planes of the component and the planes of the assembly are aligned.

4. Inserting the second component (a child) into the assembly:

- Click 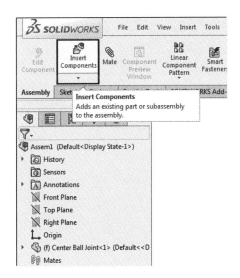 or select **Insert / Component / Existing Part/Assembly**.

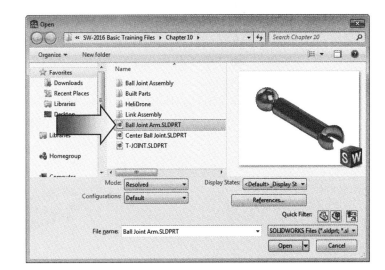

- Click **Browse** .

- Select **Ball Joint Arm.sldprt** from the Training Files folder and click **Open**.

- The preview graphics of the component is attached to the mouse cursor.

- Place the new Child component above the Parent component as shown below.

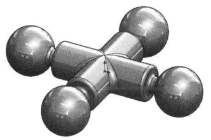

5. Mating the components:

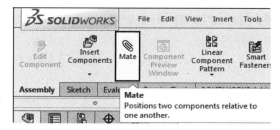

- Click 📎 or select **Insert / Mate**.

- Assembly mate options appear on the FeatureManager tree.

- Select the **two (2) faces** as indicated below.

- The **Concentric** mate option is selected automatically and the system displays the preview graphics of the two (2) mated components.

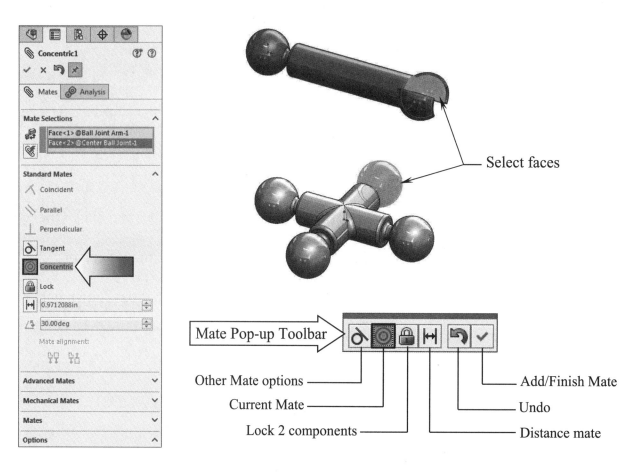

Select faces

Mate Pop-up Toolbar

Other Mate options
Current Mate
Lock 2 components

Add/Finish Mate
Undo
Distance mate

- Review the options on the Mate Pop-up toolbar.

- Click **OK** ✅.

- The **2 faces** are constrained with the concentric mate.

- The second component is still free to rotate around the spherical surface.

6. Moving the component:

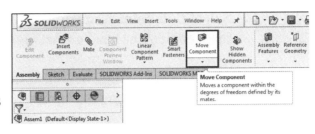

- Click **Move Component**.

- Drag the **face** as noted to see its degrees of freedom.

- Move the component to the approximate position shown.

- Click **OK** ✓.

Drag here ——

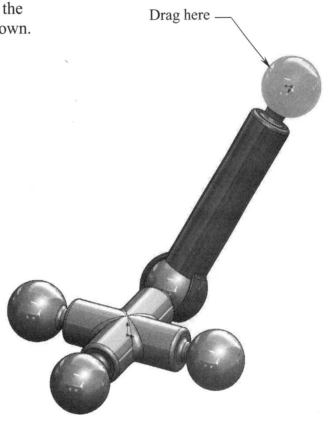

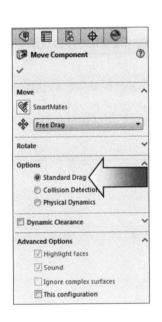

7. Inserting another instance into the assembly:

- Click 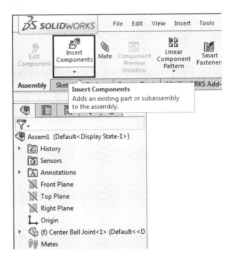 or select **Insert / Component / Existing Part/Assembly**.

- Click Browse... .

<u>NOTE:</u> *Not all assemblies are fully constrained. In an assembly with moving parts, leave at least one degree of freedom open so that the component can still be moved or rotated.*

- Select **Ball Joint Arm.sldprt** (the same component) and click **Open**.

- Place the new component next to the first one as shown.

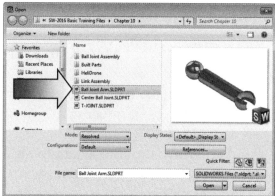

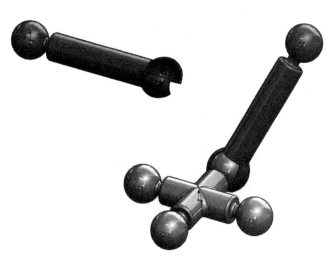

Copy Components

A quick way to make a copy of a component is to hold the Control key and drag it to a side.

8. Constraining the components:

- Click [icon] or select **Insert / Mate**.

- Select the **two faces** as shown.

- The **Concentric** mate option is selected automatically and the system displays the preview graphics of the two mated components.

- Click **OK** [icon].

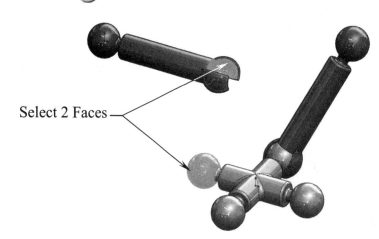

Select 2 Faces

- The two selected faces are constrained with a Concentric mate.

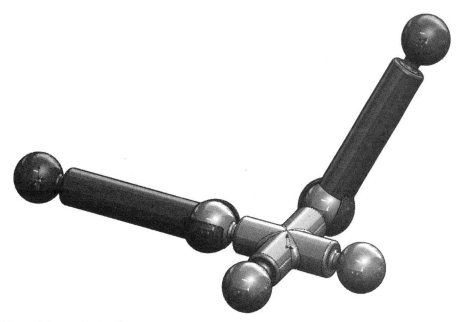

9. Repeating the step 5:

- Insert (or copy) two more instances of the **Ball Joint Arm** and add the mates to assemble them as shown.

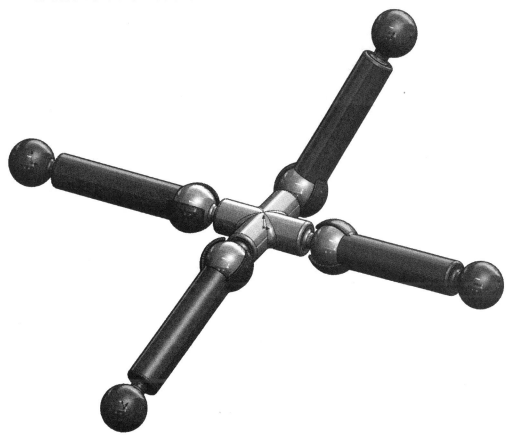

<u>**Optional**</u>:

- Insert the T-Join component (from the Training Files folder) as pictured below and mate it to the assembly.

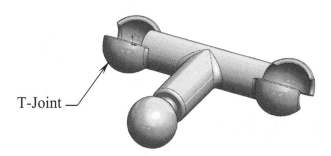

T-Joint —

- Check the assembly motion by dragging the T-Joint back and forth.

- Each component has only one mate applied; they are still free to move or rotate around their constrained geometry.

10. Saving your work:

- Select **File / Save As**.

- Enter **Ball-Joint-Assembly** for the name of the file.

- Click **Save**.

(Open the completed assembly in the training files folder to check your work against it, if needed.)

Questions for Review

Bottom Up Assembly

1. The 1st component should be fixed on the Origin.
   a. True
   b. False

2. The symbol (f) next to a file name means:
   a. Fully defined
   b. Failed
   c. Fixed

3. After the first component is inserted into an assembly, it is still free to be moved or reoriented.
   a. True
   b. False

4. Beside the first component, if other components are not yet constrained they cannot be moved or rotated.
   a. True
   b. False

5. You cannot copy multiple components in an assembly document.
   a. True
   b. False

6. To make a copy of a component, click and drag that component while holding the key:
   a. Shift
   b. Control
   c. Alt
   d. Tab

7. Once a mate is created, its definitions (mate alignment, mate type, etc.) cannot be edited.
   a. True
   b. False

8. Mates can be suppressed, deleted, or changed.
   a. True
   b. False

7. FALSE	8. TRUE
5. FALSE	6. B
3. FALSE	4. FALSE
1. TRUE	2. C

CHAPTER 10 (cont.)

Bottom Up Assembly

Bottom Up Assembly Overview
Links Assembly

- After the parts are inserted into an assembly document, they are now called components. These components will get repositioned and mated together. This method is called Bottom Up Assembly.

- The first component inserted into the assembly will be fixed by the system automatically. If it is placed on the Origin, then the Front, Top, and Right planes of the first component will also be aligned with the assembly's planes.

- Only the first part will be fixed by default; all other components are free to be moved or reoriented. Depending on the mate type, once a mate is assigned to a component, one or more of its degrees of freedom are removed, causing the component to move or rotate only in the desired directions.

- Standard mates are created one by one to constraint components.

- Multi-Mates can be used to constrain more than one component, where a common entity is used to mate with several other entities.

- This second half of the chapter will guide you through the use of the Bottom Up assembly method once again. Some of the components are exactly identical. We will learn how to create several copies of them and then add 2 mates to each one, leaving one degree of freedom open, so that they can be moved or rotated when dragged. There will be an instance number <1> <2> <3>, etc., placed next to the name of each copy to indicate how many times the components are used in an assembly.

Links Assembly
Bottom-Up Assembly

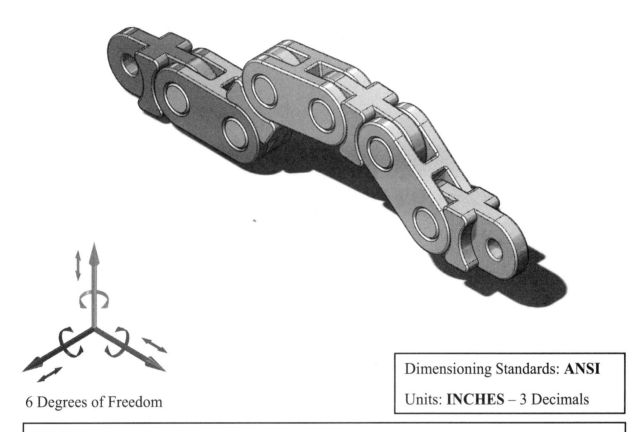

6 Degrees of Freedom

Dimensioning Standards: **ANSI**

Units: **INCHES** – 3 Decimals

Tools Needed:

📎 Mates

🖥 Insert New Component

🔄 Rotate Component

📦 Move Component

🖱 Inference Origins

🖱 Place/Position Component

Mate alignment: ⬚⬚ Align & Anti-Align

◎ Concentric Mate

⟁ Coincident Mate

1. Starting a new Assembly Template:

- Select **File / New / Assembly / OK**.

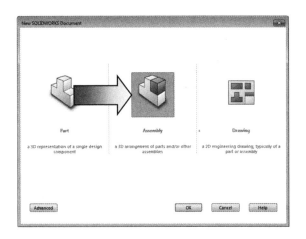
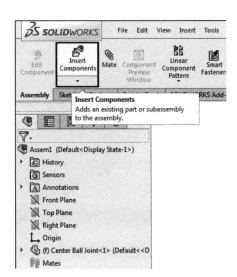

- A new assembly document is opened.

- Select **Insert Component** command from the Assembly tool tab.

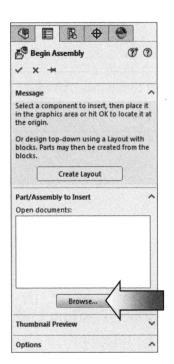
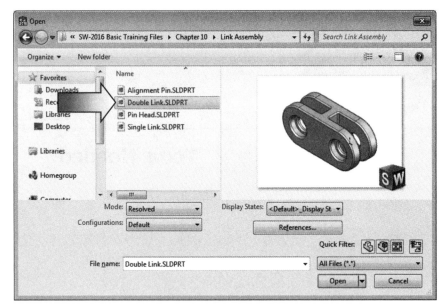

- Click the **Browse** button (arrow).

- Locate and open a part document named **Double Link.sldprt**.

2. Placing the 1st Component:

- Hover the cursor over the assembly Origin; the double arrow symbol appears indicating the part's origin and the assembly's origin will be mated coincident. Place the 1st part on the origin.

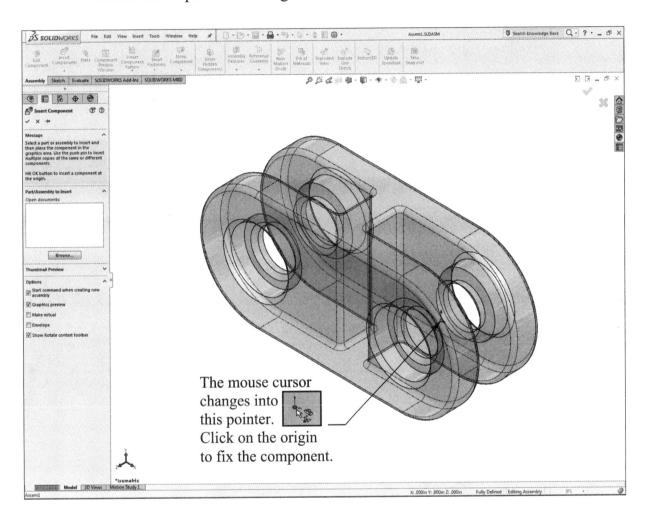

The mouse cursor changes into this pointer. Click on the origin to fix the component.

💡 "Fixing" the 1st component

- The first component inserted into the assembly will be fixed automatically by the system; the symbol (f) next to the document's name means the part cannot be moved or rotated.

- Other components can be added and mated to the first one using one of the three options:

    1. Drag & Drop from an opened window.
    2. Use the Windows Explorer to drag the component into the assembly.
    3. Use the Insert Component command.

3. Adding other components:

- Select **Insert / Component / Existing Part/Assembly** (or click 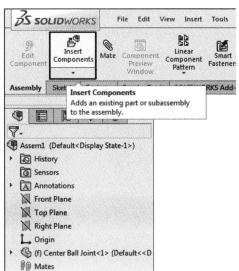) and add five (**5**) more instances of the first component into the assembly document.

- Place the new components around the Fixed one, approximately as shown.

- The Feature Manager tree shows the same name for each component but with an indicator that shows the number of times used **<2>, <3>, <4>**, etc...

- The (**-**) signs in front of each file name indicate that the components are under defined; they are still able to move or rotate freely.

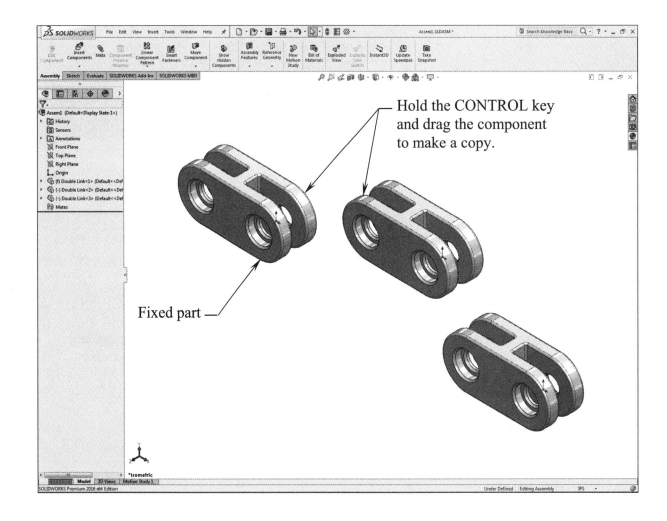

Hold the CONTROL key and drag the component to make a copy.

Fixed part

4. Changing colors:

- For Clarity, change the color of the 1st component to a different color; this way we can differentiate the parent component from the copies.

- Click the 1st component and select the **Appearances** button (the beach ball) and click the **Edit Part Color** option (arrow).

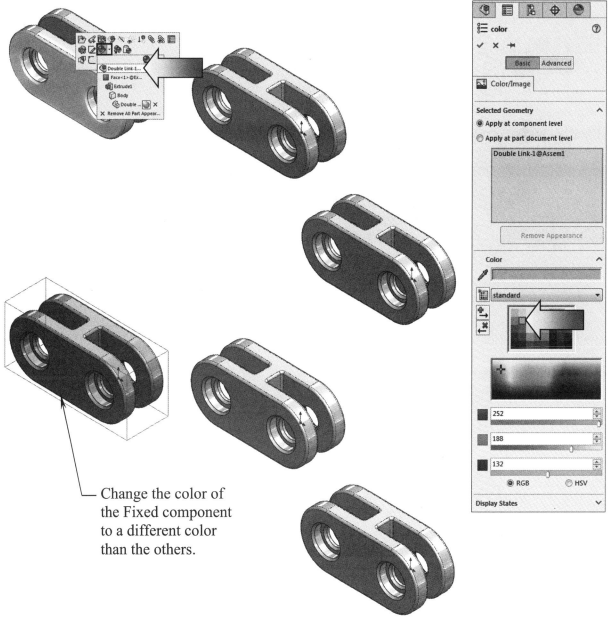

Change the color of the Fixed component to a different color than the others.

- Move the copies away from one another, approximately as shown.

- Click **OK**.

5. Inserting the Single Link into the assembly:

- Click **Insert Component** on the Assembly toolbar and select the part **Single Link** from the previous folder.

- Place the Single Link approximately as shown.

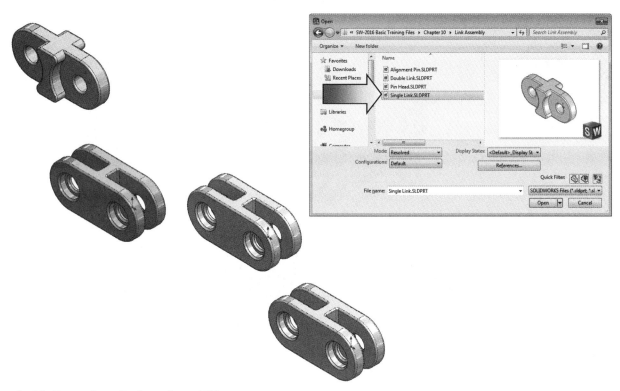

6. Using the Selection Filters:

- The Selection Filters help select the right type of geometry to add the mates such as filter Faces, Edges, Axis or Vertices, etc…

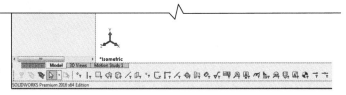

- Click **Selection Filter** icon, or press the **F5** function key.

- Select **Filter Faces** option.

Filter Faces

7. Adding Mates:

- Click **Mate** 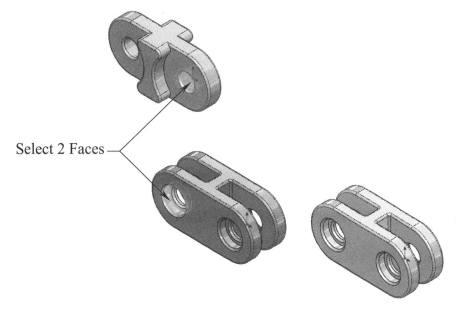 on the Assembly toolbar or select **Insert / Mate**.

- Select the faces of the **two holes** as indicated.

Select 2 Faces

- The **Concentric** mate option is selected automatically and the system displays the preview graphics for the two mated components.

- Click **OK** ✅ to accept the concentric mate.

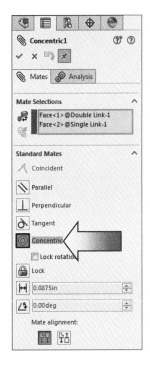

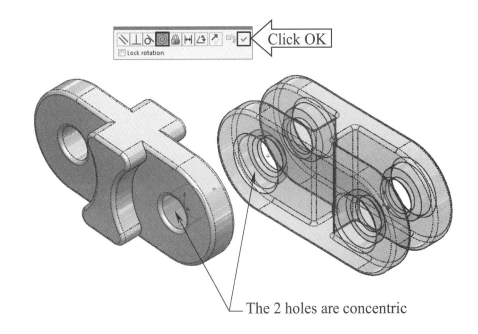

Click OK

The 2 holes are concentric

8. Adding a Width mate:

- The Width mate centers the 2 parts (width of part 1 and groove/tab of part 2).

- Click **Mate** on the Assembly toolbar or select **Insert / Mate**.

- Expand the **Advanced Mates** section and click the **Width** option.

- Select **2 faces** for **each part** as indicated. A total of 4 faces must be selected.

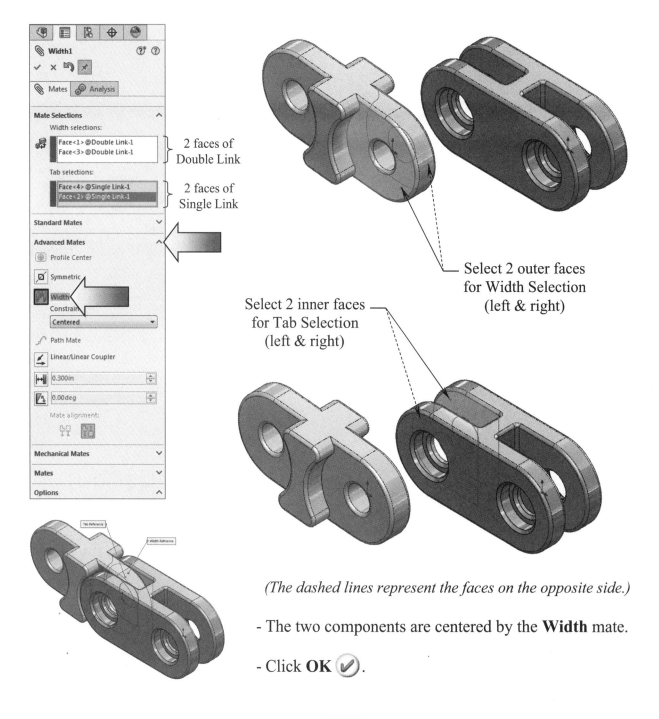

2 faces of
Double Link

2 faces of
Single Link

Select 2 outer faces
for Width Selection
(left & right)

Select 2 inner faces
for Tab Selection
(left & right)

(The dashed lines represent the faces on the opposite side.)

- The two components are centered by the **Width** mate.

- Click **OK**.

9. Making copies of the component:

- Select the part Single-Link and click **Edit / Copy**, then click anywhere in the graphics area and select **Edit / Paste** – OR – Hold down the CONTROL key, click/hold and drag the part Single Link to make a copy.

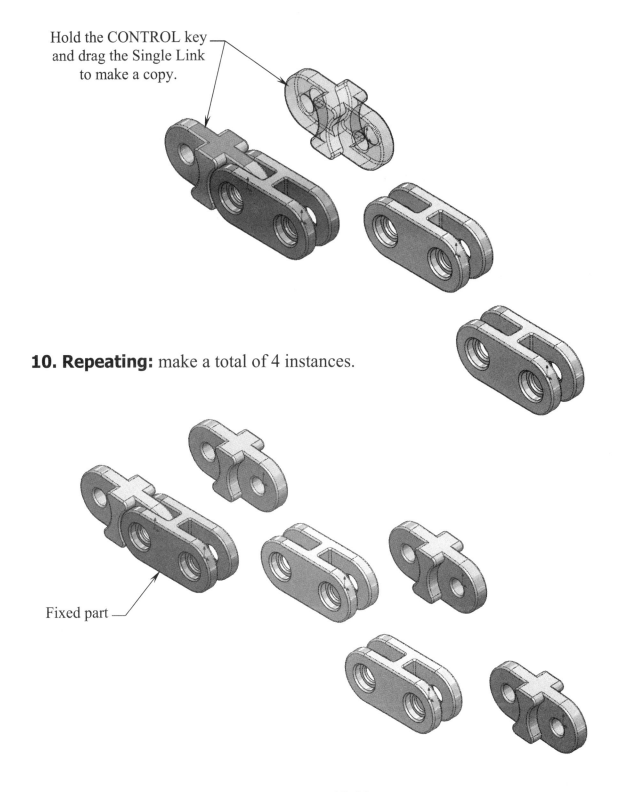

Hold the CONTROL key and drag the Single Link to make a copy.

10. Repeating: make a total of 4 instances.

Fixed part

Notes:

- The <u>correct</u> mates are displayed in Black color 📎 at the bottom of the tree.

- The <u>incorrect</u> mates are displayed with a red **X** 📎 ⊗ (+) or a yellow exclamation mark 📎 ⚠ (+) next to them.

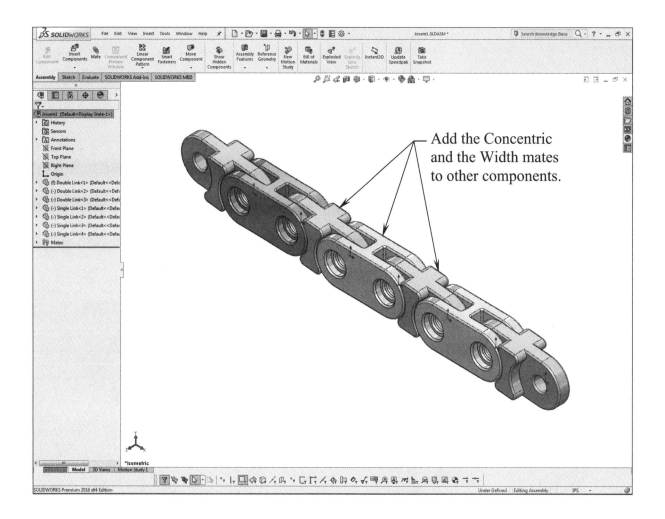

Add the Concentric and the Width mates to other components.

- Expand the Mate group 🗀 📎 Mates (Click on the **+** sign).

- Verify that there are no "Red Flags" under the Mate Group.

- If a mate error occurs, do the following:

** Right click over the incorrect mate, select Edit-Feature, and correct the selections for that particular mate - **OR** -

** Simply delete the incorrect mates and re-create the new ones.

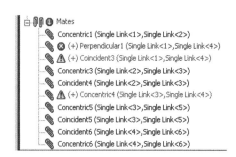

11. Inserting other components into the Assembly:

- Click or select **Insert / Component / Existing Part/Assembly.**

- Click **Browse**, select **Alignment Pin** and click **Open**.

- Place the component on the left side of the assembly as shown below.

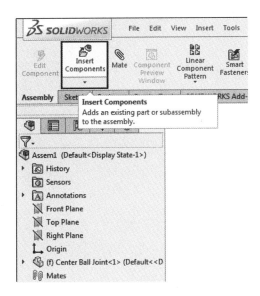

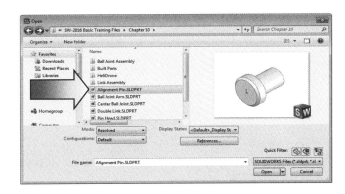

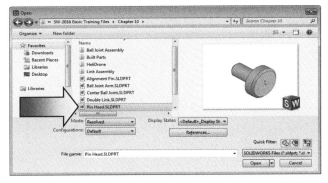

- Insert the **Pin Head** and place it on the opposite side.

12. Rotating the Pin Head:

- Select the Rotate  Component command and rotate the Pin-Head to the correct orientation.

Make 5 more copies of both the Pin-Head and the Alignment Pin.

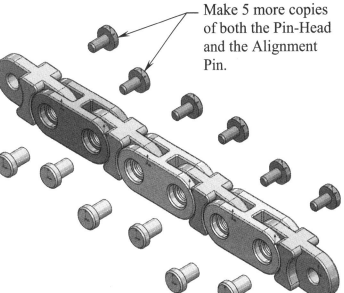

13. Constraining the Alignment Pin:

- Click 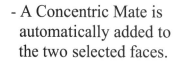 **Mate** on the Assembly toolbar.

- Select the **body** of the Alignment Pin and the **hole** in the Double Link.

- A Concentric Mate is automatically added to the two selected faces.

- Click **OK** ✓.

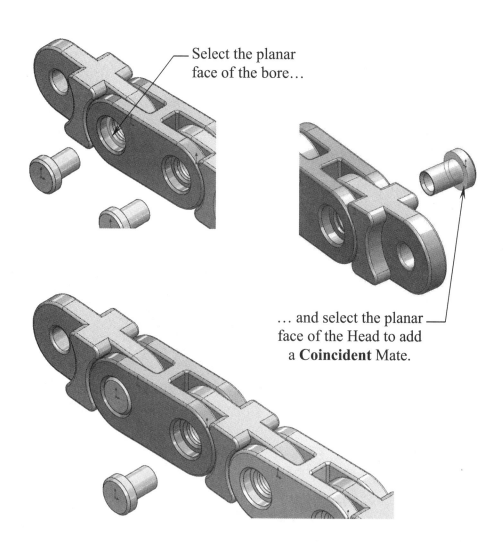

Select 2 Faces to add a **Concentric** mate.

Select the planar face of the bore…

… and select the planar face of the Head to add a **Coincident** Mate.

14. Constraining the Pin-Head:

- Add a **Concentric** mate between the Pin-Head and its mating hole.

Select the cylindrical
body of the Pin-Head…

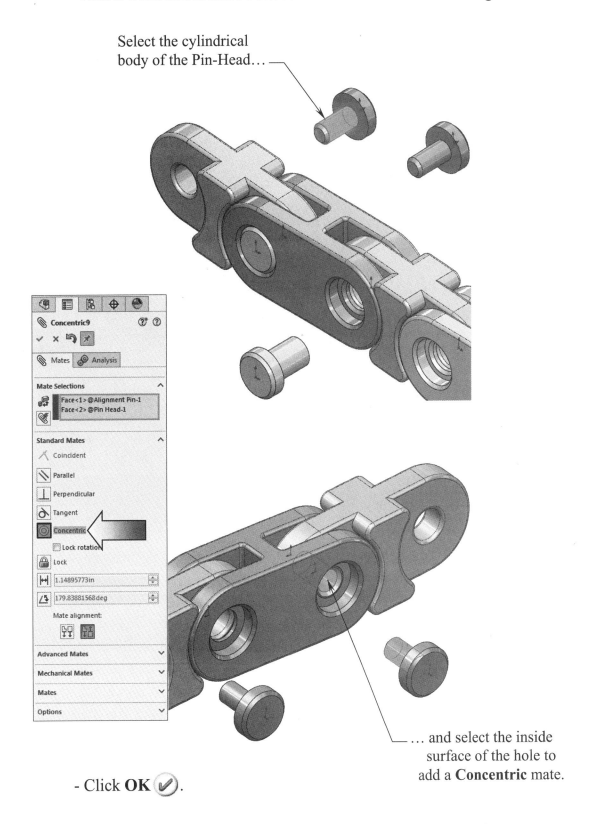

… and select the inside
surface of the hole to
add a **Concentric** mate.

- Click **OK** .

- Click 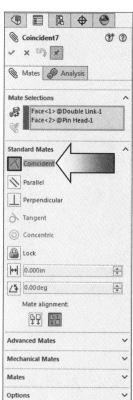 **Mate** again, if you have already closed out of it from the last step.

- Select the **two faces** as indicated to add a Coincident Mate.

Select the bottom
face of the Bore...

...and select the end face
of the Pin-Head to add a
Coincident Mate

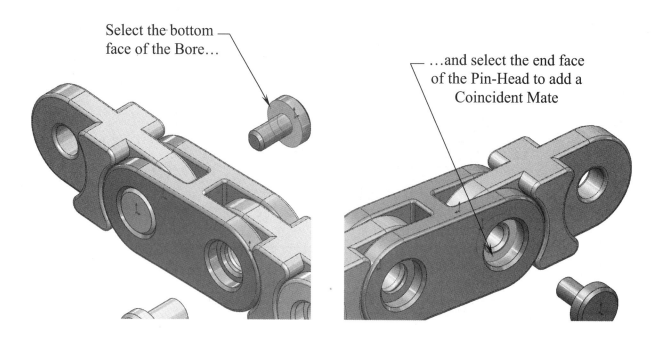

- The system adds a **Coincident** mate
  between the 2 entities.

- Click **OK** .

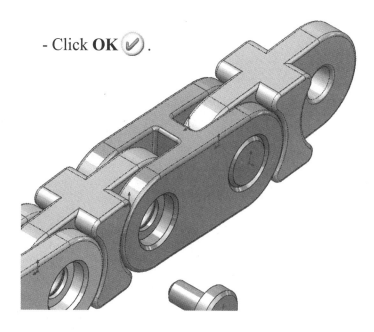

15. Using the Align & Anti-Align Options:

- When the Mate command is active, the options **Align** and **Anti-Align** are also available in the Mate dialog box.

- Use the alignment options to flip the mating component 180° .

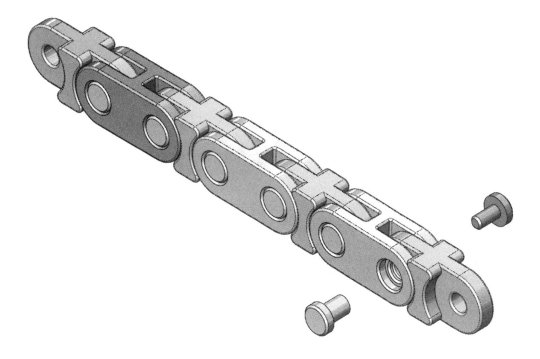

- The last two (2) pins will be used to demonstrate the use of Align and Anti-Align (see step 16).

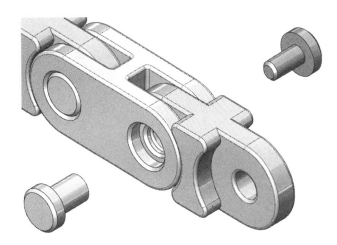

16. Using Align and Anti-Align:

- When mating the components using the **Concentric** option, the **TAB** key can be used to flip the component 180° or from Align into Anti-Align.

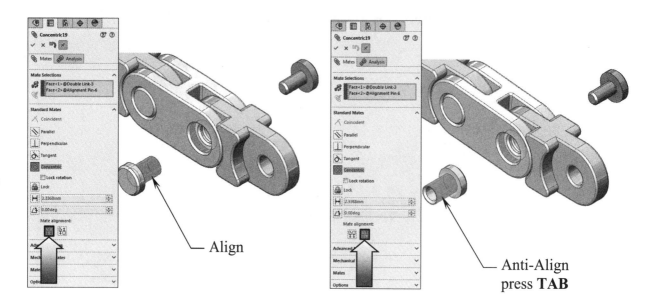

Align

Anti-Align
press **TAB**

17. Viewing the assembly motion:

- Drag one of the links to see how the components move relative to each other.

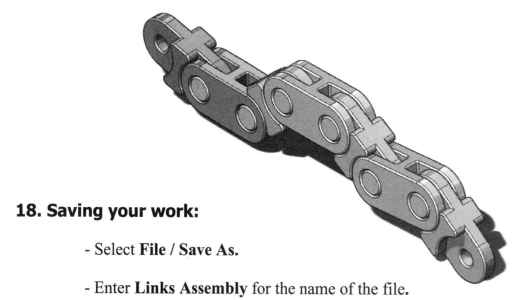

18. Saving your work:

- Select **File / Save As.**

- Enter **Links Assembly** for the name of the file.

- Click **Save**.

(Open the pre-built assembly in the Training Files folder to compare your work.)

Questions for Review

Bottom Up Assembly

1. Parts inserted into an assembly document are called documents.
    a. True
    b. False

2. Each component in an assembly document has six degrees of freedom.
    a. True
    b. False

3. Once a mate is applied to a component, depending on the mate type, one or more of its degrees of freedom is removed.
    a. True
    b. False

4. Standard mates are created one by one to constraint the components.
    a. True
    b. False

5. A combination of a Face and an Edge can be used to constraint with a Coincident mate.
    a. True
    b. False

6. Align and Anti-Align while in the Mating mode can toggle by pressing:
    a. Control
    b. Back space
    c. Tab
    d. Esc.

7. Mates can be deferred so that several mates can be done and solved at the same time.
    a. True
    b. False

8. Mates can be:
    a. Suppressed
    b. Deleted
    c. Edited
    d. All of the above

7. TRUE   8. D
5. TRUE   6. C
4. TRUE
2. TRUE
1. FALSE   3. TRUE

Exercise: Gate Assembly

Go to The Training Files folder
  Gate Assembly Folder.

1. Create an Assembly document from
   the components provided.
2. Create a Mirror plane at **26.125 in.**
   offset from the RIGHT plane.

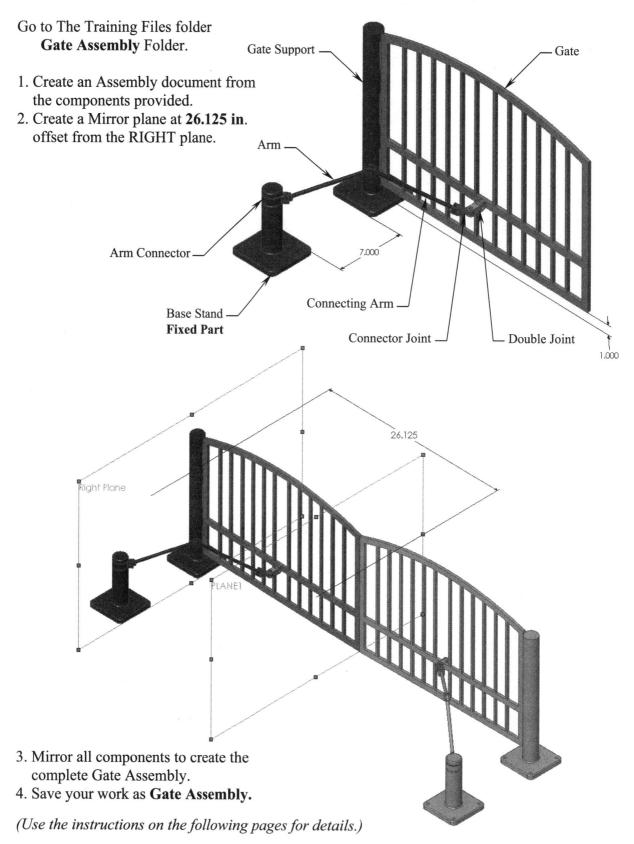

Gate Support

Gate

Arm

Arm Connector

Base Stand
Fixed Part

7.000

Connecting Arm

Connector Joint

Double Joint

1.000

Right Plane

26.125

PLANE1

3. Mirror all components to create the
   complete Gate Assembly.
4. Save your work as **Gate Assembly.**

(Use the instructions on the following pages for details.)

1. Starting a new assembly:

- Click **File / New / Assembly**.

- From the Assembly toolbar, select **Insert / Components**.

- Browse to the part **Base Stand** and place it on the assembly's origin.

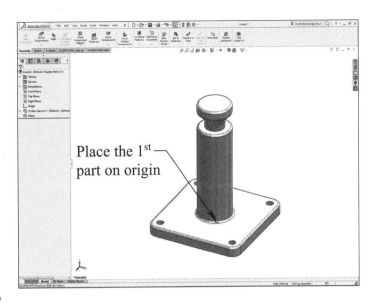

Place the 1ˢᵗ part on origin

2. Inserting other components:

- Insert all components (total of 8) into the assembly.

- **Rotate** the **Gate** <u>and</u> the **Gate-Support** approximately **180 degrees**.

- Move the Gate and the Gate-Support to the positions shown.

- By rotating and positioning the components before mating them, it helps seeing the mating entities a little easier.

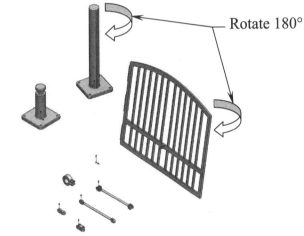

Rotate 180°

3. Adding a Distance mate:

- Click **Mate** on the Assembly toolbar.

- Select the **2 side faces** of the **Base Stand** and the **Gate-Support** as indicated.

- Click the **Distance** button and enter **7.00**in.

- Click **OK**.

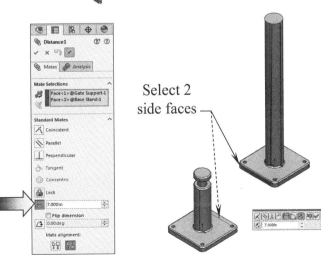

Select 2 side faces

4. Adding a Coincident mate:

- Click **Mate** on the Assembly Toolbar, if not yet selected.

- Select the **2 front faces** of the **Base Stand** and the **Gate Support** as indicated.

- The **Coincident** option is automatically selected.

- Click **OK**.

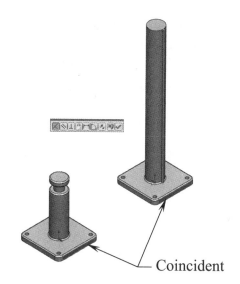

Coincident

5. Adding other mates:

- The **Mate** command should still be active, if not, select it.

- Select the **2 bottom faces** of the **Base Stand** and the **Gate Support** as indicated.

- The **Coincident** option is automatically selected.

- Click **OK**.

Coincident

Concentric

- Click the Circular Bosses on the sides of the **Gate** and the **Gate Support**; a **concentric** mate is automatically added.

- Click **OK**.

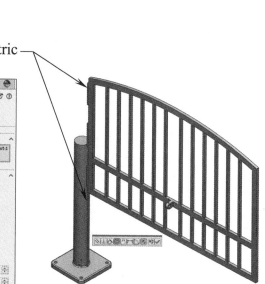
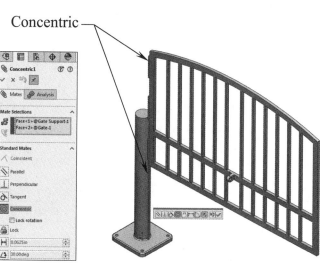

- Add a **Distance** mate of
  1.000" between the **upper
  face** of the Gate Support and
  the **bottom face** of the Gate,
  as noted.

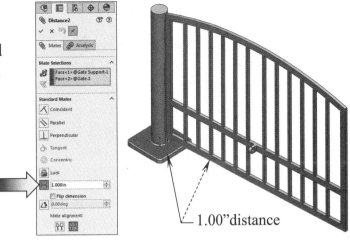

1.00"distance

- Add a **Concentric** mate
  between the **circular face**
  of the Base-Stand and
  the **center hole** of the
  Arm \Connector.

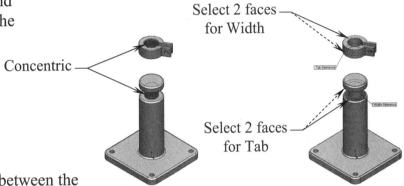

Select 2 faces
for Width

Concentric

Select 2 faces
for Tab

- Add a **Width** mate between the
  4 faces of the same components.

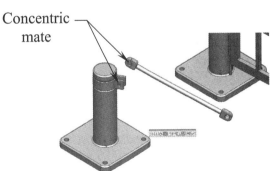

Concentric
mate

- Add a **Concentric** mate between the
  side hole of the Arm Connector and
  the hole in the Arm.

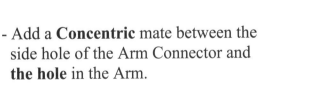

Width mate

- Add another **Width** mate between the
  4 faces of these two components.

- Click **OK**.

- Add a **Concentric** mate between
  the hole in the Arm and **the hole**
  in the Connecting Arm.

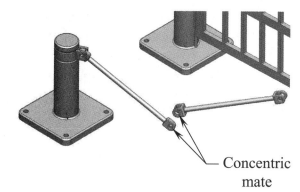

Concentric
mate

- Add a **Width** mate between the
  4 faces of the same components.

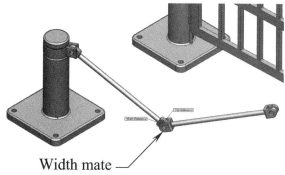

Width mate

- Add a **Concentric** mate between **the hole**
  of the Connecting Arm and **the hole** in
  the Connector Joint.

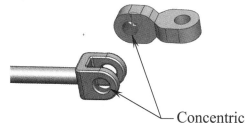

Concentric

- Add another **Width** mate between the **4 faces**
  of these two components.

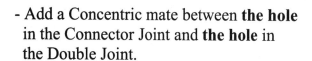

Width

- Add a Concentric mate between **the hole**
  in the Connector Joint and **the hole** in
  the Double Joint.

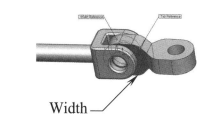

Concentric

- Add a **Width** mate between the **4 faces**
  of these two components.

Width

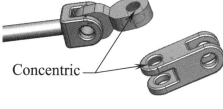

- Click **OK**.

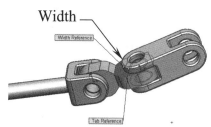

- Move the components to the position shown.

- Since the Double Joint has several components connected to its left side, this time it might be a little easier if we create the Width mate before the Concentric mate.

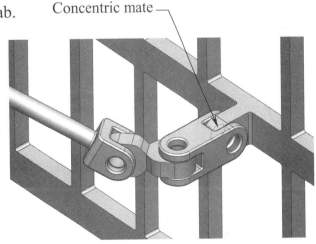

Move the components to approx. here

6. Adding more mates:

- Click the **Mate** command again, if not yet selected.

- Select the **Advanced** tab.

- Click the **Width** option.

- Select the **2 faces** of the **Double Joint** for Width selection.

- Select the other **2 faces** of the tab on the **Gate** for Tab selection.

- Click **OK**.

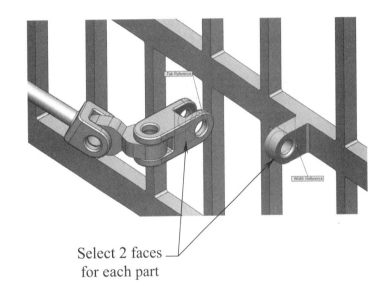

Select 2 faces for each part

- Change to the **Standard Mates** tab.

Concentric mate

- Select **the hole** in the Double-Joint and **the hole** on the tab of the Gate.

- A **Concentric** mate is added automatically to the selected holes.

- Click **OK** twice to close out of the mate mode.

7. Creating an Offset-Distance plane:

- Select the **Right** plane of the assembly and click the **Plane** command, or **select Insert / Reference Geometry / Plane**.

- The **Offset Distance** button is selected by default.

- Enter **26.125**in. for distance.

- Click **OK**.

8. Mirroring the components:

- Select the **new plane** and click **Insert / Mirror Components**.

- Expand the Feature tree and **select all components** from there.

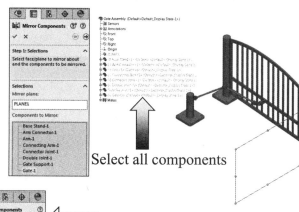

Select all components

- Click the **Next** arrow on the upper corner of the Feature tree.

- Select the part **Gate** from the list and click the **Create Opposite Hand Version** button.

- Click **OK** and drag one of the gates to test out your assembly.

9. **Save** and **Close** all documents.

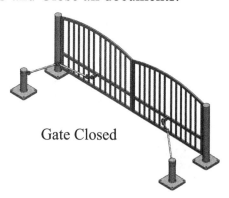

Gate Closed

Gate Open

CHAPTER 11

Using Advanced Mates

Rack and Pinion
Using Advanced-Mates

- Beside the standard mates such as Concentric, Coincident, Tangent, Angle, etc., which must be done one by one, SOLIDWORKS offers an alternative option that is much more robust called Smart-Mates.

- There are many advantages for using Smart-mates. It can create several mates at the same time, depending on the type of entity selected. For example, if you drag a circular edge of a hole and drop it on a circular edge of another hole, SOLIDWORKS will automatically create 2 mates: a concentric mate between the two cylindrical faces of the holes and a coincident mate between the two planar faces.

- Using Smart-mates, you do not have to select the Mate command every time. Simply hold the ALT key and drag an entity of a component to its destination; a smart-mate symbol will appear to confirm the types of mates it is going to add. At the same time, a mate toolbar will also pop up offering some additional options such as Flip Mate Alignment, change to a different mate type, or simply undo the selection.

- Using the Alt + Drag option, the Tab key is used to flip the mate alignments; this is done by releasing the Alt key and pressing the Tab key while the mouse button is still pressed. This option works well even if your assembly is set to lightweight.

- In addition to the Alt + Drag, if you hold the Control key and Drag a component, SOLIDWORKS will create an instance of the selected component and apply the smart-mates to it at the same time. Using this option you will have to click the Flip Mate Alignment button on the pop-up toolbar to reverse the direction of the Mate; the Tab key does not work.

- This lesson will guide you through the use of the Smart-mate options, and for some of the steps, use the standards mate options as well.

Rack & Pinion
Using Advanced-Mates

Rack & Pinion Mates

The Rack and Pinion mate option allows linear translation of the Rack to cause circular rotation in the Pinion, and vice versa.

For each full rotation of the Pinion, the Rack translates a distance equal to π multiplied by the Pinion diameter. You can specify either the diameter or the distance by selecting either the Pinion Pitch Diameter or the Rack Travel / Revolution options.

1. Open an assembly document:

- From the Training Files folder, browse to the Rack & Pinion folder and open the assembly named **Rack & Pinion mates**.

- The assembly has two components, the Rack and Gear1. Some of the mates have been created to define the distances between the centers of the two components.

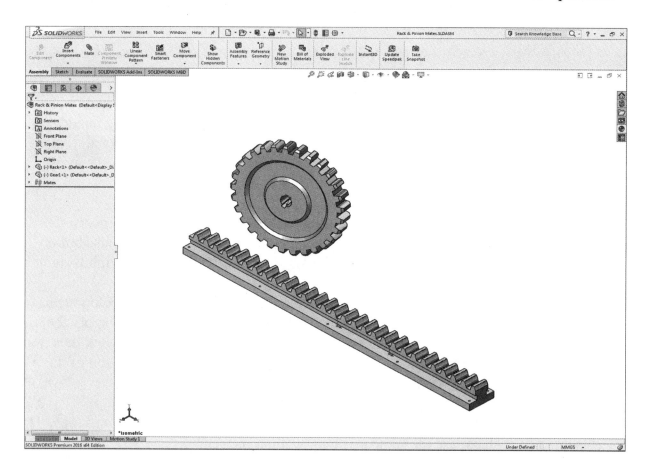

2. Adding standard mates:

- Click the **Mate** command Mate from the assembly toolbar or select **Insert / Mate**.

- Expand the FeatureManager tree and select the **Front planes** for both components. A coincident mate is automatically created for the two selected planes.

- Click **OK** .

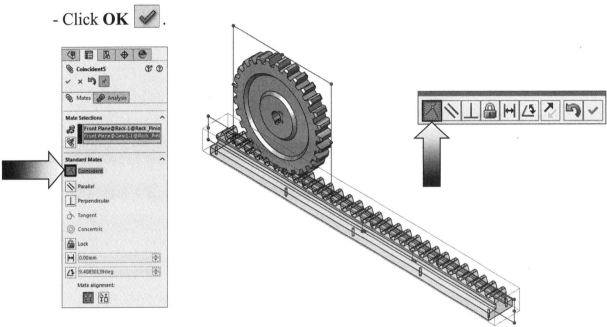

- Click the **Mate** command if not already selected.

- Select the **Right planes** for both components and click the **Parallel** mate option.

- Click **OK** .

- This mate is used to position the starting position of the Gear1, but it needs to be suppressed prior to adding the Rack & Pinion mate.

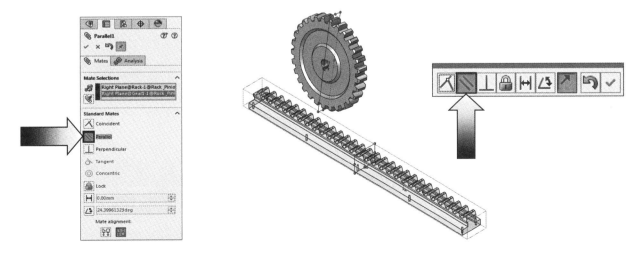

3. Suppressing a mate:

- Expand the **Mate Group** (click the + sign) at the bottom of the FeatureManager tree.

- Right click the Parallel mate and select the **Suppress** button from the pop-up window (arrow).
* *(Move the rack so that it does not interfere with the gear.)*

- The Parallel mate icon should turn grey to indicate that it is suppressed.

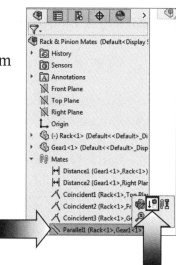

4. Adding a Mechanical mate:

- Move down the Mate properties and expand the **Mechanical Mates** section (arrow).

- Click the **Rack Pinion** button. The option Pinion Pitch Diameter should be selected already. For each full rotation of the pinion, the rack translates a distance equal to π multiplied by the pinion diameter, and the Pinion's diameter appears in the window.

- In the Mate Selections, highlight the Rack section and select the **Bottom-Edge** of one of the teeth on the Rack as indicated.

- Click in the Pinion section and select the **Construction-Circle** on the gear as noted.

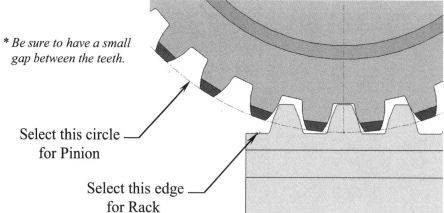

* *Be sure to have a small gap between the teeth.*

Select this circle for Pinion

Select this edge for Rack

- Enable the **Reverse** checkbox.

- Click **OK** ✓ to exit out of the Mate option.

* *If there is a collision between the 2 components, suppress the Rack & Pinion mate, move the rack to create a gap, unsuppress the mate and try again.*

5. Testing the mates:

- Change to the Isometric orientation
  (Control + 7).

- Drag either the Rack or the Gear1
  back and forth and see how the
  two components will move
  relative to each other.

- Hide the construction circle.
  Next, we will create an animation using
  a linear motor to drive the motions.

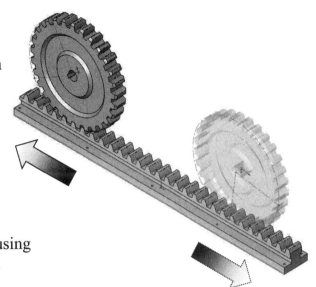

6. Creating a Linear Motion:

- Remain in the Isometric view; click the **Motion Study1** tab on the lower left
  corner of the screen.

- The screen is split into 2 viewports showing the Animation program on the bottom.

- Click the **Motor** button (arrow) on the Motion Study toolbar.

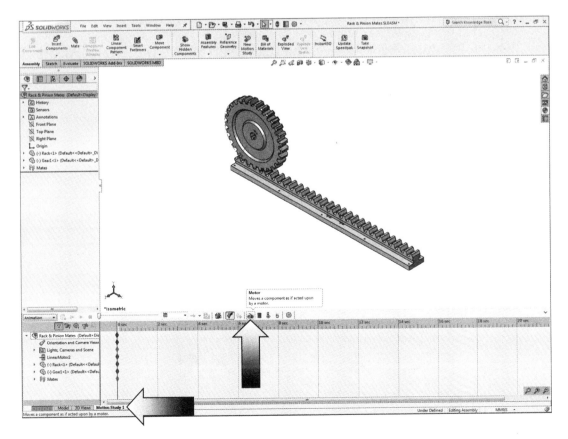

- Under the **Motor Type**, select the **Linear Motor (Actuator)** option.

- Under the **Motion** section, use the default **Constant Speed** and set the speed to **50mm/s** (50 millimeters per second).

- Click **OK** .

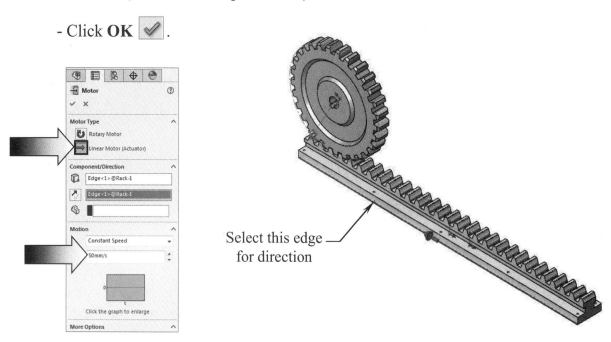

Select this edge for direction

7. Creating a Linear Motion:

- Click the **Playback Mode** arrow and select **Playback Mode Reciprocate**. This setting plays back the animation from start to end, then end to start, and continues to repeat.

- Click the **Play** button to view the animation.

- By default the SOLID-WORKS-Animator sets the play time to 5 seconds.

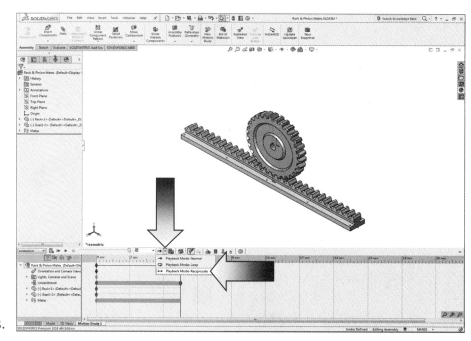

- To change the **Playback Time**, drag the diamond key to **10 second** spot (arrow).

- To change the **Playback Speed**, click the drop down arrow and select **5X** (arrow).

- Click the **Play** button again to re-run the animation.

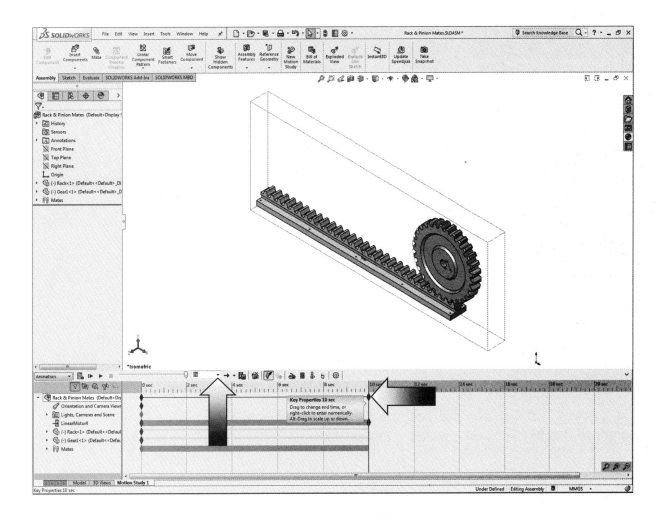

8. Saving your work:

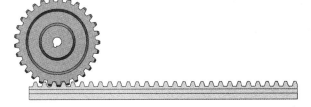

- Click **File / Save As**.

- Enter **Rack & Pinion Mates** for the name of the file.

- Overwrite the old file when prompted.

- Click **Save**.

CHAPTER 11 (cont.)

Limit & Cam Mates

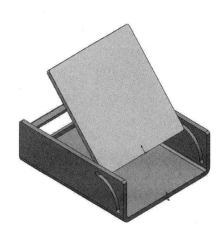

1. Opening a part file:

- Browse to the Training Files folder and open the part file named
  Limit & Cam Mates.

Limit mates: Allow components to move within a specified distance or angle. The user specifies a starting distance or angle as well as a maximum and minimum value.

Cam Mate: is a type of coincident or tangent mate. Where a cylinder, a plane, or a point can be mated to a series of tangent extruded faces.

- This assembly document has 2 components. The Part1 has been fixed by the Inplace1 mate and the Part2 still has 6 degrees of freedom.

- We will explore the use of Limit and Cam mates when positioning the Part2.

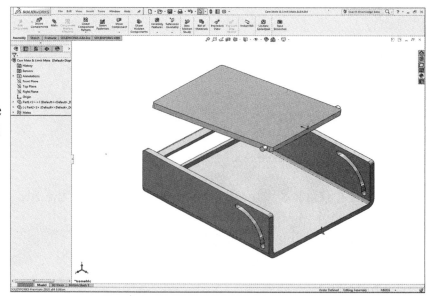

2. Adding a Width mate:

- Click the **Mate** command from the Assembly tab.

- Click the **Advanced Mates** tab and select the **Width** option.

- The Width mate aligns the two components so that the Part2 is centered between the faces of the Part1 (Housing). The Part2 can translate along the center plane of the Housing and rotate about the axis that is normal to the center plane. The width mate prevents the Part2 from translating or rotating side to side.

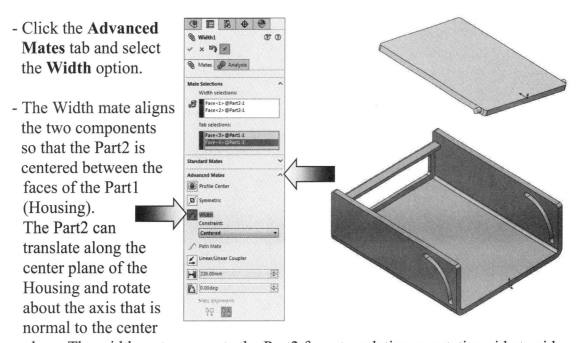

- For the **Width Selection**, select the **2 side faces** of the **Part2** (arrow).

- For the **Tab Selection**, select the **2 side faces** of the **Part1** (Housing).

- It does not matter which component you select, first or second,

just be sure to select both faces of the same part before selecting the next set.

Select the left and the right faces…

Select the left and the right faces…

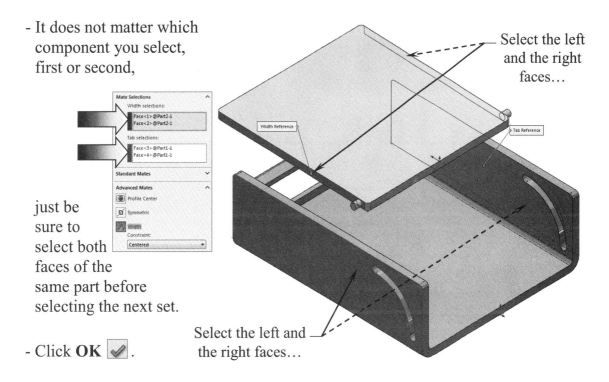

- Click **OK** ✔.

3. Adding a Cam mate:

- Click the **Mechanical Mates** tab below the Standard and Advanced tabs (arrow).

- Select the **Cam** mate button from the list.

- A Cam mate forces a cylinder, a plane, or a point to be coincident or tangent to a series of tangent extruded faces.

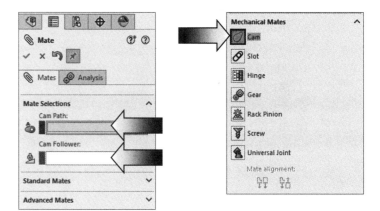

Note: The Slot-Mate can also be used to achieve the same result.

- For the **Cam Path**, select one of the faces of the slot. All connecting faces are selected automatically.

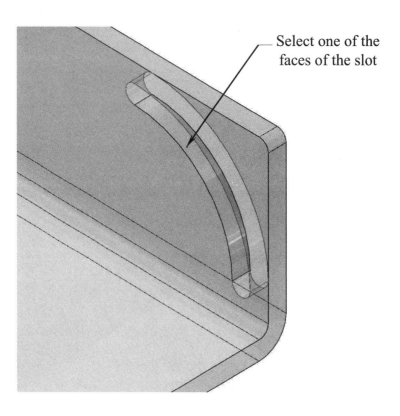

Select one of the faces of the slot

- For the **Cam Follower**, select the <u>cylindrical face</u> of one of the pins.

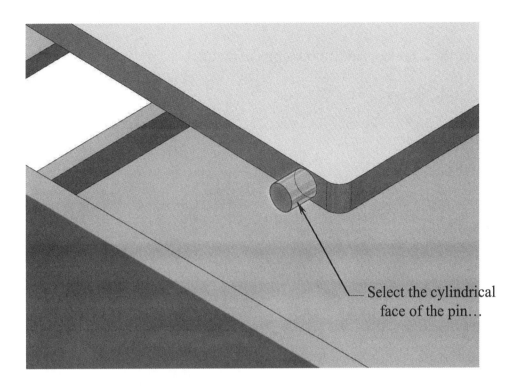

Select the cylindrical
face of the pin…

- Zoom in and check the alignment between the pin and the slot.

- Toggle
between the
2 mate
alignment
buttons
(arrow) to
make sure the two
components are
properly oriented.

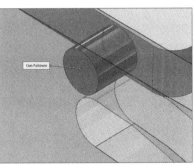

Anti-Aligned

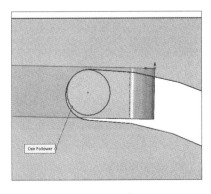

Aligned

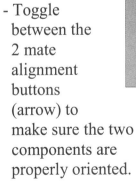

- Click **OK** .

4. Adding a Parallel mate:

- Click the **Standard Mates** tab (arrow) and select the **Parallel** option from the list.

- Select the **2 faces** as indicated to make parallel.

- Click **OK** ✔ .

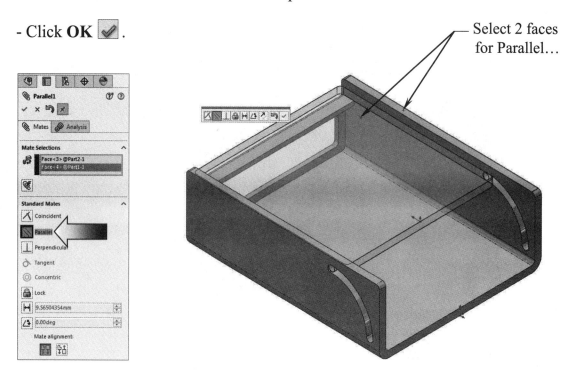

Select 2 faces for Parallel...

- The Parallel mate is used to precisely rotate the Part2 to its vertical position. But we will need to suppress it so that other mates can be added without over defining the assembly.

- Expand the Mate group by clicking the plus sign (+) next to the Mates folder.

- Click the Parallel mate and select the **Suppress** button (arrow).

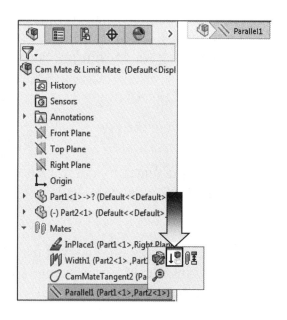

- Do not move the component, a Limit mate is going to be added next.

5. Adding a Limit mate:

- Click the **Advanced Mates** tab (arrow) and select the **Angle** option from the list.

- Select the **2 faces** of the 2 components as indicated.

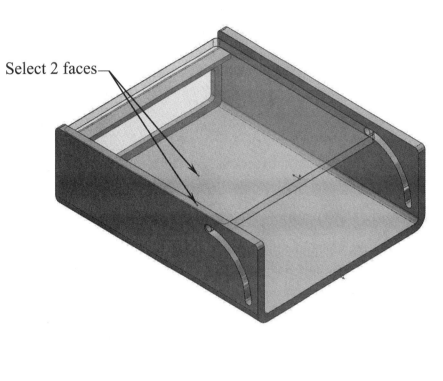

Select 2 faces

- Enter the following:

    90.00 deg for "starting" Angle.
    0.00 deg for **Maximum** value.
    0.00 deg for **Minimum** value.

- Click **OK** .

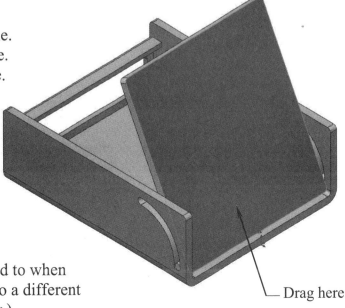

- Test the mates by dragging the Part2 up and down.

Drag here

- It may take a little getting used to when moving a cam part. (Change to a different orientation may make it easier.)

- Try pulling the right end of the Part2 downward. It should stop when it reaches the 90 degree angle.

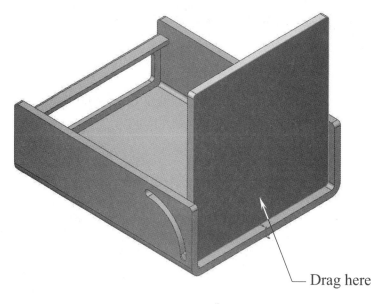

Drag here

- Let us explore some other options of dragging a cam part.

- Change to the Front orientation (Control + 1).

- Drag the **circular face** of the Pin upward. Start out slowly at first, then move a bit faster when the part starts to follow your mouse pointer.

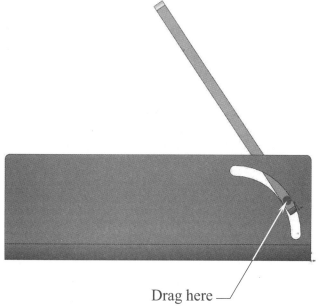

Drag here

Drag here

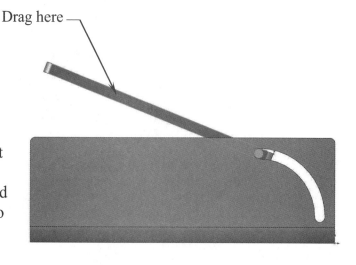

- Now try dragging the same part from the side as shown here. Also, start out slowly then speed up a little when the part starts to catch on.

6. Saving your work:

- Click **File / Save As**.

- Enter **Limit & Cam Mates** for file name.

- Click **Save**.

- Overwrite the document if prompted.

(In the Training Files folder, locate the Built-Parts folder; open the pre-built assembly and check your work against it.)

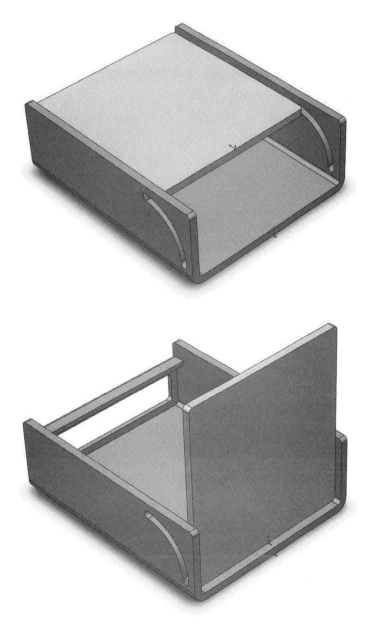

Exercise: Cam Followers*

1. Copying the Cam Followers Assembly folder:

- Go to The Training Files folder.
- Copy the entire folder named **Cam Followers** to your desktop.

A Cam-Follower mate is a type of tangent or coincident mate. It allows you to mate a cylinder, a plane, or a point to a series of tangent extruded faces, such as you would find on a cam. You can make the profile of the cam from lines, arcs, and splines, as long as they are tangent and form a closed loop.

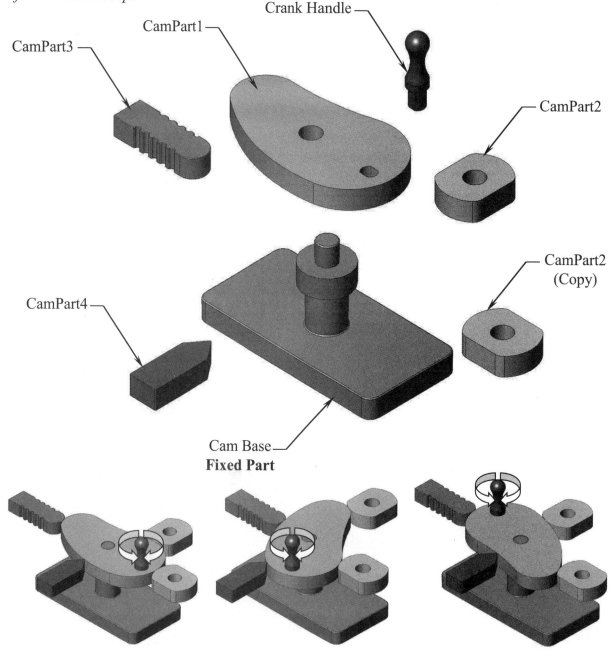

2. Assembling the components using the Standard Mates:

- Create a **Concentric** mate between the **shaft** and the **hole** as shown below.

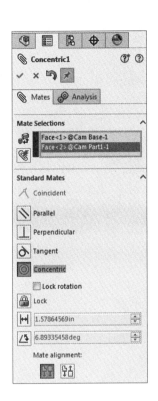

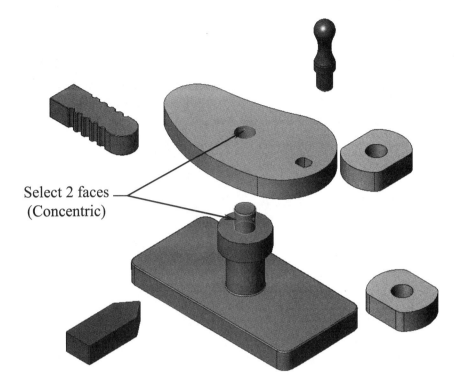

Select 2 faces
(Concentric)

- Create a **Coincident** mate between the **two faces** as shown below.

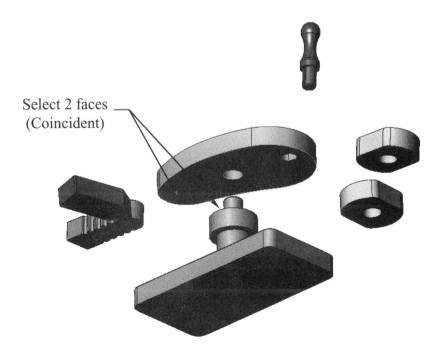

Select 2 faces
(Coincident)

- Create a **Coincident** Mate between the **2 upper surfaces** of the 2 components as indicated.

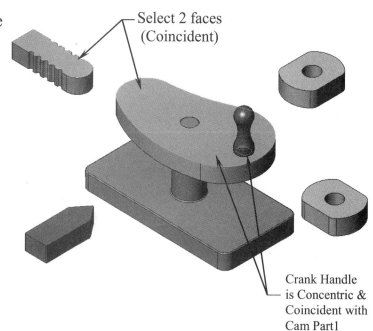

Select 2 faces
(Coincident)

- Repeat the Coincident Mates for all other parts (except for the Crank-Handle) to bring them up to the same height.

Crank Handle is Concentric & Coincident with Cam Part1

3. Using Mechanical Mates:

All Upper Faces are Coincident with the Campart1.

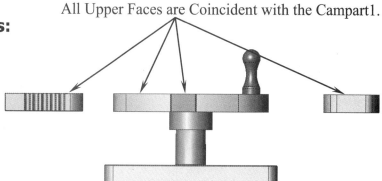

- Locate the **Mechanical Mates** section and expand it.

- Select the **Cam** option (arrow).

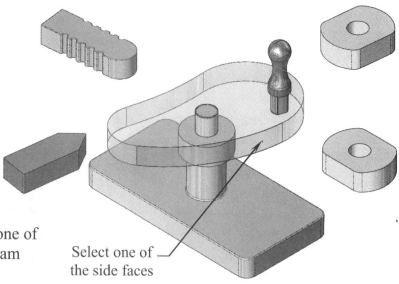

- For Cam Path, select one of the side-faces of the Cam Part as indicated.

Select one of the side faces

- For **Cam Follower**, select the curved face on the left side of the Cam Part2 as noted.

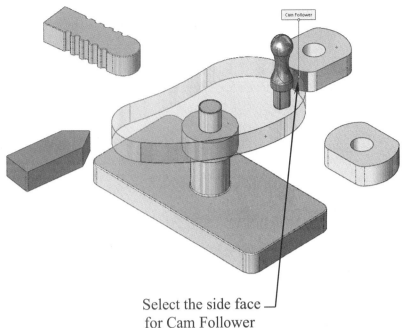

Cam Follower

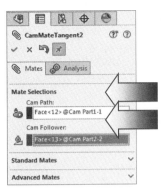

Select the side face for Cam Follower

NOTES:

- *In order for the components to "behave" properly when they're being moved or rotated, their center-planes should also be constrained.*

- *Create a Coincident Mate between the FRONT plane of the CamPart1 and the FRONT plane of the CamPart3, then repeat the same step for the others.*

4. Viewing the Cam Motions

- Drag the Crank Handle clockwise or counter-clockwise to view the Cam-Motion of your assembly.

Move the Crank Handle to test the Cam Motions

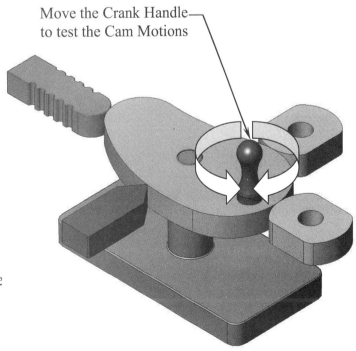

5. Saving your Work:

- Click **File / Save As**.

- Enter **Cam Follower** for the name of the file.

- Click **Save**.

Questions for Review

Using Advanced Mates

1. When adding a rack & pinion mate only a linear edge is needed for directions.
   - a. True
   - b. False

2. The rack & pinion mate will still work even if there is an interference between the components.
   - a. True
   - b. False

3. In a cam mate, more than one face can be selected to use as the cam follower.
   - a. True
   - b. False

4. In a cam mate, the alignment between the follower and the path can be toggled in or out.
   - a. True
   - b. False

5. In SOLIDWORKS Animator a motor can be used to help control the movements of an assembly.
   - a. True
   - b. False

6. Using the Angle-Limit mate, the maximum & minimum extents can only be set from zero to 90°.
   - a. True
   - b. False

7. The slot mate can also be used to achieve the same results as the cam mate.
   - a. True
   - b. False

8. After mates are added to the components their motions are restricted. They can only move or rotate along the directions that are not yet constrained.
   - a. True
   - b. False

7. TRUE   8. TRUE
5. TRUE   6. FALSE
3. FALSE   4. TRUE
1. FALSE   2. TRUE

Exercise: Bottom Up Assembly

<u>Files location</u>: Training Files folder.
                    Bottom Up Assembly Folder.
                    Copy the entire folder to your
                    Desktop.

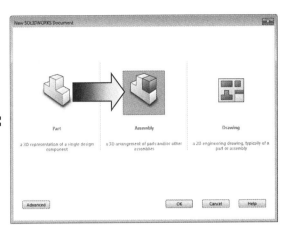

1. Starting a new Assembly document:

- Select **File** / **New** / **Assem**bly

2. Inserting the Fixed component:

- Click the **Insert Component** command
from the Assembly toolbar.

- Open the component **Molded Housing** and place it on the assembly's origin.

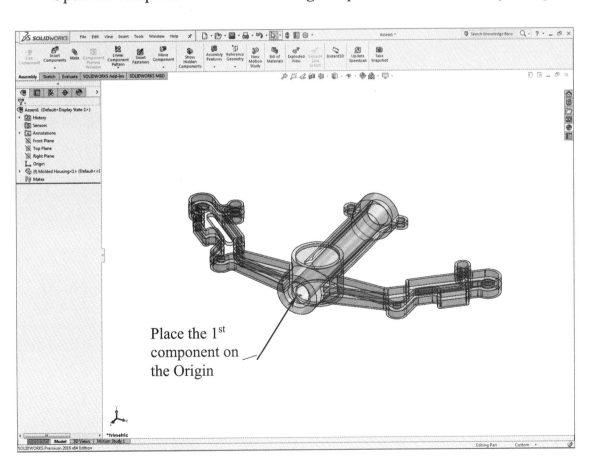

Place the 1st component on the Origin

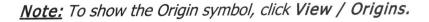

<u>Note:</u> To show the Origin symbol, click View / Origins.

3. Inserting the other components:

- Insert the rest of the components as labeled from the Bottom Up Assembly folder into the assembly.

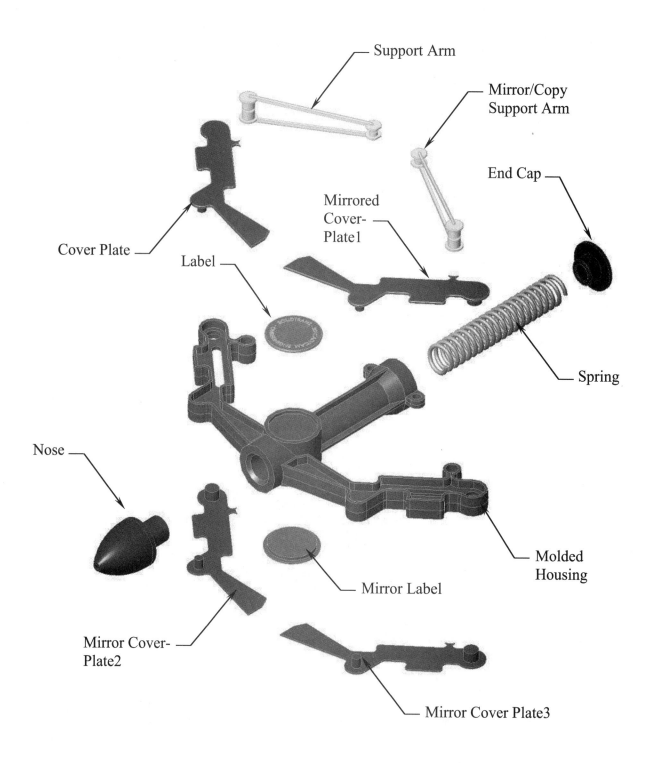

Support Arm

Mirror/Copy Support Arm

End Cap

Mirrored Cover-Plate1

Cover Plate

Label

Spring

Nose

Molded Housing

Mirror Label

Mirror Cover-Plate2

Mirror Cover Plate3

4. Mating the components:

- Assign the Mate conditions such as Concentric, Coincident, etc., to assemble the components.

- The finished assembly should look like the one pictured below.

5. Verifying the position of the Spring:

- Select the <u>Right</u> Plane and click Section View.

- Position the Spring approximately as shown to avoid assembly's interferences.

- Click-off the section view option when finished.

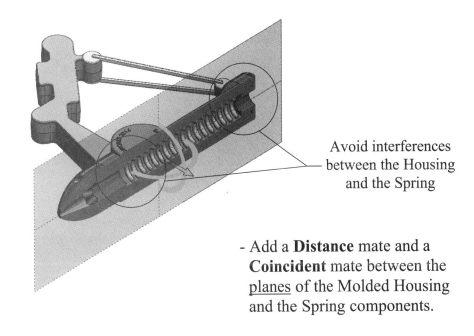

Avoid interferences between the Housing and the Spring

- Add a **Distance** mate and a **Coincident** mate between the <u>planes</u> of the Molded Housing and the Spring components.

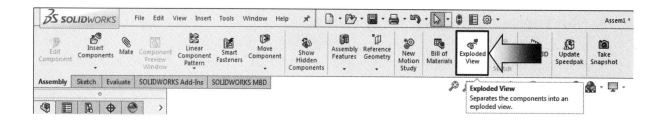

6. Creating the Assembly Exploded View:

- Click [Exploded View] or Select **Insert / Exploded View**.

- Select a component either from the Feature tree or directly from the Graphics area.

- Drag one of the three Drag-Handles to move the component along the direction you wish to move.

- Repeat the same step to explode all components.

- For editing, right click on any of the steps on one of the Explode-Steps and select Edit-Step.

- To simulate the move/rotate at the same time, first drag the direction arrow to move, then drag the ring to rotate.

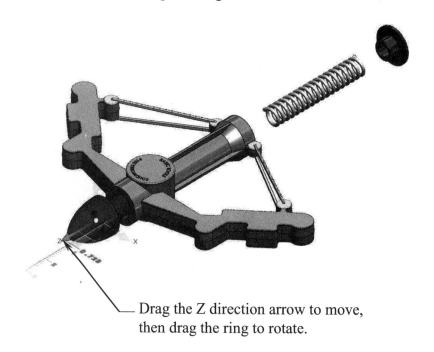

Drag the Z direction arrow to move, then drag the ring to rotate.

Note: *The completed exploded view can be edited by accessing the Configuration-Manager under the Default Configuration.*

Configuration
Manager tree

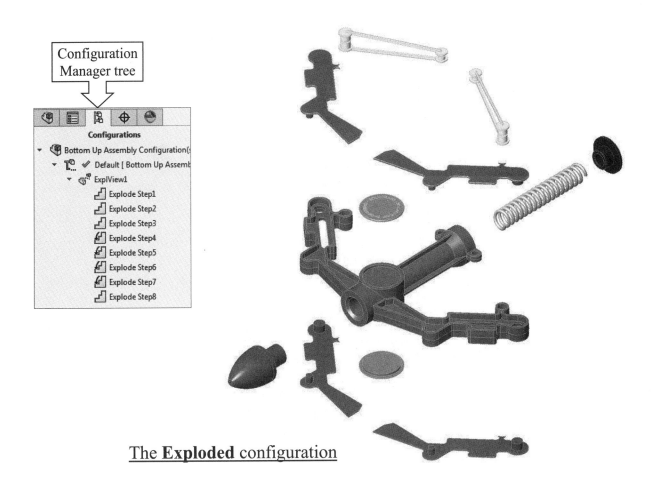

The **Exploded** configuration

The **Default** configuration

7. Saving your work:

- Select **File / Save As**.

- Enter **Bottom Up Assembly Exe** for the name of the file.

- Click **Save**.

(From the Training Files folder, locate the Built-Parts folder; open the pre-built assembly to check your work against it.)

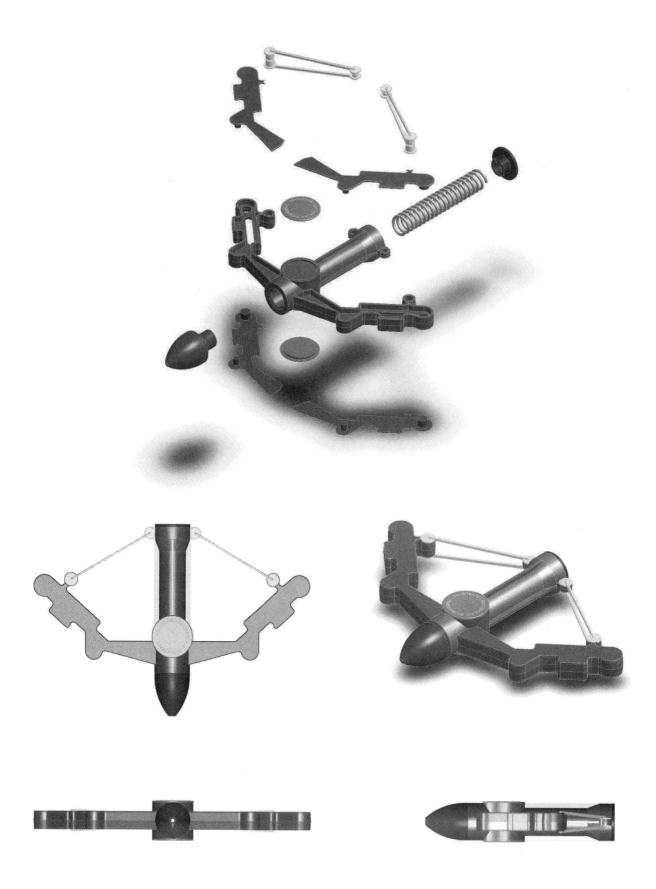

Level 1 Final Exam: Assembly Motions

1. Open the assembly document named **Assembly Motions Level 1 Final.sldasm**
2. Assemble the components using the reference images below.
3. Create an Assembly Feature and modify the Feature Scope so that only 3 components will be effected by the cut (shown).
4. Drag the Snap-On Cap to verify the assembly motions. All components should move or rotate except for the Main Housing.

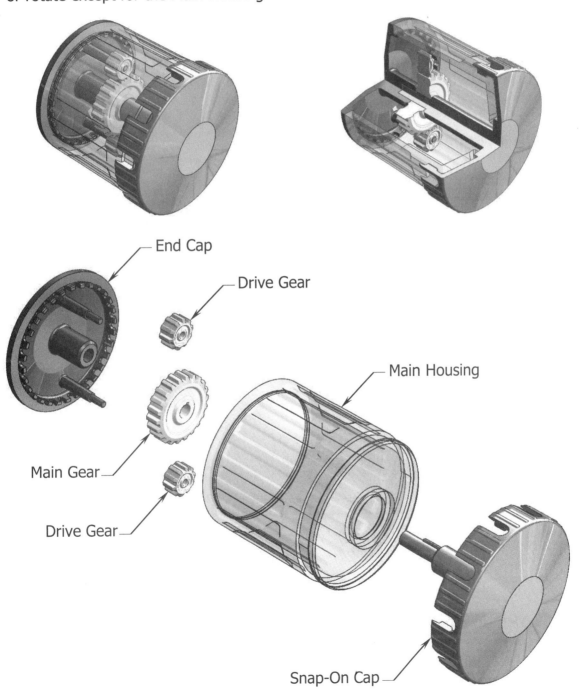

End Cap

Drive Gear

Main Housing

Main Gear

Drive Gear

Snap-On Cap

Testing the Assembly Motions:

- Drag the Snap-On Cap in either direction to verify the motions of the assembly.

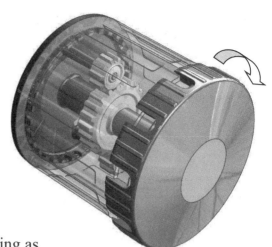

- The Main Gears, the two Drive Gears, and the Snap-On Cap should rotate at the same time.

- If the mentioned components are not rotating as expected, check your mates and recreate them if needed.

Creating a Section View:

- Open a new sketch on the <u>face</u> as indicated.

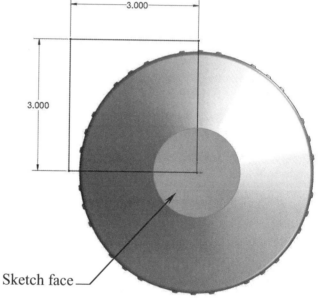

- Sketch a rectangle and add the dimensions shown.

- Create an Extruded Cut Through All components.

Sketch face

- Verify that the Keyway on the Snap-On Cap is properly mated to the Main Gear, and there is no interference between them.

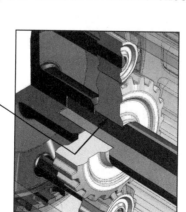

Keyway

Saving your work:

- Save your work as **Level 1 Final.**

CHAPTER 12

Layout Assembly

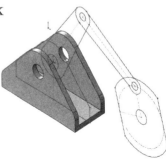

Layout Assembly

- You can design an assembly from the top-down using layout sketches. You can construct one or more sketches showing where each assembly component belongs. Then, you can create and modify the design before you create any parts. In addition, you can see the assembly motions ahead of time and how the components are going to behave when they are being moved around.

- The major advantage of designing an assembly using a layout sketch is that if you change the layout sketch, the assembly and its parts are automatically updated. You can make changes quickly and in just one place.

- In a Layout Assembly, blocks are created from each sketch to help handle them more efficiently. A block is created by grouping the sketch entities, dimensions, callouts, etc., into one unit and then saving them as a Block. A block can easily be moved, positioned, or re-used in other assembly documents.

- In layout-based assembly design, you can switch back and forth between top-down and bottom-up design methods. You can create, edit, and delete parts and blocks at any point in the design cycle without any history-based restrictions. This is particularly useful during the conceptual design process, when you frequently experiment with and make changes to the assembly structure and components.

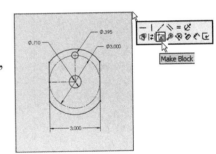

- This chapter will guide you through the use of Layout Assembly, as well as making new blocks and converting them to 3D models.

Assembly Motions
Layout Assembly

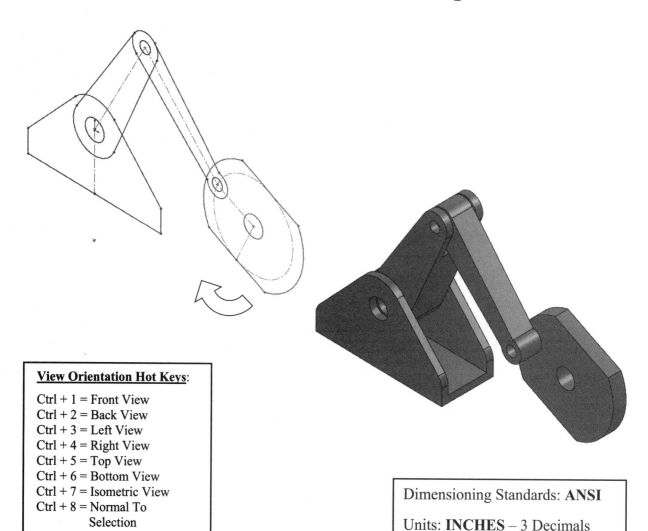

Dimensioning Standards: **ANSI**

Units: **INCHES** – 3 Decimals

Tools Needed:

Layout	Make Block	Make Part From Block
Animation Wizard	Motors	Add New Key

1. Opening an assembly document:

- Browse to the Training Files folder and open the document named **Layout Assembly.sldasm**.

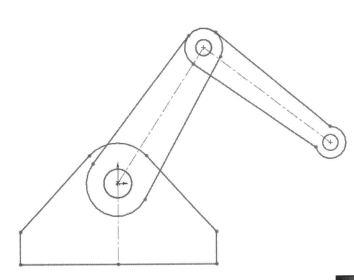

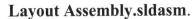

- Right click one of the tool tabs and enable the Layout option (arrow).

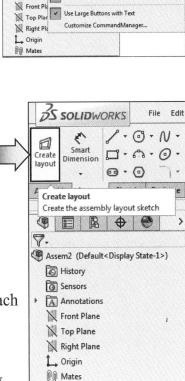

2. Activating the layout mode:

- In order to see the motions in the Layout mode, each sketch must be converted into a Block.

- In a block, a set of sketch entities and dimensions are grouped into one unit or one block so that they can be moved, positioned easily, or re-used in other assembly documents.

- Click the **Layout** button on the Layout tab next to the Assembly toolbar (arrow).

- Drag the Link component to see the motions created previously.

NOTE: *Recreate the mates if needed. All three block must be connected.*

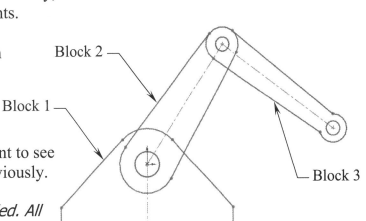

Block 2

Block 1

Block 3

3. Creating a new sketch:

- Sketch the profile below and add the dimensions as shown.

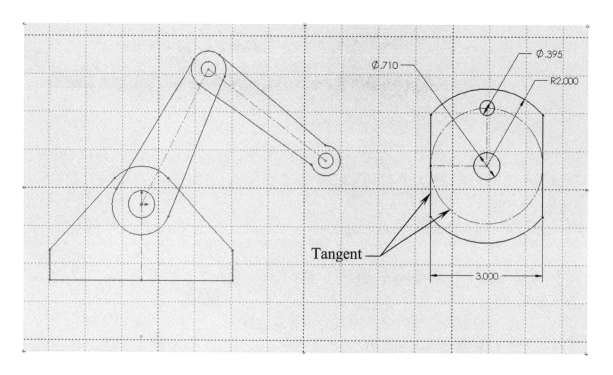

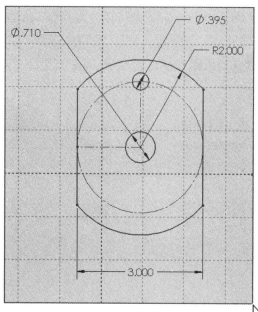

4. Making a Block:

- A block is created by grouping the sketch entities, dimensions, callouts, etc., into one unit and then saving them as a Block.

- Box-select the entire profile, click the **Make Block** button from the pop up toolbar – OR – select **Tools / Block / Make** from the pull down menus.

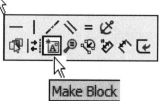

5. Setting the Insertion Point:

- Each block should have an Insertion Point (or Handle Point), which will allow the block to move and position more easily.

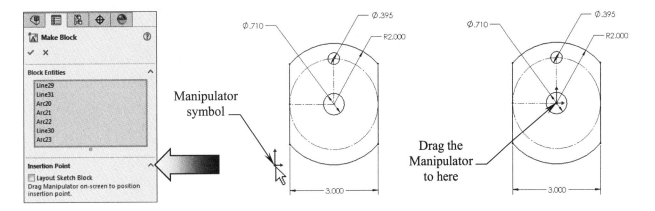

Manipulator symbol

Drag the Manipulator to here

- Expand the **Insertion Point** option (arrow) and drag the Blue Manipulator symbol and place it on the center of the middle circle.

- Click **OK** .

6. Editing a block:

- To edit a block simply double click on one of its sketch entities – OR – Right click one of the lines and select **Edit Block** (arrow).

- Click-Off the Edit Block button on the Layout tool bar when finished (arrow).

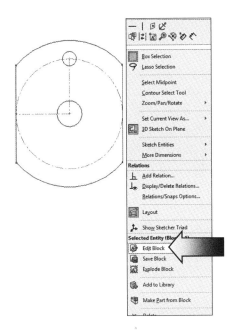

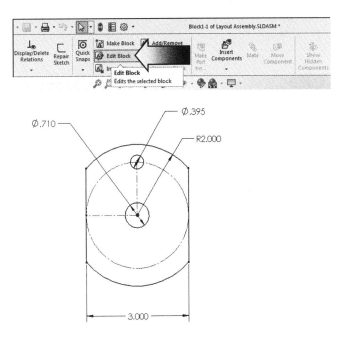

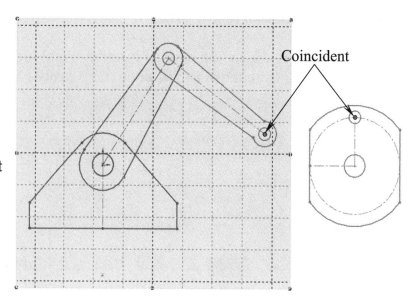

- Ensure that the
  Edit Block mode
  is off.

- Add a **Coincident**
  relation between
  the centers of the
  2 small circles as
  indicated.

Coincident

7. Adding dimensions:

- Add a **6.000 in** dimension to define the spacing between the 2 blocks.

Note: _Dimension from the vertical centerline of the 1st block to the center of the 4th block as noted below._

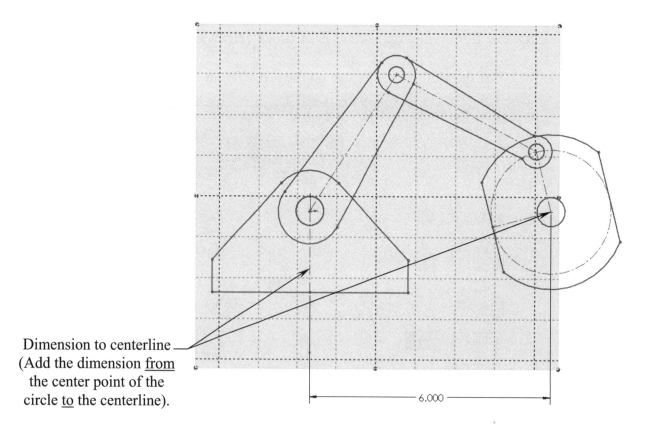

Dimension to centerline
(Add the dimension <u>from</u>
the center point of the
circle <u>to</u> the centerline).

6.000

8. Testing the relations between the blocks:

- Drag one of the vertices of the new part to see how the blocks respond.

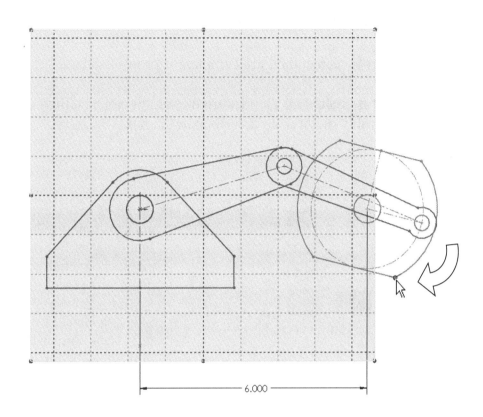

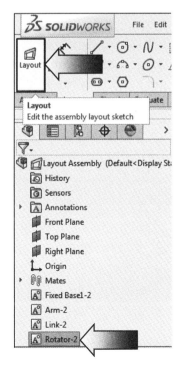

- **Click-off** the Layout command (arrow).

- Rename the new block to **Rotator** (arrow).

- So far we have 4 different blocks created as 2D-sketches in the assembly environment. The next step is to convert these blocks into 3D solid parts.

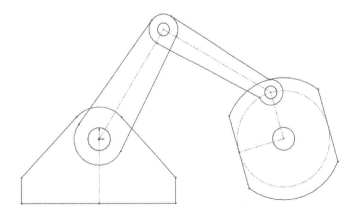

9. Converting a Block into a Component:

- Right click the name Fixed Base (the 1st block); select **Make Part from Block**.

- Select the **On Block** option under the Block to Part Constraint dialog.

- Click **OK** . Select the Part Template if prompted.

- A new part is created on the Feature tree and it can be edited using the Top-Down assembly method, as described in the next few steps.

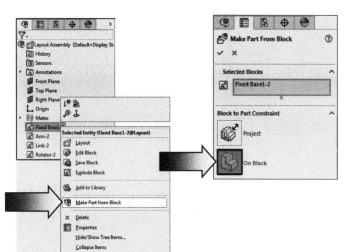

Project: Creates a part that is projected from the plane of the block in the layout sketch but not constrained to be co-planar with. In the assembly, you can drag the part in a direction normal to the plane of the block.

On Block: Constrains the part to be co-planar with the plane of the block in the layout sketch.

10. Extruding the Fixed Base:

- Select the name Fixed Base from the feature tree and click the **Edit Component** button.

- **Expand** the component Fixed Base, select the Sketch1, click **Extruded Boss/Base**, and set the following:

    * Type: **Mid Plane**   * Depth: **2.000 in**

- Click **OK** .

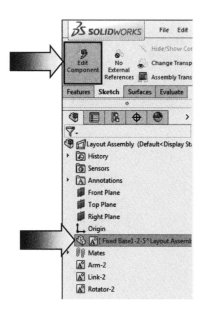

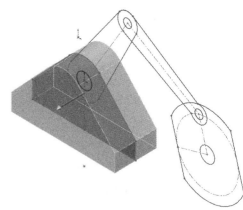

11. Adding fillets:

- Click the **Fillet/ Round** command.

- Enter **.500**in for radius.

- Select the **2 edges** as indicated.

- Click **OK** ✅.

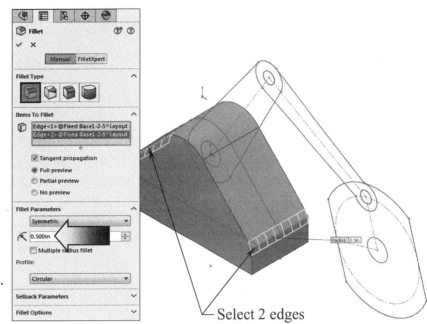

Select 2 edges

12. Shelling the part:

- Click the **Shell** command from the Features toolbar.

- Enter **.250 in** for wall thickness.

- Select the **7 faces** as noted.

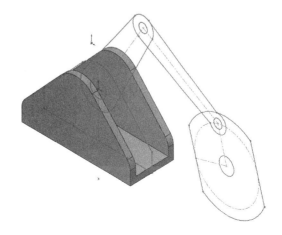

Select 7 faces on the top, left and right sides

- Click **OK** ✅.

13. Adding a hole:

- Click the **Extruded Cut** command.

- Select **Through All Both** to cut through both directions.

- Click in the **Selected-Contour** selection box and select the **circle** as noted.

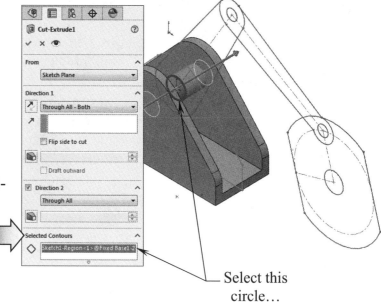

Select this circle...

- Click **OK** ✓.

- Click off the **Edit Component** command 🖱️ ; the first part is completed.

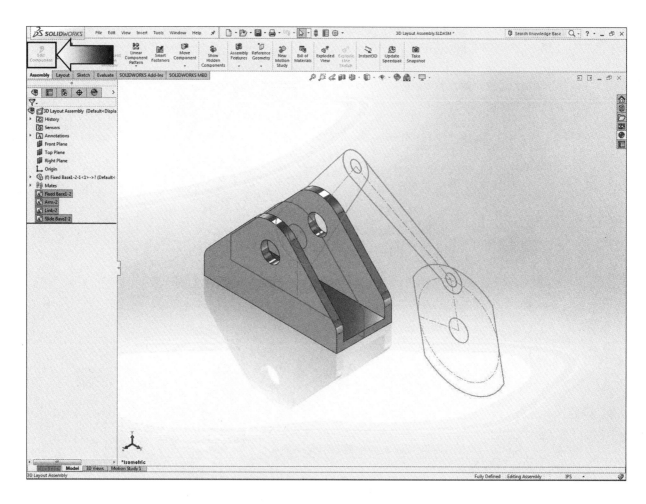

14. Converting the next block: (Repeating from step no. 8)

- Right click on the block named **Arm** and select **Make Part from Block**.

- Select the **On Block** option once again from the **Block to Part Constraint** section.

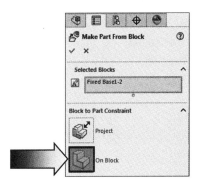

- A new part is created on the Feature tree and it can be edited using the same method as the last one.

- Click **OK** .

15. Extruding the Arm:

- Select the component **Arm** from the Feature tree and click the **Edit-Component** button.

- **Expand** the part **Arm**, select its sketch and click **Extruded Boss/Base**.

- Select the **Mid Plane** type.

- Enter **1.400**in for depth.

- Click **OK** .

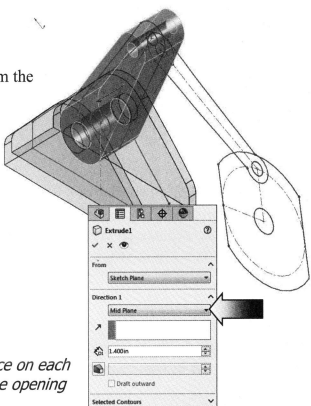

Note: _There should be a .050" of clearance on each side of this part, measured from the opening of the Fixed Base._

16. Adding a cut:

- Select the **Front** plane of the component Arm and sketch the profile as shown.

- Use **Convert Entities** if needed and add the relations/dimensions to fully define the sketch.

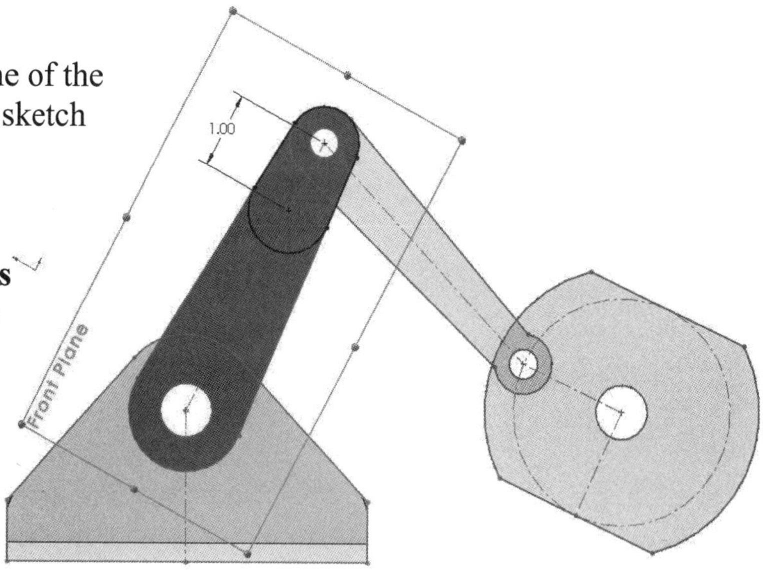

- Select the **Extruded Cut** command from the Features toolbar.

- Set the following:

    * Type: **Mid Plane**

    * Depth: **.900 in**

- Click **OK** .

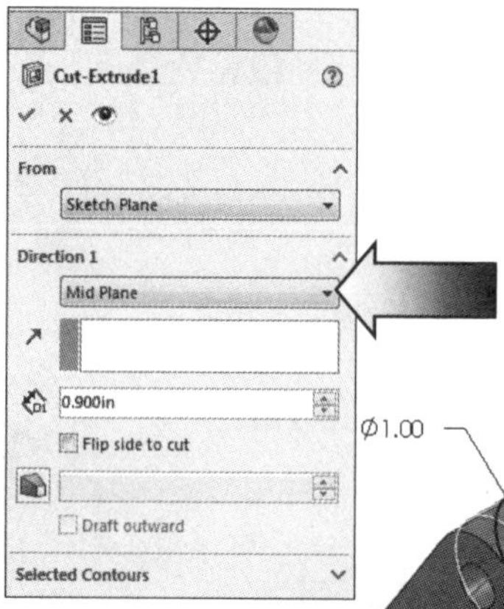

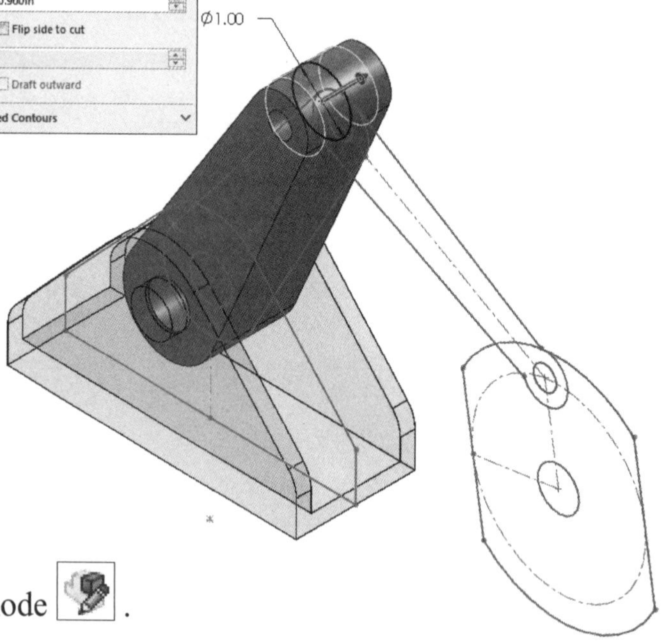

Note: *Make any adjustments if necessary to ensure proper fits between the components so that they can move freely.*

- <u>Exit</u> the **Edit Component** mode .

17. Repeating:

- Repeat either **step 8** or **step 13** and convert the next two blocks the same way.

- Make the component **Link .800**in thick as shown.

- Extrude with the **Mid Plane** type to keep the Link on the center of the Arm.

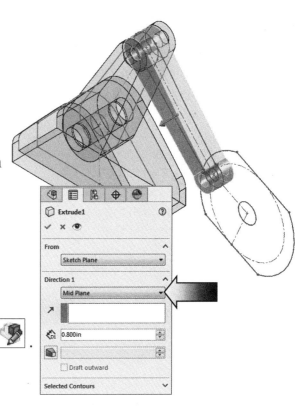

- <u>Exit</u> the **Edit Component** mode .

18. Using the Extrude-From option:

- The Extrude-From option allows a sketch to be extruded from a different location rather than from its own sketch plane. This new "reference" can either be a plane, a surface of a part, or an offset distance which the user can control.

- Select the part **Rotator** and click **Edit Component** 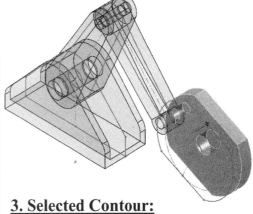.

- Set the following:

1. Extrude From:

* **Offset**

* **.400 in**

* **Reverse Direction**

2. Direction 1:

* **Blind**

* **.500 in**

* **Reverse Direction**

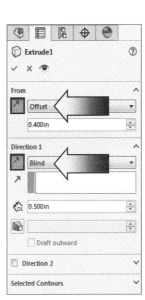

3. Selected Contour:

* Select the sketch of the **Rotator**.

* Click **OK** .

* <u>Exit</u> **Edit Component** .

19. Hiding the sketches:

- For clarity, hide all sketches of the components.

- Right click on one of the sketch entities and select HIDE.

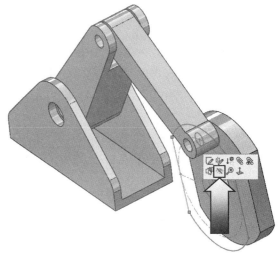

Note: *Make any adjustments if necessary to make sure the components can be moved freely.*
*Use the **Interference Detection** option and check for interferences, if any.*

20. Viewing the Assembly Motions:

- Drag the part **Rotator** back and forth to see how the components will move.

- Keep the part Fixed Base fixed and recreate any mates if necessary.

21. Saving your work:

- Save the assembly document as **Layout Assembly.sldasm**

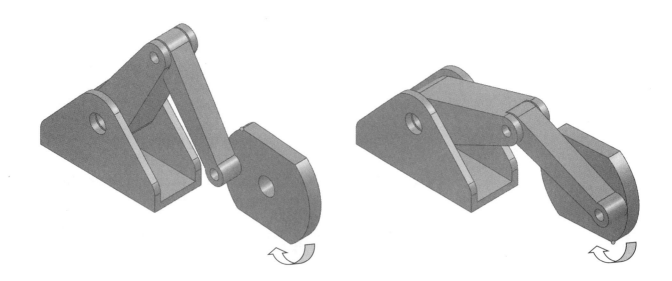

SOLIDWORKS Animator – The Basics

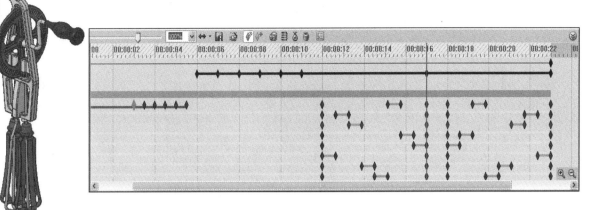

- You can use animation motion studies to simulate the motion of assemblies.

- The following techniques can be used to create animated motion studies:

    * Create a basic animation by dragging the timeline and moving components.
    * Use the Animation Wizard to create animations or to add rotation, explodes, or collapses to existing motion studies.
    * Create camera-based animations and use motors or other simulation elements to drive the motion.

- This exercise discusses the use of all techniques mentioned above.

1. Opening an existing Assembly document:

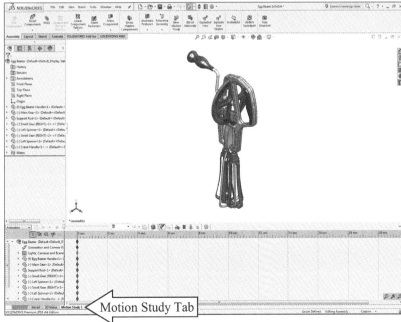

- Open the file named **Egg Beater.sldasm** from the Training Files folder.

- Click the **Motion Study** tab to switch to the SOLIDWORKS-Animation program (Motion Study1).

2. Adding a Rotary Motor:

- Click the **Motor** icon from the **Motion Manager** toolbar.

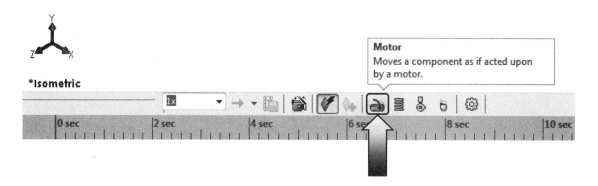

*Isometric

Motor
Moves a component as if acted upon by a motor.

- Under **Motion Type**, click the **Rotary Motor** option (arrow).

- Select the **Circular edge** of the Main Gear as indicated for **Direction**.

- Click **Reverse direction** (arrow).

- Under **Motion**, select **Constant Speed**.

- Set the speed to **30 RPM** (arrow).

- Click **OK** ✅ .

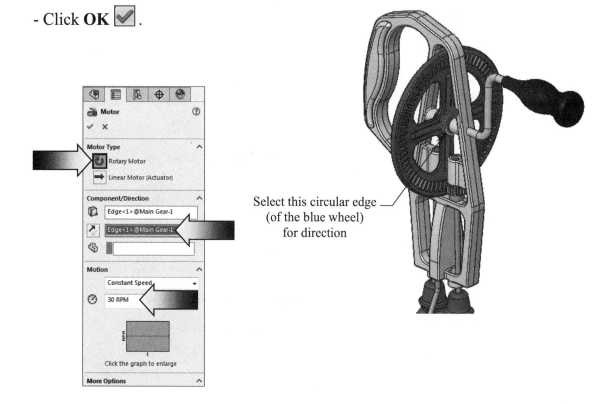

Select this circular edge (of the blue wheel) for direction

3. Viewing the rotary motions:

- Click the **Calculate** button on the **Motion Manager** (arrow).

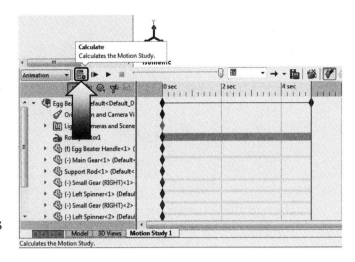

- The motor plays back the animation and by default stops at the 5-second timeline.

4. Using the Animation Wizard:

- Click the **Animation Wizard** button on the **Motion Manager** toolbar.

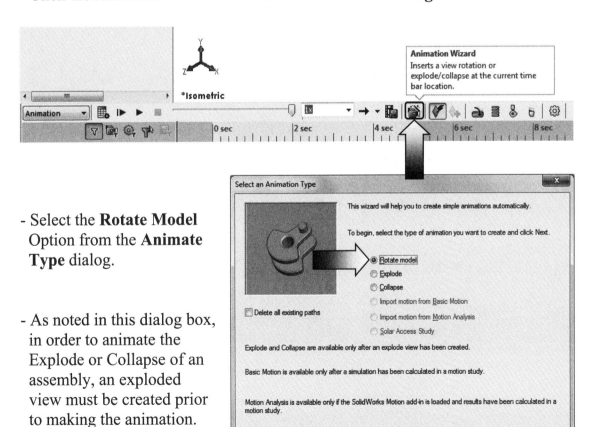

- Select the **Rotate Model** Option from the **Animate Type** dialog.

- As noted in this dialog box, in order to animate the Explode or Collapse of an assembly, an exploded view must be created prior to making the animation.

- Click **Next** Next > .

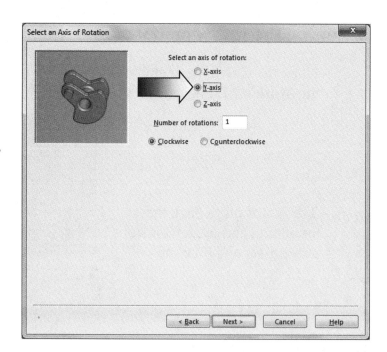

- For **Axis of Rotation**, select the **Y-axis**.

- For **Number of Rotation**, enter **1**.

- Select the **Clockwise** option.

- Click **Next** Next > .

- To control the speed of the animation, the duration should be set (in seconds).

   * **Duration: 5** (arrow)

- To delay the movement at the beginning of the animation, set:

   * **Start time: 6** seconds

- This puts one-second of delay time after the last movement before animating the next.

- Click **Finish** Finish .

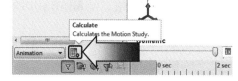

- Click **Calculate** to view the rotated animation.

5. Animating the Explode of an Assembly:

- Click the **Animation-Wizard** button once again.

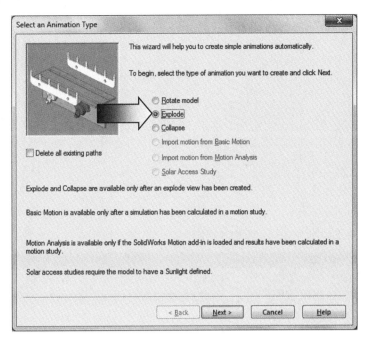

- Select the **Explode** option (arrow).

- Click **Next** Next > .

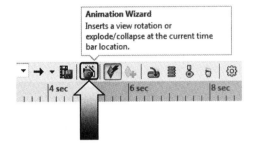

- Use the same speed as the last time.

    * Duration: 5 seconds (arrow).

- Also add one-second of delay time at the end of the last move.

    * Start Time: 12 seconds (arrow).

- Click **Finish** Finish .

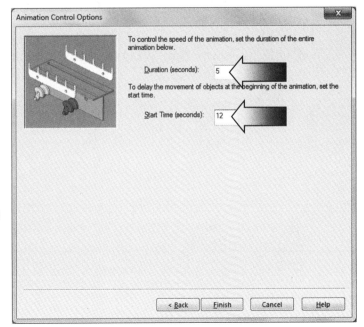

- Click **Calculate** to view the new animated motions.

- To view the entire animation, click **Play from Start**.

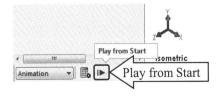

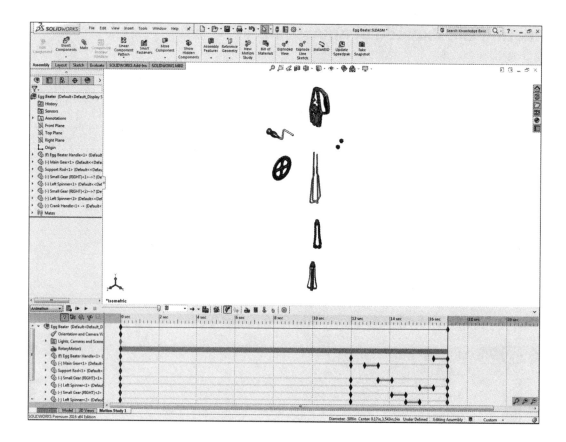

6. Animating the Collapse of the Assembly:

Animation Wizard
Inserts a view rotation or
explode/collapse at the current time
bar location.

- Click the **Animation Wizard** button on the
  MotionManager toolbar.

- Select the **Collapse** option
  from the **Animate Type**
  dialog.

Select an Animation Type

This wizard will help you to create simple animations automatically.

To begin, select the type of animation you want to create and click Next.

○ Rotate model
○ Explode
● Collapse
☐ Delete all existing paths
○ Import motion from Basic Motion
○ Import motion from Motion Analysis
○ Solar Access Study

Explode and Collapse are available only after an explode view has been created.

Basic Motion is available only after a simulation has been calculated in a motion study.

Motion Analysis is available only if the SolidWorks Motion add-in is loaded and results have been calculated in a motion study.

Solar access studies require the model to have a Sunlight defined.

< Back   Next >   Cancel   Help

- Click **Next**   Next >   .

- Set the **Duration** to
  5 seconds.

- Set the **Start Time** to
  18 seconds.

- Click **Finish** [Finish] .

- Click **Calculate** to view the
  new animated movements.

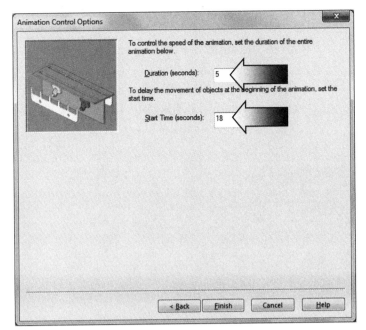

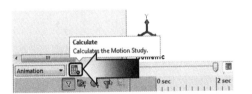

- Click the **Play from Start** button to view the
  entire animation. Notice the change in the view?
  We now need to change the view orientation.

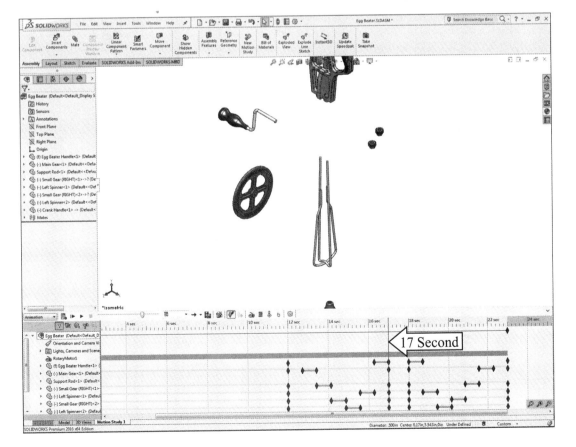

7. Changing the View Orientation of the assembly at 17-second:

- Drag the timeline to **17-second position**.

- From the MotionManager tree, right click on **Orientation and Camera Views** and un-select the **Disable View Key Creation** (arrow).

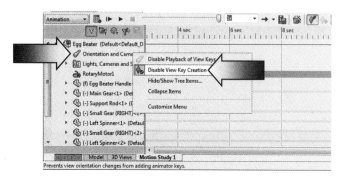

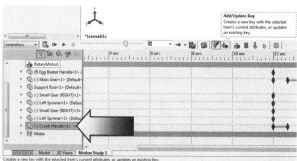

- Select the Crank Handle from the Animation tree and click the **Add/Update Key** (arrow).

- This key will allow modifications to the steps recorded earlier.

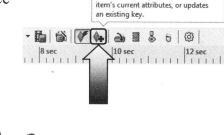

- Press the **F** key on the keyboard to change to the full screen – OR – click the Zoom to fit command.

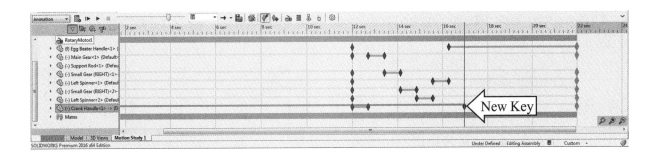

- The change in the view orientation from a zoomed-in position to a full-screen has just been recorded. To update the animation, press **Calculate.**

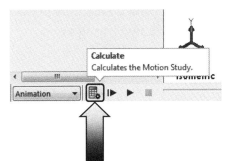

- The animation plays back showing the new Zoomed position.

Note: _This last step demonstrated that a key point can be inserted at any time during the creation of the animation to modify when the view change should occur. Other attributes like colors, lights, cameras, shading, etc., can also be defined the same way._

- When the animation reaches the 23 second timeline, the assembly is collapsed. We'll need to add another key and change the view orientation to full screen once again.

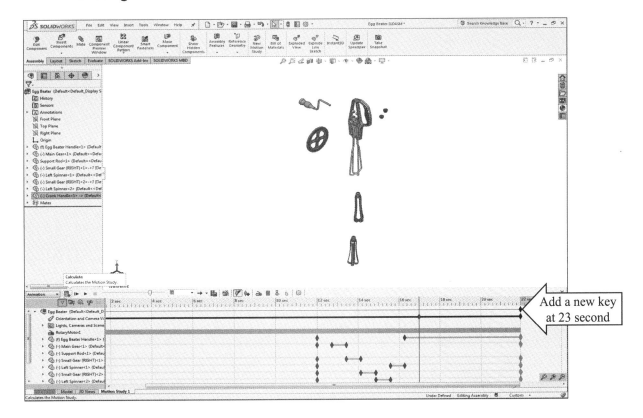

8. Changing the View Orientation of the Assembly at 23 second:

- Make sure the timeline is moved to **23 second position**.

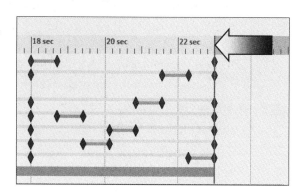

- Select the **Crank Handle** from the Animation tree and click the **Add / Update Key** button on the Motion Manager toolbar.

Note:

In order to capture the changes in different positions, a new key should be added each time. We will need to go back to the full screen so that more details can be viewed.

- Press the **F** key on the keyboard to change to the full screen or click Zoom to fit.

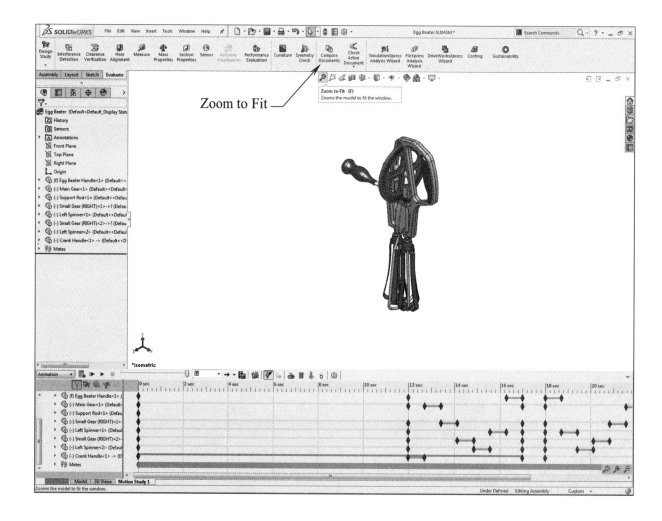

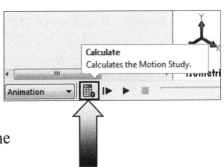

- Similar to the previous step, the change in the view orientation has just been captured.

- To update the animation, press **Calculate.**

- The system plays back the animation showing the new zoom to fit position.

- Save your work before going to the next steps.

9. Creating the Flashing effects:

- Move the timeline to **3-second position**.

- Select the **Crank Handle** from the Animation tree and click the **Add/Update Key** button.

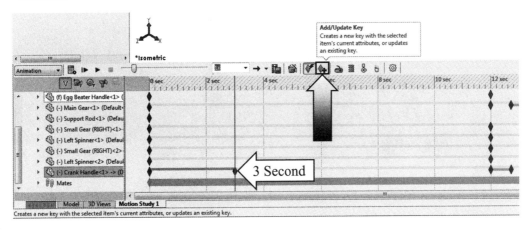

- We are going to make the Handle flash 3 times.

- Right click the part **Egg-Beater-Handle** from the Animation tree, go to **Component Display** and select **Wireframe**.

- Click **Calculate** .

- At this point, the Handle changes into Wireframe when the animation reaches the 3 second timeline and stays that way until the end.

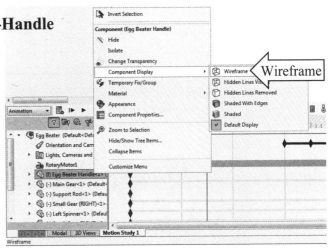

- Hover the cursor over the key point to display its key properties.

Place the mouse cursor over this key

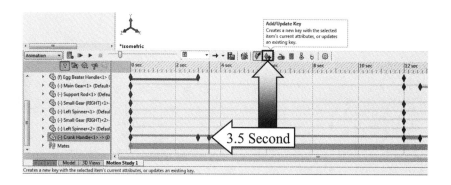

- Next, move the timeline to the **3.5 second position**. Select the **Crank Handle** and click the **Add / Update Key** button.

- This time we are going to change the Handle back to the shaded mode.

- Right click on the part **Egg Beater Handle**, go to **Component Display**, and select **Shaded with Edges**.

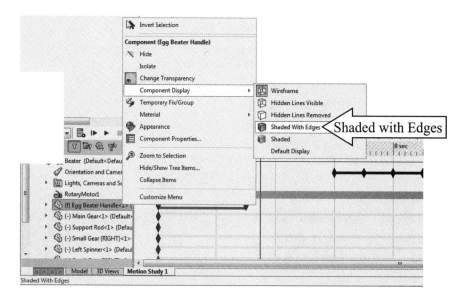

- Click **Calculate** 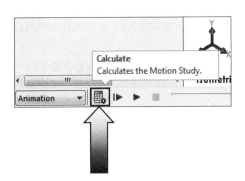.

- Since the change only happens within ½ of a
second, the handle looks like it was flashing.

- Repeat the same step a few times, to make the
flashing effect look more realistic.

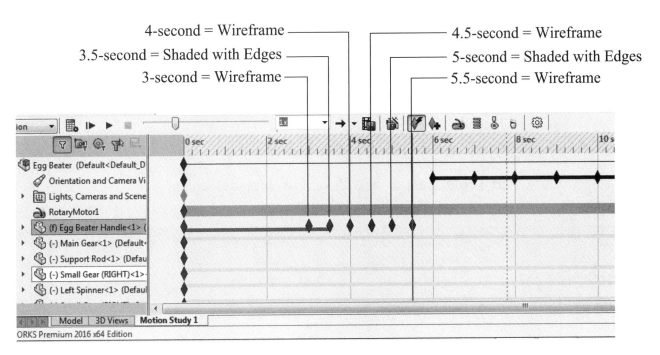

4-second = Wireframe
3.5-second = Shaded with Edges
3-second = Wireframe

4.5-second = Wireframe
5-second = Shaded with Edges
5.5-second = Wireframe

- Use the times chart listed above and repeat the step number 9 at least 3 more times.

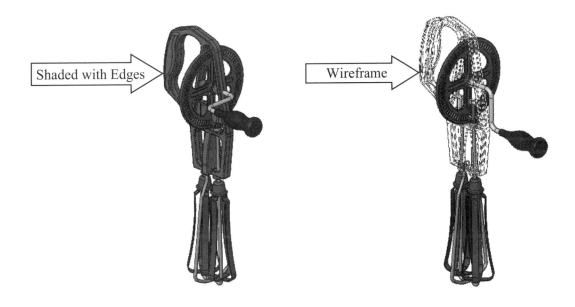

Shaded with Edges

Wireframe

10. Looping the animation:

- Click the Playback Mode arrow and select **Playback Mode: Reciprocate** (arrow).

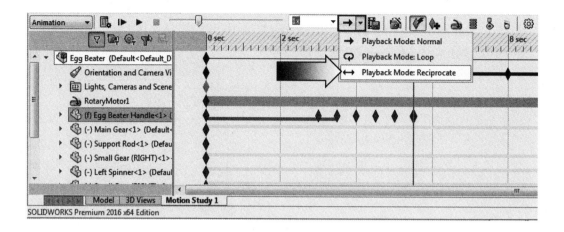

- Click **Play From Start** to view the entire animation again.

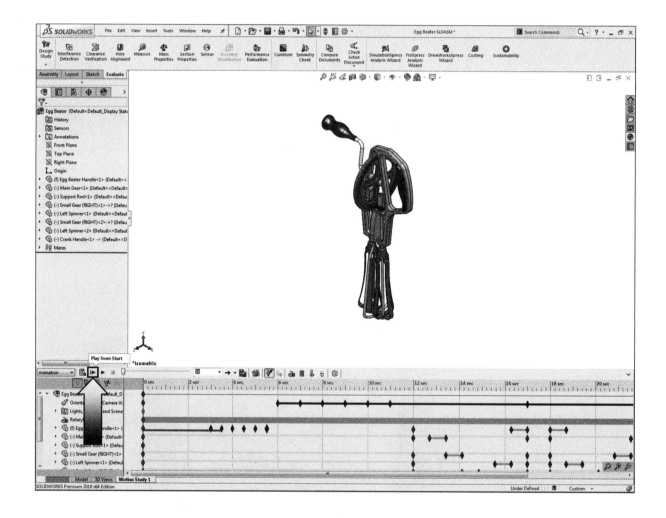

11. Saving the animation as AVI: (Audio Visual Interleaving)

- Click the **Save Animation** icon on the MotionManager toolbar.

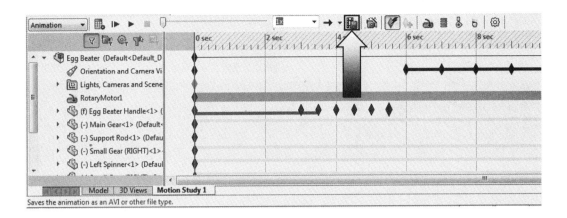

- Use the default name (Egg Beater) and other default settings.

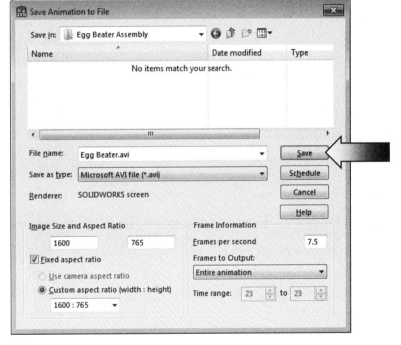

- Click **Save**.

- The **Image Size** and **Aspect Ratio** (grayed-out) adjusts size and shape of the display. It becomes available when the renderer is PhotoWorks buffer.

- **Compression** ratios impact image quality. Use lower compression ratios to produce smaller file sizes of lesser image quality. Use the default compressor.

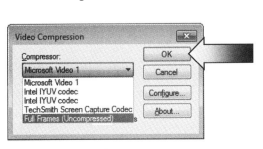

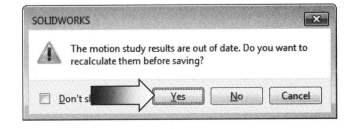

12. Viewing the Egg Beater AVI with Windows Media Player:

- **Exit** the SOLIDWORKS program, locate and launch your **Windows Media Player**.

- **Open** the **Egg Beater.AVI** from Windows Media Player.

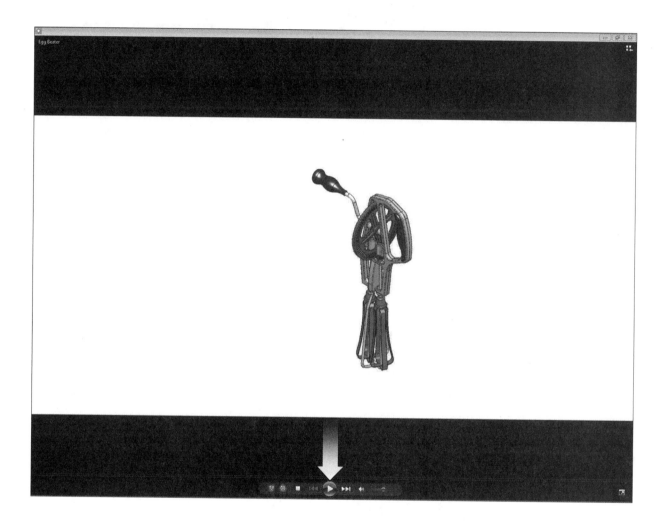

- Click the **Play** button to view the animated AVI file.

- To loop the animation in Windows Media Player, click the **Repeat** button on the controller (arrow).

- **Close** and **exit** the Window Media Player.

CHAPTER 13

Working with Sketch Pictures

Working with Sketch Pictures
Using the Spline tool

- A digital image can be used as a reference to model a part.
  Each image can be placed on its own planes, so several images can be inserted to help define the shape of the model from different orientations.

- The formats such as jpg, tif, bmp, gif, png, etc. are supported in SOLIDWORKS. They can be inserted and converted into a sketch so that a feature can be made from it.

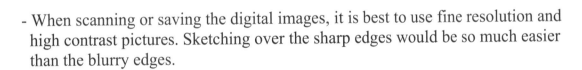

- When scanning or saving the digital images, it is best to use fine resolution and high contrast pictures. Sketching over the sharp edges would be so much easier than the blurry edges.

- Splines are often used to do the tracing of the images due to its flexibilities in manipulating the shapes, and splines offer a set of control tools to assist you with creating and maintaining the smoothness of the curves.

- The digital or scanned image can be scaled to size and repositioned with reference to the origin so that dimensions can be added for accuracy.

Working with Sketch Pictures
Using Splines

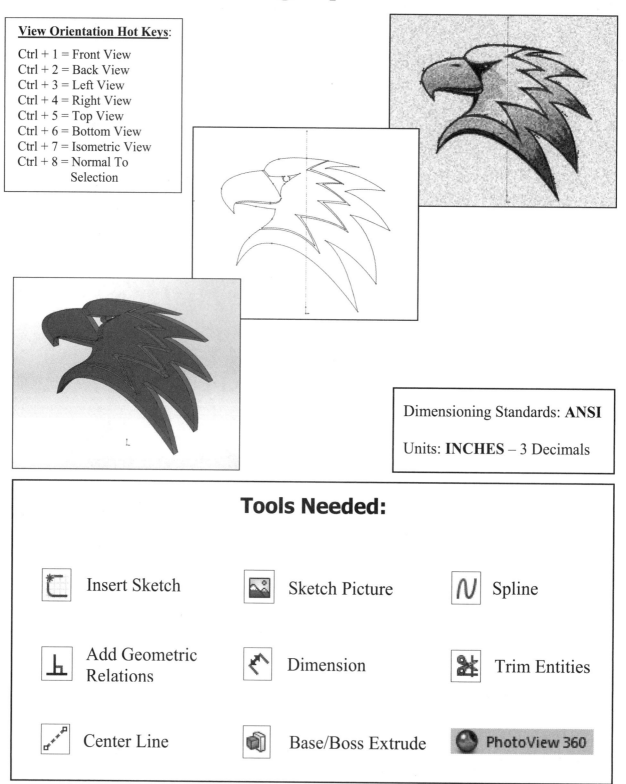

Dimensioning Standards: **ANSI**

Units: **INCHES** – 3 Decimals

Tools Needed:

Insert Sketch	Sketch Picture	Spline
Add Geometric Relations	Dimension	Trim Entities
Center Line	Base/Boss Extrude	PhotoView 360

1. Enabling Autotrace:

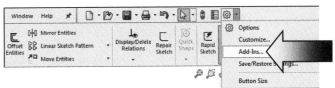

- Autotrace is an add-in that allows images such as .jpg and .bmp, .gif, or .png into sketch geometry. This add-in works best with high-contrast images or with a minimum of 300dpi.

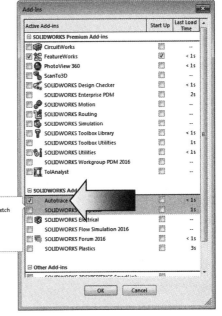

- You can apply Autotrace to part or assembly files but not to drawing files.

- The resolution is limited to 4096 x 4096. Files that exceed this limit are cut in half until both dimensions meet the limit. For example, if you insert a .tiff file that is 5000 x 3000, the file is reduced to 2500 x 1500.

- The second page of the Sketch Picture PropertyManager is available after Autotrace is enabled.

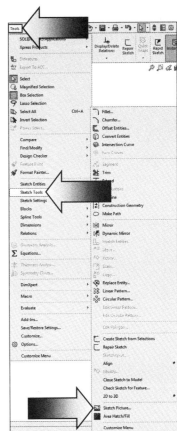

- Click **Tools** /**Add-Ins** and enable the **Autotrace** checkbox (arrow).

2. Inserting the scanned image:

- In order to use Autotrace the scanned image must be inserted into an active sketch.

- Select the <u>Front</u> plane and open a new sketch.

- From the **Tools** menu, click **Sketch Tools /** **Sketch Picture**.

<u>NOTE:</u> Go to step 6, page 13-9 if you do not have the Autotrace option available in your SOLIDWORKS version.

- Browse to the Training Files folder and select the file named **Eagle Head.jpg** and open it.

- The lower left corner of the image is placed on the origin.

- The image size and locations appear on the properties tree; we will modify those dimensions in the next step.

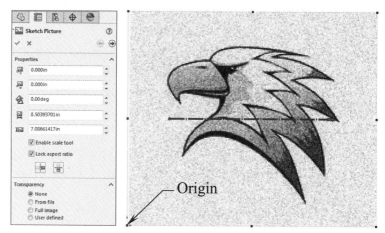

Origin

NOTE: The image was scanned with a low resolution and the colors in the background are not quite uniform. The precision of the contours may not be as high as anticipated.

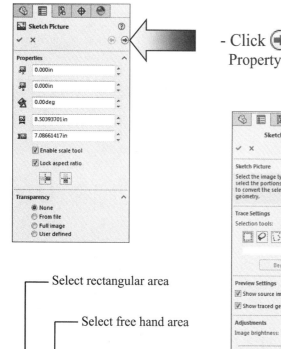

- Click ➡ to display the second page of the Sketch Picture PropertyManager (arrow).

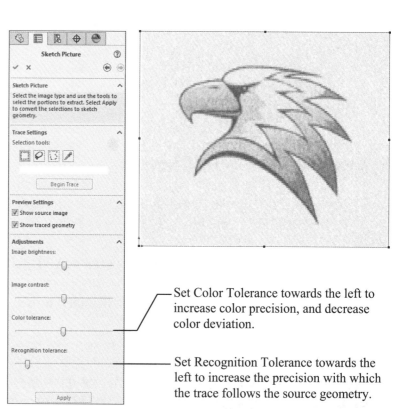

Select rectangular area

Select free hand area

Select color

Select polygonal area

Set Color Tolerance towards the left to increase color precision, and decrease color deviation.

Set Recognition Tolerance towards the left to increase the precision with which the trace follows the source geometry.

3. Using Autotrace:

- Select the Select-Rectangular tool (arrow).

- Box-select the area shown to create a border around the eagle head.

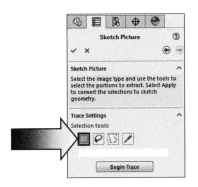

- Click **Begin Trace** Begin Trace .

- Autotrace traces the outline of the image based on the default settings.

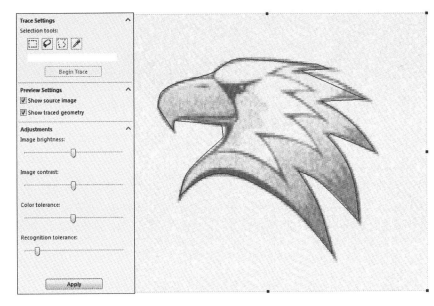

- The outline is created using a series of splines. Each spline segment can be selected and adjusted as needed. We will take a look at the different results when adjusting the image settings in the next few steps.

4. Adjusting the color tolerance:

- When the Color tolerance is set towards the left, Autotrace increases the color precision and decreases color deviation.

- Drag the slider under Color Tolerance to the <u>left</u> side, approximately as shown. Autotrace picks up the colors that it can recognize.

- Drag the same slider all the way to the <u>right</u>. Because of the busy background colors, both settings did not produce an acceptable result.

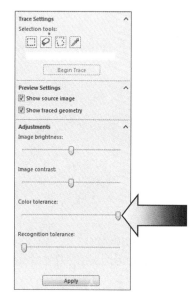

5. Adjusting the recognition tolerance:

- If the recognition tolerance is set towards the right, Autotrace decreases the precision with which the trace follows the source geometry.

- Drag the slider under Recognition Tolerance to the <u>right</u> side, approximately as shown.

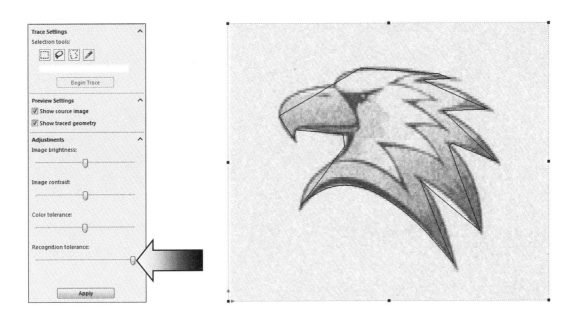

- Drag the recognition tolerance all the way to the <u>left</u>. Autotrace adjusts the degree to which the trace you created matches the geometry.
  The settings produced a little better result but still need further adjustments.

6. Applying the final settings:

- Set the Color Tolerance about half way, and the Recognize Tolerance all the way to the left as pictured.

- The eagle head image is quite complex and has such a busy background. The settings available in Autotrace can only produce an acceptable result, but more work still needs to be done afterwards.

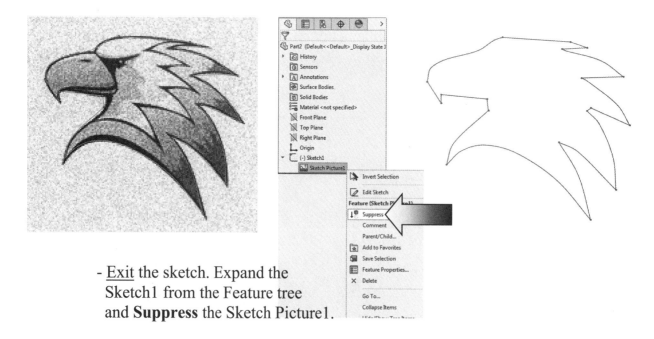

- <u>Exit</u> the sketch. Expand the Sketch1 from the Feature tree and **Suppress** the Sketch Picture1.

- Next, we will take a look at the manual trace option.

7. Positioning and sizing the scanned image:

- Double click the image to activate it.

- Enter the following dimensions to re-position and re-size the image:

  * X = **-1.825in**.
  * Y = **-0.300in**.
  * Angle = **0deg**.
  * Width = **3.600in**.
  * Height = **3.000in**.

- Be sure to enable the **Lock Aspect Ratio** checkbox (arrow).

- Click **OK**.

Splines:

- A spline is a sketch entity that gets its shape from a set of spline points. This tool is great for modeling free-form shapes that required a little more "flexibilities" than other curve tools.

- During the creation of a spline, each click creates a spline point and these points can be added or deleted when needed.

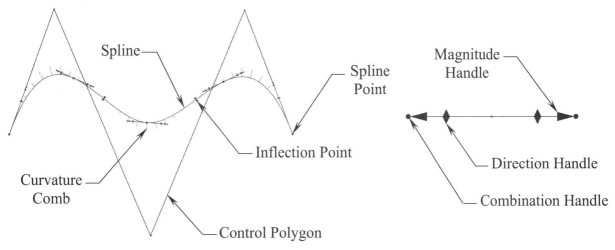

- Try to use as few spline points as possible in the general, long curving areas. Only use more spline points on tighter, smaller radiuses.

- Use the spline handles to drag freely, or hold the ALT key to drag symmetrically. The spline handles are used to change the direction and magnitude of the tangency at a spline point.

- Use the Control Polygons in place of the spline handles. Drag its control points to manipulate the spline.

- The Curvature Combs displays the curvature of the spline in the form of a series of lines called a comb. The length of the lines represents the curvature. The longer the line, the larger the curvature and smaller the radius.

- Inflection Points or Markers are used to show where the inflection changes in a spline, whether it is convex or concave.

8. Tracing the image with the spline tool:

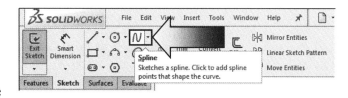

- The sketch should still be active at this time; select the Spline command from the Sketch toolbar.

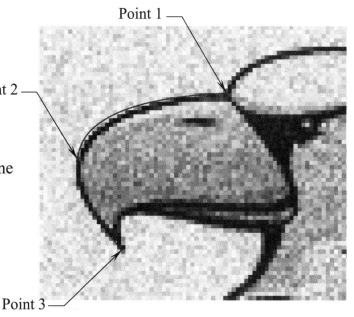

- Keep in mind that the simpler the spline, the easier to manipulate it. So we are going to create one spline with two or three spline points each time, and then adjust it to match the outline of the image as close as possible. (Zoom in a little closer.)

- Start at "point 1" and "point 2," then "point 3" as indicated.

- Push the **Escape** key when done sketching each spline.

- Zoom in even closer so that
you can adjust the spline a
little easier.

Drag the Spline-
Handles to adjust
the curvature

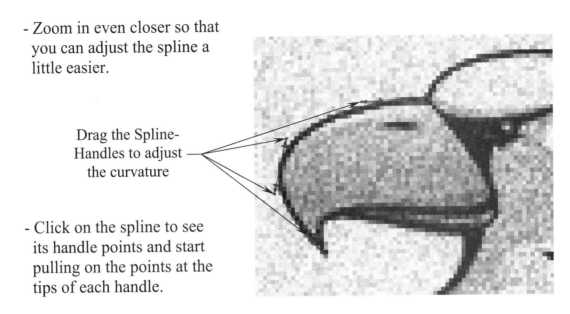

- Click on the spline to see
its handle points and start
pulling on the points at the
tips of each handle.

- It may take some getting used to, so work on a small area each time. Create
only one spline each time, and each spline should have two or three points only.

3-point
splines

2-point
splines

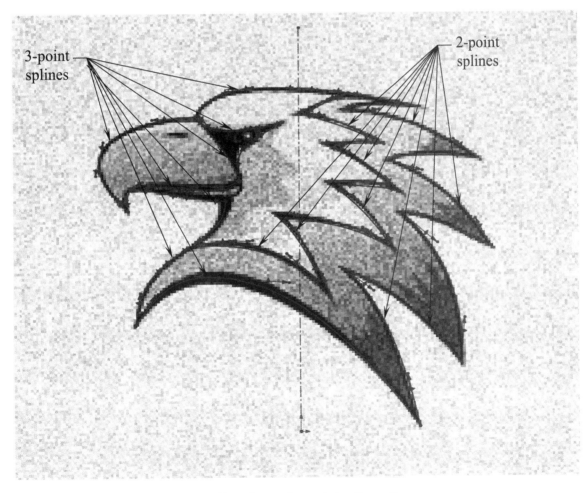

- Add a vertical centerline from the origin for reference.

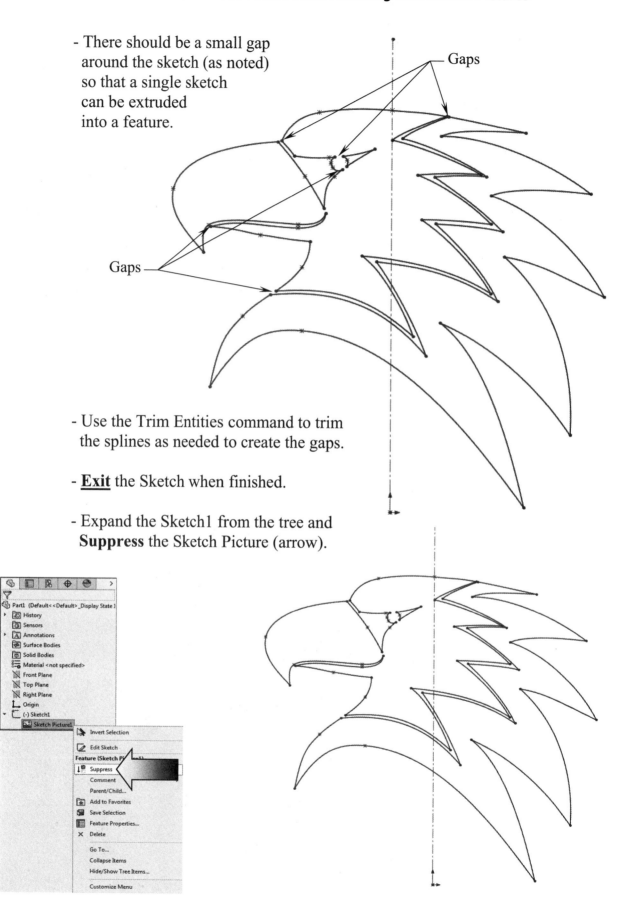

- There should be a small gap around the sketch (as noted) so that a single sketch can be extruded into a feature.

Gaps

Gaps

- Use the Trim Entities command to trim the splines as needed to create the gaps.

- **Exit** the Sketch when finished.

- Expand the Sketch1 from the tree and **Suppress** the Sketch Picture (arrow).

9. Extruding the traced sketch:

- Click **Extruded Boss-Base**.

- Use the default Blind type and enter **.125"** for thickness.

- Click **OK**.

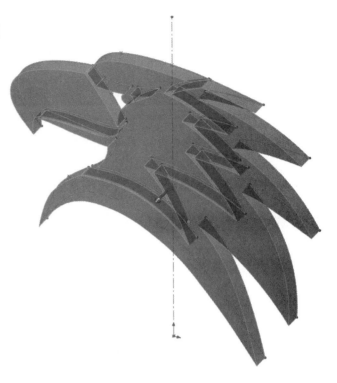

10. Optional:

- Use **Photoview 360** and render the model with the following settings:

- Appearances: **Glass / Clear Thick Gloss / Clear Thick Glass**

- Scene: **Studio Scenes / Reflective Floor Black**

- Lighting: **Green
            Brown
            Blue**

- Output Image Quality:
            1280 X 1024

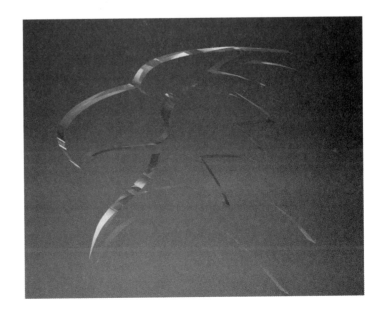

11. Saving your work:

- Save your work as **Eagle Head_Sketch Picture**.

Questions for Review

Working with Sketch Pictures

1. A digital image can be inserted into a sketch to reference a model.
    a. True
    b. False

2. Most picture formats are supported such as bmp, jpg, gif, tif, png.
    a. True
    b. False

3. A digital image can be copied and pasted into a sketch plane and used as a background for tracing.
    a. True
    b. False

4. A scanned picture that is scanned as low-resolution and has multi-colors is best for tracing.
    a. True
    b. False

5. To open a digital image, you should use the command Sketch Picture to insert it into a plane.
    a. True
    b. False

6. A digital image can be opened in SOLIDWORKS like any part or assembly file.
    a. True
    b. False

7. The spline command creates curves that are fixed and cannot be changed or manipulated.
    a. True
    b. False

8. To see the spline handles, simply click on the spline.
    a. True
    b. False

7. FALSE	8. TRUE
5. TRUE	6. FALSE
3. FALSE	4. FALSE
1. TRUE	2. TRUE

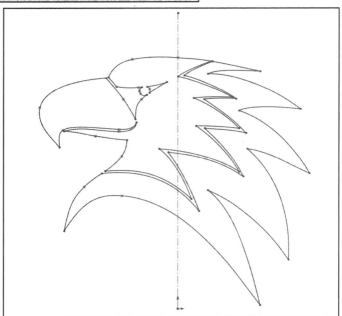

CHAPTER 13 (Cont.)

PhotoView 360 Basics

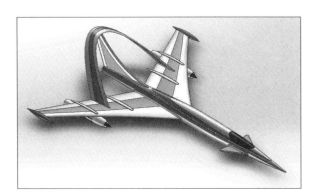
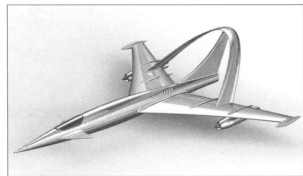

PhotoView 360 enables the user to create photo-realistic renderings of the SOLIDWORKS models. The rendered image incorporates the appearances, lighting, scene, and decals included with the model. PhotoView 360 is available with SOLIDWORKS Pro or SOLIDWORKS Premium only.

1. Activating PhotoView 360:

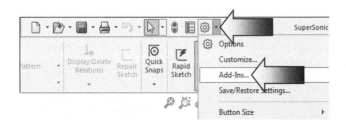

- Open the document named **Supersonic Green Aircraft** from the Training Files folder.

- Click **Tools / Add-Ins**…

- Select the **PhotoView 360** checkbox.

- Click **OK**.

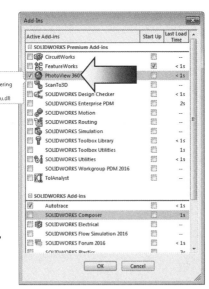

NOTE: *Enable the checkbox on the right of the PhotoView 360 add-in if you wish to have it available at startup. Otherwise only activate it for each use.*

2. Setting the Appearance: (right click the Sketch tab and enable the Render tools)

- Click the **Edit Appearance** button from the **Render** tool tab (arrow).

- The options in the Task-Pane appear on the right side of the screen.

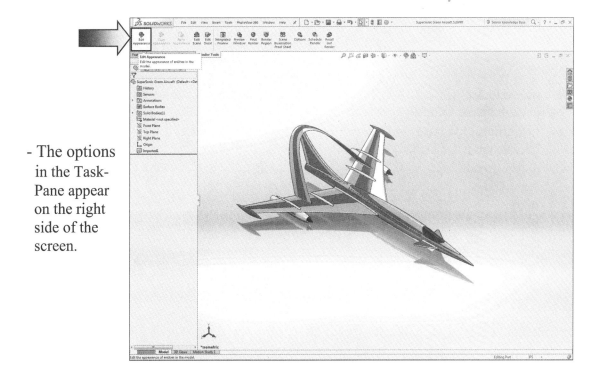

- Expand the Appearances folder, the **Painted** folder, the **Car** folder and <u>double click</u> the **Metallic Cool Grey** appearance to apply it to the model (arrows).

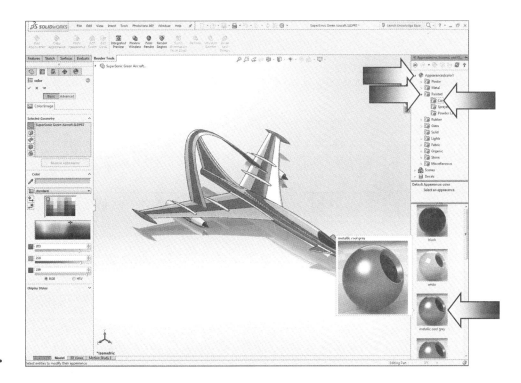

- Click **OK.**

3. Setting the Scene:

- Click the **Edit Scene** button from the Render tool tab (arrow).

- A scene is a combination of lighting, background, & foreground. It is a 2D image between the model and the scene environment.

- Expand the **Scenes** folder, the **Basic Scenes** folder (arrows) and double click the **Backdrop - Studio Room** scene to apply it. Set the other settings as noted.

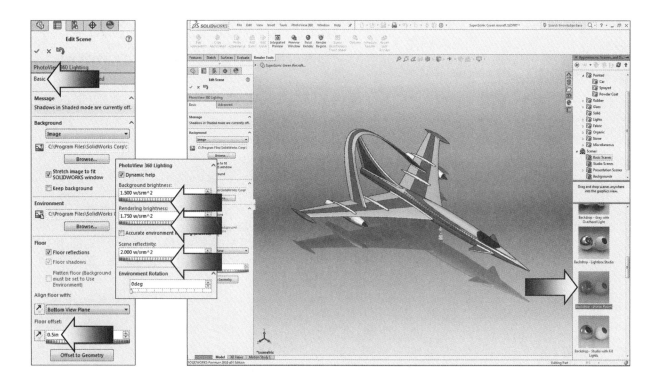

4. Setting the Image Quality options:

- Click the **Options** button from the Render tool tab (arrow).

- The Photo-
View 360
Options
Property-
Manager
controls
settings for
PhotoView
360,
including
output image
size and
render
quality.

- Set the **Output Image** to **1920x1080** from the drop down list and set the other options as indicated with the arrows. Click **OK**.

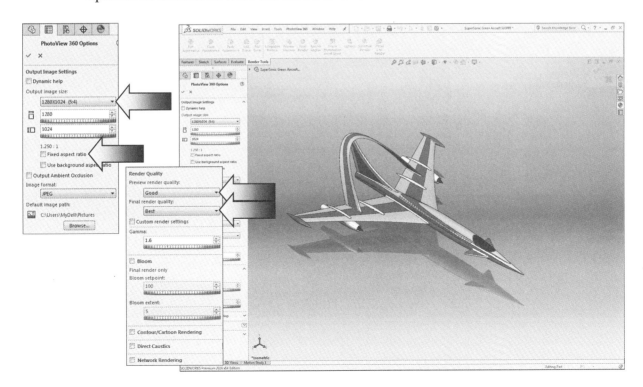

5. Rendering the image:

- Click the **Final Render** button from the Render tool tab (arrow).

- Select the **" Turn On Perspective View"** option in the dialog box. A more realistic rendering is produced with perspective view enabled.

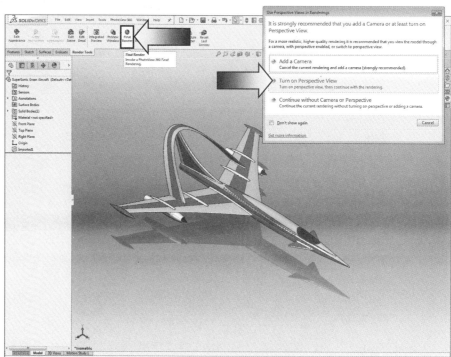

6. Saving the image:

- Select the **100%** option from the drop down list and click **Save Image** (arrows).

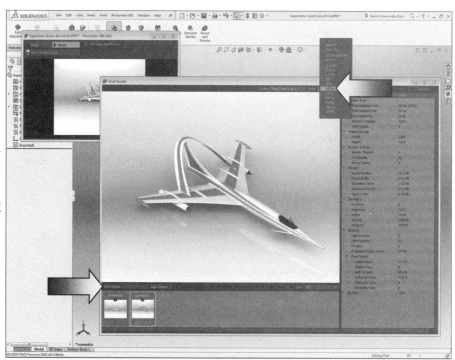

- Select the **JPEG** format from the Save-as-Type drop down list.

- Enter a file name and click **OK**.

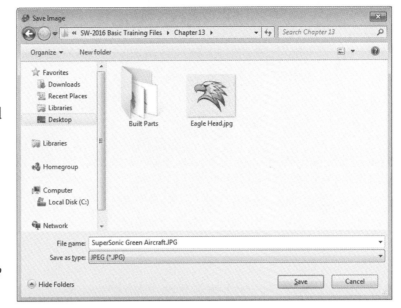

NOTE: *Different file formats may reduce the quality of the image, and at the same time, they may increase or decrease the size of the file.*

- Close all documents when finished.

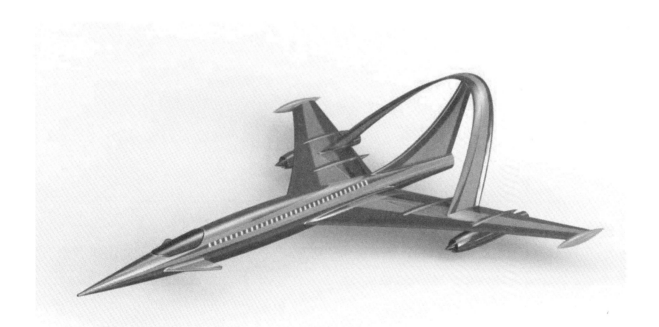

PhotoView 360 Exercise

PhotoView 360 is a SOLIDWORKS add-in that produces photo-realistic renderings of SOLIDWORKS models.

The rendered image incorporates the appearances, lighting, scene, and decals included with the model. PhotoView 360 is available with SOLIDWORKS Professional or SOLIDWORKS Premium.

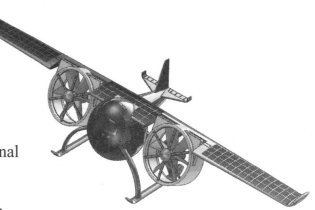

1. Opening an assembly document:

- Open an assembly document named **Helidrone.sldasm**.

- Drag/drop the **Polished Platinum** appearance to the drone's body (arrows).

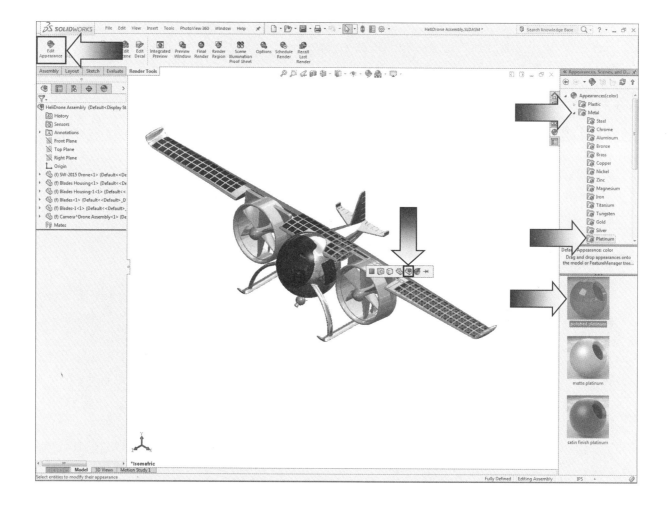

2. Applying the Scene:

- Apply the scene after the appearance is set.

- Click **PhotoView 360 / Edit Scene**.

- On the right side of the screen, expand the **Scene** and the **Basic Scene** folders.

- Double click the **Warm Kitchen** scene to apply its settings to the assembly.

- Use the options in the **Edit Scene** sections, on the left side of the screen, to modify the lightings, floor reflections, and environment rotation.

- Adjust the Background, Rendering, and Reflectivity if needed.

3. Setting the Render Region:

- The render region provides an accelerator that lets you render a subsection of the current scene without having to zoom in or out or change the window size.

- Select the **Render Region** option from the PhotoView 360 pull down menu.

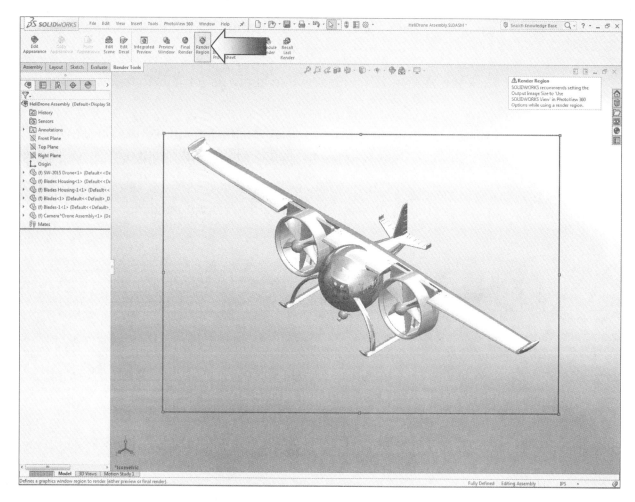

- Drag one of the handle points to define the region to render.

4. Setting the Image Size:

- Select **Options** under the PhotoView 360 pull down.

- The height and width of the render image can be selected from some of the pre-set image sizes.

- Select the **1920x1080** (16:9) from the Image Size pull down options. (The larger the image size the more time req.)

- Select **Final Render** from the PhotoView 360.

- Click **Save Image** and select the **JPEG** format to save the rendering.

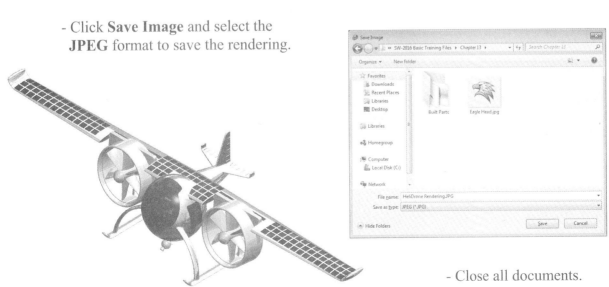

- Close all documents.

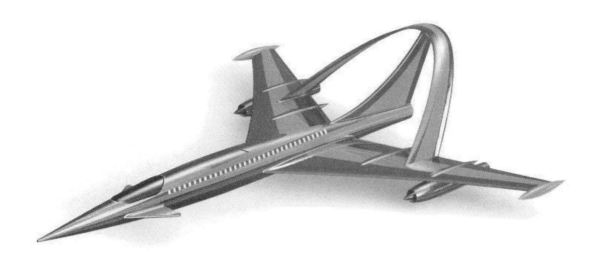

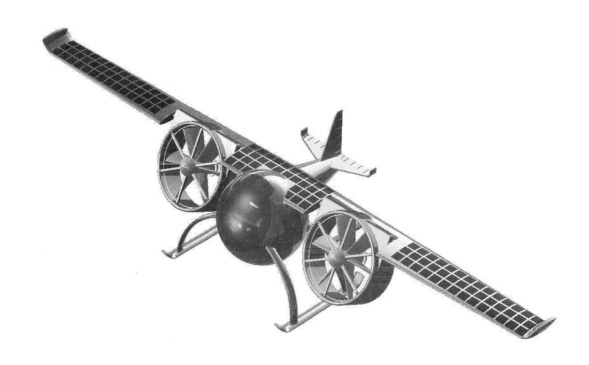

CHAPTER 14

Drawing Preparations

Customizing the Document Template

- Custom settings and parameters such as ANSI standards, units, number of decimal places, dimensions and note fonts, arrow styles and sizes, line styles and line weights, image quality, etc., can be set and saved in the document template for use with the current drawing or at any time in the future.

- All Document Templates are normally stored either in the templates folder or in the Tutorial folder:

     * (C:\Program Files\SOLIDWORKS Corp\ SOLIDWORKS\Data\Templates)
     * (C:\Program Files\SOLIDWORKS Corp\ SOLIDWORKS\Lang\English\Tutorial)

- By default, there are 2 "layers" in every new drawing. The "top layer" is called the **Sheet**, and the "bottom layer" is called the **Sheet Format**.

- The **Sheet** layer is used to create the drawing views and annotations. The **Sheet-Format** layer contains the title block information, revision changes, BOM-anchor, etc.

- The 2 layers can be toggled back and forth by using the FeatureManager tree, or by right clicking anywhere in the drawing and selecting Edit Sheet Format / Edit Sheet.

- When the settings are done they will get saved in the Document Template with the extension **.drwdot** (Drawing Document Template).

- This chapter will guide us through the settings and the preparations needed prior to creating a drawing.

Drawing Preparations

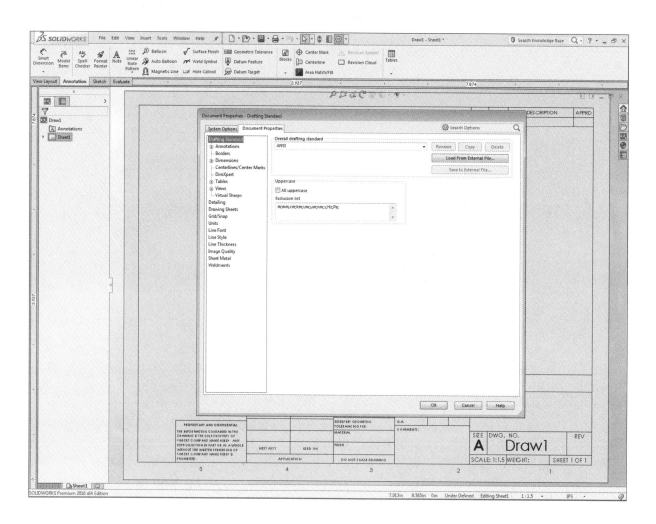

Dimensioning Standards: **ANSI**	Third Angle Projection
Units: **INCHES** – 3 Decimals	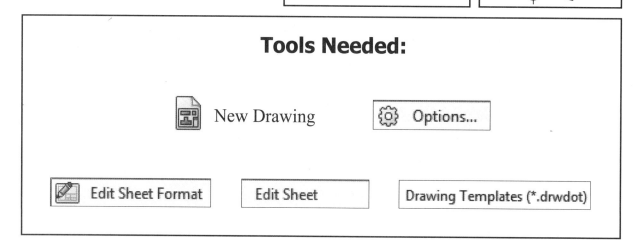

Tools Needed:

New Drawing   Options...

Edit Sheet Format   Edit Sheet   Drawing Templates (*.drwdot)

1. Setting up a new drawing:

- Select **File** / **New** / **Draw** (or Drawing) / **OK** [OK] .

- Change the option Novice to **Advanced** as noted.

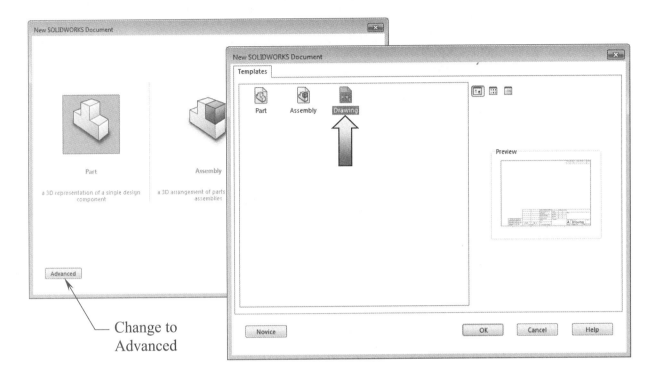

Change to
Advanced

- By selecting on either **Advanced** or **Novice** (Circled), you can switch to the appropriate dialog box to select the template.

- Set the following options:

   * **Scale: 1:2**

   * **Third Angle Projection**

   * View Label and Datum
     Label and set them both to A.

- Under Standard Sheet Size, choose
  C-Landscape.

- Uncheck the **Only Show Standard
  Format** checkbox (arrow).

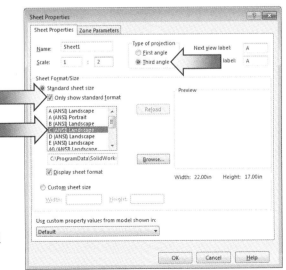

- Click **OK** [OK] .

- The SOLIDWORKS Drawing User Interface

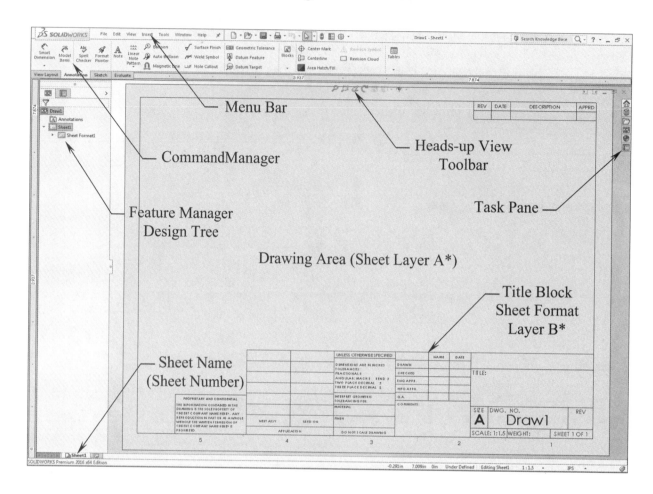

*A. By default, the **Sheet** layer is active and placed over the **Sheet Format** layer.

- The **Sheet** layer is used to create drawing views, dimensions, and annotations.

* B. The "bottom layer" is called the **Sheet Format** layer, which is where the revision block, the title block and its information are stored.

- The Sheet Format layer includes some links to the system properties and the custom properties.

- OLE objects (company's logo) such as .Bmp or .Tif can be embedded here.

- SOLIDWORKS drawings can have different Sheet Formats or none at all.

- Formats or title blocks created from other CAD programs can be opened in SOLIDWORKS using either DXF or DWG file types and saved as SOLIDWORKS' Sheet Format.

2. Switching to the Sheet Format layer:

- Right click in the drawing and select **Edit Sheet Format**.

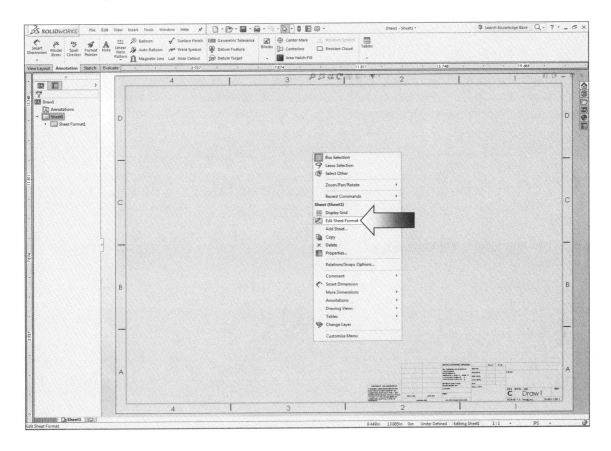

- Using the SOLIDWORKS drawing templates, there are "blank notes" already created for each field within the title block.

- Double click the blank note in the Company Name field and enter **SOLIDWORKS**.

Existing
blank note

Double click on the —
blank note to modify it…

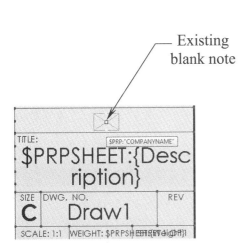

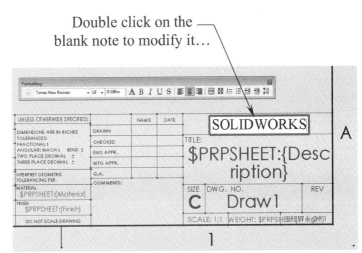

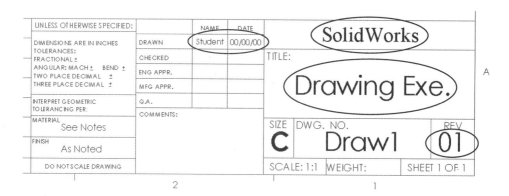

UNLESS OTHERWISE SPECIFIED:		NAME	DATE		
DIMENSIONS ARE IN INCHES	DRAWN	Student	00/00/00		
TOLERANCES:	CHECKED				
FRACTIONAL ±				TITLE:	
ANGULAR: MACH ± BEND ±	ENG APPR.				
TWO PLACE DECIMAL ±	MFG APPR.				
THREE PLACE DECIMAL ±					
INTERPRET GEOMETRIC	Q.A.				
TOLERANCING PER:	COMMENTS:				
MATERIAL See Notes					
FINISH As Noted					
DO NOT SCALE DRAWING				SCALE: 1:1 WEIGHT:	SHEET 1 OF 1

- Modify each note box and fill in the information as shown above (circled).

- If the blank notes are not available, copy and paste any note then modify it.

3. Switching back to the Sheet layer:

- Right click in the drawing and select **Edit Sheet**.

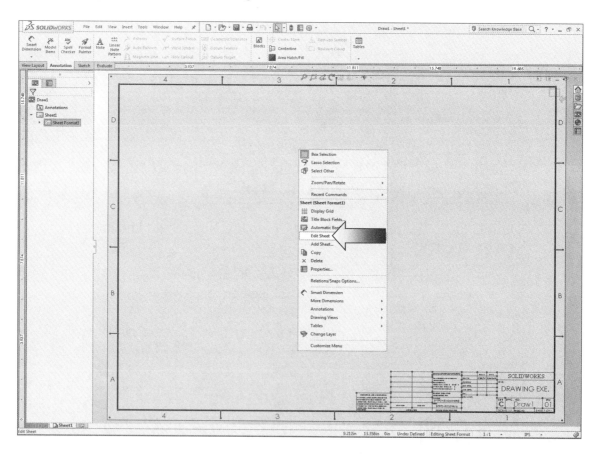

- The Sheet layer is brought to the top; all information within the Sheet Format layer is kept on the bottom layer.

4. Setting up the Drawing Options:

- Go to **Tools / Options**, or select the Options icon.

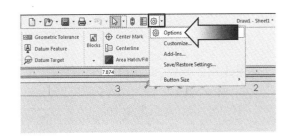

- Select the **Drawings** options from the list.

- Enable and/or disable the drawing options by clicking on the check boxes as shown below.

NOTE:

For more information about these options, refer to Chapter 2 in the SOLIDWORKS 2016 Part I - Basic Tools textbook (Essential Parts, Assemblies and Drawings).

These parameters are examples for use with this text-book only; you may have to modify them to work with your application or company's standards.

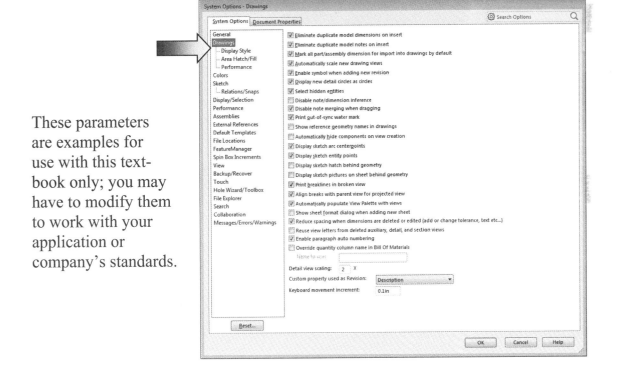

- The parameters that you are setting here will be saved as the default system options, and they will affect the current as well as all future documents.

- Once again, enable only the checked boxes as shown in the dialog above.

- Select the Display Style option (arrow).

- Set the new parameters as shown for Display-Style, Tangent Edges, and Edge Quality.

- Refer to Chapter 2 in this textbook for other settings that are not mentioned here.

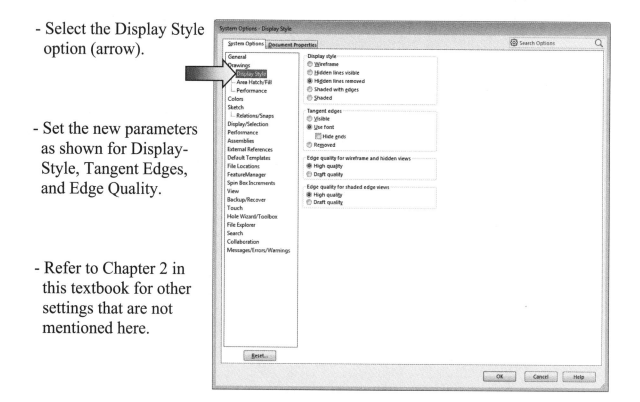

5. Setting up the Document Template options:

- Click the **Document Properties** tab.

- Select the **Drafting Standard** option.

- Change the default option to **ANSI**, which is an abbreviation of:

> **A**merican
> **N**ational
> **S**tandards
> **I**nstitute.

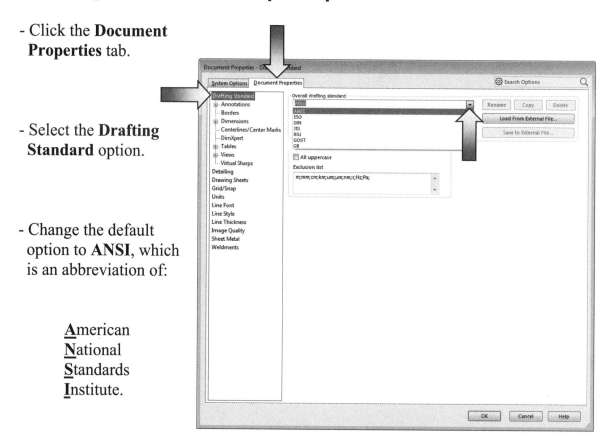

- Select the **Annotations** option (arrow).

- Set the new parameters as shown.

- Click the **Font** button and select the following:

  Century Gothic
  Regular
  13 points

- Set the Note, Dimension, Surface Finish, Weld-Symbol, Tables, and Balloon to match the settings for Annotations.

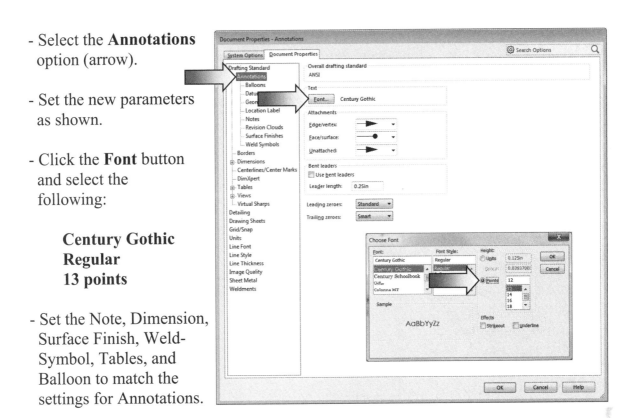

- Select the **Dimensions** option (arrow).

- Set the parameter in this section to match the ones shown in this dialog box.

- If the Dual Dimension Display is selected, be sure to set the number of decimal places for both of your Primary and Secondary dimensions.

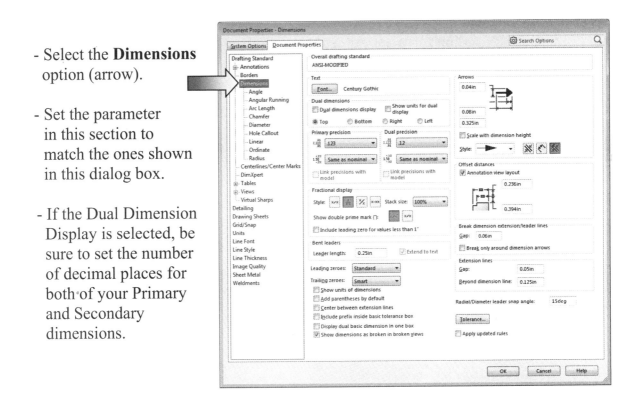

NOTE: *Skip to the Units option below if you need to change your Primary unit from Millimeter to Inches or vice versa.*

- Select the **Centerlines/ Center Marks** option.

- Set the options as indicated for Centerline Extension, Center Marks Size and Slot Center-Marks.

- Select the **Tables / Bill-of Materials** option.

- The B.O.M. is an Excel based template; set its parameters similar to the ones in Microsoft Excel such as Border, Font, Zero Quantity Display Missing Component, Leading and Trailing Zeros, etc.

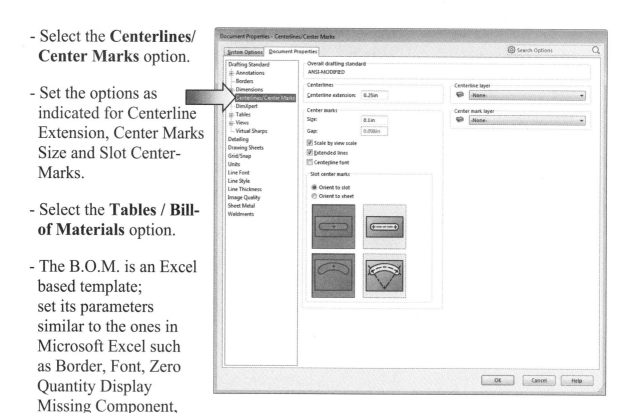

- **Leading Zeros:**
  * Standard: Leading zeros appear according to the overall drafting standard.
  * <u>Show</u>: Shows zeros before decimal points are shown.
  * <u>Remove</u>: Leading zeros do not appear.

- **Trailing Zeros:**
  * <u>Smart</u>: Trailing zeros are timed for whole metric values.
  * <u>Standard</u>: Trailing zeros appear according to ASME standard.
  * <u>Show:</u> Trailing zeros are displayed according to the decimal places specified in Units.
  * <u>Remove</u>: Trailing zeros do not appear.

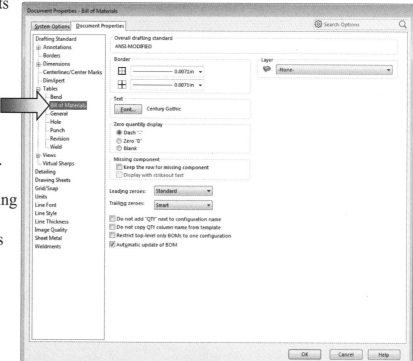

- Select the **Tables /
  Revision** option.

- Set the document-level
  drafting settings for
  revision table like
  Border, Font,
  Alphabet Numerical
  Control, Multiple Sheet
  Style and Layer.

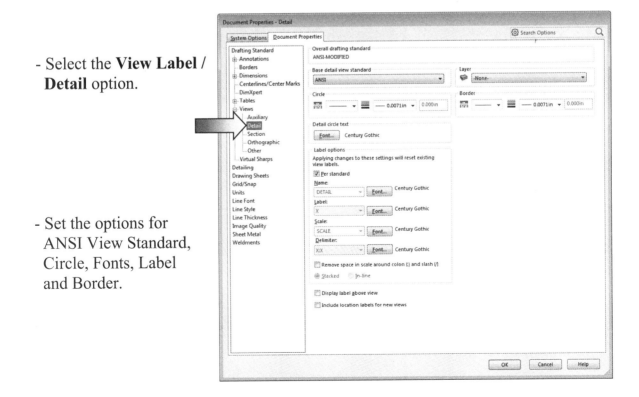

- Select the **View Label /
  Detail** option.

- Set the options for
  ANSI View Standard,
  Circle, Fonts, Label
  and Border.

- Select the **View Label / Section** option.

- Set the Line Style, Line Thickness, Fonts, Label, Scale, Layer, and Section Arrow Size.

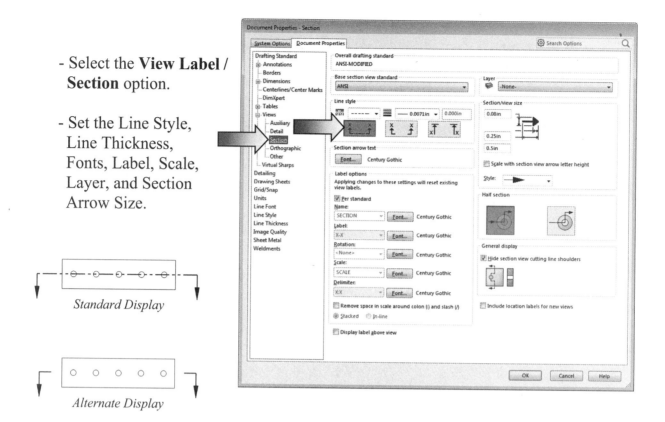

Standard Display

Alternate Display

- Select the **Detailing** option.

- Select the check- boxes for the Display Filters, Import Annotations, Auto Insert on View Creation, Area Hatch Display and View- Break Lines.

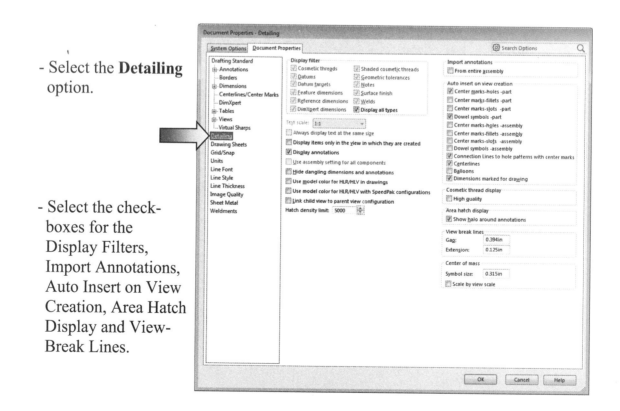

- Select the **Drawing-Sheet** option.

- Enable the check box **Use Different Sheet Format** if sheet 2 uses a different (or partial) title block.

- This property lets you automatically have one sheet format for the first sheet and a separate sheet format for all additional sheets.

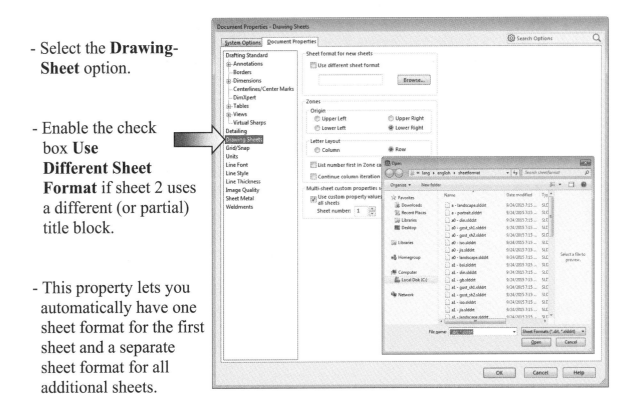

- Select the **Units** option.

- Click the **IPS (Inch, Pound, Second)** system.

- Set the Length Units to **3 Decimal Places (.123)**

- Other options can be set to meet your company's standards.

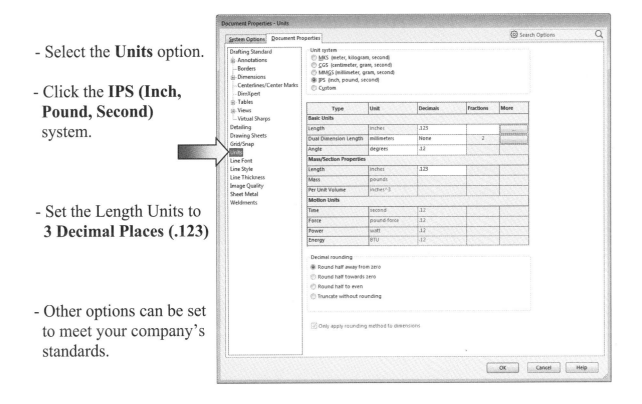

- Select the **Line Font** option.

- Set the Style and Weight of lines for various kinds of edges in drawing documents only.

- Select the **Line-Thickness** option.

- Set the **Line-Thickness** to your own preferences*.

* Normal thickness:
   Object Lines
   (outlines of the views).

* Thin: Tangent lines
   and Hidden Lines.

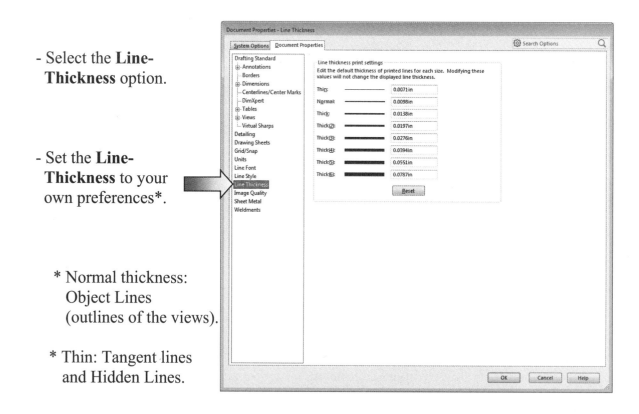

- Select the **Image-Quality** option.

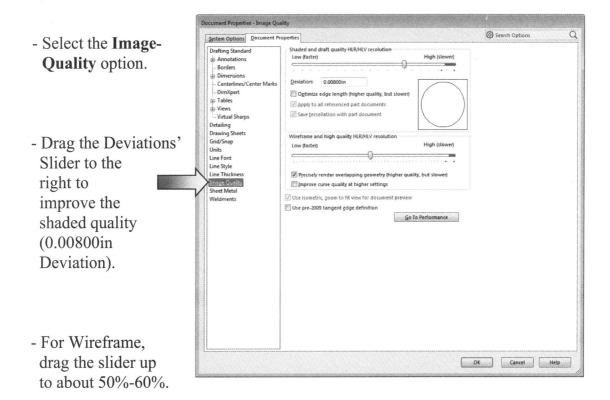

- Drag the Deviations'
  Slider to the
  right to
  improve the
  shaded quality
  (0.00800in
  Deviation).

- For Wireframe,
  drag the slider up
  to about 50%-60%.

- Select the **Sheet Metal**
  option.

- Set the colors for Bend-
  Lines, Form Features,
  Hems, Model Edges,
  Flat Pattern Sketch
  Color, and
  Bounding Box.

- Click **OK** OK .

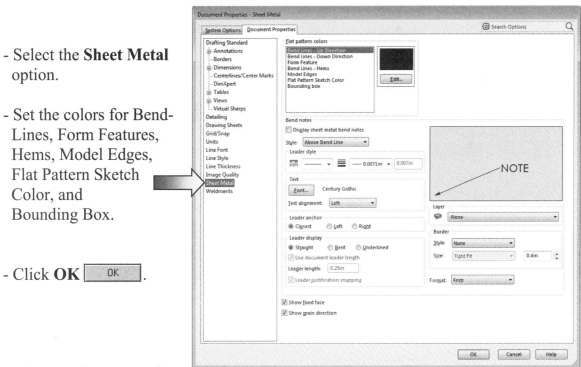

- These settings control
the tessellation of curved surfaces for shaded rendering output. A higher resolution
setting results in slower model rebuilding but more accurate curves.

6. Saving the Document Template:

- Go to **File / Save As** and change the save-as-type to **Drawing Templates** (arrow).

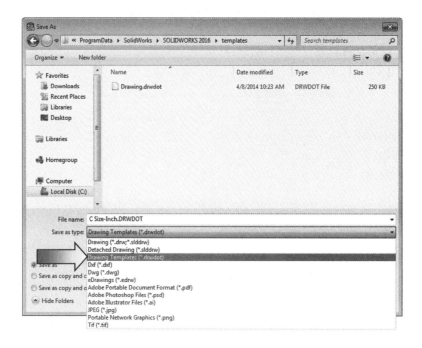

- SOLIDWORKS automatically switches to the **Templates** folder (or **Tutorial** folder), where all SOLIDWORKS templates are stored.

- Enter a name for your new template (i.e. C-Size Inch).

- Click **Save**.

- The Drawing Template can now be used to create new drawings.

- To verify if the Template has been saved properly, click **File / New**, change the option Novice to Advance, and look for the new Template (arrow).

- **Close** the document template.

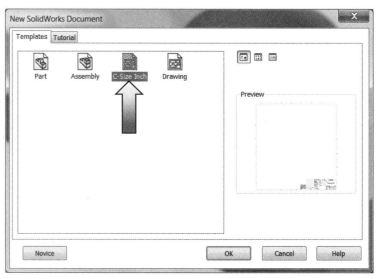

Questions for Review

Drawing Preparations

1. Custom settings and parameters can be set and saved in the Document Template.
    a. True
    b. False

2. Document Templates are normally stored either in (C:\Program Files\SOLIDWORKS Corp\SOLIDWORKS\Data\Templates) OR (C:\Program Files\SOLIDWORKS Corp\Lang\English\Tutorial).
    a. True
    b. False

3. To access the sheet format and edit the information in the title block:
    a. Right click in the drawing and select Edit Sheet Format.
    b. Right click the Sheet Format icon from the Feature Tree and select Edit Sheet-Format.
    c. All of the above.

4. The **Sheet** layer is where the Title Block information and Revisions changes are stored.
    a. True
    b. False

5. The **Sheet Format** layer is used to create the drawing views, dimensions, and annotations.
    a. True
    b. False

6. Information in the Title Block and Revision Block are Fixed; they cannot be modified.
    a. True
    b. False

7. The Document Template is saved with the file Extension:
    a. DWG
    b. DXF
    c. SLDPRT
    d. DRWDOT
    e. SLDDRW

1. TRUE 2. TRUE 3. C 4. FALSE 5. FALSE 6. FALSE 7. D

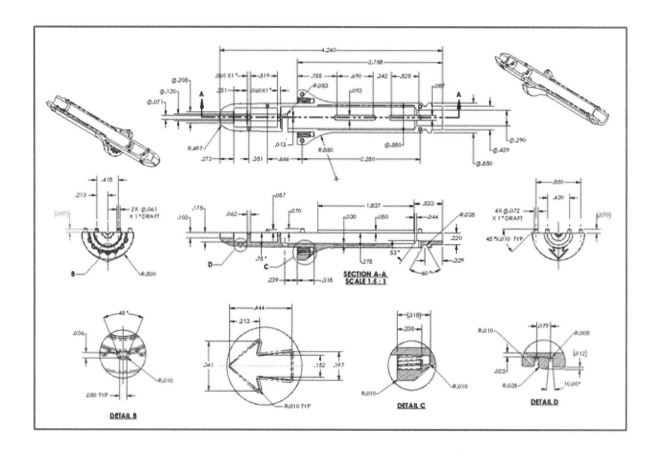

CHAPTER 15

Assembly Drawings

Assembly Drawings
Links Assembly

- Assembly drawings are created in the same way as part drawings; the same drawing tools and commands are used to create the drawing views and annotations. In an assembly drawing all components are shown together as assembled or as exploded.

- The standard drawing views like the Front, Top, Right, and Isometric views can be created with the same drawing tools, or they can be dragged and dropped from the View Pallet.

- When a cross section view is created, it will be cross hatched automatically and the hatch patterns that represent the material of the part can be added and easily edited as well.

- A parts list or a Bill of Materials (B.O.M.) is created to report the details of the components such as these:

    * Materials.

    * Vendors.

    * Quantities.

    * Part numbers, etc.

4	004-12345	Single Link	4
3	003-12345	Pin Head	6
2	002-12345	Alignment Pin	6
1	001-12345	Double Link	3
ITEM NO.	PART NUMBER	DESCRIPTION	QTY.

- The components will then be labeled with Balloons (or Dash Numbers) for verification against the Bill of Materials.

- This chapter discusses the basics of creating an assembly drawing using SOLIDWORKS 2016.

Links Assembly
Assembly Drawings

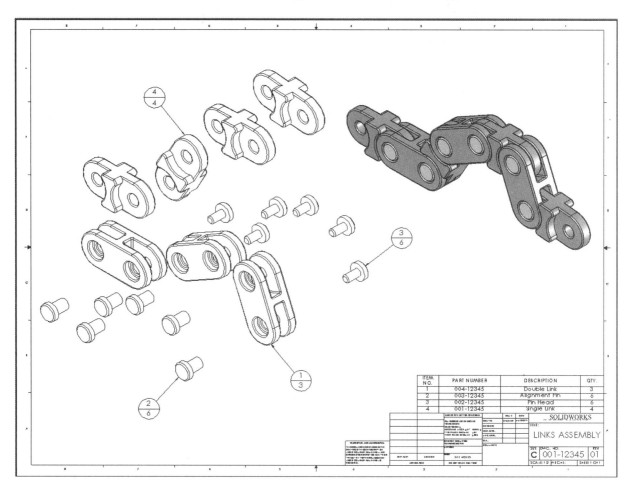

ITEM NO.	PART NUMBER	DESCRIPTION	QTY.
1	004-12345	Double Link	3
2	003-12345	Alignment Pin	6
3	002-12345	Pin Head	6
4	001-12345	Single Link	4

SOLIDWORKS

TITLE: LINKS ASSEMBLY

C | 001-12345 | 01

SCALE: 1:2 | SHEET 1 OF 1

Dimensioning Standards: **ANSI**

Units: **INCHES** – 3 Decimals

Third Angle Projection

Tools Needed:

New Drawing

Model View

Shaded View

 Balloon

Bill of Materials

Properties...

1. Creating a new drawing:

- Select **File / New / Draw** (or Drawing) / **OK**.

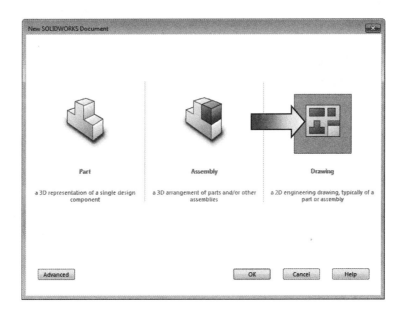

- Under Standard Sheet Size, select **C-Landscape** for paper size.

$$A = 8.5" \quad x \quad 11.00" \quad \text{(Landscape)}$$
$$B = 17.00" \quad x \quad 11.00" \quad \text{(Landscape)}$$
$$C = 22.00" \quad x \quad 17.00" \quad \text{(Landscape)}$$
$$D = 34.00" \quad x \quad 22.00" \quad \text{(Landscape)}$$
$$E = 44.00" \quad x \quad 34.00" \quad \text{(Landscape)}$$

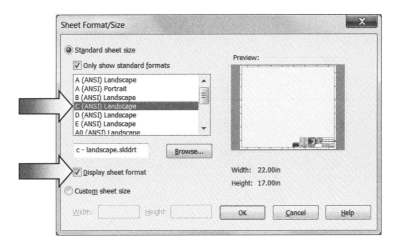

- Enable **Display Sheet Format** checkbox to display the revision and title blocks.

- Click **OK** .

- The drawing template appears in the graphics area.

- Right click in the drawing and select **Properties**.

- Set the Drawing Views Scale and Angle of Projection:

(**3rd Angle = U.S.** OR **1st = Europe & Asia**).

- Set **Scale** to **1:1** (full scale).

- Set **Type of Projection** to **Third Angle** ◉ Third angle

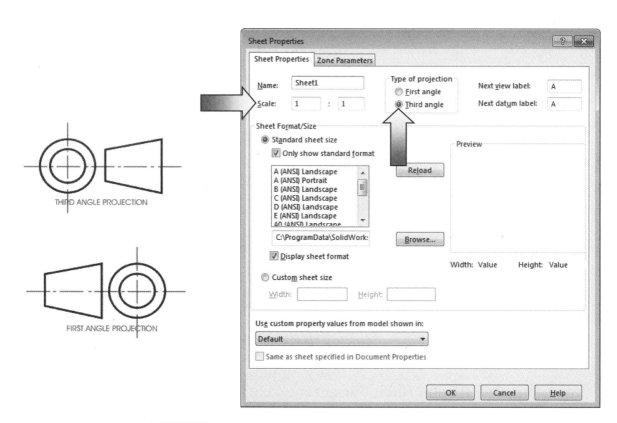

- Click **OK** [OK] .

2. Editing the Sheet Format:

- Right click inside the drawing and select **Edit-Sheet-Format**.

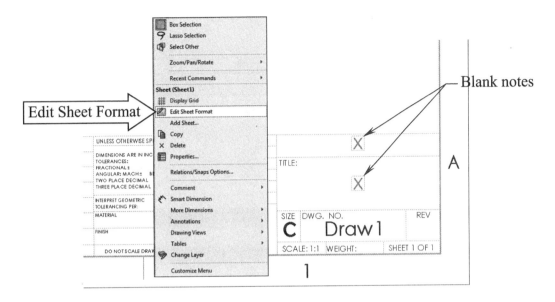

- The **Format** layer is brought up to the top.

3. Setting up the anchor point to attach the B.O.M.:

- Zoom in on the lower right side of the title block.

- Right click on the end point of the line (as shown) and select **Set-As-Anchor / Bill Of Materials.**

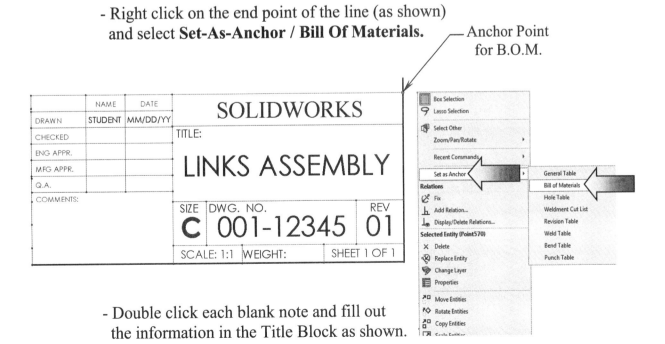

- Double click each blank note and fill out the information in the Title Block as shown.

4. Switching back to the Sheet layer:

- Right click inside the drawing and select **Edit-Sheet.**

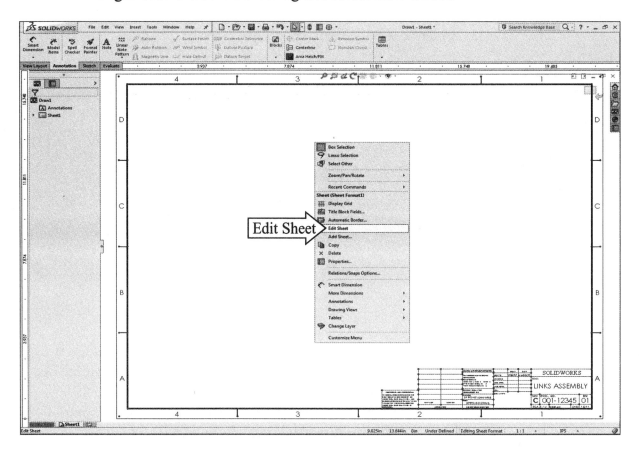

- **Change the Drawing Paper's color:**

- Select **Tools / Options / System Options / Colors / Drawing Paper Colors / Edit.**

- Select the **White** color and also enable **Use Specified Color for Drawings Paper-Color** option.

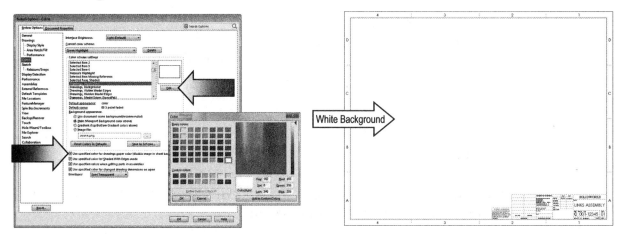

5. Opening an existing assembly document:

- Click the **Model View** command from the View Layout toolbar.

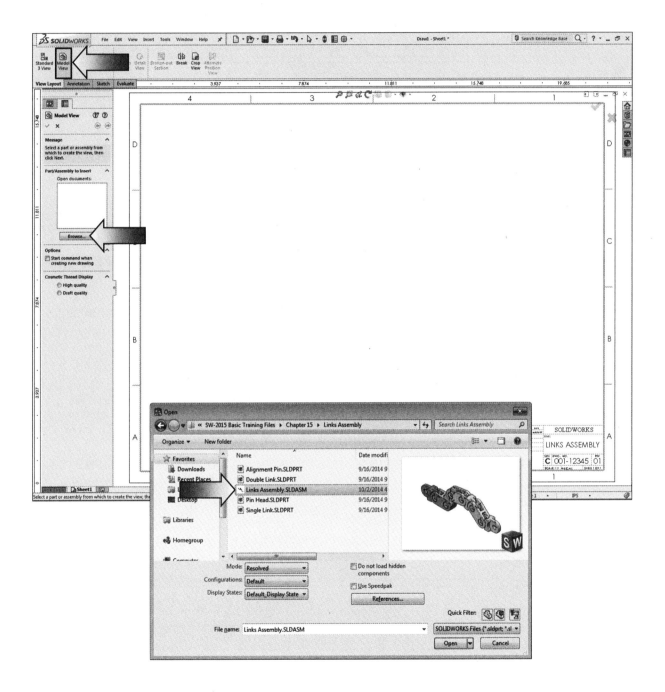

- Click the **Browse** button; locate and open the **Links Assembly** document from the Training Files folder.

- There are several different methods to create the drawing views; in this lesson, we will discuss the use of the **Model-View** command first.

- Select the **Isometric** view button (arrow) and place the drawing view approximately as shown.

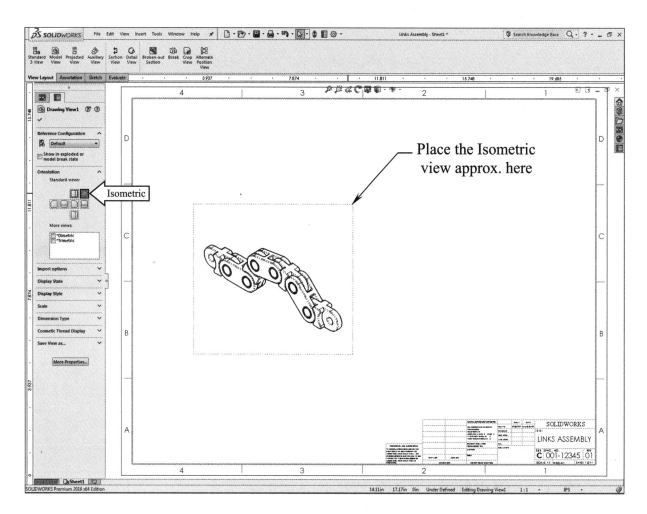

- The drawing view scale will be changed in the next couple of steps.

- The isometric view is created based on the default orientations of the last saved assembly document.

NOTE: *If the Assembly document is already opened, press **Ctrl + Tab** to toggle back and forth between the Drawing and the Assembly documents.*

6. Switching to the Exploded View state:

- You can create an exploded drawing view from an existing exploded assembly view. The actual view is a model view, usually in the isometric orientation.

- Click the drawing view's border and select the checkbox **Show in exploded or model break state** (arrow).

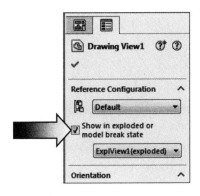

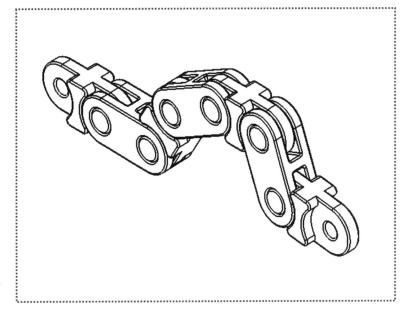

- Alternatively you can right-click the drawing view and click Show in Exploded State.

- The exploded checkbox is only available if an exploded view has been created earlier in the assembly level.

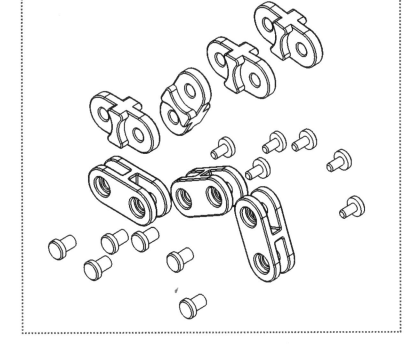

- Click **OK** .

7. Changing the Line Style:

- The tangent edges of the components should be changed to Phantom Line style.

- Right click the drawing view's border, and select **Tangent Edge, Tangent Edges With Font** (arrow).

- The tangent edges are displayed as phantom lines.

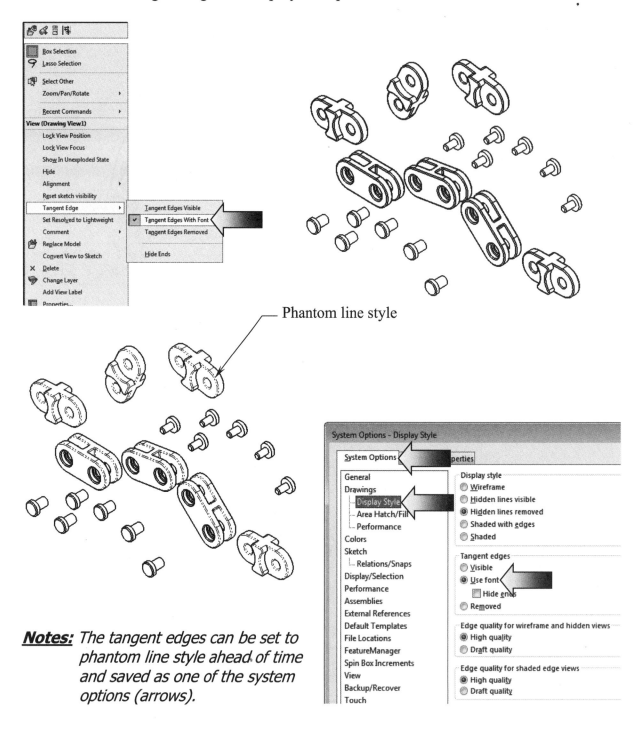

Phantom line style

Notes: _The tangent edges can be set to phantom line style ahead of time and saved as one of the system options (arrows)._

8. Using the View Palette:

- The View Palette allows a quick way to add drawing views to the drawing sheet by dragging and dropping. Each view is created as a model view. The orientations are based on the eight standard orientations (Front, Right, Top, Back, Left, Bottom, Current, and Isometric) and any custom views in the part or assembly.

- Click the **View Palette** tab on the right side of the screen (arrow).

- Click the **Browse** button [...] and open the Links Assembly document.

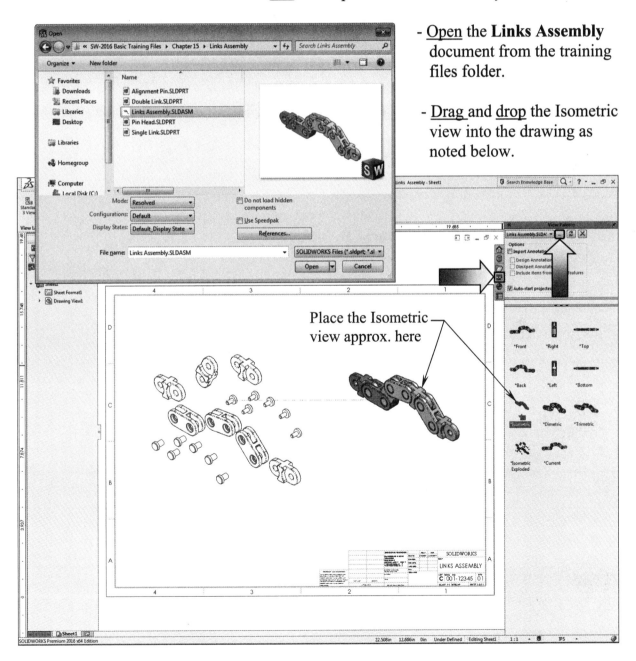

- Open the **Links Assembly** document from the training files folder.

- Drag and drop the Isometric view into the drawing as noted below.

Place the Isometric view approx. here

9. Switching to Shaded view:

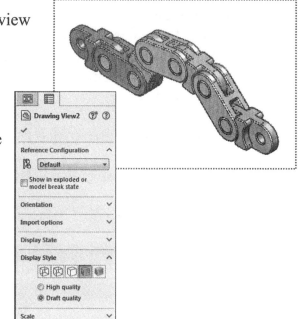

- Sometimes for clarity, a drawing view is changed to shaded instead of wireframe.

- The shaded view will be printed as shaded. To change the shading of more than one view at the same time, hold the control key, select the borders of the views then change the shading.

- Select the Isometric view's border.

- Click **Shaded With Edges** in the Display Style section.

- The Isometric view is now shown as Shaded with Edges.

10. Creating a Bill of Materials (B.O.M.):

- Click the Isometric view's border. Change to the **Annotation** tool tab.

- Click **Tables, Bill of Materials** – OR – Select **Insert / Tables / Bill of Materials**.

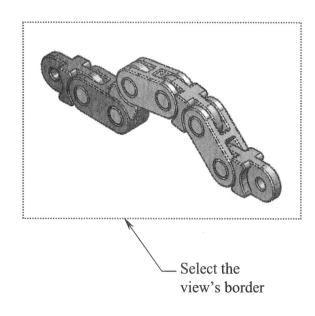

Select the view's border

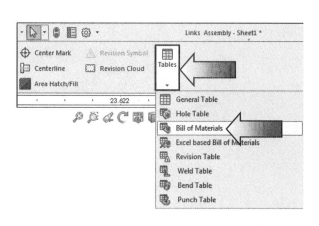

NOTE: A BOM can be anchored, moved, edited, and split into sections.

- A BOM is created automatically and the information in the assembly document is populated with item numbers, description, quantities and part numbers.

- When the Bill of Materials properties tree appears, select **Bom-Standard** (arrow) from the Table Template list and click **Open** Open .

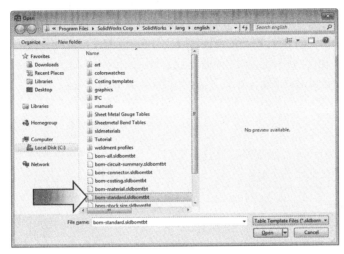

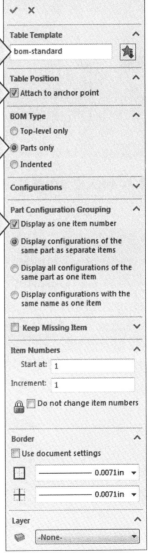

11. Selecting the B.O.M. options:

- Table Template: **BOM Standard.**

- Attach to Anchor Point*: **Enabled**.

- BOM Type: **Parts only**.

- Part Configuration Grouping **Display As One Item Number: Enabled**.

- Click **OK** ✅.

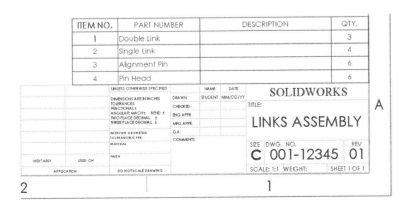

ITEM NO.	PART NUMBER	DESCRIPTION	QTY.
1	Double Link		3
2	Single Link		4
3	Alignment Pin		6
4	Pin Head		6

- The Bill of Materials is created and anchored to the lower right corner of the title block, where the anchor point was set earlier.

    * The Anchor point is set and saved in the Sheet Format layer. To change the location of the anchor point, first right click anywhere in the drawing and select Edit Sheet Format then right click on one of the end points of a line and select Set-As-Anchor / Bill of Material.

- To change the anchor corner, click anywhere in the B.O.M, click the 4-way cursor on the upper left corner and select the stationary corner where you want to anchor the table (use the Bottom Right option for this lesson).

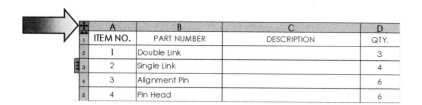

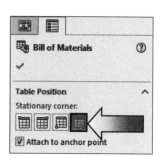

12. Modifying the B.O.M.:

- Double-click on the B.O.M. table to edit its content.

- Transfer the Part Number column over to the Description column.

- **To transfer Cell-By-Cell:**

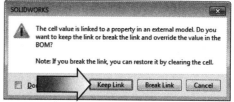

    In the Part Number column, double-click in a cell and select **Keep Link**.

    Press **Control + X** (Cut).

    Enter a New Part Number in the same cell (001-12345).

    Double-click a cell in the Description column and press **Control+V** (Paste) or simply re-enter the part name.

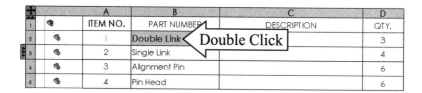

- Repeat step number 12 to change the Part Number and the Description columns to match the table shown below.

4	001-12345	Pin Head	6
3	002-12345	Alignment Pin	6
2	003-12345	Single Link	4
1	004-12345	Double Link	3
ITEM NO.	PART NUMBER	DESCRIPTION	QTY.

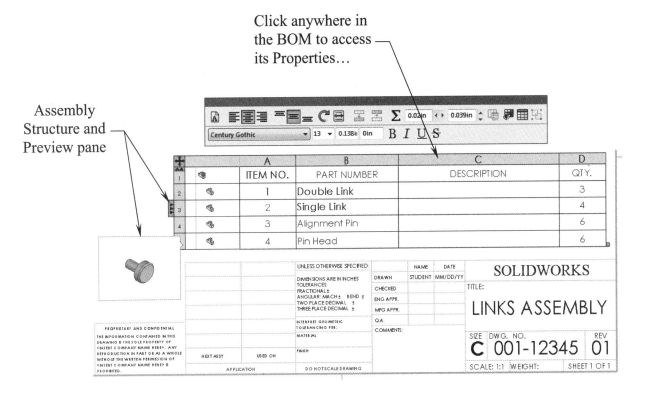

13. Reversing the column headers:

- Click anywhere in the B.O.M. table to access its **Properties**.

Click anywhere in the BOM to access its Properties…

Assembly Structure and Preview pane

		A	B	C	D
1		ITEM NO.	PART NUMBER	DESCRIPTION	QTY.
2		1	Double Link		3
3		2	Single Link		4
4		3	Alignment Pin		6
		4	Pin Head		6

- Click the Assembly Structure arrow-tab to see the preview of the components.

15-15

- The Formatting toolbar pops up on top of the BOM.

- Click the **Table Header** button to reverse it as noted.

- Click **OK** ✅.

Table Header
Top/Bottom

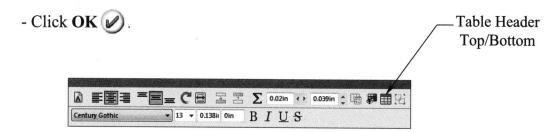

	A	B
1	ITEM NO.	PART NU
2	1	001-12
3	2	002-12
4	3	003-12
5	4	004-12

Table Header set to Top

	A	B
1	4	004-12
2	3	003-12
3	2	002-12
4	1	001-12
5	ITEM NO.	PART NU

Table Header set to Bottom

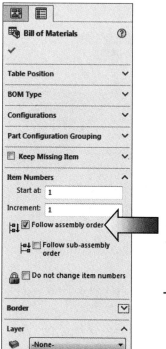

NOTE: Select **Follow Assembly Order** to reorder items in a drawing to follow the assembly from which it is created. The Bill of Materials automatically updates when a component is reordered in an assembly.

- For components with multiple instances in the Bill of Materials, the first instance appears in the order in which it appears in the FeatureManager design tree. Subsequent instances increment the quantity.

14. Adding Balloon callouts:

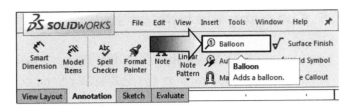

- Balloons are added to identify and label the components. They can be added manually or automatically. The item number in the balloon is associated to the assembly order. If the components are reordered in the assembly, the item number will be updated to reflect the change.

- Click ![balloon icon] or select **Insert / Annotations / Balloon**.

- Click on the **edge** of the Single-Link. The system places a balloon on the part.

- The Item Number matches the one in the B.O.M. automatically.

- Click on the Double Link, the Alignment Pins, and Pin Heads to attach a balloon to each one of them.

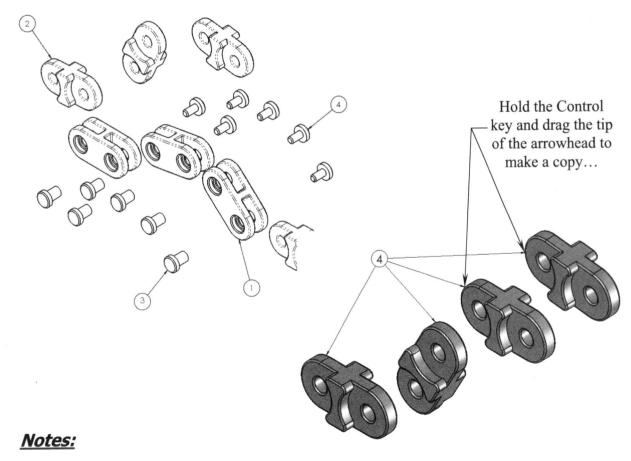

Hold the Control key and drag the tip of the arrowhead to make a copy...

Notes:

Balloons are similar to notes; they can have multiple leaders or attachment points. To copy the leader line, hold down the CONTROL key and drag the tip of one of the arrows.

15. Changing the balloon style:

- Hold down the CONTROL key and select all balloons; the balloon Properties tree appears on the left side of the screen.

- Select **Circular Split Line** under the Style menu.

- Select **2 Character** size.

- Click **OK** ✔ .

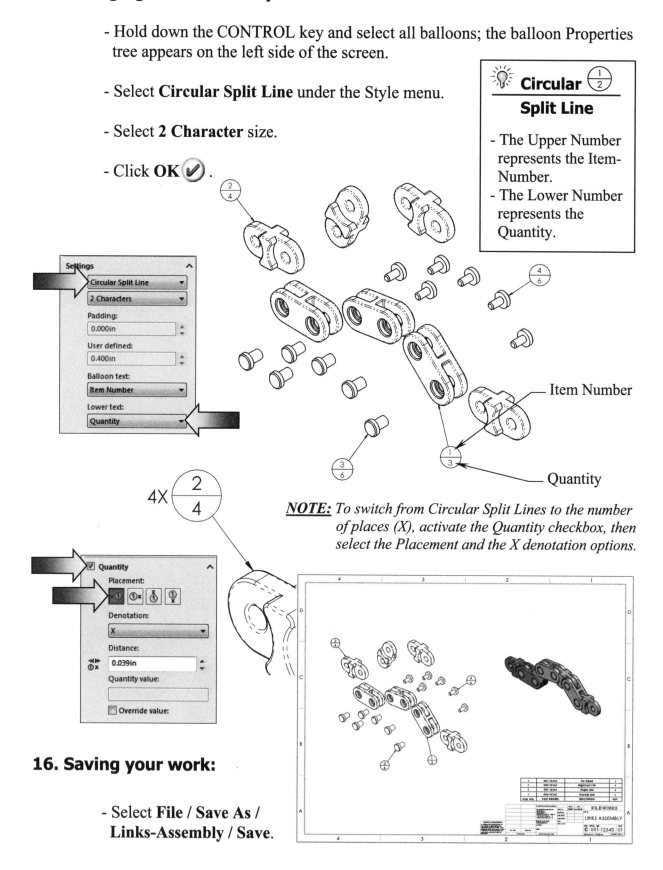

> 💡 **Circular** ①②
> _____
> **Split Line**
>
> - The Upper Number represents the Item-Number.
> - The Lower Number represents the Quantity.

Item Number

Quantity

NOTE: *To switch from Circular Split Lines to the number of places (X), activate the Quantity checkbox, then select the Placement and the X denotation options.*

16. Saving your work:

- Select **File / Save As / Links-Assembly / Save**.

Questions for Review

Assembly Drawings

1. The drawing's paper size can be selected or changed at any time.
   - a. True
   - b. False

2. The First or Third angle projection can be selected in the sheet setup.
   - a. True
   - b. False

3. To access the sheet format and edit the information in the title block:
   - a. Right click in the drawing and select Edit Sheet Format.
   - b. Right click the Sheet Format icon from the Feature Tree and select: Edit Sheet Format.
   - c. All of the above.

4. The BOM anchor point should be set on the Sheet Format, not on the drawing sheet.
   - a. True
   - b. False

5. A Model View command is used to create Isometric views.
   - a. True
   - b. False

6. The Drawing views scale can be changed individually or all at the same time.
   - a. True
   - b. False

7. A Bill of Materials (BOM) can automatically be generated using Excel embedded features.
   - a. True
   - b. False

8. The Balloon callouts are linked to the Bill of Materials and driven by the order of the Feature Manager Tree.
   - a. True
   - b. False

8. TRUE	9. TRUE
5. TRUE	7. TRUE
3. C	4. TRUE
1. TRUE	2. TRUE

Exercise: Assembly Drawings

File location: Training Files folder,
Mini Vise folder.

1. Create an Assembly Drawing
   from the components provided.

2. Create a Bill Of Materials and
   modify the Part Number and the
   Description columns as shown.

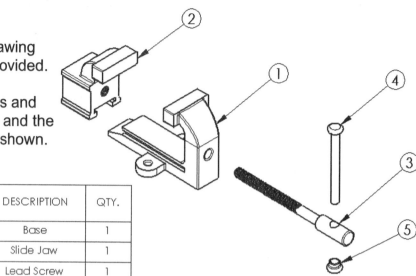

ITEM NO.	PART NUMBER	DESCRIPTION	QTY.
1	001-12345	Base	1
2	002-23456	Slide Jaw	1
3	003-34567	Lead Screw	1
4	004-45678	Crank Handle	1
5	005-56789	Crank Handle Knob	1

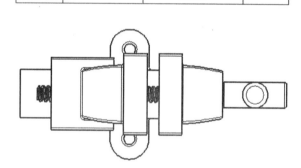

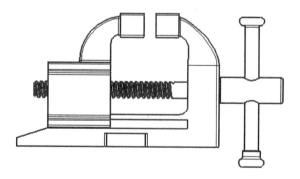

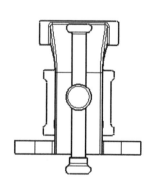

3. Save your work as **Mini Vise Assembly.slddrw**.

Exercise: Assembly Drawings

File Location:
Training Files folder
Egg Beater.sldasm

ITEM NO.	PART NUMBER	DESCRIPTION	QTY.
1	010-8980	Egg Beater Handle	1
2	010-8981	Main Gear	1
3	010-8982	Support Rod	1
4	010-8983	Right Spinner	1
5	010-8984	Left Spinner	1
6	010-8985	Crank Handle	1
7	010-8986	Small Gear (RIGHT)	1
8	010-8987	Small Gear (LEFT)	1

1. Create an Assembly
   Drawing with 5 views.

2. Add Balloons and a Bill
   Of Materials.

3. Save your work as
   Egg Beater Assembly.

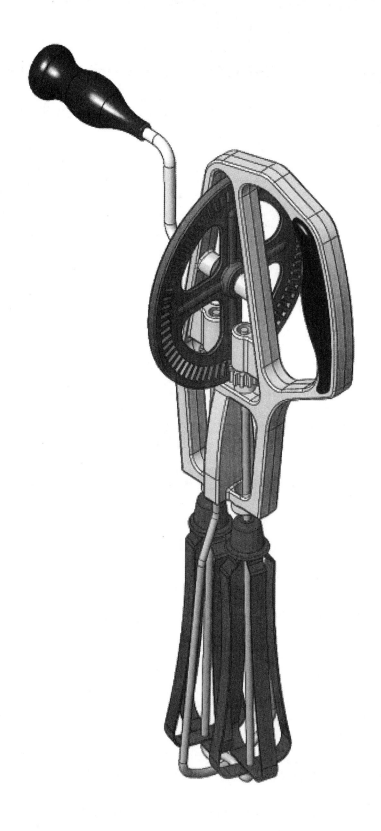

CHAPTER 15 (cont.)

Alternate Position Views

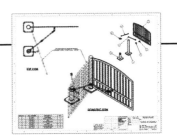

Assembly Drawings
Alternate Position Views

- Assembly drawings are created in the same way as part drawings, except for all components that are shown together as assembled or exploded.

- A Bill of Materials is created to specify the details of the components, such as Part Number, Material, Weight, Vendor, etc.

- The BOM template can be modified to have more columns, rows, or different headers.

- Balloons are also created on the same drawing to help identify the parts from its list (B.O.M). These balloons are linked to the Bill of Materials parametrically, and the order of the balloon numbers is driven by the Assembly's Feature tree.

Alternate Position Views

- The Alternate Position View allows users to superimpose one drawing view precisely on another (open/close position as an example).

- The alternate position(s) is shown with phantom lines.

- Dimension between the primary view and the Alternate Position View can be added to the same drawing view.

- More than one Alternate Position View can be created in a drawing.

- Section, Detail, Broken, and Crop views are currently not supported.

Alternate Position Views
Assembly Drawings

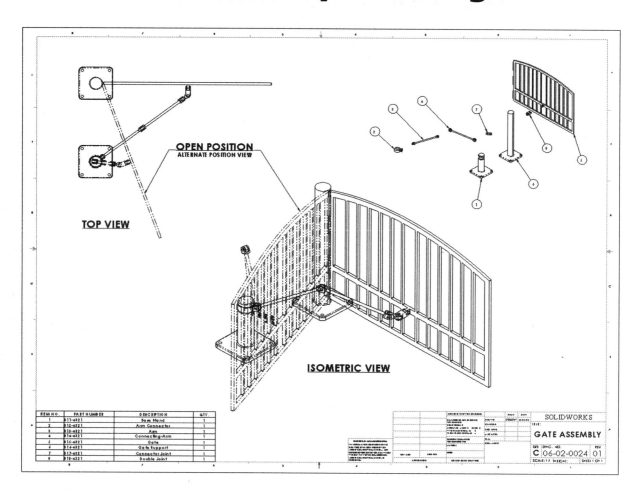

OPEN POSITION
ALTERNATE POSITION VIEW

TOP VIEW

ISOMETRIC VIEW

ITEM NO.	PART NUMBER	DESCRIPTION	QTY.
1	011-4321	Base Stand	1
2	012-4321	Arm Connector	1
3	013-4321	Arm	1
4	014-4321	Connecting-Arm	1
5	015-4321	Gate	1
6	016-4321	Gate Support	1
7	017-4321	Connector Joint	1
8	018-4321	Double Joint	1

SOLIDWORKS

TITLE:
GATE ASSEMBLY

SIZE | DWG. NO. | REV
C | 06-02-0024 | 01
SCALE:1:? WEIGHT: SHEET 1 OF 1

Dimensioning Standards: **ANSI**	Third Angle Projection
Units: **INCHES** – 3 Decimals	

Tools Needed:

Alternate Position

Model View

Note

Auto Balloon

Bill of Materials

Show in exploded or model break state

1. Creating a new drawing:

- Select **File / New / Drawing / OK**.

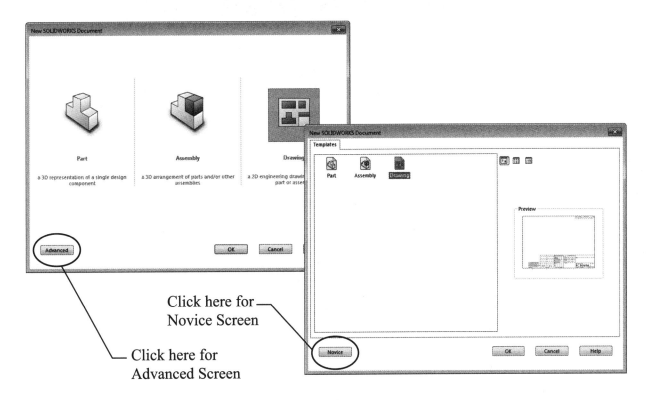

Click here for Novice Screen

Click here for Advanced Screen

- For Standard Sheet Size, select **C-Landscape**.

- Enable the **Display Sheet Format** check box.

- Click **OK**.

- Right click in the drawing and select **Properties**.

- Set **Scale** to **1:1** (full scale).

- Set **Type of Projection** to **Third Angle**.

- Click **OK**.

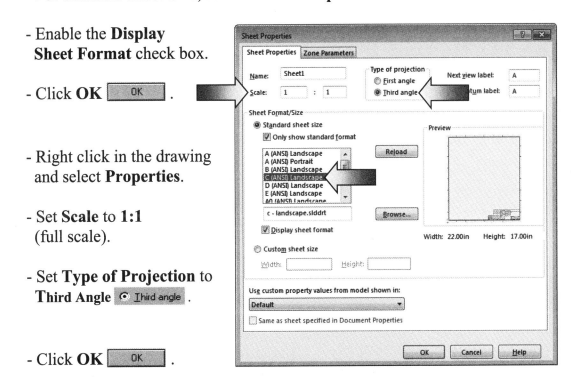

2. Creating the Isometric Drawing View:

- Switch to the **View Layout** tool tab.

- Select the **Model View** command.

- Click **Browse** and open the **Gate Assembly** document from the Training Files folder.

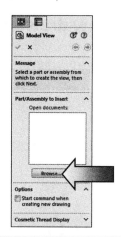

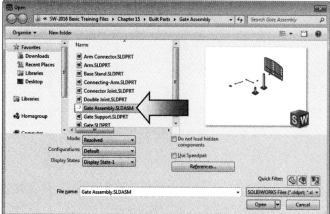

- Select the **Isometric** view from the Orientation section (arrow).

- Place the 1st drawing view (Isometric) approximately in the center of the sheet.

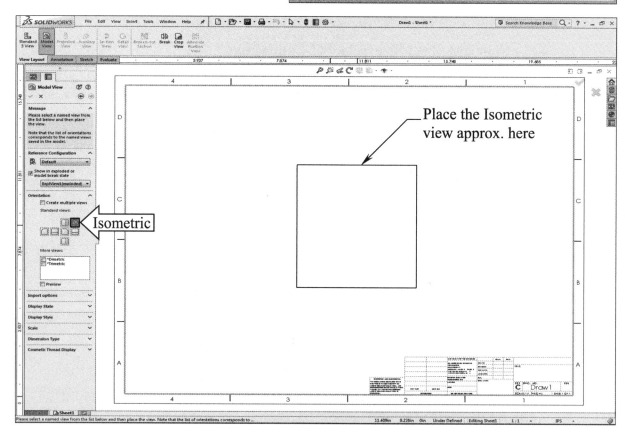

Place the Isometric view approx. here

3. Changing the Drawing View Scale:

- Click on the drawing view border and change the Scale to:

> *** Use Custom Scale**.

> *** User Defined Route**.

> *** Scale 1:3**

- Click **OK** ✅ .

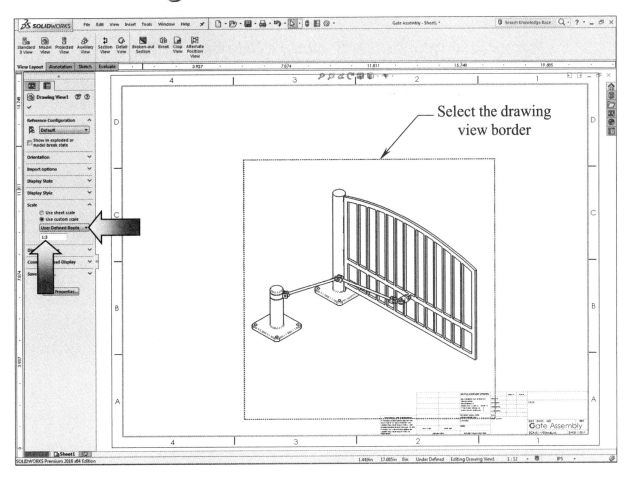

Select the drawing
view border

- The Isometric View is scaled to (1:3) or 1/3 the actual size.

- When selecting the User Defined option you can enter your own scale if
the scale option that you want is not on the list.

- The scale in the Sheet properties is linked to the scale callout in the title
block (page 14-25). Changing the scale in the Properties will automatically
update the one in the title block.

4. Creating an Alternate Position drawing view:

- Use Alternate Position Views to show different positions of the components in an assembly.

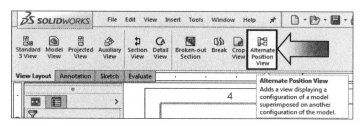

- From the View Layout Tool tab, click the **Alternate Position View** command.

- In the Configuration section, click the **Existing Configuration** option.

- Expand the drop down list and select the **Gate Open** configuration.

- Click **OK**.

- The new drawing view is shown with Phantom lines and it is superimposed over the original view.

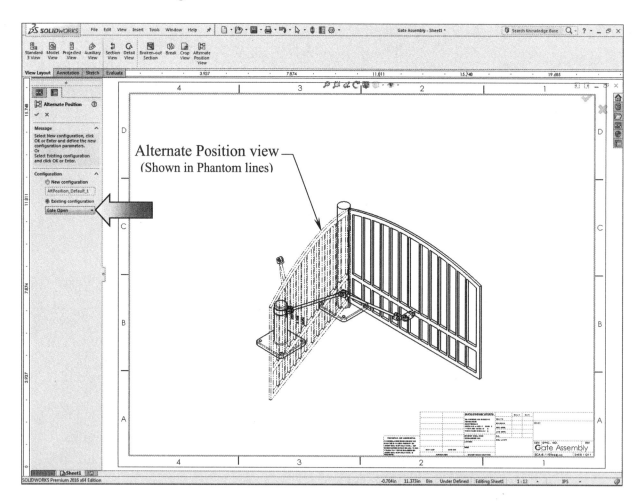

Alternate Position view
(Shown in Phantom lines)

5. Adding the Top Drawing view:

- From the View Layout tool tab, click **Model View** command .

- Click the **NEXT** arrow .

- Select the **TOP** view from the Orientation dialog.

- Place the Top drawing view approximately as shown.

- Click **OK** .

- For clarity, change the view display to **Tangent-Edges With Font**. (Right click the view's border, select Tangent Edge, and then click Tangent Edges with Font.)

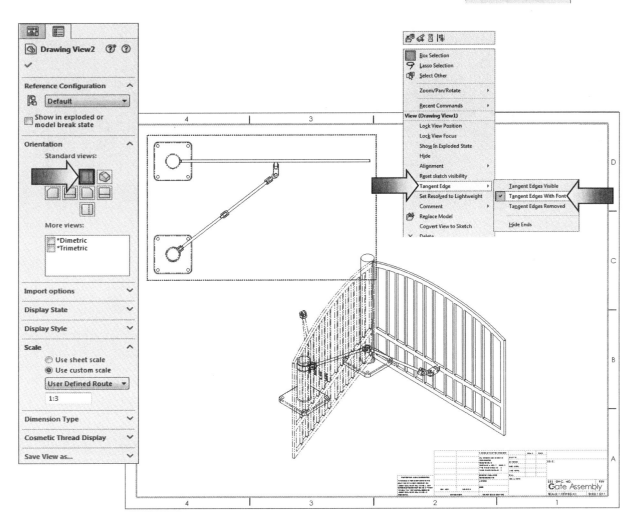

6. Creating the 2nd Alternate Position View:

- Click the top view drawing's border to activate it.

- Click **Alternate Position View** 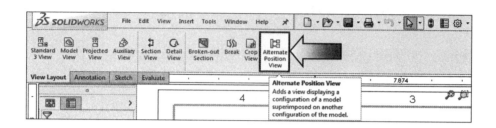 on the View Layout tool tab.

- In the Configuration section, click the **Existing Configuration** option.

- Select the **Gate Open** configuration from the drop down list.

- Click **OK** ✅.

- The new drawing view is shown in Phantom lines and is superimposed over the original view.

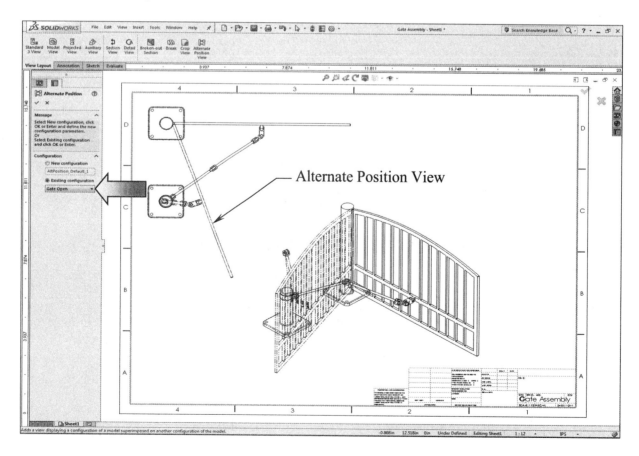

Alternate Position View

7. Adding Text / Annotations:

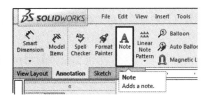

- Select the top view drawing's border and switch to the **Annotation** tool tab.

- Click the **Note** [A] command and add the notes **Top View** and **Isometric View** as shown below.

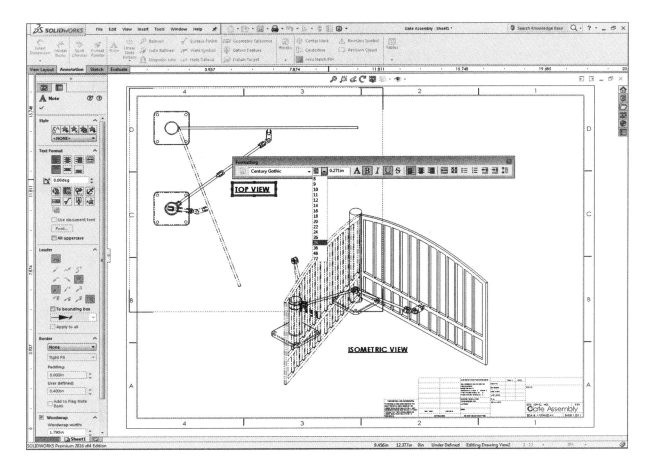

- Use the options in the Formatting toolbar to modify the text.

- Highlight the text and change it to match the settings below:

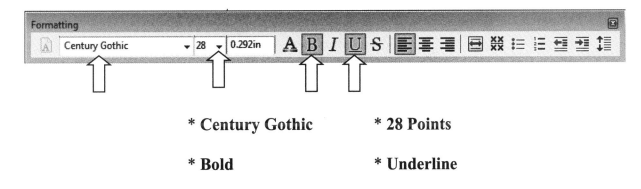

* Century Gothic	* 28 Points
* Bold	* Underline

8. Creating an Exploded Isometric view:

- Click the **Model View** command on the View Layout tool tab.

- Click the **NEXT** arrow .

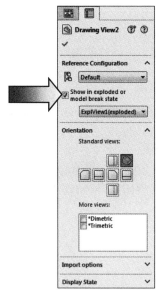

- Select the **Isometric** view button from the Orientation dialog.

- Place the Isometric view on the upper right side of the sheet.

- On the upper left corner of the Properties tree, enable the **Show-In Exploded or Model Break State** checkbox (arrow).

- Set the scale of the view to **1:8**.

NOTE:
The exploded view must be already created in the assembly for this option to be available in the drawing.

- Click **OK** .

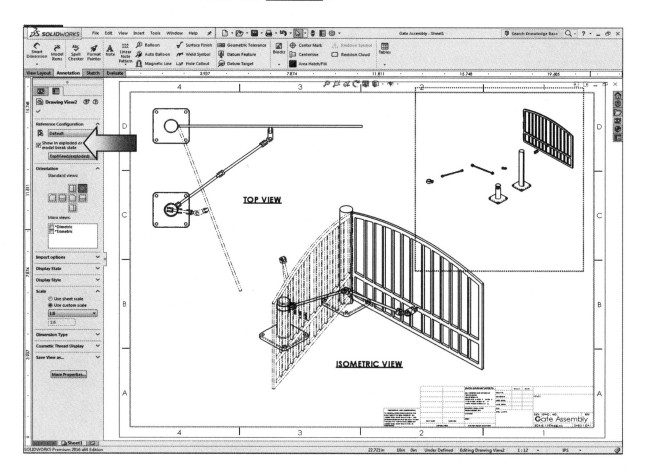

9. Adding Auto-Balloons to the Exploded view:

- Switch to the **Annotation** tool tab.

- Select the Isometric drawing view's border.

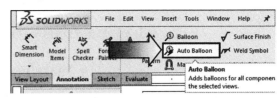

- Click 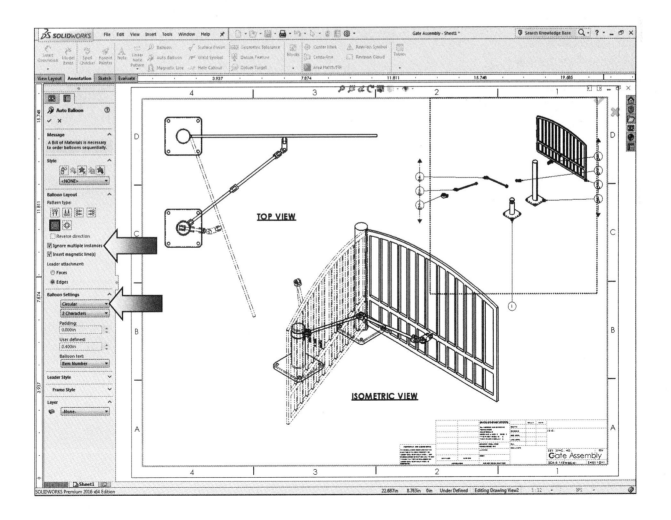 or select **Insert / Annotations / Auto Balloon**.

- In the Auto Balloon properties tree, set the following:

  * Balloon Layout: **Square**   * Ignore Multiple Instances: **Enable**

  * Insert Magnetic Line(s): **Enable**   * Style: **Circular**

  * Size: **2 Character**   * Balloon Text: **Item Number**

- Click **OK** ▭ .

10. Adding a Bill of Materials to the Drawing:

- Click **Bill of Materials** on the Annotation tool tab.

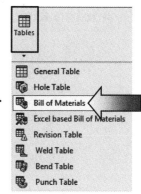

- For Table Templates select **Bom-Standard**.

- **Uncheck** the Attached to Anchor box.

- For BOM Type select **Parts Only**.

- Click **OK** OK .

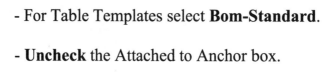

	A	B	C	D
	ITEM NO.	PART NUMBER	DESCRIPTION	QTY.
	1	011-4321	Base Stand	1
	2	012-4321	Arm Connector	1
	3	013-4321	Arm	1
	4	014-4321	Connecting-Arm	1
	5	015-4321	Gate	1
	6	016-4321	Gate Support	1
	7	017-4321	Connector Joint	1
	8	018-4321	Double Joint	1

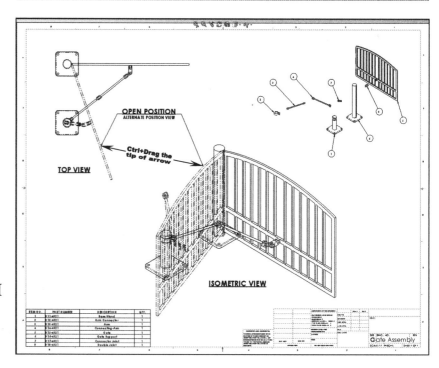

- Modify the BOM as shown to add the part numbers and descriptions.

11. Saving a copy of your work:

- Click **File / Save As.**

- Enter **Gate Assembly.slddrw** for the name of the file and click **Save.**

Questions for Review

Assembly Drawings

1. The Alternate Position command can also be selected from Insert / Drawing View / Alternate Position.
   - a. True
   - b. False

2. The Alternate Position command precisely places a drawing view on top of another view.
   - a. True
   - b. False

3. The types of views that are not currently supported to work with Alternate Position are:
   - a. Broken and Crop Views
   - b. Detail View
   - c. Section View
   - d. All of the above.

4. Dimensions or annotations cannot be added to the superimposed view.
   - a. True
   - b. False

5. The Line Style for use in the Alternate Position view is:
   - a. Solid line
   - b. Dashed line
   - c. Phantom line
   - d. Centerline

6. In order to show the assembly exploded view on a drawing, an exploded view configuration must be created first in the main assembly.
   - a. True
   - b. False

7. Balloons and Auto Balloons can also be selected from Insert / Annotations / (Auto) Balloon.
   - a. True
   - b. False

8. The Bill of Materials contents can be modified to include the Material Column.
   - a. True
   - b. False

7. TRUE	8. TRUE
5. C	6. TRUE
3. D	4. FALSE
1. TRUE	2. TRUE

CHAPTER 16

Drawing Views

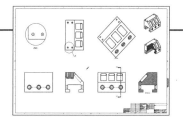

Drawing Views
Machined Block

- When creating an engineering drawing, one of the first things to do is to lay out the drawing views such as:

> * The standard Front, Top, Right, and Isometric views.

> * Other views like Detail, Cross section, Auxiliary views, etc., can be created or projected from the 4 standard views.

- Most of the drawing views in SOLIDWORKS are automatically aligned with one another (default alignments); each one can only be moved along the direction that was defined for that particular view (vertical, horizontal, or at projected angle).

- Dimensions and annotations will then be added to the drawing views.

- The dimensions created in the part will be inserted into the drawing views so that their association between the model and the drawing views can be maintained. Changes done to these dimensions will update all drawing views and the solid model as well.

- Configurations are also used in this lesson to create some specific views.

- This chapter will guide you through the creation of some of the most commonly used drawing views in an engineering drawing like 3 Standard views, Section views, Detail views, Projected views, Auxiliary views, Broken Out Section views, and Cross Hatch patterns.

Machined Block
Drawing Views Creation

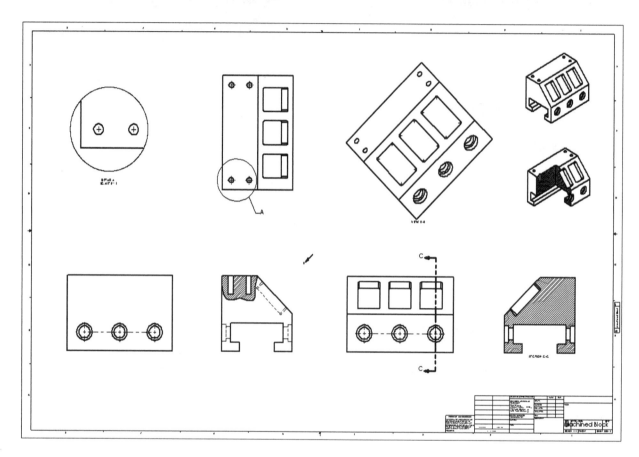

Dimensioning Standards: **ANSI**	Third Angle Projection
Units: **INCHES** – 3 Decimals	

Tools Needed:

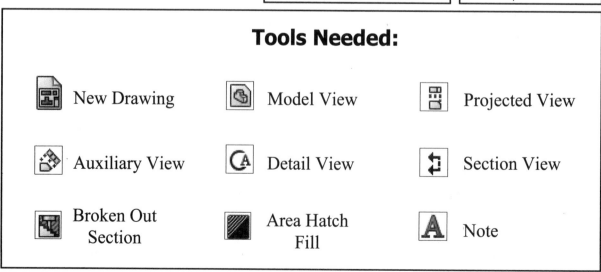

New Drawing   Model View   Projected View

Auxiliary View   Detail View   Section View

Broken Out Section   Area Hatch Fill   Note

1. Creating a new drawing:

- Select **File / New / Drawing** template.

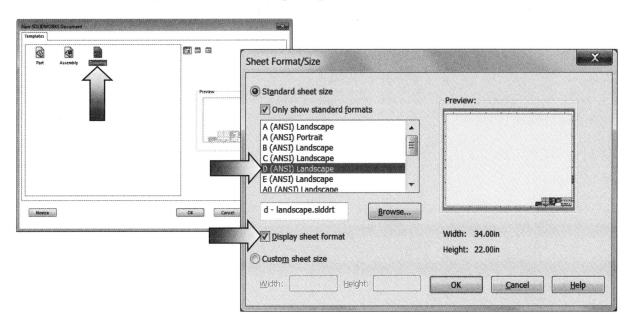

- Choose **D-Landscape*** under Standard Sheet Size (34.00 in. X 22.00 in.).

- Enable the **Display Sheet Format** check box to include the title block.

- Click **OK**.

* If the options above are not available, **right click** inside the drawing and select **Properties**.

* Select the **Third Angle** option under Type of Projection.

* Set the default view scale to **1:2**.

* The Units can be changed later on.

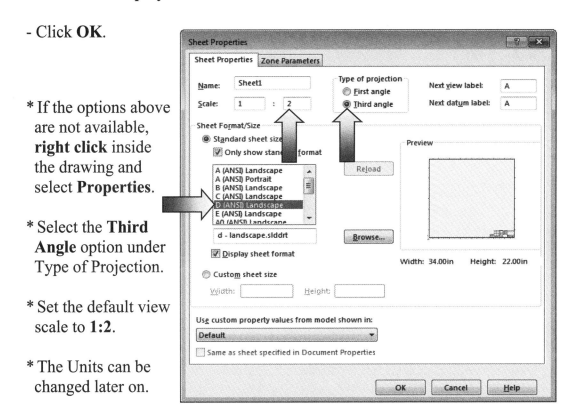

- The drawing template comes with 2 default "layers":

　　* The "Front layer" is called the **Sheet** layer, where drawings are created.

　　* The "Back layer" is called the **Sheet Format,** where the title block and the revision information are stored.

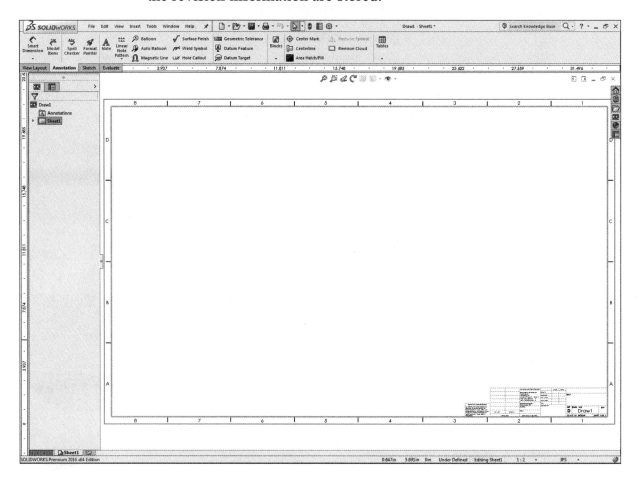

2. Editing the Sheet Format:

- Zoom in 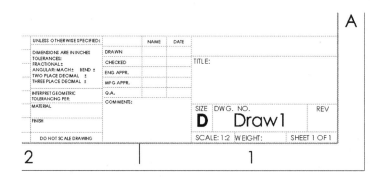 on the Title Block area (or scroll the middle-mouse-button inward). We are going to first fill out the information in the title block.

- Right click in the drawing area and select **Edit Sheet Format** (arrow).

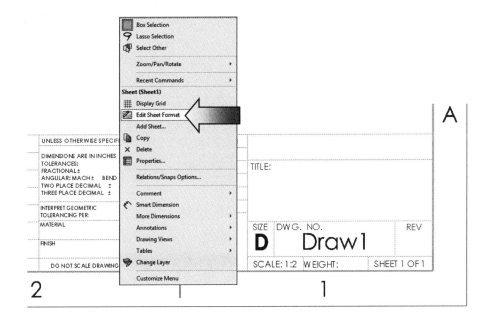

- The Sheet Format is brought up on top.

- New annotation and sketch lines can now be added to customize the title block.

- Any existing text or lines can now be modified.

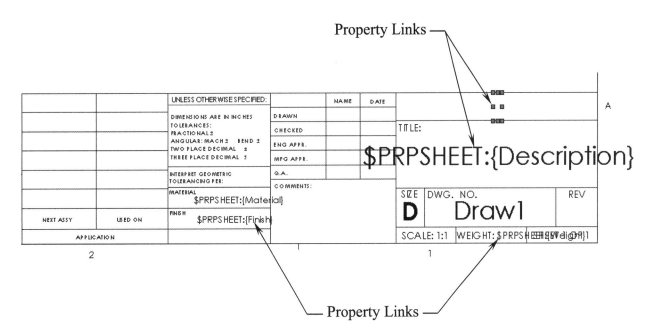

- Notice the link to properties text strings: "$PRPS." Some of the annotations have already been linked to the part's properties.

3. Modifying the existing text:

- Double click on the "Company Name" and enter the name of your company.

- Click 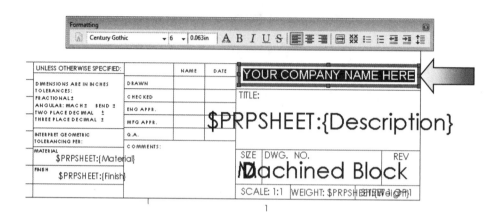 on the upper left of the Properties tree when done.

4. Adding the Title of the drawing:

- Double click on the Property-Link in the Title area ($PRPSHEET:{Description})

- Enter **Machined Block** for the title of the drawing.

- Fill out the information as shown in the title block for the other areas.

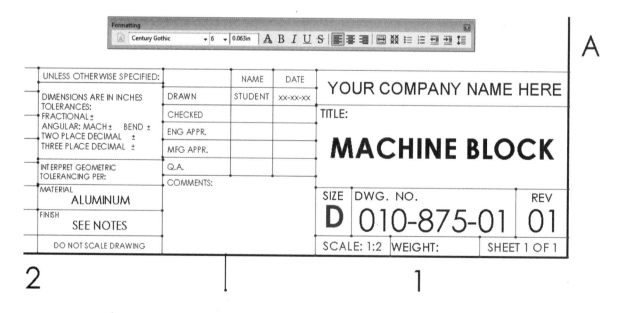

- Click **OK** ✔.

5. Switching back to the drawing Sheet:

- Right click in the drawing and select **Edit Sheet**.

- The Drawing Sheet "layer" is brought back up on top.

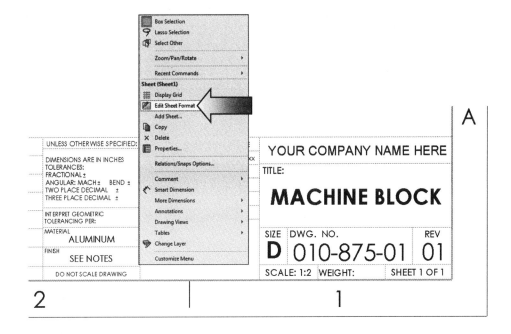

6. Using the View-Palette:

- The **View Palette** is located on the right side of the screen in the Task Pane area; click on its icon to access it.

Note: _If the drawing views are not visible in the View Palette window, click the Browse button_ ☐ _and locate and open the part Machined Block._

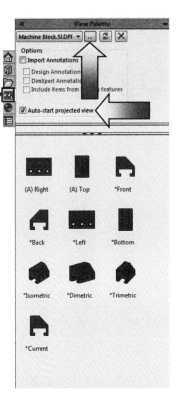

- The standard drawing views like the Front, Right, Top, Back, Left, Bottom, Current, Isometric, and Sheet Metal Flat-Pattern views are contained within the View Palette window.

- These drawing views can be dragged into the drawing sheet to create the drawing views.

- The **Auto Start Projected View** checkbox should be selected by default.

7. Using the View Palette:

- Click/Hold/Drag the Front view from the View-Palette (arrow) and drop it on the drawing sheet approximately as shown. Make sure the Auto-Start projected view checkbox is enabled (arrow).

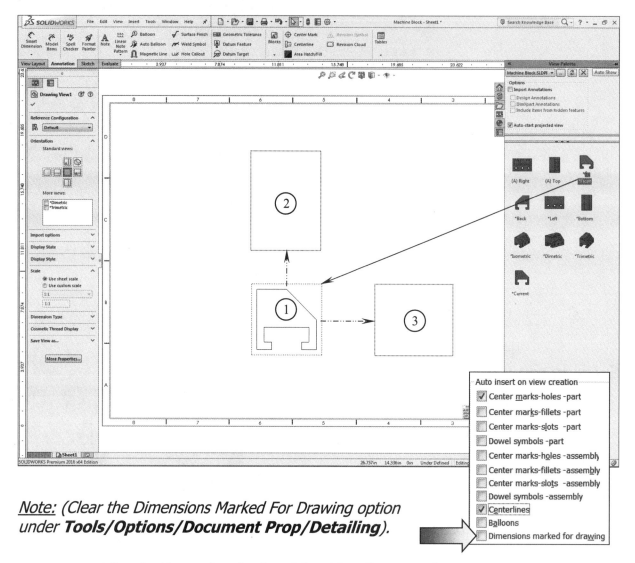

*Note: (Clear the Dimensions Marked For Drawing option under **Tools/Options/Document Prop/Detailing**).*

- After the Front view is placed (position 1), move the mouse cursor upward, a preview image of the Top view appears, click in an approximate spot above the Front view to place the Top view (position 2); repeat the same step for the Right view (position 3).

- The check mark symbol 🗎 appears next to the drawing views that have been used in the drawing.
- Click the **Refresh** button 🔁 to update the palette.

- Click **OK** ✅ when you are finished with the first three views.

8. Adding an Isometric view:

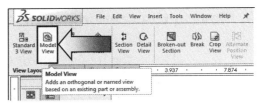

- The Isometric view can also be inserted from the View Palette, but we will look at another option to create it instead.

- Switch to the **View Layout** tab and select the **Model View** command .

- Click the NEXT arrow ➡.

- Select **Isometric** (Arrow) from the Model View properties tree and place it approximately as shown.

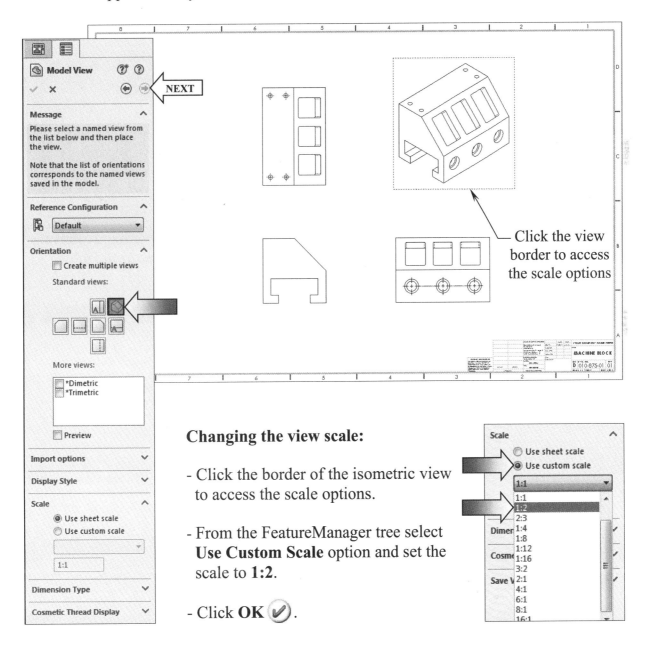

Click the view border to access the scale options

Changing the view scale:

- Click the border of the isometric view to access the scale options.

- From the FeatureManager tree select **Use Custom Scale** option and set the scale to **1:2**.

- Click **OK** ✓.

9. Moving the drawing view(s):

- Hover the mouse cursor over the border of the Front view and "Click/Hold/ Drag" to move it; all 3 views will move at the same time. By default, the Top and the Right views are automatically aligned with the Front view.

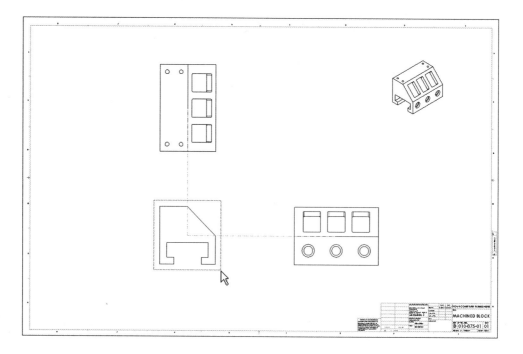

- When moving either the Right or the Top view, notice they will only move along the default vertical or horizontal directions? These are the default alignments for the standard drawing views.

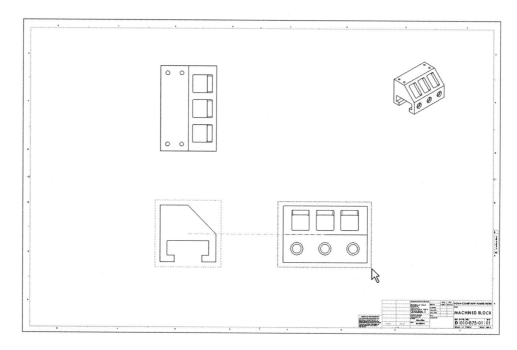

10. Breaking the alignments between the views:

- Right click inside the Top view or on its "dotted border" and select **Alignment / Break-Alignment***.

- The Top view is no longer locked to the default direction, so it can be moved freely.

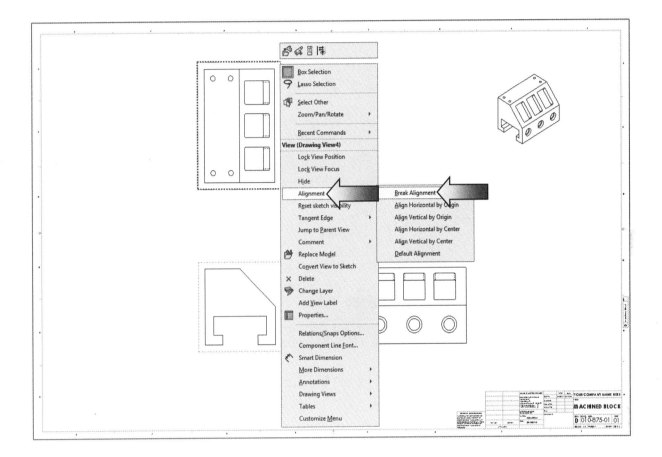

- Dependent views like Projected Views, Auxiliary Views, Section views, etc. are aligned automatically with the views they were created from. Their alignments can be broken or also reverted back to their default alignments.

- Independent views can also be aligned with other drawing views by using the same alignment options as shown above.

* To re-align a drawing view:

- Right click on the view's border and select **Alignment / Default-Alignment**.

11. Creating a Detail View:

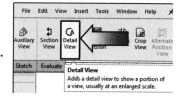

- Click or select **Insert / Drawing View / Detail**.

- Sketch a **circle** approximately as shown on the top drawing view.

- A Detail View is created automatically. Place it on the left side of the top view.

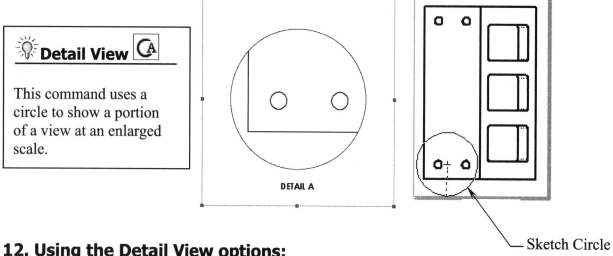

> ### 💡 Detail View Ⓐ
>
> This command uses a circle to show a portion of a view at an enlarged scale.

DETAIL A

— Sketch Circle

12. Using the Detail View options:

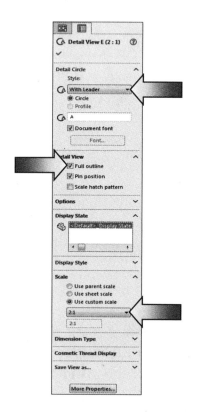

- Change Per-Standard style to **With Leader** (arrow).

- Enable **Full Outline**.

- Use Custom scale of **2:1**.

- Click **OK** ✅.

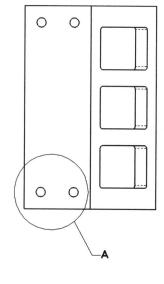

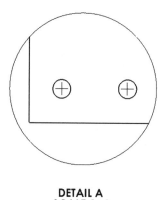

DETAIL A
SCALE 2 : 1

13. Creating a Projected View:

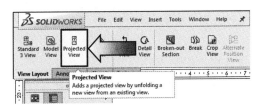

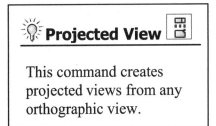

> ☼ **Projected View** ▦
>
> This command creates projected views from any orthographic view.

- Click on the Front view's border to activate it.

- Click ▦ or select **Insert / Drawing View / Projected**.

- Move the mouse cursor to the left side of the Front view and place it there.

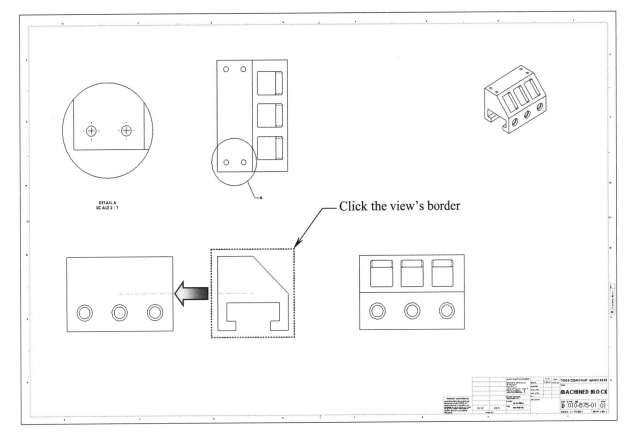

Click the view's border

- Notice the projected view is also aligned automatically to the horizontal axis of the Front view? It can only be moved from left to right.

- For the purpose of this lesson, we will keep all of the default alignments the way SOLIDWORKS creates them. (To break these default alignments at any-time, simply right click on their dotted borders and select Break-Alignment.)

(This left side view can also be dragged and dropped from the View Palette.)

14. Creating an Auxiliary View:

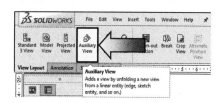

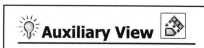

Auxiliary View

This command creates a view normal to a reference edge in an existing view.

- Select the Angled-Edge as indicated and click the **Auxiliary** command.

- Place the Auxiliary view approximately as shown below.

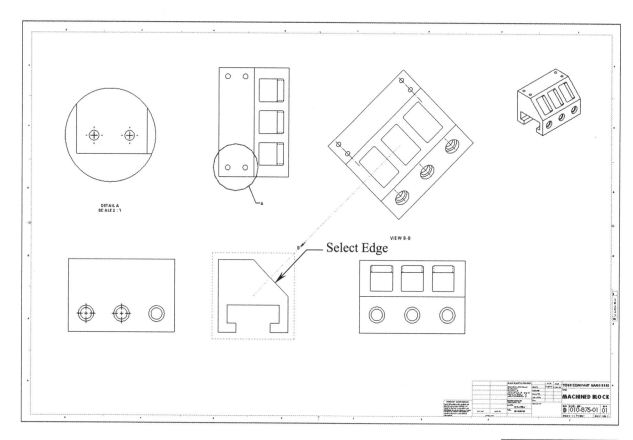

DETAIL A
SCALE 2 : 1

VIEW B-B

Select Edge

MACHINED BLOCK

D 010-875-01 01

- The Auxiliary view is also aligned to the edge from which it was originally projected.

- The projection arrow can be toggled on and off from the PropertiesManager tree (arrow).

- Use the Break-Alignment option if needed to rearrange the drawing views to different locations.

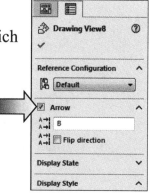

15. Creating a Section View:

- Zoom in the right view.

- Click  or select **Insert / Drawing View / Section**.

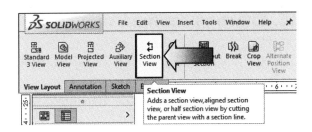

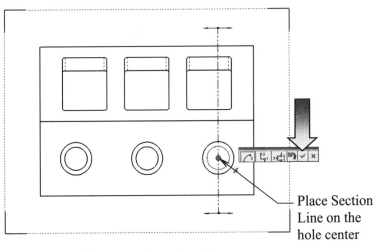

Place Section Line on the hole center

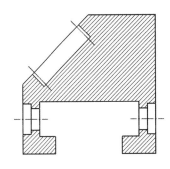

💡 **Section Views**

The Section View command creates a cut through a view, using single or multiple lines to show the interior details.
The sectioned surfaces are fully crosshatched automatically.

- Place the Section Line on the center of the hole on the right.

- The Section View Pop-Up appears; click **OK** ☑ on the pop-up and place the section view on the right side.

- The Section view is aligned horizontally with the view from which it was created and the cross-hatched lines are added automatically.

- To change the direction of the cut:

* Double Click on the section line and click Rebuild – OR –
* Enable the Flip Direction checkbox in the Feature tree (arrow).

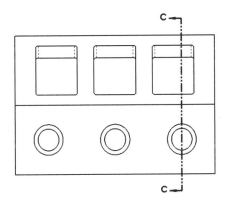

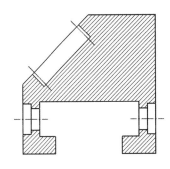

SECTION C-C

16. Showing the hidden lines in a drawing view:

- Select the Front view's border.

- Click the button **Hidden Lines Visible** under the Display Style section.

- The hidden lines are now visible.

Click the front view's border to activate it.

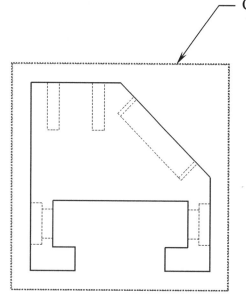

17. Creating a Broken-Out-Section:

- Switch to the Sketch tool tab and sketch a <u>closed</u> free-form shape on the view, around the Front area as shown (use either the Line or the Spline command to create the profile).

> ### Broken Out Section View
>
> Creates a partial cut, using a closed profile, at a specified depth to display the inner details of a drawing view.

Closed Profile

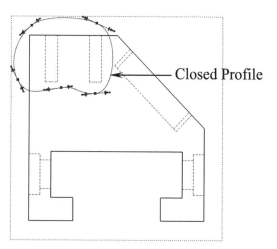

- Select the entire <u>closed profile</u> and change to the **View Layout** tool tab.

- Click **Broken-Out-Section**.

- Enable the **Preview** check box on the Properties tree.

- Enter **.500** in. for Depth.

- Click **OK** ✓.

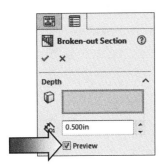

18. Adding a Cutaway view: (Previously created as a Configuration in the model)

- Click the **Model View** command 🗔.

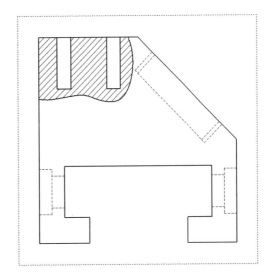

- Click **Next** → and select the **Isometric** under Orientation window; use a **Custom Scale** of **1:2**.

- Place the new Isometric view below the other isometric view.

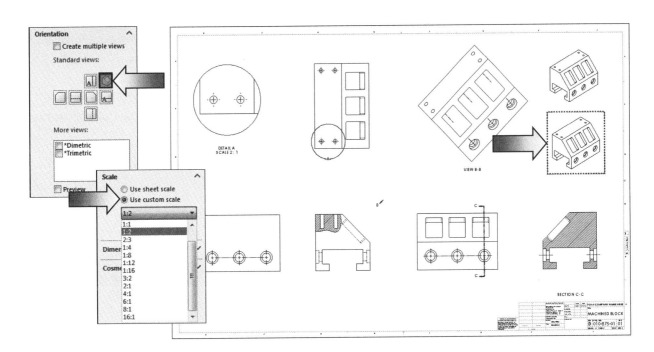

19. Changing Configurations: (From Default to Cutaway View)

- Click the new Isometric view's border.

- On the Properties tree, select the **Cutaway View** configuration from the list.

- Click **OK** ✅.

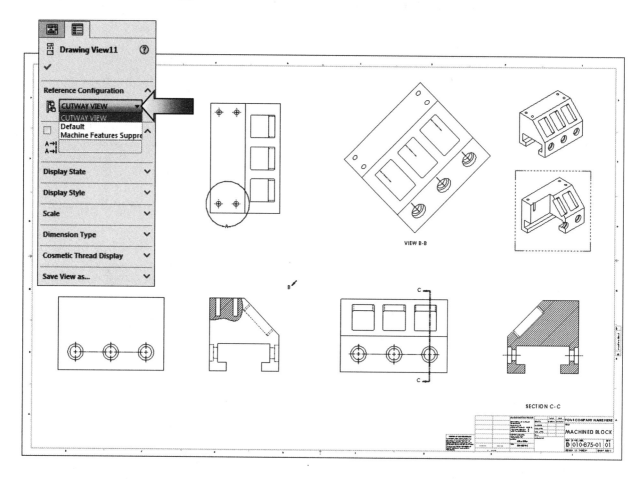

- The **Cutaway View** configuration is activated, and the extruded-cut feature that was created earlier in the model is now shown here.

- Since the cutout was created in the model, there is no crosshatch on any of the sectioned faces.

- Crosshatch is added at the drawing level and will not appear in the model.

- The hatch lines are added next...

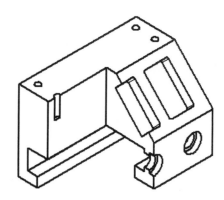

20. Adding crosshatch to the sectioned surfaces:

- Crosshatch is added automatically when section views are made in the drawing; since the cut was created in the model, we will have to add the hatch manually.

- Hold the Control key and select the 3 faces as indicated.

- Click the **Area Hatch/Fill** on the Annotation tab.

- Set the parameters indicated in the dialog box.

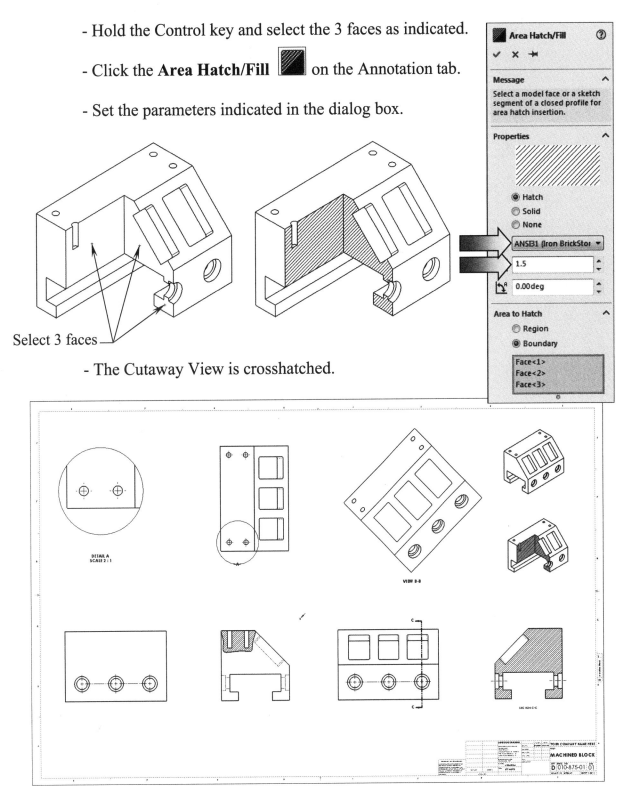

Select 3 faces

- The Cutaway View is crosshatched.

21. Modifying the crosshatch properties:

- Zoom in 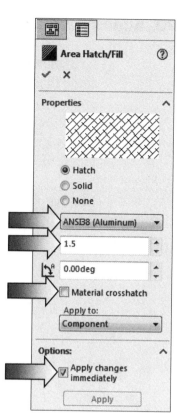 on the **Section C-C**.

- Click inside the hatch area; the **Area Hatch / Fill** properties tree appears.

- <u>Clear</u> the **Material Crosshatch** checkbox.

- Change the hatch pattern to **ANSI38** (Aluminum).

- Scale: **1.500** (The spacing between the hatch lines).

- Angle **00.00 deg**. (Sets the angle of the hatch lines).

- Enable: **Apply Changes Immediately**.

- Click **OK** ✓.

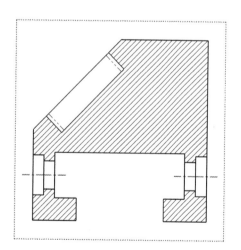

ANSI31 (Iron BrickStone)

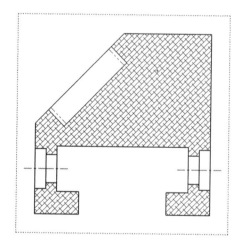

ANSI38 (Aluminum)

- When the hatch pattern is applied locally to the selected view, it does not override the global settings in the system options.

- Change to the same hatch pattern for any views with crosshatch.

22. Saving your work:

- Select **File / Save As**.

- Enter **Machine Block-Drawing Views** for file name and click **Save**.

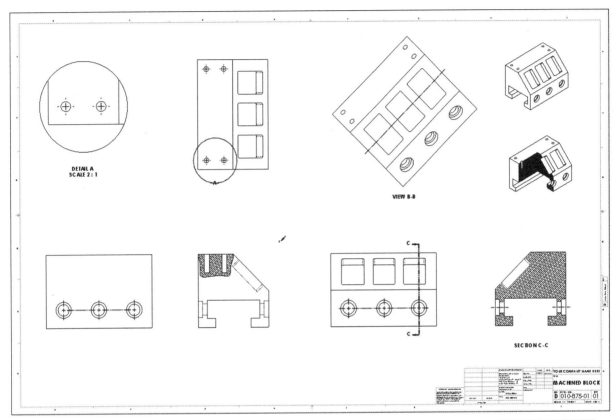

- The drawing views can also be changed from Wireframe to Shaded

- The color of the drawing views is driven by the part's color. What you see here in the drawing is how it is going to look when printed (in color).

- Changing the part's color will update the color of the drawing views automatically.

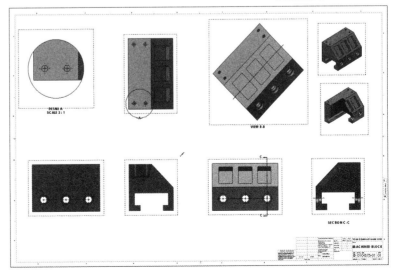

Geometric Tolerance & Flag Notes

Geometric Tolerance Symbols GCS are used in a Feature Control Frame to add Geometric Tolerances to the parts and drawings.

Symbol	Name	Symbol	Name
∠	Angularity	⊕	Position
↔	Between	⌒	Profile of Any Surface
○	Circularity (Roundness)	↗	Simple Runout
◎	Concentricity and Coaxially	↗	Simple Runout (open)
⌀	Cylindricity	—	Straightness
▱	Flatness	≡	Symmetry
⌒	Profile of Any Line	↗↗	Total Runout
//	Parallelism	↗↗	Total Runout (open)
⊥	Perpendicularity	To access the symbol libraries, select **Insert / Annotations / Note**

Modifying Symbols Library

Circle 1-99	Square 1-99	Square/Circle 1-99	Triangle 1-99
(1.) (1)	1. 1	(1.) (1)	⟨1.⟩ ⟨1⟩
Circle A-Z	Square A-Z	Square/Circle A-Z	Triangle A-Z
(A.) (A)	A. A	(A.) (A)	⟨A.⟩ ⟨A⟩

Modifying & Hole Symbols

Modifying Symbols MC

Symbol	Description	Symbol	Description
℄	Centerline	Ⓣ	Tangent Plane
°	Degree		Slope (Up)
⌀	Diameter		Slope (Down)
S⌀	Spherical Diameter		Slope (Inverted Up)
±	Plus/Minus		Slope (Inverted Down)
Ⓢ	Regardless of Feature Size	□	Square
Ⓕ	Free State	⊠	Square (BS)
Ⓛ	Least Material Condition	⟨ST⟩	Statistical
Ⓜ	Maximum Material Condition		Flattened Length
Ⓟ	Projected Tolerance Zone	ꟼL	Parting Line
Ⓔ	Encompassing	SOLIDWORKS supports **ASME-ANSI Y14.5** Geometric & True Position Tolerancing	

⊔ Counterbore (Spot face)   ∨ Countersunk   ▽ Depth/Deep   ⌀ Diameter

ASME (American Society for Mechanical Engineering)

ANSI Y14.5M (American National Standards Institute)

SYMBOLS DESCRIPTION

ANGULARITY:

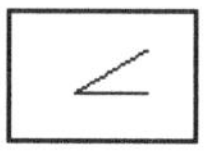

The condition of a surface or line, which is at a specified angle (other than 90°) from the datum plane or axis.

BASIC DIMENSION: 1.00

A dimension specified on a drawing as BASIC is a theoretical value used to describe the exact size, shape, or location of a feature. It is used as a basis from which permissible variations are established by tolerance on other dimensions or in notes. A basic dimension can be identified by the abbreviation BSC or more readily by boxing in the dimension.

CIRCULARITY (ROUNDNESS):

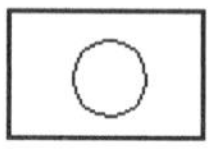

A tolerance zone bounded by two concentric circles within which each circular element of the surface must lie.

CONCENTRICITY:

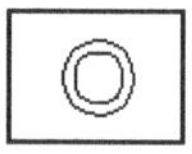

The condition in which the axis of all cross-sectional elements of a feature's surface of revolution are common.

CYLINDRICITY:

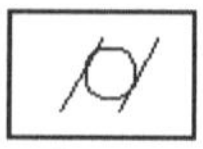

The condition of a surface of revolution in which all points of the surface are equidistant from a common axis or for a perfect cylinder.

DATUM:

A point, line, plane, cylinder, etc., assumed to be exact for purposes of computation from which the location or geometric relationship of other features of a part may be established. A datum identification symbol contains a letter (except I, C, and Q) placed inside a rectangular box.

DATUM TARGET:

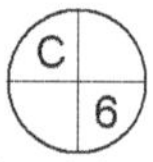

The datum target symbol is a circle divided into four quadrants. The letter placed in the upper left quadrant identifies it is associated datum feature. The numeral placed in the lower right quadrant identifies the target; the dashed leader line indicates the target on far side.

FLATNESS:

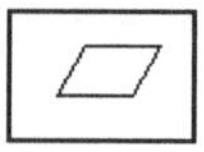

The condition of a surface having all elements in one plane. A flatness tolerance specifies a tolerance zone confined by two parallel planes within which the surface must lie.

MAXIMUM MATERIAL CONDITION: ⓜ

The condition of a part feature when it contains the maximum amount of material.

LEAST MATERIAL CONDITION: Ⓛ

The condition of a part feature when it contains the least amount of material. The term is opposite from maximum material condition.

PARALLELISM: //

The condition of a surface or axis which is equidistant at all points from a datum plane or axis.

PERPENDICULARITY: ⊥

The condition of a surface, line, or axis, which is at a right angle (90°) from a datum plane or datum axis.

PROFILE OF ANY LINE: ⌒

The condition limiting the amount of profile variation along a line element of a feature.

PROFILE OF ANY SURFACE: ⌓

Similar to profile of any line, but this condition relates to the entire surface.

PROJECTED TOLERANCE ZONE: Ⓟ

A zone applied to a hole in which a pin, stud, screw, etc. is to be inserted. It controls the perpendicularity of any hole, which controls the fastener's position; this will allow the adjoining parts to be assembled.

REGARDLESS OF FEATURE SIZE: Ⓢ

A condition in which the tolerance of form or condition must be met, regardless of where the feature is within its size tolerance.

RUNOUT: ↗

The maximum permissible surface variation during one complete revolution of the part about the datum axis. This is usually detected with a dial indicator.

STRAIGHTNESS: —

The condition in which a feature of a part must be a straight line.

SYMMETRY: =

A condition wherein a part or feature has the same contour and sides of a central plane.

TRUE POSITION: ⊕

This term denotes the theoretically exact position of a feature.

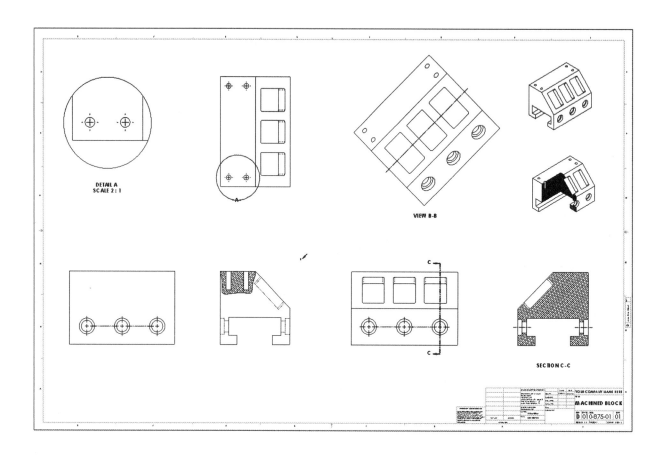

DETAIL A
SCALE 2 : 1

VIEW B-B

SECTION C-C

CHAPTER 17

Detailing

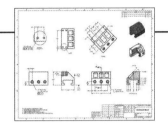

Detailing a drawing
Machined Block Details

- After the drawing views are all laid out, they will be detailed with dimensions, tolerances, datums, surface finishes, notes, etc.

- To fully maintain the associations between the model dimensions and the drawing dimensions, the Model Items options should be used. If a dimension is changed in either modes (from the solid model or in the drawing) they will both be updated automatically.

- When a dimension appears in gray color it means that the dimension is being added in the drawing and it does not exist in the model. This dimension is called a Reference dimension.

- SOLIDWORKS uses different colors for different types of dimensions such as:
    * Black dimensions = Sketch dimensions (driving).
    * Gray dimensions = Reference dimensions (driven).
    * Blue dimensions = Feature dimensions (driving).
    * Magenta dimensions = Dimensions linked to Design Tables (driving).

- For certain types of holes, the Hole-Callout option should be used to accurately call out the hole type, depth, diameter, etc...

- The Geometric Tolerance option helps control the accuracy and the precision of the features. Both Tolerance and Precision options can be easily created and controlled from the FeatureManager tree.

- This chapter discusses most of the tools used in detailing an engineering drawing, including importing dimensions from the model, and adding the GD&T to the drawing (Geometric Dimensions and Tolerancing).

Machined Block
Detailing

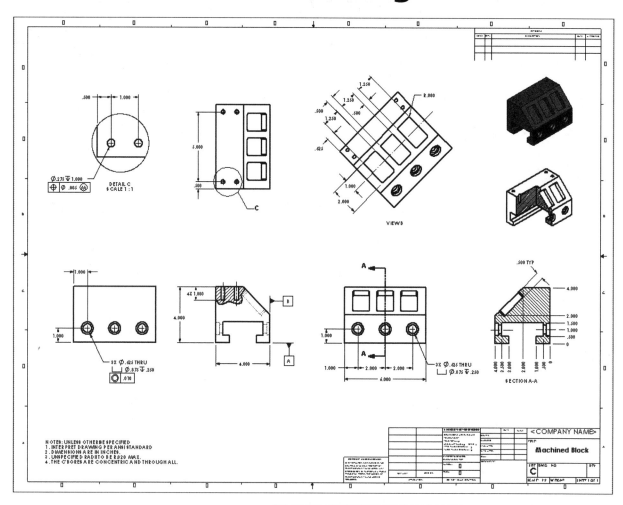

Dimensioning Standards: **ANSI**

Units: **INCHES** – 3 Decimals

Third Angle Projection

Tools Needed:

 Model Dimensions

 Geometric Tolerance

Datum Feature Symbol

 Surface Finish

 Hole Callout

Note

---

1. Opening a drawing document:

- Click **File / Open** and open the previous drawing document **Machined Block**.

2. Inserting dimensions from the model:

- Dimensions previously created in the model will be inserted into the drawing.

- Click the **Right** drawing view's border and select **Model Items** on the Annotation tool tab.

- For Source/Destination, select **Entire Model**.

- Under Dimensions, enable **Marked for Drawings**, **Hole Wizard Locations** and **Eliminate Duplicates**.

- Under Options, select **Use Dimension Placement in Sketch** and click **OK**

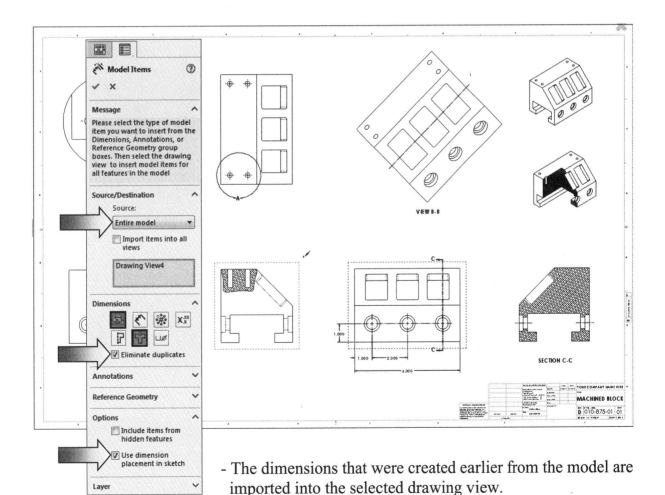

- The dimensions that were created earlier from the model are imported into the selected drawing view.

3. Rearranging the new dimensions: Zoom in  on the Right drawing view.

- Keep only the hole location dimensions and delete the others. The counterbore hole callouts will be added later.

- Use the Smart Dimension tool and add any missing dimensions manually.

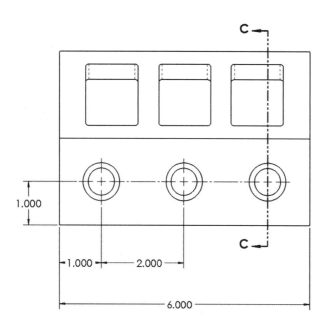

Note:

Center Marks are added automatically in the newer releases of SOLIDWORKS.

4. Inserting dimensions to the Section view:

- Select the Section view's border.

- Click 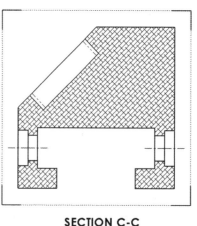 or select **Insert / Model Items**.

- The previous settings (arrow) should still be selected.

- Click **OK** ✅.

- The dimensions from the model are imported into the Section view.

- Some of the dimensions are missing due to the use of the relations in the model.

SECTION C-C

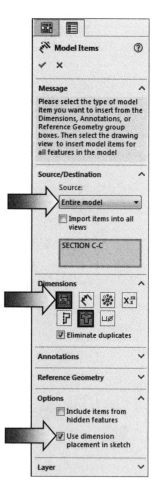

- Use the Smart Dimension tool to add any missing dimensions.

- If any of these dimensions are changed, both the model and the drawing views will also change accordingly.

- Delete the dimensions indicated; they will be added to the auxiliary view later.

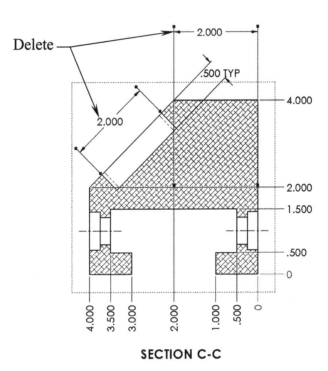

SECTION C-C

5. Repeating step 4:

- Insert the model's dimensions into the Top drawing view.

- Rearrange the dimensions and make them evenly spaced either manually or by using the options in the Align toolbar (View / Toolbars / Align).

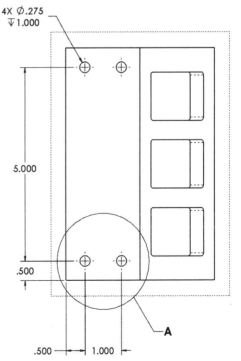

6. Adding dimensions to the Auxiliary view:

- Add any missing dimensions to the drawing view using the Smart Dimension command.

NOTE: _To add the Centerline symbol, select the Note command from the Annotation tab, click the Add Symbol button, then select the Centerline option from the list._

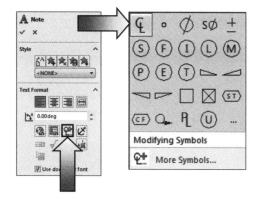

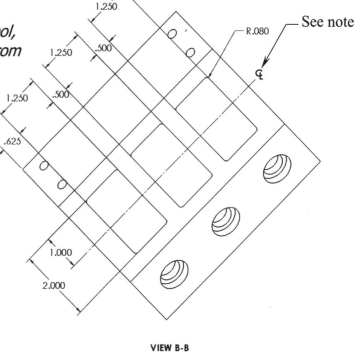

See note

R.080

VIEW B-B

1.250
1.250 .500
1.250 .500
.625
1.000
2.000

7. Adding the Center Marks:

(Skip this step if the marks are already added.)

- Zoom in on the Detail View.

- Select the **Center Mark** command on the Annotation tool tab.

- Click on the edge of each hole. A Center Mark is added in the center of each one.

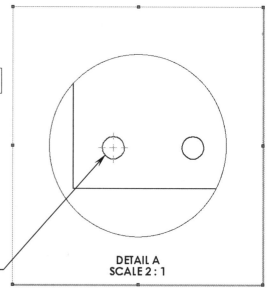

DETAIL A
SCALE 2 : 1

Click on the circular edge to add Center Mark (skip this step if the center marks are already added).

8. Adding center marks to the other holes:

- Click the **Center Mark** command 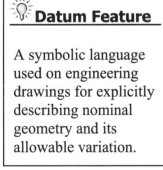 once again.

- Add a center mark to other holes by clicking on their circular edges.

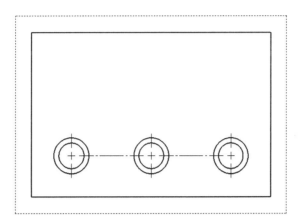

9. Adding the Datum Feature Symbols:

- Click 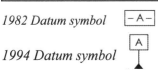 or select **Insert / Annotations / Datum Feature Symbol**.

- Select edge 1 and place **Datum A** as shown.

- Select edge 2 and place **Datum B** as shown.

💡 **Datum Feature**

A symbolic language used on engineering drawings for explicitly describing nominal geometry and its allowable variation.

1982 Datum symbol   – A –

1994 Datum symbol   A

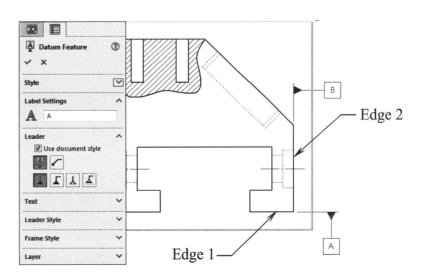

Edge 2

Edge 1

Datum Reference & Geometric Tolerance Examples

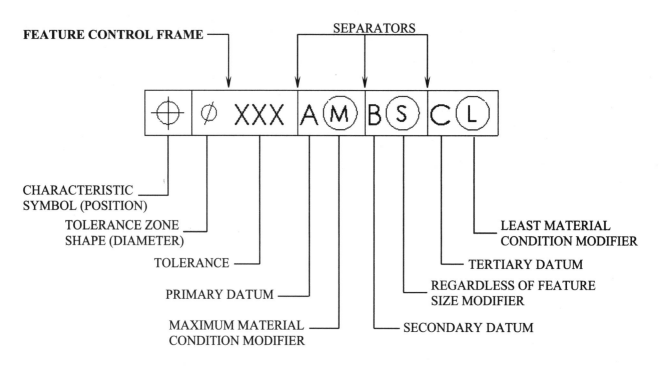

FEATURE CONTROL FRAME

SEPARATORS

CHARACTERISTIC SYMBOL (POSITION)

TOLERANCE ZONE SHAPE (DIAMETER)

TOLERANCE

PRIMARY DATUM

MAXIMUM MATERIAL CONDITION MODIFIER

SECONDARY DATUM

REGARDLESS OF FEATURE SIZE MODIFIER

TERTIARY DATUM

LEAST MATERIAL CONDITION MODIFIER

💡 FEATURE CONTROL FRAMES

A feature control frame symbolizes the tolerance requirements for a feature of a part. It can be added to a drawing note for a feature tolerance, or can be specified by running a leader line from the feature control frame directly to the feature. The box may be attached to an extension line from the feature or it can be placed on a dimension line. A feature can have more than one feature control frame, depending on its requirements.

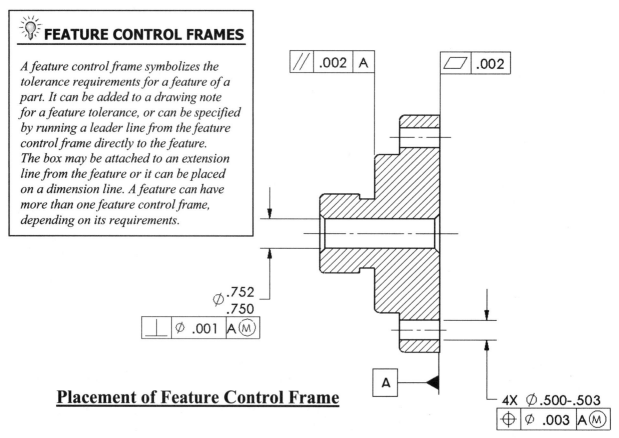

Placement of Feature Control Frame

10. Adding hole specifications using the Hole-Callout:

- Click 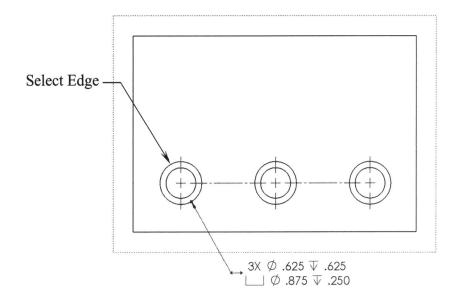 or select **Insert / Annotations / Hole Callout**.

- Select the edge of the Counterbore and place the callout below the hole.

- A callout is added as a reference dimension (gray color); it includes the diameter and the depth of the hole and the Counterbore.

Select Edge ⟶

3X ⌀ .625 ▽ .625
⌴ ⌀ .875 ▽ .250

11. Adding Geometric Tolerances:

- Geometric dimensioning and tolerancing (GD&T) is used to define the nominal (theoretically perfect) geometry of parts and assemblies to define the allowable variation in form and possibly size of individual features and to define the allowable variation between features. Dimensioning and tolerancing and geometric dimensioning and tolerancing specifications are used as follows:

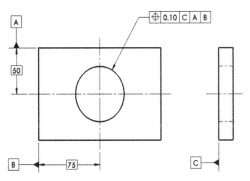

* Dimensioning specifications define the nominal as-modeled or as-intended geometry. One example is a basic dimension.

* Tolerancing specifications define the allowable variation for the form and possibly the size of individual features and the allowable variation in orientation and location between features. Two examples are linear dimensions and feature control frames using a datum reference.

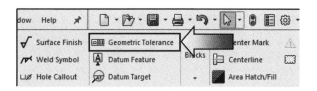

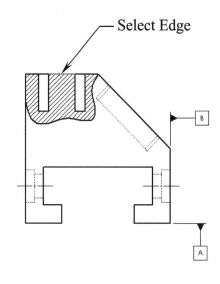

Select Edge

- Zoom in on the Front drawing view.

- Select the upper edge as shown.

- Click or select **Insert / Annotations / Geometric Tolerance**.

- The Geometric Tolerance Property appears.

- Click the **Symbol Library** dropdown list .

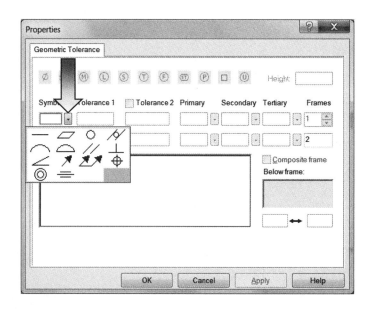

- Select **Parallelism** from the **Symbol** library list.

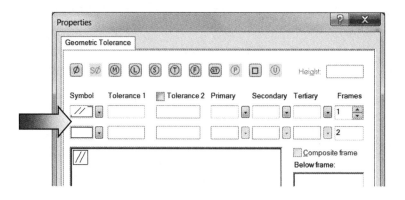

- Enter **.010** under Tolerance 1.

- Enter **A** under Primary reference datum (arrow).

- Click **OK** [OK] .

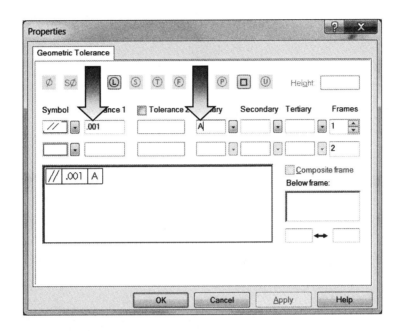

12. Align the Geometric Tolerance:

- Drag the Control Frame towards the left side until it snaps to the horizontal alignment with the upper edge, then release the mouse button.

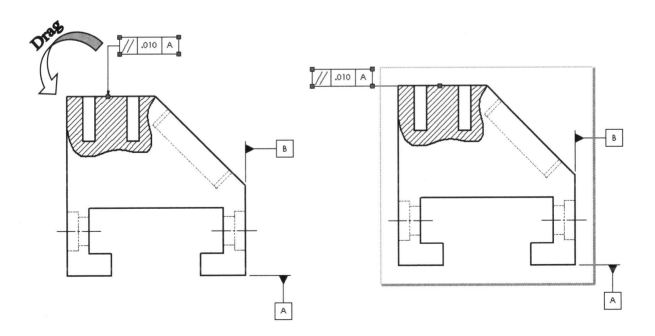

13. Attaching the Geometric Tolerance to the Driving dimension:

- Select the Counterbore dimension. By pre-selecting a dimension, the geometric-tolerance will automatically be attached to this dimension.

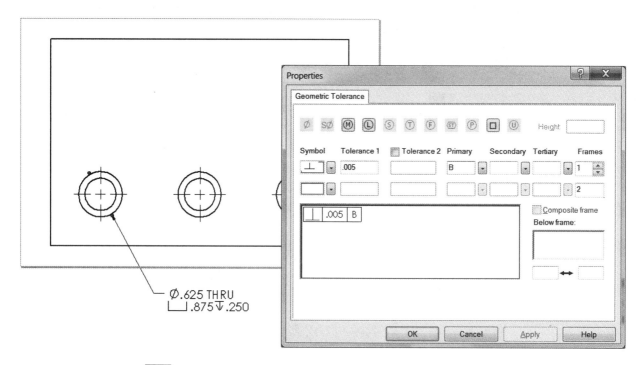

- Click or select **Insert / Annotation / Geometric Tolerance**.

- Click the **Symbol Library** dropdown list ▾ .

- Select **Perpendicularity** ⊥ from the Symbol library list.

- Enter **.005** under Tolerance 1.

- Enter **B** under Secondary reference datum.

- Click **OK** [OK] .

- The Geometric Tolerance Control Frame is attached to the counterbore dimension.

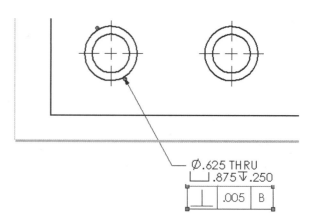

14. Adding Tolerance/Precision to dimensions:

- Select the dimension **.500** (circled).

- The dimension properties tree pops up; select **Bilateral** under the Tolerance/
Precision section (arrow).

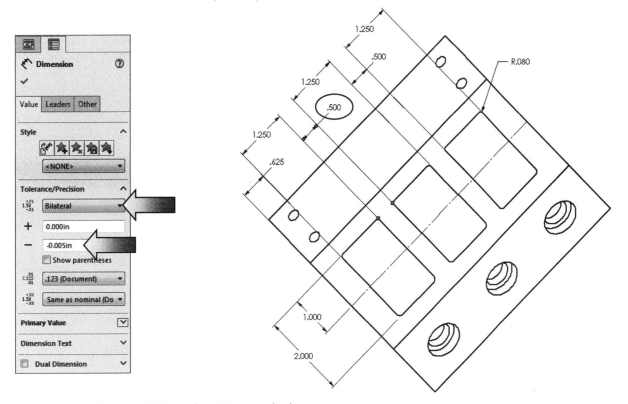

VIEW B

- Enter **.000 in**. for Max variation.

- Enter **.005 in**. for Min variation.

- Click **OK** ✅.

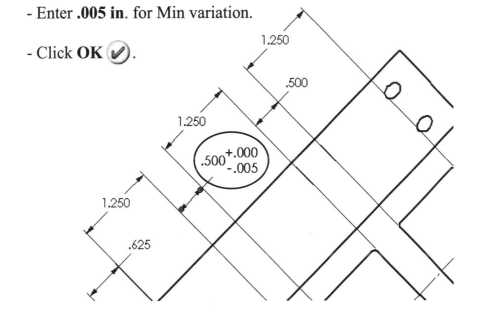

15. Adding Symmetric tolerance to a dimension:

- Click the width dimension **1.250** (circled).

- Select **Symmetric** under Tolerance/Precision list (arrow).

- Enter **.003 in**. for Maximum Variation.

- Click **OK** ✅.

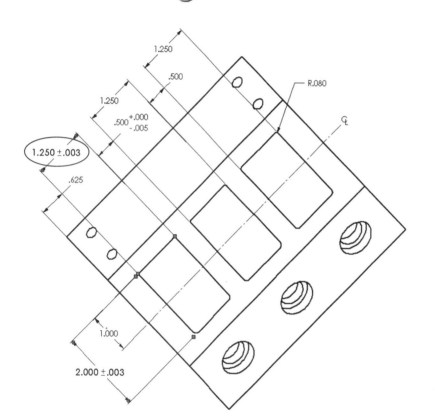

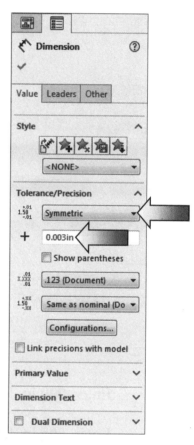

- Repeat step 15 and add a Symmetric tolerance to the height dimension: (**2.000 ±.003**).

- For practice purposes, add other types of tolerance to some other dimensions such as Min – Max, Basic, Fit, etc..

16. Adding Surface Finish callouts:

- Surface finish is an industrial process that alters the surface of a manufactured item to achieve a certain property. Finishing processes such as machining, grinding, or buffing may be applied to improve appearance and other surface flaws and control the surface friction.

- Zoom in on the Section C-C.

- Select the <u>edge</u> as indicated.

- Click the **Surface Finish** command on the Annotation tool tab.

- Choose **Machining-Required** under Symbol.

- Under **Maximum Roughness**, enter **125**.

- Under Leader, select **Bent leader.**

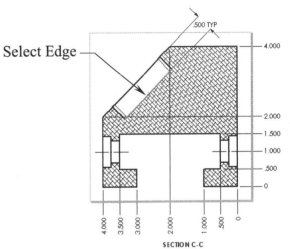

SECTION C-C

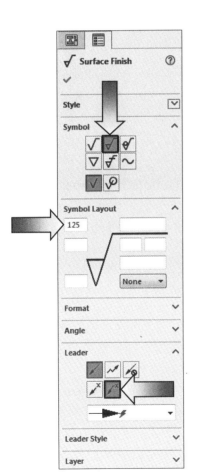

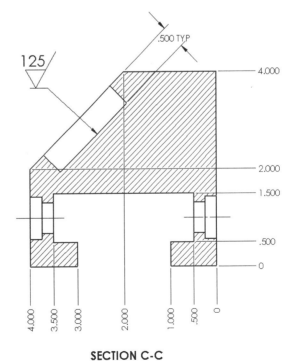

SECTION C-C

- Click **OK**.

17. Adding non-parametric callouts:

- Click **Smart Dimension**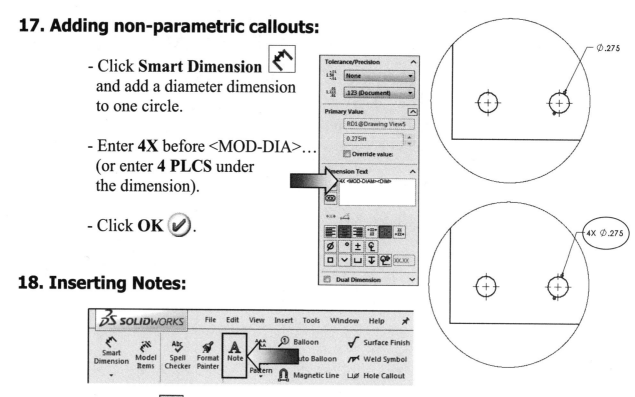
  and add a diameter dimension
  to one circle.

- Enter **4X** before <MOD-DIA>...
  (or enter **4 PLCS** under
  the dimension).

- Click **OK**.

18. Inserting Notes:

- Zoom in on the upper left side of the drawing.

- Click Note on the **Annotations** tool tab.

- Click in upper left area, approximately as shown, and a note box appears.

NOTE: *To lock the note to the sheet, right click in the drawing and select*
Lock-Sheet-Focus.

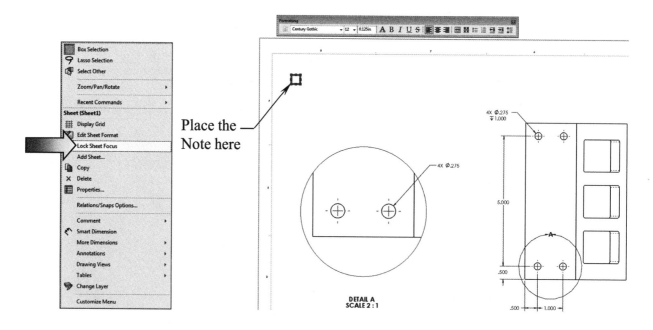

Place the Note here

DETAIL A
SCALE 2 : 1

- Enter the notes below:

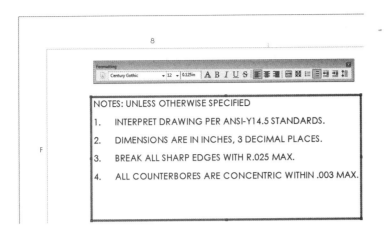

- Click **OK** when you are finished typing.

19. Changing document's font:

- Double click anywhere inside the note area to activate it.

- Highlight the entire note and select the following:

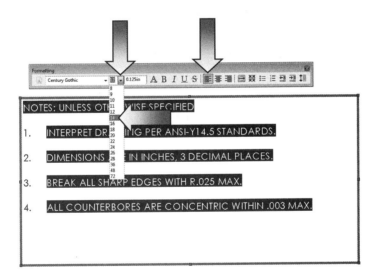

- Font: **Century Gothic**.

- Point size: **14**.

- Alignment: **Left**.

- Click **OK**.

20. Saving your work:

- Select **File / Save As**.

- Enter **Machined Block Detailing** for the name of the file.

- Click **Save**.

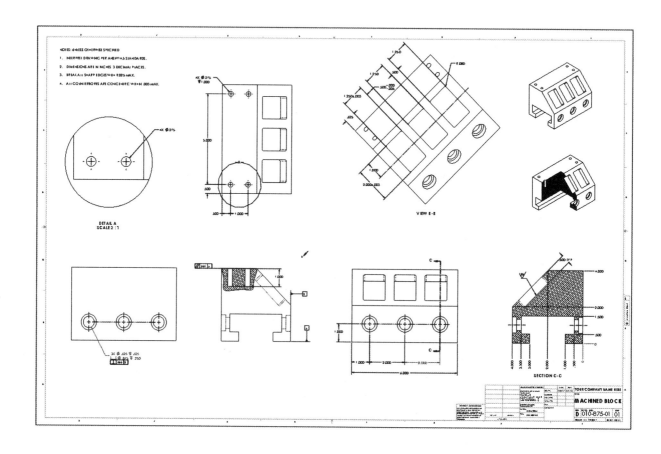

Questions for Review

Drawing & Detailing

1. Existing text in the title block can be edited when the Sheet-Format is active.
    a. True
    b. False

2. The standard drawing views can be created using the following method:
    a. Use Insert / Drawing views menu
    b. Use the Model-View command
    c. Drag and drop from an open window
    d. All of the above

3. View alignments can be broken or re-aligned.
    a. True
    b. False

4. The Detail-View scale cannot be changed or controlled locally.
    a. True
    b. False

5. The Projected view command projects and creates the Top, Bottom, Left, and Right views from another view.
    a. True
    b. False

6. To create an Auxiliary view, an edge has to be selected, not a face or a surface.
    a. True
    b. False

7. Only a single line can be used to create a Section view. The System doesn't support a multi-line section option.
    a. True
    b. False

8. Hidden lines in a drawing view can be turned ON / OFF locally and globally.
    a. True
    b. False

9. Configurations created in the model cannot be shown in the drawings.
    a. True
    b. False

9. FALSE
7. FALSE   8. TRUE
5. TRUE   6. TRUE
3. TRUE   4. FALSE
1. TRUE   2. D

Exercise: Detailing I

1. <u>Create</u> the **part** <u>and</u> the **drawing** as shown.

2. The Counter-Bore dimensions are measured from the Top planar surface.

3. Dimensions are in inches, 3 decimal places.

4. The part is symmetrical about the Top reference plane.
(To create the "Back-Isometric-View" from the model: hold the Shift key and push the Up arrow key twice. This rotates the part 180°, and then insert this view to the drawing using the **Current-View** option.)

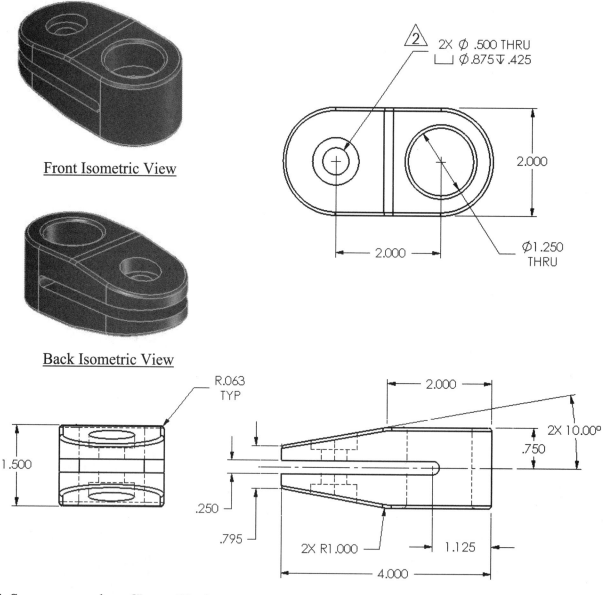

Front Isometric View

Back Isometric View

5. Save your work as **Clamp Block**.

Exercise: Detailing II

1. <u>Open</u> the part named **Base Mount Block** from the Training Files folder.
2. Create a drawing using the provided details.
3. Create the Virtual-Sharps where needed prior to adding the Ordinate Dimensions.
   (To add the Virtual Sharps: Hold the Control key, select the 2 lines, and click the Sketch-Point command.)

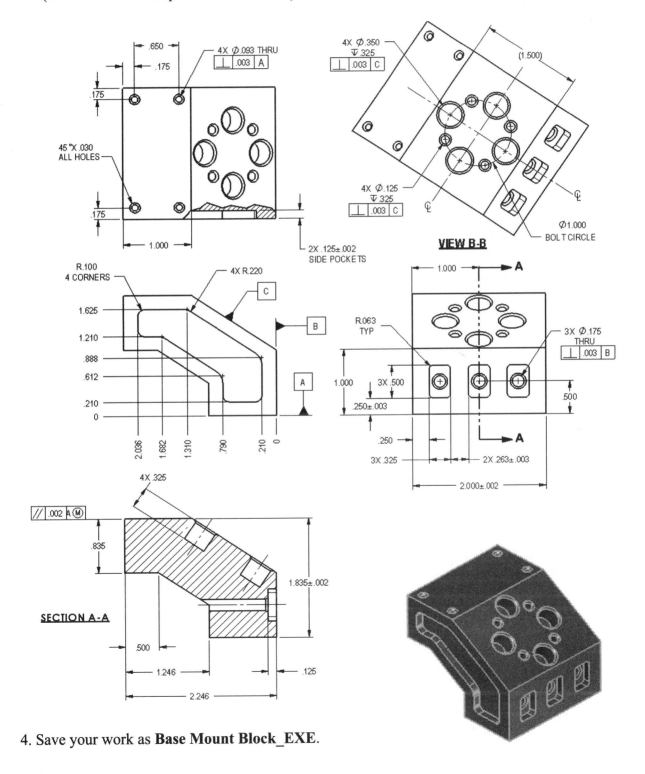

4. Save your work as **Base Mount Block_EXE**.

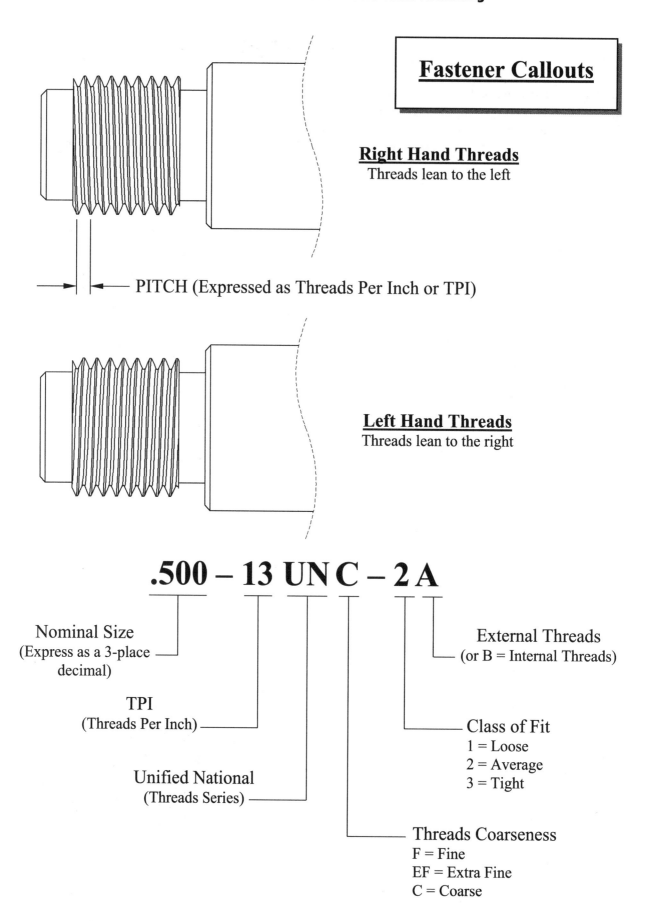

Fastener Callouts

Right Hand Threads
Threads lean to the left

Left Hand Threads
Threads lean to the right

PITCH (Expressed as Threads Per Inch or TPI)

.500 – 13 UN C – 2 A

Nominal Size
(Express as a 3-place decimal)

TPI
(Threads Per Inch)

Unified National
(Threads Series)

External Threads
(or B = Internal Threads)

Class of Fit
1 = Loose
2 = Average
3 = Tight

Threads Coarseness
F = Fine
EF = Extra Fine
C = Coarse

Thread Nomenclature

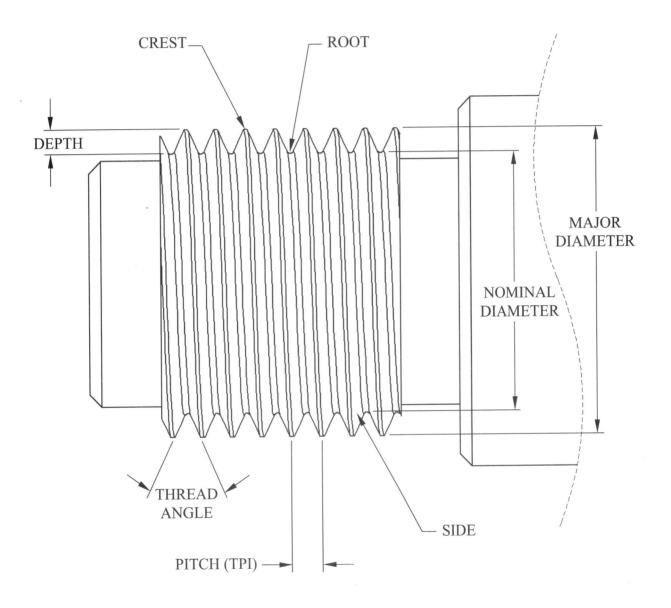

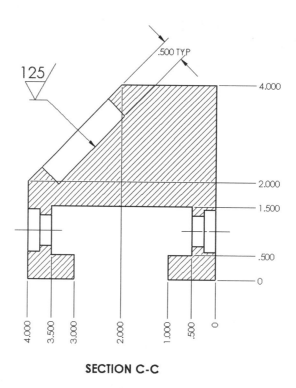

SECTION C-C

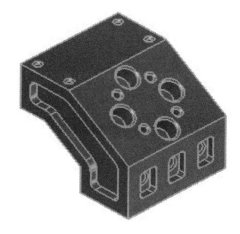

CHAPTER 18

Sheet Metal Drawings

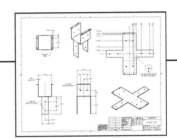

Sheet Metal Drawings
Post Cap

- When a *sheet metal Drawing* is made from a *sheet metal Part*, the SOLIDWORKS software automatically creates a Flat Pattern view to use in conjunction with the Model View command.

- Any drawing views can be toggled to show the flattened stage along with the bend lines. By accessing the Properties of the view, you can change from Default (Folded) to Flattened.

- By default, the Bend Lines are visible in the Flat Pattern but the Bend-Regions are not. To show the bend-regions, open the sheet metal part and right click the **Flat-Pattern** in the FeatureManager design tree, select **Edit Feature** and clear **Merge Faces**. You may have to rebuild the drawing to see the tangent edges.

- Both of the Folded and Flat Pattern drawing views can be shown on the same drawing sheet if needed. The dimensions and annotations can then be added to define the views.

- Changes done to the Sheet Metal part <u>**will**</u> reflect in the drawing views and the drawing itself can also be changed to update the sheet metal part as well. To prevent this from happening several options are available; refer to the Online Help from within the SOLIDWORKS software for more details.

- This exercise will guide you through the basics of creating a sheet metal drawing and the use of the Default/Flat-Pattern configurations.

Post Cap
Sheet Metal Drawings

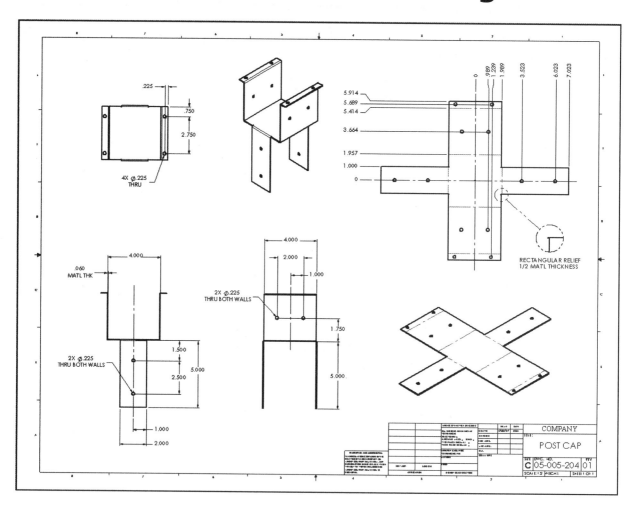

Dimensioning Standards: **ANSI**
Units: **INCHES** – 3 Decimals

Third Angle Projection

Tools Needed:

 New Drawing

 Model View

 Detail View

 Model Items

 Vertical Ordinate

 Horizontal Ordinate

1. Starting a new drawing:

- Select **File / New / Drawing**
  and click **OK**.

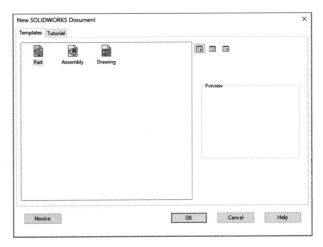

NOTE: _If you have already created and_
saved a template, you can browse
and select the same template
for this drawing.

- Click the **Cancel** button (arrow) to exit the insert part mode.
  The drawing paper size, drawing view scale, and the
  Projection angle must be set first.

- If the Sheet Properties dialog does not appear, right click in
  the drawing and select Properties.

- Set **Scale** to **1:2** and set **Type of Projection** to **Third Angle**.

- Select **C-Landscape** sheet size.

- Enable **Display Sheet Format** and click **OK** [OK] .

- Go to **Tools / Options** and
  change the **Units** to
  IPS (Inch / Pound /
  Second).

(The document units can
also be changed at the
bottom right corner of
the screen.)

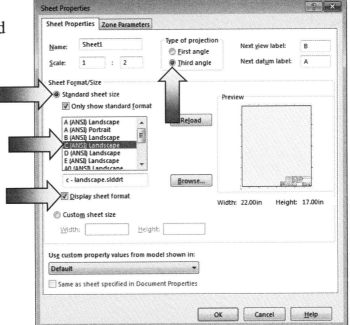

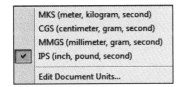

2. Creating the 3 Standard Views:

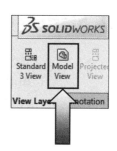

- Select **the Model View** command from the View Layout tab.

- Click the **Browse** Browse... button from the Training Files folder, and locate and open the part named **Post Cap**.

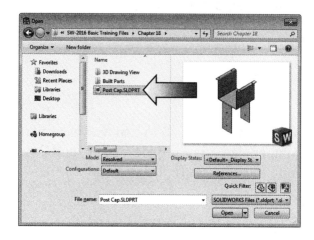

- After a part is selected SOLIDWORKS automatically switches to the Projected View mode.

- Start by placing the Front view approximately as shown and then create the other 3 views as labeled.

- Click **OK** to stop the projection.

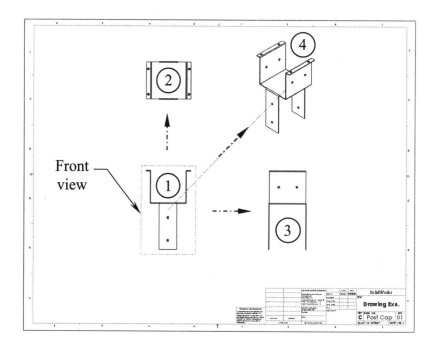

3. Rearranging the drawing views:

- Rearrange the drawing views to the approx. positions by dragging their borders. A flat-pattern view will be placed on the right side of the drawing.

4. Creating the Flat Pattern drawing view:

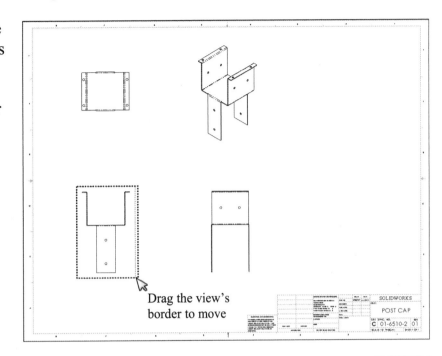

Drag the view's border to move

*NOTE: Bend Notes must be turned off <u>prior</u> to creating the Flat Pattern view: (**Tools / Option / Document-Properties / Sheet Metal**).*

- Select the **Model View** command 🖼, click Next ➡, select the **Flat-Pattern** view (arrow) from the list and place it approximately as shown.

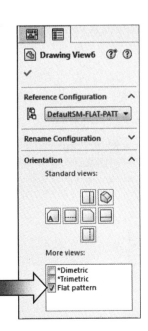

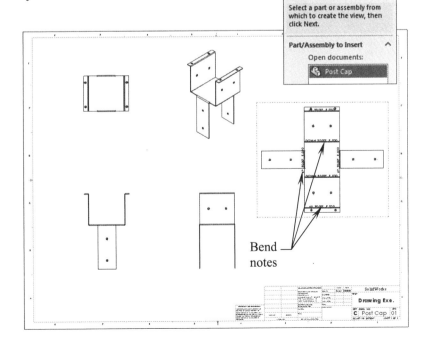

Bend notes

5. Creating a Detail view:

- Click the **Detail View** command ⟨A⟩ and sketch a Circle on the lower right Corner, approximately as shown. Also add 2 centerlines.

- Use the **Connected** option and **Custom Scale** of **2:1** (arrows).

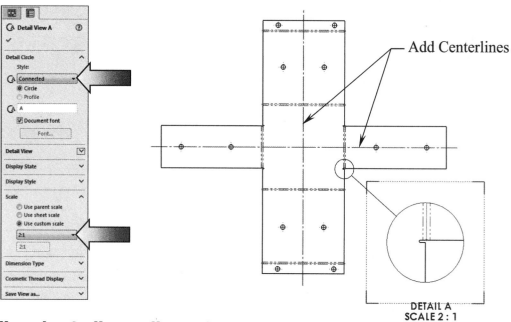

Add Centerlines

DETAIL A
SCALE 2 : 1

6. Adding the Ordinate dimensions:

- Click the drop arrow below **Smart Dimension** to access its options; select **Horizontal Ordinate Dimension** (arrow).

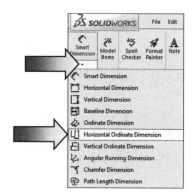

NOTE: *Ordinate dimensions are a group of dimensions measured from a zero point. When adding them in a drawing, they become reference dimensions and their values cannot be changed.*

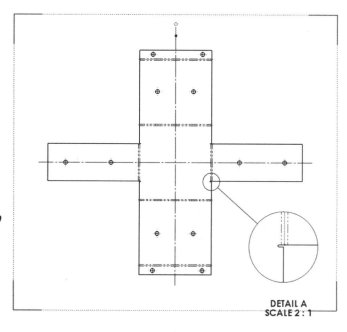

DETAIL A
SCALE 2 : 1

- Starting at the Vertical Centerline, add the Horizontal Ordinate dimensions as shown here.

- Click the drop down arrow under Smart Dimension and Select **Vertical Ordinate Dimension**.

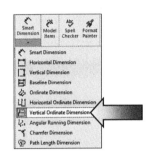

- Add the Vertical Ordinate dimensions as shown in the drawing view above.

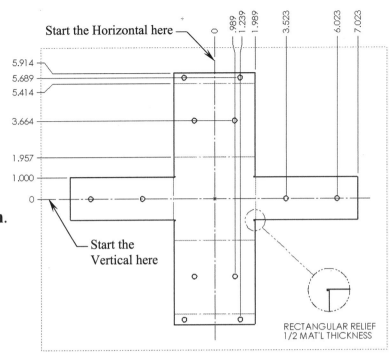

(Change the Detail View label to Rectangular Relief ½ Mat'l Thickness).

7. Adding the Model dimensions:

- Select the Front view's border to activate it.

- On the **Annotation** tab, click the **Model Items** button, and select **Entire Model** and **Eliminate Duplicates**.

- Click **OK** ✅.

- Modify the dimensions and add the depth and the thickness callouts as shown.

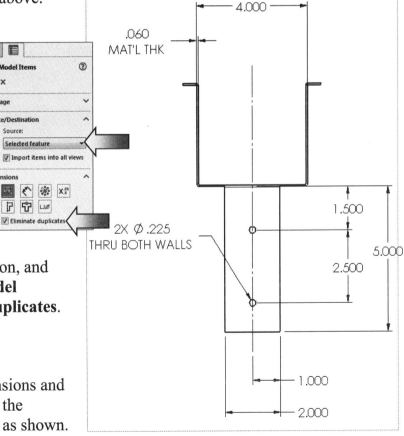

- Repeat step 6 and add the Model Dimensions to the Right drawing view.

- Add the annotations below the dimension text (circled).

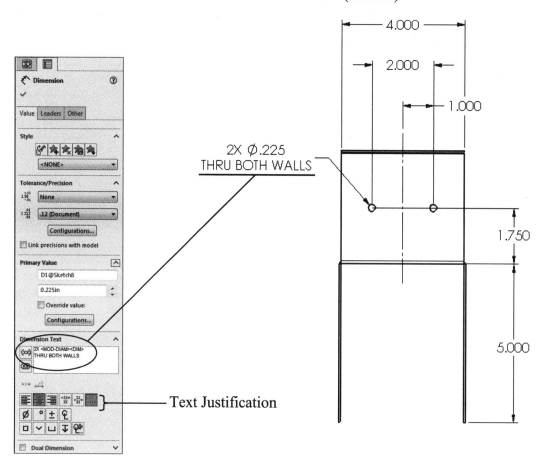

Text Justification

2X Ø.225
THRU BOTH WALLS

- Continue adding the Model Dimensions to the Top drawing view.

- Add the annotations as needed.

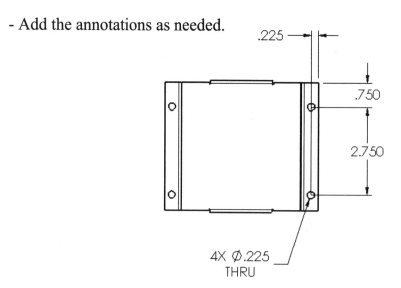

4X Ø.225
THRU

8. Creating the Isometric Flat Pattern view:

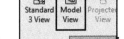

- Click the **Model View** command from the View Layout tab.

- Click the **Next button** ⊕ , select the Isometric View from the menu and place it below the flat-pattern view.

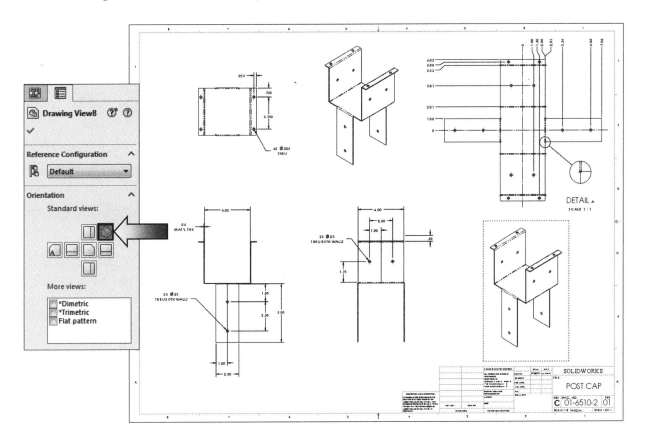

- A drawing view can also be copied and pasted using Ctrl+C and Ctrl+V.

- Under the Reference Configuration section change the **Default** configuration to **SM-Flat-Pattern** configuration (arrow).

- Click **OK** [OK] .

- The flat pattern of the sheet metal part appears. The bend lines and bend regions are also visible in this view.

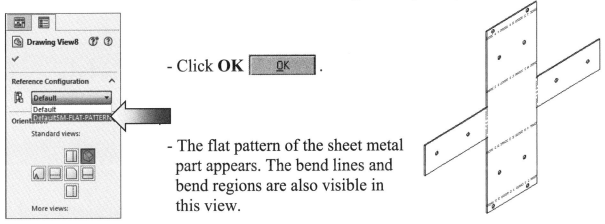

9. Showing /Hiding the Bend Lines:

- Click the DrawingManager tab (arrow), scroll down the tree and expand the last drawing view in the FeatureManager tree (click the **+** symbol).

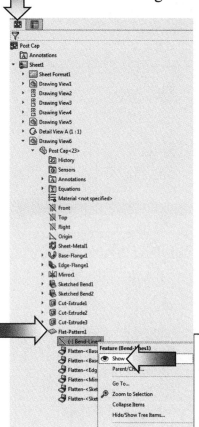

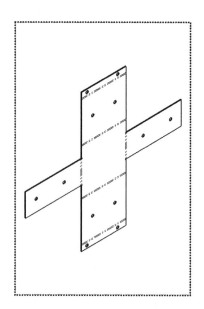

- Expand the feature Flat-Pattern1.

- Right click on Bend-Lines1 and select **Show**.

- The Bend Lines are now visible in the drawing view.

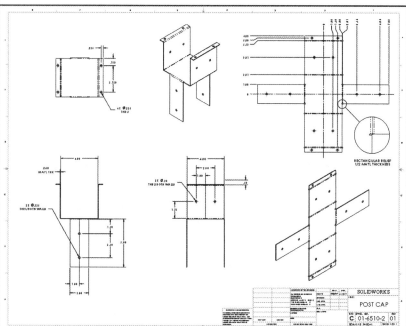

10. Saving your work:

- Select **File / Save As**.

- Enter **Post Cap.slddrw** for the name of the file.

- Click **Save**.

CHAPTER 18 (cont.)

e-Drawings

eDrawing & 3D Drawing View
Soft-lock Assembly

eDrawing:

- eDrawing is one of the most convenient tools in SOLIDWORKS to create, share, and view your 2D or 3D designs.

- The eDrawing Professional allows the user to create eDrawing markup files (***.markup**) that have markups, such as text comments and geometric elements.

- With eDrawing 2016 and SOLIDWORKS® 2016, you can create an eDrawing from any CAD model or assembly from programs like AutoCAD®, Pro/E®, and others.

- The following types of eDrawing files are supported:
    * 3D part files (***.eprt**)
    * 3D assembly files (***.easm**)
    * 2D drawing files (***.edrw**)

3D Drawing View:

- The 3D drawing view mode lets you rotate a drawing view out of its plane so you can see components or edges obscured by other entities. When you rotate a drawing view in 3D drawing view mode, you can save the orientation as a new view orientation.

- 3D drawing view mode is particularly helpful when you want to select an obscured edge for the depth of a broken-out section view. Additionally, while in 3D drawing view mode, you can create a new orientation for another model view. 3D drawing view mode is not available for detail, broken, crop, empty, or detached views.

Soft-Lock Assembly
SOLIDWORKS e-Drawing & 3D Drawing View

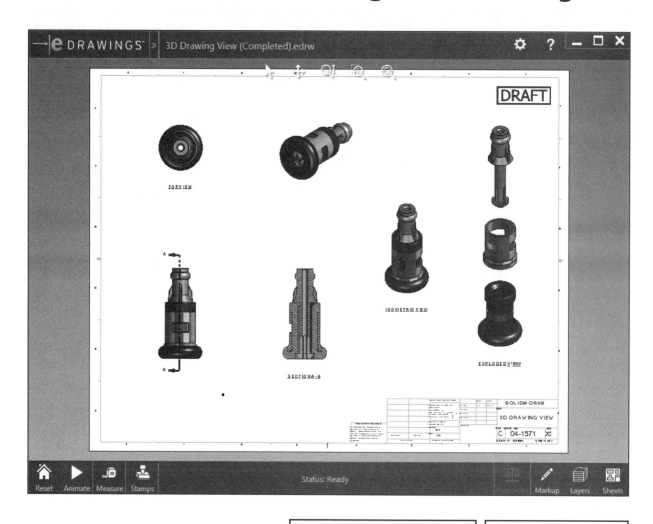

Dimensioning Standards: **ANSI**	Third Angle Projection
Units: **INCHES** – 3 Decimals	

Tools Needed:

 SOLIDWORKS e-drawing   Play Animation   Stop Animation & returns to full screen

 Rotate View   3D Drawing View

1. Opening an existing drawing:

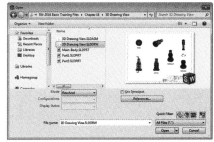

- Click **File / Open**.

- Select **3D Drawing View.slddrw** from the Training Files folder and open it.

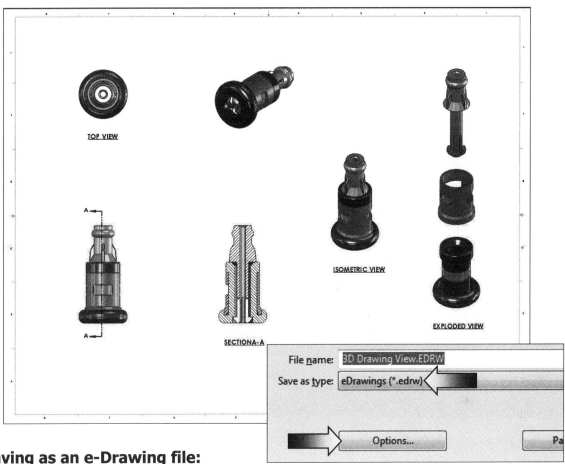

TOP VIEW

ISOMETRIC VIEW

A

A

SECTIONA-A

EXPLODED VIEW

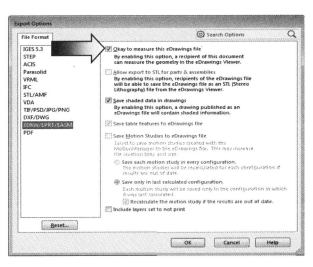

File name: 3D Drawing View.EDRW

Save as type: eDrawings (*.edrw)

Options...

Pa

2. Saving as an e-Drawing file:

- Select **File / Save As.**

- Change the file format to **eDrawing** (*.edrw).

- Enter **3D Drawing View** for the name of the file.

- Click the **Options** button and enable **OK to Measure**.

- Click **Save**.

3. Working with eDrawing:

- Exit the SOLIDWORKS application and launch the **e-Drawing** program .

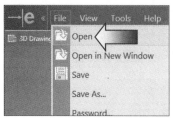

- Click **Open** .

- Select the
  document **3D-
  Drawing View
  .edrw** and click
  Open.

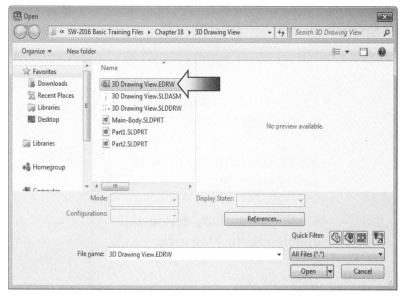

- The previously saved drawing is opened in the eDrawing window. Click the eDrawing **Options** button to see all available options.

The eDrawing Options:

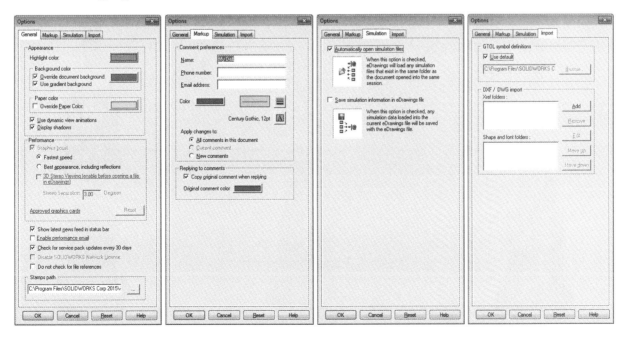

The Markup toolbar:

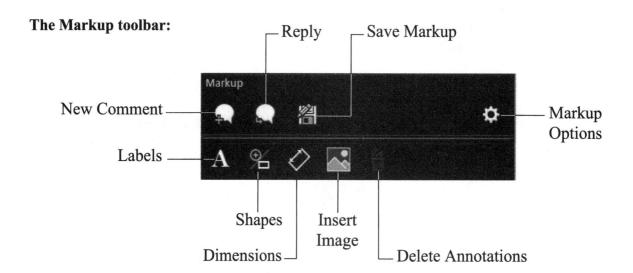

New Comment ——

Reply

Save Markup

Markup Options

Labels ——

Shapes

Dimensions

Insert Image

Delete Annotations

4. Playing the Animation:

- Click **Animate** (at the bottom left corner of the screen).

- The eDrawing animates the drawing views based on the order that was created in SOLIDWORKS.

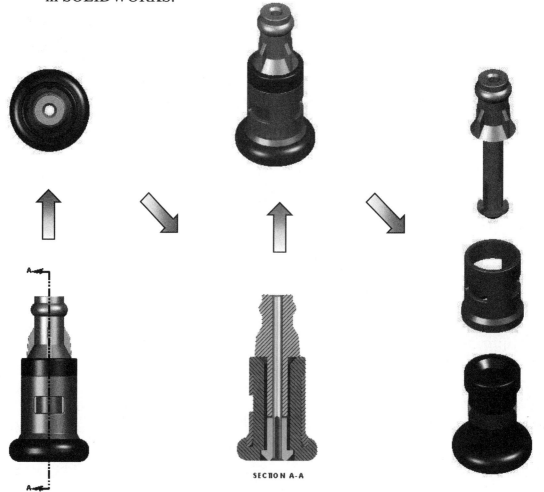

SECTION A-A

- Click **Reset** ⌂ to stop the animation.

- The Reset command also returns the eDrawing back to its full page mode.

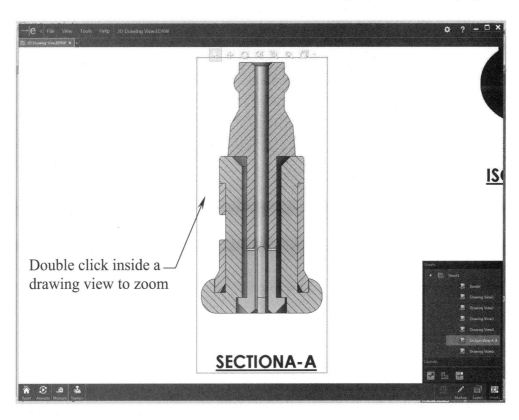

Double click inside a drawing view to zoom

SECTIONA-A

- Double click inside the Section view to zoom and fit it to the screen.

5. Adding the markup notes:

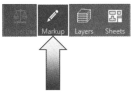

- Click the **Labels** button and select the **Cloud With-Leader** command (2nd arrow).

- Click on the **Edge** of the bottom bore hole and place the blank note on the lower left side.

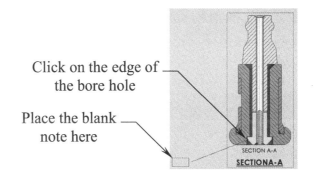

Click on the edge of the bore hole

Place the blank note here

SECTION A-A

SECTIONA-A

- Enter the note:
**Increase the Bore
Diameter by .015"**.

- Click **OK** 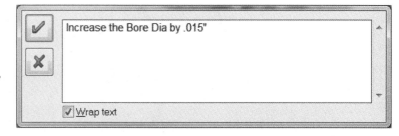.

- Zoom out a little to
see the entire note.

- Click inside the
cloud; there are 4
handle points to
move or adjust the
width of the cloud.

- Adjust the cloud
by dragging one
of the handle points.

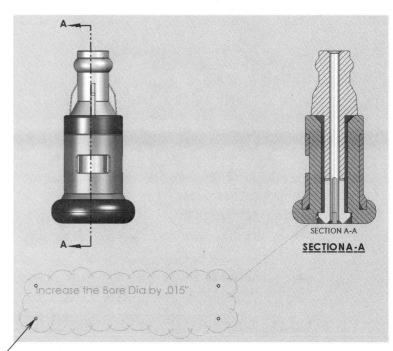

Drag handle point ⎯

6. Adding a "Stamp":

- Click the **Stamp**
button at the bottom
left corner.

- Locate the
DRAFT
stamp from the list
and drag it to the
upper right corner
of the eDrawing.

- Drag one of the
handles to resize
the stamp.

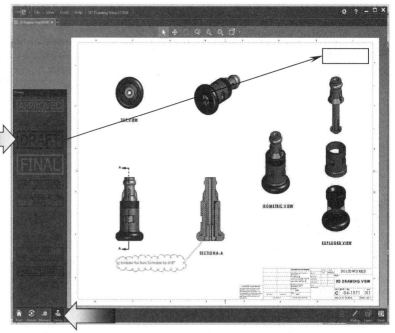

- Click the **Reset** button 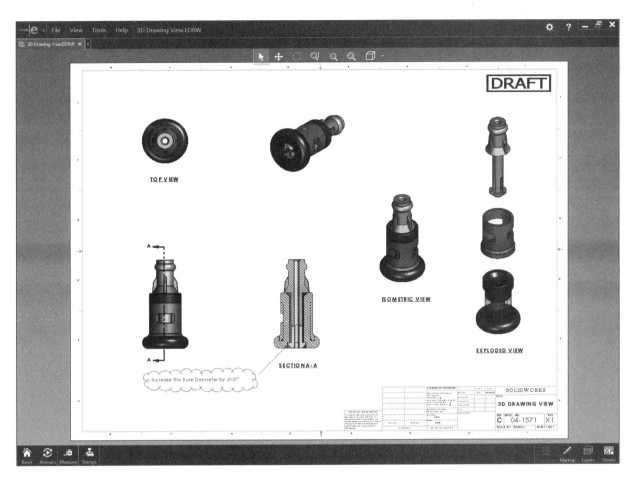 to return to the full drawing mode.

7. Saving as Executable file type:

- Click **File / Save As**.

- Select **eDrawing Executable Files (*.exe)** from the Save As Type menu.

- Click **Save**.

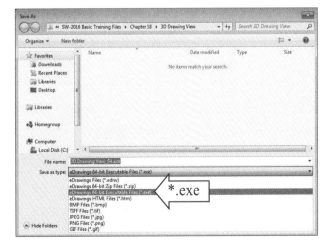

NOTES:

The .exe files are much larger in file size than the standard .edrw. because the eDrawing-viewer is embedded in the file.

The .edrw files are smaller in file size but required eDrawing Viewer or the eDrawing program itself to view.

Continue...

SOLIDWORKS 2016 - 3D Drawing View

8. Returning to the SOLIDWORKS Program:

- Switch back to the previous SOLIDWORKS drawing (press Alt+ Tab).

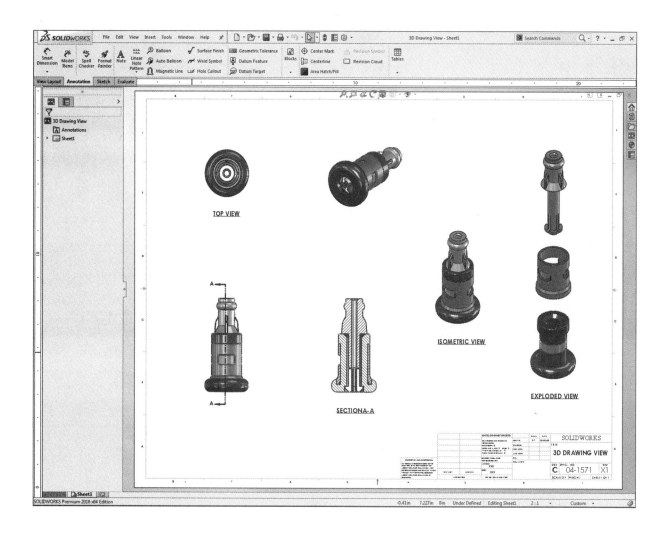

- This second half of the lesson discusses the use of the 3D Drawing View command, one of the unique options that allows a flat drawing view to be manipulated and rotated in 3D to make selections of the hidden entities.

- 3D drawing view mode is particularly helpful when you want to select an obscured edge for the depth of a broken-out section view. Additionally, while in 3D drawing view mode, you can create a new orientation for another model view.

9. Using the 3D Drawing View command:

- Create a new Front view and then click the drawing view's border to activate it.

- Click **3D Drawing View** icon 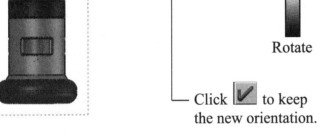 from the View toolbar (or under the **View / Modify** menus).

- Select the **Rotate** tool and rotate the Front drawing to a different position approximately as shown.

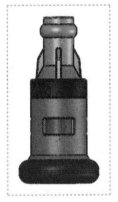

Front Drawing View

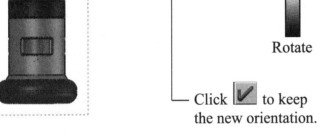

Rotate

Click to keep the new orientation.

3D Drawing View pop-up toolbar

New 3D Drawing View

10. Saving the New-View orientation:

- Click **Save** on the 3D Drawing View pop-up toolbar.

- Enter **3D Drawing View** in the Named View dialog. This view orientation will be available under **More Views** in the **Model View Property Manager** the next time you insert a model view (arrow).

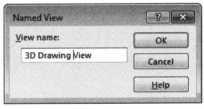

11. Saving your work:

- Click **File / Save As**.

- Enter **3D Drawing View** for the name of the file.

- Click **Save**.

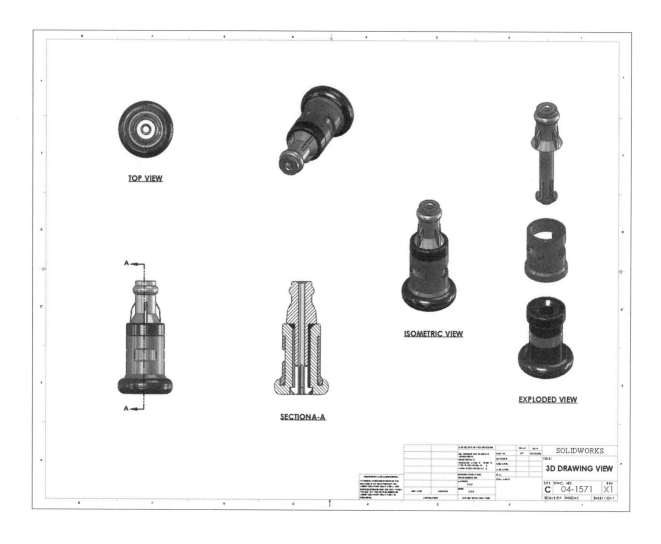

TOP VIEW

ISOMETRIC VIEW

SECTION A-A

EXPLODED VIEW

CHAPTER 19

Configurations – Part I

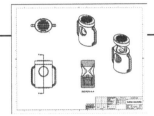

Configurations – Part I
Part, Assembly & Drawing

- Configurations is one of the unique options in SOLIDWORKS which allows the users to create multiple variations of a part or assembly within the same document.

- Configurations provide a convenient way to develop and manage families of parts with different dimensions, components, or other parameters.

- In a **Part document**, configurations allow you to create families of parts with different dimensions, features, and custom properties.

- In an **Assembly document**, configurations allow you to create:

  * Simplified versions of the design by suppressing or hiding the components.

  * Families of assemblies with different configurations of the components, parameters, assembly features, dimensions, or configuration-specific custom properties.

- In a **Drawing document**, you can display different views of different configurations that you created earlier in the part or assembly documents by accessing the properties of the drawing view.

- This chapter will guide you through the basics of creating configurations in the part assembly levels. Later on, these configurations will be called up in a drawing to display the changes that were captured earlier.

Configurations – Part 1
Part, Assembly & Drawing

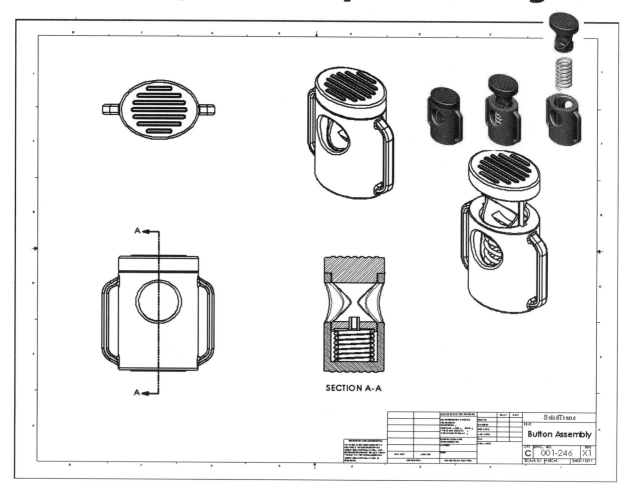

Dimensioning Standards: **ANSI**	Third Angle Projection
Units: **INCHES** – 3 Decimals	

Tools Needed:

Part document

Assembly document

Drawing document

Add Configuration...

1. Opening an Assembly Document:

<u>Go to</u>:   Training Files folder
            Button Assembly folder
            Open **Button Assembly.sldasm**

2. Using Configurations in the Part mode:

- From the FeatureManager tree, right click on **Button Spring** and select **Open Part.**

- Change to the **ConfigurationManager** tree.

- Right click over the part named Button Spring and select **Add Configuration**.

- Enter **Compressed** under **Configuration Name.**

- Under **Comment**, enter **Changed Pitch Dim from .915 to .415**

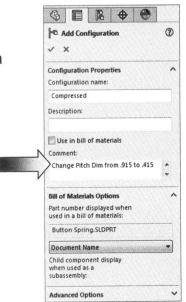

- Click **OK** ✅.

3. Changing the Pitch:

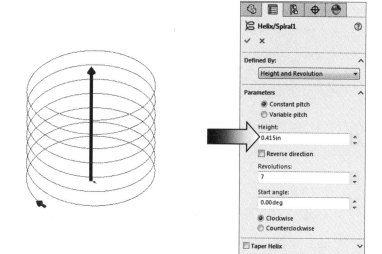

- Switch back to the FeatureManager tree (arrow).

- Locate the Helix feature on the FeatureManager tree.

- Right click **Helix/Spiral1** and select **Edit Feature**.

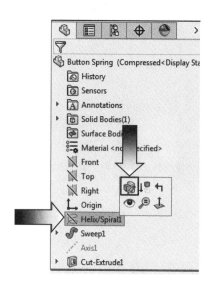

- Change the **Height** dimension to **.415** in.

- Click **OK** .

Default Configuration
(.915 Pitch)

Compressed Configuration
(.415 Pitch)

4. Creating an Assembly Configuration:

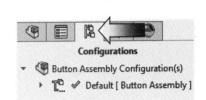

- Switch back to the Assembly document (**Ctrl + Tab**).

- Change to the **ConfigurationManager** tree.

- Right click the name of the assembly and select **Add Configuration**.

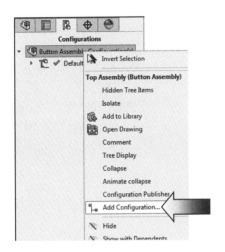
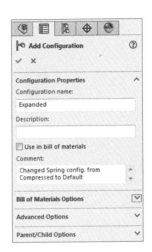

- Enter **Expanded** for Configuration Name (enter the comment for future reference).

- Click **OK** ✅.

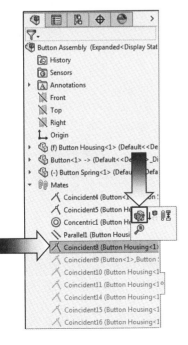

5. Changing the Mate conditions:

- Switch back to the **FeatureManager** tree and expand the Mates group.

- Right click on the mate named **Coincident8** and select **Suppress**.

- *By suppressing this mate, the Button (upper part) is no longer locked to the Housing and new Mates can be added to reposition it.*

6. Adding new Mates:

- Add a **Coincident** mate between the 2 faces of the two locking features.

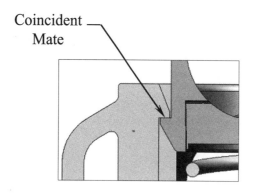

Coincident
Mate

**Compressed Assembly
Configuration**

7. Changing Configuration:

- Click the name of the part **Button Spring**; a configuration selection appears.

- Select the **Default** Configuration from the down list (arrow).

- Click the green check mark ☑ to accept the change in configuration (arrow).

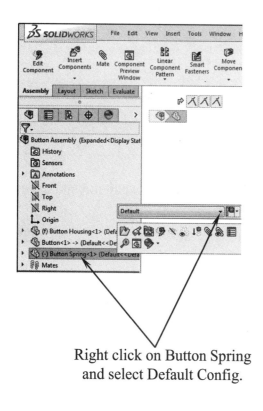

Right click on Button Spring
and select Default Config.

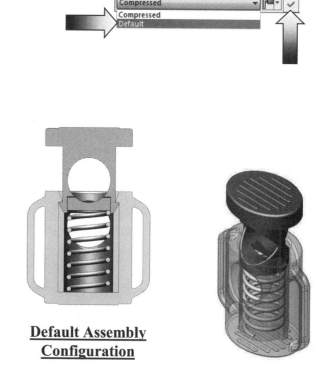

**Default Assembly
Configuration**

8. Using Configurations in a Drawing:

- Start a new drawing document; Go to **File / New / Draw** (or Drawing).

- Use **C-Landscape** paper size, **Scale: 2:1**.

- Create the 4 drawing views as shown below (using the **Default** Configuration).

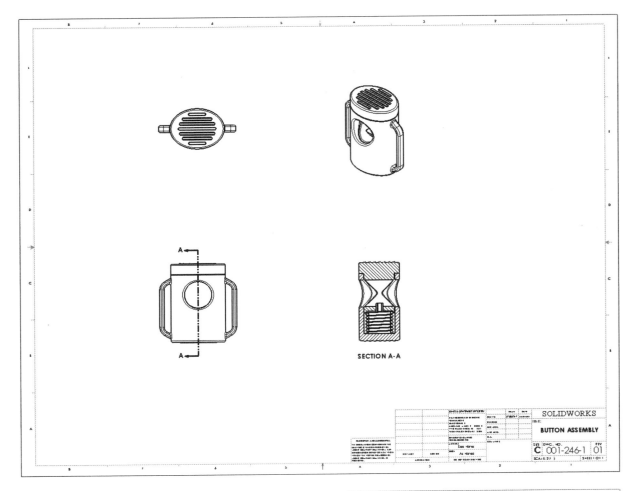

9. Creating a 2nd Isometric view:

- Create another Isometric view and place it approximately as shown.

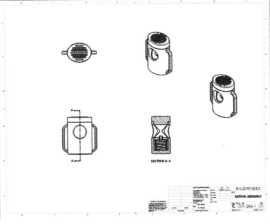

Note: *Copy and Paste also works; first select the Isometric view and press Ctrl+C, then click anywhere in the drawing and press Ctrl+V.*

10. Changing the Configuration of a drawing view:

- Click the dotted border of the new isometric view.

- Change the **Default** configuration to **Expanded** configuration (arrow).

- Click **OK** ✅.

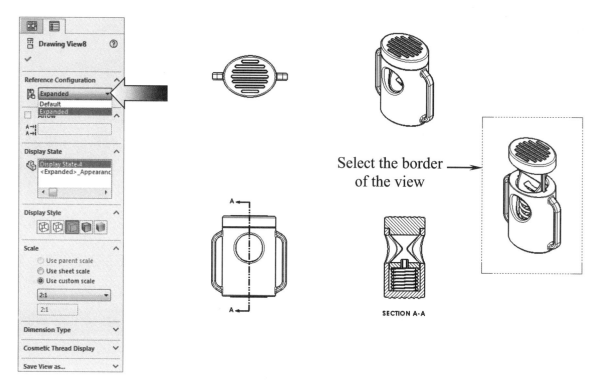

Select the border
of the view →

SECTION A-A

- The Expanded
configuration is
now the active
configuration for
this specific view.

11. Saving your work:

- Click **File / Save As**.

- Enter **Button
Assembly** for the
name of the file.

- Click **Save**.

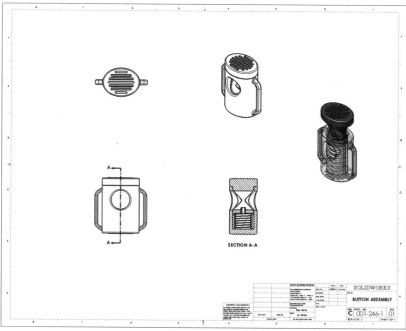

SECTION A-A

CHAPTER 19 (cont.)

Configurations – Part II

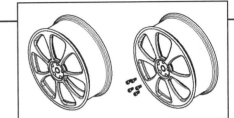

Configurations – Part II
Part / Assembly / Drawing

Configurable Items for Parts:

Part configurations can be used as follows:
* Modify feature dimensions and tolerances.
* Suppress features, equations, and end conditions.
* Assign mass and center of gravity.
* Use different sketch planes, sketch relations, and external sketch relations.
* Set individual face colors.
* Control the configuration of a base part.
* Control the configuration of a split part.
* Control the driving state of sketch dimensions.
* Create derived configurations.
* Define configuration-specific properties.

Configurable Items for Assemblies:

Assembly configurations can be used as follows:
* Change the suppression state (**Suppressed**, **Resolved**) or visibility (**Hide**, **Show**) of components.
* Change the referenced configuration of components.
* Change the dimensions of distance or angle mates, or suppression state of mates.
* Modify the dimensions, tolerances, or other parameters of features that belong to the assembly. This includes assembly feature cuts and holes, component patterns, reference geometry, and sketches that belong to the <u>assembly</u> (not to one of the assembly components).
* Assign mass and center of gravity.
* Suppress features that belong to the assembly.
* Define configuration-specific properties, such as end conditions and sketch relations.
* Create derived configurations.
* Change the suppression state of the Simulation folder in the Feature Manager design tree and its simulation elements (suppressing the folder also suppresses its elements).

Configurations – Part II
Part, Assembly & Drawing

**6 Spokes
Configuration**

**7 Spokes
Configuration**

**7 Spokes with Bolts
Configuration**

Dimensioning Standards: **ANSI**	Third Angle Projection
Units: **INCHES** – 3 Decimals	

Tools Needed:

 Part document
Part

 Assembly document
Assembly

 Drawing document
Drawing

 FeatureManager

 ConfigurationManager

Mate

Part Configurations

This section discusses the use of Configurations in the part level, where the driving dimensions of the spokes-pattern will be altered to change the number of spokes in the part.

1. Opening a part document:

       - Go to the Training Files folder, Wheel Assembly folder and open the part document named **Wheel.sldprt**

Part Configurations:

       - Change to the ConfigurationManager tree:

       - We are going to create a new configuration to capture the change in the number of Spokes.

2. Creating a new configuration:

       - Right click the name Wheel-Configuration and select **Add Configuration**.

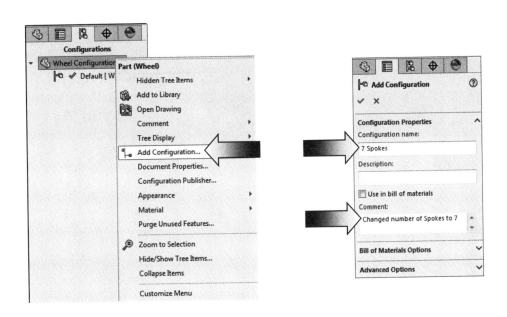

       - For Configuration Name, enter **7 Spokes** (arrows).

       - Under Description, enter **Changed number of Spokes to 7** (arrow).

       - Click **OK** .

NOTE:

To display the description next to the file name on the FeatureManager tree, do the following:

*From the FeatureManager tree, right click on the part name, go to Tree-Display, and select **Show Feature Descriptions**.*

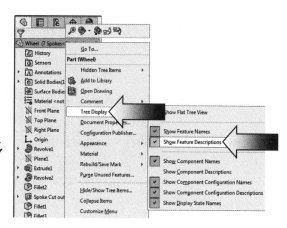

3. Changing the number of the Spokes:

- Switch back to the FeatureManager tree.

- Double click on the **Spokes Pattern** feature. Locate the <u>number 6</u> (the number of instances in the pattern) and double click it.

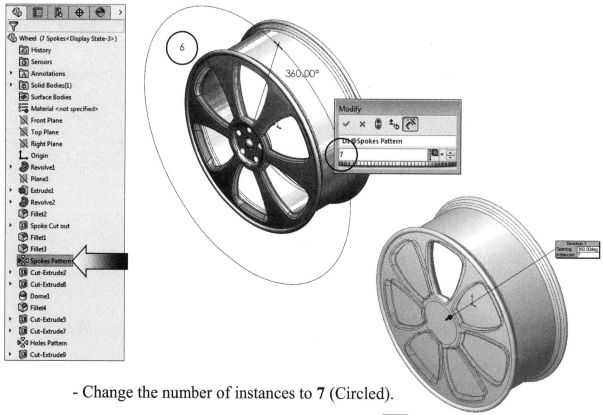

- Change the number of instances to **7** (Circled).

- Click **OK** and press the **Rebuild** button (the green traffic light) to regenerate the change.

NOTE:

Equations can be used to change the number of spokes and achieve the same result.

4. Viewing the configurations:

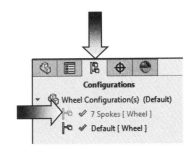

- Change to the ConfigurationManager tree.

- Double click on the **Default** configuration to see the 6 Spokes design.

- Double click on the **7 Spokes** configuration to activate it.

6 Spokes   7 Spokes

5. Saving the part:

- Save the part as a copy and name it **Wheel.sldprt**.

- Keep the part document open. It will get inserted into an assembly document in the next step and used to create new configurations in the assembly level.

Assembly Configurations

This section discusses the use of Configurations in the assembly level, where a Sub-Assembly is inserted and mated onto the Wheel as a new configuration, and any of the configurations created previously in the part level can be selected to use in the assembly level.

6. Starting a New assembly:

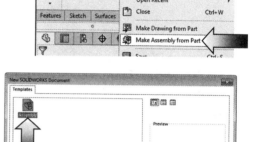

- Click **File / Make Assembly From Part**.

- Select the **Assembly Template** from the New SOLIDWORKS Document box.

- Click the Origin Point to place the component. (If the Origin is not visible, enable it from the View / Origins menus.)

- The 1st part in the assembly document is the Parent Component; it should be fixed on the origin.

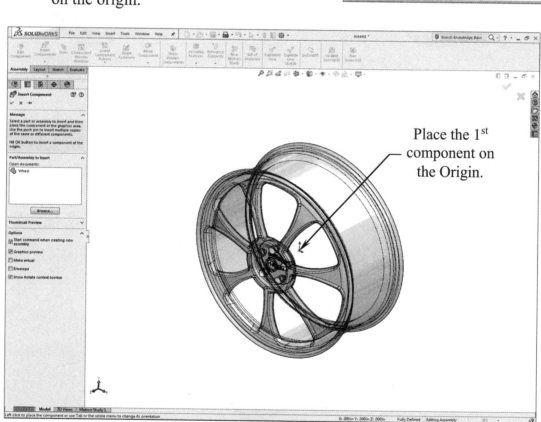

Place the 1st component on the Origin.

7. Assembly Configurations:

- Change to the ConfigurationManager tree.

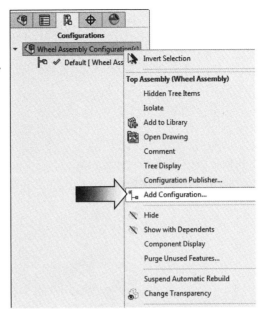

- Right click on the Assembly's name and select **Add configuration** (Arrow).

- For Configuration Name, enter **Wheel With Bolts**.

- Click **OK** .

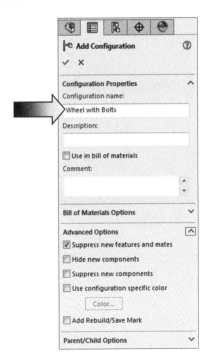

NOTE:
A set of Bolts, which have been saved earlier as an assembly document, is going to be inserted into the Top Level Assembly and becomes a Sub-Assembly.

8. Inserting the Sub-Assembly:

- Click **Insert Components.**

- Click the **Browse** button .

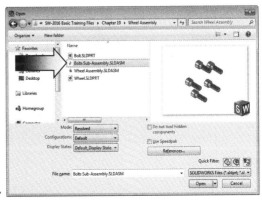

- Browse to the Training Files folder, and locate and open the **Bolts Sub-Assembly.**

- Place the 6 Bolts Sub-Assembly approximately as shown.

- For clarity, hide the origins.

Place the Bolt-Assembly
approximately here.

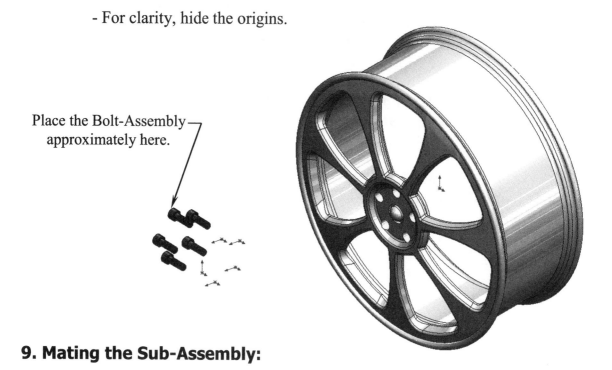

9. Mating the Sub-Assembly:

- Enable **Temporary Axis** from the **View / Hide / Show** menus.

- Click the **Mate** command on the Assembly tool tab or select **Insert / Mate**.

- Select the center Axis of one of the Bolts and the mating Holes (pictured).

Select 2 Axis

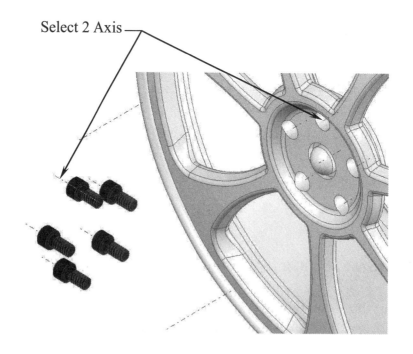

- The Coincident mate is selected automatically.

- Click either **Align** or **Anti-Align**, to flip the Bolts to the proper direction.

- Click **OK** ✅.

- Add a **Coincident** mate between the Bottom Face of one of the Bolts and its mating surface (pictured).

- Click **OK** ✅.

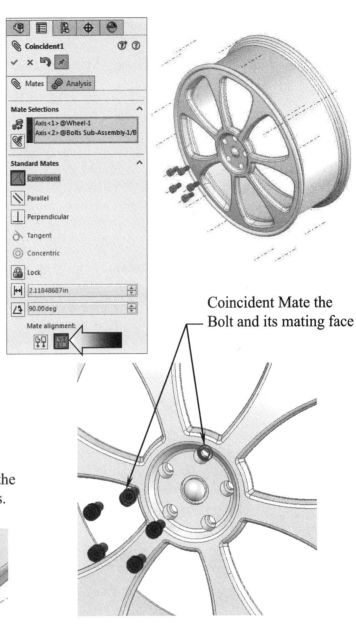

Coincident Mate the Bolt and its mating face

Coincident Mate the next 2 center Axis.

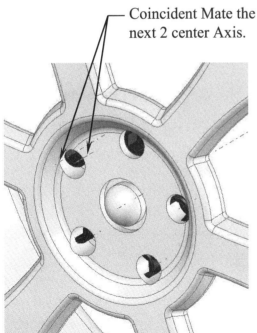

- Add another **Coincident** mate to the next 2 axes to fully center the 6 bolts.

The Completed Assembly

10. Viewing the Assembly Configurations:

- Change to the ConfigurationManager tree.

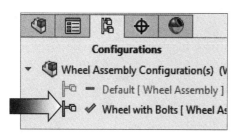

- Double click on the **Default** configuration.

Wheel With Bolts Configuration

- The Bolts Sub-Assembly is **suppressed**.

- The **7 Spokes** pattern is displayed without the bolts.

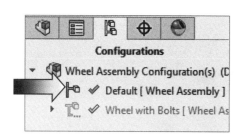

Default Configuration

- Make any necessary changes to the Number of Spokes pattern by accessing the Component's Properties and its Configurations (arrow).

- An assembly exploded view may need to be created for use in the drawing later.

11. Saving your work:

- Save as **Part_Assembly_Configurations** and close all documents.

Drawing Configurations

Change Configurations in Drawing Views.

This section discusses the use of Configurations in the drawing level, where Configurations created previously in the part and assembly levels can be selected for use in the drawing views.

- To change the configuration of the model in a drawing view, right click a drawing view (or hold down **Ctrl** to select multiple drawing views, then right click) and select **Properties**.

- In the dialog box under **Configuration information**, select a different configuration for **Use- named configuration**.

1. Creating an assembly drawing:

- Go to **File / New / Drawing**.

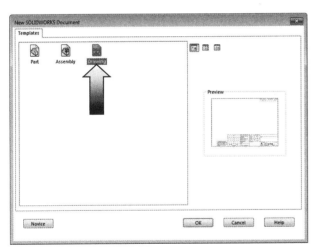

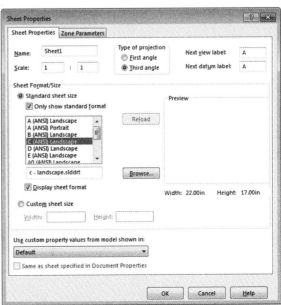

- Use **C-Landscape** paper size.

- Set **Scale** to **1 to 1**.

- Set the **Projection** to **3rd Angle**.

- Click **OK** ⬚ OK .

2. Creating the standard drawing views:

- Select **Model View** command.

- Click **Browse** [Browse...] .

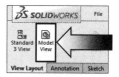

- Select the **Wheel Assembly** and click **Open**.

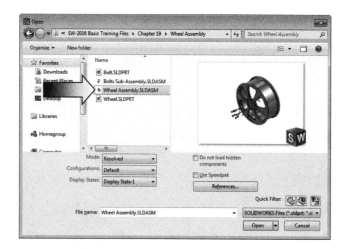

- Select the **FRONT** view [ ] from the Standard Views dialog and place it approximately as shown.

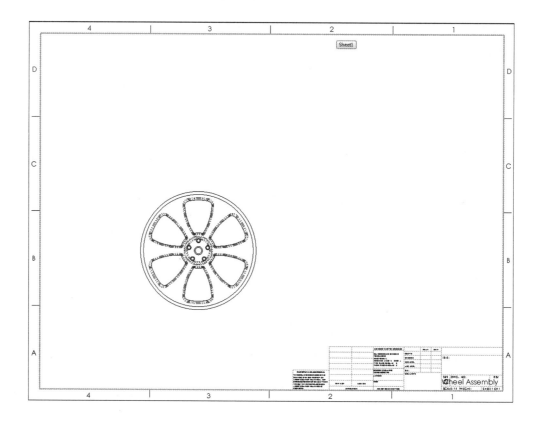

3. Auto-Start the Projected-View:

- If the option **Auto Start Projected View** is enabled, SOLIDWORKS will automatically project the next views based on the position of the mouse cursor.

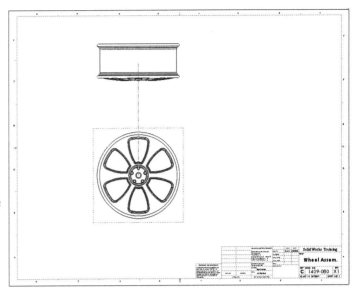

- Place the Top view above the Front view.

- Click **OK** ✅.

4. Creating the Aligned Section View:

- Select the Front drawing view's border to activate it.

- Select the **Section View** command from the View layout tool tab.

- Click the **Align** button (arrow) and create the section lines in the order shown below.

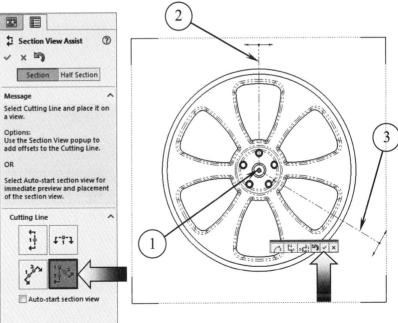

- Click **OK** ☑ on the Section Offset toolbar (arrow).

- Click **OK** to go to the next step.

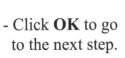

- **Section Scope**: is an option that allows components to be excluded from the section cut. In other words, when sectioning an assembly drawing view, you will have an option to select which component(s) is going to be affected by this section cut. This option is called Section Scope.

- In the Section Scope dialog box, enable **Auto Hatching**, and if needed, click the **Flip Direction** checkbox (arrow).

- Place the section view on the right side as shown.

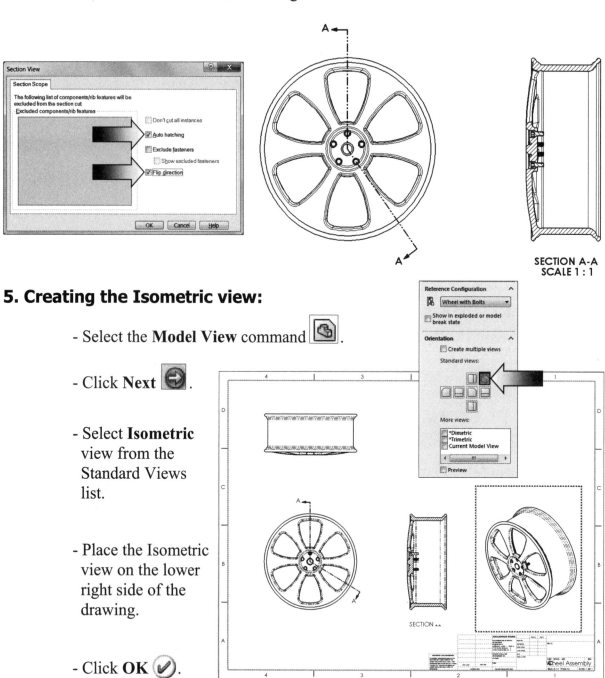

SECTION A-A
SCALE 1 : 1

5. Creating the Isometric view:

- Select the **Model View** command.

- Click **Next**.

- Select **Isometric** view from the Standard Views list.

- Place the Isometric view on the lower right side of the drawing.

- Click **OK**.

6. Displaying the Exploded View:

- An exploded view must be created from the assembly level prior to showing it in the drawing.

- Click the Isometric drawing view's border.

- Enable the **Show in Exploded or Model Break State** check box (arrow).

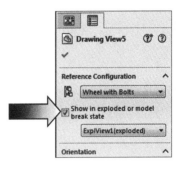

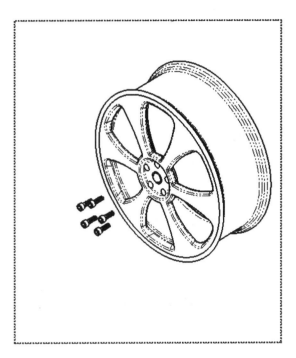

NOTE: The Exploded View option is also available when accessing the Properties of the drawing view.
(Right click the view's border and select Properties.)

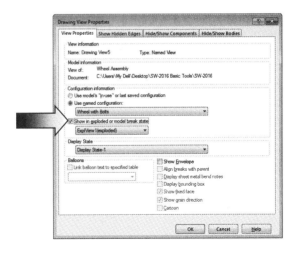

- The Assembly Exploded view is displayed.

7. Changing Configurations:

- Use the **Model View** command and create 2 more Isometric views.

- Right click on the new Isometric drawing view's border and select **Properties**.

- Select the **Default** configuration.

- Set the 2nd Isometric view to the **6-Spokes** configuration (switch to the Assembly document to modify the configurations).

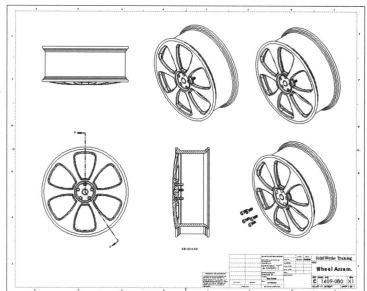

8. Adding Annotations:

- Click Note 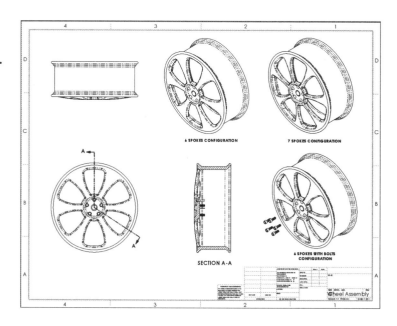 and add the call-outs under each drawing view as shown.

* 6 SPOKES CONFIGURATION.

* 7 SPOKES CONFIGURATION.

* 6 SPOKES WITH
BOLTS
CONFIGURATION.

9. Saving your work:

- Click **File / Save As**.

- Enter **Drawing Configurations** for the name of the file.

- Click **Save** and close all documents.

CHAPTER 20

Design Tables

Design Tables in Part, Assembly & Drawing

Design Table Parameters	Description (Legal values)
$PARTNUMBER@_____	- For use in a bill of materials.
$COMMENT@_____	- Any description or text string.
$NEVER_EXPAND_IN_BOM@_____	- Yes/No to expand in B.O.M.
$STATE@_____	- Resolved = R, Suppressed = S
$CONFIGURATION@_____	- Configuration name.
$SHOW@_____	- Has been obsolete.
$PRP@_____	- Enter any text string.
$USER_NOTES@_____	- Enter any text string.
$COLOR@_____	- Specifying 32-bit RGB color.
$PARENT@_____	- Parent configuration name.
$TOLERANCE@_____	- Enter tolerance keywords.
$SWMASS@_____	- Enter any decimal legal value.
$SWCOG@_____	- Enter any legal x,y,z value.
$DISPLAYSTATE@_____	- Display state name.

In a Design Table, you will need to define the names of the configurations, specify the parameters that you want to control, and assign values for each parameter. This chapter will guide you through the use of design tables in both the part and assembly levels.

Part, Assembly & Drawing
Design Tables

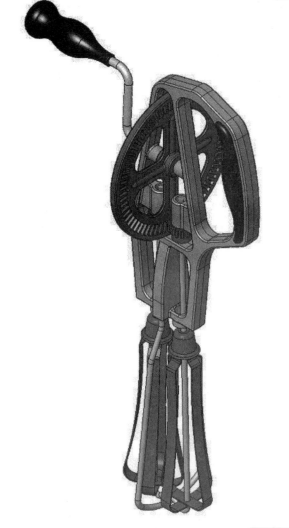

Design Table for: Egg Beater

	$state@Egg Beater Handle<1>	$state@Main Gear<1>	$state@Support Rod<1>	$state@Right Spinner<1>	$state@Left Spinner<1>	$state@Right Spinner<2>	$state@Left Spinner<2>	$configuration@Crank Handle<1>
Default	R	R	R	R	R	R	R	Default
Config1	R	S	S	S	S	S	S	Oval Handle
Config2	R	R	S	S	S	S	S	Default
Config3	R	R	R	S	S	S	S	Oval Handle
Config4	R	R	R	R	S	S	S	Default
Config5	R	R	R	R	R	R	S	Oval Handle
Config6	R	R	R	R	R	R	R	Default

Sheet1

Dimensioning Standards: **ANSI** Units: **INCHES** – 3 Decimals	Third Angle Projection

Tools Needed:

 Design Tables / Microsoft Excel

ConfigurationManager

Part - Design Tables

1. Copying the document:

- <u>Go to:</u> The Training Files folder, Design Tables folder **Part Design Table.sldprt**

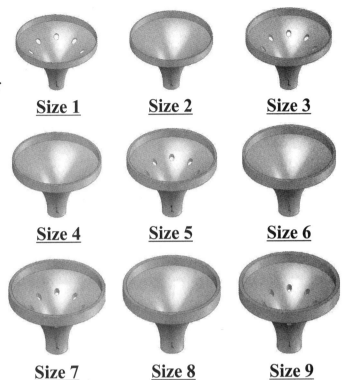

Size 1   Size 2   Size 3

- **OPEN** a copy of the part document named **Part Design Table.sldprt**

Size 4   Size 5   Size 6

- This exercise discusses the use of Changing Feature Dimensions and Feature Suppression-States in a Design Table.

Size 7   Size 8   Size 9

- The names of the dimensions will be used as the column Headers in the design table.

- From the **View** drop down menu, enable the option **Dimension Names** (arrow).

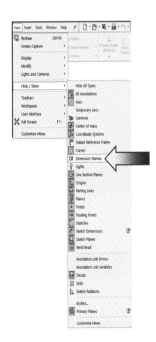

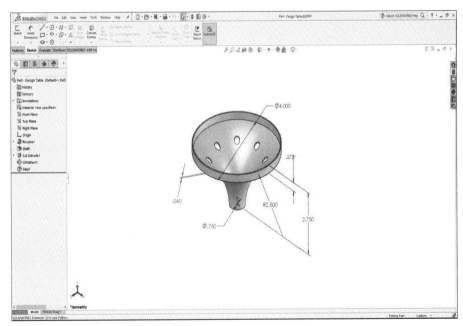

2. Creating a New Design Table:

- Click **Insert / Design Table**.

- Select the **Blank** option from the Source section.

- Enable the option **Allow Model Edits to Update the Design Table**.

- Enable the options:

    * **New Parameters**

    * **New Configurations**

    * **Warn When Updating Design Table**

- Click **OK** .

- Click **OK** in the Add Rows and Columns Dialog box.

- The Microsoft Excel Work Sheet opens up.

- The cell A1 is filled in with the part's name.

- The cell B2 is selected by default.

- The part's dimensions are going to be transferred over to the Excel Work Sheet in the next steps.

- Notice the names of the dimensions? They should be changed to what they represented, like Wall Thk, Upper Dia, Height, Radius, Lower Dia., etc.

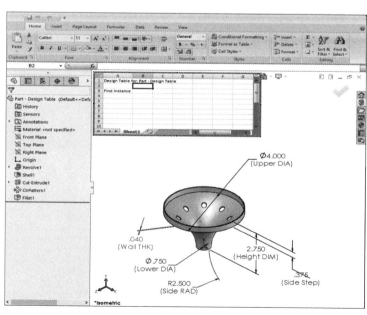

3. Transferring the Dimensions to the Design Table:

- Make sure the cell B2 is selected.

- Double click on the Height Dim **2.750**.

- The dimension is transferred over to cell B2.

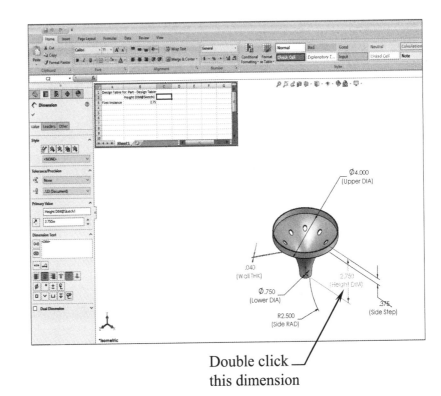

Double click this dimension

- Repeat the same step and transfer the other dimensions in the order as shown.

- Copy the formula to the cells below:

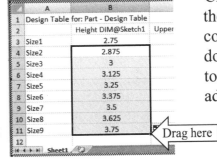

- Add configs. names: Size1 thru Size9.

	A	B	C	D	E	F	G
1	Design Table for: Part - Design Table						
2		Height DIM@Sketch1	Upper DIA@Sketch1	Lower DIA@Sketch1	Side RAD@Sketch1	Side Step@Sketch1	Wall THK@Shell1
3	Size1	2.75	4	0.75	2.5	0.375	0.04
4	Size2						
5	Size3						
6	Size4						
7	Size5						
8	Size6						
9	Size7						
10	Size8						
11	Size9						
12							

- Click and drag on the bottom right corner of cell B3, down to cell B11 to repeat the addition formula.

4. Using Excel's Addition Formula:

- Select the cell B3, type the equal sign (=), click the number **2.75** in cell B2, and then enter **+.125**.

- Copy the formula to the cells below:

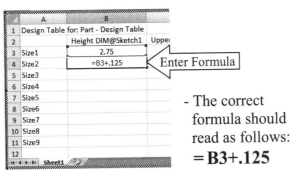

Enter Formula

- The correct formula should read as follows:
$$= B3 + .125$$

- Click and drag the bottom right corner of cell B3, down to cell B11 to repeat the addition formula.

Drag here

	A	B	C	D
1	Design Table for: Part - Design Table			
2		Height DIM@Sketch1	Upper DIA@Sketch1	Lower DIA@
3	Size1	2.75	4	0.75
4	Size2	2.875	=C3+125	
5	Size3	3		
6	Size4	3.125		
7	Size5	3.25		
8	Size6	3.375		
9	Size7	3.5		
10	Size8	3.625		
11	Size9	3.75		
12				

	A	B	C	D
1	Design Table for: Part - Design Table			
2		Height DIM@Sketch1	Upper DIA@Sketch1	Lower DIA@
3	Size1	2.75	4	0.75
4	Size2	2.875	4.125	
5	Size3	3	4.25	
6	Size4	3.125	4.375	
7	Size5	3.25	4.5	
8	Size6	3.375	4.625	
9	Size7	3.5	4.75	
10	Size8	3.625	4.875	
11	Size9	3.75	5	
12				

- In cell C4 type:

$$= C3+.125$$

and copy the formula thru cell C11.

	A	B	C	D
1	Design Table for: Part - Design Table			
2		Height DIM@Sketch1	Upper DIA@Sketch1	Lower DIA@Sketch1
3	Size1	2.75	4	0.75
4	Size2	2.875	4.125	=D3+.0625
5	Size3	3	4.25	
6	Size4	3.125	4.375	
7	Size5	3.25	4.5	
8	Size6	3.375	4.625	
9	Size7	3.5	4.75	
10	Size8	3.625	4.875	
11	Size9	3.75	5	
12				

	A	B	C	D
1	Design Table for: Part - Design Table			
2		Height DIM@Sketch1	Upper DIA@Sketch1	Lower DIA@Sketch1
3	Size1	2.75	4	0.75
4	Size2	2.875	4.125	0.8125
5	Size3	3	4.25	0.875
6	Size4	3.125	4.375	0.9375
7	Size5	3.25	4.5	1
8	Size6	3.375	4.625	1.0625
9	Size7	3.5	4.75	1.125
10	Size8	3.625	4.875	1.1875
11	Size9	3.75	5	1.25
12				

- Cell D4 thru Cell C11, type:

$$= D3+.0625$$

and copy the formula.

	A	B	C	D	E
1	Design Table for: Part - Design Table				
2		Height DIM@Sketch1	Upper DIA@Sketch1	Lower DIA@Sketch1	Side RAD@Sketch1
3	Size1	2.75	4	0.75	2.5
4	Size2	2.875	4.125	0.8125	=E3+.0625
5	Size3	3	4.25	0.875	
6	Size4	3.125	4.375	0.9375	
7	Size5	3.25	4.5	1	
8	Size6	3.375	4.625	1.0625	
9	Size7	3.5	4.75	1.125	
10	Size8	3.625	4.875	1.1875	
11	Size9	3.75	5	1.25	
12					

	A	B	C	D	E
1	Design Table for: Part - Design Table				
2		Height DIM@Sketch1	Upper DIA@Sketch1	Lower DIA@Sketch1	Side RAD@Sketch1
3	Size1	2.75	4	0.75	2.5
4	Size2	2.875	4.125	0.8125	2.5625
5	Size3	3	4.25	0.875	2.625
6	Size4	3.125	4.375	0.9375	2.6875
7	Size5	3.25	4.5	1	2.75
8	Size6	3.375	4.625	1.0625	2.8125
9	Size7	3.5	4.75	1.125	2.875
10	Size8	3.625	4.875	1.1875	2.9375
11	Size9	3.75	5	1.25	3
12					

- Cell E4 thru Cell E11, type:

$$= E3+.0625$$

and copy the formula.

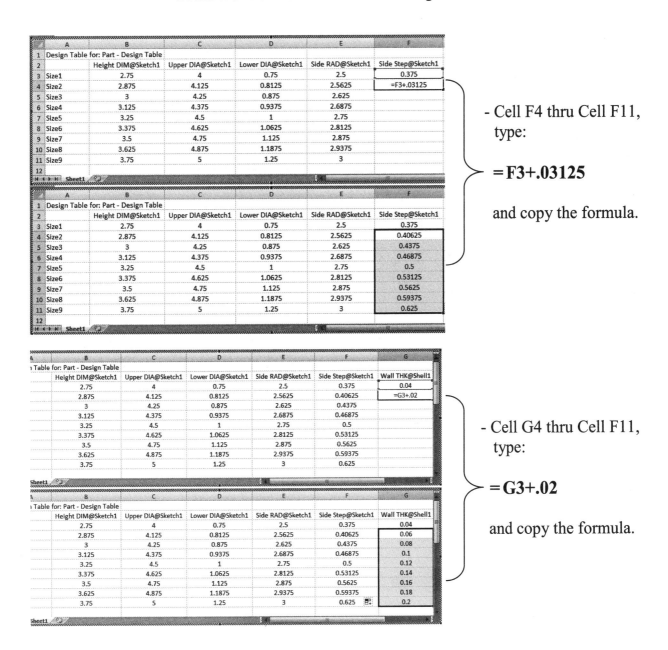

	A	B	C	D	E	F
1	Design Table for: Part - Design Table					
2		Height DIM@Sketch1	Upper DIA@Sketch1	Lower DIA@Sketch1	Side RAD@Sketch1	Side Step@Sketch1
3	Size1	2.75	4	0.75	2.5	0.375
4	Size2	2.875	4.125	0.8125	2.5625	=F3+.03125
5	Size3	3	4.25	0.875	2.625	
6	Size4	3.125	4.375	0.9375	2.6875	
7	Size5	3.25	4.5	1	2.75	
8	Size6	3.375	4.625	1.0625	2.8125	
9	Size7	3.5	4.75	1.125	2.875	
10	Size8	3.625	4.875	1.1875	2.9375	
11	Size9	3.75	5	1.25	3	
12						

- Cell F4 thru Cell F11, type:

=F3+.03125

and copy the formula.

	A	B	C	D	E	F
1	Design Table for: Part - Design Table					
2		Height DIM@Sketch1	Upper DIA@Sketch1	Lower DIA@Sketch1	Side RAD@Sketch1	Side Step@Sketch1
3	Size1	2.75	4	0.75	2.5	0.375
4	Size2	2.875	4.125	0.8125	2.5625	0.40625
5	Size3	3	4.25	0.875	2.625	0.4375
6	Size4	3.125	4.375	0.9375	2.6875	0.46875
7	Size5	3.25	4.5	1	2.75	0.5
8	Size6	3.375	4.625	1.0625	2.8125	0.53125
9	Size7	3.5	4.75	1.125	2.875	0.5625
10	Size8	3.625	4.875	1.1875	2.9375	0.59375
11	Size9	3.75	5	1.25	3	0.625
12						

B	C	D	E	F	G
Table for: Part - Design Table					
Height DIM@Sketch1	Upper DIA@Sketch1	Lower DIA@Sketch1	Side RAD@Sketch1	Side Step@Sketch1	Wall THK@Shell1
2.75	4	0.75	2.5	0.375	0.04
2.875	4.125	0.8125	2.5625	0.40625	=G3+.02
3	4.25	0.875	2.625	0.4375	
3.125	4.375	0.9375	2.6875	0.46875	
3.25	4.5	1	2.75	0.5	
3.375	4.625	1.0625	2.8125	0.53125	
3.5	4.75	1.125	2.875	0.5625	
3.625	4.875	1.1875	2.9375	0.59375	
3.75	5	1.25	3	0.625	

- Cell G4 thru Cell F11, type:

=G3+.02

and copy the formula.

B	C	D	E	F	G
Table for: Part - Design Table					
Height DIM@Sketch1	Upper DIA@Sketch1	Lower DIA@Sketch1	Side RAD@Sketch1	Side Step@Sketch1	Wall THK@Shell1
2.75	4	0.75	2.5	0.375	0.04
2.875	4.125	0.8125	2.5625	0.40625	0.06
3	4.25	0.875	2.625	0.4375	0.08
3.125	4.375	0.9375	2.6875	0.46875	0.1
3.25	4.5	1	2.75	0.5	0.12
3.375	4.625	1.0625	2.8125	0.53125	0.14
3.5	4.75	1.125	2.875	0.5625	0.16
3.625	4.875	1.1875	2.9375	0.59375	0.18
3.75	5	1.25	3	0.625	0.2

5. Controlling the Suppression-States of the holes:

- Select the cell **H2** and double click on the **CutExtrude1** to transfer to cell H2.

C	D	E	F	G	H
Table					
etch1	Upper DIA@Sketch1	Lower DIA@Sketch1	Side RAD@Sketch1	Side Step@Sketch1	Wall THK@Shell1	
	4	0.75	2.5	0.375	0.04	
	4.125	0.8125	2.5625	0.40625	0.06	
	4.25	0.875	2.625	0.4375	0.08	
	4.375	0.9375	2.6875	0.46875	0.1	
	4.5	1	2.75	0.5	0.12	
	4.625	1.0625	2.8125	0.53125	0.14	
	4.75	1.125	2.875	0.5625	0.16	
	4.875	1.1875	2.9375	0.59375	0.18	
	5	1.25	3	0.625	0.2	

Select Cell H2

Double click

	B	C	D	E	F	G	H
1	for: Part - Design Table						
2	Height DIM@Sketch1	Upper DIA@Sketch1	Lower DIA@Sketch1	Side RAD@Sketch1	Side Step@Sketch1	Wall THK@Shell1	$STATE@Cut-Extrude1
3	2.75	4	0.75	2.5	0.375	0.04	UNSUPPRESSED
4	2.875	4.125	0.8125	2.5625	0.40625	0.06	
5	3	4.25	0.875	2.625	0.4375	0.08	
6	3.125	4.375	0.9375	2.6875	0.46875	0.1	
7	3.25	4.5	1	2.75	0.5	0.12	
8	3.375	4.625	1.0625	2.8125	0.53125	0.14	
9	3.5	4.75	1.125	2.875	0.5625	0.16	
10	3.625	4.875	1.1875	2.9375	0.59375	0.18	
11	3.75	5	1.25	3	0.625	0.2	
12							

Sheet1

- In Cell H3, replace the word **Unsuppressed** with the letter **U**.

	C	D	E	F	G	H	I
1							
2	Upper DIA@Sketch1	Lower DIA@Sketch1	Side RAD@Sketch1	Side Step@Sketch1	Wall THK@Shell1	$STATE@Cut-Extrude1	
3	4	0.75	2.5	0.375	0.04	U	
4	4.125	0.8125	2.5625	0.40625	0.06	S	
5	4.25	0.875	2.625	0.4375	0.08	U	
6	4.375	0.9375	2.6875	0.46875	0.1	S	
7	4.5	1	2.75	0.5	0.12	U	
8	4.625	1.0625	2.8125	0.53125	0.14	S	
9	4.75	1.125	2.875	0.5625	0.16	U	
10	4.875	1.1875	2.9375	0.59375	0.18	S	
11	5	1.25	3	0.625	0.2	U	
12							

Sheet1

- Enter **S** for **Suppressed** in Cell H4.

- Enter **S** and **U** for all other cells as shown.

6. Viewing the Configurations generated by the Design Table:

- Click anywhere in the SOLIDWORKS graphics area to close Excel.

- Change to the **Configuration-Manager** tree.

- Double click on **Size2** to see the changes. Verify the other configurations that were created by the Design Table.

- Save your work as **Part - Design Table**.

Size 1

Size 2

Size 3

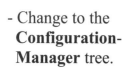
Size 4

Size 5

Size 6

Size 7

Size 8

Size 9

Assembly - Design Tables

1. Copying the Egg Beater Assembly:

- <u>Go to:</u> The Training Files folder
    Design Tables folder
    Egg Beater Assembly Folder.

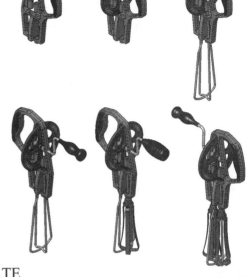

- Copy the Egg-Beater-Assembly folder to your computer.

- Open the **Egg Beater Assembly.sldasm**

- This exercise discusses the use of the STATE and CONFIGURATION parameters in a Design Table.

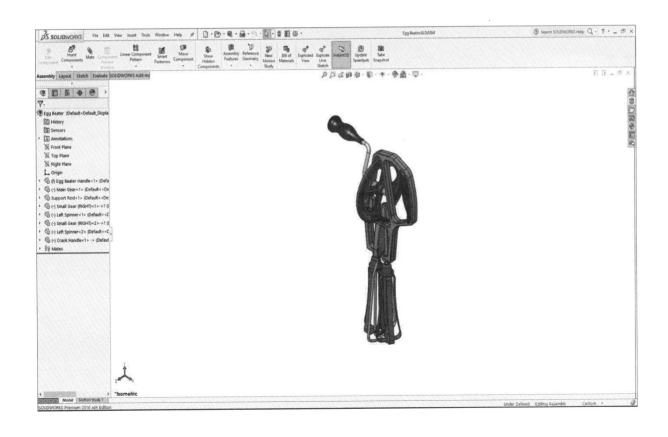

2. Creating a new Assembly Design Table:

- Select **Insert / Tables / Design Table** 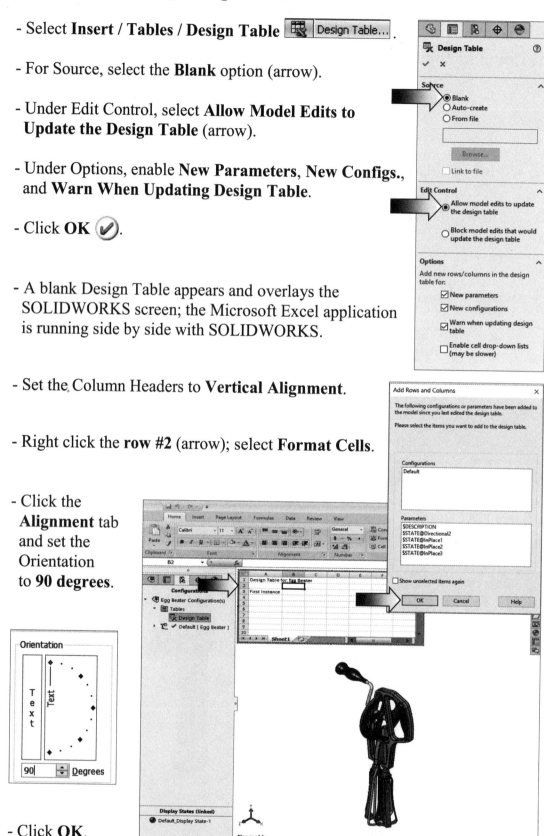.

- For Source, select the **Blank** option (arrow).

- Under Edit Control, select **Allow Model Edits to Update the Design Table** (arrow).

- Under Options, enable **New Parameters**, **New Configs.**, and **Warn When Updating Design Table**.

- Click **OK** .

- A blank Design Table appears and overlays the SOLIDWORKS screen; the Microsoft Excel application is running side by side with SOLIDWORKS.

- Set the Column Headers to **Vertical Alignment**.

- Right click the **row #2** (arrow); select **Format Cells**.

- Click the **Alignment** tab and set the Orientation to **90 degrees**.

- Click **OK**.

<u>**NOTE:**</u>
To create a design table, you must define the names of the configurations that you want to create, specify the parameters that you want to control, and assign values for each parameter.

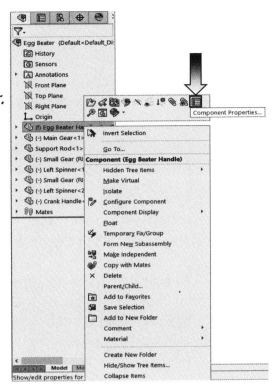

3. Defining the column headers:

- We are going to copy the name of each component and paste it to the Design Table. They will be used as the Column Headers.

- Right click on the part named Egg Beater Handle and select **Component Properties** (arrow).

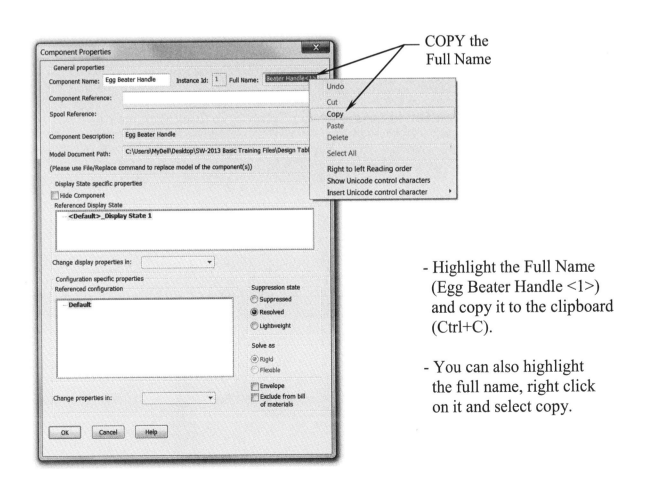

COPY the Full Name

- Highlight the Full Name (Egg Beater Handle <1>) and copy it to the clipboard (Ctrl+C).

- You can also highlight the full name, right click on it and select copy.

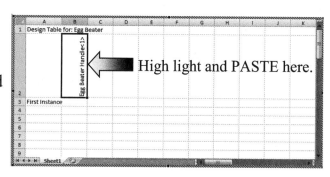

- Select the Cell C2 (arrow) and click **Edit / Paste** or press Ctrl+V.

4. Repeating step #3: (Copy & Paste all components)

- Repeat step 3, copy and paste all components into cells C, D, E, F, G, H, and I.

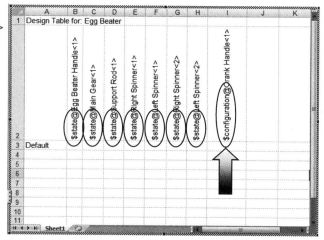

5. Inserting the Control Parameters:

- For cells **B2** thru **H2**, insert the header **$state@** before the name of each component.

Example:
$state@Egg Beater Handle<1>

- For cell **I2**, insert the header:

$configuration@

before the name of the component.

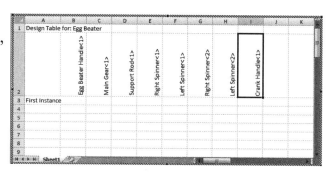

Example:
$configuration@Crank Handle<1>

6. Adding the configuration names:

- The actual part numbers can be used here for the name of each configuration.

- Starting at **Cell A4**, (below Default), enter **Config1** thru **Config5** as shown.

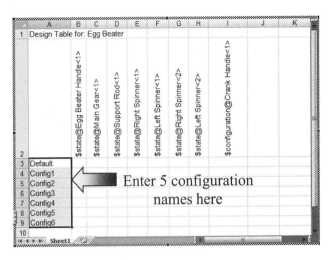

Enter 5 configuration names here

7. Assigning the control values:

- To prevent mistakes, type the letter **R** and letter **S** in each cell.

- Enter the values **R** (Resolved) and **S** (Suppressed) into their appropriate cells, from column B through column H.

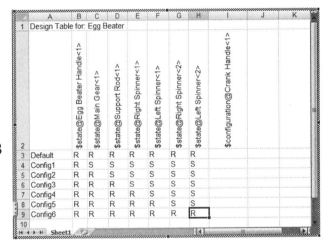

- For Column I, we will enter the names of the configurations instead.

- Select the cell **I3** and enter **Default**.

- Select the cell **I4** and enter **Oval Handle**.

- Repeat the same step for all 6 configs.

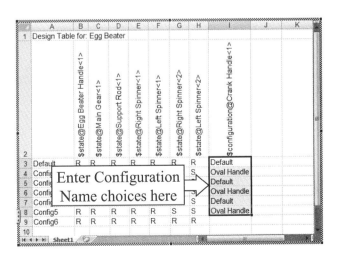

Enter Configuration Name choices here

8. Viewing the new configurations:

- Switch to the **ConfigurationManager** Tree.

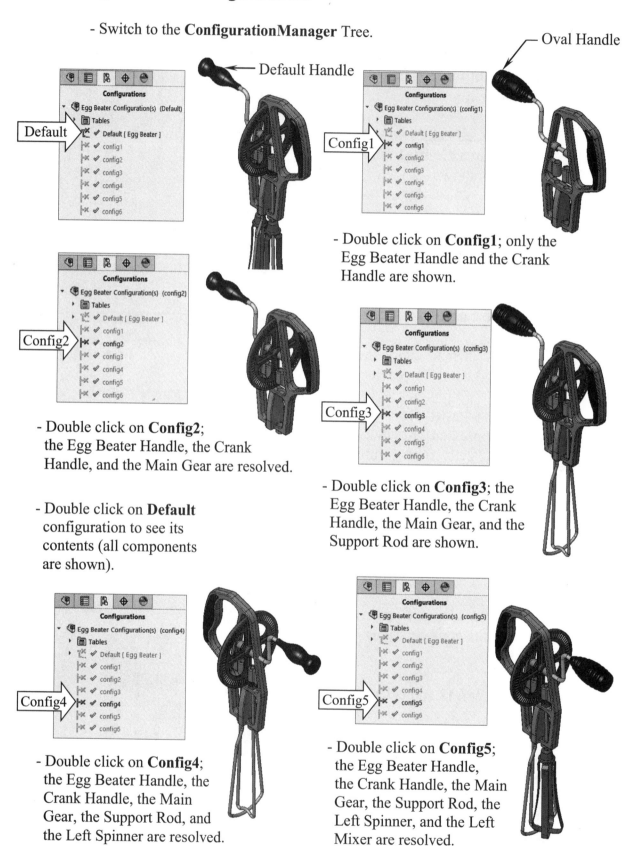

- Double click on **Config1**; only the Egg Beater Handle and the Crank Handle are shown.

- Double click on **Config2**; the Egg Beater Handle, the Crank Handle, and the Main Gear are resolved.

- Double click on **Default** configuration to see its contents (all components are shown).

- Double click on **Config3**; the Egg Beater Handle, the Crank Handle, the Main Gear, and the Support Rod are shown.

- Double click on **Config4**; the Egg Beater Handle, the Crank Handle, the Main Gear, the Support Rod, and the Left Spinner are resolved.

- Double click on **Config5**; the Egg Beater Handle, the Crank Handle, the Main Gear, the Support Rod, the Left Spinner, and the Left Mixer are resolved.

Exercise: Part Design Tables

1. Open the existing document named **Part Design Tables_EXE** from the Training folder.
2. Create a design table with 3 different sizes using the dimensions provided in the table.
3. Customize the table by merging the cells, adding colors, and borders.
4. Use the instructions on the following pages, if needed.

Design Table for: Part Design Tables_Exe									
	Lower Boss Thickness@Sketch	Upper Boss Thickness@Sketch	Center Hole@Sketch1	Upper Boss Dia@Sketch1	Lower Boss Dia@Sketch1	D1@Revolve1	Bolt Cicle@Sketch2	Hole on Flange@Sketch2	D3@CirPattern1	D1@CirPattern1
Size 1	0.25	0.25	0.5	1	2	360	1.5	0.25	360	4
Size 2	0.375	0.375	0.625	1.25	2.25	360	1.75	0.275	360	4
Size 3	0.5	0.5	0.75	1.5	2.5	360	2	0.3	360	4

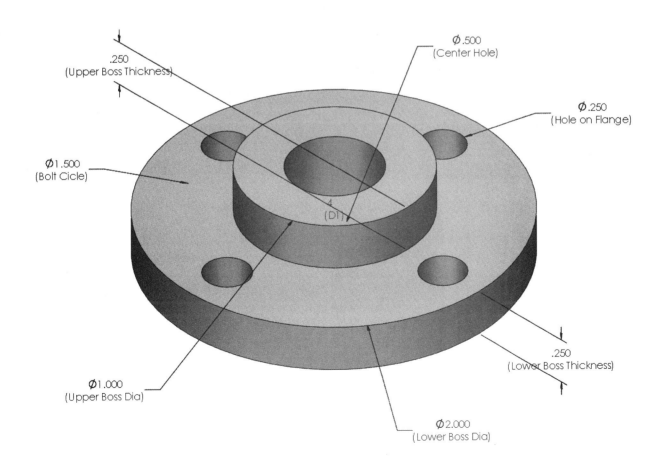

.250
(Upper Boss Thickness)

Ø.500
(Center Hole)

Ø.250
(Hole on Flange)

Ø1.500
(Bolt Cicle)

(D1)

Ø1.000
(Upper Boss Dia)

.250
(Lower Boss Thickness)

Ø2.000
(Lower Boss Dia)

1. Opening the main part file:

- From the Training Files folder, open the part named **Part Design Tables_Exe**. The dimensions in this part have been renamed for use in this exercise.

2. Inserting a design table:

- From the **Insert** menu click **Tables / Design-Table**.

- Click the **Auto Create** button (default).

- Leave all other options at their default settings.

- Click **OK**.

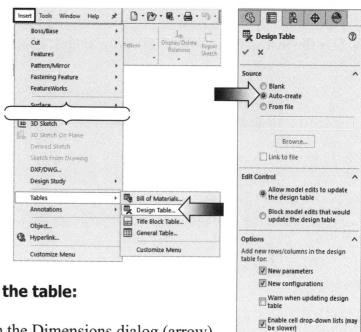

3. Adding model dimensions to the table:

- **Select all dimensions** in the Dimensions dialog (arrow).

- This option will export all dimensions from the part into the design table. Each dimension will be placed in its own column, in the same order they were created.

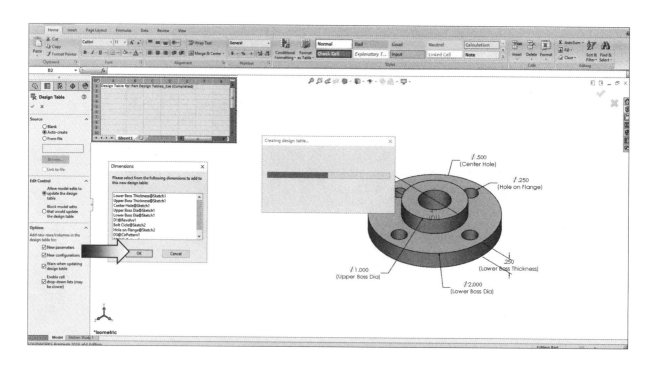

4. Changing the Configuration names:

- For clarity, change the name Default to **Size 1**.

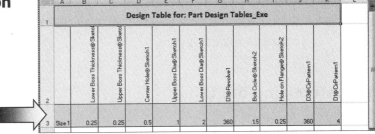

- Create the next 2 configurations by adding the names **Size 2** and **Size 3** on cell A4 and A5.

- Enter the **new dimensions** for the next 2 sizes.

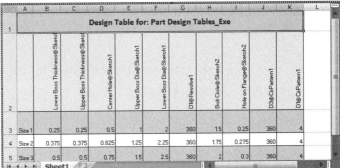

5. Viewing the new configurations:

- Click in the SOLIDWORKS background. A dialog box appears reporting 3 new configurations have been generated by the design table.

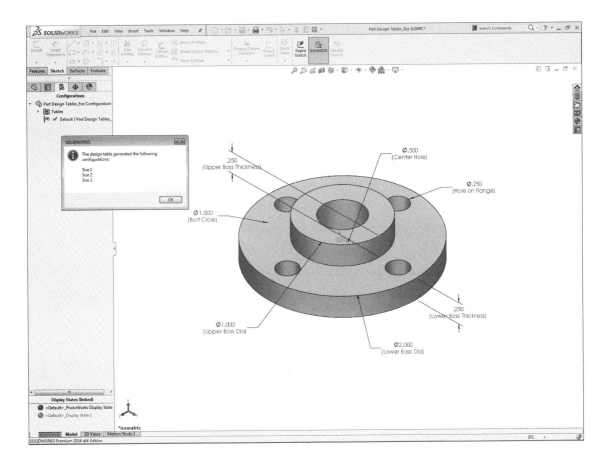

- Double click on the names of the configurations to see the changes for each size.

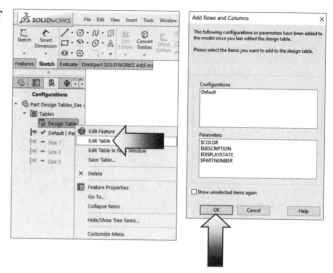

6. Customizing the table:

- Expand the **Tables** folder, right click on Design Tables and select **Edit Table**.

- Click **OK** to close the Rows and Columns dialog.

- Highlight the entire Row1 header, right click in the highlighted area and select **Format Cell**.

- Click the **Fill** tab and select a color for the Row1.

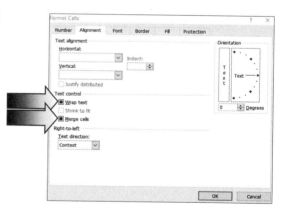

- Change to the **Alignment** tab and enable the **Wrap Text** and **Merge Cells** check-boxes.

- In the **Border** tab, select the **Outline** button.

- Click **OK**.

- Repeat step 6 for other rows.

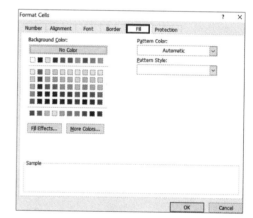

7. Saving your work:

- Click **File / Save As**.

- For file name, enter **Part Design Table_Exe**.

- Click **Save**.

- Overwrite the original document if prompted.

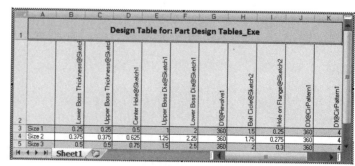

Level 2 Final Exam (1of2)

1. Open the existing assembly document named
   Assembly Motions from the Level 2 Final Exam folder.
2. Create an <u>assembly drawing</u> as shown.
3. Modify the Bill of Materials to match the information provided
   in the BOM.

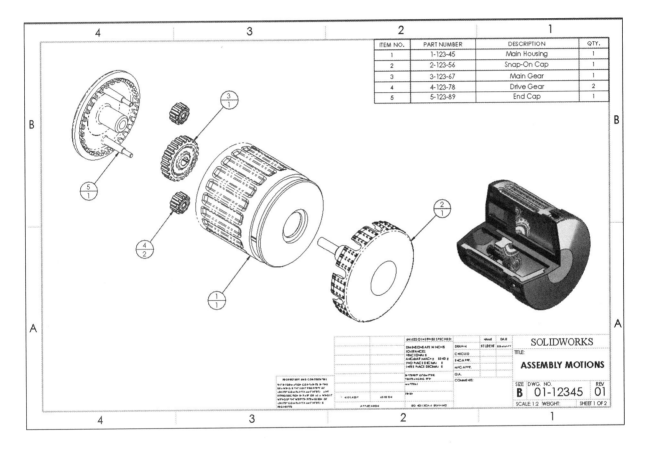

ITEM NO.	PART NUMBER	DESCRIPTION	QTY.
1	1-123-45	Main Housing	1
2	2-123-56	Snap-On Cap	1
3	3-123-67	Main Gear	1
4	4-123-78	Drive Gear	2
5	5-123-89	End Cap	1

4. Modify the Balloons to include the Quantity.
5. Fill out the title block with the information shown.
6. Save your drawing as **L2 Final Assembly Drawing**.

Level 2 Final Exam (2of2)

1. Open the existing Part document named
   Main Housing from the Level 2 Final Exam folder.
2. Create a <u>detailed drawing</u> shown below.
3. Add the dimensions as shown in each drawing view.

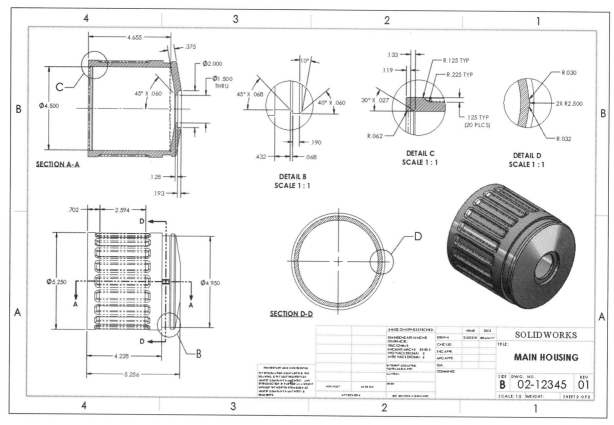

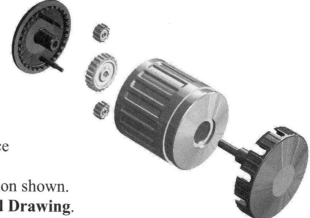

4. Add any missing dimensions as reference
   dimensions.
5. Fill out the title block with the information shown.
6. Save your drawing as **L2 Final Detailed Drawing**.

TABLE OF U.S. MEASURES

LENGTH

12 inches	=	1 foot
36 inches	=	1 yard (or 3 feet)
5280 feet	=	1 mile (or 1760 yards)

AREA

144 square inches (in)	=	1 square foot (ft)
9 ft	=	1 square yard (yd)
43,560 ft	=	1 acre (A)
640 A	=	1 square mile (mi)

VOLUME

1728 cubic inches (in³)	=	1 cubic foot (ft)
27 ft	=	1 cubic yard (yd)

LIQUID CAPACITY

8 fluid ounces (fl oz)	=	1 cup (c)
2 c	=	1 pint (pt)
2 pt	=	1 quart (qt)
4 pt	=	1 gallon (gal)

WEIGHT

16 ounces (oz)	=	1 pound (lb)
2000 lb	=	1 ton (t)

TEMPERATURE Degrees Fahrenheit (°F)

32° F	=	freezing point of water
98.6° F	=	normal body temperature
212° F	=	boiling point of water

TABLE OF METRIC MEASURES

LENGTH

10 millimeters (mm)	=	1 centimeter (cm)
10 cm	=	1 decimeter (dm)
100 cm	=	1 meter (m)
1000 m	=	1 kilometer (km)

AREA

100 square millimeters (mm)	=	1 square centimeter (cm)
10,000 cm	=	1 square meter (m)
10,000 m	=	1 hectare (ha)
1,000,000 m	=	1 square kilometer (km)

VOLUME

1000 cubic millimeters (ml)	=	1 cubic centimeter (cm)
1 cm	=	1 milliliter (mL)
1,000 m	=	1 Liter (L)
1,000,000 cm	=	1 cubic meter (m)

LIQUID CAPACITY

10 deciliters (dL)	=	1 liter (L) - or 1000 mL
1000 L	=	1 kiloliter (kL)

MASS

1000 milligrams (mg)	=	1 gram (g)
1000 g	=	1 kilogram (kg)
1000 kg	=	1 metric ton (t)

TEMPERATURE Degrees Celsius (°C)

0° C	=	freezing point of water
37°C	=	normal body temperature
100° C	=	boiling point of water

SOLIDWORKS 2016

Certified SOLIDWORKS Associate (CSWA)

Certification Practice for the Associate Examination

Courtesy of Paul Tran, Sr. Certified SOLIDWORKS Instructor

CSWA – Certified SOLIDWORKS Associate

As a Certified SOLIDWORKS Associate (CSWA), you will stand out from the crowd in today's competitive job market.

The CSWA certification is proof of your SOLIDWORKS® expertise with cutting-edge skills that businesses seek out and reward.

Exam Length: 3 hours

Minimum Passing grade: 70%

Re-test Policy: There is a minimum 30 day waiting period between every attempt of the CSWA exam. Also, a CSWA exam credit must be purchased for each exam attempt.

All candidates receive electronic certificates and personal listing on the CSWA directory when they pass *(Courtesy of SOLIDWORKS Corporation)*.

- CSWA Sample Certificate -

Certified-SOLIDWORKS-Associate program (CSWA)
Certification Practice for the Associate-Examination

> ### Drawings, Parts & Assemblies

Complete all challenges within 180 minutes

(The following examples are intended to assist you in familiarizing yourself with the structures of the exams and the method in which the questions are asked.)

Drafting competencies

Question 1:

Which command was used to create the drawing View B on the lower right? (Circle one)

A. Section View

B. Projected

C. Crop View

D. Detail

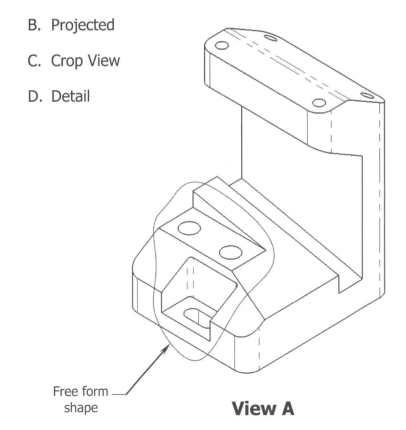

Free form shape

View A

View B

Question 2:

Which command was used to create the drawing View B below? (Circle one)

A. Section View

B. Crop View

C. Projected

D. Detail

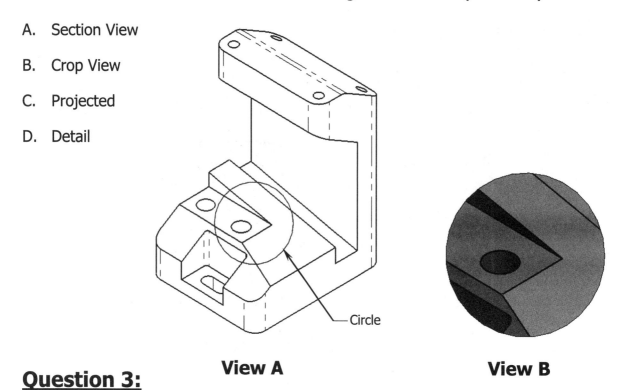

View A　　　　　　　　**View B**

Question 3:

Which command was used to create the drawing View B below? (Circle one)

A. Section View

B. Aligned Section

C. Broken-Out Section

D. Detail

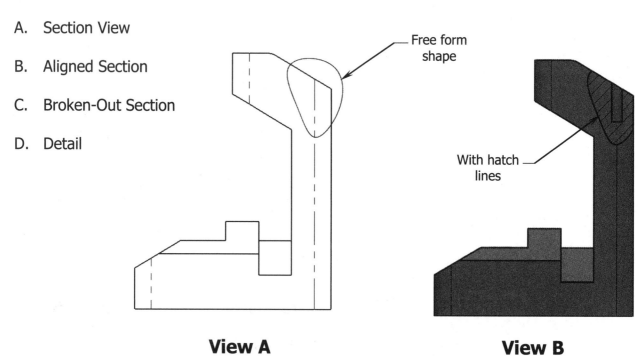

View A　　　　　　　　**View B**

Question 4:

Which command was used to create the drawing View B below? (Circle one)

A. Alternate Position View

B. Multiple Positions

C. Exploded View

D. Copy & Paste

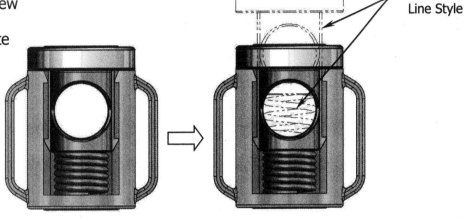

View A　　　　**View B**

Question 5:

Which command was used to create the drawing View B below? (Circle one)

A. Aligned Section View

B. Horizontal Break

C. Vertical Break

D. Broken Out Section

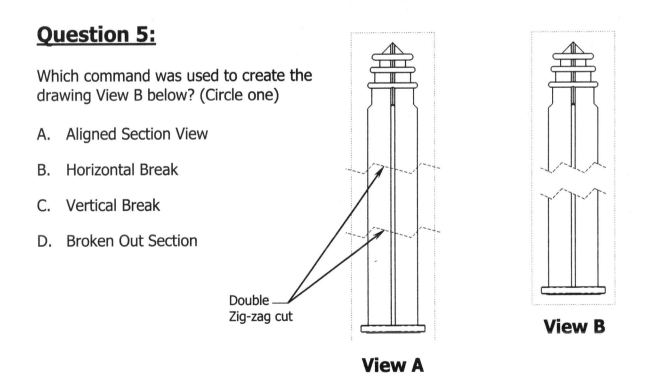

Question 6: Basic Part Modeling (1 of 4)

- Create this part in SOLIDWORKS. - Unit: **Inches, 3 decimals**

- Origin: **Arbitrary**   - Drafting Standards: **ANSI**

- Material: **1060 Alloy Steel** - Density: **0.098 lb/in^3**

(This question focuses on the use of sketch tools, relations, and revolve features.)

1. Creating the main body:

- Open a new sketch on the
  Front plane.

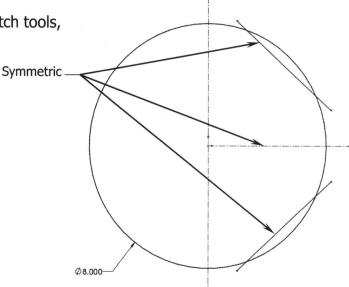

Symmetric

Ø8.000

- Sketch a circle, 2 lines, and
  2 centerlines.

- Add a **Symmetric** relation between
  the horizontal centerline and the two lines
  as noted.

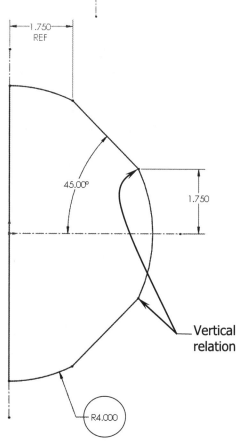

1.750
REF

45.00°

1.750

- **Trim** the left portion of the circle and the ends
  of the two lines as shown.

- Add the relations and dimensions shown to
  fully define the sketch (do not add the
  reference dimension).

Vertical
relation

- Change the 8.00 diameter dimension to a
  R4.00 radius dimension. (Use the options in
  the Leaders tab on the Properties tree.)

R4.000

2. Extruding the base feature:

- Click **Extruded Boss/Base**.

- Use **Mid-Plane** type.

- Thickness: **16.00 in**.

- Click **OK**.

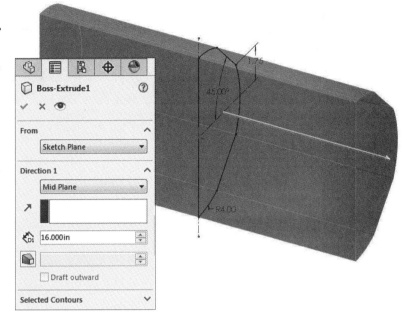

3. Creating the bore hole sketch:

- Open a new sketch on the **front face** as noted.

- Sketch the profile shown below and add dimensions/relations to fully define
  the sketch.

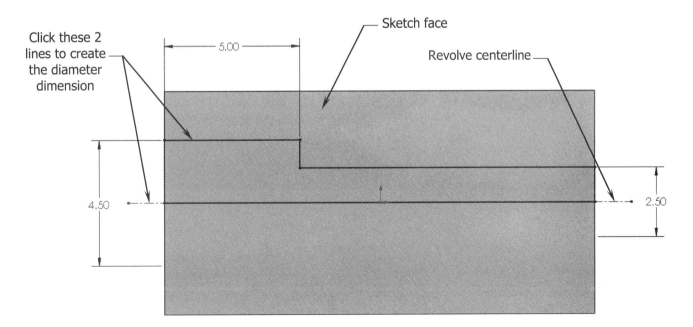

4. Creating a revolved cut:

- Click **Revolved-Cut**.

- Use the default **360°**.

- Click **OK**.

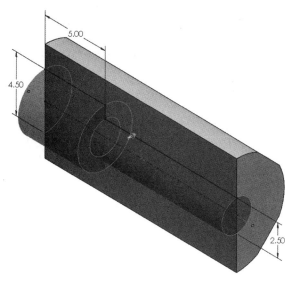

5. Adding the tabs:

- Open a new sketch on the **planar face** of the left end.

- Select the two angled edges and click **Convert Entities**.

- Add the additional lines to create two rectangles.

- Add an **Equal** relation for the Width of the rectangles, and add the **Parallels** or **Perpendiculars** relations for the others.

- Add any other dimensions to fully define the sketch.

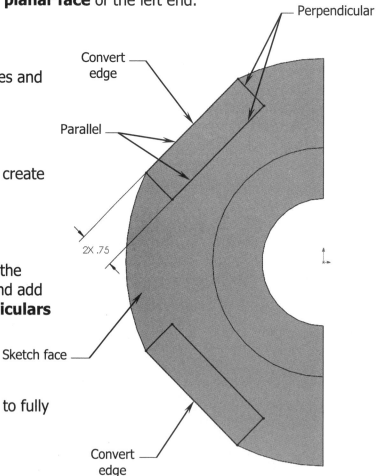

6. Extruding the tabs:

- Click **Extruded Boss/Base**.

- Use the default **Blind** type.

- Enter **1.00 in**. for depth.

- Click **OK**.

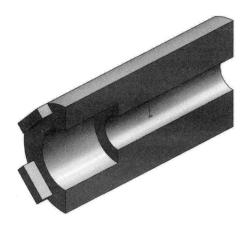

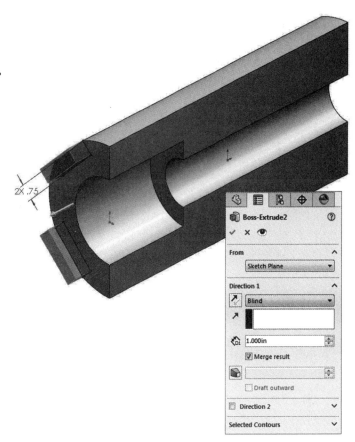

7. Creating the cut features:

- Open a new sketch on the **Top** plane.

- Sketch 2 rectangles and make the lines on the bottom **Collinear** with the edge of the model (see next page).

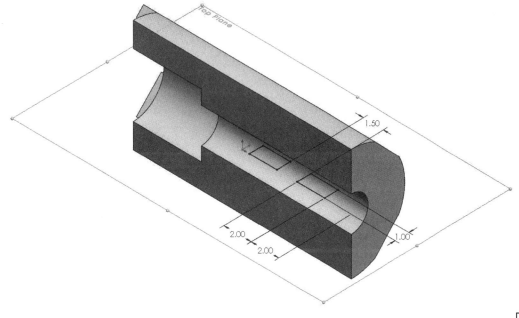

Next ⟩

- Add the relations/dimensions shown to fully define the sketch.

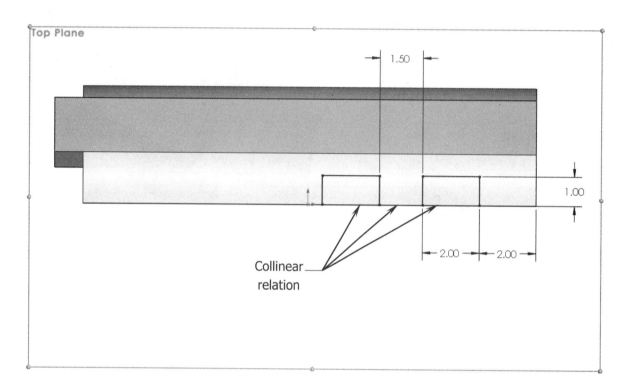

Collinear relation

8. Extruding the cuts:

- Click **Extruded-Cut**.

- Use the **Through All** type.

- Click Reverse if needed to remove the bottom portion of the half cylinder.

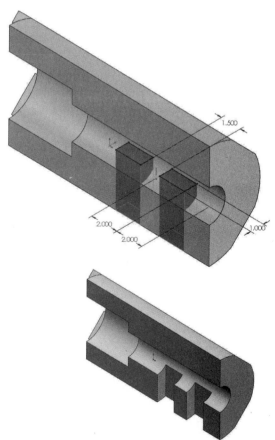

- Click **OK**.

9. Adding another cut feature:

- Open a new sketch on the **planar face** as noted.

- Sketch the profile and add the dimensions below to fully define the sketch.

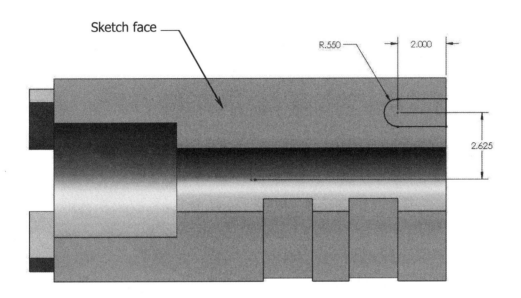

Sketch face

R.550   2.000

2.625

10. Extruding a cut:

- Click **Extruded-Cut**.

- Use the default **Blind** type.

- Enter **.750 in**. for depth.

- Click **OK**.

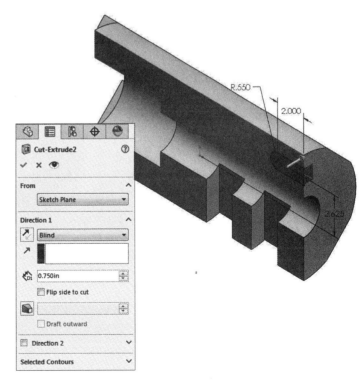

R.550   2.000   2.625

Cut-Extrude2

From
Sketch Plane

Direction 1
Blind

0.750in
Flip side to cut

Draft outward

Direction 2

Selected Contours

11. Calculating the Mass:

- Be sure to set the material to **1060 Alloy**.

- Switch to the **Evaluate** tab.

- Click **Mass Properties**.

- If needed, set the Unit of Measure to **IPS**, **3 decimals**.

- Enter the final mass of the model here:

_____ lbs.

- Save your work as **Hydraulic Cylinder Half.**

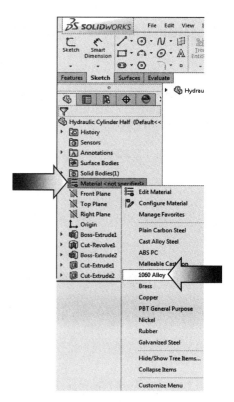

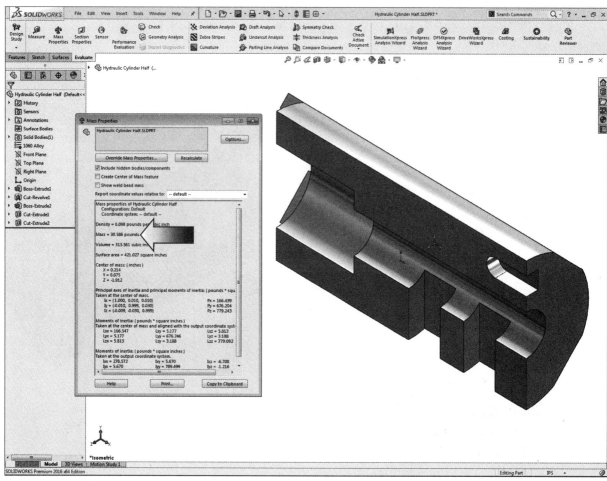

Question 7: Basic Part Modeling (2 of 4)

- Create this part in SOLIDWORKS.
- Origin: **Arbitrary**
- Material: **1060 Alloy**

- Unit: **Inches, 3 decimals**
- Drafting Standards: **ANSI**
- Density: **0.098 lb/in^3**

(This question focuses on the use of sketch tools, relations, and circular pattern feature.)

1. Creating the main body:

- Open a new sketch on the **Front** plane.

- Sketch the profile using the Mirror function to ensure all entities are symmetrical about the vertical centerline.

- Add the dimensions and relations needed to fully define the sketch.

*Note: Hold the **Shift** key when adding the 1.00" dimension.

- Add a horizontal centerline and use it as the revolve line in the next step.

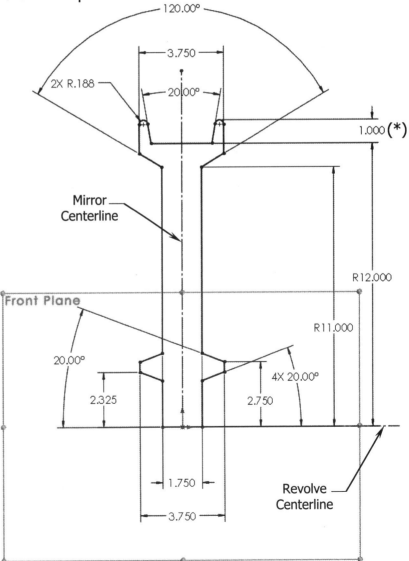

2. Revolving the main body:

- Click **Revolved Boss/Base**.

- Select the **horizontal centerline** as the Axis of Revolution.

- Use the **Blind** type and the default **360º**.

- Click **OK**.

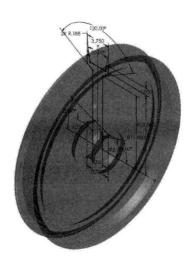

3. Creating the 1ˢᵗ cutout:

- Open a new sketch on the **face** as indicated.

- Sketch a vertical and a horizontal centerlines from the origin.

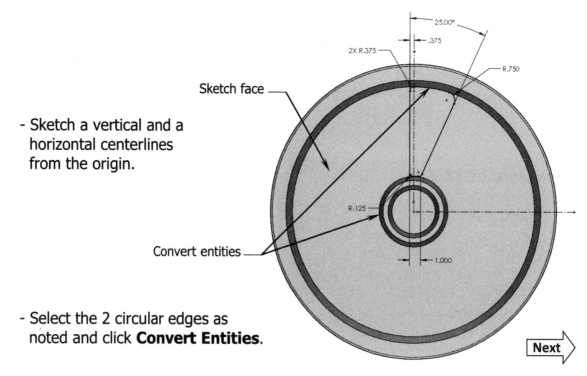

Sketch face

Convert entities

- Select the 2 circular edges as noted and click **Convert Entities**.

Next

- **Trim** the sketch entities to create one continuous closed contour.

- Add the dimensions shown to fully define the sketch before adding the sketch fillets.

- **Note:**
  There are three different fillet sizes in this sketch.

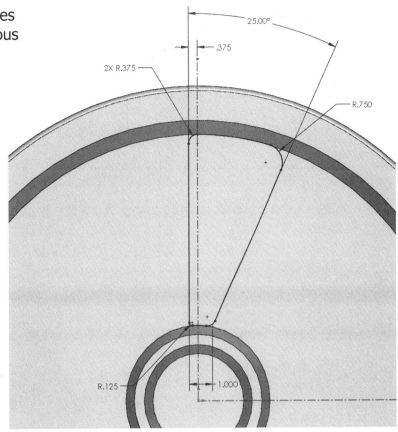

4. Extruding a cut:

- Click **Extruded-Cut**.

- Use the **Through All** type.

- Click **OK**.

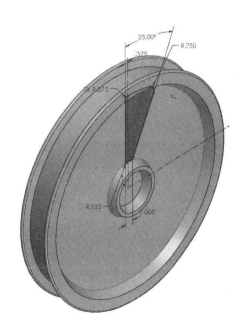

5. Creating a Circular pattern:

- Under the Linear Pattern drop down menu; select **Circular Pattern**.

- Select the **circular edge** as noted for Pattern Direction.

- Enable the Equal Spacing checkbox (**360º**).

- Enter **12** for Number of Instances.

- Select the **cutout** feature either from the graphics area or from the feature tree.

- Click **OK**.

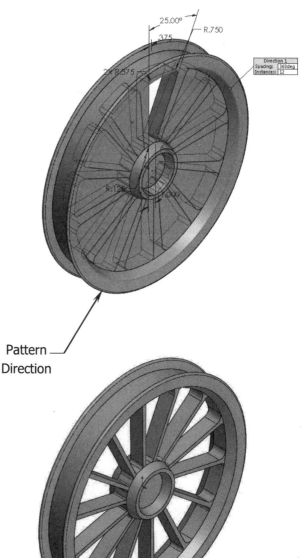

Pattern Direction

- Rotate the model and inspect the result of the pattern.

6. Calculating the Mass:

- Be sure to set the material to **1060 Alloy**.

- Switch to the **Evaluate** tab.

- Click **Mass Properties**.

- If needed, set the Unit of Measure to **IPS**, **3 decimals**.

- Enter the final mass of the model here:

_____ lbs.

- Save your work as **CSWA_Wheel**.

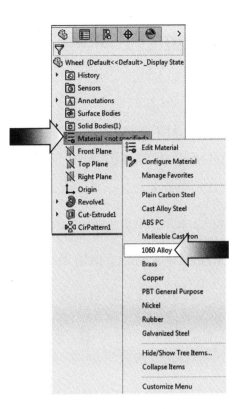

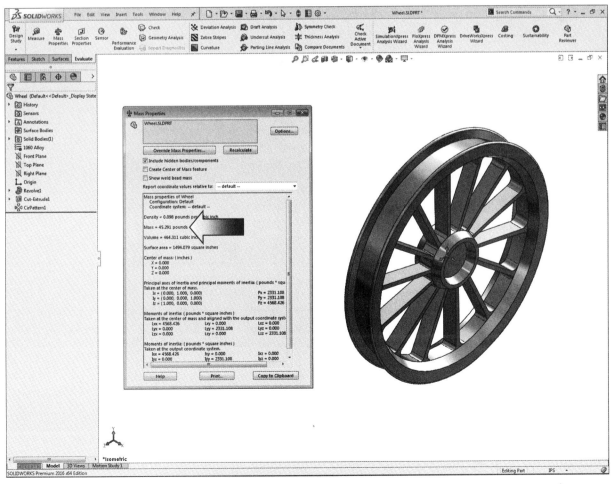

Question 8: Basic Part Modeling (3 of 4)

- Create this part in SOLIDWORKS. - Unit: **Inches, 3 decimals**

- Origin: **Arbitrary** - Drafting Standards: **ANSI**

- Material: **AISI 1020** - Density: **0.285 lb/in^3**

(This question focuses on the use of sketch tools, relations, and extrude features.)

1. Creating the main body:

- Open a new sketch on the **Front** plane.

- Sketch the profile below and only add the corner fillets after the sketch is fully defined.

- Add the dimensions and relations as indicated. Do not add the 2 reference dimensions (36 and 45.43); use them to check or measure the geometry only.

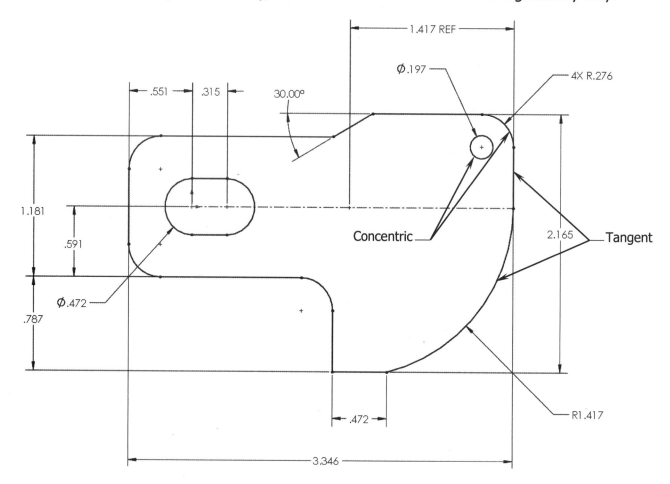

2. Extruding the base:

- Click **Extruded Boss/Base**.

- Select the **Mid Plane** type.

- Enter **1.00 in**. for depth.

- Click **OK**.

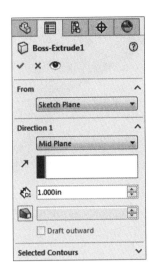

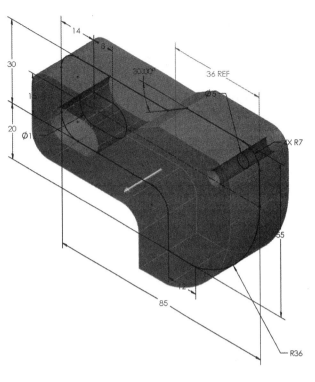

3. Creating the center cutout:

- Open a new sketch
  on the **Front** plane.

- Sketch a
  circle on the
  upper right
  corner of
  the model.

- Add the dimensions
  fully as shown to
  define the sketch.

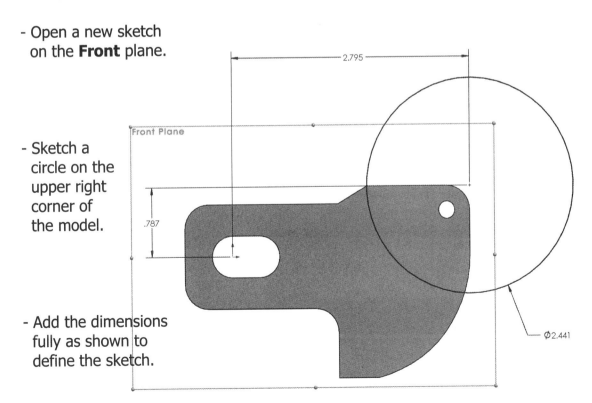

4. Extruding a cut:

- Click **Extruded Cut**.

- Use the **Mid-Plane** type.

- Enter **.475 in**. for depth.

- Click **OK**.

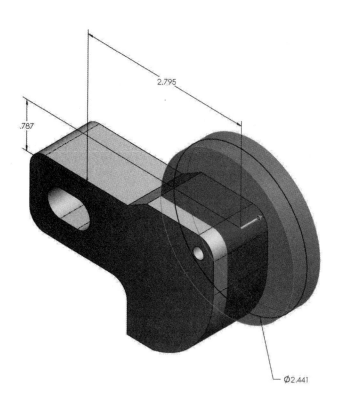

5. Creating the side cut:

- Open a new sketch on the **planar face** as noted.

- Select the **3 edges** as indicated and click **Convert Entities**.

- Extend the converted lines to merge their end points, and add 3 other lines to close off the sketch.

- Add a **Collinear** relation between the horizontal line and the model edge to fully define the sketch.

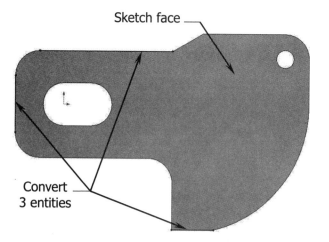

Sketch face

Convert
3 entities

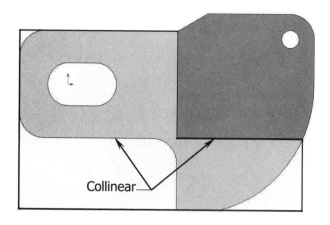

Collinear

6. Extruding a cut:

- Click **Extruded Cut**.

- Use the default **Blind** type.

- Enter **.492 in**. for depth.

- Click **OK**.

- Rotate the model to verify the result of the cut.

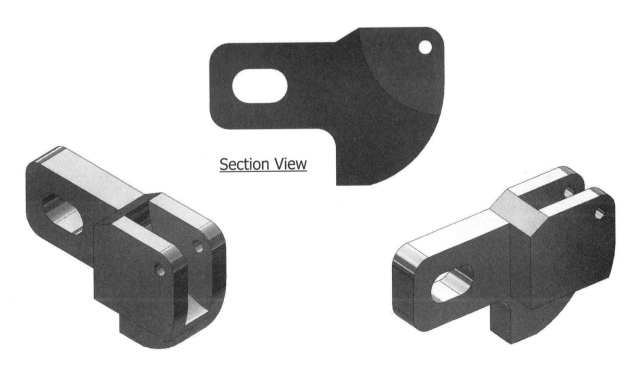

Section View

7. Calculating the Mass:

- Be sure to set the material to **AISI 1020**.

- Click **Mass Properties**.

- If needed, set the Unit of Measure to **IPS**, **3 decimals**.

- Enter the final mass of the model here:

_____ lbs.

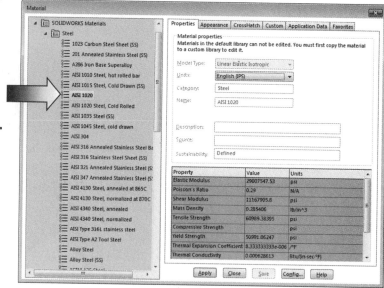

- Save your work as **CSWA Tool Block Lever.**

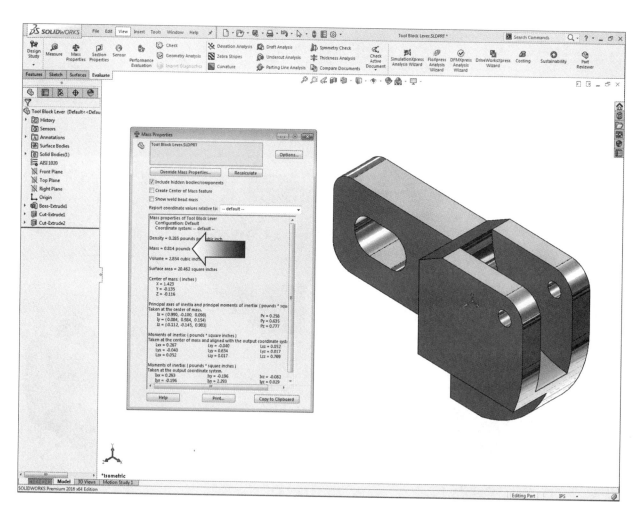

Question 9: Basic Part Modeling (4 of 4)

- Create this part in SOLIDWORKS.
- Origin: **Arbitrary**
- Material: **AISI 1020**

- Unit: **Inches, 3 decimals**
- Drafting Standards: **ANSI**
- Density: **0.285 lb/in^3**

(This question focuses on the use of sketch tools, relations, and extrude features.)

1. Creating the main body:

- Open a new sketch on the **Front** plane.

- Sketch the profile below and keep the origin in the center of the large hole.

- Add the dimensions/relations as shown to fully define the sketch.

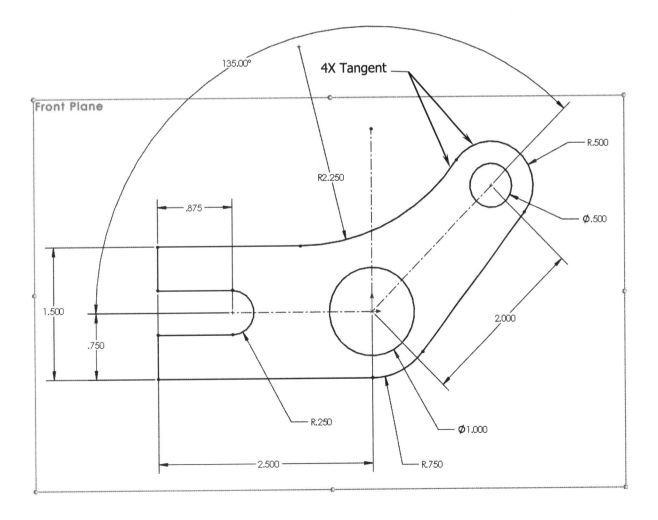

2. Extruding the base:

- Click **Extruded Boss/Base**.

- Use the **Mid-Plane** type.

- Enter **1.00 in**. for depth.

- Click **OK**.

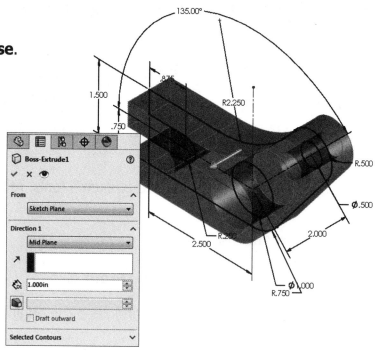

3. Creating the upper cut:

- Open a new sketch on the **planar face** as noted.

- Sketch a circle, a line, and convert 2 entities as indicated.

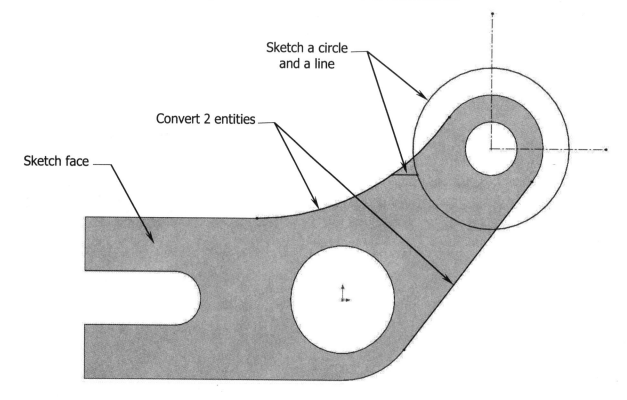

Sketch a circle
and a line

Convert 2 entities

Sketch face

- The center of the circle is coincident with the center of the existing hole.

- Trim the entities and add the dimensions shown to fully define the sketch.

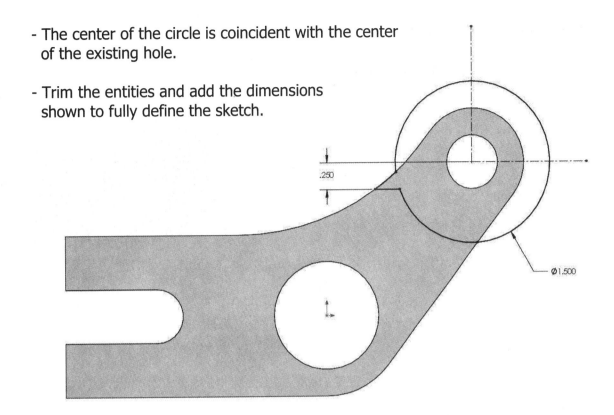

4. Extruding a blind cut:

- Click **Extruded Cut**.

- Use the default **Blind** type.

- Enter **.250 in**. for depth.

- Click **OK**.

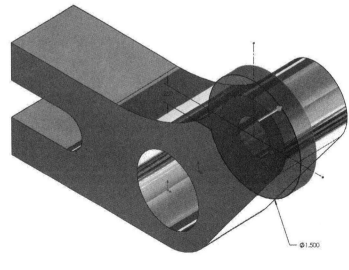

5. Mirroring the cut feature:

- Click **Mirror** from the feature toolbar.

- For Mirror Face/Plane select the **Front** plane from the feature tree.

- For Features to Mirror select the **Cut-Extrude** either from the tree or from the graphics area.

- Click **OK**.

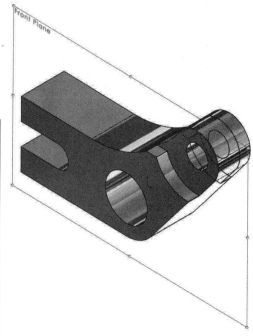

6. Creating the center cut:

- Open a new sketch on the **Top** plane.

- Sketch a rectangle approximately as shown.

- Add the dimensions/relations needed to fully define the sketch.

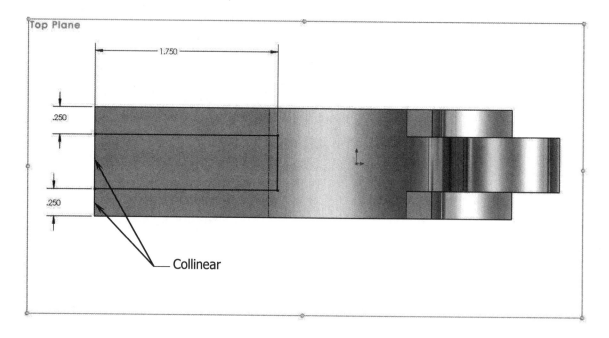

7. Extruding a through cut:

- Click **Extruded Cut**.

- Use the **Through All-Both** type.

- The 2nd direction is selected automatically.

- Click **OK**.

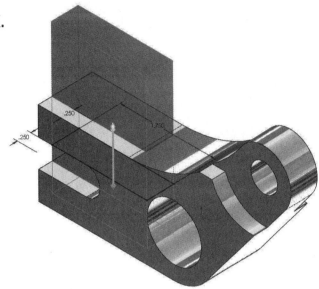

8. Creating a recess feature:

- Open a new sketch on the **planar face** as noted.

- While the selected face is still highlighting click **Offset Entities**.

- Enter **.080 in**. for offset distance and click the Reverse checkbox if needed to place the offset entities on the **inside**.

- Close the Offset Entities command.

Sketch face

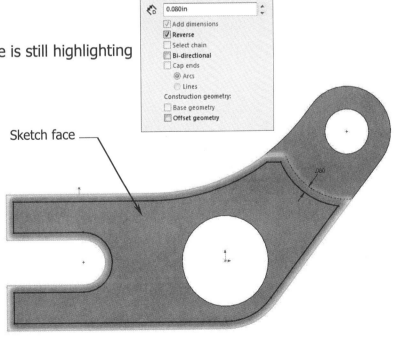

9. Extruding a blind cut:

- Click **Extruded Cut**.

- Use the default **Blind** type.

- Enter **.125 in**. for depth.

- Click **OK**.

- Rotate the model to verify the result of the cut feature.

Note: The recess feature is only added to one side. Do not mirror it.

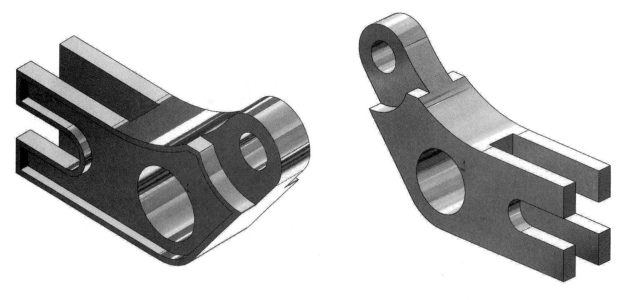

Front Isometric   Rear Isometric

10. Calculating the Mass:

- Be sure to set the material to **AISI 1020**.

- Click **Mass Properties**.

- If needed, set the Unit of Measure to **IPS**, **4 decimals**.

- Enter the final mass of the model here:

_____ lbs.

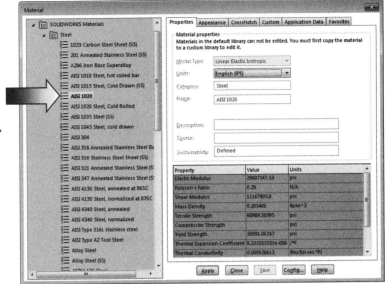

- Save your work as **CSWA Bracket**.

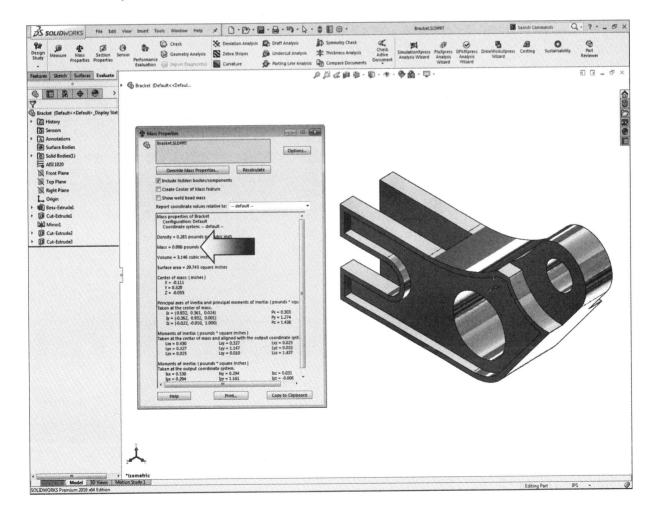

Question 10: Bottom Up Assembly (1 of 2)

- Create this assembly in SOLIDWORKS.

- Drafting Standards: **ANSI**

- Origin: **Arbitrary**

- Unit: **Inches**, 3 decimals

(This question focuses on the use of Bottom Up Assembly method, mating components, and changing the mate conditions.)

1. Creating a new assembly:

- Select: **File, New, Assembly**.

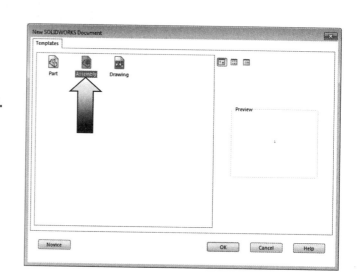

- Click the **Cancel** button and set the Units to **IPS** and the Drafting Standard to **ANSI**.

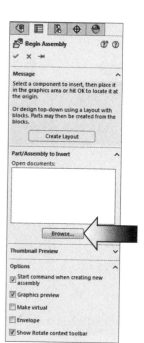

- If the Origin is not visible, select **Origins** from the View pull down menu.

- From the Assembly toolbar select **Insert Component**.

- Locate the part named **Base** from the CSWA Training Folder and open it.

- Place the 1st component on the assembly's origin.

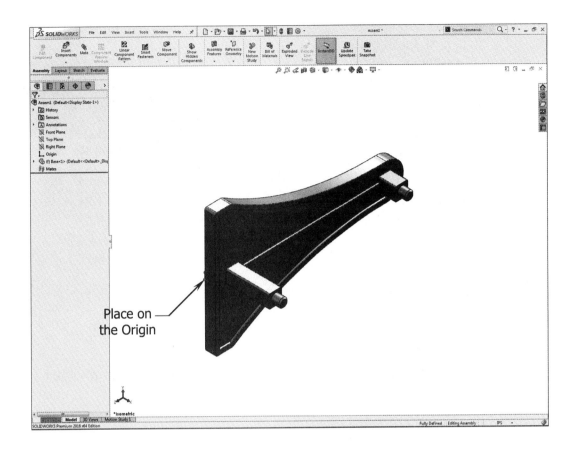

Place on the Origin

2. Inserting other components:

- Insert the rest of the components into the assembly as labeled.

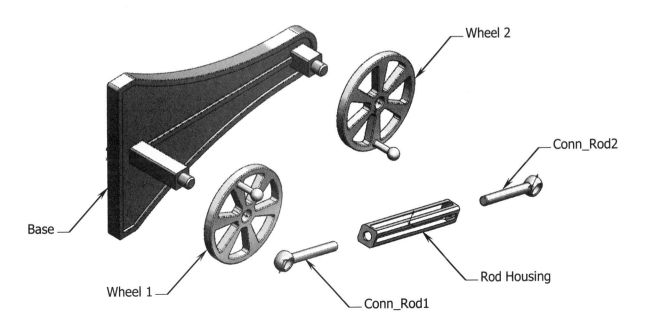

Wheel 2

Conn_Rod2

Base

Wheel 1

Conn_Rod1

Rod Housing

3. Mating the components:

- The components that need To be moved or rotated will get only 2 mates assigned to them, but the ones that are fixed will get 3 mates instead.

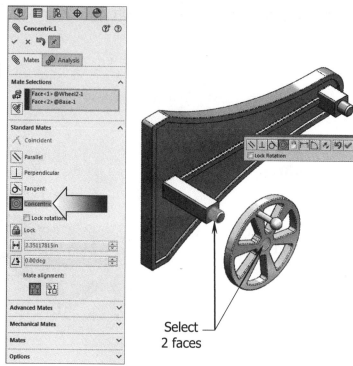

Select 2 faces

- For clarity, hide all components except for the **Base** and the **Wheel1.**

- Click the **Mate** command from the Assembly toolbar.

- Select the **cylindrical face** of the Pin on the left side of the Base and the **hole** in the middle of the Wheel1.

- A **Concentric** mate is selected automatically.

- Click **OK** to accept the mate.

- Select the **planar face** at the end of the Pin and the **planar face** on the far side of the Wheel1. (The dotted line indicates the surface in the back of the component.)

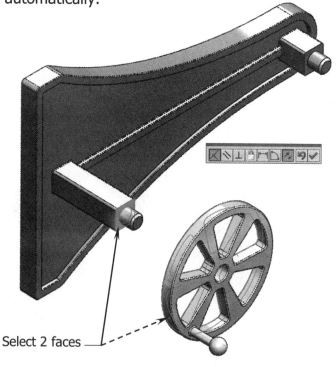

- When 2 planar faces are selected, a **Coincident** mate is added automatically.

Select 2 faces

- Click **OK** to accept the mate.

4. Mating the Wheel2 to the Base:

- Show the component **Wheel2**.

- Click the **Mate** command if it is no longer active.

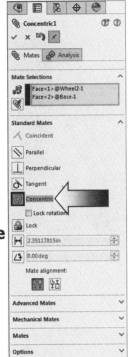

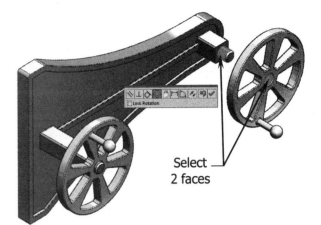

- Add a **Concentric** mate between the **cylindrical face** of the 2nd Pin and the **hole** in the middle of the Wheel2.

Select 2 faces

- Click **OK**.

- Next, select the **planar face** at the end of the Pin and the **planar face** on the far side of the Wheel1.

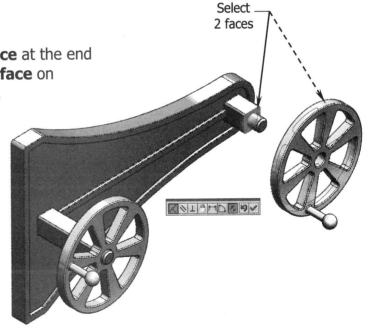

Select 2 faces

- A **Coincident** mate is added automatically.

- Click **OK**.

5. Mating the Conn_Rod1 to the Wheel1:

- Show the component **Conn-Rod1**.

- Select the **cylindrical faces** of both components, the **Wheel1** and the **Conn-Rod1**.

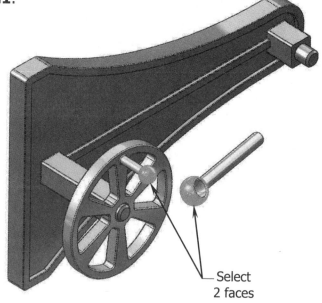

- A **Concentric** mate is added to the 2 selected faces.

Select 2 faces

- Click **OK**.

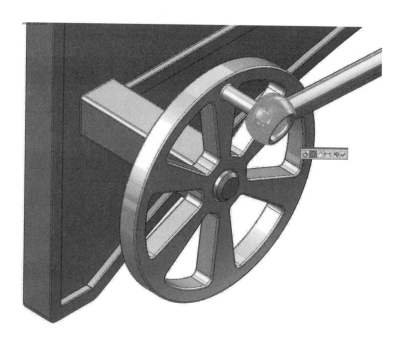

- Test the degrees of freedom of each component by dragging them back and forth.

- Move the Conn-Rod1 to a position where it does not interfere with the knob in the Wheel1 (similar to the picture above).

6. Mating the Conn_Rod2 to the Wheel2:

- Show the component **Conn_Rod2**.

- Select the **cylindrical faces** of both components, the **Conn-Rod2** and the **Wheel2** as pictured.

- Another **Concentric** mate is added to the 2 selected faces.

Select 2 faces

- Click **OK**.

- Drag the Conn_Rod2 back and forth to test it.

- Move the Conn_Rod2 to the position similar to the one pictured above.

7. Mating the Rod_Housing to the Conn_Rods:

- Show the component **Rod_Housing**.

- Select the **cylindrical face** of the Conn-Rod1 and the **hole** on the left side of the Rod_Housing.

- A **Concentric** mate is added to the 2 selected faces.

- Click **OK**.

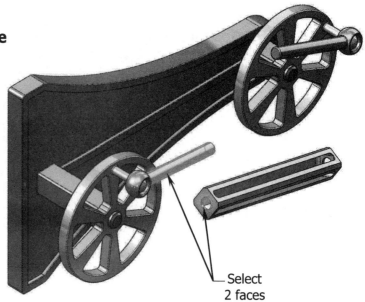

Select 2 faces

- Test the Rod_Housing by dragging it back and forth. It should be constrained to moves only along the longitudinal axis of the Conn-Rod.

- Move the Rod_Housing to a position similar to the one pictured above.

- Zoom in to the right side of the assembly. We will assemble the Conn_Rod2 to its housing.

- Click the **Mate** command if it is no longer selected.

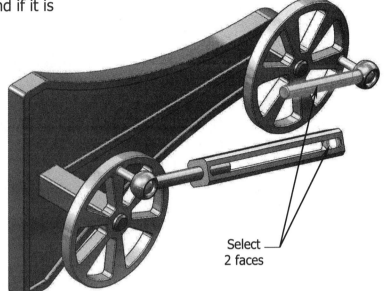

- Select the **cylindrical face** of the Conn-Rod1 and the **hole** on the right side of the Rod_Housing.

Select 2 faces

- Another **Concentric** mate is added to the 2 selected faces.

- Click **OK**.

8. Adding a Symmetric mate:

- Using the Feature tree, expand the Rod-Housing and select its **Front** Plane (A).

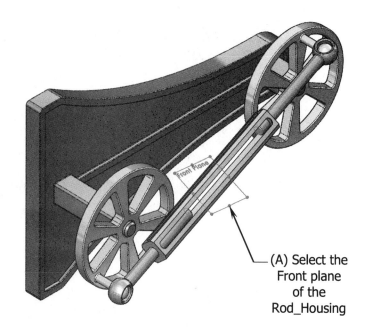

(A) Select the
Front plane
of the
Rod_Housing

- Change to the **Advanced Mates** section and select the **Symmetric** button (B).

- The 2 ends are spaced evenly. Click **OK**.

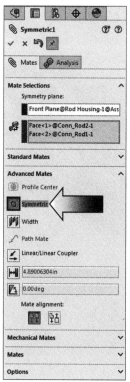

(B) Select the
2 end faces
of the 2
Conn_Rods

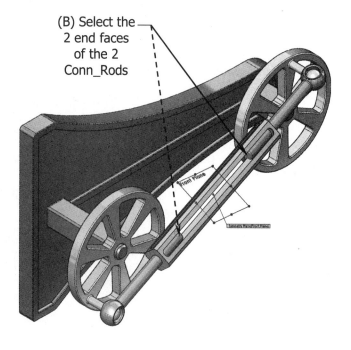

9. Testing the assembly motions:

- Exit out of the Mate mode.

- Drag the handle on the Wheel1 as indicated.

- When the Wheel1 is turned it moves the Conn-Rod1 with it, and at the same time the Rod_Housing and the Conn_Rod2 is also moved along.

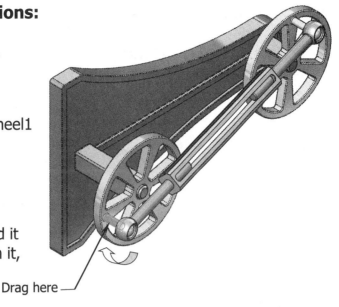

Drag here

- Without a **Limit** mate the 2 Conn-Rods will collide with each other, but since Limit mate is not part of the question, we are going to use an alternate method to test the motion of this assembly.

Longest Distance

- Drag the handles on both wheels to fully extend them to their longest distance (approximately as shown).

- Drag the handle on the Wheel2 in either direction. The Wheel2 should move both Con_Rods and the Rod_Housing with it but without any collisions.

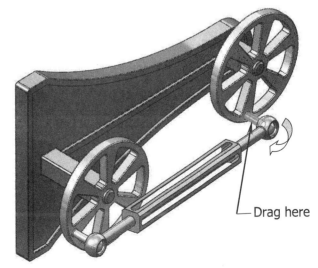

Drag here

10. Creating an Angle mate:

- Expand both components **Base** and **Conn_Rod1**.

- Click the **Mate** command again.

- Using the Feature Manager tree, select the **Front** plane of the Base and the **Right** plane of the Conn_Rod1 (arrows).

- Select the **Angle** button and enter **90º**. Click **OK**.

- The 2 planes should be perpendicular to each other.

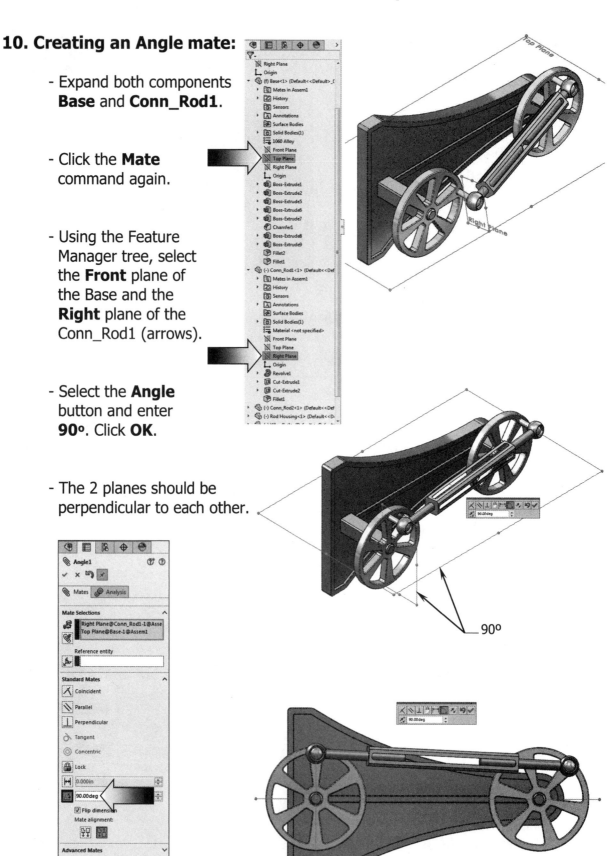

90º

11. Measuring the distance:

- Switch to the **Evaluate** tab.

- Select the **Measure** command and measure the distance between the **left end** of the Rod_Housing and the **end face** of the Conn_Rod1.

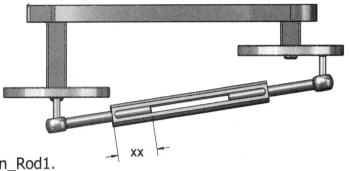

- Enter the distance (in inches) here: _____

12. Changing the mate Angle:

- Expand the **Mates Group** at the bottom of the Feature tree (arrow).

- <u>Edit</u> the **Angle mate** and change the angle to **180°.** Click **OK.**

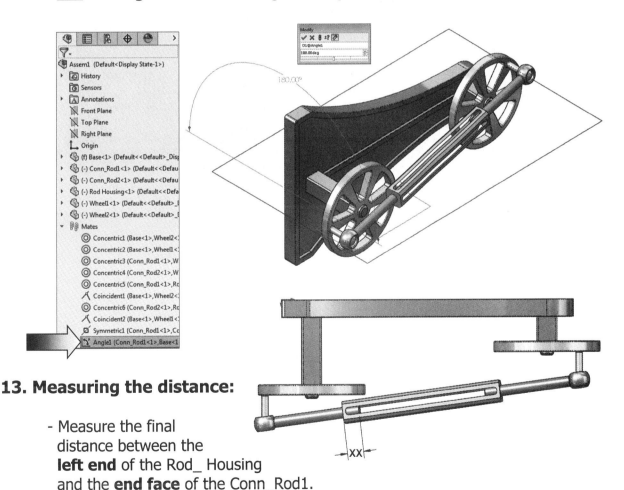

13. Measuring the distance:

- Measure the final distance between the **left end** of the Rod_ Housing and the **end face** of the Conn_Rod1.

- Enter the distance (in inches) here: _____

Question 11: Bottom Up Assembly (2 of 2)

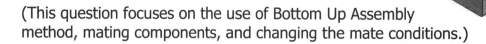

- Create this assembly in SOLIDWORKS.

- Drafting Standards: **ANSI**

- Origin: **Arbitrary**

- Unit: **Inches, 3 decimals**

(This question focuses on the use of Bottom Up Assembly method, mating components, and changing the mate conditions.)

1. Creating a new assembly:

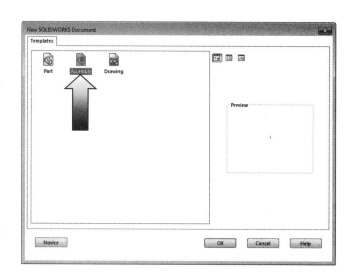

- Select: **File, New, Assembly**.

- Click the **Cancel** button and set the Units to **IPS** and the Drafting Standard to **ANSI**.

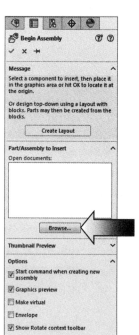

- If the Origin is not visible, select **Origins** from the View pull down menu.

- From the Assembly toolbar select **Insert Component**.

- Locate the part named **Base_Exe** from the **CSWA Assembly Exercise** folder and open it.

- Place the 1st component on the assembly's origin.

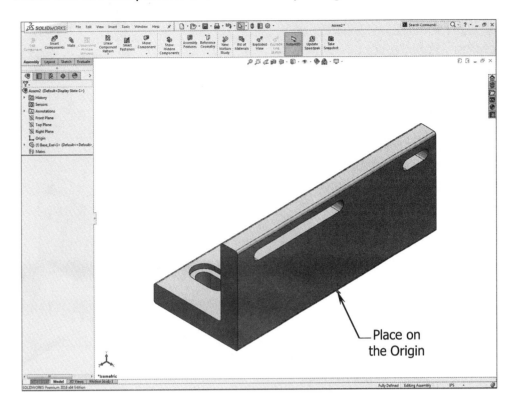

2. Inserting other components:

- Insert the rest of the components into the assembly as labeled.

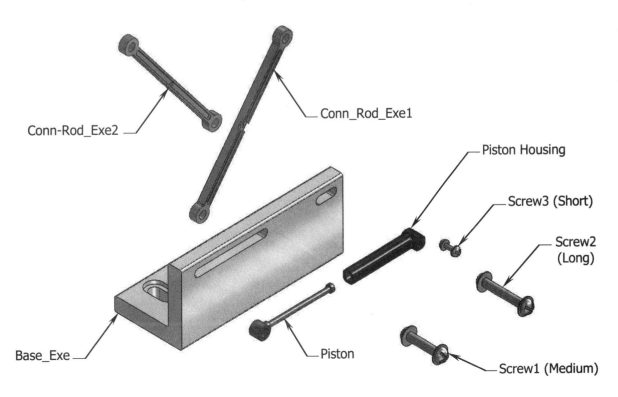

3. Changing configurations:

- The Screw contains 3 different configurations, a Long, a Medium, and a Short.

- To change configuration simply click the Screw, and in the pop-up menu select the configuration from the list and click the check mark (arrow).

- To quickly make a copy of a component, simply hold the Control key and drag it aside.

- Create a total of 3 instances of the Screw and change their configurations as labeled. Click the **check mark** after each change.

- Use the left mouse button to move a component and the right button to rotate. Rearrange the components similar to this image.

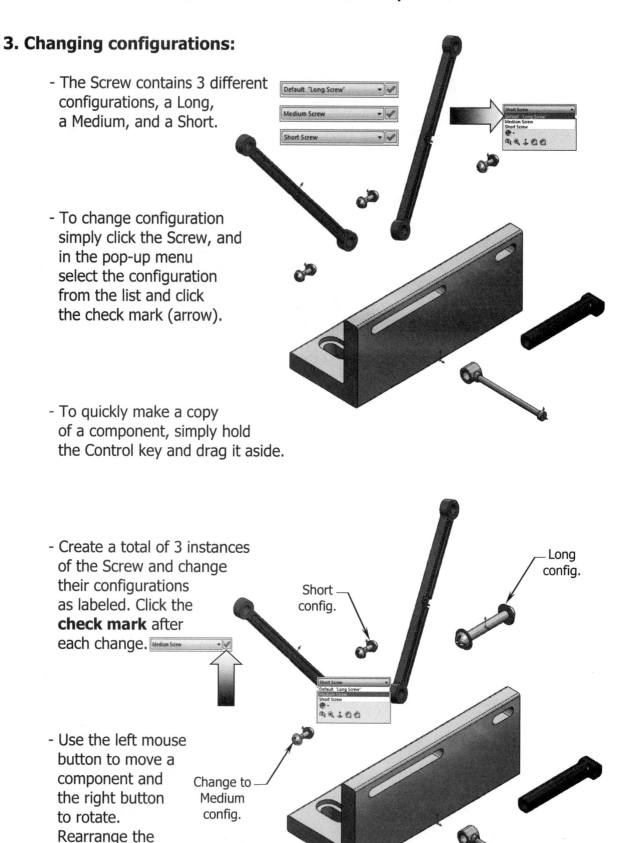

Short config.

Long config.

Change to Medium config.

4. Mating the Piston Housing:

- Click the **Mate** command again to reactivate it.

- Select the **face of the slot** of the Base_Exe and the **hole** in the Piston Housing.

- A **Concentric** mate is selected automatically for the selection.

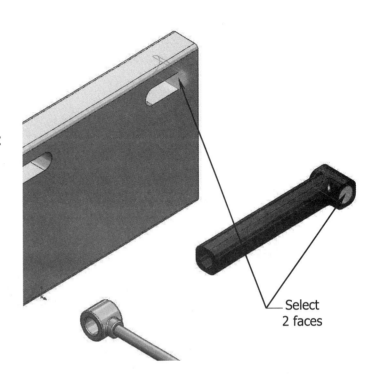

Select 2 faces

- Click **OK** to accept the mate.

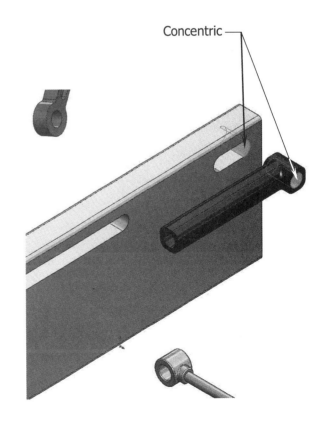

Concentric

- Select the **planar face** in the back of the
Base_Exe and the **planar face** on the
far side of the Piston Housing.
(The dashed line represents a
hidden face.)

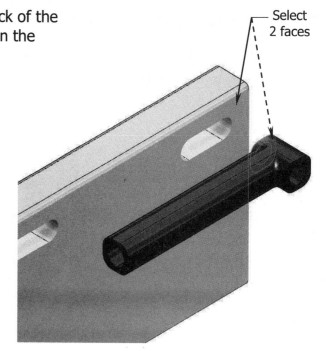

Select
2 faces

- A **Coincident** mate is selected.

- Click **OK**.

NOTE: Press the F5 function key to activate the Selection-Filters and use the Filter-Faces
to assist you with selecting the faces more precisely and easily.

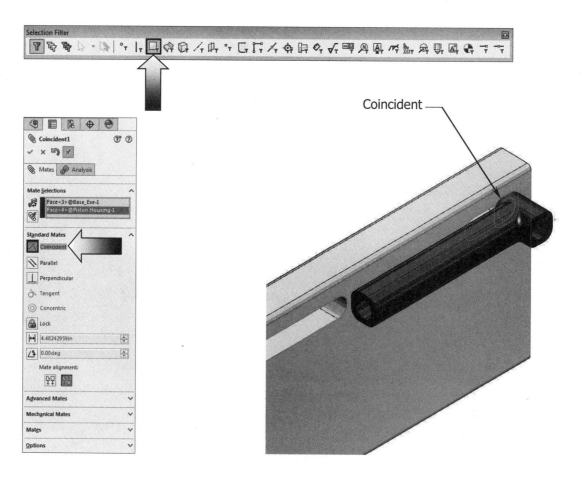

5. Mating the Conn-Rod_Exe1:

- Move the Conn-Rod_Exe1 closer to the Base_Exe as pictured; it will be mated to the Piston Housing.

- Click the **Mate** command if it is no longer active.

- Select the **hole** in the Conn-Rod_Exe1 and the **hole** in the Piston Housing.

- A **Concentric** mate is selected.

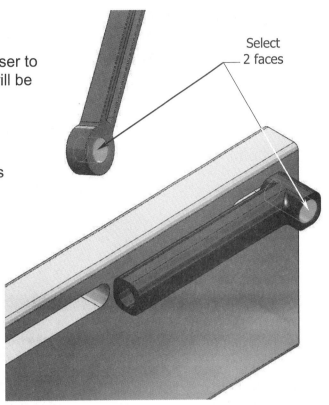

Select 2 faces

- Click **OK**.

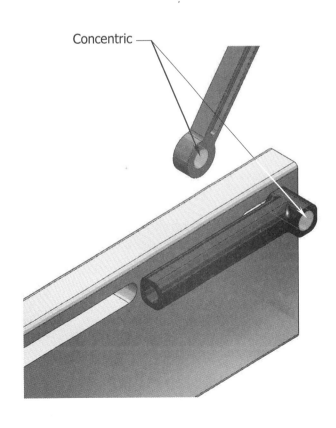

Concentric

- Select the **planar face** in the front of the
Conn-Rod_exe1 and the **planar face**
on the far side of the Piston Housing.

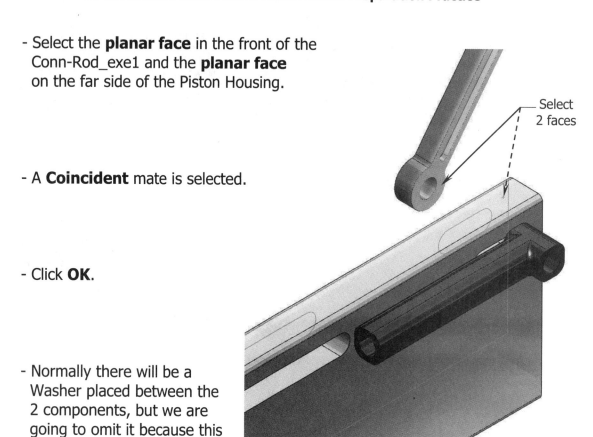

Select
2 faces

- A **Coincident** mate is selected.

- Click **OK**.

- Normally there will be a
Washer placed between the
2 components, but we are
going to omit it because this
assembly does not need one.

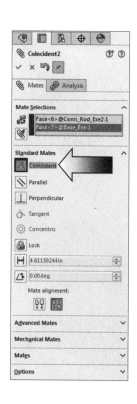

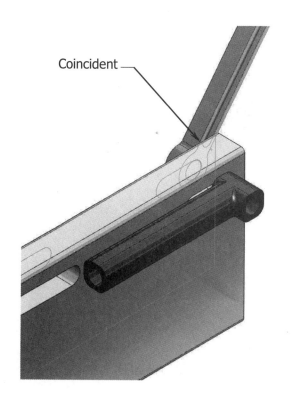

Coincident

6. Mating the Long Screw:

- Move the **Long screw** closer as pictured;
  it will be mated to the Conn-Rod_Exe1.

- Ensure that the mate command is
  still active.

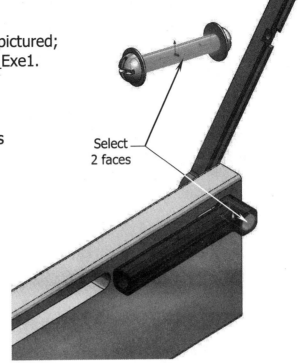

Select
2 faces

- Select the **cylindrical face** of
  the Long Screw and the **hole**
  in the Piston Housing.

- A **Concentric** mate is selected
  automatically.

- Click **OK**.

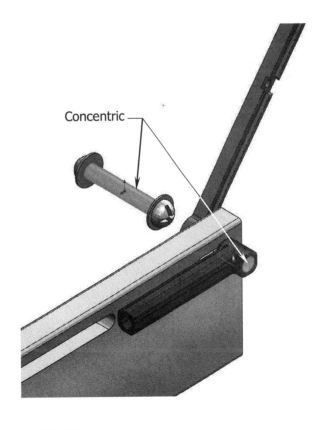

Concentric

- When 2 components need to be centered with one another, Width mate is one of the best options to do that with.

A. Select 2 opposing faces for Width

- To specify the width of each part, you will need to select two opposing faces of each one such as the faces of the tab and the faces that represent the width of the groove in which the tab will be centered.

- Expand the **Advanced Mates** section and select the **Width** option (arrow).

B. Select 2 opposing faces for Tab

A. Select the **2 opposing faces** of the Long Screw.

B. Select the **2 opposing faces** of the Piston Housing and the Conn-Rod_exe1.

- The 2 selected components are centered automatically.

- Click **OK**.

Width mate

Width Reference

Tab Reference

Width Reference

7. Mating the Piston to its Housing:

- Move the Piston closer to the Piston Housing as pictured.

- Select the **cylindrical face** of the Piston and the **hole** in the Piston Housing as indicated.

- A **Concentric** mate is selected but the alignment is incorrect.

- Locate the **Align/Anti Align** buttons (arrow) at the bottom of the Standard Mates section.

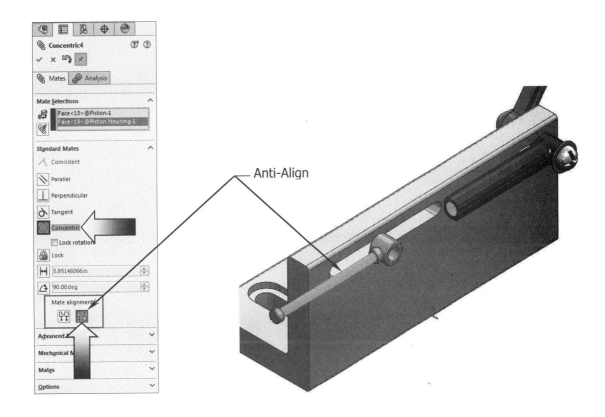

Select 2 faces

Anti-Align

- Toggle the **Align/Anti Align** buttons (arrow) to flip the Piston to the correct orientation.

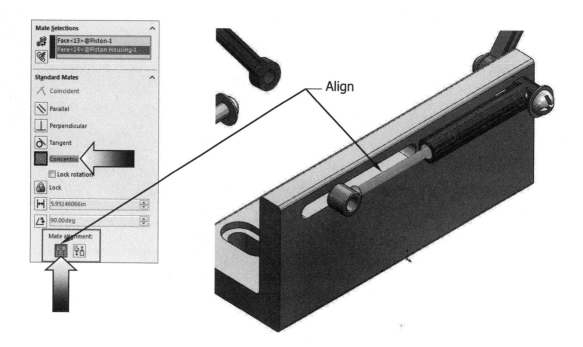

8. Mating the Conn_Rod_Exe2 to the Piston:

- Move the Conn-Rod_Exe2 closer to the Piston as shown.

- The **Mate** command should still be active; select it otherwise.

- Select the **hole** on the bottom of the Conn-Rod_exe2 and the **hole** in the Piston.

- A **Concentric** mate is selected.

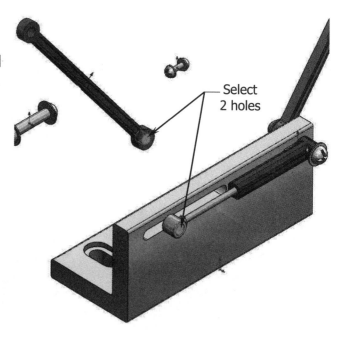

- Click **OK** to accept the concentric mate.

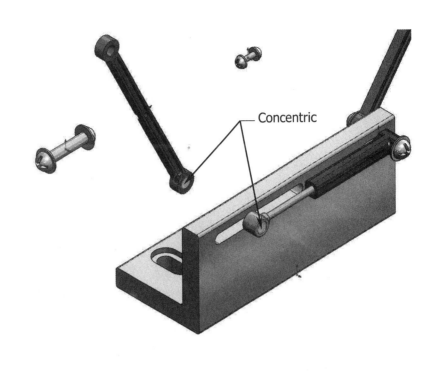

Concentric

9. Rearranging the components:

- Drag the top of the Conn_Rod_Exe2 to the right, and drag the top of the Conn_Rod_Exe1 to the left.

- From the right view orientation the 2 Conn-Rods should look similar to the one pictured below.

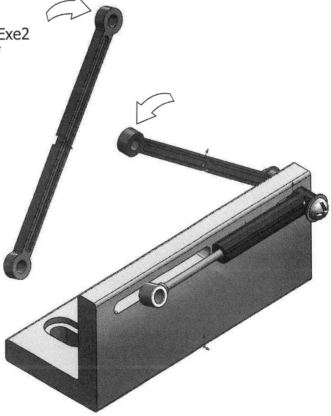

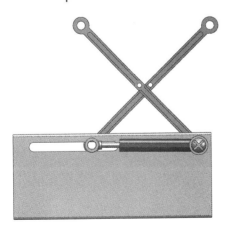

10. Mating the two Connecting Rods:

- Click the **Mate** command.

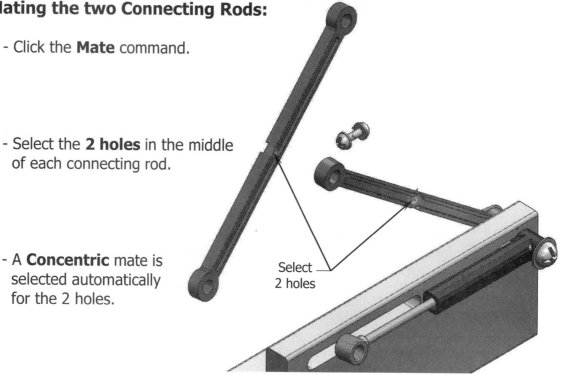

- Select the **2 holes** in the middle of each connecting rod.

- A **Concentric** mate is selected automatically for the 2 holes.

Select 2 holes

- Click **OK**.

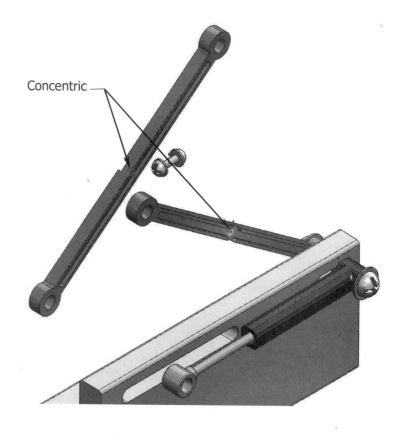

Concentric

- For the coincident mate, select **the face in the front** of the Conn_Rod_Exe2 and **the face on the far side** of the Conn_Rod_Exe1.

- The dashed line represents the hidden face on the rear of the component.

- A **Coincident** mate is selected automatically.

- Click **OK**.

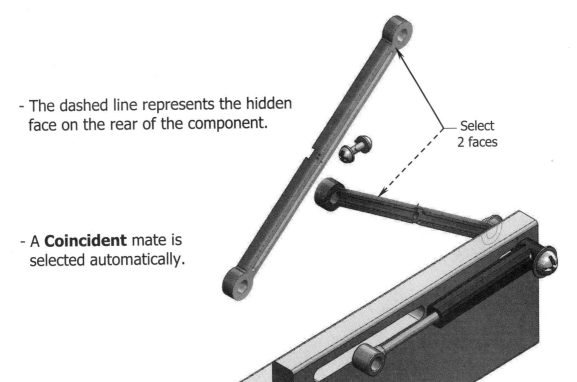

Select 2 faces

- The front face of the Conn_Rod2 moves forward and touches the back face of the Conn-Rod1.

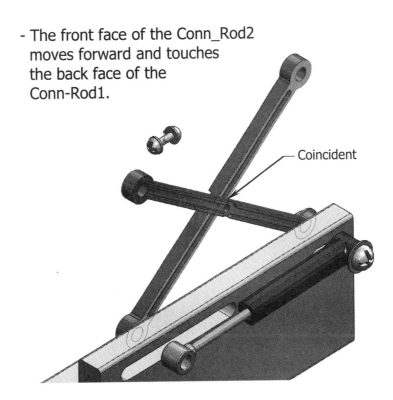

Coincident

11. Adding a Cam mate: (Note: The Slot mate option is only available in SW-2014 or newer).

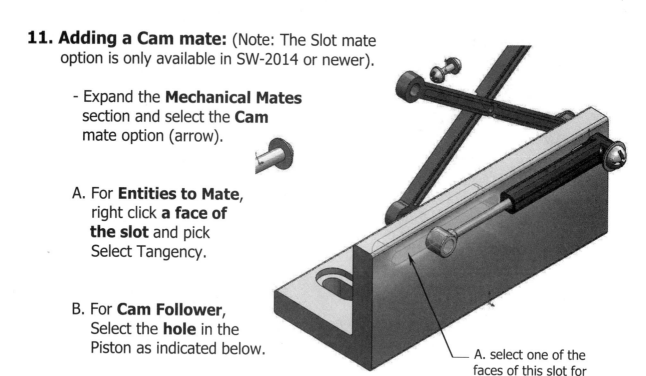

- Expand the **Mechanical Mates** section and select the **Cam** mate option (arrow).

A. For **Entities to Mate**, right click **a face of the slot** and pick Select Tangency.

B. For **Cam Follower**, Select the **hole** in the Piston as indicated below.

A. select one of the faces of this slot for **Cam Path**

- Double check the Alignment as shown below.

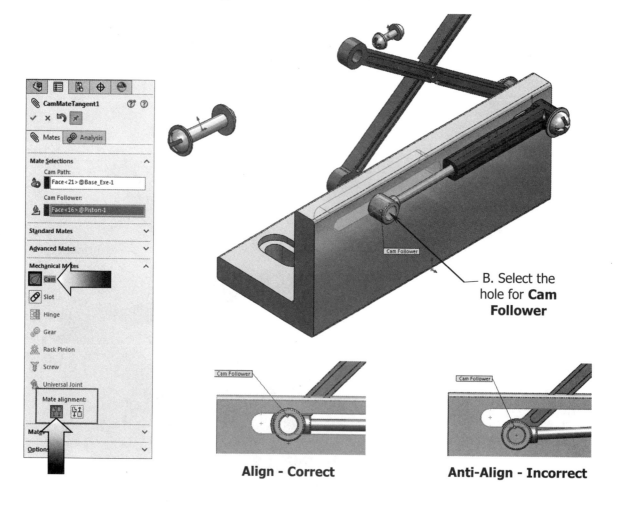

B. Select the hole for **Cam Follower**

Align - Correct

Anti-Align - Incorrect

12. Mating the Medium Screw:

- The **Mate** command should still be active.

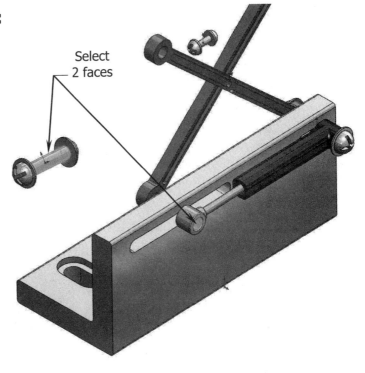

Select 2 faces

- Select the **body** of the Medium Screw and the **hole** in the Piston as indicated.

- A **Concentric** mate is selected.

- Click **OK**.

- The cylindrical body of the Medium Screw is rotated and constrained to the center axis of the hole.

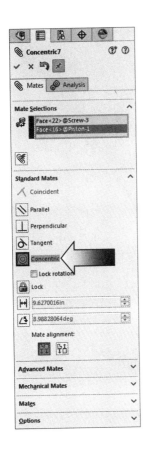

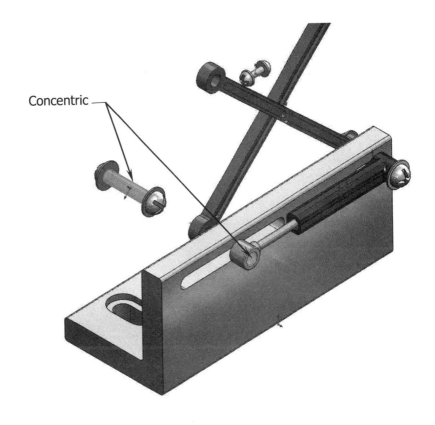

Concentric

- The **Width** mate is used to align the centers of the 2 components.

- Expand the **Advanced Mates** section and select the **Width** option (arrow).

A. Select the **2 opposing faces** of the Medium Screw as indicated.

B. Select the **rear surface** of the Conn_Rod_Exe2 and the **front face** of the Piston for Tab.

A. Select 2 opposing faces for Width

B. Select 2 opposing faces for Tab

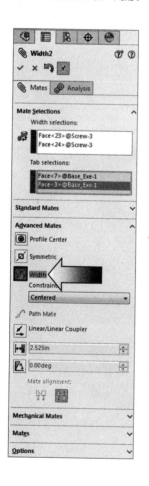

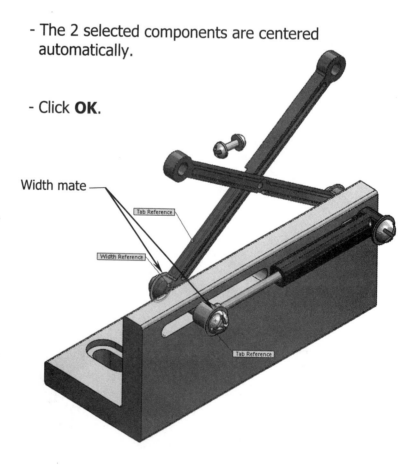

- The 2 selected components are centered automatically.

- Click **OK**.

Width mate

Tab Reference

Width Reference

Tab Reference

13. Mating the Small Screw:

- Click the **Mate** command if it is no longer active.

- Select the **cylindrical face** of the Small Screw and the **hole** in the Conn-Rod_Exe1.

- A **Concentric** mate is selected.

- Click **OK** to accept the mate.

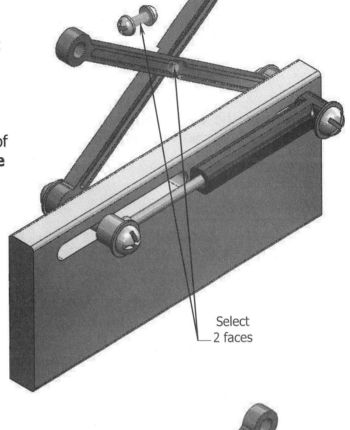

Select 2 faces

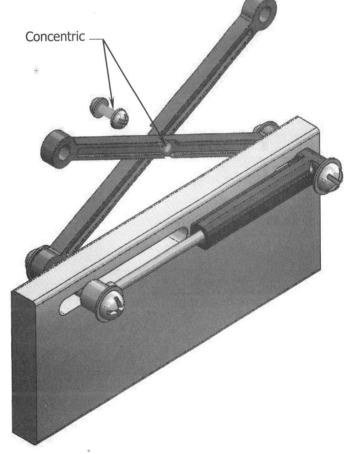

Concentric

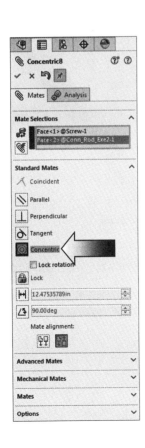

- Use the **Width** mate again to align the centers of the Small Screw and the 2 Conn-Rods.

- Expand the **Advanced Mates** section and select the **Width** option (arrow).

A. Select the **2 opposing faces** of the Small Screw as indicated.

B. Select the **rear surface** of the Conn_Rod_Exe2 and the **front face** of the Conn-Rod_Exe1 for Tab.

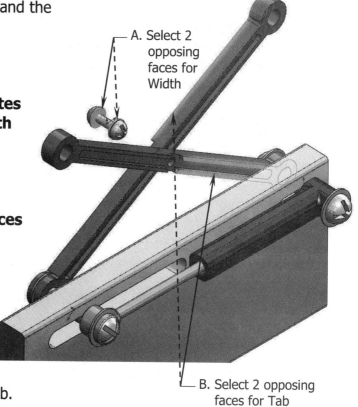

A. Select 2 opposing faces for Width

B. Select 2 opposing faces for Tab

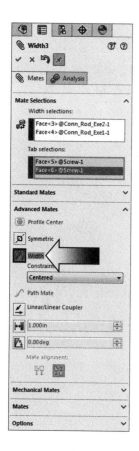

- Click **OK**.

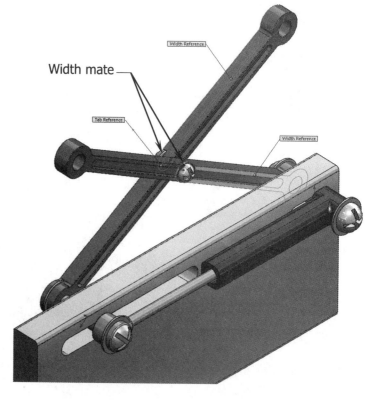

Width mate

14. Mating an Angle Mate:

- After all components have been assembled, a reference location needs to be established so that the center of mass can be measured from it.

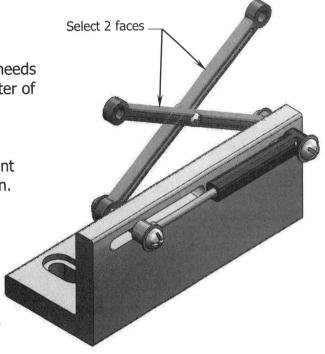

Select 2 faces

- An Angle mate is used at this point to establish the reference location.

- Click the **Mate** command if it is not active.

- Select the **2 faces** of the 2 arms as indicated.

- Click the **Angle** button (arrow) and enter **60°**.

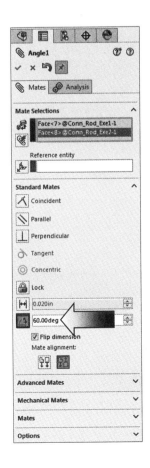

- The 2 arms move to the position similar to the image below. Click **OK**.

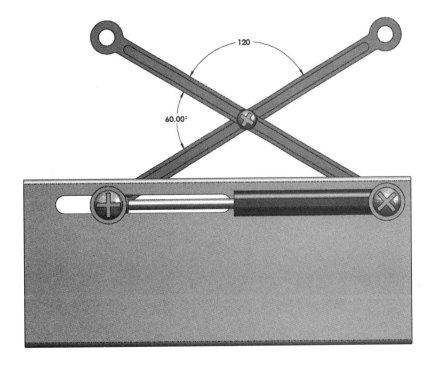

15. Measuring the Center Of Mass of the assembly:

- Click **Mass Properties** from the Evaluate tool tab.

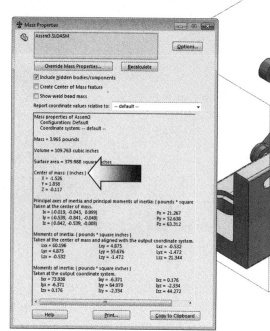

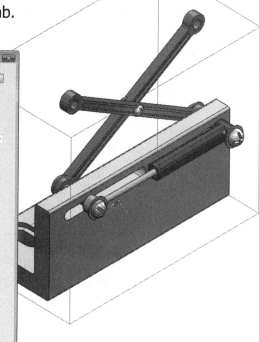

- Enter the **Center Of Mass** below (in Inches)

X = _____

Y = _____

Z = _____

16. Suppressing a mate:

- Expand the **Mates Group** and suppress the Angle mate that was done in step number 14.

- After the Angle mate is suppressed, a **Distance Mate** is needed to create another reference location.

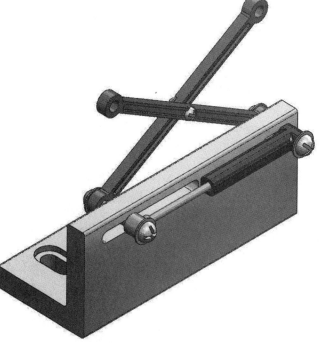

- This time a linear dimension is used instead of an angle.

17. Creating a Section View:

- Click the **Section View** command from the View (Heads Up tool bar).

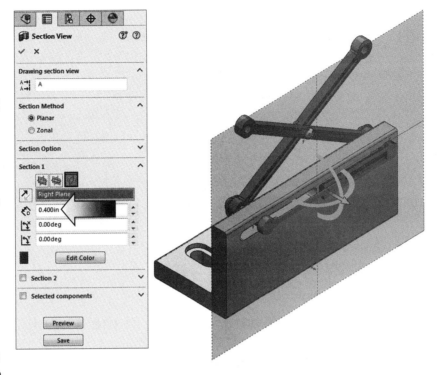

- Select the **Right Plane** as cutting Plane and enter **.400"** for **Offset Distance**.

- Click the Reverse button if needed to remove the front portion of the assembly.

- Click **OK** to close out of the section command.

18. Measuring the distance:

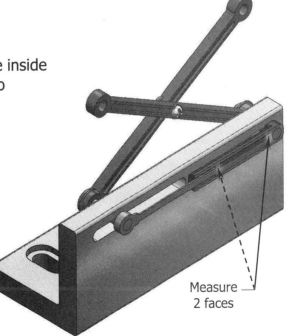

- The Section View allows us to see the inside of the Piston Housing. We will need to create a distance Mate between the end of the Piston and the inside face of the Piston Housing.

- Switch back to the Evaluate tab and click the **Measure** command.

- Measure the distance between the 2 faces as indicated.

Measure 2 faces

- Push **Esc** to exit the measure tool.

19. Creating a Distance Mate:

- Click the **Mate** command.

- Select the **2 faces** that were used in the last step.

- Click the **Distance** button (arrow) and enter **1.00"**.

- The 2 Arms move to a new position (which is equivalent to about 95.34deg).

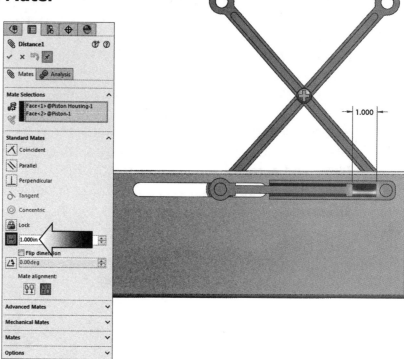

20. Measuring the Center Of Mass of the assembly:

- Click **Mass Properties** from the Evaluate tool tab.

- Enter the Center Of Mass below: (in Inches)

X = _____

Y = _____

Z = _____

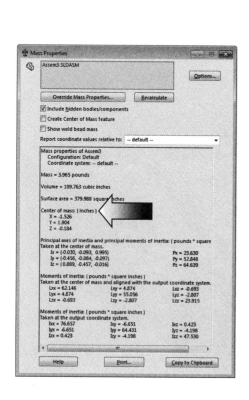

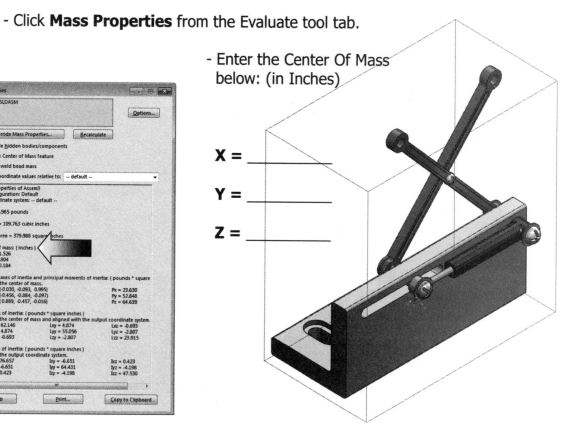

- Practice this material two or three times and time yourself to see if you could complete all challenges within a three hour time frame.

- When you are ready to take the CSWA exam, go to the web link below and purchase the exam using a credit card:
  http://www.solidworks.com/sw/support/796_ENU_HTML.htm

- The test costs $99 for a student or customer without a maintenance subscription, but the exam is free of charge for customers who have purchased the maintenance subscription. For more information, go to the quick link within the same webpage above and select *Certifications offers for subscription service customers*.

- As of the writing of this text, there are a total of **5975 Certified SOLIDWORKS Associate (CSWA)** in the USA, and **113676** CSWA world-wide.
  Go to the link below and enter your state to find out how many CSWA are in your state:
  https://solidworks.virtualtester.com/#userdir_button

- Exam Length: 3 hours

- Minimum passing grade: 70%

- Re-test Policy: There is a minimum 30 day waiting period between every attempt of the CSWA exam. Also, a CSWA exam credit must be purchased for each exam attempt.

- All candidates receive electronic certificates and personal listing on the CSWA directory when they pass. You can also update or change your log in information afterward.

- Dual monitors are recommended but not required. You could save up to 10-15 minutes for <u>not</u> having to switch back and forth between the exam and the SOLIDWORKS application.

Glossary

Alloys:

An Alloy is a mixture of two or more metals (and sometimes a non-metal). The mixture is made by heating and melting the substances together.
Example of alloys are Bronze (Copper and Tin), Brass (Copper and Zinc), and Steel (Iron and Carbon).

Gravity and Mass:

Gravity is the force that pulls everything on earth toward the ground and makes things feel heavy. Gravity makes all falling bodies accelerate at a constant 32ft. per second (9.8 m/s). In the earth's atmosphere, air resistance slows acceleration. Only on airless Moon would a feather and a metal block fall to the ground together.
The mass of an object is the amount of material it contains.
A body with greater mass has more inertia; it needs a greater force to accelerate.
Weight depends on the force of gravity, but mass does not.

When an object spins around another (for example: a satellite orbiting the earth) it is pushed outward. Two forces are at work here: Centrifugal (pushing outward) and Centripetal (pulling inward). If you whirl a ball around you on a string, you pull it inward (Centripetal force). The ball seems to pull outward (Centrifugal force) and if released will fly off in a straight line.

Heat:

Heat is a form of energy and can move from one substance to another in one of three ways: by Convection, by Radiation, and by Conduction.

- Convection takes place only in liquids like water (for example: water in a kettle) and gases (for example: air warmed by a heat source such as a fire or radiator). When liquid or gas is heated, it expands and becomes less dense. Warm air above the radiator rises and cool air moves in to take its place, creating a convection current.

- Radiation is movement of heat through the air. Heat forms match set molecules of air moving and rays of heat spread out around the heat source.

- Conduction occurs in solids such as metals. The handle of a metal spoon left in boiling liquid warms up as molecules at the heated end moves faster and collide with their neighbors, setting them moving. The heat travels through the metal, which is a good conductor of heat.

Inertia:

A body with a large mass is harder to start and also to stop. A heavy truck traveling at 50mph needs more power breaks to stop its motion than a smaller car traveling at the same speed.
Inertia is the tendency of an object either to stay still or to move steadily in a straight line, unless another force (such as a brick wall stopping the vehicle) makes it behave differently.

Joules:

The Joules is the SI unit of work or energy.
One Joule of work is done when a force of one Newton moves through a distance of one meter. The Joule is named after the English scientist James Joule (1818-1889).

Materials:

- Stainless steel is an alloy of steel with chromium or nickel.

- Steel is made by the basic oxygen process. The raw material is about three parts melted iron and one part scrap steel. Blowing oxygen into the melted iron raises the temperature and gets rid of impurities.

- All plastics are chemical compounds called polymers.

- Glass is made by mixing and heating sand, limestone, and soda ash. When these ingredients melt they turn into glass, which is hardened when it cools. Glass is in fact not a solid but a "supercooled" liquid; it can be shaped by blowing, pressing, drawing, casting into molds, rolling, and floating across molten tin to make large sheets.

- Ceramic objects, such as pottery and porcelain, electrical insulators, bricks, and roof tiles are all made from clay. The clay is shaped or molded when wet and soft, and heated in a kiln until it hardens.

Machine Tools:

Are powered tools used for shaping metal or other materials, by drilling holes, chiseling, grinding, pressing or cutting. Often the material (the work piece) is moved while the tool stays still (lathe), or vice versa, the work piece stays still while the tool moves (mill). Most common machine tools are Mill, Lathe, Saw, Broach, Punch press, Grind, Bore and Stamp break.

CNC

Computer Numerical Control is the automation of machine tools that are operated by precisely programmed commands encoded on a storage medium, as opposed to controlled manually via hand wheels or levers, or mechanically automated via cams alone. Most CNC today is computer numerical control in which computers play an integral part of the control.

3D Printing

All methods work by working in layers, adding material, etc. different to other techniques, which are subtractive. Support is needed because almost all methods could support multi material printing, but it is currently only available in certain top tier machines.

A method of turning digital shapes into physical objects. Due to its nature, it allows us to accurately control the shape of the product. The drawback is size restraints and materials are often not durable.

While FDM doesn't seem like the best method for instrument manufacturing, it is one of the cheapest and most universally available methods.

EDM
Electric Discharge Machining.

FDM
Fused Deposition Modeling.

SLA
Stereo Lithography.

SLS
Selective Laser Sintering.

SLM
Selective Laser Melting.

J-P
Jetted Photopolymer (or Polyjet)

Newton's Law:

1. Every object remains stopped or goes on moving at a steady rate in a straight line unless acted upon by another force. This is the inertia principle.
2. The amount of force needed to make an object change its speed depends on the mass of the object and the amount of the acceleration or deceleration required.
3. To every action there is an equal and opposite reaction. When a body is pushed on its way by a force, another force pushes back with equal strength.

Polymers:

A polymer is made of one or more large molecules formed from thousands of smaller molecules. Rubber and Wood are natural polymers. Plastics are synthetic (artificially made) polymers.

Speed and Velocity:

- Speed is the rate at which a moving object changes position (how far it moves in a fixed time).
- Velocity is speed in a particular direction.
- If either speed or direction is changed, velocity also changes.

Absorbed

A feature, sketch, or annotation that is contained in another item (usually a feature) in the FeatureManager design tree. Examples are the profile sketch and profile path in a base-sweep, or a cosmetic thread annotation in a hole.

Align

Tools that assist in lining up annotations and dimensions (left, right, top, bottom, and so on). For aligning parts in an assembly.

Alternate position view

A drawing view in which one or more views are superimposed in phantom lines on the original view. Alternate position views are often used to show range of motion of an assembly.

Anchor point

The end of a leader that attaches to the note, block, or other annotation. Sheet formats contain anchor points for a bill of materials, a hole table, a revision table, and a weldment cut list.

Annotation

A text note or a symbol that adds specific design intent to a part, assembly, or drawing. Specific types of annotations include note, hole callout, surface finish symbol, datum feature symbol, datum target, geometric tolerance symbol, weld symbol, balloon, and stacked balloon. Annotations that apply only to drawings include center mark, annotation centerline, area hatch, and block.

Appearance callouts

Callouts that display the colors and textures of the face, feature, body, and part under the entity selected and are a shortcut to editing colors and textures.

Area hatch
A crosshatch pattern or fill applied to a selected face or to a closed sketch in a drawing.

Assembly
A document in which parts, features, and other assemblies (sub-assemblies) are mated together. The parts and sub-assemblies exist in documents separate from the assembly. For example, in an assembly, a piston can be mated to other parts, such as a connecting rod or cylinder. This new assembly can then be used as a sub-assembly in an assembly of an engine. The extension for a SOLIDWORKS assembly file name is .SLDASM.

Attachment point
The end of a leader that attaches to the model (to an edge, vertex, or face, for example) or to a drawing sheet.

Axis
A straight line that can be used to create model geometry, features, or patterns. An axis can be made in a number of different ways, including using the intersection of two planes.

Balloon
Labels parts in an assembly, typically including item numbers and quantity. In drawings, the item numbers are related to rows in a bill of materials.

Base
The first solid feature of a part.

Baseline dimensions
Sets of dimensions measured from the same edge or vertex in a drawing.

Bend
A feature in a sheet metal part. A bend generated from a filleted corner, cylindrical face, or conical face is a round bend; a bend generated from sketched straight lines is a sharp bends.

Bill of materials
A table inserted into a drawing to keep a record of the parts used in an assembly.

Block
A user-defined annotation that you can use in parts, assemblies, and drawings. A block can contain text, sketch entities (except points), and area hatch, and it can be saved in a file for later use as, for example, a custom callout or a company logo.

Bottom-up assembly
An assembly modeling technique where you create parts and then insert them into an

assembly.

Broken-out section
A drawing view that exposes inner details of a drawing view by removing material from a closed profile, usually a spline.

Cavity
The mold half that holds the cavity feature of the design part.

Center mark
A cross that marks the center of a circle or arc.

Centerline
A centerline marks, in phantom font, an axis of symmetry in a sketch or drawing.

Chamfer
Bevels a selected edge or vertex. You can apply chamfers to both sketches and features.

Child
A dependent feature related to a previously-built feature. For example, a chamfer on the edge of a hole is a child of the parent hole.

Click-release
As you sketch, if you click and then release the pointer, you are in click-release mode. Move the pointer and click again to define the next point in the sketch sequence.

Click-drag
As you sketch, if you click and drag the pointer, you are in click-drag mode. When you release the pointer, the sketch entity is complete.

Closed profile
Also called a closed contour, it is a sketch or sketch entity with no exposed endpoints; for example, a circle or polygon.

Collapse
The opposite of explode. The collapse action returns an exploded assembly's parts to their normal positions.

Collision Detection
An assembly function that detects collisions between components when components move or rotate. A collision occurs when an entity on one component coincides with any entity on another component.

Component
Any part or sub-assembly within an assembly.

Configuration
A variation of a part or assembly within a single document. Variations can include different dimensions, features, and properties. For example, a single part such as a bolt can contain different configurations that vary the diameter and length.

ConfigurationManager
Located on the left side of the SOLIDWORKS window, it is a means to create, select, and view the configurations of parts and assemblies.

Constraint
The relations between sketch entities, or between sketch entities and planes, axes, edges, or vertices.

Construction geometry
The characteristic of a sketch entity that the entity is used in creating other geometry but is not itself used in creating features.

Coordinate system
A system of planes used to assign Cartesian coordinates to features, parts, and assemblies. Part and assembly documents contain default coordinate systems; other coordinate systems can be defined with reference geometry. Coordinate systems can be used with measurement tools and for exporting documents to other file formats.

Cosmetic thread
An annotation that represents threads.

Crosshatch
A pattern (or fill) applied to drawing views such as section views and broken-out sections.

Curvature
Curvature is equal to the inverse of the radius of the curve. The curvature can be displayed in different colors according to the local radius (usually of a surface).

Cut
A feature that removes material from a part by such actions as extrude, revolve, loft, sweep, thicken, cavity, and so on.

Dangling
A dimension, relation, or drawing section view that is unresolved. For example, if a piece

of geometry is dimensioned, and that geometry is later deleted, the dimension becomes dangling.

Degrees of freedom

Geometry that is not defined by dimensions or relations is free to move. In 2D sketches, there are three degrees of freedom: movement along the X and Y axes, and rotation about the Z axis (the axis normal to the sketch plane). In 3D sketches and in assemblies, there are six degrees of freedom: movement along the X, Y, and Z axes, and rotation about the X, Y, and Z axes.

Derived part

A derived part is a new base, mirror, or component part created directly from an existing part and linked to the original part such that changes to the original part are reflected in the derived part.

Derived sketch

A copy of a sketch, in either the same part or the same assembly that is connected to the original sketch. Changes in the original sketch are reflected in the derived sketch.

Design Library

Located in the Task Pane, the Design Library provides a central location for reusable elements such as parts, assemblies, and so on.

Design table

An Excel spreadsheet that is used to create multiple configurations in a part or assembly document.

Detached drawing

A drawing format that allows opening and working in a drawing without loading the corresponding models into memory. The models are loaded on an as-needed basis.

Detail view

A portion of a larger view, usually at a larger scale than the original view.

Dimension line

A linear dimension line references the dimension text to extension lines indicating the entity being measured. An angular dimension line references the dimension text directly to the measured object.

DimXpertManager

Located on the left side of the SOLIDWORKS window, it is a means to manage dimensions and tolerances created using DimXpert for parts according to the requirements of the ASME Y.14.41-2003 standard.

DisplayManager

The DisplayManager lists the appearances, decals, lights, scene, and cameras applied to the current model. From the DisplayManager, you can view applied content, and add, edit, or delete items. When PhotoView 360 is added in, the DisplayManager also provides access to PhotoView options.

Document

A file containing a part, assembly, or drawing.

Draft

The degree of taper or angle of a face, usually applied to molds or castings.

Drawing

A 2D representation of a 3D part or assembly. The extension for a SOLIDWORKS drawing file name is .SLDDRW.

Drawing sheet

A page in a drawing document.

Driven dimension

Measurements of the model, but they do not drive the model and their values cannot be changed.

Driving dimension

Also referred to as a model dimension, it sets the value for a sketch entity. It can also control distance, thickness, and feature parameters.

Edge

A single outside boundary of a feature.

Edge flange

A sheet metal feature that combines a bend and a tab in a single operation.

Equation

Creates a mathematical relation between sketch dimensions, using dimension names as variables, or between feature parameters, such as the depth of an extruded feature or the instance count in a pattern.

Exploded view

Shows an assembly with its components separated from one another, usually to show how to assemble the mechanism.

Export

Save a SOLIDWORKS document in another format for use in other CAD/CAM, rapid prototyping, web, or graphics software applications.

Extension line

The line extending from the model indicating the point from which a dimension is measured.

Extrude

A feature that linearly projects a sketch to either add material to a part (in a base or boss) or remove material from a part (in a cut or hole).

Face

A selectable area (planar or otherwise) of a model or surface with boundaries that help define the shape of the model or surface. For example, a rectangular solid has six faces.

Fasteners

A SOLIDWORKS Toolbox library that adds fasteners automatically to holes in an assembly.

Feature

An individual shape that, combined with other features, makes up a part or assembly. Some features, such as bosses and cuts, originate as sketches. Other features, such as shells and fillets, modify a feature's geometry. However, not all features have associated geometry. Features are always listed in the FeatureManager design tree.

FeatureManager design tree

Located on the left side of the SOLIDWORKS window, it provides an outline view of the active part, assembly, or drawing.

Fill

A solid area hatch or crosshatch. Fill also applies to patches on surfaces.

Fillet

An internal rounding of a corner or edge in a sketch, or an edge on a surface or solid.

Forming tool

Dies that bend, stretch, or otherwise form sheet metal to create such form features as louvers, lances, flanges, and ribs.

Fully defined

A sketch where all lines and curves in the sketch, and their positions, are described by dimensions or relations, or both, and cannot be moved. Fully defined sketch entities are shown in black.

Geometric tolerance
A set of standard symbols that specify the geometric characteristics and dimensional requirements of a feature.

Graphics area
The area in the SOLIDWORKS window where the part, assembly, or drawing appears.

Guide curve
A 2D or 3D curve used to guide a sweep or loft.

Handle
An arrow, square, or circle that you can drag to adjust the size or position of an entity (a feature, dimension, or sketch entity, for example).

Helix
A curve defined by pitch, revolutions, and height. A helix can be used, for example, as a path for a swept feature cutting threads in a bolt.

Hem
A sheet metal feature that folds back at the edge of a part. A hem can be open, closed, double, or tear-drop.

HLR
(Hidden lines removed) a view mode in which all edges of the model that are not visible from the current view angle are removed from the display.

HLV
(Hidden lines visible) A view mode in which all edges of the model that are not visible from the current view angle are shown gray or dashed.

Import
Open files from other CAD software applications into a SOLIDWORKS document.

In-context feature
A feature with an external reference to the geometry of another component; the in-context feature changes automatically if the geometry of the referenced model or feature changes.

Inference
The system automatically creates (infers) relations between dragged entities (sketched

entities, annotations, and components) and other entities and geometry. This is useful when positioning entities relative to one another.

Instance
An item in a pattern or a component in an assembly that occurs more than once. Blocks are inserted into drawings as instances of block definitions.

Interference detection
A tool that displays any interference between selected components in an assembly.

Jog
A sheet metal feature that adds material to a part by creating two bends from a sketched line.

Knit
A tool that combines two or more faces or surfaces into one. The edges of the surfaces must be adjacent and not overlapping, but they cannot ever be planar. There is no difference in the appearance of the face or the surface after knitting.

Layout sketch
A sketch that contains important sketch entities, dimensions, and relations. You reference the entities in the layout sketch when creating new sketches, building new geometry, or positioning components in an assembly. This allows for easier updating of your model because changes you make to the layout sketch propagate to the entire model.

Leader
A solid line from an annotation (note, dimension, and so on) to the referenced feature.

Library feature
A frequently used feature, or combination of features, that is created once and then saved for future use.

Lightweight
A part in an assembly or a drawing that has only a subset of its model data loaded into memory. The remaining model data is loaded on an as-needed basis. This improves performance of large and complex assemblies.

Line
A straight sketch entity with two endpoints. A line can be created by projecting an external entity such as an edge, plane, axis, or sketch curve into the sketch.

Loft
A base, boss, cut, or surface feature created by transitions between profiles.

Lofted bend
A sheet metal feature that produces a roll form or a transitional shape from two open profile sketches. Lofted bends often create funnels and chutes.

Mass properties
A tool that evaluates the characteristics of a part or an assembly such as volume, surface area, centroid, and so on.

Mate
A geometric relationship, such as coincident, perpendicular, tangent, and so on, between parts in an assembly.

Mate reference
Specifies one or more entities of a component to use for automatic mating. When you drag a component with a mate reference into an assembly, the software tries to find other combinations of the same mate reference name and mate type.

Mates folder
A collection of mates that are solved together. The order in which the mates appear within the Mates folder does not matter.

Mirror
(a) A mirror feature is a copy of a selected feature mirrored about a plane or planar face.
(b) A mirror sketch entity is a copy of a selected sketch entity that is mirrored about a centerline.

Miter flange
A sheet metal feature that joins multiple edge flanges together and miters the corner.

Model
3D solid geometry in a part or assembly document. If a part or assembly document contains multiple configurations, each configuration is a separate model.

Model dimension
A dimension specified in a sketch or a feature in a part or assembly document that defines some entity in a 3D model.

Model item
A characteristic or dimension of feature geometry that can be used in detailing drawings.

Model view
A drawing view of a part or assembly.

Mold

A set of manufacturing tooling used to shape molten plastic or other material into a designed part. You design the mold using a sequence of integrated tools that result in cavity and core blocks that are derived parts of the part to be molded.

Motion Study

Motion Studies are graphical simulations of motion and visual properties with assembly models. Analogous to a configuration, they do not actually change the original assembly model or its properties. They display the model as it changes based on simulation elements you add.

Multibody part

A part with separate solid bodies within the same part document. Unlike the components in an assembly, multibody parts are not dynamic.

Native format

DXF and DWG files remain in their original format (are not converted into SOLIDWORKS format) when viewed in SOLIDWORKS drawing sheets (view only).

Open profile

Also called an open contour, it is a sketch or sketch entity with endpoints exposed. For example, a U-shaped profile is open.

Ordinate dimensions

A chain of dimensions measured from a zero ordinate in a drawing or sketch.

Origin

The model origin appears as three gray arrows and represents the (0,0,0) coordinate of the model. When a sketch is active, a sketch origin appears in red and represents the (0,0,0) coordinate of the sketch. Dimensions and relations can be added to the model origin but not to a sketch origin.

Out-of-context feature

A feature with an external reference to the geometry of another component that is not open.

Over defined

A sketch is over defined when dimensions or relations are either in conflict or redundant.

Parameter

A value used to define a sketch or feature (often a dimension).

Parent

An existing feature upon which other features depend. For example, in a block with a hole, the block is the parent to the child hole feature.

Part

A single 3D object made up of features. A part can become a component in an assembly, and it can be represented in 2D in a drawing. Examples of parts are bolt, pin, plate, and so on. The extension for a SOLIDWORKS part file name is .SLDPRT.

Path

A sketch, edge, or curve used in creating a sweep or loft.

Pattern

A pattern repeats selected sketch entities, features, or components in an array, which can be linear, circular, or sketch-driven. If the seed entity is changed, the other instances in the pattern update.

Physical Dynamics

An assembly tool that displays the motion of assembly components in a realistic way. When you drag a component, the component applies a force to other components it touches. Components move only within their degrees of freedom.

Pierce relation

Makes a sketch point coincident to the location at which an axis, edge, line, or spline pierces the sketch plane.

Planar

Entities that can lie on one plane. For example, a circle is planar, but a helix is not.

Plane

Flat construction geometry. Planes can be used for a 2D sketch, section view of a model, a neutral plane in a draft feature, and others.

Point

A singular location in a sketch or a projection into a sketch at a single location of an external entity (origin, vertex, axis, or point in an external sketch).

Predefined view

A drawing view in which the view position, orientation, and so on can be specified before a model is inserted. You can save drawing documents with predefined views as templates.

Profile
A sketch entity used to create a feature (such as a loft) or a drawing view (such as a detail view). A profile can be open (such as a U shape or open spline) or closed (such as a circle or closed spline).

Projected dimension
If you dimension entities in an isometric view, projected dimensions are the flat dimensions in 2D.

Projected view
A drawing view projected orthogonally from an existing view.

PropertyManager
Located on the left side of the SOLIDWORKS window, it is used for dynamic editing of sketch entities and most features.

RealView graphics
A hardware (graphics card) support of advanced shading in real time; the rendering applies to the model and is retained as you move or rotate a part.

Rebuild
Tool that updates (or regenerates) the document with any changes made since the last time the model was rebuilt. Rebuild is typically used after changing a model dimension.

Reference dimension
A dimension in a drawing that shows the measurement of an item, but cannot drive the model and its value cannot be modified. When model dimensions change, reference dimensions update.

Reference geometry
Includes planes, axes, coordinate systems, and 3D curves. Reference geometry is used to assist in creating features such as lofts, sweeps, drafts, chamfers, and patterns.

Relation
A geometric constraint between sketch entities or between a sketch entity and a plane, axis, edge, or vertex. Relations can be added automatically or manually.

Relative view
A relative (or relative to model) drawing view is created relative to planar surfaces in a part or assembly.

Reload
Refreshes shared documents. For example, if you open a part file for read-only access while another user makes changes to the same part, you can reload the new version, including the changes.

Reorder
Reordering (changing the order of) items is possible in the FeatureManager design tree. In parts, you can change the order in which features are solved. In assemblies, you can control the order in which components appear in a bill of materials.

Replace
Substitutes one or more open instances of a component in an assembly with a different component.

Resolved
A state of an assembly component (in an assembly or drawing document) in which it is fully loaded in memory. All the component's model data is available, so its entities can be selected, referenced, edited, used in mates, and so on.

Revolve
A feature that creates a base or boss, a revolved cut, or revolved surface by revolving one or more sketched profiles around a centerline.

Rip
A sheet metal feature that removes material at an edge to allow a bend.

Rollback
Suppresses all items below the rollback bar.

Section
Another term for profile in sweeps.

Section line
A line or centerline sketched in a drawing view to create a section view.

Section scope
Specifies the components to be left uncut when you create an assembly drawing section view.

Section view
A section view (or section cut) is (1) a part or assembly view cut by a plane, or (2) a drawing view created by cutting another drawing view with a section line.

Seed
A sketch or an entity (a feature, face, or body) that is the basis for a pattern. If you edit the seed, the other entities in the pattern are updated.

Shaded
Displays a model as a colored solid.

Shared values
Also called linked values, these are named variables that you assign to set the value of two or more dimensions to be equal.

Sheet format
Includes page size and orientation, standard text, borders, title blocks, and so on. Sheet formats can be customized and saved for future use. Each sheet of a drawing document can have a different format.

Shell
A feature that hollows out a part, leaving open the selected faces and thin walls on the remaining faces. A hollow part is created when no faces are selected to be open.

Sketch
A collection of lines and other 2D objects on a plane or face that forms the basis for a feature such as a base or a boss. A 3D sketch is non-planar and can be used to guide a sweep or loft, for example.

Smart Fasteners
Automatically adds fasteners (bolts and screws) to an assembly using the SOLIDWORKS Toolbox library of fasteners.

SmartMates
An assembly mating relation that is created automatically.

Solid sweep
A cut sweep created by moving a tool body along a path to cut out 3D material from a model.

Spiral
A flat or 2D helix defined by a circle, pitch, and number of revolutions.

Spline
A sketched 2D or 3D curve defined by a set of control points.

Split line
Projects a sketched curve onto a selected model face, dividing the face into multiple faces so that each can be selected individually. A split line can be used to create draft features, to create face blend fillets, and to radiate surfaces to cut molds.

Stacked balloon
A set of balloons with only one leader. The balloons can be stacked vertically (up or down) or horizontally (left or right).

Standard 3 views
The three orthographic views (front, right, and top) that are often the basis of a drawing.

StereoLithography
The process of creating rapid prototype parts using a faceted mesh representation in STL files.

Sub-assembly
An assembly document that is part of a larger assembly. For example, the steering mechanism of a car is a sub-assembly of the car.

Suppress
Removes an entity from the display and from any calculations in which it is involved. You can suppress features, assembly components, and so on. Suppressing an entity does not delete the entity; you can unsuppress the entity to restore it.

Surface
A zero-thickness planar or 3D entity with edge boundaries. Surfaces are often used to create solid features. Reference surfaces can be used to modify solid features.

Sweep
Creates a base, boss, cut, or surface feature by moving a profile (section) along a path. For cut-sweeps, you can create solid sweeps by moving a tool body along a path.

Tangent arc
An arc that is tangent to another entity, such as a line.

Tangent edge
The transition edge between rounded or filleted faces in hidden lines visible or hidden lines removed modes in drawings.

Task Pane
Located on the right-side of the SOLIDWORKS window, the Task Pane contains SOLIDWORKS Resources, the Design Library, and the File Explorer.

Template
A document (part, assembly, or drawing) that forms the basis of a new document. It can include user-defined parameters, annotations, predefined views, geometry, and so on.

Temporary axis
An axis created implicitly for every conical or cylindrical face in a model.

Thin feature
An extruded or revolved feature with constant wall thickness. Sheet metal parts are typically created from thin features.

TolAnalyst
A tolerance analysis application that determines the effects that dimensions and tolerances have on parts and assemblies.

Top-down design
An assembly modeling technique where you create parts in the context of an assembly by referencing the geometry of other components. Changes to the referenced components propagate to the parts that you create in context.

Triad
Three axes with arrows defining the X, Y, and Z directions. A reference triad appears in part and assembly documents to assist in orienting the viewing of models. Triads also assist when moving or rotating components in assemblies.

Under defined
A sketch is under defined when there are not enough dimensions and relations to prevent entities from moving or changing size.

Vertex
A point at which two or more lines or edges intersect. Vertices can be selected for sketching, dimensioning, and many other operations.

Viewports
Windows that display views of models. You can specify one, two, or four viewports. Viewports with orthogonal views can be linked, which links orientation and rotation.

Virtual sharp

A sketch point at the intersection of two entities after the intersection itself has been removed by a feature such as a fillet or chamfer. Dimensions and relations to the virtual sharp are retained even though the actual intersection no longer exists.

Weldment

A multibody part with structural members.

Weldment cut list

A table that tabulates the bodies in a weldment along with descriptions and lengths.

Wireframe

A view mode in which all edges of the part or assembly are displayed.

Zebra stripes

Simulate the reflection of long strips of light on a very shiny surface. They allow you to see small changes in a surface that may be hard to see with a standard display.

Zoom

To simulate movement toward or away from a part or an assembly.

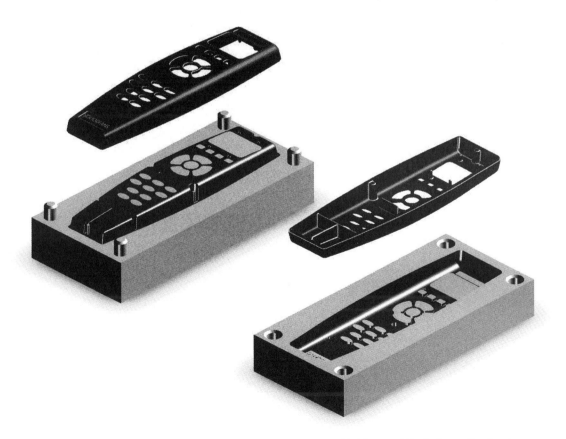

Learn Mold-Tooling Designs with SOLIDWORKS Part-III Advanced Techniques Textbook

Index

SOLIDWORKS® Quick-Guide

Quick Reference Guide to SOLIDWORKS® Command Icons & Toolbars

The STANDARD Toolbar

- Creates a new document.
- Opens an existing document.
- Saves an active document.
- Make Drawing from Part/Assembly.
- Make Assembly from Part/Assembly.
- Prints the active document.
- Print preview.
- Cuts the selection & puts it on the clipboard.
- Copies the selection & puts it on the clipboard.
- Inserts the clipboard contents.
- Deletes the selection.
- Reverses the last action.
- Rebuilds the part / assembly / drawing.
- Redo the last action that was undone.
- Saves all documents.
- Edits material.
- Closes an existing document.
- Shows or hides the Selection Filter toolbar.
- Shows or hides the Web toolbar.
- Properties.
- File properties.

The STANDARD Toolbar (Cont.)

- Loads or unloads the 3D instant website add-in.
- Select tool.
- Select the entire document.
- Checks read-only files.
- Options.
- Help.
- Full screen view.
- OK.
- Cancel.
- Magnified selection.

The SKETCH TOOLS Toolbar

- Select.
- Sketch.
- 3D Sketch.
- Sketches a rectangle from the center.
- Sketches a centerpoint arc slot.
- Sketches a 3-point arc slot.
- Sketches a straight slot.
- Sketches a centerpoint straight slot.
- Sketches a 3-point arc.
- Creates sketched ellipses.

Quick Reference Guide to SOLIDWORKS® Command Icons & Toolbars

The SKETCH TOOLS Toolbar

 3D sketch on plane.

 Sets up Grid parameters.

 Creates a sketch on a selected plane or face.

 Equation driven curve.

 Modifies a sketch.

 Copies sketch entities.

 Scales sketch entities.

 Rotates sketch entities.

 Sketches 3 point rectangle from the center.

 Sketches 3 point corner rectangle.

 Sketches a line.

 Creates a center point arc: center, start, end.

 Creates an arc tangent to a line.

 Sketches splines on a surface or face.

 Sketches a circle.

 Sketches a circle by its perimeter.

 Makes a path of sketch entities.

 Mirrors entities dynamically about a centerline.

 Insert a plane into the 3D sketch.

 Instant 2D.

 Sketch numeric input.

 Detaches segment on drag.

 Sketch picture.

The SKETCH TOOLS Toolbar (Cont.)

 Partial ellipses.

 Adds a Parabola.

 Adds a spline.

 Sketches a polygon.

 Sketches a corner rectangle.

 Sketches a parallelogram.

 Creates points.

 Creates sketched centerlines.

 Adds text to sketch.

 Converts selected model edges or sketch entities to sketch segments.

 Creates a sketch along the intersection of multiple bodies.

 Converts face curves on the selected face into 3D sketch entities.

 Mirrors selected segments about a centerline.

 Fillets the corner of two lines.

 Creates a chamfer between two sketch entities.

 Creates a sketch curve by offsetting model edges or sketch entities at a specified distance.

 Trims a sketch segment.

 Extends a sketch segment.

 Splits a sketch segment.

 Construction Geometry.

 Creates linear steps and repeat of sketch entities.

 Creates circular steps and repeat of sketch entities.

Quick Reference Guide to SOLIDWORKS® Command Icons & Toolbars

The SHEET METAL

 Add a bend from a selected sketch in a Sheet Metal part.

 Shows flat pattern for this sheet metal part.

 Shows part without inserting any bends.

 Inserts a rip feature to a sheet metal part.

 Create a Sheet Metal part or add material to existing Sheet Metal part.

 Inserts a Sheet Metal Miter Flange feature.

 Folds selected bends.

 Unfolds selected bends.

 Inserts bends using a sketch line.

 Inserts a flange by pulling an edge.

 Inserts a sheet metal corner feature.

 Inserts a Hem feature by selecting edges.

 Breaks a corner by filleting/chamfering it.

 Inserts a Jog feature using a sketch line.

 Inserts a lofted bend feature using 2 sketches.

 Creates inverse dent on a sheet metal part.

 Trims out material from a corner, in a sheet metal part.

 Inserts a fillet weld bead.

 Converts a solid/surface into a sheet metal part.

 Adds a Cross Break feature into a selected face.

 Sweeps an open profile along an open/closed path.

 Adds a gusset/rib across a bend.

 Corner relief.

 Welds the selected corner.

The SURFACES Toolbar

 Creates mid surfaces between offset face pairs.

 Patches surface holes and external edges.

 Creates an extruded surface.

 Creates a revolved surface.

 Creates a swept surface.

 Creates a lofted surface.

 Creates an offset surface.

 Radiates a surface originating from a curve, parallel to a plane.

 Knits surfaces together.

 Creates a planar surface from a sketch or A set of edges.

 Creates a surface by importing data from a file.

 Extends a surface.

 Trims a surface.

 Surface flatten.

 Deletes Face(s).

 Replaces Face with Surface.

 Patches surface holes and external edges by extending the surfaces.

 Creates parting surfaces between core & cavity surfaces.

 Inserts ruled surfaces from edges.

The WELDMENTS Toolbar

 Creates a weldment feature.

 Creates a structure member feature.

 Adds a gusset feature between 2 planar adjoining faces.

 Creates an end cap feature.

 Adds a fillet weld bead feature.

 Trims or extends structure members.

Weld bead.

The DIMENSIONS/RELATIONS Toolbar

Inserts dimension between two lines.

Creates a horizontal dimension between selected entities.

Creates a vertical dimension between selected entities.

Creates a reference dimension between selected entities.

Creates a set of ordinate dimensions.

Creates a set of Horizontal ordinate dimensions.

Creates a set of Vertical ordinate dimensions.

Creates a chamfer dimension.

Adds a geometric relation.

Automatically Adds Dimensions to the current sketch.

Displays and deletes geometric relations.

Fully defines a sketch.

Scans a sketch for elements of equal length or radius.

Angular Running dimension.

Display / Delete dimension.

Isolate changed dimension.

Path length dimension.

The BLOCK Toolbar

 Makes a new block.

 Edits the selected block.

 Inserts a new block to a sketch or drawing.

 Adds/Removes sketch entities to/from blocks.

 Updates parent sketches affected by this block.

 Saves the block to a file.

 Explodes the selected block.

 Inserts a belt.

The STANDARD VIEWS

 Front view.

 Back view.

 Left view.

 Right view.

 Top view.

 Bottom view.

 Isometric view.

 Trimetric view.

 Dimetric view.

 Normal to view.

 Links all views in the viewport together.

 Displays viewport with front & right views

 Displays a 4 view viewport with 1st or 3rd Angle of projection.

 Displays viewport with front & top.

 Displays viewport with a single view.

 View selector.

 New view.

The FEATURES Toolbar

 Creates a boss feature by extruding a sketched profile.

 Creates a revolved feature based on profile and angle parameter.

 Creates a cut feature by extruding a sketched profile.

 Creates a cut feature by revolving a sketched profile.

 Thread.

 Creates a cut by sweeping a closed profile along an open or closed path.

 Loft cut.

 Creates a cut by thickening one or more adjacent surfaces.

 Adds a deformed surface by push or pull on points.

 Creates a lofted feature between two or more profiles.

 Creates a solid feature by thickening one or more adjacent surfaces.

 Creates a filled feature.

 Chamfers an edge or a chain of tangent edges.

 Inserts a rib feature.

 Combine.

 Creates a shell feature.

 Applies draft to a selected surface.

 Creates a cylindrical hole.

 Inserts a hole with a pre-defined cross section.

 Puts a dome surface on a face.

 Model break view.

 Applies global deformation to solid or surface bodies.

 Wraps closed sketch contour(s) onto a face.

 Curve Driven pattern.

 Suppresses the selected feature or component.

 Un-suppresses the selected feature or component.

 Flexes solid and surface bodies.

 Intersect.

 Variable Patterns.

 Live Section Plane.

 Mirrors.

 Scale.

 Creates a Sketch Driven pattern.

 Creates a Table Driven Pattern.

 Inserts a split Feature.

 Hole series.

 Joins bodies from one or more parts into a single part in the context of an assembly.

 Deletes a solid or a surface.

 Instant 3D.

 Inserts a part from file into the active part document.

 Moves/Copies solid and surface bodies or moves graphics bodies.

 Merges short edges on faces.

 Pushes solid / surface model by another solid / surface model.

 Moves face(s) of a solid.

 FeatureWorks Options.

 Linear Pattern.

 Fill Pattern.

 Cuts a solid model with a surface.

 Boundary Boss/Base.

 Boundary Cut.

 Circular Pattern.

 Recognize Features.

 Grid System.

Extracts core(s) from existing tooling split.

 Constructs a surface patch.

 Moves face(s) of a solid.

 Creates offset surfaces.

 Inserts cavity into a base part.

 Scales a model by a specified factor.

 Applies draft to a selected surface.

 Inserts a split line feature.

 Creates parting lines to separate core & cavity surfaces.

 Finds & creates mold shut-off surfaces.

 Creates a planar surface from a sketch or a set of edges.

 Knits surfaces together.

 Inserts ruled surfaces from edges.

 Creates parting surfaces between core & cavity surfaces.

 Creates multiple bodies from a single body.

 Inserts a tooling split feature.

 Creates parting surfaces between the core & cavity.

 Inserts surface body folders for mold operation.

 Turns selection filters on and off.

 Clears all filters.

 Selects all filters.

 Inverts current selection.

 Allows selection of edges only.

 Allows selection filter for vertices only.

 Allows selection of faces only.

 Adds filter for Surface Bodies.

 Adds filter for Solid Bodies.

 Adds filter for Axes.

 Adds filter for Planes.

 Adds filter for Sketch Points.

 Allows selection for sketch only.

 Adds filter for Sketch Segments.

 Adds filter for Midpoints.

 Adds filter for Center Marks.

 Adds filter for Centerline.

 Adds filter for Dimensions and Hole Callouts.

 Adds filter for Surface Finish Symbols.

 Adds filter for Geometric Tolerances.

 Adds filter for Notes / Balloons.

 Adds filter for Weld Symbols.

 Adds filter for Weld beads.

 Adds filter for Datum Targets.

 Adds filter for Datum feature only.

 Adds filter for blocks.

 Adds filter for Cosmetic Threads.

Adds filter for Dowel pin symbols.

 Adds filter for connection points.

 Adds filter for routing points.

The SOLIDWORKS Add-Ins Toolbar

 Loads/unloads CircuitWorks add-in.

 Loads/unloads the Design Checker add-in.

 Loads/unloads the PhotoView 360 add-in.

 Loads/unloads the Scan-to-3D add-in.

 Loads/unloads the SOLIDWORKS Motions add-in.

 Loads/unloads the SOLIDWORKS Routing add-in.

 Loads/unloads the SOLIDWORKS Simulation add-in.

 Loads/unloads the SOLIDWORKS Toolbox add-in.

 Loads/unloads the SOLIDWORKS TolAnalysis add-in.

 Loads/unloads the SOLIDWORKS Flow Simulation add-in.

 Loads/unloads the SOLIDWORKS Plastics add-in.

 Loads/unloads the SOLIDWORKS MBD SNL license.

The FASTENING FEATURES

 Creates a parameterized mounting boss.

 Creates a parameterized snap hook.

 Creates a groove to mate with a hook feature.

 Uses sketch elements to create a vent for air flow.

 Creates a lip/groove feature.

The SCREEN CAPTURE Toolbar

 Copies the current graphics window to the clipboard.

 Records the current graphics window to an AVI file.

 Stops recording the current graphics window to an AVI file.

The EXPLODE LINE SKETCH

 Adds a route line that connects entities.

 Adds a jog to the route lines.

The LINE FORMAT Toolbar

 Changes layer properties.

 Changes the current document layer.

 Changes line color.

 Changes line thickness.

 Changes line style.

 Hides / Shows a hidden edge.

 Changes line display mode.

Did you know??

* Ctrl+Q will force a rebuild on all features of a part.

* Ctrl+B will rebuild the feature being worked on and its dependents.

The 2D-To-3D Toolbar

 Makes a Front sketch from the selected entities.

 Makes a Top sketch from the selected entities.

 Makes a Right sketch from the selected entities.

Makes a Left sketch from the selected entities.

Makes a Bottom sketch from the selected entities.

Makes a Back sketch from the selected entities.

Makes an Auxiliary sketch from the selected entities.

Creates a new sketch from the selected entities.

Repairs the selected sketch.

Aligns a sketch to the selected point.

Creates an extrusion from the selected sketch segments, starting at the selected sketch point.

Creates a cut from the selected sketch segments, optionally starting at the selected sketch point.

Evenly spaces selected dimensions.

Aligns collinear selected dimensions.

Aligns stagger selected dimensions.

The SOLIDWORKS MBD Toolbar

Captures 3D view.

Manages 3D PDF templates.

Creates shareable 3D PDF presentations.

Toggles dynamic annotation views.

The ALIGN Toolbar

Aligns the left side of the selected annotations with the leftmost annotation.

Aligns the right side of the selected annotations with the rightmost annotation.

Aligns the top side of the selected annotations with the topmost annotation.

Aligns the bottom side of the selected annotations with the lowermost annotation.

Evenly spaces the selected annotations horizontally.

Evenly spaces the selected annotations vertically.

Centrally aligns the selected annotations horizontally.

Centrally aligns the selected annotations vertically.

Compacts the selected annotations horizontally.

Compacts the selected annotations vertically.

Creates a group from the selected items.

Deletes the grouping between these items.

Aligns & groups selected dimensions along a line or an arc.

Aligns & groups dimensions at uniform distances.

The MACRO Toolbar

Runs a Macro.

Stops Macro recorder.

Records (or pauses recording of) actions to create a Macro.

Launches the Macro Editor and begins editing a new macro.

Opens a Macro file for editing.

Creates a custom macro.

The SMARTMATES icons

Concentric & Coincident 2 circular edges

Concentric 2 cylindrical faces

Coincident 2 linear edges

Coincident 2 planar faces

Coincident 2 vertices

Coincident 2 origins or coordinate systems

The TABLE Toolbar

 Adds a hole table of selected holes from a specified origin datum.

 Adds a Bill of Materials.

 Adds a revision table.

 Displays a Design table in a drawing.

 Adds a weldments cuts list table.

 Adds an Excel based Bill of Materials.

 Adds a weldment cut list table.

The REFERENCE GEOMETRY

 Adds a reference plane.

 Creates an axis.

 Creates a coordinate system.

 Adds the center of mass.

 Specifies entities to use as references using SmartMates.

The SPLINE TOOLS Toolbar

 Inserts a point to a spline.

 Displays all points where the concavity of selected spline changes.

 Displays minimum radius of selected spline.

 Displays curvature combs of selected spline.

 Reduces numbers of points in a selected spline.

 Adds a tangency control.

 Adds a curvature control.

 Adds a spline based on selected sketch entities & edges.

 Displays the spline control polygon.

The ANNOTATIONS Toolbar

 Inserts a note.

 Inserts a surface finish symbol.

 Inserts a new geometric tolerancing symbol.

 Attaches a balloon to the selected edge or face.

 Adds balloons for all components in selected view.

 Inserts a stacked balloon.

 Attaches a datum feature symbol to a selected edge / detail.

 Inserts a weld symbol on the selected edge / face / vertex.

 Inserts a datum target symbol and / or point attached to a selected edge / line.

 Selects and inserts block.

 Inserts annotations & reference geometry from the part / assembly into the selected.

 Adds center marks to circles on model.

 Inserts a Centerline.

 Inserts a hole callout.

 Adds a cosmetic thread to the selected cylindrical feature.

 Inserts a Multi-Jog leader.

 Selects a circular edge and/or arc for Dowel pin symbol insertion.

 Adds a view location symbol.

 Inserts latest version symbol.

 Adds a cross hatch patterns or solid fill.

 Adds a weld bead caterpillar on an edge.

 Adds a weld symbol on a selected entity.

 Inserts a revision cloud.

 Inserts a magnetic line.

 Hides/shows annotation.

The DRAWINGS Toolbar

Updates the selected view to the model's current stage.

Creates a detail view.

Creates a section view.

Inserts an Alternate Position view.

Unfolds a new view from an existing view.

Generates a standard 3-view drawing (1st or 3rd angle).

Inserts an auxiliary view of an inclined surface.

Adds an Orthogonal or Named view based on an existing part or assembly.

Adds a Relative view by two orthogonal faces or planes.

Adds a Predefined orthogonal projected or Named view with a model.

Adds an empty view.

Adds vertical break lines to selected view.

Crops a view.

Creates a Broken-out section.

The QUICK SNAP Toolbar

Snap to points.

Snap to center points.

Snap to midpoints.

Snap to quadrant points.

Snap to intersection of 2 curves.

Snap to nearest curve.

Snap tangent to curve.

Snap perpendicular to curve.

Snap parallel to line.

Snap horizontally / vertically to points.

Snap horizontally / vertically.

Snap to discrete line lengths.

Snap to angle.

The LAYOUT Toolbar

Creates the assembly layout sketch.

Sketches a line.

Sketches a corner rectangle.

Sketches a circle.

Sketches a 3 point arc.

Rounds a corner.

Trims or extends a sketch.

Adds sketch entities by offsetting faces; edges curves.

Mirrors selected entities about a centerline.

Adds a relation.

Creates a dimension.

Displays / Deletes geometric relations.

Makes a new block.

Edits the selected block.

Inserts a new block to the sketch or drawing.

Adds / Removes sketch entities to / from a block.

Saves the block to a file.

Explodes the selected block.

Creates a new part from a layout sketch block.

Positions 2 components relative to one another.

Projects sketch onto selected surface.

Inserts a split line feature.

Creates a composite curve from selected edges, curves and sketches.

Creates a curve through free points.

Creates a 3D curve through reference points.

Helical curve defined by a base sketch and shape parameters.

Displays a view in the selected orientation.

Reverts to previous view.

Redraws the current window.

Zooms out to see entire model.

Zooms in by dragging a bounding box.

Zooms in or out by dragging up or down.

Zooms to fit all selected entities.

Dynamic view rotation.

Scrolls view by dragging.

Displays image in wireframe mode.

Displays hidden edges in gray.

Displays image with hidden lines removed.

Controls the visibility of planes.

Controls the visibility of axis.

Controls the visibility of parting lines.

Controls the visibility of temporary axis.

Controls the visibility of origins.

Controls the visibility of coordinate systems.

Controls the visibility of reference curves.

Controls the visibility of sketches.

Controls the visibility of 3D sketch planes.

Controls the visibility of 3D sketch.

Controls the visibility of all annotations.

Controls the visibility of reference points.

Controls the visibility of routing points.

Controls the visibility of lights.

Controls the visibility of cameras.

Controls the visibility of sketch relations.

Changes the display state for the current configuration.

Rolls the model view.

Turns the orientation of the model view.

Dynamically manipulate the model view in 3D to make selection.

Changes the display style for the active view.

Displays a shade view of the model with its edges.

Displays a shade view of the model.

Toggles between draft quality & high quality HLV.

Cycles through or applies a specific scene.

Views the models through one of the model's cameras.

Displays a part or assembly w/different colors according to the local radius of curvature.

Displays zebra stripes.

Displays a model with hardware accelerated shades.

Applies a cartoon affect to model edges & faces.

Views simulations symbols.

The TOOLS Toolbar

 Calculates the distance between selected items.

 Adds or edits equation.

 Calculates the mass properties of the model.

 Checks the model for geometry errors.

 Inserts or edits a Design Table.

 Evaluates section properties for faces and sketches that lie in parallel planes.

 Reports Statistics for this Part/Assembly.

 Deviation Analysis.

 Runs the SimulationXpress analysis wizard Powered by SOLIDWORKS Simulation.

 Checks the spelling.

 Import diagnostics.

 Runs the DFMXpress analysis wizard.

 Runs the SOLIDWORKSFloXpress analysis wizard.

The ASSEMBLY Toolbar

 Creates a new part & inserts it into the assembly.

 Adds an existing part or sub-assembly to the assembly.

 Creates a new assembly & inserts it into the assembly.

 Turns on/off large assembly mode for this document.

Hides / shows model(s) associated with the selected model(s).

Toggles the transparency of components.

Changes the selected components to suppressed or resolved.

Inserts a belt.

Toggles between editing part and assembly.

 Smart Fasteners.

 Positions two components relative to one another.

 External references will not be created.

 Moves a component.

 Rotates an un-mated component around its center point.

 Replaces selected components.

 Replaces mate entities of mates of the selected components on the selected Mates group.

 Creates a New Exploded view.

 Creates or edits explode line sketch.

 Interference detection.

 Shows or Hides the Simulation toolbar.

 Patterns components in one or two linear directions.

 Patterns components around an axis.

 Sets the transparency of the components other than the one being edited.

 Sketch driven component pattern.

 Pattern driven component pattern.

 Curve driven component pattern.

 Chain driven component pattern.

 SmartMates by dragging & dropping components.

 Checks assembly hole alignments.

 Mirrors subassemblies and parts.

To add or remove an icon
to or from the toolbar, first select:

Tools/Customize/Commands

Next, select a **Category**, click a button to see its description and then drag/drop the command icon into any toolbar.

SOLIDWORKS Quick-Guide©
Standard Keyboard Shortcuts

Rotate the model

* Horizontally or Vertically:	Arrow keys
* Horizontally or Vertically 90°:	Shift + Arrow keys
* Clockwise or Counterclockwise:	Alt + left or right Arrow
* Pan the model:	Ctrl + Arrow keys
* Zoom in:	**Z** (shift + Z or capital Z)
* Zoom out:	**z** (lower case z)
* Zoom to fit:	**F**
* Previous view:	**Ctrl+Shift+Z**

View Orientation

* View Orientation Menu:	Space bar
* Front:	**Ctrl+1**
* Back:	**Ctrl+2**
* Left:	**Ctrl+3**
* Right:	**Ctrl+4**
* Top:	**Ctrl+5**
* Bottom:	**Ctrl+6**
* Isometric:	**Ctrl+7**

Selection Filter & Misc.

* Filter Edges:	**e**
* Filter Vertices:	**v**
* Filter Faces:	**x**
* Toggle Selection filter toolbar:	**F5**
* Toggle Selection Filter toolbar (on/off):	**F6**
* New SOLIDWORKS document:	**F1**
* Open Document:	**Ctrl+O**
* Open from Web folder:	**Ctrl+W**
* Save:	**Ctrl+S**
* Print:	**Ctrl+P**
* Magnifying Glass Zoom:	**g**
* Switch between the SOLIDWORKS documents:	**Ctrl + Tab**

SOLIDWORKS Sample Customized **Hot Keys**

Function Keys

F1	SW-Help
F2	2D Sketch
F3	3D Sketch
F4	Modify
F5	Selection Filters
F6	Move (2D Sketch)
F7	Rotate (2D Sketch)
F8	Measure
F9	Extrude
F10	Revolve
F11	Sweep
F12	Loft

Sketch

C	Circle
P	Polygon
E	Ellipse
O	Offset Entities
Alt + C	Convert Entities
M	Mirror
Alt + M	Dynamic Mirror
Alt + F	Sketch Fillet
T	Trim
Alt + X	Extend
D	Smart Dimension
Alt + R	Add Relation
Alt + P	Plane
Control + F	Fully Define Sketch
Control + Q	Exit Sketch

SW-Quick-Guide, Part of SOLIDWORKS Basic Tools and Advanced Techniques

SOLIDWORKS® Quick-Guide by Paul Tran – Sr. Certified SOLIDWORKS Instructor
© Issue 12 / Jan-2016 - Printed in The United State of America – All Rights Reserved